"Few stories in American history are more intriguing, or touching, than that of the bond that developed between General Washington and the Marquis de Lafayette. With verve and charm, David Clary shows how the childless Washington, who felt betrayed by many of the men who surrounded him, and Lafayette, who never knew his father and lusted for glory and the chance to help the American cause, drew close in a loving and trusting relationship. With his engaging style, Clary succeeds in bringing to life Lafayette and Washington, and also in acquainting readers with America's great and, at times, seemingly forlorn struggle for independence." —John Ferling, author of *Setting the World Ablaze: Washington, Adams, Jefferson and the American Revolution* and *A Leap in the Dark: The Struggle to Create the American Republic*

"A beautifully crafted, insightful study of the deeply intertwined lives of Washington and Lafayette, two key figures in the transforming age of revolution." —Susan Dunn, author of *Sister Revolutions: French Lightning, American Light*

"A riveting history of a tumultuous time in America and France . . . I loved this book." —Senator Kay Bailey Hutchison, author of *American Heroines: The Spirited Women Who Shaped Our Country*

"Personal friends and political allies, George Washington and the Marquis de Lafayette had one of the most important friendships of the 18th century. In this enjoyable study, Clary . . . [has] woven together grand military history with an intimate portrait of deep affection." —*Publishers Weekly*

"Well-researched . . . Clary admirably contributes to an understanding of Lafayette's importance to American independence; of the uncertainty, in Lafayette's time, of that independence; and of the private side of Washington." —*Library Journal*

"*Adopted Son* takes a fascinating peek at the emotions behind the struggle for independence of both the United States and France. We have long placed each of these men up on pedestals but rarely seen them in human form. David A. Clary provides us that glimpse." —Kerrily Sapet, BookLoons.com

"Clary's . . . portrayal of Lafayette's and Washington's bond is fascinating, lyrically told and touching." —David Rapp, AmericanHeritage.com

"Through the story told we have a new view of the Revolutionary War, as seen by an outsider—Lafayette. We gain new insights into our first president and his role as the commander of the Continental Army. Finally there is Lafayette himself, a complicated man whose impact on the Revolution has been little understood." —Marc Schulman, HistoryCentral.com

"*Adopted Son* is a most humanizing look at two mythic historical figures, one larger than life and the other nearly forgotten. The intense devotion between Washington and Lafayette seems alien in our cynical age, but that is all the more reason a book like this is so welcome." —Kim Lumpkin, Toxicuniverse.com

"Clary's narrative delves deeply inside the minds of Lafayette and Washington. We see not just what made them great historical figures, but what made them human. . . . Clary has just raised the bar for today's nonfiction authors. If authors of history books rise to the challenge, they will unleash a new genre that will capture popular attention for generations to come." —Mark Lamendola, MindConnection.com

FOURTEEN: *Vive La Fayette!*

(JANUARY 1785–DECEMBER 1791) *373*

THE HERO OF AMERICA HAS BECOME MY HERO *374*

KINGS ARE GOOD FOR NOTHING BUT TO SPOIL THE SPORT *378*

HE IS SENSIBLE HIS PARTY ARE MAD *384*

THE SCENE OF THE ONE ACTION WAS IN HEAVEN,

    THE OTHER IN HELL *393*

FIFTEEN: *The Lament of Washington*

(JANUARY 1792–DECEMBER 1799) *403*

HIS CIRCLE IS COMPLETED *404*

I HAVE ASSOCIATED YOU WITH STORMY DESTINIES *410*

COURAGE, CHILD OF WASHINGTON! *417*

THIS AFFAIR HAS MADE ME VERY UNHAPPY *425*

I HOPED THIS WOULD NOT HAVE HAPPENED *427*

ENVOI: *Le Vashington Français*

(JANUARY 1800–MAY 1834) *433*

THE SOUL HAS DISAPPEARED FROM LA GRANGE *434*

HE HAS NOT RETREATED AN INCH *439*

AFTERWORD: *Greatness of Name in the Father Oft-Times Overwhelms the Son* *450*

NOTES *453*

CHRONOLOGY OF WASHINGTON AND LAFAYETTE *518*

ACKNOWLEDGMENTS *529*

BIBLIOGRAPHY *532*

INDEX *551*

ILLUSTRATIONS

George Washington at Princeton 3

Château de Chavaniac, Lafayette's birthplace 8

Lafayette at eighteen 19

Adrienne 21

Charles Lee 63

Horatio Gates 64

Henry Knox 69

Baron de Kalb Introducing Lafayette to Silas Deane 76

Duportail 87

Johann "Baron" de Kalb 91

John Hancock 93

Washington as Lafayette first saw him 96

Lafayette as Washington first saw him 97

Alexander Hamilton 103

John Laurens 105

Lord Stirling 107

Nathanael Greene 108

Washington, Lafayette, and Greene taking shelter from a storm 111

The Battle of Brandywine 114

Lafayette Wounded at Brandywine 116

Henry Laurens 121

Daniel Morgan 125

Thomas Mifflin 134

Washington and Lafayette at Valley Forge 147

Baron von Steuben 166

Robert Morris 173

Anthony Wayne 174

Vergennes 176

Benjamin Franklin 177

John Sullivan 206

Lafayette at about the time of the Rhode Island Campaign 209

John Adams 232

John Paul Jones 235

Rochambeau 253

America's First Ally 262

La Luzerne 263

Benedict Arnold 279

Thomas Jefferson 293

Cornwallis 312

De Grasse 326

Benjamin Lincoln 333

Surrender of Cornwallis 340

John Jay 354

Washington and Lafayette at Mount Vernon 365

James Madison 367

George Washington after the war 375

Gouverneur Morris 385

Louis XVI 388

Marie-Antoinette 389

Thomas Paine 397

Lafayette at the bar of the Assembly 408

James Monroe 416

Lafayette and his family in prison 419

George Washington near the end of his life 432

La Grange 434

Adrienne after prison 435

Lafayette after his tour of America 445

MAPS

Lafayette's European World 6
Northern Theater of the American Revolution, 1776–1778 66
Battle of Brandywine 112
Campaign and Battle of Monmouth Court House 193
Southern Theater of the American Revolution, 1778–1781 292
Virginia and Yorktown Campaigns, 1781 316
Siege of Yorktown, 1781 331

A NOTE ABOUT THE LETTERS

*T*he letters and documents quoted in this book are presented as they were originally written, with one exception. I have eliminated the eccentric capitalization common during that age (when Lafayette was excited, he often capitalized every word except proper adjectives), which is tolerable in handwriting but distracting when set in type. Otherwise, spelling, grammar, and syntax are in original form, and bracketed clarifications are inserted only when necessary. Letters written in French are presented in colloquial English.

CAST OF CHARACTERS

ADAMS, John *(1736–1826), American statesman; delegate to France; president*

ANDRÉ, John *(1751–1780), British officer; Arnold's co-conspirator*

ARMISTEAD, James *(ca. 1759–1830), slave; Lafayette's chief spy in Virginia*

ARNOLD, Benedict *(1741–1801), Continental Army major general; traitor*

BAILLY, Jean-Sylvain *(1736–1793), French revolutionary*

BARRAS, Jacques-Melchior Saint-Laurent, marquis (later comte) de *(?–1800), French squadron commander*

BURGOYNE, John *(1722–1792), British general, American Revolution*

CALONNE, Charles-Alexandre de *(1734–1802), French controller of finances*

CARLISLE, Frederick Howard, Earl of *(1748–1825), head of British peace commission*

CARMICHAEL, William *(?–1795), secretary to American delegation in Paris*

CASTRIES, Charles-Eugène-Gabriel de La Croix, marquis de *(1727–1801), French minister of marine*

CHASTELLUX, François-Jean de Beauvoir, chevalier de *(1734–1788), French staff officer and writer*

CLINTON, George *(1739–1812), governor of New York; Continental Army general*

CLINTON, Sir Henry *(1730–1795), British general, American Revolution*

CONWAY, Thomas *(1733–1800?), Irish-French Continental Army general*

CORNWALLIS, Charles, Earl of *(1738–1805), British general, American Revolution*

D'AYEN, Jean-Paul-François de Noailles, duc *(1739–1824), Lafayette's father-in-law*

DEANE, Silas *(1737–1789), Connecticut lawyer; American delegate to France*

DE BROGLIE, Charles-François, duc *(1718–1804), maréchal de France*

DE BROGLIE, Victor-François, comte *(1719–1781), maréchal de France*

DE GRASSE, François-Joseph-Paul, comte, marquis de Grasse-Tilly *(1722–1788), French admiral*

DE KALB, Johann "Baron" *(1721–1789), Continental Army major general*

DE STAËL, Anne-Louise-Germaine (née Necker), madame, baronne de Staël-Holstein *(1766–1817), French writer and hostess of famous salons*

D'ESTAING, Charles-Henri-Théodat, comte *(1729–1794), French admiral*

D'ORMESSON, Henri-François de Paule Lefèvre *(1751–1807), French controller of finances*

DUPORTAIL, Louis le Bègue de Presle *(1743–1802), chief engineer, Continental Army*

FRANKLIN, Benjamin *(1706–1790), printer; American statesman; delegate to France*

FRESTEL, Félix, *George-Washington Lafayette's tutor*

GAGE, Thomas *(1721–1787), British general and colonial governor*

GATES, Horatio *(1728–1806), Continental Army major general; president, Board of War*

GÉRARD, Conrad-Alexandre *(1729–1790), first French minister to the United States*

GIMAT, Jean-Joseph Sourbader de *(1743 or 1747–1792?), French volunteer, aide to Lafayette; Continental Army colonel*

GRAVES, Thomas *(1725?–1802), British admiral, American Revolution*

GREENE, Nathanael *(1742–1786), Continental Army major general*

HAMILTON, Alexander *(1757–1804), aide to Washington; Continental Army colonel; secretary of treasury*

HANCOCK, John *(1737–1793), Massachusetts politician; president of Continental Congress*

HENRY, Patrick *(1736–1799),Virginia politician and orator*

HOWE, Richard, Lord *(1726–1799), British admiral, American Revolution*

HOWE, Sir William *(1729–1814), British general, American Revolution*

HUNOLSTEIN, Aglaé de Puget de Barbantane, comtesse d' *(1755–1796), Lafayette's mistress*

JAY, John *(1745–1829), American statesman, diplomat, jurist, abolitionist*

JEFFERSON, Thomas *(1743–1826), American politician, diplomat, president*

JOLY DE FLEURY, Jean-François *(1718–1802), French controller of finances*

JONES, John Paul *(1747–1792), American naval hero of the Revolution*

KNOX, Henry *(1750–1806), major general, Continental Army, chief of artillery*

KNYPHAUSEN, Wilhelm, Baron von *(1716–1780), German commander in America*

LA COLOMBE, Louis-Sainte-Ange, chevalier Morel de *(1755–1799), aide to Lafayette and de Kalb; New York host of George-Washington Lafayette*

LAFAYETTE, George-Washington-Louis-Gilbert du Motier, marquis de *(1779–1849), Lafayette's son*

LAFAYETTE, Marie-Adrienne-Françoise de Noailles, marquise de *(1759–1807), Lafayette's wife*

LAFAYETTE, Marie-Joseph-Paul-Yves-Roch-Gilbert du Motier, marquis de *(1757–1834), major general, Continental Army; commandant, National Guard of Paris*

LA LUZERNE, Anne-César, chevalier de *(1741–1791), French minister to United States*

LAURENS, Henry *(1724–1792), South Carolina planter and merchant; president of Continental Congress; delegate to peace talks in Paris; father of John*

LAURENS, John *(1754–1782), aide to Washington; soldier and abolitionist; son of Henry*

LEE, Arthur *(1740–1792), American diplomat, delegate to France; political troublemaker*

LEE, Charles *(1731–1782), Continental Army major general*

LINCOLN, Benjamin *(1733–1810), Continental Army major general*

LIVINGSTON, Robert *(1746–1813), American secretary of foreign affairs*

LOUIS XVI *(1754–1793), king of France 1774–1792*

LOUIS XVIII *(1755–1824), king of France 1814–1815, 1815–1824*

MADISON, James *(1751–1836), American politician; congressman; president*

MARIE-ANTOINETTE *(1755–1793), queen of France 1774–1792*

MARTIN, Joseph Plumb *(1760–1850), enlisted man, Continental Army, 1776–1783*

MAUREPAS, Jean-Frédéric Phélypeaux, comte de *(1701–1781), prime minister (without portfolio) to Louis XVI*

McLANE, Allan *(1746–1829), Continental Army cavalry officer; spy, secret agent*

MIFFLIN, Thomas *(1744–1800), Pennsylvania politician; quartermaster general of the Continental Army; member, Board of War*

MIRABEAU, Honoré-Gabriel Riqueti, comte de *(1749–1791), French revolutionary*

MONROE, James *(1758–1831), Continental Army officer, aide to Stirling; ambassador to France; president of the United States*

MONTBAREY, Alexander-Marie-Léonor de Saint-Mauris, comte (later prince) de *(1732–1796), French minister of war*

MORGAN, Daniel *(1736–1802), major general, Continental Army, risen from captain*

MORRIS, Gouverneur *(1752–1816), member of Continental Congress; ambassador to France*

MORRIS, Robert *(1734–1806), Pennsylvania speculator and financier; member of Congress; superintendent of finance for the United States; Lafayette's banker*

NAPOLEON BONAPARTE *(1769–1821), French general, dictator, emperor*

NELSON, Thomas Jr. *(1739–1789), Virginia militia commander; governor*

NOAILLES, Louis-Marie, vicomte de *(1756–1804), Lafayette's wife's cousin and brother-in-law*

O'HARA, Charles *(1740?–1802), British major general, American Revolution*

ORLÉANS, Louis-Philippe, duc d' *(1773–1850), leader of Orléanistes in the National Assembly; as Louis-Philippe,"citizen king of the French" 1830–1848*

PAINE, Thomas *(1737–1809), revolutionary pamphleteer*

PHILLIPS, William *(1731?–1781), British major general, American Revolution*

PINCKNEY, Thomas *(1750–1828), Continental Army officer; South Carolina governor; American diplomat*

POIX, Philippe-Louis-Marc-Antoine de Noailles de Mouchy, prince de *(1752–1819), cousin to Lafayette and to Lafayette's wife*

REED, Joseph *(1741–1785), aide to Washington*

ROBESPIERRE, Maximilien *(1758–1794), French Jacobin revolutionary*

ROCHAMBEAU, Jean-Baptiste-Donatien de Vimeur, comte de *(1725–1807), lieutenant general commanding French expeditionary force in America 1780–1782*

ST. CLAIR, Arthur *(1737–1818), Continental Army major general*

SAINT-GERMAIN, Claude-Louis, comte de *(1707–1778), French minister of war*

SAINT-SIMON-MONTBLÉRU, Claude-Anne de Roubroy, marquis de *(1743?–1819), French general commanding troops accompanying de Grasse to Yorktown 1781*

SARTINE, Antoine-Raymond-Jean-Gaulbert-Gabriel de *(1729–1801), French minister of marine*

SCHUYLER, Philip John *(1733–1804), New York politician; Continental Army major general*

SÉGUR, Louis-Philippe, comte de *(1753–1830), Lafayette's friend and fellow officer*

SÉGUR, Philippe-Henri, marquis de *(1724–1801), French minister of war*

SHORT, William *(1759–1849), aide to Jefferson in Paris, later chargé there*

SIEYÈS, Emmanuel-Joseph, l'abbé *(1748–1836), French revolutionary*

SIMCOE, John Graves *(1752–1806), British commander of Tory troops*

SIMIANE, Diane-Adélaïde de Damas d'Antigny, madame de, comtesse de Miremont *(1761–1835), Lafayette's mistress*

STAINVILLE, Etienne-François, duc de Choiseul, comte de *(1719–1785), French general; foreign minister*

STARK, John *(1782–1822), Continental Army brigadier general*

STEUBEN, Frederick William Augustus, "Baron" von *(1730–1794), inspector general of the Continental Army*

STIRLING, William Alexander, Lord *(1726–1783), Continental Army major general*

SULLIVAN, John *(1740–1795), Continental Army major general*

TALLEYRAND-PÉRIGORD, Charles-Maurice de *("Talleyrand," 1754–1838), French archbishop; politician; scalawag*

TARLETON, Banastre *(1754–1833), British cavalry commander*

TERNAY, Charles-Henri d'Arsac, chevalier de *(1723–1780), French commodore*

TILGHMAN, Tench *(1744–1786), Washington's aide and military secretary*

VERGENNES, Charles Gravier, comte de *(1717–1787), foreign minister of France*

WASHINGTON, George *(1732–1799), commander in chief, Continental Army*

WAYNE, Anthony *("Mad Anthony," 1745–1796), Continental Army brigadier general*

WEEDON, George *(ca. 1730–1793), Continental Army brigadier general*

An Inexplicable Charm

(JUNE 28, 1778)

> And the most glorious exploits do not always furnish us with the clearest
> discoveries of virtue or vice in men; sometimes a matter of less
> moment . . . informs us better of their characters and inclinations,
> than the most famous sieges, the greatest armaments, or the
> bloodiest battles whatsoever.

> — PLUTARCH

The air smelled like rotten eggs. The gunsmoke had settled since the end of the fighting, but its sulfurous stench hung on in the hot, humid atmosphere. To the officers of the Continental Army, it was a further reminder of an opportunity lost, thanks to the bungling (some said it was treachery) of Major General Charles Lee.

This was the aftermath of the Battle of Monmouth Court House, June 28, 1778, among the hills and hollows of central New Jersey.

More than 700 men, about half Continentals and half redcoats and Hessians, were missing or lay scattered, wounded or dead, across the sprawling battlefield. It had been the longest action of the war, over nine hours, and one of the largest. For the Americans it was also the most frustrating day's work of the whole struggle for independence. A chance to

strike a real blow against the enemy, by mauling his rear guard on its retreat across New Jersey, had been thrown away, or so the American officers believed.

As night fell over the ghastly scene, the Americans did not know that
the British were already planning to creep away. They muffled the wheels
of their wagons, abandoned their dead and many of their wounded, and
themselves were soon abandoned by hundreds of deserters. When the
sun rose the next morning—to produce another savagely hot, suffocat-
ing day with temperatures in the upper nineties—the Continental Army
would hold the field. According to the customs of war, that made the
Americans the winners.

The last cannonade ended at about five in the afternoon. The major
generals ordered their brigade commanders to round up stragglers, reor-
ganize their troops, and place them in defensive positions. Men fanned
out to plunder the dead and to retrieve American and British wounded
and take them to the rear. That night everyone who had fought collapsed
on the ground. Soldiers and officers alike were exhausted, not so much
by the fighting as by the brutal heat—many of the casualties on both sides
had fallen to sunstroke and thirst rather than gunfire.

The division commanders trudged toward headquarters, which
meant wherever the commander in chief happened to be. He was atop a
steep rise overlooking the scene of the last stages of the action. One of
them was Nathanael Greene, a sturdy, fighting Quaker and the army's
most dependable major general.

Greene found the commander in chief as dusk was turning into dark.
General George Washington was asleep on a cloak spread on the ground.
The boy, Major General Lafayette, lay curled up beside him, also asleep
on the general's cloak.

The middle-aged man and the teenage boy had met less than a year
before, at the end of another hot, stifling day—Philadelphia in August. In
the months since, they had drawn together like two orphans in a storm,
which had first blown over them in different places—one in the Old
World, the other in the New—in 1775.

The Quaker soldier shared the opinion of the American commanders
that this day would have gone better if the original plan had been followed. The young, aggressive Lafayette should have remained in command of the advance force rather than being superseded by Lee.

Washington should not have been forced to charge onto the scene and take personal command. Instead, Lafayette's energies had been wasted. Washington had found a disaster in the making and turned it into, at best, a tactical draw.

But any regrets about what might have been were banished by the touching scene before him, Washington and Lafayette asleep together. Having watched the attachment grow between these two over the months, Greene also found the youngster endearing. He had once told his wife that the boy was irresistible, owing to "an inexplicable charm." Nothing could be more charming, in these grisly, stinking surroundings, than this affectionate, familial picture— not so much two exhausted soldiers as a father and son sharing the innocent comfort of sleep.

Greene spread his own cloak under a nearby tree, vowing to drive off anyone who might disturb the slumbering pair. But the day and battle just past proved to be too much even for his iron constitution. Sleep soon settled over him, as it already had over Washington and Lafayette, together in peace amid the madness of war.

George Washington at Princeton, by C. W. Peale. This is perhaps the best painting ever done of the commander in chief, showing the easy confidence of a general who has just won two important victories. (U.S. SENATE COLLECTION)

I Was All on Fire to Have a Uniform

(SEPTEMBER 1757-DECEMBER 1775)

Of all the animals in the world,
the most unmanageable is the boy.

—PLATO

Auvergne was a region of ancient lava flows and eroded volcanic necks, an eerie landscape, rugged and heavily forested, where ghosts and monsters and strange beasts lurked. In its level spaces it supported farming on its rich volcanic soil. Sheep grazed on the gentler slopes surrounding the fields, and hogs rooted on the edges of the woodlands. Around them, the tortured, wooded mountains inspired fears. It was a land of ignorance, superstition, hard labor, and poverty.

A journey to Paris, about 200 miles north, took more than two weeks in 1757. The area had always been isolated, owing to the rugged landscape and bad roads. Those same qualities had given the province a tragic place in history. In 52 BC, the town of Alesia in Auvergne was the last stronghold of the Celtic Gauls (called the Avernii by the Romans).

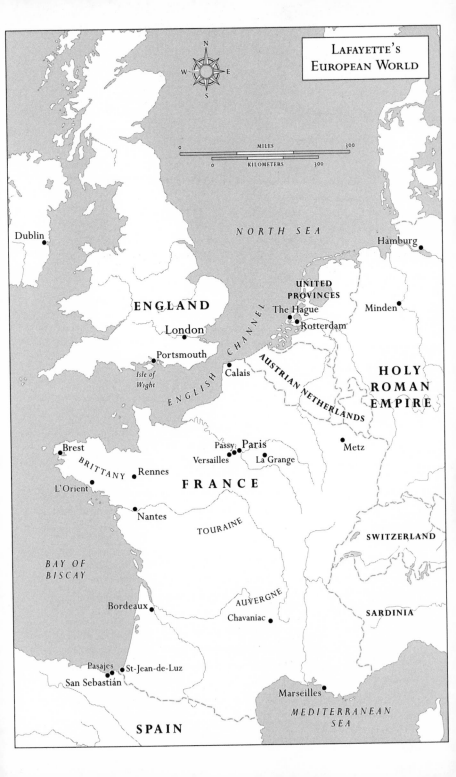

Under Vercingetorix, they had fought the conquering Roman armies through years of brutal combat. The mighty power of the Roman Empire told on the Gauls, however, until the last resisters, about 80,000 of them, were surrounded by Julius Caesar's troops and earthworks.

An army of Belgii, another Celtic nation, marched to their relief, but the Romans slaughtered them to the last man. Vercingetorix offered to surrender Alesia and offer himself as a hostage to spare the lives of his people. Caesar accepted, then ordered his troops to massacre the Gaulish soldiers and sold the people into slavery, scattering them across the Empire. He sent Vercingetorix to Rome, where he was beheaded as an *insurgentus*.

Gaul ceased to exist except as a province of the Roman Empire. Celtic was no longer spoken and was replaced by the Low Latin of the Roman soldiers. Over the centuries, that Latin became French, and what once was Gaul became France.

THE FAMILY'S MISFORTUNES IN WAR BECAME A KIND OF PROVERB

Lafayette was born on September 6, 1757, in the same room of the Château de Chavaniac as his father before him, the top-floor chamber of one of the building's corner towers. The house—built in the pseudo-castle "château style" on the foundations of a real castle that had burned down in the 1690s—was a Normanesque pile of stone with twenty large rooms and a slate roof. It was as cold as a barn in the winter despite its many large fireplaces. The château was separated from the neighboring village of Chavaniac by a moat, just as its neighborhood was separated from the rest of France by the forbidding landscape of Auvergne.[1]

The hereditary title of marquis, for a nobleman of middling rank, had been in the family for three generations, a reward for military service to the king. The clan could be traced back as far as the year 1000, and members had served in France's wars ever since. But Lafayette was descended from a line of younger sons (eldest sons inherited properties and titles), most of them Champetières who traced back to the thirteenth century. The history of Lafayette's forebears was a litany of younger sons who started out in poverty, married well, sired offspring, and went off to war

Château de Chavaniac, Lafayette's birthplace. He was born in the top room of the near tower. (LILLY LIBRARY, INDIANA UNIVERSITY)

to die young. They were close enough to Paris and Versailles to answer the call to arms but not near enough to be influential at court. They were provincial nobility, country bumpkins compared to the courtiers, glittering peacocks who surrounded the throne.[2]

Nearly all Lafayette's ancestors had been warriors of greater or lesser repute. His great-grandfather Charles, a veteran soldier with a sterling reputation, began the family's rise out of recurrent poverty, founding its permanent fortune and receiving the title marquis de La Fayette. Charles' son Edouard married very well, acquiring Chavaniac along with his bride, and expanded his land holdings. His most notable military accomplishment was to fall off his horse and crack his head in front of the king. He survived long enough to produce two sons, Jacques-Roch and Gilbert, Lafayette's father. He left behind a domain that stretched thirty-five miles across Auvergne and seventy-five miles north to south, which Jacques-Roch would inherit.

However, Jacques-Roch died in a fierce battle with the Austrians when Lafayette's father was two. That left Gilbert holding in his little hands the family name and estates. He married Marie-Louise-Julie de La Rivière, daughter of an ancient line of wealthy nobles. Her dowry extended his real estate into Brittany and gave him, for the first time in the family's history, connections to the inner circle around the king. Her grandfather, the comte de La Rivière, commanded the Mousquetaires du Roi (King's Musketeers, later made famous by Alexandre Dumas' novel *The Three Musketeers*). Known as the Black and Gray Musketeers, the outfit was the king's personal horse guard.[3]

It was a Catholic country, and infant mortality rates were high in 1757, so the newest Lafayette's prompt baptism was imperative, lest his baby soul end up in Limbo. It took place at the nearby parish church a few days after his birth, delayed to give his mother a chance to recover enough to attend. She did not make it. Neither did his father, who was away at war. His maternal grandfather, the marquis de La Rivière, had been expected, but the journey from Paris took too long. Lafayette's paternal grandmother, Marie-Catherine de Chavaniac, served as godmother, while his cousin the Abbé de Murat presided. He was baptized "the very high and very mighty lord Monseigneur Marie-Joseph-Paul-Yves-Roch-Gilbert du Motier de La Fayette, legitimate son of the very high and very mighty lord Monseigneur Michel-Louis-Christophe-Roch-Gilbert du Motier, marquis de La Fayette, baron de Vissac, lord of Saint-Romain and other places, and of the very high and very mighty lady Madame Marie-Louise-Julie de La Rivière."[4]

As this considerable mouthful of a name reflected, Lafayette's mother was a devoted Catholic, a habit that did not rub off on him. "I was baptized like a Spaniard," he said later, "and with no intention to deny myself the protection of Marie, Paul, Joseph, Roch, and Yves, I have most often called upon St. Gilbert," a wry reference not to the saint but to himself. His name, he told a correspondent, included that of every saint who might protect him in battle. So many Lafayettes had died fighting for France that "the family's misfortunes in war became a kind of proverb throughout the province."[5]

Lafayette descended from a long line of orphans, whose sires achieved fatherhood a few jumps ahead of the Fatal Bullet. He joined their ranks before he was two years old, when his father was killed on August 1, 1759, at the Battle of Minden in Germany, while serving as a colonel of grenadiers in the French army. In one of the biggest battles of the Seven Years' War, the French lost about 5,000 men killed and wounded and several thousand more captured.[6]

The elder Lafayette's commander had been ordered to keep his men below the skyline but rashly exposed them. When his immediate superior was killed, Lafayette stepped up to replace him, and as his son described it a half century later, he "was at once carried off by a ball from an English battery, commanded by a certain General Phillips."[7]

William Phillips was at the time a twenty-eight-year-old captain in the British Royal Artillery, mentioned in dispatches for his "superlative practice" at Minden. In his next battle he became the first artillerist in history to bring his guns into action at a gallop. Lafayette would run across him later. "By a strange coincidence," he said, twenty-two years later two of his cannons opened fire on the English headquarters at Petersburg, Virginia. He claimed that one shot went through a house where Phillips was, killing him outright. This comment says much about Lafayette's accuracy as a chronicler of his own career, as Phillips died of disease, although the marquis did lob a cannonball his way.[8]

FROM THE TIME I WAS EIGHT, I LONGED FOR GLORY

*L*afayette's father died, cut in two by English iron, before he had prepared a will. Young Gilbert succeeded to his feudal titles, while his widow reclaimed her dowry. Lafayette's grandmother appealed to the king for an allowance to raise him, and he granted a pension of 600 livres. Lafayette was not poor, however, because when his mother and grandmother died he could expect to receive an income of 25,000 livres. By the time he was four, an uncle died and he became future heir to the La Rivière fortune, with an annual income of 120,000 livres.[9]

The boy marquis would not starve; a board of financial guardians would see to that. His familial support was another matter. News of his father's death shattered his mother, who, consumed by her grief, abandoned him at Chavaniac and left for her family's home, the Luxembourg Palace in Paris. On April 5, 1760, barely eight months after the Battle of Minden, she gave birth to Lafayette's sister, who died less than three months later. Lafayette, growing up at Chavaniac, seldom saw his mother over the next several years.

Children often respond to the death of a parent with feelings of betrayal or abandonment and sometimes the fear that they are somehow to blame. Lafayette was too young to react that way toward his father's death, but having no fatherly presence left an empty space in his life. How he viewed his mother's absence—she off amid the splendor of Paris and Versailles, either enjoying social life or indulging in religious observance—will never be known. However much it must have affected him, in later years he was charitable rather than bitter toward her. "My mother," he said in one of his few references to her, "was a woman of lively temperament who had once had a liking for the frivolous, but after her husband's death had plunged into religion with all the strength of her character. Though she loved me devotedly it would never have occurred to her to take me away from my La Fayette grandmother, for whom she had a deep reverence."[10]

European nobles were notorious for the hands-off way they raised their children. Their marriages were arranged and often loveless, dynastic contracts between rich families to produce offspring and legitimize the transfer of titles and property between generations. The children grew up under the guidance of tutors and nurses until it became time for them to marry and for the boys to become military cadets. Lafayette was fortunate among his generation in that he was closely raised and loved by blood relations.

His *grand-mère paternelle,* Edouard's widow, had brought Chavaniac into the family as part of her dowry. She had lived in the house since 1701. Madame de Chavaniac was an unusually enlightened mistress over the family's estates, allowing the peasants to hunt and garden on her lands and to take firewood from her forests. When times were hard she made sure nobody went hungry. Moreover, she was a canny businesswoman who expanded the family's properties. She also bought out all supervising feudal rights over Lafayette, so he owed allegiance to no lord but the king.[11]

With her at Chavaniac was her spinster daughter, Madeleine, mademoiselle du Motier. When Lafayette was five, the household was joined by Madeleine's widowed sister, Charlotte Guèrin, baronne de Chavaniac, and her six-year-old daughter, Marie de Guèrin, who became like a sister to him. Lafayette, an unusually beautiful, cherubic little boy, grew up among—not under the supervision of—three generations of females, who doted on him.[12]

In fact, they let him run wild. He roamed over the estate playing games, especially war games, and dragooned peasant boys into following him in mock battles and parades. "From the time I was eight," he recalled years later, "I longed for glory." A cousin visited Chavaniac in 1768, when Gilbert was ten, and reported that he saw in the boy the "seed of self-esteem and even of ambition." The seed thus planted was of what Thomas Jefferson later described as Lafayette's "canine appetite for popularity and fame."[13]

At the age of eight, Lafayette recalled when he was twenty-two, his heart pounded when he heard of a hyena that was wreaking havoc in the neighborhood. What he referred to was the "Hyena of the Gévaudan," which showed up in the area in 1765. It killed livestock, terrorizing the region enough that the king sent royal gamekeepers to bag it. When a newspaper said that somebody named Lafayette had met the beast and run from it, he wrote a vicious letter to the editor, which his aunt intercepted.

The monster continued to roam the territory until 1787, when a hunter killed it. If it was the same animal that had appeared two decades earlier, it turned out to be either a big lynx or a wolf (accounts differ) with an inflated reputation. That was not enough for Lafayette about twenty years further on. Typically revising his early life in his memoirs, he described the "Beast of the Gévaudan" as the killer of 120 women and children along with its usual diet of sheep. He claimed that he grabbed his father's musket from the wall and headed into the forest when the monster first appeared, but his tutor and aunts made him come home.[14]

Lafayette's glorious obsessions were fueled by his education at Chavaniac. His grandmother hired his first tutor when he was five. Two years later an itinerant pedagogue, the Abbé Fayon, entered the household, and stayed to teach the young marquis and his cousin. Daily instruction emphasized reading, writing, and arithmetic, along with such broader learning as children their age could take.

This generation of young Frenchmen was saturated with the virtues of the Roman Republic, especially through the writings of Plutarch, Livy, and Tacitus. Lafayette first encountered Julius Caesar's *Commentaries* under Fayon's guidance. He gained a valuable insight from the Roman's work: a writer can brag about himself shamelessly and get away with it if he writes in the third person. The various reminiscences and memoirs that began pouring out of him in the late 1770s were often written that way.[15]

"But a child's real education," Lafayette said, "comes from the feelings and the attitude of the family in which he grows up. . . . It was but natural that I should hear much talk of war and glory among close relatives whose minds were ever filled with memories and regrets and a profound veneration for my father's memory." What he received was a combination of history from Fayon and family yarns from his *grand-maman.* Since his was a military family, it was military glory that he absorbed most.[16]

The line of soldiers whose portraits in shining armor decorated the walls of Chavaniac extended back 700 years. In 1250 Lafayettes rode in the Sixth Crusade and, according to family lore, captured the Crown of Thorns from the Saracens. In the next century Gilbert de Lafayette II fought England's Black Prince Edward at Poitiers, one of the great battles of the Hundred Years' War. In 1428, Gilbert III, *maréchal de France,* was Joan of Arc's general at Orléans, smashing the beef-eating *Anglais* and saving French independence. There was Lafayette blood shed aplenty, up to his grandfather's three wounds and his father's ghastly death.

It matters not how much of that was fact; it was accepted. But most of it was ancient history. Lafayette was more interested in the gallant death of his uncle and the senseless sacrifice of his father. He belabored his grandmother on those points, and she repeated, and embellished, the stories. She told him that the cannoneer who killed his father was named Phillips, and urged him to hate the perfidious *Anglais* in general, and that one in particular.

From Fayon he learned of Homer's *Iliad,* about two armies of proud warriors who spent ten years killing each other for the pride of their kings and the treachery of a woman. Among them were the Trojan Hector, who went to certain death for the honor of his family, and Odysseus, smartest of the Greeks, who ended the war by using his brain as well as his sword arm. After a ten-year struggle to return home, he single-handedly vanquished a mob of enemies besieging his household.

There were other heroes, including the Celtic Briton kings, those who inhabited Britannia before the Angles and Saxons and Normans became the hated *Anglais.* Among them was King Arthur, who warred against forces of darkness overrunning his homeland, leading the Knights of the Round Table. They were a brotherhood in arms, and what a noble band they were: Arthur, an orphan who became father of a new nation, his knights at his side. The greatest of them all was Launcelot du Lac (Sir Lancelot), a Frenchman, ferocious in battle and gentle in peace.

There were more recent histories, such as the French chronicles of the Hundred Years' War. In three great battles the flower of French knighthood was slaughtered by the unchivalrous *Anglais,* who had commoners rain arrows down on noble fighters rather than challenge them in manly combat, one on one. That was much like what had happened to his father.

The Battle on the Plains of Abraham took place in the year Lafayette's father died, 1759. The British general James Wolfe confronted the French general the marquis de Montcalm outside Quebec. Wolfe won, Montcalm lost, and both were mortally shot during the action. What fine, gallant deaths these handsome young generals presented (neither was really that handsome or that young, but that did not matter). The women of two countries wept at the news. West painted Wolfe's fall, Watteau Montcalm's, and engravers showed everyone the dramatic scenes.[17]

Raised on this heady brew, the young marquis developed an overwhelming urge to ride at the head of the parade, to achieve honor and fame through bravery in battle. But for the moment, he had to content himself with boyish war games, learn his lessons, and harken to the wisdom of his grandmother. Content he was until he was snatched away from the happy halls of Chavaniac and the wilds of Auvergne.

I WOULD MUCH RATHER HAVE BEEN
VERCINGETORIX

L afayette's great-grandfather the comte de La Rivière had been an outstanding soldier, so the boy inherited a martial temperament from both sides of his family. The comte was a blooded lieutenant colonel in the king's armies, holder of the exclusive Grand Cross of the Royal and Military Order of St. Louis, the king's highest military honor. La Rivière was an ancient, honorable, and powerful name in France, and in 1768 its only inheritor was the ten-year-old marquis de Lafayette. The old comte decided that the boy needed preparation for his place in society. He ordered his granddaughter to travel to Auvergne and bring him home to the Palais de Luxembourg in Paris. To start the boy on his way to the highest ranks at court, he placed him on the list of future officers of the King's Musketeers.[18]

The young marquis resisted the move. He did not want to be separated from Chavaniac, where he was the little lord of the village, or from his grandmother and aunts. He was moving to a strange, crowded world where he would be surrounded by people—men as well as women—who would view him as a rustic curiosity and a social upstart.[19]

The Abbé Fayon accompanied him, but otherwise he was cut off from everything he had known. The nobles swarming around him made it clear that they did not think he would amount to much. Nevertheless, he enrolled at the Collège du Plessis, a nursery for the sons of the most important nobles. It was supervised by the faculty of the Sorbonne, and its students typically won competitions with other schools in Paris. Its curriculum was standard for the day, emphasizing the Latin classics. Some masters also taught contemporary philosophy, theology, natural philosophy (science), and French. The students wore military-style uniforms, powdered court wigs, and child-size swords.

Fayon had prepared him well, and he received advanced placement. His chief concentration was Latin composition, and he showed a gift for languages, winning Latin contests against older boys every year. He was steeped in tales of Greek and Roman heroes, read Caesar's *Commentaries* in the original Latin, and learned about Vercingetorix's last stand in his home province. He had "a higher regard for Vercingetorix defending our mountains than for Clovis and his successors [the Franks]," he said years later. He did not know whether his distant forebears were Gauls or Franks, but he hoped he was a Gaul. "I would much rather have been Vercingetorix defending the mountains of Auvergne," he claimed.[20]

Lafayette may have had Gaulish blood in him, or Norman. In contrast to his dark-haired, dark-eyed French schoolmates, he was red-haired, blue-eyed, light-complexioned, and befreckled. That set him apart, along with his shyness and rather hostile attitude to the bustling world around him. He spent four years at Plessis, but he made no lasting friends there.

Not all the teachers took to him, either, although a rhetoric master found his boyish defiance leavened by cleverness. When the master described the perfect horse as one that would obey at the first sight of a rider's whip, Lafayette piped up that a perfect horse would be one smart enough to throw its rider at the first sight of a whip. Expecting to receive his own taste of a lash, the young marquis earned instead an amused chuckle from the teacher.[21]

While Lafayette was still a student at Plessis, returning to the Luxembourg Palace on weekends, he received a double shock in the spring of 1770. In early April, his mother died, not yet thirty-three years old. His great-grandfather followed her within a few weeks. Wealth tumbled down onto the twelve-year-old like an avalanche. Besides his own estates in Auvergne, he now owned his mother's in Brittany and a dozen other La Rivière estates. His annual income jumped by over 120,000 livres. Suddenly, he was one of the richest aristocrats—certainly the richest orphan—in France. Despite his young age, he was also the most eligible bachelor in the kingdom. Noble families quickly began to circle the marquis de Lafayette. With no one to look after him but a few indifferent uncles, he felt very alone.[22]

One of those uncles paid enough attention to decide that it was time for the boy to join the army. On April 9, 1771, he became a *sous-lieutenant* (sub-lieutenant or officer cadet) in the Black Musketeers. "I was all on fire to have a uniform," the boy soldier said later. He loved being reviewed by the king and riding to Versailles in full dress uniform.[23]

Lafayette reveled in the experience as only a glory-hound boy could. The Musketeers were the elite of all French troops, not for their battlefield record—they had none—but because their officers were from the finest families. Lafayette participated in a daily ceremony at the palace. An officer would be selected to trot up to the king to receive the day's orders, then back to the commander with the sovereign's response. Of his first time performing that duty in front of King Louis XV, the young marquis recalled, "The king told me that all was well and that he had no orders. I returned to my commanding officer to repeat words he heard repeated three hundred sixty-five days a year."[24]

Lafayette finished college in 1772, his highest distinction being his marital eligibility. His great wealth cried out for a mate, busybody friends of the La Rivières said. He should be married "as soon as nature would allow," taking into account that he was not yet fifteen years old. Self-appointed matchmakers offered one prospective bride after another; one was almost six years older than he was. His future matrimony became the business of the whole extended flock of nobles fluttering around Paris and Versailles, but nothing came of their proposals.[25]

Nothing, that is, until the Noailles family placed its bid. They were among the oldest, richest, and most powerful of the noble clans, even more than the La Rivières. The patriarch, Louis, third *maréchal,* duc de Noailles, commanded the historic regiment Dragons de Noailles (the Noailles Dragoons), a position inherited down through the family for generations. His son, *général de brigade* (brigadier general) of the king's armies, Jean-Paul-François de Noailles, duc d'Ayen, had fathered one son, who had died as an infant. The beefy, domineering general had five daughters, and he wanted them married "as soon as nature would allow." In particular, he wanted one of them to marry the marquis de Lafayette. There was a problem, however, and the duc was married to her.[26]

The doe-eyed, strong-jawed duchesse d'Ayen was unusually protective of her children, and famously stubborn to boot. She never quite got over the loss of her son, and her own recent recovery from tuberculosis had made her want to keep her family around her. She thought her babies were too young to be married. The oldest, Louise, was barely fourteen; the next, Adrienne, was twelve; and the youngest was just five. Aristocratic marriages commonly happened at a young age, but the duchesse believed that her husband was pushing things too much. They got into a notorious row, keeping the salons of Paris and Versailles abuzz.

They settled their argument in September 1772, and the duc won, though not hands down. Louise would be betrothed to a distant cousin, Louis, vicomte de Noailles, which would at least keep the name in the family. Adrienne would marry Lafayette, uniting two of the greatest fortunes in the country. But the mother demanded and won certain conditions for this union. The marriage would be deferred for two years while both children continued their educations. Neither would be told about the plan until Adrienne's mother thought fit to do so. Lafayette would move into the family palace at Versailles, and the happy couple would live there for at least a year after the ceremony.

Adrienne's father and Lafayette's uncle, with their attorneys and stewards, spent weeks drawing up the marriage contract, without either of the intendeds knowing anything about what was going on. The transaction concluded with an agreement that Adrienne's dowry would be at least 200,000 and possibly as much as 1.5 million livres. It was an enormous sum, but a small investment considering that it gave d'Ayen access to the Lafayette fortune.

The duchesse d'Ayen arranged for Adrienne and Lafayette to meet as if by accident. The marquis seemed not to notice the heart-wrenchingly pretty, dark-eyed girl with a baby-doll face. But she tumbled for the shy, awkward, skinny boy; for her, it was love at first sight. Moreover, the duchesse fell for him, as Adrienne said later, as if he were "a most beloved son."[27]

The details of the marriage contract and the dowry were worked out, and most documents signed, by February 1773. The king's approval was pending. One detail regarding Lafayette's moving into the Noailles palace was a concession to his family—he would spend the week in Versailles and weekends in Paris at the Palais de Luxembourg. He remained homeless, shuttling from place to place, with others making his decisions behind his back.

In February the fifteen-year-old Lafayette, the Abbé Fayon still with him, moved into the Noailles home. His future mother-in-law was kind, but the duc made it clear that he thought the boy pretty enough, if gangly and awkward, but otherwise of little account. He did his best with the material at hand, however. Fayon continued his private instruction, and d'Ayen hired a former army officer to tutor him in military subjects. As soon as there was an opening, he enrolled the marquis in the Académie de Versailles, a glorified riding school for princes and other high nobility. Lafayette was surrounded by young men with truly impressive lineages, and he felt out of place with his merely fourth-generation title and country ways. Moreover, he began to grow rapidly, and became clumsy.[28]

Lafayette was lonely. He was not at home among his future in-laws, who seemed to keep him as a house pet. D'Ayen never failed to let him know that he was worthless except for his title and fortune, a drone who required constant pushing to amount to something. The duc arranged his appointment as a full lieutenant in the Noailles Dragoons in April 1773, the better to keep an eye on him. The marquis, being an adolescent, seethed at the leashes being strapped onto him.

The match, made not in heaven but in a lawyer's office, approached. Adrienne's older sister, Louise, married Noailles in the fall of 1773. A date for Adrienne's own wedding was set for just after Easter the next spring. Still she did not know, although Lafayette received the news that winter. Problems with the inventory of his property—essential to determine what would become joint tenancy under the marriage contract—delayed the plans a bit. Although Adrienne was the last to know what was coming, when she heard about it she was delighted because she was really in love with her betrothed. There was no sign that he returned her affection, but he would do his husbandly duty. He could not fail to see how pretty she was.

Lafayette at eighteen, captain of dragoons, all arms and legs. Portrait by Boilly. (LILLY LIBRARY, INDIANA UNIVERSITY)

On March 14, the duc and duchesse de Noailles presented Lafayette and Adrienne at court, and King Louis XV signed the marriage contract. Their wedding took place on April 11, 1774, in the chapel of the Hôtel de Noailles in Paris. The same abbé who had baptized Lafayette presided; he was now the archbishop of Paris. There was a houseful of high nobility in attendance for the big event. Afterward, the royal family and hundreds of aristocrats flooded the place for a feast of more than one hundred courses and forty-six desserts. When it was all over, the duchesse sent the newlyweds off to their separate apartments. They were too young to consummate the marriage, in her opinion; the groom was sixteen, the bride fourteen.

As a wedding present, the duc promised Lafayette promotion to the rank of captain, with command of a company in the Noailles Dragoons. He arranged that in May. A few days after the wedding, the frustrated bridegroom rode off to Metz for summer training with his regiment.[29]

I DID NOT HESITATE TO BE DISAGREEABLE

*L*afayette wrote to Adrienne occasionally that summer. Expressing no more than ritual affection, his letters dripped with adolescent self-absorption, whining that she did not write to him often enough. Her feelings did not seem to concern him.[30]

He did not lack diversion. He made his first real friends, two fellow officers in the Noailles Dragoons, both about his age. The dominant one was his brother-in-law, the vicomte de Noailles, who cut a dashing figure in uniform. A hard rider, harder drinker, and even harder gambler, he was a natural leader among the teenagers. The other was Louis, comte de Ségur, who, like Lafayette, was a follower, trotting after the wild Noailles. Their revels continued after they returned to Versailles in the fall.[31]

They returned from Metz in September 1774 to find a smallpox epidemic raging in Paris and Versailles. Lafayette decided to do something that was not generally approved—receive "inoculations" against the disease. That involved scratching the skin and painting the wound with secretions taken from a pustule of an infected person. It was potentially as dangerous as it was curative, and because the church frowned on the practice, it had to be done in secret. Adrienne and her mother supported this medical rebellion. He rented a small house in the Paris suburb of Chaillot, where he and Adrienne stayed for the two weeks it took for the inoculation to prove itself. It worked, while the newlyweds spent their first time together outside the d'Ayen household—suitably chaperoned, however. The duchesse was not about to take any chances.[32]

That reinforced Lafayette's frustration at not being allowed to sleep with his beautiful bride. Noailles and Ségur urged him to follow the road customary among the French nobility—have an affair. He tried. "I shall spare you also the confession of an unedifying youth," he wrote a few years later, "and even of the story of two romances dedicated to beauties who were then very celebrated, in which my head had a larger part than my heart. The first, scarcely begun, broke against the obstacles of jealousy with which I collided head-on. The other . . . I pursued, despite long interruptions, on every possible occasion."33

The identity of the first lady remains a mystery. The second was probably Aglaé, comtesse d'Hunolstein, a married noblewoman. Court gossip linked him with her when he was in America in 1778, and he definitely connected with her later. She was beautiful and unusually promiscuous, even for her time and place.

When Lafayette panted up her trail for the first time she was the mistress of the duc de Chartres, son and heir to the duc d'Orléans, so she spurned him at first. The duc was a

Madame de La Fayette

From a Miniature in the possession of the Family

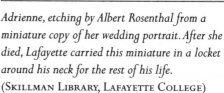

Adrienne, etching by Albert Rosenthal from a miniature copy of her wedding portrait. After she died, Lafayette carried this miniature in a locket around his neck for the rest of his life.
(SKILLMAN LIBRARY, LAFAYETTE COLLEGE)

member of the royal family, so the marquis could not challenge him to a duel over the lady's affections. Instead, he showed up drunk at his friend Ségur's place one night, and took him on. His fellow officer recalled that Lafayette spent the whole night "in a fit of jealousy, trying to persuade me to fight with him, swords drawn, for the heart of a beauty on which I had no claim."34

Those with modern standards of sexual propriety may be shocked by the escapades of the nobility during the eighteenth century, for whom affairs were a normal, and expected, escape from arranged, often loveless marriages. Lafayette was the product of his time as well as his place, and he was at a stage in a boy's life when his hormones boiled over. Rebelling against the restrictions imposed by his in-laws, during the winter of 1774–75 he began to sneak into Adrienne's apartment. Soon it was a nightly habit, demonstrating (as he put the best face on it) his "tender and stable affection" for his wife. In the spring of 1775, Adrienne wrote him that she was pregnant.[35]

When they were not chasing ladies, Lafayette, Noailles, Ségur, and other young bloods raised merry hell. Louis XV had died the previous summer, and the new king, Louis XVI—and especially his lusty queen, Marie-Antoinette—had attracted a younger set to the social whirl of Versailles. The boys showed youthful rebellion, parading around in costumes from the early fifteenth century. The queen and the younger courtiers were amused, while the older ones were visibly annoyed, which was the point of it all. With Noailles in the lead, the youngsters established a fad for horse racing; the old-clothes fashion wore away, but the turf sport remained.

The young set called themselves the Court Club and adopted yet another diversion, making the rounds of new cafés springing up on the Right Bank of the River Seine through Paris, abandoning the Left Bank hideouts favored by their elders. When the boys were in their cups, they put on exaggerated plays and declamations. They stirred up political trouble by appearing to oppose royal absolutism, and more seriously by making fun of the high courts known as les Parlements. All over Paris and Versailles, noble elders wailed their version of humankind's oldest refrain: "What's the matter with kids these days?"[36]

These boyish hijinks were not a sign, let alone a cause, of the approaching decline and fall of France, but a youthful reaction to a process already under way. "Through centuries of strife and vicissitude," said the historian Francis Parkman, "the French monarchy had triumphed over nobles, parliaments, and people, gathered to itself all the forces of the State, beamed with illusive splendors under Louis the Great, and shone with the phosphorescence of decay under his contemptible successor; till now, robbed of prestige, burdened with debt, and mined with corruption, it was moving swiftly and more swiftly towards the abyss of ruin."[37]

The rotten heart of this decaying realm was Versailles, the seat of court a few miles outside Paris. It had begun in the 1660s as a love nest for Louis XIV and expanded into an elaborate assembly of buildings and gardens that became a sort of gilded cage for the aristocracy. There its complex set of social hierarchies trapped them in endless competition for preferment and enrichment. Its ornate marble bathing rooms introduced and made fashionable the taking of baths, reinstating a habit abandoned a thousand years before. Less positively, Versailles established a tradition of excessive expenditure by the royal families who succeeded the Great Louis. Everything about Versailles and its inhabitants showed the grossest self-indulgence, at the expense of the country, on the part of royalty and nobility.[38]

When Louis XIV moved his court from Paris to Versailles, requiring the aristocracy to join him there, it was part of a comprehensive plan to establish his "absolute" control over the country. That required taming the nobility, the chief rivals for the king's power, because they had their own armies, or resources to hire mercenaries. He dared not go so far as to tax them—that burden remained on the peasants—but he could redirect their energies. Palaces at Versailles, in addition to their homes, drained their income, as did expensive entertaining. Their propensity for troublemaking was restricted by their presence at Versailles under the king's eye. It was also diverted into backstabbing and gossip, through competition for such silly honors as determining who would sit nearer the king at the next banquet. When Louis saw how slavishly the once rebellious nobility followed his lead, he donned outlandish costumes, which the nobles had to copy, spending their resources on cloth and tailors and wigmakers.

To tame the nobles' sons, he ended mercenarism, perfected the "regular" army (meaning it was under the king's control), and sent the boys to become officers in royal regiments. The rising, educated middle class was tamed by sending its sons to military academies to study engineering, artillery, and logistics. Instead of rebels, the young men became loyal subjects, thinning their own ranks by leading troops in battle.

Such was the world Lafayette entered in the fall of 1774. He did not fit in. "I have still less to tell you of my entry into society," he said later, "and of the unfavorable opinion that I incurred through my silence, because I did not heed and scarcely listened to things that did not appear to be worthy of discussion. That ill effect . . . was not moderated by the awkwardness of my manners, which, without being improper on great occasions, never succumbed to the graces of the court or to the charms of a supper in the capital."[39]

In this instance he was an honest judge of his own behavior. "Lafayette always seemed so distant," Ségur recalled. He had "a cold, solemn look." He seemed awkward, danced badly, and spoke little.[40]

It was not that Lafayette did not try to fit in, at least in the beginning, when the duchesse d'Ayen took her married daughters and their husbands to social events. It had one lasting effect on him—he became a clotheshorse. His own clothing was hopelessly out of fashion when he made his first appearance among the swiftly changing styles of the court. For the rest of his life, even when he was broke, he made sure that he dressed in the finest of garb.

A distant cousin observed Lafayette trying to keep up with his profligate friends in gambling, horse racing, and drinking. He also saw him at court and in the Versailles salons. The marquis, he remembered, "carefully sought what he believed to be the most fashionable, both in people and in things, but despite his taste for fashion, he was altogether awkward; he was terribly tall, his hair was red; he danced without grace, rode poorly." As if that was not enough, when Marie-Antoinette saw Lafayette trying to dance at one of her balls, he was "so awkward and gauche that the Queen could not help laughing." It was worse than that: he tripped and fell on his face. Given the customs of the servile court, everyone else in the place also laughed at him. He was humiliated as only a seventeen-year-old could be.[41]

The marquis was taller than the average Frenchman, but he was not too tall; he topped out eventually at about five feet nine inches. He gained his height rapidly during his teen years, and that made him clumsy. Nor was his hair too red; rather, it was a light red, strawberry blond. In an environment where fashion was obeyed slavishly, being different in any way made him feel outcast. There was more: in Auvergne he had mixed happily with peasant boys, a galaxy away from him on the social scale, but here he was among his own kind. This was a conclave of nobles presided over by an ineffectual king who let his queen run wild. Even the king's mistress went out of her way to shock and embarrass him.[42]

Lafayette started to rebel against the forces hemming him in, beginning with his father-in-law. The man who might have been like a father to him was instead, in his youthful mind, a tyrant bent on curbing his behavior, denying him the freedom to live his own life. If the duc d'Ayen loved anything about Lafayette, it was his fortune. Otherwise, he seemed to assume that the young marquis would achieve nothing on his own. With the best of intentions, he tried to win Lafayette a place as a retainer of the comte de Provence, the king's brother. That would have been a significant social advance, but Lafayette thought the honor would make him a permanent lackey at court. He sabotaged the duc's plans by deliberately insulting Provence in a private conversation. As he explained later, "I did not hesitate to be disagreeable to preserve my independence."[43]

The only career still open to him was as a soldier, but that was what he had wanted all along. He did not entirely look the part, all arms and legs, no shoulders or hips, so slender that he appeared frail, but that was deceptive. He had a heart-shaped face, owing to a wide forehead broadened by an already receding hairline, with a rather pointed chin. It was bisected by a long, straight nose. Big hazel eyes sparkled under arched brows, and he had a lush mouth, a ruddy complexion, and a sprinkling of freckles. He was no longer as beautiful as he had been, but he was still attractive. The ladies thought so, anyway. He was about to discover that older men also could find him appealing, although not in the same way. It was his puppylike charm, which later would be called "inexplicable," the endearing radiance of someone young, vulnerable, trusting, loyal, a threat to no one.

Lafayette was likable, at least to his peers and to commoners. He liked people, and he wanted to be liked. He wanted approval, especially from those he could respect, and he wanted the applause of the many. He wanted a father, someone he could honor. The duc d'Ayen had not measured up.

THE DESTINIES OF FRANCE AND HER RIVAL WERE BOTH TO BE DECIDED

Then Lafayette met Charles-François, duc de Broglie, commander of the Army of the East. The young captain of the Noailles Dragoons came under his command—though separated by layers of senior officers who stood between the lowly company leader and the highest general—when his regiment reported to Metz for its annual training in late spring 1775.

De Broglie was a well-padded man with a chubby face, wide, deep eyes, and a kindly expression, which flattered someone who had been a fighting soldier all his life. He had been victorious during the Seven Years' War, under the command of his brother, Victor-François, comte de Broglie, until the incompetence of others at Minden erased their gains against the Prussians. He was also a relentless schemer and plotter who had been active in the secret intrigues of Louis XV's government, especially in Poland. He had lost influence since the war ended in 1763, but in the 1770s he was regaining it as a relentless advocate of a renewed war against England. De Broglie had the worst instincts of a pirate and the best talents of a cutthroat. Thomas Jefferson saw him riding at the head of troops in Paris in 1789 and aptly described him as "a high-flying aristocrat, cool and capable of everything." His ample exterior cloaked his sinister nature. In person he was friendly, hearty, and indulgent to the young.[44]

The general knew that he had under him junior officers whose military rank did not reflect the power of their family connections. Nor had it escaped his notice that Lafayette had a lot of money. De Broglie was grand master of a traveling (military) lodge of the Freemasons. In that capacity he invited Lafayette, Noailles, Ségur, and a few other young officers to join. Flattered, they found themselves for the first time in a real "brotherhood." It was especially intriguing for the country boy from Auvergne. The Masons were a social organization, but they talked about the equality of men and the rights of all—loaded political ideas in an absolutist monarchy. That was a message congenial to a young Frenchman schooled in the ideals of the Roman Republic and exposed to fiery notions about the "social contract" preached by the latest philosophers.

Fighting had broken out in America in the spring of 1775, and the news touched off a frenzy among soldiers in France. The young ones, fired by Enlightenment ideas, hungered for a taste of the action. The elders wanted revenge against England for the French defeat in 1763. It was a popular subject at meetings of the military lodge, where Lafayette and the other boys first heard about American leaders such as George Washington and Benjamin Franklin—with the additional news that they were Masons.

In August 1775, the Duke of Gloucester, brother of Britain's King

George III, passed through Metz. De Broglie invited him to a dinner with fellow Masons, including Lafayette and his friends. Gloucester expressed his sympathy for the Americans and his opinion that his brother was being boneheaded about it all. Here, the boys agreed, was an opportunity for glory, and for revenge against the *Anglais,* all in a good, even noble cause.[45]

De Broglie had plans of his own for the American Revolution, but he did not let the young officers in on them. He hoped that when they returned to Versailles and Paris at the end of the summer they would influence public and court opinion in favor of French intervention into Britain's colonial troubles. He knew that an official shift in policy toward the Americans would not happen overnight, but he was as patient as he was crafty. He might seem fatherly to Lafayette and the others, but he was really taking advantage of their connections and their youthful sympathies for the American struggle.

Lafayette later claimed that he was won over immediately. "Such a glorious cause," he said in his memoirs, "had never before rallied the attention of mankind." Waving his pen like a sword, he concluded, "I gave my heart to the Americans and thought of nothing else but raising my banner and adding my colors to theirs."[46]

That was written decades later to present Lafayette in hindsight as a democratic republican from the outset. In 1775, however, he was still a French aristocrat, uncomfortable in Versailles but not opposed to the form of government that it represented. He had been raised to hate the *Anglais* and was infected by the rage for *revanche* (vengeance) that permeated the French army after the Seven Years' War. Above all else, he was consumed with a boyish desire for glory in battle. The uprising in America was not to him a beacon of freedom. It was the only military game in town, and he wanted to take a hand in it.

He was more objective when he wrote about these matters earlier, in 1779. "At the same time the destinies of France and her rival were both to be decided," he said. England was in danger of losing much of her commerce, a quarter of her subjects, and half the British territory. On the other hand, if she reunited with the thirteen colonies, "[t]hat would have been the end of our Antilles and our possessions in Africa and Asia, of our maritime commerce, and . . . ultimately of our political existence."[47]

Lafayette and his friends talked up the American cause, and the logic of French participation in it, when they returned to the capital in the fall of 1775. They joined *sociétés de pensée* (thinking groups, direct ancestors of the political clubs that would appear during the French Revolution), which were multiplying in Paris. Those were forums for vigorous debate on political questions, not viewed tolerantly by the government. They paralleled the Masons and often had identical memberships with the lodges, but they were not outgrowths of Masonry. The latter, however, had proven itself congenial to young officers with unconventional views, and it offered a tradition of secrecy—nothing said in a lodge meeting was to be repeated outside the room. The day after Lafayette's daughter Henriette was born on December 15, he, Noailles, and Ségur joined the Masonic Lodge Saint-Jean de la Candeur, in Paris.[48]

There they fell under the spell of a defrocked Jesuit priest, the Abbé Guillaume Raynal, who spouted tedious harangues against kings, priests, and slave owners. Nobody paid much attention to him until the government banned his tirades, making him popular in Masonic lodges, where the king's agents could not hear him. In those chambers he ranted against a multitude of evils incarnate, including royalty, nobility, and the church, and extolled the "rights of man." Young Lafayette was greatly impressed, and late in life he called the Jesuit windbag the greatest writer of the eighteenth century.[49]

Lafayette thereby began an association with a loose network of organizations, the Freemasons, that would continue on and off for the rest of his life. He was never a prominent or especially active member, but time and again he found it useful to take advantage of connections that Freemasonry offered. For an ambitious teenager, the very notion of belonging to an exclusive group, with rituals and signs known only to the select, was its own attraction. That behind it lay a socially tolerant philosophy of "liberty, equality, fraternity" was added cachet. Besides, there were all those American revolutionaries who were said to be Masons. Even before Lafayette met Washington, what was good enough for the older man was good enough for him.[50]

The young French captain wanted to enlist in the American cause, even if his understanding of what that cause was all about was vague. He wanted to go to *l'Amérique*. But he was a French soldier and bound to his duty in France, so unless his country joined with the Americans against the British, the chances of his fighting in America appeared slim.

Nevertheless, somehow or other he would find a way to escape from the house of Noailles and his domineering father-in-law. He would serve under General Washington.

T W O

So Young and Inexperienced
a Person

(FEBRUARY 1732-JUNE 1775)

What creature goes about on four legs in the morning, on two legs at noon,
and on three legs at the end of the day?

—THE RIDDLE OF THE SPHINX

Tidewater Virginia was worn-out farmland in 1732. Indians had farmed the area for millennia, keeping it fertile by mixing their crops. English settlers had worked the land for only a century, but they had mined the soil, wearing it out by farming the same crops year after year. For the soil, the most debilitating crop was tobacco. For the farmers, the most rewarding crop was also tobacco. It required so much labor that small farmers could raise no more than an acre of the stuff, devoting the rest of their land to wheat, corn, flax, and other consumables. Large planters had another solution to tobacco's demands for labor—slaves. The crop was living gold, giving the poor farmer the only cash he ever saw, making the rich farmer even richer.

Tobacco had created a class society in the Tidewater. An emerging aristocracy controlled the greater share of land, wealth, and political power. Below it stood two underclasses: free farmers struggling for survival and at the bottom slaves and indentured workers, who had little control over their own condition.

Ships sailed up the rivers, unloading cargoes at plantation or county wharves, taking on tobacco. Most goods came from England, along with books and schoolmasters, although the wealthier Virginians often sent their sons over the sea for their education. Virginia was a land of opportunity for the hungry, the greedy, the ambitious. They need only look west.

Or they could look next door. In Virginia's Northern Neck, near the fall line where the Tidewater gave way to the Piedmont, two plantations overlooked the Potomac River. One was Epsewasson, part of the Washington family's extension of its ambitions to the frontier. Its main building was a common timber farmhouse, a place to sleep between days of hard work carving a farm from the wilderness, built by its occupants and their slaves. The other was Belvoir, headquarters of an immense royal grant of land to Lord Fairfax, a grand mansion imported from England, filled with luxurious furnishings, a place to entertain and to impress, paid for by income from His Lordship's estates back home. Together they represented a divide in Virginia's future.

KEEP TO THE FASHION OF YOUR EQUALS

$\mathcal{G}$eorge Washington was born into this English-Virginian world on February 22, 1732, at Popes Creek Plantation, a snow-covered tobacco farm overlooking a wide, sparkling tributary of the lower Potomac. He was part of the fourth generation of Washingtons in Virginia, a succession of orphans who married well, expanded their landholdings through skill and hard work, and died young to leave something for their own orphans.

John Washington, homeless at age eleven, arrived in 1657 at age twenty-five, amassed over 10,000 acres, and died when his son, Lawrence, was a teenager. Lawrence left a tidy sum behind for his son, Augustine, then four years old, when he died in 1698. "Gus" grew up to buy Popes Creek Plantation, Epsewasson upriver, and Ferry Farm across the Rappahannock from an iron mine he had bought near Fredericksburg. He married in 1715 and produced three sons (one of whom died an infant) and a daughter before his wife died in 1729. He married again in 1731, to Mary Ball, who gave him four sons and a daughter who survived. The first child was George. He in turn lost his father, Augustine, when he was eleven years old, after the family had moved to Ferry Farm.[1]

Gus left an estate that included over 10,000 acres of land in seven tracts, forty-nine slaves, and the iron mine. George's eldest half brother, Lawrence, got the lion's share, including the mine and Epsewasson. George's inheritance included Ferry Farm, half interest in a useless tract of 4,360 acres, ten slaves, three small lots in Fredericksburg, and part of the residuary estate.[2]

It was not much, and it fell under the control of George's mother, Mary, until he reached legal age. She was not the type to let go of anything once she had her hands on it; George battled her for thirty years before he gained title to his own inheritance. Mary was a selfish, tyrannical woman and a terror to the neighborhood. The boy's home life was miserable.[3]

The situation also made the young Washington independent and self-reliant. Whenever he could, he stayed with his half brothers, and he went farther afield to visit distant relatives. His chief refuge was Lawrence, a tall, charming, scholarly man, who took on the role of protector and adoptive father to George. He had been educated in England, then returned to Virginia, only to leave again to serve as an infantry captain in an expedition against the Spanish in the Caribbean. The fleet was ably commanded by Admiral Edward "Old Grog" Vernon. Incompetent generalship in the land force, however, brought the campaign to grief. Lawrence returned disgusted by British generals and their contempt for Americans, although he had great admiration for the admiral, in whose honor he renamed his estate Mount Vernon.[4]

George spent much of his youth at Mount Vernon, where his elder brother looked for ways to rescue him from Mary. They included enlistment as a midshipman in the Royal Navy, a scheme Mary loudly scotched. More important was Lawrence's encouragement of George's self-instruction, and his introduction to a wider world. The two of them formed a tight bond, and George looked to Lawrence for the guidance their father's death had deprived him of. They were together much of the time, and George drank in his brother's stories of his military adventures and his views of the British government and its empire. Lawrence's dignity and sheer decency were powerful examples for the younger brother to follow.

The boy's education was indifferent, involving a tutor and a country school, and it was over by the time he was fifteen. Its most positive result was a broad foundation in mathematics. Otherwise, he read whatever came to hand. Lawrence gave him some guidance in the classics and encouraged what became a lifelong interest in self-education by reading. He also received pointers in behavior. His most famous work in his childish hand was copying out 110 maxims called "Rules of Civility and Decent Behavior in Company and Conversation." These lacked the piety that laced most advice to the young in those days—religion would not be among Washington's major concerns until late in his life.

Beginning with the first rule ("Every action done in company ought to be with some sign of respect to those that are present"), George learned to treat people considerately. He was taught to show courtesy toward inferiors, equals, or superiors, kindness to the first, and deference to the last. As for the middle, "[k]eep to the fashion of your equals." The maxims drummed into Washington the importance of maintaining personal dignity and honor, qualities that so distinguished Lawrence.[5]

George's brother gave him free run of Mount Vernon's stables, and he became a superb horseman—more than one admirer during the Revolution described him as the best they had ever seen. When Lawrence's in-laws, the Fairfaxes, imported a pack of foxhounds, Washington developed a passion for fox hunting. He harbored a passion of another kind—a volcanic temper, which more than anything else he feared losing control of. He cultivated an outward reserve, even iciness, and trained himself (with only partial success) not to take offense at what others said or did. Equally, he acquired a hunger for approval from others. He wanted to be admired, respected, but not necessarily liked. He was socially awkward, owing to his rural upbringing, and he had few friends. Standing a rawboned six feet three inches tall, however, he was easy to notice.

Washington's main stab at a social life came in November 1752, when he was initiated into the Masonic Lodge at Fredericksburg, although he was below the required age of twenty-one. He attended twice more, until he reached the Sublime Degree of Master Mason ("Third Degree") in August 1753, then only twice again, that year and in 1755. Freemasonry—which in America was more social than political—became important to him late in life, but he never was diligent about going to meetings.[6]

The young man was more interested in improving himself, socially and economically. He had inherited the land hunger of his family and his class and began a lifelong quest to own more. His chief distinction from other Virginia planters in this was a parallel interest in learning how to farm without wearing the soil out. The Washingtons had, over four generations, acquired thousands of acres, but they never counted among the grandees of Virginia. All their houses were small, rustic, crowded, and fitted out with necessities, not luxuries. That was true of Mount Vernon when Lawrence owned it. Its house was not the large mansion George would turn it into, but a cramped timber farmhouse.

Things were different next door, at Belvoir, the manor house of the 5 million Virginia acres owned by England's Lord Fairfax and managed by his nephew William, a model gentleman who introduced George to the history of Republican Rome and taught him that the highest achievement was to earn the applause of his countrymen through honest deeds.

Belvoir was splendid. The parlor at Ferry Farm served as an extra bedroom, but in the Fairfax mansion that room was filled with mahogany furniture and dominated by an enormous—and enormously expensive—mirror above the mantel. Majestically overlooking the Potomac, the house was like nothing else Washington had ever seen. Unlike the timber houses of his own family, he said, Belvoir was "of brick, two stories high, with four convenient rooms and a large passage on the lower floor; five rooms and a large passage on the second; servant's hall and cellar below." Other buildings around the house included offices, stables, and a coach house, surrounded by a large garden yielding "a great variety of fruits all in good order."[7]

Washington wanted to live like that. He also wanted to go through life dressed as well as the Fairfaxes, and he became meticulous about his clothing. Proper dress and grooming contributed to the commanding presence and air of dignity, even nobility, that everyone who saw him during the Revolution would notice.

In 1748, when Washington was sixteen, William Fairfax hired a surveyor to subdivide some of his lands in the Shenandoah Valley. Washington and Fairfax's son George went along. It was a rough trip into the wilderness, and he reveled in every minute of it, even his first night's lodging in a squatter's shack. "I, not being as good a woodsman as the rest of my company," he wrote in his journal, "stripped myself very orderly and went in to the bed, as they called it, when to my surprise, I found it to be nothing but a little straw matted together, without sheets or anything else, but only one threadbare blanket, with double its weight of vermin, such as lice, fleas, etc. . . . I put on my clothes, and lay as my companions [on the floor]." The next night was better, he recalled: "We had a good dinner prepared for us, wine and rum punch in plenty, and a good feather bed with clean sheets, which was a very agreeable regale."[8]

During more than a month in cold, early spring weather, Washington discovered that he loved being beyond the frontier. He bore hardships well and learned how to survey. When he returned, he became the Fairfaxes' surveyor and soon earned his license as a public surveyor. He had discovered something else during his first trip: surveyors were ahead of the market when it came to finding valuable lands. Over the next three years, Washington made repeated trips west, claiming land for others and himself. He became an agent of the Ohio Company, a scheme put together by a syndicate of English and Virginian aristocrats to wheedle the king into giving them large grants of land beyond the Appalachians.

While George explored the frontier, his brother Lawrence came down with tuberculosis. He decided to go to Barbados to recuperate, taking George with him. Lawrence's improvement was only temporary, however, and while there George contracted smallpox, scarring his face but giving him immunity to this plague. After they returned to Mount Vernon, Lawrence died of his disease. He had appointed George executor of his estate and residuary heir to his property, including Mount Vernon, which George received title to in 1761.

Washington was orphaned again, deprived of the guidance and sterling example Lawrence had given him. But whatever inward doubts he harbored, outwardly he was ready to challenge the world. In 1753, the world challenged him.

A YOUTH OF GREAT SOBRIETY,
DILIGENCE, AND FIDELITY

*E*ngland and France had been at war with each other for centuries, and their colonists in America sometimes were drawn into the conflict. They provided troops and supplies, invaded enemy territory, and incited Indians to do their butchery for them. The Indians—arrayed in groups varying from isolated bands to multitribal confederations—played the two white tribes off against each other, promising allegiance to whichever offered the best tribute. As a general rule, the Indians favored the French, because their population was smaller and they paid the best bribes. By the 1750s the English were clearly a greater threat to native well-being. Their growing population displaced eastern tribes westward, where they collided with other tribes. In response, they attacked frontier settlements and farms. The French in Canada encouraged them with firearms, ammunition, and plenty of liquor.

In 1752 and 1753, French authorities in Canada sent expeditions to the Ohio River Valley to post markers of their king's sovereignty. In the spring of 1753 they extended a line of military posts from the eastern end of Lake Erie toward the Forks of the Ohio, where Pittsburgh now stands. That not only challenged British claims to the country but threatened the future profits of the Ohio Company. Its investors had plans of their own to build a post at the Forks, trade with the Indians, and claim the lands beyond.

Robert Dinwiddie, lieutenant governor of Virginia, was a Scottish tycoon and, along with the Fairfaxes, a heavy investor in the Ohio Company. News of three new French posts in what is now western Pennsylvania, forming a line aimed at the Forks, alarmed him. He complained to his government in London about this invasion, and suggestively asked for instructions. In October 1753, King George II's orders arrived. Virginia should build forts on the Ohio and send an emissary to confirm whether the French had invaded English soil. If that was the case, the officer should "require of them peaceably to depart." If they refused, "[w]e," said the king, "do strictly command and charge you to drive them out by force of arms."[9]

King George did not understand that this order committed his government and its British and American taxpayers to doing the Ohio

Company's work for it. Since Virginia's Assembly (House of Burgesses) would have to pay the major part of the bills, the conniving Dinwiddie kept it in the dark. He summoned the King's Council (the appointed upper house) and urged it to authorize an expedition to drive the French out, and build a post at the Forks. He had just the candidate to lead the enterprise—the twenty-one-year-old George Washington.

Washington confessed, "It was deemed by some an extraordinary circumstance that so young and inexperienced a person should have been employed on a negotiation with which subjects of the greatest importance were involved." But he was "used to the woods," said one of Dinwiddie's business partners, and "a youth of great sobriety, diligence, and fidelity." Besides, he could be trusted not to feather his own nest while serving the interests of the Crown, so thoroughly mixed up with those of the Ohio Company.[10]

On October 30 Dinwiddie ordered Washington to venture into the West, contact friendly Indians, and proceed to the French forts. There he was to present a nicely phrased ultimatum from Dinwiddie, politely inviting the "frog-eaters" (as the English called the French) to clear out. While awaiting their reply, he was also supposed to gather as much intelligence as he could about the other side's strength, dispositions, and intentions.

Washington trekked into a literally howling wilderness—winter roared in ahead of schedule. He was accompanied by Ohio Company trader Christopher Gist; Jacob van Braam, a Dutchman who claimed to speak French; a scalawag who said he could interpret the Indians' languages; and four others who eventually deserted him. With Gist's help, Washington enlisted a few Indian allies, slogged through rain and sleet, forded torrential rivers, and reached Fort LeBoeuf (Erie, Pennsylvania) on December 11, 1753. The local commander received him with great courtesy. He invited Washington to cool his heels for three days as he prepared a reply to Dinwiddie's ultimatum, which he forwarded to his superiors in Canada.

The French officers wined and dined the Virginian. He reported later that the wine, which they drank by the gallon, loosened their tongues. They told him "that it was their absolute design to take possession of the Ohio, and, by G——, they would do it; for that although they were sensible the English could raise two men for their one, yet they knew their motions were too slow and dilatory to prevent any undertaking of theirs." Or at least that was how the message came through the Dutchman's translation; Washington spoke no French. He understood well enough, however, that the "*rosbifs*" (as the French called the English) were being told to go to hell. The official letter to Dinwiddie said much the same, but more politely.[11]

Washington hurried back to Virginia's capital, the muddy little village of Williamsburg. His horses were worn out, so he decided he could make better time on foot. Leaving the rest of his party behind, he and Gist set out through storms and hostile Indians. Twice he came close to drowning, and once he narrowly dodged a musket ball. Gist became crippled by frostbite, and Washington left him at an Ohio Company post. He pressed on alone to Williamsburg, where he reported to Dinwiddie in early February 1754.

There he wrote a formal report to the lieutenant governor. After many pages of chipper boasting, its ending betrayed youthful uncertainty and hunger for approval. "I hope what has been said," Washington pleaded, "will be sufficient to make your Honour satisfied with my conduct; for that was my aim in undertaking, and chief study throughout the prosecution of it." Dinwiddie was satisfied; he ordered the report published, along with his praise of it, to justify the war he was starting.[12]

Dinwiddie was in over his head and not bright enough to realize it. France and England were at peace, and he was about to blunder them into war. Moreover, Virginia had not mounted a military expedition since the previous century. Nobody in the province understood what a campaign would involve, let alone what it would cost. Nevertheless, the lieutenant governor called the Assembly into session to get it to pay for a war the burgesses did not want. They debated until April, when the Assembly voted some money, but not enough. Meanwhile Dinwiddie sent emissaries to the Indian tribes, and to other colonies, appealing for support. He did not get much.[13]

The lieutenant governor appointed Washington a lieutenant colonel of the militia, and commander of the expedition. Meanwhile, in early spring Dinwiddie had dragooned about forty carpenters and militiamen into going to the Forks to build a fort. In April 1754, Washington, wearing a tailor-made uniform, set out from Alexandria at the head of 160 underpaid, disgruntled militiamen and wagoneers. He had been authorized

200, but he was lucky to assemble the force he did. As his little army cut its way through the forest at a rate of two or three miles a day, it became apparent that Washington also was in over his head, but not mature enough to realize it.

The men at the Forks faced starvation, because the Delawares refused to provide food. That was a sensible move on the Indians' part, because early in May about a thousand French soldiers arrived at the Forks with eighteen cannons. The forty Virginians surrendered and headed home. The French started building a professionally engineered fortification, named Fort Duquesne.

Washington was encamped in a grassy valley split by a swift stream, called Great Meadows. He ordered his men to cut timber and erect a circular stockade, which he called Fort Necessity. It was not big enough to enclose even his small complement, so he surrounded it with a ring of shallow trenches. The whole thing was commanded by wooded hills all around, where the French could pepper it with musketry and bombard it with cannonballs.

The commander at Fort Duquesne kept an eye on Washington's progress through Canadian and Indian scouts. In late May he sent out a party of about thirty-five, commanded by a young, popular, and well-connected ensign, Joseph-Coulon de Villiers de Jumonville. His instructions were to deliver an ultimatum telling the Virginians to leave the country. When Washington first learned from Indians of Jumonville's approach, he sent half his force off in the wrong direction. Receiving further information, he took forty-seven men—half of what he had left at the fort—and went looking for the French party at night in a driving rain.

Before dawn the next day, May 28, the Virginians reached a friendly Indian camp, less seven men who had gotten lost in the dark. The rain had stopped, and Washington ordered his men to reload their muskets, while Indians scouted the location where they believed the French were camped. It was a rocky glen, and as the French were rousing from their sleep, Washington posted his troops around three sides of the hollow while the Indians closed off the only way out. Exactly what happened next has been the subject of debate ever since, but it is certain that Washington had no control over the events.

A shot rang out, then the Virginians fired at least two volleys down into the Frenchmen, who tried to retreat into the surrounding woods but were halted by the Indians. Washington had given no order to fire, but when a French officer called for quarter, he ordered a cease-fire. Resistance had been ragged, and only three Virginians were wounded and one dead; fourteen Frenchmen, including Jumonville, lay wounded at the bottom of the glen. The bleeding ensign tried to explain, through an interpreter, that his mission was peaceful, but before he could present his ultimatum an Indian leader tomahawked him, reached into his open skull, and pulled out the young officer's brain. That was the signal for the other Indians to begin slaughtering the wounded, scalping, beheading, and dismembering their helpless victims.

Washington, who had been a passive observer rather than a commander, came to himself and ordered his troops to surround and protect the French survivors, one wounded, the others not. He hustled twenty-one prisoners out of the glen while the Indians finished their work. A French fugitive who reached the Forks claimed that Washington had fired on a flag of truce—an atrocity of war. The massacre shook the young Virginian commander to his core. He sent a terse report back to Dinwiddie, papering over what had really happened, but he was fully aware that he had entirely lost control of a situation he assumed he could command by virtue of his rank alone.

Washington could more rightly be described as amateurish than as atrocious. When new arrivals just after the skirmish raised his manpower to about 400, he set out through the forest to attack Fort Duquesne and its garrison, grown to more than 2,000 men. For the next two weeks his little army struggled to move baggage, supplies, and nine swivel guns, and got nowhere. Wagons broke down, horses died, the men wore out, and the last Indian allies went home. On June 28, Washington learned that a large French and Indian force was headed his way, and he turned back. The retreat was worse than the advance, the men carrying whatever stuff could be salvaged after the last of the horses died. The whole force collapsed on the ground at Fort Necessity on July 1, 1754.

The next night it began to rain. Few of the men had any shelter while the valley turned into a swamp. By the morning of the third, fewer than 300 men were fit for duty. The enemy, about a thousand strong, attacked in late morning, led by a savvy veteran named Coulon de Villiers, Jumonville's older brother. Washington expected a conventional infantry slugfest of volleys and bayonet charges, but the French and Indians dispersed into the surrounding cover and blasted the Virginians with musket fire. The rain resumed, drowning the Virginians' muskets. The French, under trees, kept their powder dry and poured hell onto Fort Necessity. Musket balls smacked into its timbers, splatted into the sodden ground, and thunked into human flesh. Washington walked untouched through the storm of lead, not knowing what to do.

His lack of control became obvious at nightfall. Discipline disintegrated, and soldiers broke in to the rum supply. Over half of them were soon falling-down drunk, thanks to their fatigue and empty stomachs. De Villiers called on him to surrender and leave the territory. Using as intermediary the same Dutchman who had been with him at Fort LeBoeuf, Washington signed articles of surrender at midnight. He did not realize that he had just confessed to the murder of Jumonville—van Braam was not much of a translator.

Out of the 300 combatants at his disposal on July 3, Washington had lost thirty killed and seventy wounded, many severely; French and Indian losses were negligible, only three dead. The exhausted, hung-over survivors of Fort Necessity carried their wounded out of the place and prepared to drag themselves back to Virginia. The defeat was total. "Whatever may have been the feelings of Washington, he has left no record of them," the historian Francis Parkman observed. "His immense fortitude was doomed to severer trials in the future; yet perhaps this miserable morning was the darkest of his life. He was deeply moved by sights of suffering; and all around him were wounded men borne along in torture, and weary men staggering under the living load. His pride was humbled, and his young ambition seemed blasted in the bud. It was the fourth of July."[14]

I WISH EARNESTLY TO ATTAIN SOME KNOWLEDGE OF THE MILITARY PROFESSION

Leaving his bleeding and destitute corps at an Ohio Company post, Washington went on to Williamsburg, where he arrived in the middle of July, begging for supplies and medical care. He discovered that he was a Virginia hero despite the defeat. His performance had not been discreditable, given his inexperience and the meager support he had received from his government. He had demonstrated a remarkable ability to get men to follow him in impossible circumstances. Later he showed an equal talent for learning from experience. In the short run, the burgesses refused to cough up any more money, and other Virginians ignored Dinwiddie's calls to join new military units.

Dinwiddie appealed to other colonies to join in a renewed campaign against Fort Duquesne. They also ignored him. The governor ordered Washington to renew the attack, despite his protests that mere rumors that the campaign would resume caused men to desert. In the end, everyone still alive went home, with few exceptions. Washington went back to Mount Vernon, not returning to Williamsburg until the fall, for the regular meeting of the Assembly. There he learned that Major General Edward Braddock would arrive in the spring of 1755, with two regular regiments behind him. He would command all regular troops already in the colonies, along with all colonial levies. Some money and supplies already had reached Virginia.

The ambitious Dinwiddie was not about to wait for the professionals. With the governors of Maryland and North Carolina, he cooked up a plan for a campaign against Duquesne that fall. Maryland's governor, Horatio Sharpe, a veteran of the regular army, would command. Claiming he was following orders from London—this was a lie— Dinwiddie told Washington that the Virginia Regiment would be disbanded into its separate companies, to be attached to other units. Washington would drop in rank to captain. His pride wounded, he resigned and stormed back to Mount Vernon. Sharpe realized that Washington was the best military talent Virginia had. If he wanted to lead a campaign into the wilderness, with winter approaching, he needed the young fellow's knowledge and experience. He wrote to Mount Vernon, offering face-saving conditions to get Washington to rejoin, but the proud young man would not budge. Sharpe cancelled the expedition.[15]

When Braddock arrived in Virginia in late February 1755, Washington wasted no time skirting around Dinwiddie. "I must be ingenuous enough," he told Braddock's chief of staff, "to confess that . . . I wish earnestly to attain some knowledge of the military profession and, believing a more favourable oppertunity cannot offer than to serve under a gentleman of General Braddock's abilities and experience." When the

British commander and his aides met him, he charmed them with his eagerness and his knowledge of the western country. Washington got what he was after. Braddock, an aide wrote him, would be happy to take him along as a volunteer aide-de-camp, treated as if he were a colonel.[16]

Braddock was a squat, elderly soldier whose military experience had been mostly on the parade ground. He was a blunt, foul-mouthed officer who loved to argue for the sake of arguing. He was always short of money but scrupulously honest and as brave as a lion. "Desperate in his fortune, brutal in his behavior, obstinate in his sentiments," as a contemporary said of him, "he was still intrepid and capable." Benjamin Franklin remarked after his death that the general was a brave man who might have done well in a European war. "But he had too much self-confidence; too high an opinion of the validity of regular troops; too mean a one of both Americans and Indians."[17]

Braddock liked Washington and encouraged him to consider going after a commission in the regular army. During the course of the campaign he ensured that the Virginian understood its technical details, and they spent a remarkably large amount of time together. Stubborn as the general was, he invited suggestions from the young man, knowing that Washington possessed information about the country that he lacked. Braddock was the best teacher Washington ever had. From him the Virginian learned not only how to do things militarily but also how not to do them.

By May 1755, when Washington joined him at Frederick, Maryland, Braddock had assembled over 2,000 men, about half colonial and half regulars. The force included an artillery train, a baggage train, about 2,500 horses, and specialists in engineering and artillery. They were supported by hired teamsters, and trailed by a horde of camp followers. When the column set out for the mountains, it stretched nearly six miles, and it was in trouble from the outset. Braddock's brusque manners had alienated colonial authorities, and he had difficulty raising supplies and, especially, horses. American horses were not the purpose-bred draft animals he was used to in Europe and were too small and weak to haul the heavy artillery. The burden of clearing a road to Fort Duquesne, already a nearly impossible challenge, was doubled by the extra work—reducing hills, filling gullies—needed for the horses.

Braddock campaigned as he would have in Europe. He was going to besiege and assault a fort designed and built by professional engineers. He would need big guns and plenty of ammunition, a lot of men and horses, and food and supplies for all of them—all to be hauled along. Washington tried to talk the commander into sizing up the enemy and matching his plans to the landscape. He attempted, he wrote years later, to impress the general and his officers "with the necessity of opposing the nature of his defense to the mode of attack which, more than probably, he would experience from the *Canadian* French and their Indians." It was no use. "But so prepossessed were they in favor of *regularity* and *discipline,* and in such absolute contempt were *these people held,* that the admonition was suggested in vain."[18]

As the expedition entered the forested mountains, headway slowed to under two miles a day. By the middle of June men all along the column were dropping from dysentery, scouts and deserters were turning up dead and scalped, horses were giving out. Cursing the green hell he was trying to hack his way through, Braddock concluded that it would take another month to reach Duquesne. He called a council of war to decide what to do next. First, however, he asked Washington's advice. The Virginian proposed detaching about 1,200 light troops, taking the minimum supplies and artillery, to speed ahead. The rest of the army would follow with the wagons and heavy baggage. Braddock presented the proposal to the council, which ratified the plan but increased the numbers of guns, wagons, and beef cattle making the trip.

Washington then nearly collapsed from dysentery, aggravated by hemorrhoids. Braddock ordered him to bed, promising to summon him when it was time to engage the enemy. The old general marched out with the striking force. Washington, borne on a wagon, caught up with him on July 8, 1755, two miles from the Monongahela and twelve from Duquesne. Still shaky, the next morning he strapped some pillows to his saddle and rode up to join Braddock, who had sent the engineers across the river to make a road on the far bank. In early afternoon, he led the army across, Washington at his side. Their road was a narrow track flanked by dense underbrush and overhung by towering hardwood forest. Braddock's arrangements would have been perfect if this had been the open country of Europe. In this jungle he should have sent out scouts.

Instead, he strung small battalions of flank guards on either side. Closer in, the main bodies of troops marched in close-order columns of two, on either side of the central convoy of artillery, the artillery wagons, and the beef on the hoof. In the lead was a guide party, a few foot soldiers, and six horsemen. They were about twenty yards ahead of the advance party, consisting of a company and then a battalion in columns of three. They were followed by a work party, engineers and sappers who would rush ahead of the advance to clear any obstructions. Braddock and Washington rode behind this group, ahead of the main column. A strong battalion served as a rear guard.

All trudged along in good order until a ragged popping of musketry erupted in front of the column. It grew into a continuous roar that spread from the van down the length of the army, invisible musket fire from the woods on both sides. Braddock, with Washington close behind, rode forward to see what was afoot. They ran into the guides and the vanguard, fleeing back until they collided with the advance party and scrambled its ranks. Then the advance turned and ran, overtaken by panic.

A party of about 600 Indians and 300 French and Canadians had set out from Duquesne to find the British. They and Braddock's advance had stumbled into each other on the dark, narrow track. The advance had panicked, while the French and Indians coolly dispersed to flank the British column.

The officers drew their swords and ordered the fleeing redcoats to stop and re-form, "with as much success," Washington recalled, "as if we had attempted to have stopped the wild bears of the mountains." Ranks forming up in the column were driven into confusion, men literally falling over one another, when the fugitives from the advance ran into them. Balls tore into the tangled mass and took out officers on horseback.

Washington's horse dropped under him, and he caught another. The British regulars were so panic-stricken that they could not hear commands. After the initial stampede, they did what they had been trained to do—stand their ground and keep fighting—but they were haphazard about it. Most casualties, Washington thought, "received their shot from our own cowardly English soldiers who gathered themselves into a body, contrary to orders, ten or twelve deep, would then level, fire, and shoot down the men before them."[19]

The Virginians plunged into the woods on either side, to engage the enemy on his own terms, from behind trees and in open order. A British officer interpreted these maneuvers as desertion and ordered the colonials to re-form ranks and rejoin the center of the column. Seeing that his fellow Virginians had the solution to the army's problem, Washington offered to lead the provincial troops into the forest to take the fight to the enemy. Braddock, however, had other ideas.

The heaviest fire came from a rise on the column's right, and the general decided to charge the slope with bayonets. The officers restored some order, but the men refused to advance. One by one, including Braddock, the officers went down. Washington's second horse collapsed with a gunshot wound, and a ball carried away his hat. By this time his coat was thoroughly perforated. When he caught another mount, he was the senior officer on the scene still standing. The wounded Braddock summoned him and gave permission to charge the woods with the Virginians.

Washington sent the general to the rear on a cart, then remounted to consider the situation. The narrow road and the woods around it were choked in thick, stinking gunsmoke. He could see that he was losing more Virginians to British fire than to the enemy. The redcoats shot blindly into the woods, assuming that anyone there was the foe, although most of the colonials were just inside the treeline. There was nothing to do but order a retreat. The troops formed their depleted ranks and backed up, fighting, to the rear guard. That unit covered the army as it recrossed the river, and Washington posted the remaining men on a rise on the other side. The Battle of the Monongahela—which most Americans would call "Braddock's Defeat"—was over.

It was one of the worst catastrophes ever to befall British arms. Of the 1,200 men engaged, over 900 were dead or wounded. They littered the forest floor along with dead and dying horses and cattle and abandoned equipment. On the other side, twenty-three French and Canadians were dead, sixteen wounded; Indian figures likely were at the same low level. Already the blowflies, vultures, and scalping knives were hard at work.[20]

Washington was worn down by dysentery, exhaustion, and despair, but Braddock had work for him as night fell on July 9. He ordered him to ride forty miles eastward to where the second division was bringing up the heavy baggage, to get relief for what was left of the striking force. For the first few miles he rode through the battle's human refuse. "The shocking scenes which presented themselves in this night march are not to be described," he remembered. He rode past the dead and the dying, hearing "groans, lamentations, and cries." It was a journey of "gloom and horror" made more frightful by the darkness imposed by the thick forest cover.[21]

Washington reached the camp early in the morning of July 10, 1755, but news of the catastrophe had beaten him to the place. Officers and men were consumed by terror. Many privates were already deserting as fast as their legs could carry them, leaving behind a trail of dropped muskets and accoutrements. Washington ordered some relief wagons sent back, then collapsed with weakness.

Braddock—swaying on horseback because the men refused to carry him—appeared with the shattered striking force late in the day. He had only one thing in mind: to get out of this forested hell on earth. Anything that could not be carted off was destroyed. Ammunition, wagons, food, equipment, and other baggage were put to the torch, cannons smashed. The army then marched eastward as fast as it could haul itself.

The old general died just past the ruins of Fort Necessity, on the third day after the battle. Washington buried him in the road, then trooped the army over the grave to hide it from the Indians. "Thus," the Virginian mourned, "died a man whose good and bad qualities were intimately blended. . . . His attachments were warm, his enmities were strong, and, having no disguise about him, both appeared in full force."[22]

Never again would Washington find an older patron to offer the guidance and protection he had received from his half brother, from William Fairfax, and from the flawed but caring Braddock. He was twenty-three years old.[23]

THE CONSCIENCE OF A SOLDIER HAS SO LITTLE SHARE

Washington studied the military arts for the rest of his life. His starting point was Braddock's Defeat. It amazed him that such a large, strong, and well-trained army could have been so thoroughly shot to pieces. He had high praise for the British and colonial officers because of their steadfast bravery. The Virginian privates "behaved like men and died like soldiers." The fault for the catastrophe, he thought, rested on the regular British infantry, who performed like a mob of cowards.

The Virginia colonel was too hard on them. Their behavior grew out of the way they had been trained, combined with their being in a situation for which they had not been trained. Regulars had been drilled to stand in close order just yards from an enemy arrayed the same way. It took a stern kind of bravery to stand still while the enemy fired volleys into their ranks. Sergeants stalked back and forth keeping the lines straight, closing up vacancies left by dead or wounded. When so ordered, the soldiers would load and fire and step off into a bayonet charge toward a mass of enemy firing or charging back. All that took place amid blinding smoke and dying friends and deafening blasts of gunfire.

Regular soldiers spent a lifetime, under brutal discipline, learning to follow their orders as tight formations, not as individuals. When the officers went down at the Monongahela, the enlisted men did not know how to think for themselves, and had been trained not to. American soldiers had never had the kind of training and discipline that it took to make a regular. They saw themselves as individuals more than as cogs in a military machine, and believed they could figure out what to do without excessive supervision. The contrast between the two styles would vex Washington in his next war.

The young officer also drew conclusions about the importance of discipline to an army. He had imposed none at Jumonville's Glen or Fort Necessity, and the result was catastrophe. At the Monongahela, redcoat discipline had evaporated, causing another disaster. Orders from commanders, Washington decided, would not be obeyed unless they were enforced. An army had to be controlled ruthlessly, to produce unquestioning obedience in any situation.

There was something else: Braddock had proved disastrously that commanders did not have a monopoly on good ideas. He had been unusually receptive to suggestions from subordinates, but most often he dismissed their ideas and stood firm with his own original notions, because in European regular warfare, seniors gave orders and juniors obeyed them. Somewhere in the back of his mind, the young man absorbed a lesson in leadership—the commander should be willing to listen before making a final decision.

Washington returned to Virginia to find himself a famous man—not just locally but across the colonies and even in England. He was already well-known in France as the villain who had committed murder under a flag of truce. But the cool way he had ridden back and forth through the Battle of the Monongahela, untouched while his horses died and his coat was shredded, impressed friend and foe alike. He seemed as charmed a man as he was brilliant a leader, salvaging something from the catastrophe. He became known around the world as the "hero" of Braddock's Defeat.

Washington's transformation from British hero to American patriot began on August 14, 1755, when Dinwiddie commissioned him "Colonel of the Virginia Regiment and Commander in Chief of all forces now raised in the defense of His Majesty's Colony." He received authority to exercise his own judgment to "act defensively or offensively." This implemented an act of the Virginia Assembly, which voted £40,000 to raise and maintain a regiment of 1,000 men, along with 200 frontiersmen organized into four companies of "rangers," as irregular Indian fighters were called.[24]

Virginia faced catastrophe on a western frontier extending nearly 350 miles, as the Indians raided farms and settlements in the Shenandoah Valley. The remaining British regulars had marched off to Philadelphia as leaders in London and in the colonies considered what to do next. Over the next year the main theater of the war in America shifted northward toward Canada, while the killing of Jumonville grew into a world war, called the French and Indian War in America and the Seven Years' War everywhere else. The major powers of Europe entered the fray, their armies and navies fighting on that continent, and in India, the world's oceans, and the Caribbean islands.

Washington believed his province had been abandoned by London. But he would accept his new position only if the conditions were "honorable." He complained that he had "suffered much in my private fortune besides impairing one of the best of constitutions," meaning his health. The Assembly granted him £300 for his past expenditures, a salary of 30 shillings per day, £100 a year for expenses, and a 2 percent commission on all official purchases he made.[25]

Satisfied, Washington ordered new uniforms for himself, then designed those of the Virginia Regiment—blue with scarlet facings and silver trim—and placed orders for them also. He raised the thousand men and appointed the officers. He declared that officers would receive commissions by merit and not through influence, although he had to give in on that point in a few cases. Finally, he raised the ranger companies and ordered the construction of about two dozen small timber forts along the frontier.

It was a fine school for a budding commander in chief (Washington was the first American to carry that title). He sent out patrols against Indian raids, demonstrating that white Virginians could be every bit as savage as their native opponents. He ordered the lash and the occasional hanging for desertion and other infractions. He smoothed out conflicts between officers when the sexual customs of his own planter class ran up against the proprieties of the middle class. A typical case involved an officer who had poached another's servant girl and made her his mistress.

Washington instituted a training and disciplinary regimen for the Virginia Regiment that made it the finest body of light troops in America, pursuing open-order tactics, fast movements, and marksmanship. Its ways suited American conditions better than those of the line (heavy) troops that Braddock had led across the Monongahela. The Virginia rangers, who saw more action than the regiment, were as effective as those led by Robert Rogers farther northeast.

Washington quickly became discouraged, however, owing to lack of support and respect from British authorities. He concluded that he and his province had little stake in the war he had helped to start. It was just one of "the usual contests of empire and ambition." Virginians were pawns in somebody else's squabble, in which "the conscience of a soldier has so little share that he may properly insist upon his claims of rank, and extend his pretensions even to punctilio."[26]

Washington threatened to resign but was urged to visit higher commanders to clarify his position, and that of his troops, as members of the British army. He got nowhere on that score during his first trip in 1756, but the journey introduced him to the America that lay beyond Virginia. He visited the first cities he had ever seen, including Philadelphia, Boston, and Newport. He was overwhelmed by the goods available in those places, and spent beyond his means for his increasingly fine personal uniforms.

The commander in chief returned to Virginia after several weeks to find the war on the frontier raging, and decided not to resign. He took rangers and some militiamen out to meet Indians marauding through the Shenandoah. He could claim success in the bush, but most of his men were holed up in forts where they were of little use against the mobile enemy. Too often they were unpaid, ill-clad, and ready to quit. However, Washington's chief frustration was the refusal of London to grant him and his officers commissions in the royal army.

"If it should be said," he complained to Dinwiddie, "that the troops of Virginia are irregulars, and cannot expect more notice than other provincials, I must beg leave to differ." All they needed to make them regulars were commissions in the royal army. He and his men, he believed, were better at the American kind of war than any English snob in a red suit. It was therefore especially insulting that his officers and privates were paid less than British regulars who could not perform as well. "We cannot conceive," he railed, "that because we are Americans, we shou'd therefore be deprived of the benefits common to British subjects."[27]

Still Washington soldiered on, stemming the Indian tide from the west. He wanted to campaign against Fort Duquesne, the fount of the Indian war, but he could not do it with Virginia's resources alone. Finally, in April 1758 he learned that help was on the way. General John Forbes, a thirty-year veteran of British service, arrived in Pennsylvania with a regular force twice the size of the one Braddock had commanded, accompanied by his second in command, General Henry Bouquet. Their target was Fort Duquesne.

Washington offered his services and his troops, as well as Cherokee and Catawba allies he had enlisted in the Carolinas. Indians, Washington told Forbes, were "the only troops fit to cope with Indians on such ground." Forbes and Bouquet liked that idea and just about everything else Washington proposed to them. They appeared to regard the Virginians as the real professionals in this bloody business, and replaced their men's red coats with Virginia ranger uniforms. They also adopted Washington's bush-fighting tactics and put the Virginia Regiment in the vanguard of the expedition westward. They bought Washington's argument that "from long intimacy, and scouting in these woods, my men are as well acquainted with all the passes and difficulties as any troops that will be employed."[28]

The Virginian did not have his way in everything. He proposed that the approach to Duquesne should follow Braddock's road northwest out of Virginia. It was already cut and needed only minor clearing. What he was really after was to protect Virginia's interest in being the gateway to the West, realizing his and the Ohio Company's ambitions for land and profit over the mountains. He was not about to let Pennsylvania reap that harvest at Virginia's expense.

Forbes and Bouquet were competent and experienced, and they enjoyed the services of excellent engineers and quartermasters. Washington could and did learn a lot from them about campaign logistics. Their army was based at Carlisle, Pennsylvania, so it would be easier to cut a new road west than to move the whole affair south, then back north. Bouquet invited Washington to Carlisle to make his case, assuming that he would accept the final decision, whichever way it went. In the end, the British generals decided on a route west from Carlisle.

Washington had no choice but to go along. Privately he exploded in a blizzard of insubordinate letters to officials in Williamsburg and officers of the Ohio Company. The campaign, he claimed, was doomed. As the expedition crawled westward through the fall, his language became inexcusable. He accused Forbes and Bouquet of incompetence. The march was too slow, and the army would be caught by snows in the mountains. It would never reach the French fort. If there was another massacre, it would not be Washington's fault. It was a disgraceful performance, as he understood years later, when it appeared that insubordinate officers were plotting against him. And he was wrong on every count.

The lead elements of the column reached the vicinity of Fort Duquesne early in November, with no snow falling. Braddock's ghost hovered over the expedition, as Forbes called a council of war to decide what to do next. Washington counseled against an immediate attack, owing to lack of intelligence. Forbes agreed to postpone action. Washington smugly wrote to Williamsburg that the campaign was stalled, just as he had predicted.

On November 12, 1758, the Virginians stumbled into a patrol out of the fort and became disorganized, companies firing on each other. Washington knocked muskets aside with his sword in a hail of lead that brought down dozens of his men. The French patrol hightailed it for home after the Virginians captured three of them. The prisoners described the fort as deteriorating, undermanned, and ripe for the picking. Forbes ordered an advance, with the Virginians in the lead. They found the place abandoned and partly destroyed. Leaving behind a small guard, the Forbes-Bouquet expedition returned to its various homes. Washington led his Virginians down Braddock's road, then rode on to Mount Vernon.

With the French gone from the Forks and their fortunes falling toward the loss of Canada to the British in 1760, the Indians lost support for their raids on the frontier. They had backed the wrong horse in a war whose scale they could not have imagined. The Virginia borderlands became more peaceful, settlers returned, and others ventured across the mountains to carve out homesteads.

Washington resigned his commission at the end of December 1758. His regimental officers regretted "the loss of such an excellent commander, such a sincere friend, and so affable a companion!" They remembered, "In our earliest infancy, you took us under your tuition, trained us up in the practice of that discipline which alone can constitute good troops." They praised his impartiality, justice, and ability to recognize and reward merit, which encouraged them to succeed. "How rare it is to find those amiable qualifications blended together in one man!" they raved. "How great the loss of such a man!" His service in the regiment, he replied modestly, would always be "the greatest happiness" of his life, which would in the future give him "the most pleasing reflections."29

I AM NOW EMBARKED ON A
TEMPESTUOUS OCEAN

Washington suggested that any progress in the war made without his help could be credited to chance. "The scale of fortune in America," he said of the fall of Quebec in 1759, "is turned greatly in our favor, and success is become the boon companion of our fortunate generals." As for himself, "I am now, I believe, fixed at this seat with an agreeable consort of life, and hope to find more happiness in retirement than I ever experienced amidst a wide and bustling world."30

This "seat" was Mount Vernon. He had already begun to expand it into the stately mansion familiar to later generations, but it was some years yet in the building. The "consort" was his new bride, Martha Dandridge Custis, the richest widow in Virginia, whom he married on January 6, 1759. She was not the first potential wife he had courted, but she best suited him, affectionately as well as economically. She was a small, pretty woman with a rounded figure, tiny hands and feet, a noble brow and equally noble Roman nose, a strong chin, and large eyes beneath wide eyebrows. She had a retreating, almost timid manner, which cloaked steadfast courage. She bore up through a lifetime of personal losses and George's frequent absences.

After Washington died, at his request Martha burned their personal letters. All third-party evidence suggests that the two of them learned early on to love each other deeply. That was normal then, when love followed rather than preceded most marriages. Their union lasted forty years. George was a loving and devoted husband and an affectionate guardian to her two children. They had no children together, although she was obviously fertile. By the time she was past childbearing age, he had concluded that he was sterile. That gnawed at him, but he stoically accepted it. Instead, he indulged her children, grandchildren, and nieces and nephews.

Martha's chubby boy, John Parke ("Jackie") Custis, grew up spoiled, provided with everything George had lacked in his own childhood. Washington gave the youngster a wealth of material goods and excellent tutors and formal education. Never having to struggle for anything, he refused to put out much effort on his own behalf, and failed in college. He married well at age nineteen, in 1773, and Washington set the couple up on one of the inherited Custis estates. The boy ran it into the ground and died in 1781. He left behind grandchildren whom George and Martha adopted.

The girl, Martha Parke ("Patsy") Custis, was a sadder story. She suffered epileptic seizures from an early age. Despite her stepfather's best efforts to provide care through physicians and spas, one of the seizures killed her in 1773, when she was seventeen. Martha was devastated and wore mourning clothes for the next year.

Besides the children, Martha brought to the marriage three plantations along the York River totaling 18,000 acres, worked by over 200 (eventually 300) slaves; she was worth at least £30,000. The marriage made Washington the owner of one of these "dower" plantations and, as guardian of the children, the manager of the other two. Added to Mount Vernon's 3,000 acres, which he enlarged to 6,500 acres by 1775, the property made the Washington family one of the wealthiest in Virginia.

Like his forebears, George had married up in the world, and like them, his lust for real estate kept him land-poor.

Washington's hunger for other goods did not help his situation. He went on a multiyear spending spree, outfitting Mount Vernon with the latest in luxuries imported from London. He kept Martha and himself elegantly clothed in English fashions. His lavish tastes outspent his income from tobacco sold on consignment in England, and by 1765 he was in arrears to his London agent. It was a rude awakening. Besides curbing his spendthrift ways, it made him think about the relation between Britain and her colonies. The economic system known as mercantilism, he concluded, was designed to exploit the colonists and keep them in debt.

In 1766 Washington ceased to plant tobacco at Mount Vernon, although he continued to grow it on the Custis plantations. He turned to the production of wheat, corn, and flax and built a gristmill to produce flour and income from milling for others. He bought fishing boats and built a salting plant. He acquired sheep and set up a weaving mill to produce and sell linsey-woolsey, part linen (flax) and part wool. He even bought a small ship to carry his produce overseas, and systematically weaned himself from dependence on the mother country.

This process had a political dimension. Washington claimed his veteran's rights to land warrants west of the mountains, and bought warrants from other veterans. He helped to found the Mississippi Land Company, and made other ventures into wilderness real estate. He looked into opening a route to the West via the Potomac River. These activities ran afoul of King George III's Proclamation of 1763, forbidding English settlement west of the Appalachians. "I can never look upon that proclamation in any other light," Washington rightly observed, "than as a temporary expedient to quiet the minds of the Indians."[31]

The royal government declared the land between the mountains and the Mississippi River a vast Indian reservation, to end a widespread Indian war that had broken out even before the end of the Seven Years' War in 1763. Settlers had crossed the mountains in growing numbers, and agents for speculators such as Washington also showed up in the West. The first to rise against the white tide were the Cherokees in the Carolinas. Soon there was a general war involving many tribes and nations, some of them in a confederation organized by the Ottawa leader Pontiac. To the government, Indians killing individual settlers was bad enough, but the power of the uprising was such that it wiped out several military posts. Pontiac came close to taking Detroit in the winter of 1763–64.

The proclamation was supposed to reassure the Indians, but the renewed peace was short-lived, and it provoked American disrespect for the king's authority. Washington was not the only colonial who treated this attempt to stop history as a joke. He and others proceeded with their plans in the West, the Indians be damned. By 1770 he had claimed 20,000 acres in the Great Kanawha River valley, and sent settlers there to hold the land.

The king's standing in America was further eroded by a series of parliamentary blunders that began in 1765 with the Stamp Act. Each in turn was defied in the colonies and had to be repealed. The home government, heavily in debt from the Seven Years' War, was desperate to raise money and had gone about as far as it could in Britain without provoking rebellion there. The colonists were told that they must help pay for the war and for their own defense. They believed that they had already paid their share, in blood and treasure alike. Moreover, they did not feel themselves obliged to honor taxes imposed on them without their having a say in Parliament—the "taxation without representation" issue.

By the late 1760s, people in several colonies were attacking tax collectors. Parliament reacted to suppress colonial unrest, but each time it retreated, making the situation worse. Washington served in the Virginia Assembly during the whole period. In May 1769, he submitted a proposal for a colony-wide boycott of trade with England. The law passed, but it was not widely observed.

Washington emerged as a conscience of his colony. Men worried about Britain's colonial policies gravitated toward Mount Vernon. British backpedaling on nearly all its acts postponed a crisis, until in 1773 the Boston Tea Party defied one revenue measure that Parliament had not repealed. In 1774, to punish the home of that riot, the government passed what became known as the Intolerable Acts. They closed the port of Boston, imposed martial law on Massachusetts, and sent an occupation force.

Washington, along with other Americans—they were becoming that at this point—was outraged. He told George Fairfax that "the cause of Boston . . . ever will be considered as the cause of America." There was a conspiracy, he alleged, "to fix the right and practice of taxation" on the colonists. To Fairfax's brother he charged that the government planned to "make us as tame, & abject slaves, as the blacks we rule over with such arbitrary sway." He knew slavery firsthand and did not want to be reduced to it.[32]

Washington was by August 1774 a leader of the protest movement in Virginia and could be counted on to do the right thing. He became one of seven delegates from the province to the First Continental Congress in Philadelphia. There he mostly kept his silence during the debates, as he had in the House of Burgesses, but he opposed the Intolerable Acts and favored as retaliation a continent-wide boycott of British imports. Before he left town, he looked into the price of muskets, bought new trim for his uniforms, and ordered some military books.

Back home at Mount Vernon, Washington tended to his affairs, pursued his claims in the West, and sent a party of slaves to start dredging the upper Potomac. In March 1775 a second Virginia Convention assembled, heard Patrick Henry deliver his "liberty or death" tirade, and sent Washington to the Second Continental Congress, which considered how to respond to the British invasion of Massachusetts. Wearing his uniform, he sat on Congress' military committees, and gave his professional advice.

Shooting broke out at Lexington and Concord in Massachusetts on April 19, 1775. On May 10, renegade forces under Ethan Allen and Benedict Arnold seized Fort Ticonderoga, in northern New York, from its British caretakers. Alarmed delegates wanted it returned to royal authorities. Members from New England blocked that—Ticonderoga sat on the main invasion route from Canada to their territory.

Congress considered the appointment of a commander in chief—the title was Washington's suggestion—to lead colonial resistance. Various colonies were sending volunteers to Massachusetts, but what became the Continental Army had not yet been settled on. Besides Washington, there were not many candidates for the post. Washington had the background, the costume, and the bearing—John Adams pointed out that he was the tallest man in the room. In addition, a Virginian commander would make Massachusetts' struggle a continental one.

On June 14, 1775, Congress authorized the first parts of what would become the Continental Army—six companies of frontier riflemen from

Pennsylvania, Maryland, and Virginia. Adams moved that Washington be appointed commander in chief, debate began, and Washington modestly retreated to his boardinghouse. The next day he was unanimously elected commander. He returned to Congress on the sixteenth and learned that Congress had assumed control "of the forces raised and to be raised in the defense of American liberty." Then he was asked if he would accept "supreme command."

Washington rose, took a paper from his pocket, and read his acceptance. He pledged to fulfill his duties to the full extent of his powers. "But," he cautioned, "lest some unlucky event should happen, unfavorable to my reputation, I beg it may be remembered, by every gentleman in this room, that I, this day, declare with the utmost sincerity, I do not think myself equal to the command I am honored with." He concluded by refusing to accept pay, asking only that Congress reimburse his expenses.[33]

This display of modesty overwhelmed its audience. When it was printed in the newspapers it electrified the world. This was no self-appointed rebel general, waving a flag and howling for blood. This was George Washington, leader of his people, talking in a voice they trusted, ready to defend their homes, forced to do so against his better nature.

It took Washington two days to work up enough nerve to tell Martha what he had agreed to, and apologize for the burdens it would put on her. He did not know how long it would be before he returned home.

"I am now embarked on a tempestuous ocean," the commander in chief told another relative, "from, whence, perhaps, no friendly harbor is to be found."[34]

THREE

This Great Military Arrangement

(JULY 1775-JUNE 1777)

There were a king with a large jaw and a queen with a plain face on the
throne of England; there were a king with a large jaw and a queen with a fair
face on the throne of France. In both countries it was clearer than crystal
to the lords of the state preserves of loaves and fishes that things
in general were settled forever.

—CHARLES DICKENS

Washington reached the army around Boston on July 3,
1775. It was strung along an arc from the Mystic
River above Charlestown on the left to the
Dorchester Heights southeast of Boston on the right.
After the Battle of Bunker Hill two weeks earlier, the British commander,
General Thomas Gage, was not inclined to make another sally. Washington
had known Gage during the Monongahela campaign, where he commanded a battalion. Now the English general had become passive. That
was difficult to understand, because the British faced not an army but
a mob.

To begin with, there was the unmilitary way the Americans housed
themselves, in holes in the slopes or in "booths and huts of various shapes
and sizes" scattered among the earthworks. As one of them described the

rebel quarters, some were made of boards or sailcloth or a combination of the two, others of stone and turf, yet others of brush. "Some are thrown up in a hurry," he said, "and look as if they could not help it."[1]

The commander in chief needed to know how many men lived in the slovenly housing. He had been told to expect 24,500 troops. He asked for an exact figure and heard that somewhere between 18,000 and 20,000 men were on hand. He insisted on a precise count and kept insisting. There were 16,600 enlisted men, but only 14,328 were present and fit for duty. "Could I have conceived," he roared, "that what ought, and, in a regular army, would have been done in an hour, would employ eight days," he would have reported his strength to Congress immediately. Instead, he had been "drilled on from day to day" until he was "ashamed to look back at the time which has elapsed."[2]

The truth hit him like a rock: this was going to be either a very short war or a very long one.

THEY WERE BRIBED INTO THE PRESERVATION OF THEIR LIBERTIES

The day after he arrived Washington announced that the "Troops of the United Provinces of North America" were thereafter under the authority of the Continental Congress. Congress' appointed commander in chief was taking charge.[3]

He gave early attention to uniforms. "To prevent mistakes" in telling officers apart, he ordered that the general officers and their aides each wear a "ribband" across his breast, between his coat and waistcoat. Each rank had its own specified color. Until Congress provided clothing, the "ribbands" (sashes) were as far as he could go on uniforms.[4]

On July 25, the ten companies of frontier riflemen authorized by Congress began to arrive in camp. They were as tough as men came— some had marched 600 miles in three weeks. Their weapons—rifles rather than smoothbore muskets—caused a sensation. They were slow to load, but their balls traveled more accurately and three times as far as a musket ball.[5]

The riflemen's long arms were not what impressed Washington, however. Rather, it was their clothing—off-white, knee-length frocks called "hunting shirts," made of linen or linsey-woolsey, topped off by wideawake hats. On August 7, 1775, he asked Congress to give each man a hunting shirt, and spent the next few years badgering the legislature to outfit the army in the practical frocks. They were replaced officially after 1779 by the familiar blue-and-buff uniform, but until late in the war if the Continental Army had any uniformity at all, it was hunting shirts.[6]

Washington's greater problem was to make an army out of a mob. The New England troops were mostly militiamen, accustomed to electing and firing their own officers. He recast them into something resembling military formations and fired and appointed regimental officers on his own. Congress had granted him a modified version of Britain's articles of war, and he imposed fierce discipline. He ordered improvements to the fieldworks, and foot and boat patrols. He issued orders for drills and other training, with indifferent results. The low quality of the officer corps hampered him at every step. Congress let him appoint his own staff, but it retained the power to commission general officers; they were a mixed bunch throughout the war. Washington's own military experience was in the past, and he pored over books and treatises, trying to become a proficient supreme commander.[7]

Before he left Philadelphia Washington talked two men into joining his personal staff, the first of thirty-two aides who would serve him during the war. Joseph Reed, a well-educated Philadelphia lawyer, became his military secretary. Thirty-four years old, he was intelligent, energetic, and a craftsman with the language. But he was torn between the army and his family and business at home. He came and went until he became adjutant general in June 1776. A few months later, he became the first trusted officer to betray his commander in chief.[8]

Thomas Mifflin was Washington's first aide-de-camp. From a family of Philadelphia merchants, he was thirty-one when he accompanied the general to Boston. His business experience caused Washington to appoint him quartermaster general in August, but he turned out to be incompetent. A born schemer and an ambitious politician, he too betrayed his commander.[9]

Washington soon became a better judge of character in choosing his closest aides. He surrounded himself with much younger, bright, energetic assistants. Known as "His Excellency's boys," they were loyal to a fault, captured by the general's commanding personality. Some of them caused him problems, however.

Aides he could appoint. His senior generals were out of his hands, because Congress kept to itself the power to hire and fire general officers. It told the commander in chief to hold councils of war with them over every major decision. He was also required to consult directly with committees of Congress.[10]

The second in command at Boston, Major General Artemas Ward, forty-eight years old, was a stern-looking man, medium tall, with a stout body and a slow way of speaking. A Harvard graduate, his military experience was a failed attack on Fort Ticonderoga in 1758. He directed the Battle of Bunker Hill from a sickbed and felt insulted when Washington superseded him. Products of alien cultures, they fired nasty darts at each other until Ward resigned a year later.[11]

Third in command was Major General Charles Lee, the most experienced soldier in the American army, and also the strangest. Tall and so thin that he looked as if he could stay dry in the rain, he had a startling hooked nose that parted the air before him. He was unusually dirty even for his time, looking as if he had been dragged by a tornado, smelly, and swarming with fleas. He was a constant talker and an entertaining one despite a shockingly obscene vocabulary.

Born in England in 1731, Lee served as a lieutenant in Braddock's expedition, where Washington first met him, then as a captain in the Mohawk Valley. He was seriously wounded during the attack on Ticonderoga but returned to his regiment for the capture of Niagara and Montreal. He rose to lieutenant colonel through several campaigns in British service, became a major general in the service of the king of Poland, and earned another wound. Lee migrated to Virginia in 1773 and bought an estate in western Virginia. There he built a timber farmhouse as bachelor quarters for himself, two slaves, and an unruly pack of dogs. For the rest of his life, his dogs were with him, orbiting him like a mob of barking planets.

Lee became an effective pamphleteer for the American cause. He was witty, charming, and intelligent and knew the latest liberal ideas, winning him fans in Congress. He was suggested for commander in chief, and he wanted the post, but he was British. Washington welcomed him into the Continental Army to take advantage of his military experience. At Boston, Lee fulfilled his promise, riding the whole length of the American lines daily, calling himself the "scamperer-general."[12]

Washington's other two major generals in the summer of 1775 were, like him, experienced mostly as Indian fighters in days past. Philip Schuyler of New York and Israel Putnam of Connecticut were appointed for geographical balance. They were competent enough, Putnam especially as a recruiter, Schuyler for his political influence in New York. But both Putnam, at fifty-seven, and Schuyler, forty-five, were softened by age and comfortable living.[13]

Charles Lee, a contemporary caricature. A talented, erratic, and maligned man, he was recognized at the time as the strangest general in the war. (AUTHOR'S COLLECTION)

The eccentric Lee was a bomb waiting to go off in Washington's headquarters. So was another British veteran of the Braddock campaign, Horatio Gates. The bastard son of a British duke and his housemaid, he served with distinction in the Seven Years' War but could not rise above major in an army dominated by aristocrats. At Washington's urging, he moved to Virginia in 1772. Congress made him adjutant general, with a brigadier's rank. Gates was forty-seven years old, squat, with a stooped posture, ruddy cheeks, thinning gray hair, and spectacles perched at

Horatio Gates, by C.W. Peale, 1782. As a general Gates got lucky once at Saratoga, became involved in intrigues against Washington, and ended his career with a spectacular disaster at Camden.
(INDEPENDENCE NATIONAL HISTORICAL PARK)

the end of his long nose. His manner was that of a fussy schoolmaster, and the troops called him "Granny Gates." Like Lee, he thought that he should have been appointed to the top command. He was an unenergetic man who as a general got lucky once, turned on Washington, and ended his career with a notorious disaster.[14]

Using the material at hand, Washington set out to organize the army. As troops from other states arrived, the Continental Army fielded thirty-eight regiments of varying size (600 to 1,000 men). Washington reorganized them into six brigades (usually of six regiments each) and into divisions of two brigades each. Brigades, divisions, and regiments were terms identifying administrative headquarters. The tactical designation of the regiment was "battalion"; it was the main unit of maneuver in an army that Washington intended would fight as a tactical whole. He followed European doctrine, as presented in the treatises he read.[15]

Washington tried to mold his army into shape by harsh means, copying British practice. Trials were frequent, and punishments were severe. Almost any infraction earned the lash. As far as his privates were concerned, he was a hard man.[16]

"An army," Napoleon famously remarked, "marches on its stomach." Washington would have agreed, because too often his services of supply failed him. Supply was the most chaotic operation of the Continental Army throughout the war. Except for small arms, artillery, and ammunition, the troops wanted for nearly everything. They suffered from short-ages of food, forage, fuel, straw, clothing, blankets, shoes, and vehicles. America was not ready for war and never became so. The supply problems arose from unsound currencies, limited domestic manufactures, wavering popular support, congressional and state interference or inaction, and plain ineptitude. Competent staff officers moved to line commands, because capable commanders were in even shorter supply. Departments of the quartermaster, purchasing, clothing, and subsistence collided with each other. Medical services were poor.[17]

Supply shortages were especially galling around Boston, because Massachusetts was a land of plenty. Yet local and state authorities were noticeably uncooperative in meeting the army's needs, and in recruiting state troops they competed with Congress. They gave higher bonuses and fatter rations, especially of spruce beer and rum, than offered by the Continental Army. When the New England troops neared the ends of their enlistments late in 1775, most planned to go home or join the state forces, so Congress raised the Continental ration. "Never," Washington addressed the men, "were soldiers whose pay and provision have been so abundant and ample [as now provided]. . . . There is some reason to dread that the enemies to New England's reputation may hereafter say . . . that they were bribed into the preservation of their liberties."[18]

Washington aggravated his difficulties by failing to get along with New Englanders. He was a provincial Virginian and their ways were alien to him, while they resented his intruding into their territory and their war. Above all, New England egalitarianism was contrary to Washington's patrician beliefs. He wanted to build an army founded on a strict hierarchy from commander down through the ranks to privates. New Englanders tended to be democratic about everything. He unwisely derided them at his dinner table and in letters, and his remarks leaked, causing an uproar in Congress, until he promised to "reform" himself.[19]

The commander in chief had a larger problem with the quality of officers, wherever they came from. Washington believed that military status should reflect social status, with "common" men serving in the ranks and middle- and upper-class officers supervising them. Unfortunately, few officers had any supervisory experience, military or otherwise. That was reflected in the poor quality of the winter housing in the early years of the war. It was not for want of skills. The difficulty was a failure to

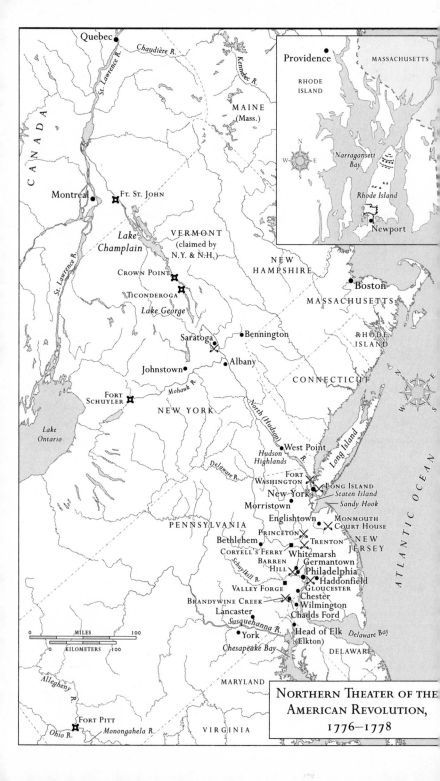

NORTHERN THEATER OF THE
AMERICAN REVOLUTION,
1776–1778

organize and direct the work, because company officers left everything to unsupervised sergeants, following the British example.[20]

The weaknesses in the officer corps left the Continental Army substantially untrained. Men could learn from each other how to load and fire a musket, but performing maneuvers as units was on another plane altogether. There were no standard tactical manuals, although they would have been of little help without a tradition of supervised training.[21]

The mob hoping to become an army stared across the harbor at the British, who stared back. Neither side was willing or able to attack the other. Washington—lonely, unhappy in this strange place, and pining for Mount Vernon—was thoroughly discouraged. Such army as he had was about to dissolve around him at the end of 1775, when most enlistments expired. He offered Congress a goal of a 20,000-man Continental Army—identified as such, and not with the states. That was a reasonable number to hope to recruit for 1776, but by November only about a thousand of the present army had proved willing to sign on for the long term. Washington would have to disband one army and form another in the face of the enemy.[22]

He complained to Reed about the "dearth of public spirit and want of virtue" to be found "in this great military arrangement." He added, "Could I have foreseen what I have, and am likely to experience, no consideration upon earth should have induced me to accept this command."[23]

Washington talked like that when he was depressed, but he was not one to abandon any responsibility. He would carry on. He needed something to get the war moving, a dramatic gesture that would inspire men to stay with him, and others to join him. Or maybe he needed a miracle.

A miracle is what he got, in the roly-poly figure of Henry Knox.

I THINK THE GAME IS PRETTY NEAR UP

$\mathcal{T}$he stalemate around Boston bid fair to go on forever. Washington hatched one complicated plan after another for an attack on the city, only to meet objections from the other generals. The rebels needed to find a way to outgun the enemy, so the twenty-five-year-old Knox went to Washington with an idea.

Knox was the biggest general in the war, tipping the scale at 300 pounds. He was agile enough, but hard on horses. He was as jolly as the proverbial fat man, with a megaphone voice, hearty personality, genteel manners, and fancy dress, and had lost two fingers of his left hand when his shotgun blew up during a bird hunt.

Knox had witnessed the Boston Massacre of 1770 and hated the British. He had joined a Boston militia company at age eighteen, began importing books, and opened a shop he called the London Book-Store, which attracted redcoat officers. There he kept his ears open, learning as much as he could about military affairs in general, and about the occupiers' intentions in particular, to pass on to rebel leaders in the city. He fought at Bunker Hill and accompanied Ward to the siege lines around Boston. He kept reading, concentrating on the art and science of artillery, and became a pioneer in field artillery tactics. He had another valuable military talent—he was a born scrounger.[24]

Knox told Washington that there were about five dozen big guns and mortars at Fort Ticonderoga, and volunteered to go get them. On November 17, 1775, Washington appointed him colonel of the (nonexistent) Continental Regiment of Artillery and sent him on his way. Knox left Cambridge a few days later with a small escort and reached Ticonderoga on December 5 in head-high snow. He selected forty-three heavy cannons, fourteen mortars, and two howitzers, at a total weight of nearly 200,000 pounds, to which he added shot and a barrel of flints. He and his men felled trees and built forty-two heavy sledges, and he rounded up eighty yoke of oxen. They dragged it all to the southern end of Lake George by January 7, 1776, with 300 miles yet to go. Always impatient, Knox pulled his train east through steep grades and heavy snows in the Berkshire Mountains at a remarkable rate. He had his "noble train of artillery" in Cambridge by the twenty-fifth of January.[25]

His work was not done. The best place to put the guns was the Dorchester Heights, which commanded the city and harbor. Getting them emplaced there involved a prodigy of construction, hauling, and heavy lifting in an area exposed to enemy fire. Virtually all this work took place secretly in one night, March 4, and the British woke up to find themselves literally under Knox's guns. Delayed only by a storm, Major General Sir William Howe, who had replaced Gage, sailed away with his army on March 17, 1776. Washington had driven the enemy out of Boston.[26]

That triumph accompanied a disaster for the American cause—the invasion of Canada. Congress hoped that 80,000 French *habitants* in Quebec would welcome rescue from British occupation. Most of them would not.

Schuyler launched the campaign during the summer of 1775. Slowed by ill health and not knowing what he was doing anyway, he sent about a thousand men under Brigadier General Richard Montgomery, a veteran soldier from New York, toward Montreal, then on to Quebec. Washington sent another thousand under the pugnacious Brigadier General

Henry Knox, by C.W. Peale, 1784. A bookseller turned soldier, Knox was a pioneering genius in field-artillery tactics, and the largest general in the war. (INDEPENDENCE NATIONAL HISTORICAL PARK)

Benedict Arnold of Connecticut, who took along a company of riflemen under a Virginian captain, Daniel Morgan, to approach Quebec through the Maine woods. Both expeditions were poorly planned and supplied, through nearly impassable country, while most soldiers' enlistments would expire at the end of the year.

A series of horrendous ordeals brought one small success after another, until Montgomery took Montreal, where he learned that Arnold was on his way to Quebec. They met there in December and besieged the place in howling winter weather with supplies running out. On New Year's Eve, they assaulted the works at night during a blizzard. Montgomery's face was shot away, Arnold took a ball in the leg, and Morgan stormed the place almost single-handedly and was captured. The disaster was compounded by Congress' determination to send thousands more troops northward. When the ice broke and British ships landed troops in Canada in May 1776, the American armies retreated. The campaign had cost 5,000 casualties, along with tons of supplies and money.[27]

The evacuation of Boston was the last good news the American cause received for nearly a year. Congress passed a series of laws to give Washington his 20,000-man army, but the measures made recruitment more difficult. Washington's manpower hovered around 9,000 men through the summer. After they were kicked out of New York, however, "the contagion of desertion . . . raged after the manner of a plague," in Washington's words. He was down to just over 5,000 men at the end of November, and half of them were slated to go home the next day. Unless the new army was recruited quickly, Washington warned Congress, "*I think the game is pretty near up.*"[28]

Few people, despite the Declaration of Independence on July 4, wanted to join an army with a record of defeats and disasters. After the British left Boston, Washington marched to New York to face 30,000 redcoats and Hessians, as well as a large fleet commanded by General Howe's brother, Admiral Richard Lord Howe. Washington unwisely placed the majority of his troops on Long Island, in front of a superior opponent who commanded the sea. On August 27, 1776, the enemy assaulted the American lines. Washington's position was too long, and his left flank hung in the air. The British turned it, capturing a new major general, John Sullivan.

The American army should have been trapped, but a change in weather allowed Washington to evacuate under cover of night and fog and reestablish himself on Manhattan. His officers disagreed about whether to stand there, or retreat. Lee—recently returned from a successful defense of Charleston, South Carolina, against a British attack earlier in the summer—and another new major general, Nathanael Greene, wanted to get onto solid ground north of the island. In the middle of September, a British force under Sir Henry Clinton landed on Manhattan and drove the Americans northward to Harlem Heights. There entrenched resistance and murderous fire from Pennsylvanian riflemen stopped the advance. Among Clinton's subordinates was General Charles Lord Cornwallis, a veteran of Minden.

As the enemy continued probing, Washington evacuated Manhattan except for Fort Washington at its northern tip. He kept a garrison there at the urging of Greene, who had changed his mind about making a stand on the island. Cornwallis' redcoats and Hessians attacked in November 1776, suffering heavy casualties before they overran the rebel position. Afterward, infuriated Hessians bayoneted many of the prisoners. Washington and Greene watched the disaster from Fort Lee on the New Jersey shore. Greene raged. Washington wept, "with the tenderness of [a] child," said another officer.[29]

It appeared that the cause was lost. The dwindling army retreated across New Jersey, desertion rampant. The militia simply disappeared. Washington was down to about 5,000 men before he got out of the state.

Meanwhile, Gates (now a major general) and Lee became rebellious. Gates openly criticized Washington's alleged lack of competence, Lee his indecisiveness. Lee had led part of the army toward Morristown, and once the retreat began Washington ordered him to rejoin the main body. First Lee ignored the orders, then responded with excuses. Finally he headed toward Trenton. On December 13, he and the dogs were captured by British dragoons, betrayed by loyalists in a tavern where he spent the night.[30]

Lee left behind another bitter blow for the commander in chief. On November 29, Washington received a letter from Lee addressed to his adjutant general, Joseph Reed, and opened it expecting some news of Lee's whereabouts. Instead, Lee thanked Reed for an "obliging, flattering letter." He agreed with Reed's complaints about "that fatal indecision of mind which in war is a much greater disqualification than stupidity." The words were Lee's, but clearly they echoed Reed's, and they referred to Washington. He forwarded the letter to Reed and apologized for opening it accidentally. He knew that the younger man would resign out of embarrassment.

The wound Washington suffered from this betrayal was still bleeding years later. He explained to the belatedly apologetic Reed that his "unreserved manner" toward the aide entitled him to his honest advice, and Reed's censuring his conduct to another was so disloyal that he "was not a little mortified at it." At the time, he wondered whether he could trust anybody around him.[31]

There was disagreement in the British command on what to do after Washington retreated across the Delaware in early December 1776. Clinton wanted to go all out to obliterate the Continental Army and take Philadelphia. But supply lines reached all the way back to England, and the troops were short of everything, so the Howes contented themselves with taking New Jersey out of the war. British and Hessian troops fanned out over the state, ousting people from their homes amid looting, murder, burnings, and gang rapes. Where formerly the Crown had retained a fair measure of loyalty, now New Jersey was ready to rise in fury.

In a fit of panic, Congress authorized a fantastic army of eighty-eight regiments, over 60,000 men. Washington was optimistic enough to detach officers and men to oversee recruitment, but after he had consolidated his forces between Philadelphia and Trenton, he faced more expiring enlistments along with desertions. Unless something happened, he would be down to about 1,500 men on January 1, 1777.[32]

Washington solved his problem with his most dramatic action of the war. On Christmas night he led the troops across the ice-choked Delaware River north of Trenton, then down the east bank to attack the Hessian garrison there at dawn. His plan of attack was too complicated, with too many elements supposed to separate and come together on schedule. But he was still learning—and demonstrating that he could learn. The men performed splendidly, and surprise was complete. There was a sharp fight in the streets, shortened by Knox's gunnery. The Americans bagged hundreds of prisoners, along with small arms, ammunition, cannons, and supplies, which they ferried back across the river.[33]

Washington's success at Trenton was electric. The German troops withdrew from all their posts on the Delaware, while Cornwallis left New York to set things right. He had no chance, because a general uprising began across the state, provoked by the savage occupation. The American cause was reinspired, and volunteers flocked to Washington's camp. He received authority to appoint and dismiss all officers below brigadier, to impress supplies, and to offer incentives for men to reenlist for the duration. About half of them did, and with them and partisan support he shot up a British detachment at Princeton on February 3, 1777. Cornwallis gave up most of New Jersey and returned to New York.[34]

The Continental Army went into winter quarters at Morristown. From the New Jersey hills, Washington watched the redcoats and Hessians huddled around New York. Near the end of May 1777, his spies brought him word that the enemy was up to something, possibly an attack on Philadelphia, so he marched his troops toward the capital. In midsummer, it appeared that the redcoats would move into southeastern

Pennsylvania, so Washington rode into the city to confer with members of Congress. One of the subjects he wanted to talk about was something he had complained about before. American agents had been sending too many European, mostly French, officers to join his army. Except for some of the younger ones, and technical experts such as engineers, most of them had been nothing but trouble.

I HAVE FOUND A UNIQUE OPPORTUNITY
TO DISTINGUISH MYSELF

News of the American uprising swept through France in 1775. The newspapers exaggerated American strength, raved about the superior fighting abilities of American militia, and painted all Americans as hardy frontiersmen. Frenchmen believed in the "noble savage" as the ideal human in original form. These Americans were most certainly *sauvage,* and definitely noble, with the added attraction of being white.[35]

American attitudes toward the French also had changed since 1763. France had been a traditional enemy, and it was a Catholic country with an absolutist government. Once the shooting started, however, Americans looked to France for support. At first they wanted commercial relations, and soon they desired military help as well. But they did not want to trade one colonial master for another.[36]

Americans did not appreciate how great was French interest in their situation, nor how far back it went. In 1761 Etienne-François Choiseul, comte de Stainville and foreign minister of France, looked for ways to strip Britain of its colonial trade, reduce its weight in the balance of power, and restore France to primacy in Europe. He needed time to rebuild his country's army and navy and to seal up the "Family Compact" with Spain. In 1763 he started to send secret agents to all thirteen colonies. He enlarged his spy service in London, developed colonies in the West Indies, and added Corsica and Lorraine to the kingdom.[37]

In 1768, Stainville sent de Broglie's aide Johann de Kalb to America. De Kalb was a French army officer, born a Prussian commoner, who had dubbed himself a "baron" in order to rise in rank. A big bear of a man, he had a lantern jaw, a prominent nose, and a talent for languages and mathematics to cap his splendid combat record. He spent several months in

America and picked up a great deal of information about the people and their politics. What he learned persuaded high officials of the French government that Americans were growing restless under British rule and that there might arise an opportunity for France to take advantage of the situation to strike a blow at the hated enemy.

Stainville lost his position in 1770 and was succeeded by Charles Gravier, comte de Vergennes, who became foreign minister in 1774. Then fifty-seven years old, he had been a diplomat all his life. He looked the part, a tall, dignified man with a comfortably lined face. A noble nose separated thoughtful, deep-set eyes, while a straight mouth sat quietly above a strong jaw. His expression was of someone wise and kind, like a favorite uncle.

That benign face masked a fierce hatred of the *Anglais*. When the American uprising broke out, he saw possibilities for renewing the war with Britain and restoring French prestige. Until things became clear, however, he wanted any aid to the rebels to be secret. Over the next two years he pushed his government toward the brink of war and found ways to get supplies and French officers to America. By 1777 he was ready to go all the way, but the Americans had suffered reverses, and it seemed possible that they might make peace with their mother country. Vergennes waited for an American triumph, after which he would lead his country into war.[38]

The foreign minister found a channel into the American rebellion in the spring of 1776, when a forty-year-old Connecticut lawyer named Silas Deane arrived in Paris as Congress' agent. His instructions were to sound out French attitudes toward the Revolution and try to round up material assistance. While he was at it, Congress also wanted him to find some French officers willing to serve in America. Deane was too gullible to be a diplomat. Vergennes took him under his wing, and other Frenchmen found him easily impressed. He created a mess that Benjamin Franklin had to straighten out when he took over the Paris mission the following year. Deane also exceeded his authority in various ways, among them hiring a known pyromaniac to burn English dockyards.

Less loony but still annoying was Deane's granting of high commissions in the Continental Army to French officers and his involvement in a plot to supersede Washington as commander in chief. More positively, although it was more Vergennes' doing than Deane's, the king granted

1 million livres to buy goods for the Americans, funneled through a sham trading company. Cannons, muskets, tents, ammunition, and clothing poured into America in 1777, including 90 percent of the powder used by the Continental Army that year.[39]

The plot to replace Washington began with de Broglie, who thought that an expanded war in America might give him a chance to rise to higher rank. After de Kalb briefed him on the American situation, he went to Vergennes. Washington's reverses around New York suggested that the rebel cause could use some professional guidance. He wanted to be appointed a generalissimo, or supreme general, to exercise political as well as military control over the Americans. His model was the "state-holders" ruling the Netherlands. They were military dictators on behalf of their kings without the formality of annexing the subject provinces. Vergennes liked the idea.

King Louis XVI, never a bold man, resisted open involvement in Britain's struggles with her colonies. At twenty years old, however, he could not stand up to the determined Vergennes. France, the minister declared, had the right to influence "all great affairs." Since England was the blood enemy, "all means to reduce the power and greatness of England . . . are just, legitimate, and even necessary, provided they are efficient." Louis caved in.[40]

De Broglie and de Kalb became Deane's principal recruiters in 1776. Because of a reorganization of the French army, there were many officers looking for work. Among them was Lafayette, reduced to the reserve list on June 11, because the new war minister was disbanding or reorganizing the old family regiments. The marquis was out on the street, crushed. Already a social misfit in Versailles, he was adrift. His father-in-law, d'Ayen, made no secret of his disappointment.[41]

When word got out that de Broglie and de Kalb were looking for officers to join the American army, Lafayette and his friends Noailles and Ségur applied to de Kalb. De Broglie, his plans at risk if too many talkative young nobles came aboard, stepped in. Before they could go to America, he said, they needed permission from their families, because they were underage. De Broglie told Lafayette that he had witnessed his father's death at Minden, and he would not "be accessory to the ruin of the remaining branch of your family."

The boys asked permission. D'Ayen flatly rejected any such nonsense for Noailles and Lafayette, and Ségur's father also put his foot down. Ségur gave up trying, and soon Noailles backed out. Lafayette, as an orphan, thought himself independent of family restraints—besides, he was rich and could do as he pleased. He pressed de Broglie, who finally relented in order to shut him up. He sent him back to de Kalb, who introduced him to Deane.[42]

Baron de Kalb Introducing Lafayette to Silas Deane, *an engraving (1856) based on an earlier painting by Alonzo Chappell.* (Lilly Library, Indiana University)

De Broglie had already made his own move with the American agent. In November 1776, Vergennes formally proposed that the French general become supreme commander of the American army. He summoned de Broglie to Paris to meet Deane, and de Kalb went along as translator. "A military and political leader is wanted," the general said. Such a man would carry the weight of authority in the colonies, unite their parties, and, most important, attract a large following of "brave, efficient, and well educated officers, who confide in their superior, and repose implicit faith in him." He suggested sending de Kalb to America to explain it all to Congress.[43]

Deane was struck by the idea and told Congress it should not pass up the chance to recruit de Broglie, "a person of so much experience, and who is by every one recommended as one of the bravest and most skilled officers in the kingdom." He thought such a proven European general "would give a character and credit to your military, and strike perhaps a greater panic in our enemies."[44]

Blithely unaware that his proposal insulted Washington in particular and the very idea of an American rebellion in general, Deane again exceeded his instructions. De Kalb had given him a list of sixteen officers, and Deane enrolled them at fat salaries and high ranks, appointing de Kalb a major general.[45]

De Broglie commandeered two frigates to carry de Kalb and his gang to America, telling de Kalb that his first order of business would be to visit Congress. The main point of his mission was to explain "the absolute necessity of the choice of . . . a generalissimo."[46]

Then Lafayette, who knew nothing about any of this, showed up on Deane's doorstep, and the scheme began to unravel. Deane and his assistant William Carmichael were impressed with his enthusiasm and his pedigree. Lafayette turned on the charm and on December 7, 1776, reached an agreement with the Americans. Deane prepared a contract, probably drafted by de Kalb, making the teenager a major general in the American army. "His high birth," the document said, "his alliances, the great dignities which his family holds at this court, his considerable estates in this realm, his personal merit, his reputation, his disinterestedness, and above all his zeal for the liberty of our provinces" justified the rank.[47]

Of all the officers Deane sent over the ocean, only in Lafayette's case did he mention nonmilitary assets, such as noble birth and connections.

Lafayette himself sweetened the offer in his addendum to the contract, promising "to depart when and how Mr. Deane shall judge proper, to serve the United States with all possible zeal, without any pension or particular allowance, reserving to myself the liberty of returning to Europe when my family or my king shall recall me." None of Deane's other recruits traveled with conditions governing their departure or return, and no other officer agreed to serve without pay. But then, none of the others was as rich as Lafayette.[48]

Appended to the agreement was a list of twelve officers—all but one part of de Broglie's advance party—with the ranks they should expect on arrival in the United States. They ranged from major general ("le Baron de Kalb") to two lieutenants. Entirely without knowing it, Lafayette had just hijacked the best-laid plans of the would-be generalissimo, de Broglie.[49]

Lafayette's "zeal" was not so much for American liberty as his boyish hunger for glory and for a chance to fight the *Anglais*. He was smugly proud of himself. "When I presented myself to Mr. Deane I was just nineteen years old," he wrote a couple of years later. "The secrecy of those negotiations and of my preparations was truly miraculous. Family, friends, ministers, French spies, English spies, all were blind to them."[50]

The marquis conveniently forgot the ensuing uproar. Like most triumphant youngsters, he could not keep his mouth shut. He told Noailles and Ségur about his plans, and they again asked their families for permission to join him. As de Kalb and the other officers prepared to board ship at Le Havre, news of this juvenile escapade spread. The British ambassador heard about it, lodged a formal protest, and threatened to break diplomatic relations and blockade French ports.

It was one thing for Deane to send individual adventurers to join the American army. Three noble sons of prominent families were another matter. Vergennes was furious, telling the prime minister that what Lafayette had done was "a hostile act" and an insult to the king. To appease the British he closed French ports to American ships, banned the sale of goods to America, stopped the departure of de Broglie's ships, and ordered the arrest "with plenty of publicity and severity" of any French soldiers claiming that the French government had ordered them to go to America. The British fleet blockaded the French ports anyway. The disgusted de Broglie recalled de Kalb and the others to Paris, and Vergennes ended French aid to America. Deane worried that he would be ordered home in disgrace.[51]

The duc d'Ayen stormed at his sons-in-law for embarrassing the family, outraged that Lafayette would even think of abandoning his duties as husband and father. To cool him off, Lafayette agreed to go to London to visit the marquis de Noailles, the duc's uncle, just appointed ambassador to Great Britain. He was still determined to cross the ocean but now realized that he would have to be sneaky about it.

The marquis visited de Broglie, proposing to buy his own ship and finance the expedition himself. De Broglie, seeing another chance to take Washington's job, agreed and sent his procurement officer to purchase a cargo ship in Bordeaux. "Our young marquis does not despair," his secretary told de Kalb. "He still has the greatest desire to go." Lafayette told Deane, "Until now, sir, you have only seen my zeal for your cause," but now that he was buying a ship, "we must feel confidence in the future, and it is especially in the hour of danger that I wish to share your fortune." Deane was reassured.[52]

Lafayette kept his head down, playing the dutiful husband to Adrienne, who was pregnant again. On February 11, 1777, he learned that the agent in Bordeaux had bought the cargo ship *Victoire* (Victory), with two guns and a crew of thirty. He wrote a note to cover the deposit on the vessel, and told Carmichael that, in a month at the latest, he would "take to your country the zeal that animates me for their happiness, their glory, and their liberty."[53]

The young warrior left Paris for London on February 17 without bothering to say goodbye to Adrienne. After he got to the big city he sent her a series of letters that ended with empty expressions of love, full of self-pity because he had received no letters from her. He thoughtlessly wrote things that must have hurt her. "At the ball tonight we shall see all the ladies. . . . I am very impatient to see all the young women, and the famous Duchess of Devonshire," he said on the twenty-fifth. Early in March he complained, "I was quite distressed, dear heart, not to receive any news from you for two posts. Fortunately, I know that you are not sick but only lazy." He was enjoying himself with "some truly charming women." He ended with, "If I needed new proof to convince myself how tenderly I love you, it would be the pain I have felt in not receiving any letters from you when I have had them from all of my friends. Good day."[54]

Lafayette was having a high time in the British capital, where he was a celebrity, owing to the uproar over his earlier attempt to leave for America. He was presented to King George, his nights were filled with dinners, balls, and receptions, and he had the company of willing young ladies. At the opera he met General Sir Henry Clinton, who was in England consulting with the government. He later claimed, "I often defended the Americans; I rejoiced at their success at Trenton."

In the second week of March, the teenager skipped a ball in his honor and returned to France. He hid out in de Kalb's house so his father-in-law could not order him to rejoin his regiment, which would make him a deserter if he left the country. He lied to de Kalb and de Broglie, telling them that he had received the blessings of his family. In fact, his suspicious father-in-law and his pregnant wife had no idea where he was or what he was doing.[55]

De Kalb went ahead with plans for the voyage, and Deane and Carmichael gave him letters of introduction to Congress. He ordered the officers from the Le Havre group to leave for Bordeaux by night, and on the night of March 16 he and Lafayette rode out to join them.[56]

Lafayette had written Adrienne a letter, which he sent after he left town. The adolescent wallowed in his own situation, indifferent to its effects on his wife. "I am too guilty to vindicate myself," he said, "but I have been too cruelly punished not to deserve a pardon. If I had expected to feel my sacrifices in such a frightful manner, I would not be at present the unhappiest of men. But I have given my word, and I would die rather than go back on it. . . . If you knew how painful this is, you would surely be more sorry for me than you will ever be."[57]

Adrienne had fallen in love with this self-absorbed boy at first sight, and she stayed in love with him, whatever he did. Her mother consoled her by praising his character and predicting a great future for him. The older woman knew nothing about conquests or glory, Adrienne recalled, but in her heart was sure that he would achieve both. The pregnant girl needed no reassurance—she felt the same way.[58]

Her father learned what Lafayette was up to in another tardy letter. "You will be astonished, my dear Papa, by what I am about to tell you," it said. "I have found a unique opportunity to distinguish myself, and to learn my profession." As a general officer in the American army, he was "overjoyed" at having a chance to show what he was made of.[59]

Elsewhere in this letter, the teenage general promised to visit d'Ayen while he was in Paris. Instead, he delayed mailing it. He had stuck his finger into his father-in-law's eye, and he was afraid to face him. This was not the stuff of a hero in the making. Not surprisingly, Lafayette soon began to have second thoughts.

D'Ayen set out for Versailles, where Vergennes was in high dudgeon, fearing that the boy's action would provoke a war before France was ready. He had embarrassed the government and compromised Ambassador Noailles. Louis expressed royal shock and forbade all French officers from serving in the British colonies. He ordered any who arrived there, "notably Monsieur le marquis de la Fayette," to leave immediately and return to France. Vergennes announced that the king had issued a *lettre de cachet* (a royal warrant) for Lafayette.

As this volcano erupted in their wake, Lafayette and de Kalb rode to Bordeaux. Soldiers pursued them with orders to report to Marseilles, but they became lost. Word of what the impetuous marquis was doing spread around the country, and people celebrated. In Paris, a mob cheered in the streets. He became an instant hero, a picture of gallant soldiery even before he boarded the ship. Plays were written and performed about his valor. The British ambassador was outraged, reporting home that there was general opposition to the government's attempts to stop him.[60]

Lafayette, de Kalb, and the others boarded *Victoire* under assumed names, unaware of what was going on in the capital. De Kalb had some premonitions, for he urged the marquis to write de Broglie's brother, giving him cover. "I have the honor to inform you, M. le comte," he said, "that I leave for the country you know, and for that adventure which you counseled me not to risk. . . . I have not even wished to discuss it with you again because . . . you would have opposed my desires, and I already had enough obstacles to overcome."[61]

De Broglie and the government used this pack of lies to counter claims by the British government that the comte had arranged Lafayette's move to America on behalf of the French ministry. To the ambitious duc de Broglie, however, that was of small moment. Lafayette had unhorsed him again. Thanks to the political and diplomatic storm the boy had kicked up, de Broglie would never become an American generalissimo.

His rear was not the only one needing protection. Lafayette confessed to de Kalb that he had acted without the knowledge of his family. De Kalb told Deane that he hoped this would not cause trouble for either of them, "for we both were confident that all was done in that matter by the advise & consent of his nearest relations." A few months later he defended himself to the government against charges that he had encouraged the boy to defy his family. "I was utterly astounded," he said, claiming that he had advised Lafayette to go home and face the music.

Instead, the ship sailed for the Spanish Atlantic port of Los Pasajes, where the news from home caught up with it. "The letters from my family were terrifying," Lafayette remembered, "and the *lettre de cachet* was peremptory: 'You are forbidden to go to the American continent, under penalty of disobedience, and enjoined to go to Marseilles to await further orders.'" He knew the consequences of disobeying the king (imprisonment) and dreaded "the power and the wrath" of the royal government. Curiously, as Lafayette's escapade made him fear for his safety, it heartened the American delegation in Paris, because of its effect on public opinion. "All Europe is for us," Franklin and Deane told Congress.[62]

L'affaire Lafayette was the talk of two cities. Edward Bancroft, Deane's secretary and also a spy for the British, told London all about it, and provided a list of the officers with him. Tongues wagged at the French court and in Paris. When d'Ayen demanded that Deane write to Washington, asking him to revoke Lafayette's commission, he did so. Then he set off a round-robin of blame that almost universally pointed at de Broglie. Justifying himself to Vergennes, Deane referred the foreign minister to de Broglie. To the British ambassador, Lord Stormont, Vergennes disavowed any official complicity in Lafayette's departure, alleging de Broglie's intrigues. Stormont first told his superiors in London to soft-pedal their reaction, saying the boy was responsible. A few days later, he joined the chorus and shifted the blame to de Broglie.[63]

The saddest case involved the marquis de Noailles, ambassador to London, who had showed Lafayette around the court there. He wrote an anguished letter to the prime minister, the comte de Maurepas, wailing that he had been "extremely shocked" to learn that the boy had left for America, although his age might excuse his thoughtlessness. "Why,

Monsieur le comte," he asked in pain, "should incidents that are independent of political affairs, damage my reputation?"[64]

Vergennes told the ambassador that "by the greatest good luck, the project has not been completed," and no one would ever blame him anyway. The foreign minister was relieved, the prime minister was relieved, Deane was relieved, and d'Ayen also was relieved, asking Deane not to send the letter to Washington. Stormont crowed, "Lafayette's expedition has been a short one indeed!" Lafayette was back in France.[65]

The boy had gotten cold feet. On April 1, 1777, the day after his ship reached Spain, he was overcome with indecision. De Kalb demanded that he choose between the call of his family or going ahead with the expedition, so he bought a horse and rode back to France. The other officers wanted to sail without him, but de Kalb reminded them that Lafayette owned the ship. So they sat and waited.

Lafayette rode into Bordeaux on the third. There were no troops standing by to arrest him, and the local commander advised him to report to Marseilles to await orders. Instead, Lafayette wrote to the prime minister, begging for a revocation of the king's warrant. Then he sat and waited.

De Broglie, his hopes of becoming generalissimo dissolving, sent a hard-riding aide to talk Lafayette into returning to the ship. He told him that everyone in Paris except d'Ayen was with him in his plans, that there really was no *lettre de cachet* on him, that de Broglie was close to Vergennes, and that the government was secretly behind him. Lafayette swallowed the whole story, some of which may have been true. When the Bordeaux commandant threatened to arrest him if he did not go to Marseilles, the teenage swashbuckler pretended to obey, hired a coach, and headed east with army officers on his tail. When the coach stopped to change horses, he put on a disguise, rented a horse, and galloped off toward the Spanish border. When his minders picked up his trail, he sweet-talked an innkeeper's daughter into pointing them in the wrong direction.[66]

Having conquered that challenge on his own, Lafayette became more sure of himself, and his swagger returned. He ordered the ship made ready as soon as he reached Los Pasajes. De Kalb wrote Deane that Lafayette had returned, and everything had been sorted out. Lafayette told Carmichael, "On the whole, this affair has produced all the éclat I desired, and now that everyone's eyes are on us, I shall try to be worthy of that celebrity." He predicted that after he departed everyone would agree with him, and "once I am victorious, everyone will applaud my enterprise." He hoped to become a good general "as readily as I have become a good American."[67]

The night before he sailed, Lafayette penned a farewell to his pregnant wife. Another self-focused whine, it complained that "they" would not give him two weeks' leave to see her. "My heart is broken," he said. "If you do not send word to me that you still love me, that you forgive me . . . I shall be in despair."[68]

Victoire sailed with the tide on April 20, 1777. She carried the spearhead of a crumbling plot to make de Broglie a generalissimo, and the scheme's unwitting paymaster, the marquis de Lafayette.[69]

As soon as the ship hit the ocean swells, the young adventurer discovered something about himself: he could not go on the water without becoming violently seasick.

A GENEROUS RECEPTION WILL DO US INFINITE SERVICE

*A*s Lafayette heaved his guts over the gunwale, his family calmed down. Adrienne and her mother prevailed on d'Ayen to cut the boy some slack. He had tried to close off his son-in-law's access to his own fortune and failed. Lafayette, although a minor, could spend whatever he wanted of his own money, according to his financial guardians. The point of the arranged marriage between his child and the marquis now lost, d'Ayen agreed to let his wife forward expense money secretly.

Also secretly, the whole family went to see Deane and Franklin, looking for a covert way to make sure that Lafayette wanted for nothing. The boy had been spending money heavily and would likely continue to do so. They believed that he had no sense when it came to economy, and feared that he would be taken advantage of. This set off a remarkable series of letters to Congress, Washington, and others. Franklin asked the commander in chief to advance whatever sums Lafayette needed against his draft, which the Noailles family would honor. As the letters poured out of the American delegation, Lafayette's future position in America was transformed. He became a valuable national commodity, and Washington was entrusted with his care.[70]

Franklin and Deane knew that Congress was reluctant to accept any more of their recruits, but they believed that Lafayette should be an exception, because they had fallen for the notion that he went to America with the government's secret approval. They argued that the boy would be a real asset to the American cause and that he should be protected accordingly. "The Marquis de Fayette [*sic*]," they advised, "is exceedingly beloved, and every bodys good wishes attend him. We cannot but hope he may meet with such a reception as will make the country and his expedition agreeable to him." Even those who disapproved of his actions applauded his spirit, and a welcome reception in America would boost the United States' interests, because it would please both the court and "the whole French Nation." For the sake of the "beautifull young wife big with child" Lafayette had left behind, the ambassadors hoped that "his bravery and ardent desire to distinguish himself will be a little restrain'd by the Generals [Washington's] prudence; so as not to permit his being hazarded much but on some important occasion."[71]

Deane separately wrote to Robert Morris, the most renowned money man in America, future superintendent of finance for the Revolution. He explained that because of Lafayette's connections, "[a] generous reception will do us infinite service." The marquis wanted no pay and had a distinguished military pedigree, but his relatives were "afraid his generous disposition may be abused by avanturiers of his own country." Deane had assured them that he would "recommend him to the care & oversight of one who would be as a father to him on every occasion . . . He is expected to live in character, & his friends wish it, but they are apprehensive on the score I hinted at." All the young man wanted was glory, and everyone in France thought he was bound for it. "You may think it makes a great noise in Europe, & at the same time see that well managed it will greatly help us."[72]

So Lafayette was coming to America, bringing the force of his connections with him. He was a powerful addition to the cause, but so gullible that somebody should watch out for him like a "father." He was a soldier from a noble line of soldiers, but Washington should make sure that he was not put where he could be shot at.

F O U R

The Confusion Became Extreme

(JUNE-SEPTEMBER 1777)

There was a most infernal fire of cannon and musketry; smoke; incessant
shouting, "Incline to the right!" "Incline to the left!" "Halt!" "Charge!" &c. The
balls ploughing up the ground; the trees cracking over one's head; the
branches riven by the artillery; the leaves falling as in autumn,
by the grape shot. The affair was general.

— JOHN LAURENS

*I*n February 1777, Washington complained to Congress about the
"distress" he suffered from the number of French officers wanting
commissions in his army. "This evil," he said, "is a growing
one . . . they are coming in swarms." They could not speak the
language and therefore could not meet the first duty of a battalion officer—recruiting men. Moreover, "our officers . . . would be disgusted if
foreigners were put over their heads." He did not receive a reply.[1]

Deane and Franklin were besieged by European officers wanting to
get into the American conflict. The Continent swarmed with unemployed soldiers looking for adventure and glory, along with high military
rank and peacetime nobility. Some of them were amazingly persistent.
Franklin told one, "If, therefore, you have the least remaining kindness

for me . . . for God's sake, my dear friend, let this your twenty-third application be your last."[2]

The foreign officers the American commissioners sent overseas were not all bad. Franklin arrived in Paris late in 1776 with a request from Washington to find some competent military engineers. Among those he located was Louis le Bègue de Presle Duportail, who arrived in February 1777. The thirty-four-year-old son of a noble family, he was rising fast in the French service when the court "loaned" him to the United States. He became Washington's chief engineer in July, and today he is honored as the father of the Army Corps of Engineers.[3]

Louis le Bègue de Presle Duportail, by C.W. Peale, early 1780s. As Washington's chief engineer, Duportail designed the siege of Yorktown and became the father of the U.S. Army Corps of Engineers. (INDEPENDENCE NATIONAL HISTORICAL PARK)

Many French officers showed up at Washington's headquarters on their own. They were often supercilious and refused to learn English. Deane's gifts to the cause created the most trouble, because frequently he offered them high rank, and Congress felt it had to go along, alienating native officers. In May the commander in chief exploded. "These men have no attachment nor ties to the country," he complained to Congress. He was "disgusted" by the lawmakers' habit of "giving rank to people of no reputation or service." This time, his words were heard.[4]

The last straw was a pompous ass named Philippe-Charles-Jean-Baptiste Tronson du Coudray. Born in 1738, he was an artillerist and the author of textbooks. He was well connected at court—his brother was Marie-Antoinette's lawyer. In September 1776 Deane promised him a commission as major general and chief of artillery and engineers in the American forces. That superseded Knox, already chief of artillery, and outranked Greene and Sullivan; all three threatened to quit. The Frenchman's personality prevented any friendly solution to these conflicts. Used to having his own way, he was arrogant, overbearing, and a veteran of thirty duels, who arrived in June 1777 with a retinue of eighteen officers and ten sergeants. Washington protested, and Duportail told him that the man was not the military engineer he claimed to be.

Congress appointed a commission to deal with him. It was fishing around for titles by which to honor Deane's commitments to these characters without placing them over American officers, and had already appointed an "inspector-general of cavalry," who did not last long. It offered the same favor to Tronson du Coudray, making him "inspector-general of ordnance and military manufactures." He received the rank of major general "of staff," meaning he would command no line officers, but inserting him into Washington's army was a prescription for trouble. He solved the problem in September by galloping his horse onto a ferry so fast that he landed in the water on the other side and drowned. As Lafayette put it later, "the loss of that troublemaker was perhaps a fortunate accident."[5]

HE REQUIRED NO PENSION
NO SPECIAL COMMAND

*A*s *Victoire* pounded across the Atlantic, Lafayette had no idea that he was sailing in Tronson du Coudray's wake. He had no idea about anything in the first weeks out of port, because he was seasick. The trip was miserable, as all sea voyages were then. Passengers were confined to their cabins, small, dark, damp, smelly holes infested with bugs and decorated only by mold. Rations were short and nasty, the water was foul, and the weather was often rough.

The marquis began to recover near the end of May and started a letter to Adrienne. It was another self-pitying lament, wondering whether she had forgiven him, wishing for a letter from her, and complaining about his seasickness. "[B]ut I could have given myself the consolation of the wicked, which is to suffer in a numerous company." Then he reassured her—or himself. "Once I arrive," he said, "I am sure that I shall have acquired the hardiness that will assure me perfect health for a long time. Do not fancy, dear heart, that I shall run great risks in my service here. The post of general officer has always been regarded as a warrant for long life."

On June 7 Lafayette complained about "this dreary plain, dear heart, and it is so dismal that one cannot make any comparison with it." D'Ayen's attitude bothered him, and he hoped that his service in America would win his father-in-law's respect. Then he added a curious plea, asking her, for his sake, to "become a good American. Besides, it is a sentiment made for virtuous hearts. The welfare of America is intimately connected with the happiness of all mankind." Hoping that landfall was near, he said he had been studying English from books. His last installment was written from "Major Huger's house." He was in America.[6]

The passengers worried about the reception they would meet. One of them told Lafayette before they landed that it would be mixed, and that "we French must be detested by them, when, as people who come to offer knowledge superior to theirs, we hurt their pride in general and arouse their envy in particular. Don't worry, though, it will be politic to welcome you."[7]

On June 12 the ship neared Charleston, South Carolina, and met an American vessel whose captain warned of British frigates blockading the harbor. *Victoire* headed north. On the thirteenth, she dropped anchor off North Island, at the entrance to Georgetown Bay, about sixty miles from Charleston. Lafayette, de Kalb, and four other officers were rowed ashore and met some black oystermen, who led them to the home of their master, Benjamin Huger, a rice planter. He told them that Georgetown Bay was too shallow for their ship. Offering to find a pilot to guide her past the blockade into Charleston, he proposed sending the officers overland.

When he felt American soil under his feet for the first time that night, Lafayette claimed later, his first words were "an oath to conquer or die for America's cause." It is more likely that his first words proclaimed joy that the terrible voyage was over. He was in an exotic land, eating such strange foods as cornbread and sweet potatoes. Everything was new to him, he recalled, "the room, the bed draped in delicate mosquito curtains, the black servants who came to me quietly to ask my commands, the strange new beauty of the landscape; outside my windows, the luxuriant vegetation—all combined to produce a magical effect and fill me with indescribable sensations."[8]

Lafayette bubbled with boyish enthusiasm, enchanted by his great adventure. His companions were not so happy. One of them complained about trekking overland on hot sands and through thick woods, most of them walking because they had only three horses. They could not walk in their riding boots, so they went barefoot. They reached Charleston after three days, he said, "looking very much like beggars and brigands." They were "received accordingly."[9]

The bedraggled soldiers received a municipal cold shoulder until *Victoire* crept into port the next day. She and her cargo raised the French party's reputation—anyone who owned such a fine ship (actually, she was a tub) must be important. Lafayette introduced himself as a Mason at the local lodge, and the city's dignitaries welcomed him as a "brother." He and the other officers enjoyed eight days of feasts and celebrations.[10]

It was impossible, Lafayette wrote to an uncle, "to be received with more enthusiasm, cordiality, or pleasantness than that with which I have been received by the American people and all the officials of this country." By boosting his American reputation, he hoped to raise his standing in France as well. He gave Adrienne his impressions so far. Americans, he said, "are as likable as my enthusiasm has led me to picture them. A simplicity of manners, a desire to please, a love of country and liberty, and an easy equality prevail everywhere here." The richest man and the poorest, he said, treated each other as equals. In general, the country reminded him of England, "but there is more simplicity, equality, cordiality, and courtesy here than in England." Charleston was "one of the most beautiful and well built of cities," and its inhabitants were among "the most agreeable people" he had ever met. American women were "very pretty, totally unaffected, and maintain a charming neatness." Finally, he was happy to report that he could at least converse in "broken English."[11]

There was a flaw in this land of liberty, and the starry-eyed Lafayette was blind to it. That was slavery. In America there were no paupers, he told Adrienne, "or even the sort of people we call peasants." Everyone had "property, a considerable number of Negroes, and the same rights as the most powerful proprietor in the land." During his first year in

America he became a slaveowner, and later proposed an attack on the British West Indies, "where the Negroes would pay the cost of the enterprise." He meant to round up the slaves and sell them.[12]

Lafayette's journey out of Charleston almost did not start. He had planned to sell *Victoire* and her cargo to pay off what he still owed on her, and to finance his time in America. The shipping company's agent would not allow that without clearance from the Bordeaux office because he was a minor, which in his country meant under twenty-five years old. The ship left for France and sank on the way. Insurance from that paid off his note, and the whole business was a loss to him. He borrowed against his accounts at home, but de Kalb had to cosign the note for 28,000 livres, again because of his age.[13]

On June 26, 1777, Lafayette, de Kalb, and five others set out on a grueling trip over 900 miles, through bad roads, swamps, and mosquitoes, headed for Philadelphia. The rest of the party decided to go by sea.

Lafayette proved what his relatives had feared— that he had more money than sense. He bought a train of carriages that would have been fine in the city but were not up to cross-country travel, pulled by horses with the same shortcomings. By the fourth day, some of the carriages were in splinters, and several of the horses were dead or lame. Replacing them used up all the party's money. The officers were forced to leave part of their baggage behind, and some of it was stolen. They traveled much of the way on foot, sleeping

Johann "Baron" de Kalb, by C.W. Peale. De Kalb went from being de Broglie's fixer to become an American patriot who died heroically at Camden. (INDEPENDENCE NATIONAL HISTORICAL PARK)

in the woods, as one of them recalled, "starving, prostrated by the heat, and some of us suffered from fever and dysentery." He claimed that "no campaign in Europe could be more difficult than this journey."[14]

Another member of the group was even more sour. "We endured abominable heat in South Carolina, and to refresh ourselves at the end of each day we had to accept horrible lodgings and detestable water," the chevalier du Rousseau de Fayolle groused. Things in America were not as they had been described in France. The people were not united in their common cause, and he did not think they would ever "do anything spectacular." He thought Americans were vain, all wanting to be officers rather than soldiers, and were "no better as one than as the other."[15]

Lafayette, in contrast to the others, remained chipper. He studied the language and local customs, and saw products and methods of cultivation wholly new to him. "Vast forests, immense rivers—nature adorns everything in the land with an air of youth and majesty," he sang. He resumed writing to Adrienne along the way, and a self-deprecating humor suddenly emerged in him. "I departed most handsomely in a carriage," he told her; "you will now learn that we are all on horseback after having broken the carriages, according to my laudable custom, and I expect to write to you in a few days that we arrived on foot." The farther north he went, the more he liked both the country and its people, who showered him with courtesies and "kind attentions." On July 17, at Annapolis, he sent his mail off on a ship bound for France. The group boarded another boat and sailed to Philadelphia, reaching the rebel capital on July 27.[16]

They cleaned themselves up and went to the Pennsylvania State House (now Independence Hall), where Congress met. The doorkeeper would not let them in. A delegate told them that French officers were "very forward" to come without being invited. America did not need their services. They were stunned. "Our reception by the Congress . . . was not what we expected," one of them complained; "on the contrary, it could not have been more uncivil. It even made us suspect that they were very surprised to see us."[17]

The Frenchmen had walked into a hornet's nest stirred up by the obnoxious Tronson du Coudray. Congress had formed a Committee on Foreign Applications, to send foreign soldiers packing. There were also suspicions about de Broglie's plot. De Kalb was known to be the general's man, and some delegates assumed Lafayette was also. On the other hand, the letters from Deane and Franklin about him also had arrived, so he could not be brushed off lightly. No one knew he was a fugitive from the French king's law, because the commissioners failed to mention that.

Lafayette and de Kalb approached the president of Congress, John Hancock, and the marquis offered to serve at his own expense. Hancock liked the price, at any rate, and sent a member to interview him. In his halting English, Lafayette read aloud a note he had written. "After the sacrifices I have made," it said, "I have the right to exact two favors: one is to serve at my own expense, and the other is to begin to serve as a volunteer." The congressman recommended his recruitment.[18]

On July 31, 1777, Congress proclaimed, "Whereas the Marquis de la Fayette, out of his great zeal to the cause of liberty in which the United States are engaged, has left his family & connexions & at his own expense come over to offer his service to the United States without pension or particular allowance, and is anxious to risque his life in our cause: RESOLVED That his service be accepted and that in consideration of his zeal, illustrious family and connexions, he have the rank and commission of major general in the army of the United States."

John Hancock, by S. F. B. Morse, after John Singleton Copley, ca. 1816. Hancock recommended that Congress appoint Lafayette as a "volunteer" major general, and later calmed the uproar in Boston caused by the arrival of the French fleet from Rhode Island.
(INDEPENDENCE NATIONAL HISTORICAL PARK)

This was a highly unusual resolution, because it stressed Lafayette's connections and his willingness to serve for free; his services were "accepted." Appointment of a general officer, foreign or domestic, almost always was a one-sentence resolution, creating the position and naming the person voted into it.[19]

The other officers were turned aside on the grounds that they did not speak English and had misunderstood Deane. Lafayette promised to lobby for them. In the meantime, a major general needed aides, so he appointed the two youngest of the group as his aides-de-camp. Jean-Joseph Sourbader de Gimat and Louis-Sainte-Ange, chevalier Morel de La Colombe, thus joined the Continental Army.[20]

Congress clearly intended his commission to be honorary. Much of the discussion before the resolution emphasized his service as a "volunteer," which was why his offer was "accepted." In other words, the lawmakers thought they were getting his labor in America and influence in France for free. He would not clamor for a command over American generals. Congressman Henry Laurens thought this was a terrific bargain for the United States. "He required no pension no special command," just a chance to serve under Washington and, Laurens told a friend, to show his "zeal for the glorious cause of American freedom." The risk was small compared to the possible benefits. Laurens predicted that "this illustrious stranger" would "have a short campaign & then probably return to France & secure to us the powerful interest of his high & extensive connections."[21]

Neither Lafayette nor the lawmakers understood each other. Congress heard "volunteer," meaning free labor, thinking he would be satisfied with an empty commission. The marquis heard "*volontaire*," which in the French army meant a young noble attached to a general officer as a military apprentice, who performed the duties of an aide-de-camp. He had no official position until he moved on to a staff assignment—or a line command. There were many volunteers in the Continental Army, who often became regular staff officers. A volunteer who was also a major general was, to say the least, highly unusual on either side of the Atlantic.[22]

Lafayette assumed that he was entering a period of preparation under the commander in chief, before getting a command in the line. When Washington was informed of the appointment, he believed that he had acquired a glamorous supernumerary with a purely decorative rank.

What, the commander in chief wondered, was he going to do with the marquis de Lafayette?

I HAVE COME HERE TO LEARN

The British were determined to smash the American Revolution. A two-pronged invasion of northern New York out of Canada had started. Clinton sat in New York with a large force. The Howes had left that city, destination unknown. Fearing an attack on Philadelphia, the commander in chief had marched his army toward the capital. When word arrived on August 4, 1777, that the British fleet was off the Delaware capes, the question was whether its target was Philadelphia or a southern port.

Washington rode into the city to consult with Congress. On the evening of the fifth, some of the members hosted him for dinner at City Tavern. The group crowded into a dining room on the second floor, the windows open to relieve the heat, the atmosphere made smoky by lamps and tapers. Everyone's attention was distracted by the figures at either end of the table. Washington was not the only guest of honor, because the delegates had brought along Lafayette.

Washington dominated the room, as he always did. As Lafayette recalled his first sight of "this great man" in the crowded room, "the majesty of his figure and his height were unmistakable." His friend Ségur was more descriptive four years later. "His presence almost foretold his history," he said, "simplicity, grandeur, dignity, calm, kindness, firmness were stamped upon his face and upon his countenance as well as his character. His figure was noble and tall; the expression on his face was pleasant and kind; his smile was gentle, his manners simple without being familiar. . . . He inspired rather than commanded respect," the awestruck young officer concluded.[23]

Washington contemplated the nineteen-year-old at the opposite end of the table, this French marquis whose trip to America had kicked up a diplomatic storm, British protests and threats flying. Lafayette in the flesh—what there was of it—was a skinny boy in a fancy but trail-worn suit. Washington noticed that his slight body trembled with anticipation,

George Washington, by James Peale, after C.W. Peale. The "great man" as he appeared when Lafayette first met him. (INDEPENDENCE NATIONAL HISTORICAL PARK)

as he had seen high-strung horses do. The boy was modest, eager to please, and trying to talk in English.[24]

Everyone in the place was taken with Lafayette, and his puppy-dog charm was in full flower. Most appealing was his drop-jawed admiration for the commander in chief. He was overwhelmed by the legendary general at the other end of the table and could not conceal his awe. The more reserved Washington later said that he had felt from first sight that the boy was worthy of "esteem and attachment."[25]

For the moment, the general had partly decided what he would do with the marquis. The scene remained vivid in Lafayette's mind a half century later. He presented it, as he often described his own life, in the Caesarian third person: "Washington took Lafayette aside, spoke to him very kindly, complimented him upon the noble spirit he had shown and the sacrifices he had made in favor of the American cause, and then told him, that he should be pleased if he would make the quarters of the commander in chief his home, establish himself there whenever he thought proper, and consider himself at all times as one of his family." The older general warned that he could not promise him the luxuries of a court, "which his former habits might have rendered essential to his comfort," but he was confident the young general would "submit with a good grace to the customs, manners, and privations of a republican army."[26]

One word in that invitation struck Lafayette like a bolt: "family." As had happened with "volunteer," Washington and the young Frenchman began their connection with a misunderstanding. Lafayette heard *famille,* French for blood relations. Washington, following English practice, meant his military staff. Lafayette assumed that he was being adopted into the older man's personal household. Washington had no idea that was the way his statement could be interpreted.[27]

Lafayette learned better soon enough, but this use of "family" remained a novelty to the French in America. The chevalier de Chastellux—who spent the last half of the war in America as both tourist and sometime staff officer, then in a delightful memoir explained the New World to the Old—met Washington in 1780 and described this linguistic curiosity to his French audience. "He presented me to the generals," he wrote, "and to his *family* . . . for in England and America, the aides-de-camp, adjutants and other officers attached to the general, form what is called his *family*."[28]

Lafayette at twenty, by Corcelli. The marquis as Washington first saw him. The "inexplicable" puppy-dog charm of the best-dressed soldier in North America is evident in this view. (Lilly Library, Indiana University)

Washington invited Lafayette into his military family to keep an eye on him. He soon received another letter from Franklin and Deane. The marquis' bills had begun showing up, *Victoire* was lost, and the family still fretted that he did not handle money well. The commissioners asked Washington to find somebody who would put the teenager on an allowance. There were a lot of people in France, they reminded the general, "who interest themselves in the welfare of that amiable young nobleman."[29]

Babysitting could wait, because Washington had a more immediate problem involving his staff. Congress had authorized him four aides-de-camp, and three of the positions were filled. He needed another aide, but he had to hold the slot open until Lafayette's position became clear. John Laurens, son of the next president of Congress, Henry Laurens, had applied for the aide's job on August 4. Washington knew that he could be as useful militarily as politically.

After meeting Lafayette, he wrote to young Laurens. For reasons "unnecessary to mention" he could not appoint a fourth aide, but he invited him to join the family "as an extra aide." Laurens was wealthy, so serving without pay was no obstacle to him. He accepted, and after Lafayette's status shook itself out, on October 6 Washington formally gave Laurens the position.[30]

Washington returned to camp, but Lafayette had unfinished business in Philadelphia. He lobbied Congress for the other officers. On August 13, he thanked the lawmakers for his own commission. He promised, "I schall neglect nothing on my part to justify the confidence which the Congress of the United States has been pleased to repose in me. . . . I wish to serve near the person of General Washington till such time as he may think proper to entrust me with a division of the army." This was the first letter Lafayette wrote personally in English, and an early sign that his interpretation of his "volunteer" status differed from everyone else's. He closed by saying, "It is now as an american that I'l mention every day to Congress the officers who came over with me," because he thought they also deserved commissions.[31]

It was to no avail. Nearly all were broke, so Lafayette offered to pay their way home. Most of them left over the following months, and Congress eventually coughed up the cost of their passage.

De Kalb was not about to leave, however. Early in August he petitioned Congress forcefully. "What is deemed genérosity in the marquis de la Fayette would be downright madness in me, who am not one of the first rate fortunes," he pointed out. "I am heartily glad you granted his wishs, he is a worthy young man, and no one wil outdo him for enthusiasme in your cause of liberty and independence." However, they had come to America as military men with the same assurances, and "preference, if there was to be any, was due to me," owing to his thirty-four years of military service.

The Prussian-Frenchman promised to sue Congress for breach of contract in French courts if he went home without a command. This was a serious threat—it would drag into the open France's covert support for the American uprising, and its tolerance of Deane's recruiting. He did not stop there, suggesting that giving him a lesser rank in the American army would also produce bad effects on opinion in the French government and among military men. Congress gave in to this blackmail and offered him a commission as a major general with one day's seniority over the marquis. Satisfied, he asked for the same date as Lafayette's commission and got it. [32]

De Kalb gave de Broglie the bad news, that his plot had been unhorsed for the last time. He explained that it would be "impossible to succeed in the grand project . . . it would be regarded as a crying injustice against Washington and an outrage on the country." No longer de Broglie's front man, de Kalb had become an American. [33]

Lafayette's other errand was to prepare himself to be a major general in the Continental Army. On August 4, an admiring Philadelphian bought him a slave to be his driver and servant. He spent about two weeks outfitting himself and his aides, buying a carriage and a wagon, horses and furnishings, arms, tents and camp equipage, and accoutrements. Much of the time went to tailors, boot makers, and leather workers turning out magnificent uniforms for the three young Frenchmen. By the time they reached Washington's camp outside the city, on August 20, they were the best-dressed soldiers in North America.

When this dazzling display of martial splendor appeared before the commander in chief, Washington came as close as he ever did to a chuckle. "I suppose," he said, "we ought to be embarrassed to show ourselves to an officer who has just left the French forces." The marquis replied with pride and innocence, "I have come here to learn, *mon général,* not to teach." [34]

Lafayette's education began sooner than he had expected, when Washington hustled him into a private space in his quarters. The marquis had said that he expected command of a division, and had pestered the general about it. Preparing for his arrival at camp, the elder man relayed his concerns to Benjamin Harrison, a member of Congress, suggesting that perhaps Lafayette "has misceived the design of his appointment, or Congress did not understand the extent of his views, for certain it is, if I understand *him,* that he does not conceive his commission is merely honorary; but given with a view to command a division of this army. True, he has said that he is young, & inexperienced, but at the same time has always accompanied it with a hint, that so soon as *I* shall think *him* fit for the command of a division, he shall be ready to enter upon the duties of it." The commander in chief wanted a clarification of the marquis' status and how Congress expected him to treat his new major general.[35]

Washington was thoroughly confused. Harrison told him he should not be, reminding him that he had said earlier that Lafayette's commission was "merely honorary." He and every other member of Congress understood that "his chief motive for going into our service was to be near you, to see service, and to give him an eclat at home, where he expected he would soon return." He could not have obtained his commission on any other terms. "Congress never meant that he should have [a command], nor will not countenance him in his applications."[36]

Washington and Lafayette sat down for what the marquis would always call their "great conversation." The older man promised that he would be treated with all respect due to a major general. He wanted him in his headquarters and would involve him in every military activity. It was a fact of life, however, that Congress would not give a foreigner a command over American generals. There was no point in continuing to expect such an assignment or to ask for it. But, Washington said, he held Lafayette in high regard. He would be happy to have his confidence as his "friend and father."[37]

Lafayette took the news well. But Washington did not suspect the reaction going on inside the boy toward his "friend and father." The orphan of Auvergne, exiled, timid behind his swagger, found what he had missed all his life. He set out to be a dutiful son to "this great man." He fell completely under Washington's influence, seeking his approval, wanting to do things as his hero would do them. Washington would have been surprised at this point to know that Lafayette had set him up as a life model. When he realized it later, however, he was more than pleased. Others saw it. Many years later the French politician Talleyrand observed that Lafayette's "ambition, and his efforts to distinguish himself, do not seem his own, but rather to have been taught him. Whatever he does seems foreign to his nature, he always acts as though he follows someone else's advice."[38]

Lafayette continued to drop hints about his desire for a line command, and the elder man gently turned them aside. The two were together often over the next few months, the junior presenting one idea after another for campaigns and operations, for his senior's approval. As Washington evaluated each one, gradually the marquis appreciated the commander in chief's military methods, so unorthodox from a European perspective. Lafayette became the general's chief military student during the war. More important, the two of them could understand each other because both knew how to learn from experience. Other young men for whom Washington showed fondness sooner or later turned on him. Lafayette never did.[39]

LA FAYETTE IS THE SOLE EXCEPTION

Whatever starry-eyed images Lafayette had of the Continental Army, his first tour of its camp gave him a shock. This was not what the word "army" brought to the mind of a French officer. "About eleven thousand men, poorly armed and even more poorly clothed, offered a singular spectacle," he recalled. "In that motley and often naked array, the best garments were *hunting shirts.* . . . As for tactics, it suffices to say that, for a regiment formed in battle order to advance on its right, instead of a simple turn to the right, the left had to begin an eternal countermarch. They were always formed in two ranks, with the small men in the front; no other distinction as to height was ever observed."[40]

Lafayette had little direct contact with the army during the next few weeks, because he was part of Washington's family. The gulf between them and other general officers, on the one hand, and the men and officers of the regiments, on the other, was wide—socially, militarily, and materially. Generals and the family usually occupied houses or great pavilions in the field. Lesser souls lived in huts or tents.

Washington was no Spartan. He worked hard, and he ended the day in grand style. His dining habits were English, the main meal being a "dinner" late in the afternoon, followed by a "supper" a few hours afterward. Wine and rum were downed by the gallon, with meals and in toasts to this personage or that. Chastellux found these customs amazing. "The repast was in the English fashion," he said, "consisting of eight or ten large dishes of butcher's meat, and poultry, with vegetables of several sorts, followed by a second course of pastry, comprized under the two denominations of pies and puddings. After this the cloth was taken off, and apples and a great quantity of nuts were served, which General Washington usually continues eating for two hours, *toasting* and conversing all the time." He described the conversation as "calm and agreeable."

About half past seven the party arose from the table, which servants shortened for a smaller group. "I was surprised at this manoeuvre, and asked the reason of it; I was told they were going to lay the cloth for supper." Chastellux protested the extra trouble, which he assumed was for his benefit, but Washington told him he was accustomed to take something in the evening. He invited the Frenchman to join him and the family, eat some fruit, and participate in the conversation. He "desired nothing better." The supper offered three or four light dishes, some fruits, "and above all a great abundance of nuts, which were as well received in the evening as at dinner." After that, the waiters put "a few bottles of good claret and Madeira" on the table. "This supper or conversation, commonly lasted from nine to eleven, always free, and always agreeable."[41]

Claude Blanchard, a French quartermaster, also was impressed. "The table was served in the American style," he reported, "and pretty abundantly: vegetables, roast beef, lamb, chickens, salad dressed with nothing but vinegar, green peas, puddings and some pie, a kind of tart . . . all this being put upon the table at the same time." There were no separate courses: everything was served on the same plate. Madeira wine followed the eating, consumed "whilst drinking different healths."[42]

Except for the *anglais* custom of eating beef roasted rather than boiled, Lafayette found himself in congenial surroundings. Because he was a major general, he did not share the crowded quarters of Washington's aides, but otherwise he was folded easily into the "family." Reigning quietly over all was a tall, slender, handsome businessman with an honorary rank of lieutenant colonel, Tench Tilghman. He had joined Washington as his military secretary at the age of thirty-two in August 1776 and would remain until the end of the war. He was a born bureaucrat who kept the army's paperwork flowing smoothly. He also kept the younger aides in order and their minds on their jobs. Self-effacing, entirely dedicated to his duties, he was a rock in a swirling storm.[43]

Before Lafayette's arrival, the youngest of the family was Alexander Hamilton, a few months older than he was. The bastard son of a Scottish trader and a West Indian woman, he was orphaned early—his father abandoned the family before he was eleven, his mother dying soon after. He grew up on the slave-holding islands of St. Croix and Nevis, supporting himself into his teen years as a self-taught clerk and then business manager for a trading company. He so impressed his employers that they sent him to New York for a college education in 1773, but he soon devoted himself to revolutionary pamphleteering. When the shooting started, he became captain of a New York artillery battery and later served with distinction at Trenton. Washington talked him into becoming an aide in March 1777, with the rank of lieutenant colonel.

Hamilton was a small, frail young fellow, less than five and a half feet tall, with a tendency to fall into a sickbed after times of stress. He was reasonably handsome but self-conscious about an odd bump near the top of his nose. There was fire in his fiercely blue eyes. He was a dynamo of lightning-bright intelligence, wide-ranging

Alexander Hamilton, by C.W. Peale, early 1790s. Hamilton, Lafayette, and John Laurens formed a triangular friendship that endured until their deaths. (INDEPENDENCE NATIONAL HISTORICAL PARK)

knowledge, quick temper, and raging passions. He possessed the self-assurance that came with knowing he was smarter than other people, which included almost everyone he met. He was a good writer and spoke several languages.

He could be cold. He admired Washington, as almost everyone did, and instinctively understood what power meant in human affairs. The commander in chief was a powerful man, but he was also a childless one who adopted a paternal attitude toward youngsters in his charge. The orphaned bastard from the West Indies might have wanted a father figure to give his life the stability he had never known, but he was ferociously independent. When he joined the family, he resolved that if Washington offered any "advances" of personal friendship toward him, he would receive them "in a manner which showed at least I had no inclination to court them, and that I wished to stand rather on a footing of military confidence than of private attachment."[44]

Lafayette and Hamilton formed a lifelong friendship. That became a triangle at the end of August with the arrival of John Laurens. Twenty-three years old, he also was a slender young man, whose head seemed large for his body. It carried a handsome face with a high brow, noble nose, and strong chin. His wide eyes, as blue as Hamilton's, were set deep. His full mouth seemed always on the verge of a smile, from either amusement or arrogance, depending on the situation. He was almost as brilliant as Hamilton, but his mind was of a different order. While the one wanted to build a model world as if it was an engineering project, Laurens was on a crusade to improve mankind. He shared Hamilton and Lafayette's lust for glory on the battlefield. Reckless as they were, neither matched Laurens' tendency to lunge into the fight without thinking. They survived the war. He did not.

Laurens was from South Carolina, son of a prosperous Huguenot (Protestant) family that had fled religious oppression in France a century earlier. His father owned large plantations and hundreds of slaves, and had once been a slave trader before going into politics. Remarkably, Henry Laurens became increasingly uneasy about the injustice of slavery as the younger Laurens was growing up. When John's mother died in his sixteenth year, Henry took him and his brothers to Europe for their education. After a year in London, John and one brother spent the next three in Geneva, a hotbed of radical ideas about the equality of men and the logic of republican government. Besides those heady notions, Laurens acquired a wide grounding in the classics, philosophy, and languages—he became a master of several. His father sent him back to London to read law in 1775, but the uprising in America distracted him. He had a passing affair with the daughter of a wealthy family and got her pregnant. He married her but never bothered to tell his father about that.

Abandoning his little family early in 1777, John went to Paris, met Franklin, and made his way back to America. Once he joined the army, Washington developed a great deal of fondness for the younger man. Laurens, although he had a loving father of his own, returned the regard, accepting friend-

John Laurens, by C.W. Peale. The Latin inscription around this miniature echoes the epitaph on Laurens' gravestone, and means "It is sweet and fitting to die for your country." He did, in a skirmish in 1782, after he had opened Lafayette's mind to the injustices of slavery and religious intolerance. (INDEPENDENCE NATIONAL HISTORICAL PARK)

ship where Hamilton spurned it. Not even he, however, could match the place in the elder man's heart that Lafayette filled.[45]

Laurens and Hamilton hit it off. Hamilton showed a strong attachment to the South Carolinian that he never demonstrated even to the woman he later married. When Laurens was absent, Lafayette filled his place in Hamilton's affections. The three wrote gushy letters to each other. Hamilton routinely addressed Laurens as "my dear" and vowed his "love." Such language was usual in their time, the age of "Sentiment." Letter writing was almost a sport and flowery talk was the norm, especially for young fellows burning with passions for war and politics.[46]

Hamilton, with his penetrating mind and gift for argument, and

Laurens, with his fierce beliefs and crusading zeal, made great impressions on Lafayette. They talked about things that had never before crossed his mind—what was justice, what was the basis of government, what was right and wrong. Laurens especially broadened the Frenchman's thinking—and he could do it in flawless French—on two subjects. One was religious intolerance. The other was slavery. Laurens had returned from Europe a dedicated abolitionist. Eventually he aroused similar sentiments in Lafayette.

The relation between them was not all one-way, as Lafayette turned Laurens into a clotheshorse. After his arrival in the army, John wrote his father continually to ask him to send articles of clothing, hair powder, and other adornments. He had never before been so conscious of his appearance, and Henry was mystified. If he had visited the camp, he would have seen the explanation. John wanted to match the marquis' splendid appearance.[47]

Before Lafayette and the family became fully acquainted, on August 21 Washington invited him to a council of war. The generals decided that the Howes were probably taking their fleet and army to South Carolina, and agreed to ask Congress for permission to leave Philadelphia and challenge Clinton in New York. Lafayette signed the minutes along with the other major generals present, and above the brigadiers. Although he had been too junior to have attended a council of war in the French army, he recognized that this meeting was nothing like what a French general would have conducted. In Europe, commanders did the talking, and subordinates listened and agreed. Washington let everyone speak his mind, guiding the discussion but aiming for the broadest possible agreement, because he remembered from Braddock's example that he did not have a monopoly on good ideas. He did not know it at the time, but his conduct of councils of war gave Lafayette another example to follow in the future.[48]

There were two other major generals present, the rest of them being on detached duty. Lafayette charmed both of them. The oldest general in the army, at age fifty-one, was "Lord" Stirling, from New Jersey. He was named William Alexander but claimed to be the rightful Earl of Stirling. Authorities in Scotland did not agree, but his American colleagues called him and his wife Lord and Lady Stirling. The same courtesy extended to their pretty daughter Lady Kitty, who made Lafayette's head spin when he met her. His sexual escapades were not as frequent in America as in France, but his appetites were undiminished. He tried but failed to conquer "the most charming Miss Ketty," as he called her.

Stirling was a portly man with gray hair, who had married into wealth and built more. Much of his fortune had been destroyed by the British since the start of the war, and he seemed determined to spend what remained before he left the planet. He was a bluff, hard-drinking, and courageous man. Chastellux said, "[H]e is accused of liking the table and the bottle, full as much as becomes a lord, but more than becomes a general." The chevalier did not like him much, calling him "old and rather dull." His American colleagues thought otherwise. In a fight he was stone sober and energetic, inspiring confi-

William Alexander, Lord Stirling, by Bass Otis, after an earlier engraving, 1858. A hard drinker and a harder fighter, Alexander was Washington's oldest major general. His daughter "Miss Ketty" made Lafayette's head swim, but he never conquered her. (INDEPENDENCE NATIONAL HISTORICAL PARK)

dence in his men and fellow generals. He had built the fortifications of New York City and was captured on Long Island. After he was exchanged, he fought ably in several actions. He was staunchly loyal to Washington and was one of the first to integrate Knox's field artillery innovations into his own tactics. In the fight or out, he could be relied upon to do the right thing. Lafayette liked him immensely.[49]

The other major general was Nathanael Greene, a thirty-seven-year-old rising star in the army. He was a man of average height, slope-shouldered, with a broad, friendly face and wide-set eyes. The marquis impressed him with his boyish enthusiasm, modesty, deference to his elders, courteous adherence to military etiquette, open idolization of Washington—and "inexplicable charm," as he told his wife. As the commander in chief became an adoptive father to Lafayette, Greene stepped into the role of Dutch uncle, and the young fellow responded.

Nathanael Greene, by C.W. Peale, 1783.
Washington's best major general, Greene became the first in a succession of "uncles" who looked out for Lafayette when he was away from his adoptive father. (INDEPENDENCE NATIONAL HISTORICAL PARK)

Greene walked with a slight limp from a stiff leg he had been born with. The son of prosperous Rhode Island Quakers, he grew up in the family business of mills, forges, and merchandising. As a boy he developed an interest in the Latin classics and mathematics, which offended his strict parents. In 1773 he began studying military treatises and memoirs, and he helped revise the state militia regulations. When he tried to join the militia, he was rebuffed because of his gimpy leg, and expelled from his pacifist Friends meeting. In 1774 he married outside the denomination.

Greene raised his own militia company and started a friendship and intellectual partnership with Henry Knox. He became a brigadier general of state forces by May 1775, and a month later a brigadier in the Continental Army. During the siege of Boston he demonstrated twin

talents as an organizer of supplies and as a diplomat soothing the jealousies between officers from various states. He became a major general
in August 1776. Despite his fault in the Fort Washington disaster, Greene
became the commander in chief's most trusted adviser—to the extent
that he was accused of "dominating" his superior. He proved at Trenton
and in later campaigns that he was as brave as he was smart, an effective
leader, and an outstanding strategist.[50]

Lafayette's simple decency set him apart from other European officers who had invaded the Continental Army, and he got along even with
them. De Kalb acknowledged that when he complained about the bicker-
ing among the other French officers. "These people," he raged, "think of
nothing but their incessant intrigues and back-biting. . . . La Fayette is
the sole exception. . . . La Fayette is much liked, he is on the best of
terms with Washington."[51]

WE DON'T CARE HOW SOON HE
BEGINS THE FROLICK

*L*afayette had joined a perilous cause. Washington's army remained
deficient in tactics, intelligence, and supplies, while its leader was
still learning to command. The initiative in 1777 rested with the British.
Washington could not make the first move as long as the enemy controlled the sea and could go where it pleased. The redcoats had decided
to put down the American rebellion by force, and so they had to take the
offense. Washington was content to let them do that, reacting so far as
was within his army's abilities. The British accommodated him. Rather
than go after the Continental Army, the redcoats set out to conquer the
map, and cast off their advantages of size, experience, and logistical support by dividing their forces and miring them down where they could
not support each other.

The two-pronged invasion of upper New York under General John
Burgoyne was so hopeless that Washington felt little concern about it. It
was a British disaster from the outset. When Burgoyne dispatched a
Hessian brigade to raid Bennington, Vermont, militia swarmed to the
scene, surrounded the enemy, and captured several hundred Hessians in
the middle of August. Soon afterward, an invading army paralleling

Burgoyne's to the west ran for home when it heard a rumor that a large corps under Benedict Arnold was on its way.[52]

That left the main force under "Gentleman Johnny" Burgoyne, a notorious London dandy, who burdened his column with his mistress and wagons full of luxuries. The rugged terrain of forests, swamps, and mountains would bring him to grief, Washington knew. The commander of the Northern Department, Schuyler, cut trees and threw every conceivable obstacle in the way as Burgoyne's army gnawed through the landscape at the rate of under a mile a day. Congress, deciding that Schuyler was not aggressive enough, replaced him with Gates, who continued to prolong Burgoyne's ordeal, not rushing into a fight.

William Howe had spent months jousting with Washington, mostly in eastern New Jersey. But the "sly fox," as he called the American, would not let himself be forced into an all-out battle, and after both armies had marched themselves nearly barefoot, he gave up. He should have gone north to help Burgoyne, but instead had a fixation on taking Philadelphia. Leaving Clinton behind in New York with vague orders to support Burgoyne but not enough resources to do it, the Howes sailed away with their main army and 260 ships and disappeared. They dithered away most of the campaign season sailing to and fro. Washington concluded that they posed no threat to the capital city, because it made no sense to take it. The American rebellion was lodged not in a place but in an army and a government, and they could be anywhere. Besides, if Howe wanted Philadelphia, he need only sail up the Delaware and walk into town. Instead, he had last been seen off the Delaware capes.

On August 22, 1777, the day after Lafayette's first council of war, Washington learned that the British had sailed into Chesapeake Bay. Howe was headed for Philadelphia after all, and from an unexpected direction. On August 25, the enemy began landing at Head of Elk, the upper end of navigation on the bay. The Americans formed up to meet them. "I am in hopes," Greene wrote his wife, "Mr. How [*sic*] will give us a little time to collect, and then we don't care how soon he begins the frolick."[53]

Lafayette, close beside Washington, rode out to do righteous battle.

THE AMERICAN FIRE WAS MURDEROUS

*A*lerting Major General John Sullivan, detached with his division in New Jersey, Washington assembled his main body and set out for Wilmington, Delaware, to see what Howe was up to at Head of Elk (now Elkton, Maryland). His route of march was through Philadelphia. Lafayette rode on Washington's right, the rest of the family following. "With their heads adorned with green branches," the marquis recalled, "and marching to the sound of drums and fifes, these soldiers, despite their nakedness, presented a pleasing spectacle to the eyes of all the citizens. The general shone at their head."[54]

Washington, Lafayette, and Greene taking shelter from a storm near Wilmington, before the start of the Brandywine Campaign. (LILLY LIBRARY, INDIANA UNIVERSITY)

The army settled into position at Wilmington early in September, and Sullivan caught up with it, raising its total to about 11,000 men. Enemy numbers were about 12,500. Wanting a closer look, Washington, Greene, and Lafayette rode forward, spent a long day considering the prospects, then headed back to camp as dark fell. A sudden storm overtook them, and they sought shelter in a farmhouse, despite Greene's

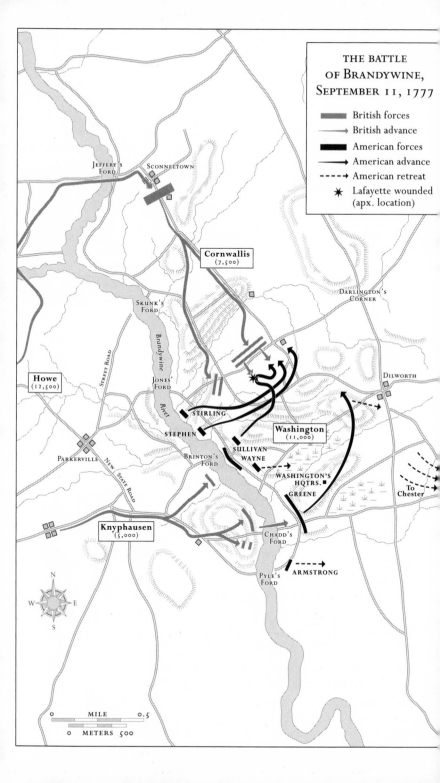

THE BATTLE
OF BRANDYWINE,
SEPTEMBER 11, 1777

British forces
British advance
American forces
American advance
American retreat
Lafayette wounded
(apx. location)

JEFFERY'S FORD
SCONNELTOWN

Cornwallis
(7,500)

DARLINGTON'S CORNER

SKUNK'S FORD

Brandywine

Howe
(12,500)

STREET ROAD

JONES' FORD

DILWORTH

STIRLING

STEPHEN

River

Washington
(11,000)

PARKERVILLE

NEW STATE ROAD

BRINTON'S FORD

SULLIVAN
WAYNE

WASHINGTON'S HQTRS.

GREENE

To Chester

Knyphausen
(5,000)

CHADD'S FORD

PYLE'S FORD

ARMSTRONG

N
W E
S

0   MILE   0.5
0   METERS   500

objections that Washington could be captured. They spent a forlorn night trying to dry off before a fire and returned to camp in the morning. When they rode out at dawn, Lafayette said, Washington "admitted that a single traitor could have betrayed him."[55]

Washington declined to tackle Howe in the open. When the redcoats and Hessians began their march, they angled to the left, planning to enter Philadelphia from the west. Washington moved between the enemy and the city and sent Greene out to find a good place to stop the invasion. Brandywine Creek seemed a likely bet. It was swift and deep, passable only at a series of shallow fords, flanked on either side by steep, wooded hills and ridges.[56]

Washington had not yet developed a good tactical intelligence system. He had few cavalry and used them as flank guards rather than as scouts. The Americans did not know just how many fords crossed the creek, and they confused the names of ones they did know. Howe and Cornwallis did better. The majority of citizens fled before them in panic, but loyalists stayed, providing information and drawing maps.

Washington established his headquarters east of Chadds Ford on September 10, 1777. There he placed two brigades and Greene's division, with a detachment of 800 men across the creek. He told a Pennsylvania militia brigade to cover his left, along with some mounted men. He ordered Sullivan to cover all fords north of Chadds with his division, and sent two other divisions to the east where they could support either Greene or Sullivan. It was not a bad plan, except that there were more fords north of Sullivan than he knew.

The morning of the eleventh dawned in thick fog, masking sight and sound until the sun burned through, making the day hot and steamy. Howe had moved out before five in the morning, sending out scouts in all directions, and divided his force, a risky maneuver. About 5,000 men under the Hessian general Wilhelm von Knyphausen headed for Chadds, drove the advance party back across the creek, then stood still while his cannons lobbed balls toward American gunners on the other side, who returned the favor. Neither side had much effect except to push the opposing infantry behind the treeline. Washington waited for Knyphausen to attack, and lost a good opportunity to attack him instead.

General Cornwallis' "grand division" of about 7,500 men, with Howe along, marched to the west, hidden by the terrain, covering seventeen miles in less than eleven hours. By the time they opened their part of the battle, Washington's line extended almost ten miles. The enemy showed him how to concentrate forces where they were needed.

Just before noon Washington received word of Cornwallis' movements and ordered Stirling and General Adam Stephen to shift their divisions north to Birmingham Meeting House, to block the road to Chadds Ford. He could have brought superior force to bear, with Sullivan's and Greene's divisions, against the enemy across Chadds, except that he began receiving contradictory information. He countermanded Stirling and Stephen's orders and waited to see what developed. Early in the afternoon, he received a frantic warning that he had been encircled. He renewed his orders to Stirling and Stephen and about four-thirty sent Sullivan to the north, where he assumed command of the whole right flank. Meanwhile, Knyphausen's gunners stepped up their cannonade, pinning Washington down.

The Battle of Brandywine, contemporary woodcut. This represents Sullivan's division beginning to break as Cornwallis' Hessians storm in from the left.
(LILLY LIBRARY, INDIANA UNIVERSITY)

Hell erupted to the north. Sullivan had been in this position before, on Long Island a year earlier. There he had also held a flank, which Howe swallowed after a jab at the army's center, earning him a few months in captivity. His luck and his scouting were no better this day. Before he could get his division fully deployed to Stirling's left, Cornwallis' army stormed into him, having crossed an unknown ford far upstream. The sudden roar of British fusillades and the ragged crackle of Americans firing individually, punctuated by the thump of cannons, were heard at Washington's post four miles away. Sullivan deployed, and the American troops gave as good as they got. Knox's artillery, distributed to "stiffen" the infantry, was especially effective. But the enemy was superior in numbers and in technique. The redcoats and Hessians drove a wedge between Sullivan and Stirling, and soon Sullivan's and Stephen's men began to falter.

Then Lafayette arrived on the smoke-filled battlefield. As Washington had been ordering Greene to move to Sullivan's support, the marquis asked if he could ride up to observe the situation. Distracted, the commander in chief agreed.

When the marquis got there, he said, "Milord Cornwallis' men suddenly emerged from the woods in very good order. Advancing across the plain, his first line opened a very brisk fire with cannon and muskets. The American fire was murderous, but both their right and left wings collapsed." Separating Stirling's division from the other two on its flanks and advancing across an open field despite heavy losses, the redcoats concentrated their fire on the center. "The confusion," said Lafayette, "became extreme."[57]

Greene's division, having crossed four miles of goat hills in forty-five minutes, stormed onto the scene at about six o'clock, Washington close behind. Sullivan's battalions were breaking, some scattering, some just falling back. Lafayette reacted instinctively and charged the fleeing men, riding his horse back and forth and shouting at them. Finally he dismounted and began shoving some to turn them around, slapping others on the back with the flat of his sword. By sheer force of will, he imposed order on his part of the line. Laurens also lunged into the fray, doing the same, getting himself soundly smacked in the ankle by a ricocheting musket ball. Even Lafayette was amazed at his friend's recklessness. "It was not his fault that he was not killed or wounded," he said, "he did every thing that was necessary to procure one or t'other."[58]

The noise was tremendous, and the young marquis' blood was up. He did not feel it when an enemy ball, probably from a Hessian rifle, punched through his left calf. He and other officers kept trying to reverse the tide, but the enemy pressure was too great. Greene deployed his men, letting the retreating soldiers pass through. He stabilized the front, stopping the enemy advance.

The generals and aides halted the fugitives behind a treeline in the rear. The army and its guns retreated behind Greene's shield as darkness fell, and the exhausted redcoats and Hessians collapsed onto the ground. Human bodies, dead horses, and splintered trees covered the dimming, smoke-shrouded field. Meanwhile, in Washington's absence Knyphausen had crossed Chadds Ford and driven back the Americans there. The militia on the left ran for home. Washington lost about 1,200 men, 400 of them prisoners. The enemy lost 577 killed and wounded, six missing.[59]

The American army was defeated but not destroyed. Washington retreated toward Chester. At about that time, Lafayette's aide Gimat saw blood seeping from the young general's boot, found a horse, and hoisted him aboard. He rode along with the retreating army, helped only by a

Lafayette Wounded at Brandywine, *an engraving by C. H. Jeens after an early-nineteenth-century painting by Alonzo Chappell. This echoes contemporary depictions of the deaths of Montcalm and Wolfe, which set a fashion for such scenes. The officer helping Lafayette is Gimat, while the figure on horseback may represent Lafayette's slave, name unknown.* (LILLY LIBRARY, INDIANA UNIVERSITY)

makeshift bandage Gimat had tied on him. At the Chester bridge he deployed troops to defend the crossing, and by the time Washington found him, the marquis was reeling in his saddle. The general summoned his surgeon, Dr. John Cochran, who applied first aid.

Cochran, Lafayette's aides, and Stirling's aide Captain James Monroe (a future president) carried him to a nearby church for further dressing of the wound. Monroe had been wounded at Trenton, and consoled him on that score while giving his French some exercise. The marquis retained his sense of humor. He later claimed that other officers, looking very hungry, entered the room where he was resting on a table, and he asked them not to eat him.

Washington arrived and ordered that he be put on a boat to Philadelphia. "Take care of him as if he were my son," Lafayette remembered the general saying, "for I love him the same."[60]

If Washington actually said such a thing, there is only Lafayette's word to go by. He had every reason to be worried. He was already fond of the young man and feared for his well-being. Moreover, the marquis had been in the sort of danger Washington was supposed to keep him out of.[61]

Lafayette was weak from loss of blood, not to mention his frenetic activity. He was a hero, and he had the wound to prove it. If this was martial glory, *très bien*. But did it have to hurt so much?[62]

I Am Now Fixed to Your Fate

(SEPTEMBER 1777-JANUARY 1778)

And at last his eyes seemed to open to some new ways. . . . He knew that
he would no more quail before his guides wherever they should point.
He had been to touch the great death, and found that, after all, it was
but the great death. He was a man.

— STEPHEN CRANE

ashington spent the winter learning from the
Roman general Fabius, of the third century BC. The
Carthaginian Hannibal had invaded Italy and in
three brutal battles wiped out 150,000 Roman sol-
diers. Fabius, who assumed command of the defense, knew that he could
not challenge Hannibal directly without taking another bloody beating,
and made Hannibal chase him all over southern Italy. Sneering Romans
called him Fabius Cunctator (Fabius the Delayer). After thirteen years,
Hannibal gave up and left the country. Fabius became Fabius Maximus
(Fabius the Greatest).

Fabian tactics were never popular among armchair generals. When
Washington declined to rush to upstate New York to meet Burgoyne,
he heard carping from members of Congress. Hamilton explained that

protecting any given place was less important than "preserving a good army" to "waste and defeat the enemy by piecemeal." In the long run, that would pay off. "Every new post they take, requires a new division of their forces, and enables us to strike with our united force against a part of theirs." The British could not suffer another Trenton without losing the war.[1]

After Brandywine Washington retreated, and on September 26, 1777, the British marched into Philadelphia. Lafayette and the other wounded were shipped off to Bethlehem, in northeastern Pennsylvania. Congress decamped for Lancaster, then York, and criticisms of Washington increased.

The general still hoped to defeat the enemy in a stand-up battle, and gave in to temptation when Howe put 9,000 men in an unfortified position at Germantown, seven miles northeast of Philadelphia. Four columns, two militia and two Continentals, were supposed to converge after a night march that began the evening of October 3. Everything went wrong. The militia failed to show up. Sullivan's unsupported division drove the British outposts back in confusion, but Greene's division had gotten lost, arriving late. Part of Sullivan's force had diverted to flush several redcoat companies out of a stone house and failed. Adam Stephen, who was drunk, attacked Anthony Wayne's brigade. British reinforcements arrived, and a thick fog swallowed everything. Washington lost a thousand men that day, twice the enemy's casualties. It looked like a disaster. Yet Washington realized that his army had made victory costly for the enemy.[2]

The following spring the commander in chief asked his generals what strategy to adopt in the fourth year of the war, and his chief engineer, Duportail, offered him a history lesson. Washington, he advised, should model himself on Fabius. What he said about that ancient conflict was familiar. "Fabius however commanded Romans," he explained, "but these Romans had been thrice defeated; they were disheartened, dreaded the enemy, and were nearly reduced to the condition of new and unformed troops." Fabius avoided general battles, despite bitter criticism in the capital. He knew that "the event would determine his reputation in the world," so he stuck to his plan, "and by his firmness which was crowned with success, he merited the appellation of Savior of Rome." His ego tickled, Washington became the American Fabius.[3]

ADVISE ME, DEAR GENERAL,
FOR WHAT I AM TO DO

*T*he night after Brandywine Washington sent a quick report to the president of Congress, commending Lafayette, whose actions probably saved Sullivan's division. The boy general had become popular among the other officers, and a hero to the troops. The commander in chief ended optimistically. "Notwithstanding the misfortune of the day," he said, "I am happy to find the troops in good spirits, and I hope another time we shall compensate for the losses now sustained."[4]

Lafayette had turned twenty years old five days before the battle. His behavior reminded Washington of himself when he was twenty-three. At the Monongahela he also had acted on his own in a hail of lead. Both battles had been defeats, but youthful energy and quick thinking kept the losses from being worse than they were.

The marquis awoke in Philadelphia on September 12, discouraged, in shock and pain, but he had heard from Adrienne at last. "I shall begin," he told her, "by telling you that I am well, because I must end by telling you that we fought in earnest yesterday, and we were not the victors. Our Americans, after holding firm for a considerable time, were finally routed. While I was trying to rally them, the English honored me with a musket shot, which wounded me slightly in the leg." The wound, he said, was "nothing," and all he had to do for it to heal was to lie on his back for a while, which put him "in very bad humor." He knew that whatever he wrote to her would be passed on to others, but he ended on a gloomy note. "This battle will, I fear, have unpleasant consequences for America; we must try to repair the damage, if we can."[5]

Lafayette did not know that his own reputation was taking a beating in France. Gossip connecting him with Mme. d'Hunolstein swirled through Paris and Versailles, his financial affairs were a mess, and newspapers repeated stories in the British press that he had been killed months earlier. Adrienne's mother had taken her to the country to keep the bad news from her. His letter would not reach her for two months.[6]

The marquis was soon moved to the hospital at "Bethlehem, a Moravian settlement, where the mild religion of that brotherly people and the community of goods, education, and interests among that large and simple family made a striking contrast to the scenes of carnage and the convulsions of civil war," as he put it afterward. Continuing in the third person, he said, "The good Moravian brothers loved him, and lamented his warlike folly; while listening to their sermons he dreamed of setting both Europe and Asia ablaze." He took the time to improve his English, and to read. He had never before read the *philosophes,* the Enlightenment French philosophers whose radical political ideas were on the march in America, and John Laurens' father, Henry, had supplied him with their books. Bedridden and hurting, the boy also spent time feeling sorry for himself, and became a letter-writing addict. [7]

Henry Laurens had escorted Lafayette to Bethlehem. He saw the political value of friendship with the father who had endowed John with his slender build, good looks, and thoughtful mind. On September 25, 1777, the marquis told him, "My leg is about in the same state and without your kindness would be in a very bad one." His English was improving, but it was loaded with literal translations of French idioms. "Troublesome it will be to you," he said, "for ever to have been so kind with me, because it

Henry Laurens in the Tower of London, 1781. John Laurens' father became a lifelong friend to Lafayette, and another of his "uncles." (U.S. SENATE COLLECTION)

seems me now that I became in right by my first obligations, of disturbing you for my businesses." Two days later he congratulated Laurens, "and myself with you for the good niews which we heared about the colonel's of the queen's light dragoons rgt army. *His royal* Master will not be very much satisfied with the conduct of that noble instrument of his justice, and I hope that we schall make too a proclamation one day or another before the walls of Quebec." [8]

Nearly all his letters to congressmen over the following years urged the commissioning or promotion of French soldiers in the army. Laurens answered indulgently but without promising anything. This letter also contained Lafayette's first mention of his hope for an American and French conquest of Canada. Then there was his reference to the colonel of the Queen's Light Dragoons, none other than Gentleman Johnny Burgoyne.

The long picnic Burgoyne, his officers, and their women had enjoyed ended dramatically on September 19, 1777, at Freeman's Farm on the upper North (now Hudson) River. Killings of civilians by his Indian allies had brought out hordes of militia, and Washington had sent Daniel Morgan's riflemen to lend Gates a hand. The frontier rifles and the aggressive tactics of Benedict Arnold finished the enemy off. There was another fight at Bemis Heights and then a ghastly siege. British and Hessian soldiers fell one after another amid the rotting corpses of their fellows. Burgoyne gave up on October 17. As buzzards circled overhead, an entire British army became prisoners of Horatio Gates, near the village of Saratoga.[9]

News of Freeman's Farm was a tonic to Lafayette. Again he told Adrienne about his "very slight wound in the leg," sounding very chipper about it. He did not know how he received it, he said; "in truth, I did not expose myself to enemy fire," a white lie. "It was my first battle, so you see how rare battles are." As for the wound itself, "[t]he surgeons are astonished by the rate at which it heals; they are in ecstasy every time they dress it, and maintain that it is the most beautiful thing in the world. I myself find it very foul, very tedious, and rather painful; there is no accounting for tastes." Maturity and humor were surfacing in the young general. "But, finally, if a man wished to be wounded just for his own amusement, he should come and see my wound and have one just like it."

This provided an excuse to brag about being close to Washington: "All the physicians in America" were looking after Lafayette, because his friend had told them to. That friend was Washington. "This estimable man," he continued, "whom I at first admired for his talents and qualities and whom I have come to venerate as I know him better, has become my intimate friend. His affectionate interest in me soon won my heart." The two of them lived together "like two brothers in mutual intimacy and confidence," and their close friendship made him as happy as he "could possibly be in this country. When he sent his chief surgeon to care for me, he told him to care for me as though I were his son, for he loved me in the same way."[10]

The wound was slow to heal, and Lafayette was eager to talk to Washington. A letter would have to do, but it would be difficult to write, and he put it off until October 14. "My dear general," he began, "I do not do myself the honor of wraïting to you as many times as I would chuse, because I fear to disturbe your important occupations." He beat around the bush for a while, until he got to what was really on his mind. "Give me leave, dear general," he begged, "to speack to you about my own business with all the confidence of a son, of a friend, as you favoured me with those two so precious titles. My respect, my affection for you, answer to my own heart that I deserve them on that side as well as possible." Since their "last great conversation," the marquis had not asked again about taking command of a division. Washington had been too busy, and so had Congress, so he had contented himself with fighting. "Now that the horable. Congress is settled quiete," he went on, "and making promotions, that some changements are ready to happen in the divisions, and that I endeavoured myself the 11 september to be acquainted with a part of the army and known by them, advise me, dear general, for what I am to do."

Instead of petitioning Congress for a command, "dear general I'l conduct myself by your advices." He asked Washington to consider that Europe and particularly France were watching him. He wanted "to do some thing by myself, and justify that love of glory which I left be known to the world in making those sacrifices which have appeared so surprising, some say so foolish. Do not you think that this want is right?" It might have been best that he had not received a division earlier because he did not know the army, but that had changed on September 11, at Brandywine. In any case, he would do whatever Washington "will think proper."

"You know I hope, with what pleasure and satisfaction I live in your family," Lafayette continued. "Be certain that I schall be very happy if you judge that I can stay in America without any particular employement." But if he stayed without a chance to distinguish himself, he would earn jeers from his friends and family—his reputation worried him more than anything else. "I do not tell all that to my general, but to my father and friend," he said. "I schall conduct myself entirely by your advices, and if you say that some thing is proper I'l do it directly——I desire only to know your opinion."

There was more in that line until he wound it up. He hoped to be in camp in three or four days, he said, where he would "speack to your excellency about all my businesses. I beg your pardon for being so tedious—— it is for you a disagreable and troublesome proof of my confidence——but that confidence is equal to the affection and respect which I have the honor to be with your excellency's the most obedient servant The Mquis. de Lafayette."[11]

The marquis' nervousness showed in his writing. His English had improved, and letters he wrote to others around the same time compared well with those of native speakers. But he was putting his adoptive father on the spot at the same time as he begged his approval. Washington had told him he would never get a line command and should stop asking for it, so it is not surprising that his hand and his language were both shaky. He fretted for four days. Fearing that he may have offended Washington, he wanted to see him in person. On October 18, although his wound was still open, he told Laurens that he had decided to go home to the army. He recommended promotion of a French friend to brigadier, "the rank to be in my family when I'l get a division of the army."[12]

Lafayette rode to Washington's camp northeast of Philadelphia. Because of his wound, he would not be able to pull on a boot for several weeks, but he was as game as ever. He was also popular. His fans included those who liked him, such as Greene (who called him "one of the sweetest-tempered young gentlemen") and even those who did not. Not only was he adorable, but he had bled for the American cause. Several people pointed that out to Washington.[13]

Among them was Sullivan, who asked for the young Frenchman's help. Thirty-six years old, he was a rawhide frontier lawyer and politician from New Hampshire. A burly, energetic man, his graceful manners hid a prickly ego, and he owned the proverbial Irish temper to go with his parentage. He said things in the heat of the moment that he later regretted and apologized for. He was a scrapper but not a natural general. Having grown up on a frontier ravaged by Indian raids, he had no love for either Indians or their former sponsors, the French, excepting Lafayette. He came into his own later in the war when he led campaigns against Indians.[14]

There were attempts to scapegoat him for losses in New York and at Brandywine. Congress had ordered a court of inquiry, the general solicited testimonials, and Lafayette offered his support. Although he thought Sullivan's character was beyond question, it was "with the greatest pleasure" that the marquis declared "how sensible" he had been "of his bravery at the affair of Brandiwine the 11 7bre [September]. I can assure him that such courage as he shewed that day will alwaïs deserve the praises of every one." Sullivan was cleared by the court.[15]

Another new friend was Colonel Daniel Morgan. Lafayette had been fascinated with the idea of American savages before he left France. Here was a *sauvage* in the flesh, and the two of them became lifelong friends. At forty-one, Morgan was as tough as any officer. Over six feet tall, over 200 pounds in bulk, he was known as the "Old Wagoner" because of his experience as a teamster during the French and Indian War. In that conflict he survived 500 lashes for punching a British officer, and the loss of all the teeth on one side when an Indian musket ball hit him in the face. Since then he had become a prosperous frontier farmer. He had raised the first of the Virginia rifle companies to reach Boston, was a hero at Quebec, a prisoner of the British for a year, and a hero again at Saratoga. He was a born soldier, and Lafayette held him in awe.[16]

Daniel Morgan, by C.W. Peale, 1794. The "Old Wagoner" fascinated Lafayette as an American sauvage, and Morgan's rifle tactics were important to the light-troop strategies that the marquis carried back to Europe. (INDEPENDENCE NATIONAL HISTORICAL PARK)

As the marquis continued to pester Washington for a line command, in late October he decided to cover his bases. If he could not lead American troops, maybe he could command French forces. Hoping to rehabilitate his standing in his own country, he sent de Broglie's secretary an ambitious plan for a campaign against the British West Indies, along with suggested actions in Asia and Canada. He explained why he had rank but no command in the American service, and so would be available to lead other campaigns. "The opportunities for doing something outstanding . . . are rare for a foreigner," he said. "This situation always causes jealousy or stifles the good that one can do in any country in the world; at least, that is what the French who are employed here are saying, and they are shrieking like devils," complaining about the conduct of the war. "As for the rest, among all the accusations and injustices, I hope that we always except General Washington, my friend, my intimate friend, and since I like to choose my friends, I dare say that to give him that title is to praise him."17

Lafayette sent an even more elaborate proposal to the French prime minister, the comte de Maurepas. He wanted to lead an expedition, to be authorized by Congress under Maurepas' influence. He proposed going to the West Indies to recruit pirates, with whom he would raid English shipping in the China and India trades. He repeatedly mentioned his youth and inexperience, as if this juvenile scheme needed any such explanation. He showed a boyish fascination with secret messages. Assuming his offer was accepted, "[i]n such a case, an order from the king, deigning to *recall me for a while to my family and friends* without *forbidding me to return, would signal me* to arm myself with American Continental commissions."

Lafayette wanted to be an American hero, and also a French one who urged his native country to enter the war against the *Anglais.* "Without giving myself the airs of a prophet in current affairs," he told the prime minister that "to inflict harm on England is to serve (do I dare say revenge?)" France. His proposal would do both, he suggested. As for his own situation, he had come to America without permission; he served "without any approbation" from the French government "but that of silence"; and he could allow himself "another little voyage without authorization." However his proposal worked out, "the flames of the smallest English settlement" would satisfy his heart.18

This was the voice of the vainglorious boy who had led his little army of peasant youths in campaigns around Chavaniac. If Washington had known about the letter, he might have hesitated to do what he did next. He was overwhelmed with problems, not knowing what Howe would do, his supply system collapsing. Moreover, he had set the legal wheels turning to cashier the drunkard Stephen and was drawing up lists of other officers who should be sacked. He needed division commanders with energy and ability. Greene had been urging him to give Lafayette a chance. He hesitated, because he feared that his affection for the marquis clouded his judgment. Lafayette's letter from Bethlehem prodded him, however.

On November 1 the commander in chief recommended a division command to Congress. Although he felt himself "in a delicate situation" with respect to Lafayette, considering "his illustrious and important connections—the attachment which he has manifested to our cause, and the consequences, which his return in disgust might produce, that it will be adviseable to gratify him in his wishes." This was especially important because "several gentlemen from France, who came over under some assurances, have gone back disappointed in their expectations." Lafayette had urged them not to complain when they got home, "and in all his letters has placed our affairs in the best situation he could." Besides, the young general was "sensible—discreet in his manners—has made great proficiency in our language, and from the disposition he discovered at the Battle of Brandy Wine, possesses a large share of bravery and military ardor."[19]

Lafayette did influence other French officers and had earned the undying loyalty of de Kalb. In a formal report to the war ministry, the baron explained: "The friendship with which he has honored me since I made his acquaintance, and that which I have vowed to him because of his personal qualities, oblige me to have that deference for him. No one is more deserving than he of the consideration he enjoys here. He is a prodigy for his age; he is the model of valor, intelligence, judgment, good conduct, generosity, and zeal for the cause of liberty for this continent." Regarding Lafayette's spendthrift ways, de Kalb said he had involved himself in them "only to advise economy." Even though the marquis was rich, de Kalb had advised him to "exercise more control over his generosity and liberality. I have not failed to speak of this to him often."[20]

Lafayette was defensive about his spending. He had heard about the alarm his bills raised at home. On November 6 he wrote Adrienne, for the first time addressing his wife with the intimate *tu* (you) instead of the formal *vous.* His financial problems he blamed on the loss of *Victoire* and her cargo. Although everything was expensive in America, it was worth it. He enjoyed the love of all Americans and especially "a tender union, sustained by a reciprocal confidence, with the most respectable and admirable of men, General Washington."[21]

The young general presumed on his connections with Laurens' father to promote the army's well-being. "Thoug I am near a very hot fire," he said, "howeer as my eyes fall in this moment upon three poor quite nacked fellows, it congeels in my blood and obliges me to tell you again how happy I would be if our army was drest in a comfortable manner." He had heard rumors that France might go to war against England. "How many reasons I have to wish it of all my heart," he crowed, "it would be too long to explain."

Two days later he announced that he was marching out with a detachment under Greene's command. "I hope my wound w'ont be much hurted," he said. "I shall never reproach myself loosing any occasion of doing some thing, as far as it can be for my present situation, or to speak better the inaction I am in." He was excited, as his language reflected.[22]

One foot booted, the other wrapped in a blanket, Lafayette again rode off to do righteous battle.

THE MARQUIS IS DETERMINED TO BE IN THE WAY OF DANGER

Cornwallis had expanded his reach over southern New Jersey, and the American Fabius saw a chance to raid an outpost, kill a few of the enemy, steal some livestock, and spread alarm. He and Greene cooked up a plan, and when Lafayette heard about it he volunteered to go along. Greene was happy to have him. They rode out on November 20, 1777, headed for a militia camp at Haddonfield.

Greene gave the marquis command of about 350 men, militia and a detachment of Morgan's rifles, and ordered him to reconnoiter toward Gloucester, where Cornwallis was encamped. On the twenty-fifth, Lafayette, still limping, crept toward an outpost. He could have been shot or captured, except, as he put it, "those who had the chance to kill him . . . counted too much on the dragoons, who should have taken him prisoner." There were about 350 Hessians and two cannons at the outpost. He deployed flankers to harry them, and led his screaming men straight at the enemy center, which fell back in disorder and kept falling back even when redcoat reinforcements showed up. Afterward, Cornwallis moved his troops across the river. Lafayette's action cost the enemy about sixty officers and men killed, wounded, or captured. He lost one officer killed and five enlisted men wounded. He retired to Haddonfield and reported to Greene.[23]

It had been a splendid little engagement, and he knew it. So did Greene, who reported to Washington hoping that his remarks would support Lafayette's case in Congress. After recounting the facts of the action, Greene concluded with the observation that Lafayette and his men "drove the enemy about half a mile and kept the ground until dark," a clear sign of victory. He ended with a flourish: "The marquis is determined to be in the way of danger."[24]

It was the first battlefield command of Lafayette's career, and he could not settle down. He hopped around on his good foot, as happy as he was excited. He could not wait to go to White Marsh to tell Washington. Greene suggested that he write a report, promising to send it along with his own.

"I want to acquaint your excellency of a little event of last evening," Lafayette began, "which tho' not very considerable in itself will certainly please you on account of the bravery and alacrity a small part of ours showed in that occasion." He had a gift for blowing his own horn by saluting others. The conduct of the soldiers was "above all praises." He had never seen men "so merry, so spirited, so desirous to go on to the enemy what ever forces they could have as that little party was in this little fight. . . . I returned to them my very sincere thanks this morning. I wish *that this little success of ours* may please you—tho' a very trifling one I find him [it] very interesting on account of the behaviour of our soldiers."

Lafayette knew that his actions would meet with Washington's approval. If he had had any doubts, his English would not have been so readable, although Greene may have helped him. In any event, the message overflowed with infectious enthusiasm. It also furthered his reputation for modesty, by downplaying his own achievement. He said of Greene,

"I should have been very glad if circumstances had permitted me to be useful to him upon a greater scale." He signed off with "the most tender affection and highest respect."[25]

The young soldier had done so well that Washington did not wait for him to get back to camp to forward Greene's report to Congress, renewing his request to award a division to Lafayette. There were vacancies in the army, and the marquis had earned it. "I am convinced," the general said, "he possesses a large share of that military ardor which generally characterizes the nobility of his country. He went to Jersey with Genl. Greene, and I find that he has not been inactive there."[26]

Congress was impressed with Greene's report, especially the observation that "[t]he marquis is determined to be in the way of danger," and ordered it published in several newspapers. The Continental Army could use generals with that kind of spirit. President Laurens already favored a line command. Lafayette gave him a nudge, at Washington's prompting. "His excellency has been pleased to let you know a very small engagement on the other side of Delaware," he observed. The skirmish was "very trifling in itself," and no merit could be assigned to himself, "the general officer who was by chance with them." However, he had the greatest pleasure to see "with what bravery and alacrity a little reconnoitring party" had beat up the Hessians. "I was there nothing almost but a witeness, but I was a very pleased one in seeing the behaviour of our men."[27]

Congress resolved "[t]hat General Washington be informed, it is highly agreeable . . . that the marquis de La Fayette be appointed to the command of a division in the Continental Army." On December 4, 1777, Washington announced that he had been appointed to "command of the division lately commanded by General Stephen." It was Lafayette's lucky day, because the division he took over was from Washington's home state, and he also learned of the birth of his second daughter, Anastasie.[28]

Lafayette was polite and deferential to his superiors. He sent Laurens his personal thanks. "I am very sensible of the mark of confidence I received from Congress in being appointed to a division of the army," he said, promising to deserve it by his own and the division's conduct on all occasions. His "tenderest and warmest attachement for our respectable and great general" made him especially grateful to command Washington's fellow Virginians.[29]

Word of Brandywine reached France in October, followed by news of Lafayette's wound, the defeat at Germantown, and the victory at Saratoga. The marquis became caught up in French joy over England's defeat. Newspapers had him single-handedly routing a British regiment at Brandywine, Voltaire praised him, street minstrels sang ballads about his bravery, even English mothers read stories about him to their children—and his father-in-law forgave him. "The very persons who had blamed him most for his bold enterprise now applauded him," Lafayette's friend Ségur recalled. "The court showed itself almost proud of him and all the young men envied him. Thus, public opinion, turning more and more toward the war, made it inevitable and dragged a government too weak to resist in the same direction." The fugitive from the king's warrant now carried the glory of France on his slight shoulders. [30]

The British prime minister, Lord North, worried that the marquis' celebrity would push France into the war. In December he sent an envoy to Paris to negotiate with Franklin, Deane, and a new American agent, Arthur Lee, but they spurned him. They told Congress that King Louis was determined to acknowledge American independence and "make a treaty with us of amity and commerce." Besides the king's "real good will to us and our cause," it was in France's interest that English power be diminished by the loss of its American colonies. "There is every appearance of approaching war." There was more good news, a pledge of an additional grant to the United States of 3 million livres. Spain promised an equal sum. [31]

As Americans used Lafayette to boost their interests in France, so did Vergennes. He had to overcome Maurepas' resistance; the prime minister was shy about war, and he thought the marquis' proposal to hire pirates was silly. The foreign minister, however, passed around Lafayette's accounts of the military situation and claims of close connection to Washington. With the collapse of de Broglie's plot, the boy general was the highest French officer with any potential to become generalissimo. It was a fading dream, but it lingered. The marquis created public sentiment that boosted Vergennes' hopes of *revanche* for his country's defeat in 1763.

Lafayette reinforced it all with a long letter to d'Ayen in December 1777. It was time to claim his father-in-law's respect. His rise to a divisional command provided the pretext, along with an introduction for

John Adams, on his way to Paris to replace Deane. He offered a glowing account of the military situation and of his participation in events. He also dropped names and promoted France's formal entry into the war. "America is most impatiently expecting us to declare for her," he said. France, he hoped, would "decide to humble the pride of England." The Americans were not, he confessed, as strong as he had expected, but with the help of France they would "win the cause" he so cherished "because it is just, because it honors humanity, because it is in the interest of my nation, and because my American friends and I are deeply committed to it." The American cause was to squash the divine right of kings, although he had not yet recognized that. His words must have given his father-in-law, a pillar of royalist society, a chill.

The marquis admitted that he had intended to lead a division from the outset, but went the whole summer without a command. He had spent that time "in General Washington's household [*là chés le Gal. Vashington*], just as though I were in the home of a friend of twenty years." After his victory in New Jersey, Lafayette claimed, Washington had offered him his choice of troops to command, and he had taken a division composed entirely of the general's fellow Virginians. He predicted that America would win its war because of "the superiority of General Washington . . . Our general is a man formed, in truth, for this revolution, which could not have been accomplished without him." The marquis saw the general "more intimately than any other man" and could testify that he was "worthy of the adoration of his country." His warm friendship for Lafayette and his "complete confidence" in him in "all things military and political, large and small," let the marquis "share everything he has to do, all the problems he has to solve and all the obstacles he has to overcome. Every day, I learn to admire more his magnificent character and soul."[32]

Lafayette had no intention of returning to the Hôtel de Noailles, however. "Don't you think, my dear heart," he asked Adrienne, "that after my return we shall be mature enough to establish ourselves in our own house, where we shall be happy together, receive our friends, establish an easy freedom, and read the foreign newspapers without having the curiosity of going to see for ourselves what is happening?"[33]

Claiming to be an American hero, Lafayette wanted to be a French one as well, and enlisted Adrienne's help. Sending his joy at the birth of their second daughter, he asked her to aid his cause and show American envoys around. He gave Adams a letter of introduction to her because "I thought it would not be disagreeable to you if I would desire Madame de la Fayette . . . to introduce you to some of my other friends." He thrust his shy, lonely bride onto the stage of world affairs at the age of eighteen.[34]

HE LIKES TO CONSULT ME ABOUT THE MOST IMPORTANT MATTERS

R obert Morris became Lafayette's private banker and financial manager. Morris put him on an allowance, which he usually exceeded, and forced him to ask for "loans" against his own account for anything extra. The system worked, more or less, but once Lafayette had his own troops he could not resist dipping into his purse to buy them food and clothing. He spent "very generously," one of his aides said, buying everything he could find to equip and arm his soldiers. "This war has cost him enormous sums of money."[35]

"Your condescension Sir to take notice of the naked condition of our soldiery," Henry Laurens told Lafayette, "is a mark of paternal regard for those your adopted sons." He said he was "morally certain" of sending him a large supply of blankets and clothes before Christmas. They did not arrive.[36]

The supply system of the Continental Army had collapsed by late fall 1777. The quartermaster general, Thomas Mifflin, fell out with Washington over the loss of Philadelphia, but he had been notably unhelpful anyway. The quartermaster's department was in "a most wretched condition," Greene complained, because Mifflin had not been seen with the army since it entered Pennsylvania. In November, Washington forced him to resign. Mifflin then had a grievance against the commander in chief, and he nursed it. The burden of army supply fell increasingly on Greene, whom Washington persuaded to become quartermaster general late in the winter.[37]

There was a separate commissary general of subsistence, to provide the army's food, but transportation was the responsibility of the quartermaster, and Mifflin had neglected it. The army's suffering that winter was

*Thomas Mifflin, by C.W. Peale, 1783–84. The
failed quartermaster general nursed a grudge
against Washington that played a large role in the
"Conway Cabal."* (INDEPENDENCE NATIONAL
HISTORICAL PARK)

due to a shortage of wagons and draft animals, without which nothing could be hauled even if it had been procured. The Continental Army suffered from bad currencies, which shippers and suppliers would not accept, and competition from the British in Philadelphia, who paid in hard cash.[38]

A delegation from Congress visited Washington early in December 1777, urging him to attack Philadelphia and drive the British out. He asked his council of war for advice, and Lafayette echoed the other generals. Attacking fortified positions would invite unacceptable casualties, he said. The terrain posed obstacles, such a movement could not be kept secret, the militia was nowhere to be seen, and supplies were short. He advised going into winter quarters.[39]

John Laurens was outraged that Congress would suggest such a thing. "Our army in particular requires exemption from fatigue in order to compensate for their want of clothing," he railed at his father; "relaxation from the duties of a campaign, in order to allow them an opportunity of being disciplined and instructed; warm quarters, that it may appear in the spring with undiminished numbers and in the full powers of health; etc. Besides it is urged that the hardships which our soldiers undergo discourage men from enlisting."[40]

Nobody wanted to join an army that looked, as one private described it, "not only starved but naked." The greater part of the men were not only shirtless and barefoot but "destitute of all other clothing, especially blankets." The Continental Army was "as disheartened as need be." When the troops reached their winter quarters a few days before Christmas, "[i]n our miserable condition, to go into the wild woods and build us habitations to *stay* (not to *live*) in, in such a weak, starved and naked condition, was apaling in the highest degree."[41]

On December 19, 1777, the army went into winter quarters at Valley Forge, twenty miles northwest of Philadelphia. It actually was a steep ridge overlooking the Schuylkill River, a windswept, inhospitable place. Its only natural comforts were an abundant water supply and nearby forests to provide firewood and building materials. Washington selected it because it was defensible and because it stood between the British army and York, where the disgruntled Congress sat. De Kalb suggested that the place had been chosen on the advice of a speculator, a traitor, or a council of ignoramuses. Nobody argued with him.[42]

The sufferings of the army at Valley Forge have become legendary, but they were real enough. Everything was in short supply. Fatigued and underfed men labored to erect huts of fence rails and tree trunks chinked with clay, moss, or straw. Even in that they were defeated, as straw was in short supply. Many thatched roofs went unfinished, and many men— crowded twelve to each small room—slept on brush or bare ground. The hovels quickly attracted bedbugs and other vermin, and the chimneys were so poorly built that they filled the rooms with smoke. A third of the 9,000-man army was unfit for duty by the end of December, and cries of "No meat! No meat!" echoed through the camp.[43]

Lafayette remembered that the soldiers lacked everything. "Their feet and legs turned black with frostbite, and often had to be amputated." The lack of hard money deprived them of food as well as clothing. He and his aides lived in a commandeered house and usually ate better than the privates. Another French officer observed, "We, who lived in good quarters, did not feel the misery of the times, so much as the common soldiers, and the subaltern officers; yet we had more than once to share our rations with the sentry at our door."[44]

The situation in the camp was so bad, said Brigadier General James Mitchell Varnum, "that in all human probability the army must soon dissolve." Washington begged Congress for relief. "What then is to become of the army this winter," he asked, "and if we are as often without provisions now, as with it, what is to become of us in the spring," when he hoped to campaign before the enemy could be reinforced.[45]

Lafayette did what he could to improve his men's condition. He pestered Henry Laurens when the promised clothing and blankets did not arrive, because they were, "I am told, detained in York town and confined in a dark jail. Consider, if you please, that they are innocent strangers, traveling thro' this state, and very desirous of meeting the Virginian regiments they belong to. If they are detained only for exerting the most respectable rights of hospitality receive here my thanks in the name of Virginia. But if it is possible, I do not want they should be entertained longer." He raised the subject again two weeks later when the goods had still not reached camp, without the humor, and badgered Governor Patrick Henry to get Virginia to meet its quotas for recruitment and supply.[46]

When Duportail outlined field fortifications to defend the camp, Lafayette, Stirling, and Greene rotated as "major general of the day," supervising the work. The others grumbled, but the marquis complained only about the shortage of tools. He stayed on-site as the labor went forward, to show his men that he ate the same poor rations and suffered the same conditions as they did. That did not impress them, but when he reprimanded an officer for making soldiers work before they had eaten, they enjoyed it.[47]

Lafayette spent part of almost every day with Washington and wrote him personal letters, either when he could not see Washington or when the spirit moved him. They were formal military messages, but he signed off with unmilitary salutations such as "with the tenderest respect and highest admiration." He was not afraid to challenge his commander when he thought he was in the wrong. Once he reported two officers who separately left their posts. Lafayette and Washington disagreed on what to do about them, and the commander in chief held them for court-martial over the marquis' objections. One was acquitted, the other convicted and discharged.

Lafayette protested, feeling that the trials were not justified in either case. He wanted the guilty verdict overturned, and lost that argument also. So he wrote a long letter for the record, beginning, "I schall make use in this particular instance of the liberty you gave me of telling freely every idea of mine which could strike me as not being useless to a better order of things." He ended with this: "There are reasons against court martials, when there is not some considerable fault to punish. According to my affair I am sorry in seeing the less guilty being the *only one punished*. However, I shall send to court martials but for such a crimes, that there will be for the judges no way of indulgence and partiality."[48]

Direct challenges like that made the young general nervous, and it showed in his English. More often, he begged for Washington's approval, as in a long, unsolicited letter recommending all manner of things. "Is it not very importune and even very impertinent," he asked, "to lay before you my young and unexperienced ideas about what is to be done? But if they are unjudicious and unacceptable, I hope at least that you will not miss the sentiment which dictate them. I am very far from thinking myself able to give any advice in this army, but I dare hope that my warmest wishes for the good and right could inspire me some times with some tolerable ideas, and as I have no pretentions in it I'l see myself deceived by false ones without being surprised at all."[49]

However often Lafayette asked for Washington's reassurance, to his audience in France he emphasized how much the elder man depended on him. Telling Adrienne once more why he could not come home, he said his presence was "more necessary to the American cause at this moment" than she could imagine. There was much at stake, because "General Washington will be truly unhappy if I speak to him of leaving. His confidence in me is greater than my age allows me to admit. In his position, he is surrounded by flatterers and secret enemies. He finds in me a trustworthy friend to whom he can open his heart, and who always tells him the truth. Not a day passes that he does not have long conversations with me or write me long letters, and he likes to consult me about the most important matters. At this moment there is a particular matter in which my presence is of some use to him; this is not the moment to speak of leaving."[50]

Lafayette flattered himself, but in this case he was right. He had just done something for his adoptive father that nobody else could have. The commander in chief suffered one of the greatest crises of his career, and the young general helped him through it.

I ENTERTAIN SENTIMENTS OF THE
PUREST AFFECTION

$\int$ aratoga was a serious military loss for Britain, and a worse political one. Howe's hostile reception farther south showed that there was no widespread loyalist support in the middle states. Washington had met tactical defeat, but his soldiers had fought stoutly enough to give the enemy a hard shock. The Continental Army was still together.

Some members of Congress were not so sure, because the positive aspects of the Main Army's defeats were not obvious to anyone who was not a soldier. It was also easy to draw a contrast between Washington's setbacks and Gates' victory. Discontent in high places made for grumbling and encouraged change for the sake of change. That was fertile ground for the seeds of personal ambitions, and no one had more ambition than Brigadier General Thomas Conway, another of Silas Deane's gifts to the American cause. Born in 1735 in Ireland, he grew up in France, where he entered the army in 1749. He saw service during the Seven Years' War and rose to colonel by 1772. He made his way to America in April 1777, carrying Deane's promise of a brigadier general's commission.

A large man with a chinless, rather pop-eyed face, Conway was much given to posturing and intrigue. He encouraged civilians to believe that he owned great military talents, but he wore out his welcome in the army with his pomposity and ceaseless bragging. "It is a maxim with him to leave no service of his untold," Washington snorted. Conway established himself as a thorn in Washington's side, one of the few people the general ever expressed personal animosity toward. Hamilton called him "one of the vermin bred in the entrails of this chimera dire. . . . There does not exist a more villainous calumniator or incendiary."[51]

At first Lafayette admired Conway, swallowing his claims to military genius and his proffers of friendship. The Irish-Frenchman saw the marquis' closeness to Washington and his moderating influence over other French officers. He wanted to win the young general over to his side, helping him draw up his plans for expeditions against the British, which Conway presented to Congress as his own. When Henry Laurens mentioned them in a letter, Lafayette volunteered to present them to the French government. Hence his pirate proposal to Maurepas.[52]

Conway would use anybody or anything to advance his own interests, and when it came to feathering his own nest he was no slacker. He often left his brigade to push his case among the delegates to Congress, hinting that he should be promoted to major general. Rumors that he was about to have his way hit the army in the middle of October 1777, and Washington cut the ambitious brigadier off. If there was any truth in a report he had received, he told Richard Henry Lee, that Congress had appointed or was about to appoint Conway a major general, it would be "as unfortunate a measure as ever was adopted. I may add (and I think with truth) that it will give a fatal blow to the existence of the Army." Conway's talent, said Washington, "exists more in his own imagination, than in reality." He was also the junior brigadier. To promote him over the heads of all the others would cause most of them to resign, and with good reason. In conclusion, he said, "I have been a slave to the service: I have undergone more than most men are aware of, to harmonize so many discordant parts; but it will be impossible for me to be of any further service, if such insuperable difficulties are thrown in my way." There were limits to how much interference in his command he would put up with.[53]

Washington believed that he had scuttled Conway's project, and turned his attention to the condition of his army. It was still woefully untrained, so he needed an additional staff officer to supervise training and maneuvers and to prepare regulations. European officers in his camp had made him familiar with the role of inspectors general in foreign armies.

The commander assembled a council of fourteen generals on October 29, 1777, and asked them, "Will the office of inspector-general to our army, for the purpose principally of establishing one uniform set of maneuvers and manual, be advisable as the time of the adjutant-general seems to be totally engaged with other business?" The generals answered that "such an officer was desirable, the manual of regulations to be first agreed upon by the commander in chief, or a board of officers appointed for the purpose." By that statement, they reminded him that the inspector must be subordinate to the commander, who should issue any regulations. The new officer would superintend the training of the whole army, imposing a common set of tactics, under the commander in chief's authority. Washington sent the record of the meeting to Congress and asked it to establish the inspector general's position.[54]

Congress passed his request to its Board of War, established in June.

It was supposed to handle all military matters and correspondence, and supervise recruitments and supplies in the thirteen states. Because the board had been ineffective, Congress appointed the victorious Gates as its chairman. He was soon joined by the disgruntled former quartermaster general, Thomas Mifflin.

Conway was present at the meeting on the proposed inspector general and signed the report. He let Congress know that he would like the new job, which carried a major general's rank. He believed that Gates' fortune was on the rise after Saratoga, and Washington's was about to fall, so he hitched his wagon to Gates' star and wrote him a flattering letter that disparaged Washington. There were grumbles in Congress that the cause might be better served with the victor of Saratoga in command, instead of the loser of Germantown. They remained nothing more than idle mutters, and not even Gates put much stock in them.

Major James Wilkinson, Gates' aide, saw Conway's letter to his general and was greatly amused. He stopped at Lord Stirling's headquarters at the end of October. As one drink led to another, Wilkinson began to talk. Hearing what Conway had been up to, Stirling sobered up and passed the news to Washington.[55]

Conway had crossed the boundaries of military decency. On November 9, Washington confronted him bluntly: "Sir: A letter which I received last night, contain'd the following paragraph. In a letter from Genl. Conway to Genl. Gates he says: 'Heaven has been determined to save your country; or a weak general and bad councellors would have ruind it.' I am Sir Yr Hble Servt. George Washington."[56]

As November passed, Washington's generals and aides saw signs of a plot in Congress to replace him with Gates. There was no organized conspiracy, but there were those—Mifflin in particular—who saw fit to advance Gates' case, and for various reasons, Conway's name popped up often. Hamilton and John Laurens urged Washington to head it all off. The commander in chief made it well-known near the end of the month that he wanted to hear the last of Conway. Lafayette seemed blind to the growing unrest, praising Gates when others criticized him. But he began to have doubts about Conway.[57]

The petulant Irish-Frenchman had developed a habit of threatening to resign if he did not get his way. Lafayette observed this in passing in a letter to Henry Laurens, which alarmed congressmen who believed that

Conway was an asset. Laurens told Lafayette that to lose Conway "would be a circumstance extremely mortifying to a few persons here who hold themselves to be of the best friends to the United States. . . . We have something in view which we hope will hold the general longer in America."[58]

"Something in view" became clear on December 13, 1777, when Congress authorized two inspectors general, "essential to the promotion of discipline in the American Army." Instead of being the eyes and ears of the commander in chief, Congress wanted the officers to be political commissars. They were to send their reports to the Board of War, not the commander, and forward any complaints or grievances to Congress. As Hamilton put it, this measure "conferred powers which could not fail to produce universal opposition in the army," and by requiring the approval of the Board of War before the introduction of every regulation, it introduced delays that would "defeat the usefulness of the institution." It erected a political wall between the commander and his own army. Even worse than that, Congress appointed Conway to one of the positions (it never filled the other) and promoted him to major general.[59]

Lawmakers believed that this inspectorate, proposed by Washington himself, would improve the army. There may have been a few who hoped that appointing Conway would force Washington to resign, but they were few. The majority believed Conway's self-professed reputation as a military expert and accepted his concept—he had helped draft the bill—as the recommendation of an authority. They did not understand that they had imposed an inspectorate that directly challenged Washington's control of his army. They were equally unaware that every high officer at Valley Forge saw the office and Conway's appointment as a plot to unhorse the commander in chief.[60]

All the generals and virtually all the colonels rose in outrage. The brigadiers threatened to resign en masse, and Greene, ever diplomatic, tried to calm them down. He noticed Lafayette and other French officers giving Conway the cold shoulder when he reached camp late in December 1777. He also decided that there really was a "cabal," organized by Gates, to drive Washington out of the army, so he took it upon himself to write to Congress, calling for the discharge of all foreign officers. Greene excepted only Lafayette, because of "this nobleman's generous, disinterested conduct, his sacrifices to our cause, and his great merit." He explained why so many officers were upset at what they saw as favoritism for one who had not earned promotion. Sullivan drafted a letter, which all the generals signed, making the same demand, and also excepting Lafayette. Sullivan advised Washington to withhold announcing any recent promotions, meaning Conway. Washington agreed.[61]

When Conway presented himself, ready to take up his duties, the commander in chief gave him an icy reception. He observed that the Board of War's instructions said that the board would furnish a set of regulations. When he asked if Conway had those instructions with him, the inspector general said that he did not. Washington told him that he could not possibly serve in his new office until the regulations arrived, and had an aide show the fuming Irish-Frenchman the door.

Conway complained to Gates, "I have been coolly received at my arrival here," and returned to York. Washington wrote to Congress opposing Conway's appointment, sending along the minutes of the October meeting to show that his version of the inspectorate was not what had been recommended. He wrote again when he heard Conway's complaint about their meeting. "If General Conway means," he said, "by cool receptions . . . that I did not receive him in the language of a warm and cordial friend, I readily confess the charge. I did not, nor shall I ever, till I am capable of the arts of dissimulation. These I despise, and my feelings will not permit me to make professions of friendship to the man I deem my enemy and whose system of conduct forbids it. At the same time truth authorizes me to say, that he was received and treated with the proper respect to his official character, and that he has had no cause to justify the assertion, that he could not expect any support for fulfilling the duties of his appointment."[62]

Lafayette finally tumbled to what was going on, and learned that Conway had implicated him and de Kalb in his dealings with the board and Congress. When he asked Washington about it, the general showed him Lord Stirling's letter. He was shaken to the core, spied a plot to destroy the revered Washington, and feared that the general might think he had been in on it. Conway was the enemy, and so was Gates. They had played him for a fool and made him look like a traitor to his adoptive father. He had to do something.[63]

On December 29 the marquis went to headquarters. The general was too busy to see him, so he spent all night writing Washington a letter. He was so overcome by emotion that it mangled his English, and his hand shook enough to make his writing hard to read. He poured his young heart out. "My dear general," he began, "I don't need telling you how I am sorry for all what happens since some time. It is a necessary dependence of my most tender and respectful friendship for you, which affection is as true and candid as the other sentiments of my heart and much stronger than a so new acquaintance seems to admit. But an other reason to be concerned in the present circumstances is my ardent, and perhaps enthusiastic wishes for the happiness and liberty of this country. I see plainly that America can defend herself if proper measures are taken and now I begin to fear that she could be lost by herself and her own sons."

When in Europe, Lafayette continued, he thought that in America "almost every man was a lover of liberty and would rather die free than live slave." He was therefore astonished to hear Toryism (support of the king) professed as openly as Whiggism (opposition to the king). He had believed "that all good Americans were united together" and that the confidence of Congress in Washington was "unbounded." He "entertained the certitude that America would be independant" so long as Washington was in command. "Take a way for an instant," he told his adoptive father, "that modest diffidence of yourself (which, pardon my freedom, my dear general, is sometimes too great, and I wish you could know as well as myself, what difference there is betwen you and any other man upon the continent), you shall see very plainly that if you were lost for America, there is nobody who could keep the army and the revolution for six months." There were "oppen dissentions in Congress, stupid men who without knowing a single word about war undertake to judge you, to make ridiculous comparisons."

He went on to state his surprise at the creation of the Board of War and its interference in the army, and said that the promotion of Conway was "beyhond all my expectations." He confessed to being fooled by Conway, who "says he is entirely a man to be disposed of by me, he calls himself my soldier, and the reason of such behaviour for me is that he wishs to be well spoken of at the french court . . . but since the letter of Lord Stirligg I inquired in his caracter." Lafayette had found him to be an ambitious and dangerous man who had done all he could "by cunning maneuvres to take off my confidence and affection for you. His desire was to engage me to leave this country." Observing that all the generals had rebelled against Congress, he worried, "Such disputes if known by the ennemy, can be attended with horrid consequences. . . . I wish indeed those matters could be soon pacified. I wish your excellency could let them know how necessary you are to them."

Apologizing for his "very useless and even very importune" letter, Lafayette expressed shock that a Frenchman could behave so badly. "But, sir, besides Connway is an Irishman. . . . That gentleman had engaged me by entertaining my head with ideas of glory and shining projects, and I must confess for my shame that it is a too certain way of deceiving me." He rambled some more and concluded: "My desire of deserving your satisfaction is stronger than ever, and every where you'l employ me you can be certain of my trying every exertion in my power to succeed. I am now fixed to your fate and I shall follow it and sustain it as well by my sword as by all means in my power."[64]

This was an expression of absolute love and loyalty. Washington had never in his life received anything like it. Beset by troubles all around, betrayed by one officer after another, not knowing if he could trust anyone, he now knew there was one person in the world who would never turn on him. He told him so: "My dear marquis, Your favor of yesterday conveyed to me fresh proof of that friendship and attachment which I have happily experienced since the first of our acquaintance, and for which I entertain sentiments of the purest affection. It will ever constitute part of my happiness to know that I stand well in your opinion, because I am satisfied that you can have no views to answer by throwing out false colours, and that you possess a mind too exalted to condescend to dirty arts and low intrigues to acquire a reputation. Happy, thrice happy, would it have been for this army and the cause we are embarked in if the same generous spirit had pervaded all the actors in it."

As for Conway, "[h]is ambition and great desire of being puffed off as one of the first officers of the age, could only be equalled by the means which he used to obtain them; but finding that I was determined not to go beyond the line of my duty to indulge him in the first, nor, to exceed the strictest rules of propriety, to gratify him in the second, he became my inveterate enemy; and has, I am persuaded, practised every art to do me an injury. . . . How far he may have accomplished his ends, I know not, and, but for considerations of a public nature, I care not. For it is well known, that neither ambitious, nor lucrative motives led me to accept my present appointment; in the discharge of which, I have endeavoured to observe one steady and uniform conduct, which I shall invariably pursue, while I have the honour to command, regardless of the tongue of slander or detraction."

Washington never told anyone else how hurt he had been by Conway and his allies. Sharing that secret, he went on to assure Lafayette that the dissension he had complained about would be headed off. "The fatal tendency of disunion is so obvious," he said, that he had "in earnest terms" urged officers who were complaining about Conway's promotion "to be cool and dispassionate in their decision upon the matter." He hoped that they will not "suffer any hasty determination to injure the service. At the same time, it must be acknowledged that officers' feelings upon these occasions are not to be restrained, although you may controul their actions."

He closed with some fatherly advice. "The other observations contained in your letter," he said, "have too much truth in them, and it is much to be lamented that things are not now as they formerly were; but we must not, in so great a contest, expect to meet with nothing but sunshine." He had no doubt "but that every thing happens so for the best; that we shall triumph over all our misfortunes, and shall, in the end, be ultimately happy; when, my dear marquis, if you will give me your company in Virginia, we will laugh at our past difficulties and the folly of others; where I will endeavour, by every civility in my power, to shew you how much and how sincerely, I am, your affectionate and obedient servant."[65]

Lafayette was overwhelmed with happiness. He answered at once, "I must tell you that I received this favor with the greatest satisfaction and pleasure. Every assurance and proof of your affection fills my heart with joy because that sentiment of yours is extremely dear and precious to me." Then he tried to restrain himself. "A tender and respectful attachement for you," he resumed, "and an invariable frankness will be discovered in my mind the more as you will know me better—but after those merits I must tell you that very few are to be found. I never wish'd so heartily to be intrusted by nature with an immensity of talents, than on this occasion where my frienship could then be of some use to your glory and happiness as well as to mine own."

He was still a glory-hunting boy. "What man do not join the pure ambition of glory with the other ambitions of advancement rank and fortune[?]" he asked. As an "ardent lover of laurels," he could not "bear the idea that so noble a sentiment should be mixed with any low one. In your preaching moderation to the brigadiers upon such an occasion, I am not surprised to find your virtous character. As I hope my warm interest is known to your excellency, I dare entertain the idea that you will be so indulgent as to let me know every thing concerning you when ever you will not be under the law of secrecy or particular circumstances. With the most tender and affectionate friendship with the most profond respect."[66]

Once Washington gave Conway the stiff-arm, the generals and aides launched an all-out campaign to discredit him, Gates, and Mifflin. Greene, Knox, Sullivan, Stirling, Laurens, Hamilton, Tilghman, and others bombarded the world with angry letters, attacking the "cabal" and defending Washington. None showed as much outrage or was as energetic in his commander's defense as Lafayette. "If Washington were lost," he asked Henry Laurens, "what would become of American liberty?" He had plenty of company: all the commander in chief's men united to destroy the opposition. "I am happy that the work is done," Greene said; "I do not care who does it."[67]

Words such as "conspiracy," "faction," and "cabal" were loaded terms in America. Washington's supporters made sure that important people knew about Conway's letter to Gates. Thereafter few members of Congress would touch the inspector general. As one of them expressed their collective shock at the uprising: "I always before heard him mentioned as having great military abilities, and this was all I had ever heard concerning him. The kind of correspondence he carried on with General G—— was not known at the time of his promotion." If Congress had known about that, it would not have appointed him. "A dissension among the principle officers of the army must be very injurious to the public interest," he said. "The authority & credit of the commander in chief must be supported."[68]

Henry Laurens ended the uproar late in January 1778. He looked into the affair and interviewed Conway and Gates. He wrote John, who showed his letter to Washington and the other officers. The whole thing was mostly idle talk from a handful of malcontents, with only Conway and Mifflin showing any real malice to Washington. That ended the talk about cabals and plots among his officers. It did not stop them from claiming victory, however. "The poor and shallow politicians," Greene crowed, "unmasked their batteries before they were ready to attempt execution." Hamilton predicted that the conspiracy would go underground. "All the true and sensible friends to their country," he warned, "and of course to a certain great man, ought to be upon the watch to counterplot the secret machinations of his enemies."[69]

There had never been a plot against Washington, however much his partisans claimed there was. The turmoil had some positive effects, among them leaving Washington almost immune from criticism for the remainder of the war. Nor would Congress again try to impose a high officer he did not want in his camp. The lawmakers became so sensitive about interfering in his command that its committees hesitated to visit Valley Forge.[70]

Washington and Lafayette at Valley Forge, engraving by Hall from an earlier painting by Chappell. No other depiction conveys so well Washington's paternal regard for his adopted son. (LILLY LIBRARY, INDIANA UNIVERSITY)

De Kalb had rallied around Washington with the rest of the officers. It occurred to him that when the news of the controversy reached France, it might inspire de Broglie, generalissimo *manqué*. Forget it, he advised. There was no commander in America but Washington. "He will rather suffer in the opinion of the world than hurt his country," he said; "he did and does more every day than could be expected from any general in the world . . . and I think him the only proper person . . . to keep up the spirits of the army and people, and I look upon him as the sole defender of his country's cause."[71]

Washington emerged from the "Conway Cabal" solidly in control, with the commander in chief established as the sole military authority accountable to the civil power, founding a strong American tradition of separation between the military and political spheres. If the politicians wanted to know about the army, they would have to see him first.

Lafayette would be at his side. Washington suffered all the grievances that have plagued senior commanders since the Trojan War: prima donna generals, uncooperative politicians, obnoxious foreigners interfering in his command, incompetent or unlucky subordinates, orders gone astray or misinterpreted or simply ignored, shortages of men and food and ammunition, temperamental allies, adored protégés who turned rebellious, uncertain support from the people, separation from his home and family, plots against his powers of command—all in the face of a resourceful and sometimes overwhelming enemy. Through it all, Lafayette gave him unwavering loyalty, truly filial devotion.

Oh American Freedom
What Schall Become of You!

(JANUARY-APRIL 1778)

I think that we Americans, at least in the Southern colonies cannot contend
with *a good grace* for liberty, until we shall have enfranchised our slaves. How
can we whose jealousy has been alarmed more at the name of oppression
than at the reality reconcile to our spirited assertions of the rights of
mankind the galling abject slavery of our negroes?

—JOHN LAURENS

*L*afayette, Laurens, and Hamilton killed time at Valley Forge
by arguing into the night. Laurens was afire with beliefs
about the rights of man and erupted in youthful outrage
over the hypocrisy of his elders. Hamilton picked and
chose his targets. Those that bothered Laurens the most, religious intolerance and slavery, were of little interest to him. He had crusades of his
own, mostly against British tyranny. To him, "slavery" meant the injustices
the London government wanted to impose on Americans. What
Americans did to Africans did not trouble this young fellow, who had
grown up in the West Indies, where slavery was at its worst.[1]

Hamilton's Anglo-Saxon passions struck Lafayette as cold and technical. Laurens' Gallic outrage was something else. His storms against
wrongs done to people struck a chord with the boy who had felt outcast

in Versailles. He could understand the social pain of others, because he still wallowed in his own, and Laurens made him think about things that had never crossed his mind. Religious intolerance was a case in point. He was a nominal Catholic, but mostly he was indifferent. Laurens raged against persecution of people for their beliefs. His Huguenot forebears in France had suffered oppression until the Edict of Nantes in 1598 granted limited tolerance. Louis XIV revoked that in 1685, driving hundreds of thousands of Protestants, including his family, out of the country. It shocked Lafayette to learn that there were people in his homeland persecuted over things that he did not take seriously.

Laurens compared every such situation to the Declaration of Independence and urged Lafayette to think about what he was really fighting for. The continuation of slavery, Laurens maintained, was the greatest hypocrisy when measured against the Declaration. Lafayette actually owned a slave, and when French troops took the West African slave factory of Senegal, he was elated. That victory over the British, he declared, was good news for America, because southerners had complained to him that British control of Senegal had interrupted "the Nigrò trade for that part of the United States."[2]

Laurens told him that America betrayed its own cause. He had learned much from his father, who had abandoned the slave trade in 1763 and often railed against its injustice, although he did not know how to free himself from the hundreds of slaves he owned. John described himself as not "one of those who dare trust in Providence for defence and security of their own liberty while they enslave and wish to continue in slavery thousands who are as well entitled to freedom as themselves."[3]

Slavery compromised American standing in Europe. "How is it that we hear the loudest yelps for liberty among the drivers of negroes?" the English curmudgeon Samuel Johnson asked. He had a point, Laurens believed. The American army also needed troops. By 1777 the northern states had expanded the recruitment of black men, offering freedom to them and compensation to their owners. Thousands of blacks served in the army during the war, and by its end the northern states were beginning to outlaw slavery.[4]

On January 1, 1778, John Laurens sent his father two startling proposals. One was that he be authorized to return to South Carolina to recruit slaves for the army, to receive freedom at the end of the war. He would start with a company of forty men raised from Henry's own plantations. The second was to prove to other southerners that their plantation economy could get along without slavery. He would lease a plantation from his father and operate it with free black labor. John told Lafayette about all this, and he kept it in mind.[5]

John kept pressing his father, and in March 1779 Congress sent him south to recruit 3,000 slaves for the army, with Congress compensating their owners. Hamilton offered to help his friend out, giving abolitionist congressman John Jay his one significant statement on slavery. He thought that "in the present state of southern affairs" Laurens' proposal made sense. He did not see how enough troops could be raised in the region otherwise. Liberation of the recruits was just an inducement to enlistment, giving them "their freedom with their muskets." This would "secure their fidelity, animate their courage, and I believe will have a good influence upon those who remain."

Hamilton thought slaves would make good soldiers, but not because of human equality. "It is a maxim with some great military judges, that with sensible officers soldiers can hardly be too stupid." He thought that black men's "want of cultivation (for their natural faculties are probably as good as ours) joined to that habit of subordination which they acquire from a life of servitude, will make them sooner become soldiers than our white inhabitants. Let officers be men of sense and sentiment, and the nearer the soldiers approach to machines perhaps the better." There would be resistance to Laurens' scheme, he predicted. However, "it should be considered, that if we do not make use of them in this way, the enemy probably will."[6]

So slaves would make good soldiers not because they would fight for liberty. Instead, they were available, might otherwise be lost to the enemy, and—most important—they had been beaten into the kind of obedience Hamilton believed soldiers must have.

Laurens' plans to raise a slave army were hopeless. Slave owners in South Carolina and Georgia refused to go along. He got himself elected to the Assembly but had no more success as a member. Eventually he returned to the army, but he never lost hope. In 1782 he tilted at the windmill again, but he died before anything could come of his renewed proposal.[7]

Not long after he and Lafayette joined Washington's headquarters,

Laurens began pestering the commander in chief as well as his father on the slavery issue. Lafayette listened, but it was still too new to him. The time would come, however, when he also would bother his adoptive father on this subject. [8]

I DO NOT ENTERTAIN MYSELF ANY IDEA
OF LEAVING YOUR ARMY

Congress heard late in 1777 that the French *habitants* in Canada were ripe for revolt against the British. As with yarns that had justified the invasion in 1775, these stories were false, but there were delegates who would not let go of their hope to add the northern provinces to the thirteen insurgent colonies. In January 1778 they plunged ahead with their enterprise, which would be independent of Washington's Main Army, inspiring a belief in Washington's camp that it was another round of the Conway Cabal. The Irish-Frenchman and his backers Gates and Mifflin were alleged to have cooked up the expedition as a way to separate Washington from his most ardent defender, Lafayette. In reality, many delegates honestly believed there was a chance for success and that French Canadians would welcome an invasion led by a French general. Two officers who met that description were Lafayette and Conway. [9]

Lafayette learned about the project from Conway's aide on January 20. He said that Conway had been summoned to York by Gates and Mifflin to command the invasion. "They will laugh in France," Lafayette told Washington, "when they'l hear that he is choosen upon such a commission out of the same army where I am," because the man was Irish, and Canadians would expect a Frenchman to liberate their country. He reassured his adoptive father that "I mention that only as a remark of theyr folly, Sir. I do not entertain myself any idea of leaving your army." [10]

The marquis heard from Henry Laurens on the twenty-second that he, not Conway, would command the "irruption," and Washington advised him to hurry to York. Congress authorized the expedition with the marquis in command, Conway second in command, and New Hampshire general John Stark in third place. Lafayette visited Gates and imposed conditions before he would accept the job. First was that Conway not be part of it. Second was that an American ought to be his deputy. Third was that he be allowed to pick his own officers. Finally, and most important, he would serve only under Washington, not as an independent commander. Orders must come to him from the Board of War through the commander in chief.[11]

Gates and the board said they agreed. They told him he would find 2,500 men waiting for him at Albany, a "large body" of militia at Coos, $200,000 in paper money, some silver money, and "the means for crossing the ice of Lake Champlain." After he burned the British flotilla, he should "fall upon Montreal and act there as the situation required." Gates told him, "The Board flatter themselves that the officers appointed by Congress to cooperate with you in this matter will be acceptable."[12]

Gates and the board assumed that the young general would accept a march to glory on any terms, even if Conway was along for the ride. Back at Valley Forge, on January 24 Lafayette thanked Laurens, asking that Congress permit him to regard himself only as detached from Washington's army, remaining under his immediate command, rather than as an agent of the Board of War. As for his second, he said, "Mr. Connway is the most disagreeable to me. . . . How can I support the society of a man who has spocken of my friend in the most insolent and abusive terms, who has done, and does every day all his power to ruin him?

"On the other hand," he continued, "I am very certain that every one who can find one single reason of refusing düe respect and love to Gal Washington will find thousand ones of hating me to death." He sputtered with rage, and his English showed it. He charged that Conway would "sacrify honor, truth, and every thing respectable to his own ambition and desire of making a fortune. What engages me to despise him more is that he is with me as submist, as complaisant, and low than he is insolent with those he do'nt fear."[13]

Members of Congress were in camp meeting with Washington. Lafayette showed his letter to one of them, Gouverneur Morris, before he sent it. Morris told Laurens that he supported Lafayette's request for an American second in command, preferably the tough old fighter General Alexander McDougall. The marquis also shared his letter with John Laurens, who took it to Washington. John disapproved of the Canada project, but he stood behind Lafayette's position. Washington tacitly concurred.[14]

The expedition was not off to a happy start. "We have now in motion an irruption into Canada," Henry Laurens said, "under the command of Marquis de Lafayette, provided he will condescend to accept of Mr. Conway for his second. If I may judge from his letters to me in which he speaks of this officer with the utmost abhorrence, he will not."[15]

Washington's supporters were suspicious about the motives behind the enterprise, about which the commander in chief had not been formally notified. Lafayette also suspected that he was being set up for a fall. The expedition would be allowed to fail, he would go back to France in disgrace, and Conway would replace him. In truth, the Board of War appeared malevolent when it was just clumsy. It wanted Conway on the campaign to get him away from York.[16]

Washington's notification and Lafayette's instructions arrived with Conway on January 27. The Irish-Frenchman sent an ingratiating note to the marquis, and the younger general boiled over again. Conway, he sneered to Laurens, said "he feels a much greater pleasure to be under me than if he was commander in chief, too happy, says-he, if he can by every exertion in his power contribute in some thing to my reputation." He also objected to Congressman William Duer as the board's representative to the expedition because he believed that Duer was a Trojan horse plotting against Washington.[17]

Lafayette wanted to lead the invasion, but he did not want to be a patsy. Just as important, he wanted no one to undercut Washington's powers of command. The commander in chief decided to watch the crazy affair work itself out and refused to give his professional opinion. Because he knew nothing about either the aim or the logistical arrangements for the expedition, he advised Gates, he declined to pass judgment on the subject. "I can only sincerely wish," he said, "that success may attend it, both as it may be advancive of the public good and on account of the personal honor of the Marquis de la Fayette, for whom I have a very particular esteem and regard." This was a veiled warning. The boy had defended him, and he would defend the boy.[18]

Lafayette played on congressional interest in Canada to spike Conway's guns, because he believed the Conway Cabal was still at work. Washington let the marquis have his head in this affair, so that he could learn to rise above any future challenge. The young general could be exasperating, however, even to the indulgent Henry Laurens, who told him to cool off. The president knew how to tell good motives from bad, and "as I judge charitably I would endeavour to act circumspectly even with such characters, who divested of the spirit of party may be valuable men in community." In other words, Duer would stay with "Your Excellency."[19]

Lafayette spent January 30 with Laurens, and they came to terms. Then he visited Gates and the board to clarify his instructions. Lafayette wore down the opposition and got his way. Unless Conway was replaced by McDougall (or de Kalb if McDougall was too sick, which he was), and unless Congress commissioned a list of French officers he presented, he would lead all the French officers home. There they would explain why he, they, and Washington were disappointed at the situation in America. The board and Congress caved in, but the objective of the campaign now was to seize or destroy enemy boats and supplies. It was a raid, in other words, and no longer a conquest. That was a letdown, but he took it in stride. Besides, Conway had been dropped to third in command. The important thing was that Lafayette would ride at the head of the only troops scheduled to move this winter.[20]

While the marquis prepared to leave York in early February 1778, President Laurens received a visit from a downtrodden Henry Gates, who wanted the president to help him heal his differences with Washington. Conway had become an albatross, and Gates disavowed him. Laurens passed this news on to his son John, who told Washington. The commander in chief decided that Gates had not been his enemy after all, and the two of them reconnected in a stiff, formal way.[21]

THE WORLD HAS THEYR EYES FIXED UPON ME

On February 3 Lafayette told Adrienne, "The love of my calling and an inclination to be something in the military line . . . together with my friendship for General Washington and an estimable president [Laurens] now at the head of Congress, plus the advances I have already made for this American cause—these are the reasons that send me so far in the winter." He looked forward to acclaim at home. "The idea of liberating all of New France and freeing it from a heavy yoke is too splendid to stop there," he crowed. He expected his success in Canada to attract a great many Frenchmen to the American cause. Lest anybody in France believe his assignment was piffling, "[t]he number of troops I shall have under me, which would be negligible in Europe, is considerable in America."[22]

Lafayette greatly admired Greene, an iron man notorious for going many days without sleep, spending nights on campaign doing paperwork and writing letters. The marquis, already addicted to letter writing, emulated him. Letters poured out of his tent nightly, most of them designed to cover his political rear—he had learned a thing or two from the backstabbing court at Versailles. He penned a farewell to Henry Laurens, buttering him up, and adding, "Indeed my dear Sir you must have a great indulgence for me if you pardon *mon griffonage* [my scrawl]." The next day he defended Washington. "I was thinking of the title of that man going to Canada," meaning himself. He did not want to be called commander in chief, but "only general and commander of the northern army," so as not to undercut Washington's authority.[23]

Lafayette needed political protection, because he did have a Trojan horse in his camp. It was not Duer, as he suspected, but Gates' chief of staff, Robert Troup. They butted heads first at Valley Forge, where Lafayette was waiting for the roads to clear before heading out, and Troup insisted on going on. Gates' agent sent his chief a stream of reports running him down. "I left the marquis at Lancaster," he began. "He seems to be strongly tinctured with the Fabian principles of head-quarters." He thought that Lafayette would reach Albany too late in the season to do anything. Troup rode ahead and met Conway, who believed that "the cabal at head quarters" wanted to replace him with de Kalb to prevent Conway from receiving his share of glory.[24]

Lafayette knew something was going on behind his back. He also learned that the men, money, and supplies promised him would not be there when he reached Albany. Assuming that the Conway Cabal was setting him up for failure, he counterattacked, making Gates liable for any future blame. "This project is yours, Sir," he told him on February 7, "therefore you must make it succeed. If I had not depended so much on you I would not have undertaken the operation."[25]

Lafayette trudged toward his destination, his doubts growing with each step. "I go on very slowly sometimes pierced by rain, sometimes covered with snow, and not thinking many handsome thoughts about the projected *incursion* into Canada," he told Washington on the ninth. "Lake Champlain is very cold for producing the least bit of laurels, and if I am neither drawned neither starv'd I'l be as proud as if I had gained two battles." Then he burst out in homesickness. "Could I believe one single instant," he wailed, "that this *pompous command of a northern army* will let your excellency forget a little an absent friend, then i would send the project to the place it comes from. But I dare hope that you will remember me sometimes. . . . It is a very melancholy idea for me that I ca'nt follow your fortune as near your person as I could wish."[26]

Lafayette's friends in Congress had started to cover his rear. On February 11, while he was slogging through the snow, the Committee of Conference voiced its "deep concern" about the Canadian expedition. If it failed, "it would produce desertion among the troops . . . disgrace to our arms, and all its consequences upon our money, upon our people, upon our friends in Europe, and upon the enemies we have in our own bowels. . . . The army in Canada tho crowned with laurels must . . . undoubtedly starve." On February 24 Congress told Lafayette to conduct himself "according to the probability of success."[27]

When the marquis had reached Albany on the seventeenth, he had found nothing waiting for him except fewer than 1,200 underfed men. The militia was nowhere in sight, because Stark had not been notified. He asked the acting quartermaster for a full report, and the officer shot back that he had everything lined up, so his department could not be faulted if the expedition failed. Lafayette asked town officials in Albany for help getting men and supplies. He heard from McDougall, who said he was not healthy enough to serve with him and offered advice on how to avoid Burgoyne's fate. Ten days later, McDougall told Greene that the project was a disaster in the making and that Lafayette was being set up to take the blame.[28]

Albany officials told him that the troops lacked winter clothing. There was no chance of getting any, or enough men, or other supplies. Although the state had given the quartermaster authority to impress supplies, there simply were not enough in the neighborhood. The people of Albany would help in any way they could, meaning not much.[29]

Lafayette sent a stiff rebuke to Conway, complaining that he had not heard from him. "All these circumstances, besides your military knowledge, & experience enable you to advise me better than any body" and help the expedition succeed.[30]

Conway thought the situation was a mess, telling Gates that the number of men was far short of what was expected by the Board of War, they were poorly clothed and supplied, and they had not been paid for five months. "The intelligence from Canada is not encouraging," he added. "Indeed I found here a general aversion to the expedition." He told Lafayette that his instructions did not mean that he must go ahead with the invasion with too few men, but if the marquis ordered him to march anyway, he would.[31]

Lafayette recognized that the invasion could not happen and decided that the whole thing had been planned to embarrass him in France. He turned to Laurens, to "explain my heart to my friend, and let him know which hell of blunders, madness and deception I am involved in." The situation was so bad that not even Conway could be blamed for it. Feeling betrayed, he warned, "The world has theyr eyes fixed upon me." People would laugh at him, and he would be almost ashamed to show his face in public. "I'l publish the whole history," he vowed, "I'l publish my instructions *with notes* through the world, and I'l loose rather the honor of twenty Gates and twenty boards of war, than to let my own reputation be hurted in the least thing."[32]

The boy general appealed to Washington for comfort. "Why am I so far from you," he cried, "and what business had that board of war to hurry me through the ice and snow without knowing what I schould do, neither what they were doing themselves?" He had learned that the leaders of the 1775 invasion had warned against trying it again. He had been "schamefully deceived by the board of war," he charged. His reputation worried him the most, because his friends in Europe knew that he was in command. "The people will be in great expectations, and what schall I answer?" Again, being laughed at was his greatest fear, and he asked Washington to bail him out and give him a real shot at glory.[33]

Lafayette made sure everyone knew that he had been misled. "I do not make any complaints," he told Congress, then offered several pages full of them. He threatened again to publish the truth for the world to see. "What my perhaps too quick and too warm heart must feel after being so much deceived, every sensible man must have some idea of."[34]

"I am sorry," he told Gates, "that a so displeasant affair came through your hands, but I am not in any doubt that you were fully convinced of every thing you induced me to built my hopes upon." To the governor of New York he claimed that all would have gone well if he had been allowed to start the campaign earlier. If proper orders had been given, proper money spent, and proper measures taken on time, he "schould have been able to do great and useful things." Nobody could blame Lafayette for any part of the mess.[35]

Lafayette was responsible for one of his difficulties, however. He spent about $50,000 out of his pocket while he was in Albany, then lost the receipts. This interfered with getting compensation from Congress until he found and forwarded some of the receipts in April. The expedition was a personal loss to him in every way.[36]

The marquis told Laurens how "distressed and unhappy" he was, because of "a deception, a treachery, what you please . . . Certainly there is some villainy." Alleging that Gates and Conway were plotting evil, he dreaded what the newspapers were saying, and asked the president to send him clippings.[37]

Once again Lafayette turned to his adoptive father. "I meet with an occasion of wraïting to your excellency which I wo'nt miss by any means," he began, "even schould I be affraïd of becoming tedious and troublesome. But if they have sent me far from you for I do'nt know what purpose, at least I must make some little use of my pen to prevent all communication be cut of[f] between your excellency and me. I have writen lately to you my distressing, ridiculous, foolish, and indeed nameless situation." The boy who had been laughed at on the queen's dance floor did not want that to happen again. "I confess, my dear general, that I find myself of very quick feelings whenever my reputation and glory are concerned in anything. It is very hard indeed that such a part of my happiness without which I ca'nt live, would depend upon the schemes of some fools. . . . I am more unhappy than I ever was." He wished Washington was with him "to give me some advices. . . . I am at a loss how to act, and indeed I do'nt know what I am being here myself."[38]

Having gotten that out of his system, Lafayette took up his responsibilities, reorganizing the troops and instituting training and disciplinary regulations. He paid off most of the army's bills and lit a fire under his quartermaster, and some supplies rolled in. But he heard nothing from

Congress or the Board of War. The only good news was that de Kalb had joined him.[39]

While Lafayette fretted in the snows of New York, Laurens tried to bail him out. The marquis' letters had reached York by the end of February and were passed around. When some delegates assumed that Lafayette was under Gates' orders rather than Washington's, Laurens stepped in. Gates had violated all agreements by ordering Lafayette to report directly to him rather than through Washington. The president persuaded Congress on March 2 to give Lafayette permission to call the whole thing off. To soothe his wounded feelings, the resolution would "at the same time, inform him that Congress entertain a high sense of his prudence, activity and zeal, and that they are fully persuaded nothing has, or would have been wanting on his part, or on the part of the officers who accompanied him, to give the expedition the utmost effect."[40]

Henry Laurens had taken on the role of uncle where the prickly marquis was concerned, because he understood that the boy general was lonely, uncertain, and far from home. It cost nothing to give him praise, reassurance, a pat on the back now and then—or a whack on the head when that was in order. Laurens wanted to keep him from making decisions that he would regret later, such as returning to France in a huff.

"I would be criminally silent were I not to declare," the president told him, "the intentions of Congress respecting your Excellency's honour & merits, are altogether one." He declined to answer Lafayette's insinuations about Gates and others. "But I would deal gently with those whose errors are of the head," he advised, "whose general tone speaks the public good." He wanted to avoid "every whisper which may tend to fan the flame of party." Then he laid it on thick, enough to make the boy's head spin: "If ever man stood on a firm base, you do my dear general, you are possessed of what Bacon calls the 'vantage ground of Truth'—from whence you may look down upon the crooked vales & paths below." He was horrified at the idea that Lafayette would leave the United States at a critical time. The marquis' record, he assured him, and the resolves of Congress both guarded his reputation. "Fall the blame of the late abortion where it ought or where it may . . . not the smallest spark or speck of censure can possibly light on the Marquis de Lafayette; that general has performed every thing which had been prescribed to him."[41]

Laurens knew as well as Washington that the young general needed continual reassurance. The president had better communications to Albany, so while Lafayette was detached on the Canadian project he stepped into Washington's place. "Once more," Laurens told him on March 6, "be assured you have gained great reputation in this country." The Board of War planned to recall Lafayette and de Kalb to Valley Forge, and Conway would remain where he was. "Do not dear marquis suffer this to discompose you." Gates said that should be agreeable to "your Excellency" because "there is no command yonder worthy of you." That was a quiet way of saying that they knew that Lafayette had been fishing for a chance to salvage his reputation by attacking New York.[42]

Some in Congress feared that a recall to Valley Forge might embarrass Lafayette, so the delegates postponed instructions until they had heard from him. Laurens advised him to show some discretion, telling him how properly to address the legislature. Lafayette should ask "how you are to be disposed of & so forth, in which your Excellency needs no hint or information from me. Permit me to intreat you sir . . . avoid disclosing that kind of resentment which may bring on disagreeable altercation." He should "make a sacrifice to peace by passing quietly over the bagatelle." In other words, let sleeping dogs, like Conway and Gates, lie.[43]

Washington received Lafayette's letters from Albany on March 10. As always, he knew what to say. "I . . . hasten to dispel those fears respecting your reputation, which are excited only by an uncommon degree of sensibility," he advised. "You seem to apprehend that censure proportioned to the disappointed expectations of the world, will fall on you in consequence of the failure of the Canadian Expedition." But the mere fact that he "had received so manifest a proof of the good opinion and confidence of Congress as an important detached command" would read well in Europe. Moreover, "I am persuaded that everyone will applaud your prudence in renouncing a project, in pursuing which you would vainly have attempted physical impossibilities. . . . However sensible your ardour for glory may make you feel this disappointment, you may be assured that your character stands as fair as it ever did, and that no new enterprise is necessary to wipe off this imaginary stain."

Washington counseled against attacking New York, because it was bound to fail. Mounted from so far away, an attack could not be kept secret. The American Fabius wanted to wait for the enemy to present an opportunity, "and success would principally depend upon the suddenness

of the attempt." As for the rest of Lafayette's situation, "[y]ou undoubtedly have determined judiciously in waiting the farther orders of
Congress. Whether they allow me the pleasure of seeing you shortly or
destine you to a longer absence, you may assure yourself of [my] sincere
good wishes."[44]

Lafayette did not see this, or the advice from Laurens, for some time.
He was off among *les sauvages*.

KAYEHEANLA

With de Kalb on hand, the marquis felt free to leave Albany to answer a request for help from General Philip Schuyler. Congress
had appointed Schuyler a commissioner to negotiate with the Iroquois
and allied tribes, and Schuyler thought the Frenchman could play on
their old ties to France and get the tribes to transfer their allegiance from
Britain to the United States. Lafayette, Schuyler, and other commissioners traveled by sleigh forty miles northwest to Johnstown to meet with
the Six Nations at Mohawk River. British agents had been bribing the
Indians to raid farms and settlements on the northern frontier. Lafayette
heard very lurid stories involving scalping and cannibalism. "'It is thus,'"
as he put it, "the Indians were told as they drank at their council fires,
'that you must drink the blood of the rebels.' "[45]

When the commission arrived, Lafayette was pleased that the
sauvages knew who he was. They were impressed by his good looks, his
bearing, and his magnificent uniform, and they enjoyed the gifts he
handed out, including mirrors, rum, brandy, and gold coins called *louis
d'or*. The Frenchman had never seen anything like the spectacle before
him: "Five hundred men, women, and children, gaudily painted and be-
decked with feathers, their ears pierced, their noses ornamented with
jewels, and their nearly naked bodies marked with various designs, attended these councils. As the old men smoked, they discoursed very well
on politics. The balance of power would be their goal, if their drunkenness with rum, like drunkenness with ambition in Europe, did not often
divert them from it."[46]

One of Lafayette's aides was not so impressed. "Europe's beggar
seemed less disgusting than America's savage," he growled. But then he

had not been adopted into their nation, as Lafayette was. They called him Kayeheanla, after a great warrior of their past. Compared to fancy British goods, the presents the commissioners handed out were piddling, but the Indians signed a treaty with the Americans. As Lafayette wryly concluded, "[A] few of the Indians observed it; the troubles were at least suspended."⁴⁷

The marquis ordered that a scattering of small posts be built to guard the frontier. He also headed off a mutiny at Johnstown by giving the men their back pay out of his own money. He had returned to Albany by March 11, annoyed that he had heard nothing from Gates or Congress. "I expect with the greatest impatience letters from the Board of War where I'l be acquainted of what I am to do," he fired off to Gates. "We want monney, sir, and monney will be spoken by me till I will be enabled to pay our poor soldiers." He told Laurens that the troops were in an uproar over not being paid. Without money or clothes they could not have soldiers, he declared.⁴⁸

Letters from Laurens and Gates, ending the campaign, arrived the next day. Gates ordered Lafayette and de Kalb to Valley Forge, to resume their former duties. Lafayette was instructed to turn over his command to Conway, and he took that as an insult. He exploded again, threatening to lead all the French officers back to France. His hatred of Conway knew no bounds.⁴⁹

On March 13, 1778, as if the members expected such an outburst, Congress authorized Washington to recall Lafayette and de Kalb to the Main Army. Lafayette, having received his adoptive father's and Laurens' cautionary advice, realized that he had overstepped his bounds. He told Washington, "I must confess you, my dear general, that I have been too hasty" in earlier letters. He had since learned that Congress had been "kind enough as to expect knowing my sentiments before making any disposition of general officers. I assure you, my dear general, that I will do very chearfully ever thing they will propose to me in such a manner— you know too well my heart to be in any doubt but I schall consider myself very happy to service with you. . . . Farewell, my most dear and beloved general, do'nt forget your northern friend, and be certain that his sentiments for you will end with his life."⁵⁰

Lafayette promised not to lead the other officers back to France, and a week later he apologized to Laurens for his hotheadedness. The same day, March 20, he sent a formal report to the president, thanking Congress for its approval and offering to remain in America and serve the cause in any capacity. He feared that his temper could have cost him his commission.[51]

On March 20, Washington formally ordered Lafayette and de Kalb to return to the Main Army and resume divisional commands. "I anticipate the pleasure of seeing you," he closed. Two days later Lafayette heard rumors to that effect from York, and told his adoptive father how pleased he was about it. "I seize with the gretest pleasure the first occasion of telling you how happy I have been to see in your last favor a new assurance of those sentiments of yours so dear to my heart."[52]

As couriers galloped through the spring rains and mud, Laurens wrote Lafayette on March 24. Congress, he told him, did not mean to insult him when it asked that he turn over his command to Conway. Instead, the lawmakers had not yet "resolved on a disposition for General Conway." The Irish-Frenchman had been sent off to Peekskill to serve under McDougall. Laurens chided Lafayette for his intemperate remarks and demanded that the young fellow show courtesy and decorum in his correspondence.[53]

Before he received that, and still fretting that he had overdone it, Lafayette wrote to Washington again. He could not refrain from another jab at the Board of War. "Oh american freedom what schall become of you, if you are in such hands!" He told his adoptive father that he had given up the idea of attacking New York and his only desire was to rejoin the general. The sole condition he had made in accepting the northern command, he said, had been not to be under any orders but those of General Washington. "I seem to have had an anticipation of our future friendship, and what I have done out of esteem and respect for your excellency's name and reputation, I schould do now out of mere love for General Washington himself."[54]

Lafayette received his orders to rejoin Washington at last. He and de Kalb packed up on April 1, 1778, and headed home to Valley Forge. So ended the "irruption" into Canada, a botched enterprise that never should have started. Despite his temper tantrums, the marquis emerged from the mess with his reputation intact, even heightened by his good judgment in not going forward without enough resources. His star had risen along with Washington's, while Gates' was on the wane. As for Conway, his light grew dimmer by the day.

Conway had tried to cozy up to Lafayette and others, but the remarks that started the "cabal" controversy had been unforgivable. He was a pariah—in his own words, "ordered from place to place." He blundered one last time, again offering his resignation. On April 28, 1778, Congress voted overwhelmingly to accept it. He exploded to Gates, "I had no thoughts of resigning," then spent the next several weeks in deranged attempts to persuade Congress to reconsider, to deny his resignation, to resign again, to ask for reinstatement—all to no avail. For reasons that never became clear, he challenged General John Cadwalader to a duel, and on July 4, 1778, the Irish-Frenchman took a bullet in the mouth. He claimed to be on his deathbed, and wrote to Washington to express his "sincere grief for having done, written, or said anything disagreeable to your Excellency." The unforgiving commander in chief did not answer. Conway did not die; he just went back to France.[55]

THE PROPEREST MAN WE COULD CHOOSE

*L*afayette and de Kalb reached Valley Forge on April 8 and found the place transformed. It was still the grimy collection of hovels that they had left over two months earlier, but Greene had made headway on the supply problem. The men were eating better, although their clothes were still rags. The biggest changes, Henry Laurens told the marquis, were because "Baron Stüben is making great improvements and giving much satisfaction to every body."[56]

Lafayette looked forward to meeting this man, with whom he had already exchanged letters. He knew that the newcomer had been spending a lot of time with Washington and was probably headed for a high commission, so he was jealous. Within a year Lafayette gave him a left-handed compliment as "an old Prussian whose methodical mediocrity perfected the organization and tactics of the army."[57]

Frederick William Augustus von Steuben, as he called himself in America (he changed his names often), was also known as Baron von Steuben. He had arrived in Washington's camp on February 23, 1778,

Frederick William Augustus, Baron von Steuben, by C. W. Peale, 1781–82. The Prussian drillmaster not only overhauled the army's drill and tactics, permitting the successes at Barren Hill and Monmouth, but he created the first regulations of the American army, some elements of which survive in today's regulations. (INDEPENDENCE NATIONAL HISTORICAL PARK)

preceded by letters of introduction that described him as a former lieutenant general in the Prussian army, almost right-hand man to Frederick the Great. It was all a fraud, as Washington knew before he arrived. The forty-seven-year-old officer had risen no higher than captain on the Prussian general staff, although Frederick had commended him. Since the end of the Seven Years' War, he had wandered among minor German states as a military adviser to their rulers. One had presented him with a knighthood and the honorary title of *Freiherr,* so he had some right to call himself a baron. His inflated résumé was the work of two comedians in Paris—Franklin and Caron de Beaumarchais, chief conduit of French supplies for America, better known as the author of *The Barber of Seville.*[58]

Steuben was a far cry from some of the earlier European volunteers. The American agents and the French war minister instinctively recognized that he held great promise, and they promoted him to lieutenant general to cover the fact that he was really an unemployed fugitive from debt collectors. Washington greeted him cautiously. After long discussions with him about the army's problems the commander in chief decided to see what he could do. Within a month, the newcomer earned the role of acting inspector general and Washington's recommendation that Congress commission him as major general. John Laurens told his father that Steuben "would be the properest man we could choose for the office," in place of the "obnoxious" Conway.[59]

Steuben was a large man, impressive in the saddle, but once he dismounted it was apparent that his height was all above the waist. His comically short legs were as disarming as the friendliness that no Prussian discipline could erase from his broad face, with its potato nose, ruddy complexion, and twinkling eyes. He was a man of winning good humor, and his entourage was likewise affable. It included his translator, Pierre-Etienne Duponceau, a small, owlish schoolteacher so nearsighted that he bumped into trees. Steuben could not maintain the stern, aloof manners expected of a Prussian general. There was a lot of bluster in his makeup, but his storms were mostly noise. He simply liked people, especially Americans, and he was fond of the young and mixed with them easily. In an army where the gulf between senior and junior had always been wide, Steuben became as popular as he was respected.

Washington asked the baron to look over the situation in the army. "Matters had to be remedied," Steuben said later, "but where to commence was the great difficulty. . . . The arms at Valley Forge were in a horrible condition," the men were "literally naked, some of them in the fullest sense of the word." As for discipline, "I may safely say that no such thing existed. In the first place there was no regular formation."[60]

Things were even worse than they looked. There was no uniform organization, returns were usually incomplete, and the army lost between 5,000 and 8,000 muskets in every campaign, carried away by deserters and by men at discharge. The troops were poorly managed, "scattered about in every direction."[61]

Steuben saw more clearly than Washington that European methods could not simply be imposed on Americans, and he observed, "In our European armies a man who has been drilled for three months is called a recruit; here, in two months I must have a soldier." He planned to simplify the drill manuals, developing a new system that softened British rigidity with French and Prussian practicality. In another departure from Old World practices, he said inspectors must examine financial accounts. At least, someone should do that for the Continental Army.[62]

He began with drill, because the army knew neither how to drill nor how to march, limiting its performance in battle. Giving the Prussian his head, on March 17, 1778 Washington ordered an additional hundred men assigned to his own guard. Training the formation began two days later.

Steuben spoke no English at first and relied on pantomime and personal demonstration. He trained one squad first, then supervised assistants who trained others. Once the squads were trained, he drilled them as a company. After the model guard company was ready, he extended his system to battalions, then brigades, and in three weeks maneuvered an entire division for Washington's review. With the commander in chief's backing, he forced the officers to supervise their own troops, instead of leaving it to sergeants.[63]

Steuben's lack of English caused him problems. He wrote his drill regulations in French, which Duponceau translated into literary English. The translator was no military man, so Laurens and Hamilton edited them into military parlance, and Steuben memorized the text as well as his broken English allowed. Nevertheless, the phrasing of his orders sometimes scrambled the ranks. He vented his frustration with explosions of French and German profanity punctuated with loud bursts of "goddam," his first English word.

The problem was solved quickly when Captain Benjamin Walker volunteered to translate on the drill field. Steuben's gift for profanity remained. Walker recalled something that happened often: "When he had exhausted his artillery of foreign oaths, he called to his aides, 'My dear Walker and my dear Duponceau, come and swear for me in English. These fellows won't do what I bid them.' A good-natured smile then went through the ranks and at last the maneuver or the movement was properly performed."[64]

The training extended across the army. Steuben galloped all over the camp, flying off in "whirlwinds of passion" whenever he did not like what he saw. His eruptions could be shocking at first. "You hallooed and swore and looked so dreadfully at me once," a captain told Steuben, "when my platoon was out of place, that I almost melted into water." The Prussian blushed and said, "Oh fie, *donc,* fie, *Capitaine!*"[65]

Civilians gathered to watch the spectacle. Germans were always objects of curiosity to Americans, and Steuben was especially so throughout the war. He recalled that so many people came to see him that he felt like "a rhinoceros on display."[66]

Supervising drill was just part of what Steuben accomplished. More important were the regulations that provided the basis for drill and everything else. His were a masterpiece of improvisation. With no printing presses at Valley Forge, Steuben and any available Francophone officers—Duponceau, Laurens, Hamilton, Lafayette, Greene, Walker, and others—drafted the instructions a chapter at a time. Brigade inspectors wrote out copies, which were entered into orderly books of brigades and regiments. From the orderly books copies were made for each company, from which each officer and drillmaster made his own copy. It took two to three days for each chapter to be fully distributed.[67]

Steuben also overhauled the army's organization. Few regiments were ever full enough to serve as training units, and turnover in the ranks made continuous training necessary. He divided the brigades into training battalions, subdivided into companies and platoons, and redistributed the officers. The regiments no longer matched the battalions, but the battalions became uniformly known quantities able to maneuver with calculable results. Steuben's organization made it possible to muster effective units for battle no matter how depleted the army was.

American troops had difficulty going from column of march into line of battle, because of their customary marching formation of a single column of files ("Indian file"), stringing the force out. That was why many units had arrived late at Brandywine and Germantown. Steuben cured that bad habit, training battalions to occupy no more road space than they would require room in battle. At his suggestion, on April 10 Washington outlawed the column of files. From then on, all units marched exactly as they were taught on the drill field. The result was an army that marched and deployed faster.[68]

The army had to fight as well as march, and that required weapons instruction. Steuben taught a simplified manual of arms, with many fewer movements than those of European armies, and replaced difficult battalion volleys with platoon fire. He also emphasized use of the bayonet, the essential infantry assault weapon of his day, and turned his soldiers into fiercely confident bayonet fighters, as they later demonstrated.[69]

Steuben transformed the army, and he did it in short order. He not only trained it but taught it how to train itself. His regulations showed the men everything from how to stand at attention to how to maintain camp sanitation. His inspection system stopped the loss of muskets and other supplies bleeding out of the army, causing Knox to say that Steuben was worth an arsenal all by himself. The financial accounts were cleaned up, and Washington could know in an instant how many men he had fit for duty. Most important, this Prussian whirling dervish had given the Continental Army a confidence it had never known before. Officers and men alike hungered, at the end of April, for a chance to show what they could do.

Lafayette may have resented Steuben's entrance onto the scene, but he could not help admiring what the man accomplished, making the Continental Army tactically equal to the army he had known in France. He sometimes joined the nightly gathering of young officers at the baron's hut and regaled the others with colorful stories about his adventures in New York, "which his hearers found as good as a play," according to Greene.[70]

The marquis was more often at Greene's house, where the general's wife, Kitty (also called Katy or Caty), presided. Duponceau remembered her as a "handsome, elegant, and accomplished woman." She attracted the foreign officers because she spoke French and was well versed in French literature. There was trouble in the Greene household that spring. Having abandoned her children to the care of friends six months earlier, she flirted with the French officers, especially Lafayette. She practically threw herself at Anthony Wayne, then in an unhappy marriage, and commissary general Jeremiah Wadsworth, a prosperous Philadelphia merchant. Both of them became her lovers after Nathanael died, but how far she went at Valley Forge remains a mystery.[71]

Kitty Greene claimed, after her husband died, that she had had a passionate affair with Lafayette at Valley Forge. The marquis was silent about the matter. His appetites had not declined since he arrived in America, and during the Canadian campaign he had continued his long-distance flirtation with "Miss Ketty." He later offered some wistful comments about the distaff side of America. "The women are devoted to their families," he said, "and delight in making a comfortable home for them. One speaks of love to the girls, and their flirtatiousness is as amiable as it is modest." This strange new world was very different from what he had known. "In the marriages of convenience that are made in Paris, a wife's fidelity is often repugnant to nature, reason, and even the principles of justice. In America one marries one's sweetheart; to break that valid agreement would be like having two lovers at the same time, because the two parties understand why and in what manner they are bound to each other."[72]

That may have been a lament about his limited romantic life in the New World. But if he had Kitty Greene in mind when he wrote it, the marquis was protesting too much.

In any event, spring had cleared the roads. Good news was expected from France. The campaign season was about to open. Mars, not Venus, would rule the mind of the marquis de Lafayette, as it did that of General Washington.

They Will Not Be Fond of Fighting Us

(APRIL-JULY 1778)

Come out, ye Continentalers!
We're going for to go
To fight the red-coat enemy,
Who're plaguy "cute," you know . . .
Charge bagnet!—that's your sort, my boys;
Now quick time!—march!—that's right;
Just so we poke the enemy
If they were but in sight.

— "The Song of the Awkward Squad"

he richest orphan in France was broke. He had been spending money recklessly and had borrowed heavily from Henry Laurens and Robert Morris during the Canada expedition. Lafayette turned to Beaumarchais' agent in America, Lazare-Jean Théveneau de Francy, asking him to arrange a loan for him at home, settle his debts to Morris and Laurens, and take over all his accounts. Since most of his outlays were for military expenses, he was entitled to compensation from Congress. Through Beaumarchais' company, the French government could repay his costs when the American lawmakers were slow, charging them against loans and grants to the insurgent government.[1]

The new arrangements helped some, but by war's end he was in the hole for about a quarter million dollars. He was his own worst enemy. When Washington asked him to organize a network of spies in Philadelphia, he hired an agent named Allan McLane and sent him off with a bag of coins. As if that did not cost enough, he provided for the widows and children of officers, through intermediaries so the source would remain unknown.[2]

SUFFER HIM TO RETURN TO HIS EMPLOYERS

Washington was above challenge politically by the spring of 1778, and Congress acted toward the army only as he asked it to do. He extended his reach into political affairs and assigned new duties to trusted officers, making Lafayette his chief of "foreign affairs." The marquis increased his correspondence to France, boosting the American cause. He said later that he did everything he could to draw the two peoples closer together.[3]

His heaviest burden was petitions from officers wanting commissions in the Continental Army. He had brought that load on himself, because his adventures had inspired legions of soldiers to cross the Atlantic. The worst sort of pretenders had ceased to make the trip, but few of the newcomers spoke English. The French army had learned how to

Robert Morris, by C. W. Peale, 1782. The superintendent of finances for the revolution, as Franklin and Deane asked him to, tried to control Lafayette's spendthrift ways, putting him on an allowance. It did not work. (INDEPENDENCE NATIONAL HISTORICAL PARK)

Anthony Wayne, by James Sharples Senior, 1796.
"Mad Anthony" and Lafayette became friends
during the Monmouth Campaign and were
partners through the Virginia Campaign. Wayne
was the army's most aggressive combat leader.
(INDEPENDENCE NATIONAL HISTORICAL PARK)

employ foreigners. With Washington's backing, the marquis formed several "corps of strangers," as he literally translated *corps d'étrangers* (bodies of foreigners). One of his fellow voyagers from *Victoire* commanded an all-French cavalry battalion, one of several such units. Thanks to Lafayette's efforts, the Polish patriot Casimir Pulaski formed his "legion," as a mixed force of infantry and cavalry was called.[4]

Also in the range of "foreign affairs" were the Iroquois Lafayette had courted in New York. In April, he sent a French officer to round up reliable warriors who had promised to join him at Valley Forge. About fifty of them showed up early in May and hung around camp, hoping to see action under Kayeheanla's leadership.[5]

Lafayette wanted to see his whole country enter the struggle against Britain, beyond sending supplies and volunteers. He had learned the hard way that he could be undiplomatic, so he asked Henry Laurens for advice. Since he was going to write to friends and relatives "who may have some influence in a certain court," he told Laurens, he took the opportunity to ask "in which terms and stile" he should present his ideas.

The Frenchman had some advice for the president. "I beg also leave to observe," he piped up, that the American ambassadors in France had spoken "in too high terms of the strenghts [*sic*] of America." He was afraid that exaggerating American power would undercut his own efforts to draw French military forces into the war.[6]

Lafayette did not know that the crafty Franklin had been at work. Vergennes had been all for allying with America since Saratoga, but his king was reluctant, and other members of the ministry were opposed. After British peace emissaries had arrived in Paris in December 1777, Franklin played the two great powers against each other. If the British granted independence, the English-speaking countries might cooperate in seizing France's colonies in the West Indies. On the other hand, if France joined the war, she might gain Britain's share of the Indies. This was dead serious, because the sugar islands were the single greatest source of wealth on the planet.

Vergennes brought the king and cabinet around. The Americans had asked for a "treaty of amity and commerce," calling for a free flow of goods and money to support the war. They were not enthusiastic about inviting a French army across the Atlantic, but Vergennes was as slick as Franklin, and a better poker player. He insisted on adding a "conditional and defensive alliance" to the pact, authorizing French military action. The United States guaranteed that the French would keep their islands in the West Indies, while France guaranteed American independence. Each side would retain its territorial gains during the war, except that France disavowed any interest in Canada. There would be no separate peace—both sides would keep fighting until independence had been won. After some delays to gain Spanish agreement (required under the "Family Compact" between the two Bourbon kingdoms), on February 6, 1778, the treaties were signed in Versailles. The Americans were presented to King Louis, who was in his bed praying. Then they enjoyed the "privilege" of standing all evening while they watched Marie-Antoinette play cards.[7]

On May 1, 1778, Simeon Deane—brother to and messenger for Congress' agent in Paris, Silas Deane—galloped into Valley Forge. Washington summoned his officers and read the words of Franklin and Deane. "The great aim of this treaty," they told Congress, "is declared to be 'to establish the liberty, sovereignty, and independency, absolute and unlimited, of the United States, as well in matters of government as commerce'; and this is guaranteed to us by France." Tears in his eyes, aflame with Gallic ardor, Lafayette threw his arms around Washington

Charles Gravier, comte de Vergennes, engraving by Holloway after a painting by Collet, 1786. Longtime foreign minister of France, Gravier capitalized on Lafayette's adventures to take his country into the war against Britain. He also was an "uncle" when the marquis was away from Washington. (SKILLMAN LIBRARY, LAFAYETTE COLLEGE)

and kissed him on both cheeks. That shocked everyone, because no one ever touched His Excellency. It would happen again, however, and the general would learn to return his adopted son's hugs.[8]

Washington told Congress that he had "mentioned the matter to such officers as I have seen, and I believe no event was ever received with more heart felt joy." The camp went wild, officers and men expecting money, clothing, and supplies to pour in from abroad. Lafayette was ecstatic, believing that the treaty was his doing, sure that Washington agreed with him. He returned to his quarters and began writing letters.[9]

"Be so good as to present to the Congress of the United States," the marquis told the president formally, "my very sincere felicitations for the great intelligences lately arrived from France. I am myself fit to receive as well as to offer congratulations in this happy circumstances." Privately, he told Laurens, "Houza, my good friend, now the affair is over, and a very good treaty will assure our noble independence."[10]

Lafayette later wanted the world to believe that at this point he was fighting for liberty. Actually, he remained a patriotic Frenchman consumed with hatred for the *Anglais,* and independence for the United States would humiliate Britain. His letters home to France spoke of the glory and honor of his homeland, while those to Americans used the same terms about the United States. News of the treaty tore him between two loyalties. On one hand, he talked about rejoining the French army. "If my compatriots are making war in any corner of the world, I shall fly to their colors," he told de Francy. On the other, he was devoted to Washington. In the end, he decided to stay with his adoptive father, but only after an internal struggle.[11]

As a patriotic Frenchman, Lafayette feared that the Americans would make a separate peace. He told de Francy that it was up to the Frenchmen at the cap-

Benjamin Franklin, by an unidentified French artist, after Joseph Siffred Duplessis, late nineteenth century. Lafayette was the most effective aide Franklin ever had, and in return he became a surrogate grandfather to the youngster, who had never really known his own. (INDEPENDENCE NATIONAL HISTORICAL PARK)

ital to prove to the Americans that their salvation lay in France's protection. He loved their cause, he said, but he "would be quite annoyed and dismayed should it succeed in a way that were disadvantageous to my own much beloved, much adored country." The French agent should press Congress to stay in the war and "dismiss any idea of listening to England."[12]

Lafayette put on a white scarf, symbol of Bourbon France, and led a group of French officers through the celebrating Americans. Deane had also brought him letters from home, telling him that his daughter Henriette had died the previous fall, yet he waited a month and a half to write to his wife. "How dreadful our separation is!" he cried. "Never have I so cruelly felt how horrible this situation is. My heart is tormented with my own grief and with yours, which I was not able to share." In case word of his joining the festivities had reached her, he explained that the sad news had reached him immediately after that of the treaty, and while his heart "was consumed with sorrow," he had to "receive and take part in public celebrations."[13]

Congress ratified the treaty on May 4, 1778, and Washington ordered a grand review to honor the king of France. With Greene absent, honors for leadership went in order of seniority. The brigades, the commander in chief ordered, were to march to their places in the line of battle as indicated by Steuben's aides. The right wing of the first line would be commanded by Stirling and the left wing by Lafayette. De Kalb commanded the second line. To get the troops into the right mood, "[e]ach man is to have a jill of rum."[14]

On the evening of May 6, before a large crowd of civilians, Steuben paraded the army while Washington and his family stood in review. The disciplined force greatly impressed the crowd. The high point came with the *feu de joie* (fire of joy). Three times, after Knox's cannons fired a thirteen-gun salute, running musket fire started from one end of a long line and ran to the other, after which the troops shouted, "Long live the king of France!" It was an impressive display, showing the kind of discipline the army had been lacking. Robert Morris told Washington, "Our independence is undoubtedly secured; our country must be free."[15]

A newspaperman overheard a report that there was a British spy among the spectators. An officer said, "Suffer him to return to his employers, as they must feel more pain from his account of the army, than grief on hearing of his detection and death." Washington was overjoyed, issuing an order to the army expressing his "highest satisfaction."[16]

The grand show caused members of Congress to beg Washington to attack Philadelphia. His army had grown to over 13,000 men, and they faced just 10,000 British troops in the former capital. He had already put out a questionnaire to all general officers, asking their advice on three options—attack New York, Philadelphia, or Rhode Island. They ratified his Fabian strategy, as he told Congress, "to remain on the defensive and wait events, and not attempt any offensive operation against the enemy."[17]

THE GENERAL WELL KNEW WHAT HE WAS ABOUT

$\mathcal{T}$he French alliance gave the British a basketful of troubles. For the first time, Britannia was in a world war without major allies, and it would get worse if Spain joined in. The need to protect the West Indies and India dominated strategic thinking, as did the threat of a French invasion of the British Isles. The London government limited military commitments to the colonies, ordered Howe to leave Philadelphia, and redirected forces to New York and Rhode Island. Troops in Canada would stay on the defensive, and there would be an effort to detach the southern states from the United States. There were so many potential theaters of war that it could become mostly a naval one, with the Royal Navy controlling the American coasts and the Caribbean islands. There was a peace commission in New York, headed by the Earl of Carlisle, but its mission was futile unless it granted independence. It was not allowed to do that.

A French fleet could close the mouth of the Delaware River, taking Admiral Howe's ships out of the war. That would strand General Howe unless he opened a supply line through hostile territory to New York. The card games and parties among Philadelphia's loyalist elite were at an end. By the middle of May 1778, the Howes had decided to clear out, and orders arrived for the general to return to England, turning his command over to Clinton.

Lafayette's spies in the city and scouting parties out of Valley Forge reported that the British were up to something. Lafayette had showed that he could operate independently and prudently in the Canada incursion, his tantrums notwithstanding. On May 18 Washington gave him another chance to prove himself, putting him in command of about

2,200 men and five cannons. They were mostly light infantry from across the army, the rest 600 militia and scores of Morgan's riflemen. The Iroquois warriors tagged along.

Washington's orders were unusually long and explicit, and definitely fatherly. He was taking a big chance by putting so much of his command in the hands of a twenty-year-old. The detachment, he said, was "designed to answer the following purposes—to be a security to this camp and a cover to the country between the Delaware and Schuylkil [*sic*]—to interrupt the communication with Philadelphia—obstruct the incursions of the enemies parties, and obtain intelligence of their motions and designs." He offered an emphasis that would have insulted a more experienced general. "This last is a matter of very interesting moment, and ought to claim your particular attention. You will endeavor to procure trusty and intelligent spies, who will advise you faithfully of whatever may be passing in the city; and you will without delay communicate to me every piece of material information you obtain."

Washington explained that a variety of intelligence made it probable the enemy was preparing to evacuate Philadelphia. "This is a point which it is of the utmost importance to ascertain; and if possible the place of their future destination." If Lafayette had a chance to attack the enemy's rear while the redcoats were withdrawing, he should do so. "But this will be a matter of no small difficulty, and will require the greatest caution and prudence in the execution. Any deception or precipitation may be attended with the most disastrous consequences."

Washington warned the young general not to lunge headlong into battle. "You will remember," he lectured, "that your detachment is a very valuable one, and that any accident happening to it would be a severe blow to this army. You will therefore use every possible precaution for its security, and to guard against a surprise. No attempt should be made nor any thing risked without the greatest prospect of success, and with every reasonable advantage on your side." The commander in chief was not too pedantic, however. "I shall not point out any precise position to you," he said, "but shall leave it to your discretion to take such posts occasionally as shall appear to you best adapted to the purposes of your detachment." He advised that in general "a stationary post is unadviseable, as it gives the enemy an opportunity of knowing your situation and concerting successfully against you. In case of any offense [move]ment against this army, you will keep yourself in such a state as to have an easy communication with it and at the same [time] harrass [the] enemy's advance."

The commander concluded with two items typical of his other orders. "Our parties of horse and [foot] between the rivers are to be under your command and to form part of your detachment," he said, clarifying Lafayette's authority. And looting would not be tolerated.[18]

As Lafayette marched at the head of his detachment, across and then along the north bank of the Schuylkill, he should have clearly understood that he was to gather intelligence but avoid being detected. The best way to do that was not to spend too much time in any one spot. Above all, he was to keep in touch with the Main Army, making sure that he was not cut off. But the day was warm, the greenery was sprouting, the birds were singing, and he was so full of himself that he forgot what Washington had told him. After marching eleven miles downriver, about halfway to Philadelphia, he reached the top of a broad rise called Barren Hill. As he recalled in Caesarian terms later, it "was on a good elevation, with some rocks and the river on his right, some excellent stone houses and a small wood on his left, his front supported by five pieces of well-placed cannon, and some roads to his rear. He was expecting 100 dragoons who did not arrive in time, so he posted 600 militiamen on his left at Whitemarsh."[19]

The place had a nice view of Germantown and the road to Philadelphia, and it was a good base from which to send out scouting parties and dispatch spies into the city. He ordered his men to camp there. Despite Washington's warnings, he stayed for two nights, and on the evening of May 19 the enemy found him. General Howe was at his own farewell party when word arrived that the marquis was on the near side of the Schuylkill with a large force. He promised the ladies that they would soon dine with the famous marquis de Lafayette, before he was sent to London as a prisoner. Howe and Clinton set out into the night with 8,000 men, aiming to bag "the boy."[20]

Major General James Grant led 5,000 men and fifteen guns to an intersection just over a mile north of Barren Hill. Major General Charles Grey marched 2,000 grenadiers and a troop of dragoons up the Germantown road to land on Lafayette's left (east) flank. Howe and

Clinton drove their detachment straight at the marquis' southern front. Encircled on three sides by superior forces, trapped against the bluffs above the river, the boy would have to surrender.[21]

The marquis and his men had been having a pleasant encampment. The Indians spent the first evening shooting at all sorts of things and stirred up a nest of bats in an old church. Otherwise, things were peaceful, and Lafayette let his guard down. On the morning of May 20, he was "chatting with a young lady," he admitted later, explaining that she was willing to go to Philadelphia to spy for him. While they chatted, a messenger informed him that some redcoat dragoons were at Whitemarsh. That, he said, "was the uniform of those whom he was awaiting."

He was about to be cut off. When he asked for more information, he heard that a column was marching toward his left. He shifted his front and covered it with the houses, a little woods, and a cemetery. No sooner had he done that than he learned he had been cut off in the rear by Grant on the road to Swede's Ford. At the same time, he also heard that Howe, Clinton, and the rest of the army were advancing along the road from Philadelphia.[22]

Lafayette should not have stayed in the place two nights and should have had more pickets farther out. He had, however, a narrow avenue of escape along the river, so he ordered his men to form up and head out there. He sent out small detachments of infantry and riflemen to snipe at the advancing enemy, then fade into the woods. This slowed the encircling forces enough that the army retreated smartly behind its rear guard.

Private Joseph Plumb Martin, a young Connecticut volunteer who served in the Continental Army from the beginning of the war to the end, was there. "The quick motion in front kept the rear on a constant trot," he remembered. There were two pieces of artillery in front and two in the rear of the detachment. The enemy had nearly surrounded the Americans by the time they began their retreat, but the road they were on was "very favourable," because it ran through small woods and copses. When Martin and his unit were about halfway to the river, he saw the redcoat right wing across a meadow about half a mile away, "but they were too late; besides, they made a blunder here,—they saw our rear guard with the two fieldpieces in its front, and thinking it the front of the detachment, they closed in to secure their prey; but when they had sprung their net they found that they had not a single bird under it." The British columns ran into each other, the rebels nowhere in sight.[23]

The redcoats did not know what had happened to them. They had been fooled into thinking they were up against a larger force than Lafayette had. Sometime during the confusion, the marquis said, his Indian allies collided with a troop of British dragoons. "The war cries on one side and the appearance of the cavalry on the other surprised the two parties so much that they fled with equal speed." The noise raised an alarm at Valley Forge, where Washington ordered three cannon shots fired, adding to Grant's confusion. Lafayette led his army to safety across the river, and the exhausted British trudged back to the city.[24]

His feints and dodges completely flustered the forces closing in on him. Private Martin thought the marquis had performed splendidly. "If any one asks," he explained, "why we did not stay on Barren Hill till the British came up, and have taken and given a few bloody noses?—all I have to answer is, that the General well knew what he was about; he was not deficient in either courage or conduct, and that was well-known to all the revolutionary army."[25]

Washington agreed, praising him in his report to Congress. His failure to complete his mission and his nearly letting himself be trapped were forgotten, erased by the brilliance of the retreat. Making the redcoats look like fools more than made up for his errors.

John Laurens had been an aide to the marquis during the expedition. "I make you my warmest thanks to have progenited a son like yours," Lafayette told John's father. The younger Laurens had been so helpful, "and tho' you dint think much of me when you did get him, I however acknowledge myself under great obligatons to you for that so well performed work of yours."

Henry answered that racy compliment by saying, "Your Excellency's notice of the young man, does himself & his father, too much honor." The elder Laurens raved about the "applause" being heaped on Lafayette at the capital and said he had sent an account to the newspapers. The young general replied modestly that if there was something to be praised in the late retreat, it was much more "owing to the intelligence and exertions of the officers, to the spirit and good order of the soldiers" than to any merit of his own. With men like that, he crowed, "I schall willingly meet the best english troops upon equal terms."[26]

The "good order of the soldiers" reflected the wonders worked by Steuben. There was a general feeling at the time that the sterling performance of the Continental Army at Barren Hill, and later at Monmouth, was owing to Steuben's efforts. That was the case, but it can be exaggerated, because most of the troops he trained were experienced. He simplified and imposed uniformity on their maneuvers. When Lafayette gave his commands, the troops knew instantly what to do, and they did it compactly. The old straggling columns would never have dodged the British trap, and "the boy" would have dined in Philadelphia.[27]

Lafayette himself deserved the major credit for what happened at Barren Hill. Even more than at Gloucester, he showed a talent for handling light troops. Washington asked Congress to order several reorganizations of the army in May 1778, one to expand the light infantry. Under Steuben's influence, the commander in chief abandoned the idea of modeling his army on the British one, and the light infantry doctrine of the American army marked a sharp departure from European practices. Those provided for some light troops, mostly as skirmishers, but held that they should also be trained as line (heavy) troops, because they were expected to fall back into the line once the main action began. Washington's army now trained all its infantry as both line and light, and expanded the part of the army formally designated as light. Their tactics were open and flexible.

Private Martin transferred to the light infantry later that summer and complained that the duty there was the hardest while in the field of any troops in the army, "if there is any *hardest* about it." When the army was in the field the light troops were always nearest the enemy, "and consequently always on the alert, constantly on the watch." Marching and keeping guard, along with all the other duties of troops on campaign, fell "plentifully to *their* share." He concluded ruefully, "There is never any great danger of light infantry men dying of the scurvy." The kind of independent deployment he described would have been unthinkable for rigidly disciplined European regulars.[28]

The use of light troops would have profound effects on the outcome of the war. And Lafayette, with his gift for that kind of fighting, took his tactics to Europe afterward and set off a chain of developments that would change how battles were fought there.[29]

HIS COUNTRYMEN SOON FIND
ACCESS TO HIS HEART

Washington's warm approval after Barren Hill was the action's most satisfying result for Lafayette. The acclaim pouring down on him from Congress, other soldiers, and the citizenry inflated an ego that did not need more air. The boy general got out of line, prescribing diplomatic and military actions for the United States and France, formally telling the president of Congress about his proposal for a pirate campaign in the West Indies. Suggesting that it appeared the French government would go along, he passed along his correspondence with the governor of Martinique. At the same time, he sent a personal letter to Laurens, asking, "Do'nt you think that if the king agrees to it, the scheme could be very advantageous to your country on every respect?"[30]

Two days later the marquis had second thoughts. He warned that his correspondence with the governor should not be interpreted as approval by the French government. The governor would find himself "compromised in some respects if his majesty had right by an answer of Congress to believe that the governor has anticipated his orders." Lafayette suggested that Laurens present the idea to Congress as his own.[31]

Laurens had already answered his first messages. "You have encouraged me to this freedom of address," he said, setting Lafayette up for a fall. "One of your letters is so very comical, I can't attempt a particular reply, if I did, there would follow such a mixture of laughter & serious reflecsion as would detain a very short letter an hour." He had consulted another member on whether to present Lafayette's proposal to Congress, and "he advises, not for the present." Once he received the marquis' cautionary letter, he complimented his "determination to withhold that which relates to the West India enterprise." Still hoping that he might yet sail with the pirates of the Caribbean, the deflated Lafayette bowed to "[w]hatever you will think proper, my dear sir."[32]

The young soldier was still torn in his loyalties between France and Washington. He had started his whole American adventure wanting to earn glory in France. Now that his country was in the war, he told de Francy, he hoped for a recall from the king. If he did not receive one, he felt free to do what he pleased. In that case he would not hesitate to join the French army wherever in the world he could fight on their side. His ego needed some stroking from home, and he refused to go back unless he was invited. He feared the British peace commission and did not trust Congress to resist Lord Carlisle's advances. He would "be annoyed" if peace were made "without obtaining Canada," a subject that was gradually becoming an obsession with him.[33]

Lafayette's desire to stay with Washington also was growing. He was grateful for the Barren Hill assignment and expected more. At some point it dawned on him that the alternative was to be a little frog in the great pond of the French army. But he pictured himself as the sole defender of France's honor, which would be stained if the Americans made a separate peace. The great enemy of both countries was Carlisle's mission, so he set out to discredit its members. He scorned their offer of a pardon to all American rebels. "Ay, my dear sir," he warned Laurens, "never suffer such a people to approach you." He told Adrienne he could not return home because he was needed to fight the commission. "Besides, my heart has always been completely convinced that in serving the cause of humanity and that of America, I was fighting for the interests of France."[34]

Laurens calmed him down, showing no irritation at his lack of confidence in Congress. He told the marquis that the members had rejected any offers from the British government short of full independence and the withdrawal of all military forces. The answer from Congress to the commissioners was "a fine peace [*sic*]," Lafayette acknowledged.[35]

The marquis continued recommending French officers for commissions in the army, so often that he annoyed many in Congress. Just before turning the presidency over to Gouverneur Morris, Laurens asked him to stop it. Washington also was irritated, but not by Lafayette. The foreigners were a constant headache, and Steuben had begun pestering him for command of a division. Washington told Morris that he objected to promoting men who first said they wished for nothing more than "the honor of serving so glorious a cause as volunteers," then asked for rank without pay, next wanted money advanced to them, finally wanted further promotions, and were "not satisfied with any thing you can do for them." Since the French entry into the war, the problem had grown. "I do most devoutly wish," he declared, "that we had not a single foreigner among us, except the Marquis de Lafayette, who acts upon very different principles from those which govern the rest."[36]

Lafayette backed off, but not entirely. The problem with French officers eased after a French plenipotentiary arrived and discouraged their ardor for the American cause. Morris gave Washington that happy news, and he also complained about Lafayette's gullibility. The commander in chief apologized for his young friend. "His countrymen soon find access to his heart," he explained, "and he is but too apt afterwards to interest himself in their behalf, without having a sufficient knowledge of their merit."[37]

Lafayette returned from Barren Hill to find another foreign officer at Valley Forge, the British-born Charles Lee, exchanged from captivity. Washington had learned during the winter that Lee had campaigned to take his place during the Conway fracas and had otherwise disparaged him. There were also suspicions, later confirmed, that he had tried to collaborate with the British. Now he was back, the highest ranking major general, asserting his right to be second in command under Washington. But he had changed during his captivity. He was often depressed, and even the dogs seemed subdued. He said that American soldiers could not stand up to British regulars. Lafayette disagreed. He said Lee's "whole appearance was entirely peculiar," but he got along with him. They had a few meetings in which the strange general displayed his biting wit, but their friendship did not last. A year later Lafayette explained that "as one of them was a violent Anglomaniac and the other a French enthusiast, their relationship was never peaceful."[38]

FIGHT, SIR

*T*he differences between the two foreign officers became apparent in mid-June 1778, after Clinton evacuated Philadelphia. Because shipping space was short, he sent only his heavy equipment, his invalids, and about 3,000 Tories downriver. Before sunrise on June 16, he removed his artillery from its positions around the city and began sending infantry regiments across the Delaware River. By the eighteenth he had evacuated his entire force of about 10,000 men, encumbered by baggage, guns, and more loyalists. At Haddonfield, New Jersey, he assembled a slow-moving train nearly twelve miles long before Washington tumbled to what had happened.[39]

Sensing that Clinton was up to something, the commander in chief had sent a list of questions to his generals on the sixteenth, asking for advice. The next day they hashed it out at a council of war. Lee dominated the discussions, and most of the others deferred to his forceful presentation and his experience. He advised against attacking the British with amateur American troops. Lafayette suggested at least harassing the redcoats if they crossed New Jersey. "I am of opinion that theyr army is as precious to them as ours is to us," he said, "and that they will not be fond of fighting us, but upon equal grounds." Greene, Wayne, and Pennsylvania militia general John Cadwalader agreed with him, while Hamilton and Laurens cheered from the sidelines. Washington bowed to the majority and decided that the army would stay at Valley Forge until Clinton's intentions became clear, postponing a final decision for forty-eight hours.[40]

Washington had 13,500 men under him and could count on about 2,000 New Jersey militia, who mobilized when the redcoats entered the state. Clinton, with his smaller force and heavy baggage, was a great temptation. The decisive engagement of the war could lie ahead of both generals. Clinton was bogged down with few roads to choose from, and Washington might destroy his entire army. On the other hand, if he lost, he could ruin the American cause.[41]

Clinton could be attacked while in column rather than formed for battle. The roads ahead of him were scarcely worth the name, the militia had already begun to block them, and the bridges were destroyed. Once he reached Bordentown he had two choices. He could move through Trenton and Princeton to Brunswick, from which he could march to Amboy with his flank protected by the Raritan River and then proceed by ferry to Staten Island. The other route lay northeast to Raritan Bay, where the fleet could meet him. As Washington tried to figure out where Clinton would go, the British general's decision depended on what the American army did.

Thanks to Steuben's efforts, the Americans moved fast. They began marching out of Valley Forge on June 18, and the place was empty soon after midnight. Washington reached Coryell's Ferry on the twenty-first, still lacking enough information to tell where Clinton was headed; he assumed that it would be northward. Scout reports the next day said that he had guessed right. He ordered the militia to step up their harassment and sent Morgan's riflemen to snipe at Clinton's east flank. Other troops,

militia and Continentals, barked at the redcoats' heels. On the twenty-
third Washington reached Hopewell, east of Princeton, where he learned
that the British and Hessians were south of Bordentown. His most critical guessing game began in earnest. He must have troops on any road the
British might use, but he could not scatter his divisions enough to keep
him from assembling a striking force once Clinton's route of march became clear. He called a council of war for the twenty-fourth.[42]

It was one of the most heated meetings Washington ever presided
over. The decision to be made was whether to strike at Clinton or just
follow him across New Jersey. Lee, as usual, started it off. He wanted to
postpone any engagement until reinforcements arrived from France. He
"very eloquently," in Lafayette's opinion, "argued that we should provide
a *pont d'or* [golden bridge, a graceful way out] for the enemy to reach
New York . . . that the British army had never been as disciplined and as
strong." Most of the others agreed with him. Lafayette, Greene, Steuben,
Cadwalader, and Wayne did not. Lafayette said that "it would be disgraceful for the army command and humiliating for our troops to permit them
to travel the length of New Jersey with impunity." Washington asked all
of them what they thought. "Fight, sir," said Wayne, and the other four
echoed the sentiment.[43]

Washington compromised. He would avoid a general engagement
but send a force of 1,500 men to annoy Clinton's flanks and rear.
Lafayette, Greene, Steuben, and Wayne protested, and Wayne refused to
sign the minutes of the meeting, although the others did. "People expect
something from us," Greene thundered, "and our strength demands it. I
am by no means for rash measures but we must preserve our reputations
and I think we can make a very serious impression without any great risk
and if it should amount to a general action I think the chance is greatly in
our favor." Hamilton muttered that the decision "would have done honor
to the most honorable body of midwives and to them only."[44]

Washington sent Colonel Charles Scott off with 1,500 men to harry
Clinton's rear and right, and Morgan's riflemen to snipe at the other
flank. He was taken aback by the sharp divisions, and he was about to
hear more. Steuben and Duportail cornered Lafayette after the meeting
and asked him, because his English was better, to explain to Washington
"how distressed they were to see that we were going to loose an occasion
which may be repented as one of the finest ever offered." Greene,

Hamilton, and Wayne joined the trio and begged the marquis to use his personal influence with the commander.[45]

Instead of a formal protest, Lafayette wrote Washington a personal letter and handed it to him. He had signed the minutes, he began, because he had been told he should sign it, and because almost all the others who agreed with him also signed. The main disagreement was whether 1,500 or 2,500 troops should be sent to harass the retreating enemy. Arguing for the larger figure, he said the main part of the army should maintain contact with Clinton, to take advantage of any opportunity. The enlarged advance force would be able to attack "some part of the ennemy with advantage—of even beating those tremendous grenadiers if they fight with them." Six generals agreed with him, he said.

"In a word," he continued, "I think the measure consistent with prudence, military principles, with the honor of the american army and every one in it. . . . I have perceiv'd my dear general, that you were rather inclind to follow the same way I so ardently wish for, and I would a council of war would never have been call'd." He closed with a personal touch: "But I forgot that I write to the general, and I was ready to speack freely to my friend."[46]

Lafayette was right, and Washington knew it. This was the time for bold action, not half-measures. The marquis urged him to give in to his own inclinations, and he did. Almost immediately, new scout reports suggested that the redcoats were in a bad way. The temperatures hit nearly 100 degrees every day, and the air was suffocatingly humid when it was not raining, which it did often. Both armies faced the same conditions, but the Americans traveled light. Clinton's overloaded men were literally dropping dead from the heat as they slogged through mud and sand at about six miles a day.

Washington decided to fight, hoping to tear a piece off the redcoat column's rear. Instead of 2,500 men, he raised the figure to 4,000 Continentals and militia, big enough to need a major general to supersede Scott. Since Lee was senior, Washington offered the post to him. He declined it because he opposed the project in general and because a vanguard was not lofty enough for his dignity. Washington gave the command to Lafayette, with Wayne his second.

Lafayette was to use "the most effectual means for gaining the enemys left flank and rear," Washington told him in the small hours of June 25, "and giving them every degree of annoyance. All continental parties that are already on the lines will be under your command and you will take such measures . . . as will cause the enemy most impediment & loss in their march." Instead of the fatherly caution of the Barren Hill orders, he granted the discretion that a proven general deserved. "For these purposes," he said, "you will attack them as occasion may require by detachement, and if a proper opening shd. be given by operating against them with the whole force of your command."[47]

Clinton had been last reported heading from Cranbury toward Monmouth Court House on a road nineteen miles long, deep sand all the way. Lafayette and Wayne rounded up their troops and headed off by forced march. After they left, Lee reappeared in Washington's office and behaved in a manner that Hamilton scorned as "truly childish." He had declined command of the advance thinking that it would amount to 1,500 men, but since he had learned its true size he had changed his mind.[48]

Washington was exasperated. He had to bow to Lee's demands because seniority required that he have his way. Washington knew Lafayette would be disappointed, so he ordered a deal that both generals agreed to. Clinton had shifted his best troops to the rear of his column, where Lafayette would face them. Reinforcements were necessary, and he sent them with Lee. When he joined the marquis, he could take command by virtue of seniority. Until that point, they were separate commands, and Lee could not take over if Lafayette was in action. When Lee did catch up with the younger general, he was not yet engaged. "My future and my honor are at stake," he told Lafayette. "I place them in your hands." The marquis agreed to hand over command, provided he was not in battle within twenty-four hours.[49]

In solving one problem, Washington had created two others. One was that his action was controlled by a general who opposed the plan and its tactics. The other was that he had given Lafayette every incentive to rush into battle. The marquis reported that he had taken off toward the enemy, marching as fast as he could and "without waïting for the provisions tho' we want them extremely." Hamilton was with him, scouting ahead. By late on June 25 he had located the enemy approaching Monmouth Court House, and Morgan had skirmished with them. Lafayette wanted to push on and fired off appeals for supplies. "We want to be very well furnish'd with spirits as a long and quick march may be found necessary," he told Washington.[50]

The weather was brutal, like "the mouth of a heated oven," Joseph Plumb Martin remembered; "it was almost impossible to breathe." Washington feared that Lafayette would march his men into the ground. "Tho' giving the enemy a stroke is a very desirable event," he cautioned, "yet I would not wish you to be too precipitate in the measure or to distress your men by an over hasty march." If he pushed the troops too hard, many of them would become unfit for action. Washington then set out with the main force on Lafayette's trail.[51]

The marquis had to stop because of his men's hunger and exhaustion. He bombarded Washington with messages, begging for supplies, lathering to get into action. At Robins' Tavern, on the road to Monmouth, he held his own council of war and told the commander in chief that his officers wanted to strike the enemy immediately. The redcoats were just four miles off and fading away from heatstroke and desertion. He believed "an happy blow would have the happiest effect, and I'll alwaïs regret the time we have lost by want of provisions," he complained. Washington answered that his own force was bogged down by mud and thunderstorms, so Lafayette should hold off until Washington was close enough to support him. Then new intelligence caused him to divert the advance toward Englishtown. "I am persuaded you will," Washington said hopefully (and perhaps nervously), "on every occasion observe the greatest circumspection."[52]

Lafayette had done his level best to get into battle before he had to turn his command over to Lee. The heat, the supply shortages, and straying communications defeated him. He told Washington that his order had arrived too late to execute. He would march out at two o'clock the next morning, June 27, headed for Englishtown, to join up with Lee. The discouraged marquis, once he gave up his position, was again a volunteer without a division, but when he offered to serve under Lee, the older general welcomed him to his command.

Later on the twenty-seventh, Washington summoned his generals to discuss the coming action. The enemy was encamped around Monmouth Court House, ready for a fight. If they did not face one, they soon would be safe behind the heights at Middletown, a ten-mile hike to the east. Lee must attack Clinton early the next day, and Washington would come up

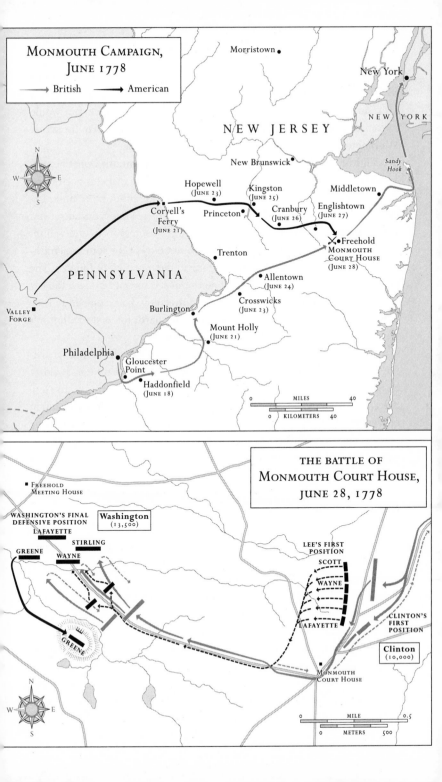

MONMOUTH CAMPAIGN, JUNE 1778

→ British   → American

Morristown

New York

NEW JERSEY

NEW YORK

New Brunswick

Sandy Hook

Hopewell (June 23)

Kingston (June 25)

Middletown

Coryell's Ferry (June 21)

Princeton

Cranbury (June 26)

Englishtown (June 27)

Trenton

Freehold Monmouth Court House (June 28)

PENNSYLVANIA

Allentown (June 24)

Crosswicks (June 23)

Burlington

VALLEY FORGE

Mount Holly (June 21)

Philadelphia

Gloucester Point

Haddonfield (June 18)

MILES 40

KILOMETERS 40

THE BATTLE OF MONMOUTH COURT HOUSE, JUNE 28, 1778

Freehold Meeting House

WASHINGTON'S FINAL DEFENSIVE POSITION

Washington (13,500)

LAFAYETTE

LEE'S FIRST POSITION

STIRLING

SCOTT

GREENE

WAYNE

WAYNE

LAFAYETTE

CLINTON'S FIRST POSITION

GREENE

Clinton (10,000)

MONMOUTH COURT HOUSE

MILE 0.5

METERS 500

to support him. Yet when Lee returned to his own commanders, all he told them was that the commander in chief desired no disputes over rank. In the absence of intelligence, he had no plan of attack, but would move cautiously and make it up as he went along. Then he wrote Washington that he expected the enemy to attack *him*.[53]

Clinton occupied a strong position around Monmouth Court House, a building at a crossroads about five miles southeast of Lee's position at Englishtown. Washington with the main force was about three miles behind Lee. Clinton was ready to defend, attack, or resume marching away, and had spent the twenty-seventh expecting Washington to attack him. Not disappointed that the day had been quiet except for some skirmishing, he planned to leave the camp at four in the morning of June 28. The night before, Washington ordered Lee to put scouts out to watch the enemy, but he did not do so until six in the morning. The scouts found the British camp empty, except for a strong rear guard; the rest of Clinton's force and its baggage were already on the road.[54]

Lee set out at about seven in the morning to cut off the rear guard. He demonstrated from the beginning that he meant what he had said— he had no plan. He also had not properly scouted the terrain, had too few aides, had shifted commanders around without remembering who was in charge of what, and did not tell his subordinates or Washington what he was doing. He had opposed the whole business from the outset and gained no enthusiasm for it as the sun rose. A confusing swirl of orders and counterorders, marches and countermarches, advances and withdrawals scrambled the 5,000-man force. All he accomplished was to alert Clinton that his rear guard was in danger, so the British commander turned Cornwallis' division around.

Lee's advance had made contact with Clinton's rear, but his main force did not come onto the scene until ten o'clock. The landscape was varied—farm fields, hills, ravines, hedges, and a steep ridge to the west. Lafayette had asked for orders before dawn, and Lee told him to take charge of Wayne's and Scott's troops. He set off toward the courthouse, but Lee stopped him because of conflicting intelligence; he had also forgotten where his own men were. The two spent much of the morning arguing. Lafayette wanted to attack. Lee could not make up his mind.

Finally, Lee told the marquis to take three of Wayne's battalions and some guns and strike the enemy's left (south) flank. Lafayette jumped forward, ended up exposed in a hollow with rough ground ahead of him, and looked for a better place to begin an assault. As he maneuvered to another line of departure, other commanders mistook his movements for a withdrawal. There had never been a good line formed anyway, and one after another American units fell back until a cascading retreat developed, some battalions in good order, others disorganized. Lafayette and the men under him came under fire from a British battery on his right.

The marquis pulled back. His men became confused, and his guns got tangled in some brush before their crews could get them to safety, across a creek and onto a hill to the west. He wanted to make a stand there, but the whole force was falling back around him. Lafayette claimed later that he had not intended to retreat, just re-form his ranks, but he really did not know what was going on. There had not been any serious fighting yet, because Cornwallis' real muscle had not reached the scene. Lee tried to form a line, ordering Lafayette to anchor himself on a Quaker meeting-house overlooking a ravine the enemy had to cross to strike the American right. It was not a good position, and the redcoats began to advance. Although Washington was not far to the rear, Lee retreated again. Skirmishing broke out as men on both sides dropped from heat and thirst. "I presume every one has heard of the heat of that day," Private Martin declared, "but none can realize it that did not feel it. Fighting is hot work in cool weather, how much more so in such weather as it was."[55]

Martin was not in the battle yet, because he was in the advance of the main force moving up with Washington. After his unit was ordered to take a break, he watched something interesting: "[W]e sat down by the road side;—in a few minutes the Commander-in-chief and suit[e] crossed the road just where we were sitting. I heard him ask our officers 'by whose orders the troops were retreating,' and being answered, 'by Gen. Lee's;' he said something, but as he was moving forward all the time this was passing, he was too far off for me to hear it distinctly; those that were nearer to him said that his words were—'d—n him;' whether he did thus express himself or not I do not know, it was certainly very unlike him, but he seemed at the instant to be in a great passion, his looks if not his words seemed to indicate as much." After passing Martin, Washington rode forward to observe and "remained there some time upon his old English charger, while the shot from the British artillery were rending up the earth all around him." He rode back, deployed two brigades behind a fence, and told them to hold the enemy until the main force and its guns reached the scene.[56]

Earlier, at about noon, Washington had heard some cannon fire from the direction of the courthouse, but no musketry indicating a battle. Hamilton rode up with a report that Lee was about to engage. As the general continued advancing, Knox sent a message that Lee's troops were in disorder and that Washington ought to take steps to prevent a reverse. Next he encountered a fugitive soldier, then elements of two retreating Continental battalions. They were exhausted, almost staggering, but in good order. Their commanders told Washington that they had retired on orders from Lee. This was probably the encounter that Martin witnessed.

What happened next has become so entangled in legend as to be unknowable in fact. Washington galloped forward and found Lee about 400 yards east of a bridge across a ravine. According to Tench Tilghman, who was there, the commander in chief asked, "What was the meaning of this?" Lee answered that he had received conflicting intelligence, his orders were not being followed, the troops had fallen into confusion, and he was retreating to high ground to re-form. Besides, he said, he had been against the attack from the beginning. "General Washington answered," said Tilghman, "whatever his opinion might have been, he expected his orders would have been obeyed, and then rode on to the rear of the retreating troops." One of Lee's officers remembered that he said, "Sir, these troops are not able to meet British grenadiers," to which Washington replied, "Sir, they are able, and by God, they shall do it!"[57]

Thanks to two officers who were not present, a yarn arose that Washington exploded in a violent outburst and ordered Lee from the field; both invented their stories decades later. One was Lafayette, who said that Washington called Lee a "damned poltroon" and sent him to the rear. Scott invented a more colorful tale, praising the commander in chief's swearing, which was so thunderous that "the leaves shook on the trees." Hamilton, who also was not present, said that Lee later thought that his sanity had been questioned, and asked him to record that he was in possession of his faculties. Exactly what passed between Washington and Lee will never be known. It is not likely that the commander had time for a temper tantrum, with disaster about to overtake his army.[58]

His behavior the rest of the day was a model of determined self-possession. He sent back orders to bring up the main body, then galloped forward to take over Lee's disintegrating advance. He filled the men who saw him with admiration. "I never saw the general to so much advantage," Hamilton wrote a few days later. "His coolness and firmness were admirable. He instantly took measures for checking the enemy's advance, and giving time to the army, which was very near, to form and make a proper disposition. He then rode back, and had the troops formed on a very advantageous piece of ground. . . . By his own good sense and fortitude, he turned the fate of the day. Other officers have great merit in performing their parts well, but he directed the whole with the skill of a master workman."[59]

Lafayette also was awed. "During this whole business," he said, "which was so badly prepared but ended so well, General Washington seemed to arrest fate with a single glance. His nobility, grace, and presence of mind were never displayed to better advantage."[60]

Such battle as had opened before Washington galloped to the front had been like a barroom brawl, individual units slugging at individual units. Clinton had not wanted a general engagement, but when he saw Lee's disorder, he deployed his troops in two lines and advanced against the rebels. He was stopped when Washington ended the retreat and formed a temporary line. Using a hedgerow to stabilize the line, and sending artillery to keep the enemy from crossing a bridge, he organized a stouter defense on higher ground to the rear. He sent Stirling to the left and put Lafayette behind him in charge of a second line. Lafayette was "sadly disappointed," his future aide James McHenry reported. "He had flattered himself, from his advanced situation under General Lee, with the first laurels of the day." Now Washington had sent him to form in the rear of the army, to provide support in case of a retreat. He did well there. When Clinton tried to turn the American left, Lafayette advanced against him, and the redcoats backed off without firing a shot.[61]

Once Washington gave up the hedgerow, Clinton took it over and planted several batteries there. Greene had taken over the right, and with Wayne holding in front, Washington told the fighting Quaker to set up his guns to enfilade the British pieces along the hedgerow. The British pulled back, and Greene's and Wayne's infantry pushed them farther with two attacks. The day ended with a standstill, the two sides lobbing cannonballs at each other.

The artillery was really the star of the day. Knox was all over the field, even more than Washington. He had already turned field artillery into a branch of infantry by imaginative placement of his guns, dispersing some among the battalions to "stiffen" the line. Where sloping terrain permitted, he put his cannons behind the infantry line, firing over the heads of the foot soldiers. Canister, grape, and solid shot blasted into the enemy lines, while other batteries targeted British guns. The noise was deafening, and thick smoke spread over the whole area.

Washington, as always, lived a charmed life on the battlefield. His coat was holed, but he was unscratched. He had another big white horse die under him, but it fell to heatstroke rather than enemy fire. The weather was "almost too hot to live in," Private Martin said. By the later stages of the fight, troops on both sides huddled in shade wherever they could find it. [62]

Monmouth Court House was the longest battle of the war, almost sunrise to sundown. It turned out to be the last major engagement in the north, and the last time Washington would command troops in action until 1781. Tactically it was a draw, but it marked the arrival of the Continental Army as a force equal to its enemy. Each side matched the other in the stamina and courage that it took to fight so hard in the blistering heat.

About 365 Americans were lost—72 killed, 161 wounded, and 132 missing. Many of the missing had collapsed from the heat and rejoined their units when they recovered. At least 37 men died from sunstroke. Clinton lost 358 killed and wounded, about 60 of the dead from sunstroke. His total losses were over 1,200, because over the next several days part of his army evaporated. Over 600 deserters, 440 of them Hessians, plodded into Philadelphia by July 6. [63]

Lafayette gained a new friend during the Monmouth campaign. The hard-charging Brigadier General Anthony Wayne, thirty-three years old, was one of the most experienced fighters in the army, so aggressive that he was known as "Mad Anthony." His strong chin, Roman nose, and thoughtful eyes hid his background as a successful Pennsylvania tanner, but his broad shoulders and powerful build did not. In war, he never passed up a fight. He had argued with Lee as the retreat began, and after Washington took over he moved ahead of the main line and held back British attacks on the center. He and the marquis had not had their last adventure together. [64]

THE GENERAL AND HE SLEPT
ON THE SAME CLOAK

*T*he bond between Washington and Lafayette strengthened further after the battle. It was increasingly apparent even to men in the ranks
that the two were becoming ever closer in their affections; one private, in
Lafayette's detachment, told a friend that a few days afterward. He also
called him a "French nobleman of extraordinary abilities [whose] conduct
is highly approved by His Excellency."[65]

Expecting to resume battle the next day, the exhausted Washington
spread his cloak on the ground, atop the ridge behind Lafayette's lines.
Lafayette lay down beside him. There Greene found them both asleep
and spread himself out under a nearby tree. Writing about this in the first
version of his memoirs, the marquis said, "The general and he slept on
the same cloak and discussed Lee." That seems unlikely, given their
weariness, and Washington did not discuss the shortcomings of others
behind their backs. At this point, he was disappointed in Lee's behavior,
not angry with him. Lafayette's memory was colored by something that
happened the next day.[66]

Both armies were exhausted, and when Washington awoke on June 29
he found that Clinton's whole army, less its casualties and deserters, had
decamped during the night. The American commander saw nothing to be
gained in pursuing his enemy in the brutal heat. Instead, the Continental
Army escorted Clinton out of New Jersey, keeping in touch at a leisurely
pace. That morning each man received a gill of rum, Private Martin remembered, but nothing to eat. They then joined their regiments in the line
"and marched for Hudson's river." They advanced by what was called "easy
marches," striking their tents at three o'clock in the morning, marching
ten miles, and then encamping at about one or two o'clock in the afternoon. They rested every third day. The army reached the river at King's
Ferry on July 15, the second line under Lafayette crossed on the nineteenth, and the army camped at White Plains to keep an eye on New York.
Besides the heat, Lee's court-martial had slowed the march.[67]

The morning after the battle, Washington received a letter from Lee,
complaining about the "very singular expressions" the commander in
chief had directed to him. He accused Washington of "cruel injustice"
based on misinformation "instigated by some of those dirty earwigs who

will forever insinuate themselves near persons in high office." He demanded "some reparation for the injury committed." The commander promised Lee a hearing, but the latter did not have sense enough to let well enough alone. He sent two more letters, even more obnoxious than the first, the same day, sneering at Washington's "tinsel dignity." The commander in chief took Lee's communications as deliberate insults, placed him under arrest, and ordered a court-martial. Lee's conduct during the battle would scarcely have rated a court of inquiry, and Washington did not raise even that idea until Lee forced him to. Now the erratic general faced three formal charges. The first was disobedience of orders in not attacking the enemy on June 28, as instructed. The second was misbehavior before the enemy by making an "unnecessary, disorderly, and shameful retreat." The third was disrespect to the commander in chief, in his letters.

Lord Stirling was appointed president of the court on July 1, 1778, and he began hearings the next day. They dragged on until August 9, because almost every field and general officer who had been at or near Monmouth testified. Their accounts suggested that Lee did not follow orders to advance and make contact with the enemy. They also demonstrated that he lost control of the action as it developed. The case of disrespect was evident to everyone. On the other hand, everyone who had seen Lee during the battle testified that he had shown great personal courage. Lee conducted his own defense, but he was not good at it.

The court found him guilty on all three counts on August 9 and suspended him from command for twelve months. Nobody believed that he was really guilty on the first two charges; if they had, the proper sentence would have been outright dismissal. Instead, the remarks that had earned him the third charge were so offensive that his insubordination after the battle backfired into a finding of guilt during it.

The unstable Lee had brought it all down on himself with his undisciplined pen. He used the same weapon, along with his tongue, to bring about his final ruin. Washington sent the verdict to Congress on August 16, but the lawmakers did not begin discussing whether to approve it until October 23. Lee spent three months in Philadelphia writing and talking too much, abusing Washington to anyone who would listen. By the time he was done, Congress could not bail him out without it looking like a vote of no confidence in the commander in chief. The lawmakers upheld the verdict on December 5, 1778.[68]

While Lee let his mouth run loose, Steuben threatened to challenge him to a duel, but cooler heads intervened. John Laurens and Anthony Wayne did throw down the gauntlet. On December 3, Lee was slightly wounded in a pistol duel with Laurens. He was ready to trade shots again, but Hamilton and other seconds called it off. The wound was bad enough that he could not accept Wayne's challenge. He and his dogs went back to the Shenandoah Valley until the end of his suspension. When he heard that Congress planned to dismiss him altogether, he wrote the lawmakers a letter so obnoxious that they made his dismissal unanimous. He returned to Philadelphia to lobby for reinstatement. There the strangest general of them all, talented, unstable, and maligned, died in 1782. He had loved, and been loved by, only his dogs. Only they mourned him.[69]

Lafayette, obsessed with the notion that there were conspiracies afoot against Washington, thought Lee was a traitor. He told Henry Laurens, "You have heard [a] good deal, I dare say, of the court against Gal. Lee," he said. "I am very unwillingly an evidence in it but am happy enough as to have nothing material to say. This Gal. Lee is very much prejudic'd in favor of his english nation. If he is condemn'd, certainly he must be guilty of some thing very ugly."[70]

Wherever Lee's prejudices lay, Lafayette's own loyalties, to his adoptive father and to his homeland, were about to be tested. A French fleet was approaching the American coast.

I Hope Your French Friend
Will Ever Be Dear to You

(JULY 1778–JANUARY 1779)

> This story shall the good man teach his son . . .
> But we in it shall be remembered,—
> We few, we happy few, we band of brothers;
> For he to-day that sheds his blood with me
> Shall be my brother . . .
>
> —WILLIAM SHAKESPEARE

harles-Henri-Théodat, comte d'Estaing, was a tall man. His sailors said he was six foot two in peace and six foot four in battle. He was aggressive in a fight, but he often showed up late to start one. Like Lafayette, he was born in Auvergne, twenty-eight years before the marquis. They were cousins, and it showed. D'Estaing was very slender, all arms and legs, with a teardrop face, broad forehead, receding hairline, pointed chin, long nose, and wide eyes under arched brows.

Most of his career had been in the army, where he became a brigadier at twenty-seven. He was captured by the British during the Seven Years' War, then paroled, and he fought in naval actions before his exchange. Captured again, he was abused by his keepers. In April 1778 Louis XVI appointed him to command all French forces in America, with a dual rank of lieutenant general in the army and *lieutenant-général des armées navales* (rear admiral) in the navy. Career naval officers did not approve.

"Brave as his sword," said a French naval historian, "d'Estaing was always the idol of the soldier, the idol of the seaman; but moral authority over his officers failed him on several occasions, notwithstanding the marked protection extended to him by the king." He was no sailor. "Had the admiral's seamanship equaled his courage," snorted one of his captains after a bungled action, "we would not have suffered four dismasted vessels to escape." Louis could not have picked a worse choice for the first commander to serve beside his American allies.[1]

AT LEAST WE SHALL GET A GOOD DINNER

D'Estaing sailed from Toulon on April 13, 1778, with twelve ships of the line, five frigates, and 4,000 marines, taking along Silas Deane, recalled by Congress, and Conrad-Alexandre Gérard, the first minister of a foreign country to be accredited to the United States. His orders were to head straight to Delaware Bay to bottle up Admiral Howe. He took eighty-seven days to cross the Atlantic, stopping to chase English privateers, and missed Howe, who had sailed to New York. When d'Estaing was spotted off Maryland on May 5, Washington asked him to sail up the New Jersey coast to Sandy Hook to trap the British fleet in New York Harbor.

After replenishing his food and water and treating scurvy among his men, the comte arrived off New York on July 11. His ships of the line were too big to clear the bar at the harbor mouth, because they drew more water than the enemy ships sitting safe inside. "It is terrible to be within sight of your object, and yet to be unable to attain it," d'Estaing said.[2]

Anticipating an attack on New York, Lafayette hired Elias Boudinot to recruit spies in the city. He promised a hundred guineas to any spy who returned important intelligence. "I beg you would send a legion of spies among theyr troops and theyr fleet, no sum of monney will be thought too much by me if such intelligences are got that we might depend upon them." A few days later he said, "Any sums of monney they may cost I schall very willingly pay." He still had more funds than sense.[3]

The marquis believed that he was still out of favor with the court of France. The last news he had had from anybody in an official position was the order for his arrest when he left the country. Now, as self-appointed liaison to the French fleet, he wanted to restore his standing back home. His cousin the general-admiral might offer him a way to do that.[4]

Lafayette was not Washington's first emissary to d'Estaing. John Laurens was. The commander in chief sent him to the French commander with a welcome, an analysis of the military situation, and a letter of introduction from Lafayette, laced with bluster, much of it in the vein of "May you, Monsieur le Comte, defeat [the British], sink them to the bottom, lay them as low *as they have been insolent;* may you begin the great work of their destruction by which we shall trample upon their nation; may you prove to them at their expense what a Frenchman, and a Frenchman from Auvergne, can do; and may you do them as much harm as they wish to do us."

He told the comte that he would be hearing from Washington, who would share intelligence with him. D'Estaing could trust the American commander "as a man devoted to the French alliance and as the man on this continent who is the most disgusted with England." He also claimed that, however happy he was in America, he had always thought that he would "rather be a soldier in the French service than a general officer anywhere else." He said he planned to leave immediately for the Antilles, Europe, even the East Indies if France was waging war in one of those parts of the world. "Monsieur le Comte, send me your orders," he urged.

The marquis was not a man of divided loyalties, but a patriotic Frenchman who wanted to return to his own country's flag. He was so busy waving that flag that he almost forgot the point of his letter, which was to introduce Laurens. He did that in a postscript, suggesting that d'Estaing would "greatly please the general and Congress by receiving him with distinction and *that will have many good effects.*" In this, Lafayette overstepped his bounds, because he presumed to volunteer diplomatic advice to his superior.[5]

Lafayette would not be upstaged by Laurens for long. Once an attack on New York became impossible, Washington proposed a joint assault on the 6,000 British troops at Newport, Rhode Island, to drive the last enemy forces from New England. But there was a problem—Sullivan commanded the 3,000 Continentals in Rhode Island, along with 6,000 Massachusetts militia under Governor John Hancock. Sullivan and Lafayette were friends, but the Irishman's hatred for all other Frenchmen was well-known. To make sure that he got along with the new allies, on July 22 Washington sent Lafayette to Rhode Island with two brigades and another detachment to serve under Sullivan as liaison to the French fleet.[6]

The young general was delighted, telling Sullivan how pleased he was to serve under him. "I both love and esteem you, therefore the moment we'll fight together will be extremely pleasant and agreable to me." He worried that he would miss the show. "For God's sake, my dear friend," he pleaded, "do'nt begin any thing before we arrive."[7]

Laurens returned from d'Estaing with an invitation for Lafayette to command the marines in his fleet, and any sailors he put into the land force, making him both an American and a French officer. He was ecstatic, he told his cousin, at the chance "to seem worthy to you of being a French soldier and of serving in this capacity under your orders."[8]

Off he marched, firing letters daily to Washington, Henry Laurens, d'Estaing, Sullivan, and others, reporting his progress and his enthusiasm. His advance was slow because of muddy roads and difficulty in getting provisions. He wanted Washington to know that he had learned from Monmouth and was not pushing the soldiers too hard. As for his enthusiasm, he cried to Sullivan, "For God's sake, in the name of your own love of glory, do not begin before we arrive! I avow that if I were to arrive too late I should like to hang myself!"[9]

Washington knew that Lafayette was tempted to return to French service. He also decided that more troops would be needed at Newport, so he sent them under Greene, who was from Rhode Island. The commander in chief told Sullivan to divide all his troops into two divisions under Lafayette and Greene, and gave Lafayette more explanation than was necessary, assuring him that the rearranged command would "not be less honorable" than the original assignment.

Privately, Washington told Sullivan, he did not know whether d'Estaing would land any troops. If he did, there was no way to predict whether they would be under American or French command. He closed by warning the explosive Irishman to control himself. "Harmony and the best understanding between us should be a capital and first object," he advised, reminding Sullivan that d'Estaing was "a land officer and of the high rank of Lt. General in the French Army."[10]

Lafayette did not learn about the change of orders until Greene caught up with him near Newport. He told the commander in chief that anything he ordered or even wished, "schall alwaïs be infinetly agreable to me, and I

John Sullivan, by Richard Morrell Staigg, after John Trumbull, 1876. The volcanic commander at Rhode Island nearly broke up the alliance with France, but he and Lafayette emerged from the uproar still friends. (INDEPENDENCE NATIONAL HISTORICAL PARK)

will alwaïs feel happy in doing any thing which may please you or forward the public good." Washington, who had worried about the young fellow's reaction, breathed a sigh of relief. His letter, he told him, "afforded a fresh proof of the noble principles upon which you act; and has just claim to my sincere & hearty thanks." Lafayette's "chearful acquiescence to the measure," after being appointed to command the brigades that marched from the Main Army, "gave me singular pleasure."[11]

That was about the last "chearful" news anyone would hear from Rhode Island. The comte reached the coast on July 29, 1778, and began an exchange of stiff notes with Sullivan. From the outset, they did not get along. Sullivan treated his ally as a subordinate, and his requests sounded like orders. D'Estaing, who could be gracious or arrogant as the mood hit him, was offended. He told Lafayette on the thirtieth that he looked forward to seeing him "with the most extreme impatience." The marquis was "the one who will have won over the opinion and assistance that were essential needs." He groused about the shoal waters on the American coast and was clearly not enthusiastic about the whole enterprise. Lafayette arrived on August 2 and walked into an international dogfight.[12]

D'Estaing's arrival sent the British into near panic, and they beached or blew up their ships and boats to prevent capture. But the comte was pessimistic. His protracted crossing of the Atlantic had left many of his marines and sailors sick or dead from scurvy; he put some of them ashore on an island to recover. He kept looking out to sea, afraid that Howe would show up and blockade him in Narragansett Bay. Sullivan pressed him to land in force for a joint operation on Rhode Island—the island where Newport stood gave the colony its name—then told him to wait until Hancock arrived with the Massachusetts militia.

The allied commanders were about to throw down gauntlets at each other, so Lafayette went out to d'Estaing's ship to mediate. His cousin greeted him icily, mentioning his "political anxiety about receiving a French officer who had violated the king's orders not to leave for America." Feeling slapped, the marquis replied that he "had come to fight the English to learn to serve his master [King Louis]." The comte accepted that and later graciously told his superiors that "no one is in a better position than this young general officer to become an additional bond of unity between France and America." The marquis and the admiral worked up a plan of action that thoughtlessly disregarded Sullivan's. The French would land two battalions of marines under Lafayette's command to support an attack on the island, while the ships moved in with their guns against the British works.[13]

Lafayette returned to camp to outline the plan to Sullivan and Greene. They did not like it. Sullivan wanted to wait for more militia and did not want to detach troops to cover the landing of the French marines. The marquis reacted defensively, and the American officers were taken aback. John Laurens thought that his "private views withdrew his attention wholly from the general interest," favoring the French party too much. His hunger to command anything from the French forces instead of a division in the American ones also annoyed them. Complaining that the others wanted the French fleet to play only a "humiliating secondary part," he told d'Estaing that they acted out of jealousy. It was truly "irksome for certain people to see the beautiful scenes of a play performed by foreign actors," he sniffed. He felt that "the French will overshadow their neighbors a bit."

Instead of furthering cooperation between the two allies, Lafayette was hindering it. D'Estaing smoothed Sullivan's feathers by bowing to the American plan of campaign but ruffled them again by mildly rebuking the general for being too hard on the marquis. He could be tactful when he wanted to be, however, and offered a plan satisfactory to everybody, including Lafayette, who would command an American detachment cooperating with the French. The admiral would run his fleet into the channel, past the British shore batteries, on the night of August 8. On the night of the ninth, Sullivan would cross over to the northeastern tip of the island, prepared to move on Newport at the southern end. The next morning d'Estaing would land his marines on the island to support him.[14]

Early on August 9, 1778, Sullivan learned that British general Robert Pigot had withdrawn from the northern end of the island to the fieldworks around Newport. Without telling d'Estaing, he crossed his American troops over to take the northern positions. When the French commander protested, Sullivan sneered that the comte was "unduly sensitive and punctilious." John Laurens told his father, "The French officers sounded like women disputing precedence in a country dance."[15]

Things got worse. Lord Howe had sailed from New York, and he appeared offshore on August 9, by which time d'Estaing was inside Narragansett Bay. The French admiral wanted to sail out and confront the enemy before he was bottled up. On the island, Sullivan called a council of war. If the fleet left him, his men would be exposed. The council decided to ask d'Estaing to stay. Lafayette snitched to his cousin that Sullivan promised to provide subsistence to the naval force and did not think the French ships were in any danger. He said undiplomatically "that the *Americans do not find your situation dangerous,* but it is easy to make plans of attack and defense when one is ashore and not responsible for anything."[16]

D'Estaing was trapped in the bay throughout the ninth, because the winds were southerly. They shifted to the north during the night, and the comte retrieved his sick and sailed out. Howe was downwind of an enemy who outnumbered and outgunned him. As the two fleets jockeyed for advantage, on the night of August 11 an extremely violent storm hit and blasted them for three days. The ships were scattered and heavily damaged. D'Estaing's flagship, *Languedoc,* was completely dismasted and lost her rudder. When the storm blew itself out on the fourteenth, Howe took his leaking ships back to New York. The French fleet straggled into Narragansett Bay, the crippled *Languedoc* under tow.[17]

Lafayette had assumed command of the American left before d'Estaing sailed out. Sullivan's troops were still full of fight, and the capture of Pigot's army seemed like a sure thing. The Americans pushed down the island toward Newport after the big storm. The town was stoutly defended by two lines of redoubts and batteries, bristling with abatis, both flanks against the water. Ahead of the two lines of redoubts was a ravine, which would have to be

Lafayette at about the time of the Rhode Island Campaign, by C. W. Peale, 1779–80.
(Independence National Historical Park)

crossed. The Americans dug trenches and gun emplacements, sure that with the French fleet's help they could overrun the enemy.[18]

Sullivan was happy to see the ships back in the bay, no matter how beat-up they looked. Allied messenger boats passed each other between shore and ship. The Americans wanted to resume the attack. The French wanted to leave for Boston, to repair their damage. When Sullivan assured the general-admiral that Providence, at the north end of the bay, offered all needed facilities, d'Estaing rebuffed him. So on August 20 the American commander sent Greene and Lafayette to the flagship to make the case in person. "If we fail in our negotiation," Greene said as they were being rowed out, "at least we shall get a good dinner."[19]

PEOPLE CENSURE THE ADMIRAL
WITH GREAT FREEDOM

As soon as they were hoisted aboard *Languedoc,* Greene lost his appetite, becoming violently seasick, although Lafayette, surprisingly, did not. When he recovered, Greene outlined the importance of a renewed offensive against Newport and described the shipyards at Providence, which could meet the fleet's needs. The comte turned the decision over to a council of his captains, and Lafayette later told Sullivan that he thought his combative cousin would have stayed and fought if not for their objections. They had no confidence in the foot-soldier admiral, who had let Howe outsail him before the storm. Their fleet was wounded, and they wanted to find a refuge before he got them into a worse mess.[20]

"[T]he devil has got into the French fleet," Greene roared, "they are about to desert us, and go round to Boston. I am afraid our expedition is now at an end; to evacuate the island is death; to stay may be ruin." Sullivan, Hancock—who had arrived with his militia—and Lafayette appealed to the admiral to change his mind. He told his cousin that he had "never seen these gentlemen so certain about the facilities you will find here and about the hopes for our success." This time, Lafayette agreed with the Americans.[21]

The fleet sailed on the morning tide. Sullivan had spent the night preparing a nine-item memorandum, signed by all the generals except Lafayette, arguing against the voyage to Boston. It included language that was bound to inflame the allies, one point being, "Because the honor of the French nation must be injured by their fleet abandoning their allies upon an island, in the midst of an expedition agreed to by the Count himself. This must make such an unfavorable impression on the minds of Americans at large, and create such jealousies between them and their hitherto esteemed allies, as will in great measure frustrate the intentions of His Most Christian Majesty and the American Congress." When d'Estaing received this, he underlined "their hitherto esteemed" twice.[22]

Lafayette blew up, insulted for his country and personally. The American generals recoiled at his outburst and tried to mollify him. He was too hot to calm down, however, and sent his own letter along with the nine points, confessing that he had lost his temper. "Would you believe," he asked the admiral, "that they dared summon me to a council where they protested against a measure taken by the French squadron? I told those gentlemen that my country was more dear to me than America, that whatever France did was always right, that M. le Comte d'Estaing was my friend, and that I would support those sentiments with a sword," meaning a duel. He ranted on and on. "Monsieur le Comte, judge my situation: from now on, every word that is uttered may be the one I think I must avenge." His loyalties were never more split than at that moment.[23]

Lafayette was not the only one being childish. Sullivan's general orders for August 24 said that "Americans will prove by the event able to procure that by their own arms which their allies refuse them assistance in obtaining." Soon the whole camp was talking about d'Estaing's "desertion," and Lafayette was even more hurt and angry. He went to Sullivan's headquarters, while rumors swirled that he planned to challenge the general to a duel. The volcanic Irishman realized that he had overdone it. He apologized to his young friend and promised to correct his statement in the next orders.[24]

Sullivan's orders for the twenty-sixth weakly bandaged the wound. "It having been supposed by some persons that . . . the Commander in Chief meant to insinuate that the departure of the French fleet was owing to a fixed determination not to assist in the present enterprize," he said, "as the Genl. would not wish to give the least colour for ungenerous and illiberal minds to make such unfair interpretations, he thinks it necessary to say that as he could not possibly be acquainted with the orders of the admiral he . . . therefore did not mean to censure an act which the admirals orders might render absolutely necessary." That was limp, and it was too late.[25]

Like Achilles of old, Lafayette sulked in his tent, nursing his wounded pride. He refused to associate with the other generals or attend councils of war. Nearly all the militia had gone home, and Sullivan lacked the manpower to challenge Pigot.

Hancock wanted to go back to Boston to help d'Estaing get his ships repaired, and asked Lafayette for an introduction. He sent two letters, one formal, the other private. The formal one told d'Estaing that Hancock was "a Brutus in the flesh, and this one's role in the revolution should make him as interesting to persons in the present age as he will be to posterity." Hancock was a true friend of France, he said.[26]

Privately, the marquis snorted that Hancock was "a Jesuitical twist: the man has only the wit necessary to get him out of difficulty wherever he goes, and his vanity equals the reputation that has so readily been given him in Europe; yet he is all-powerful in Boston. . . . Fear of English vengeance will make him a loyal ally of our country; he is a man to be treated entirely with respect in the town whose assistance is unfortunately essential to you."

Lafayette's hypocrisy grew out of his anger. He had expected that the fleet's departure would ruffle American feathers, he told the comte, but the scale of the uproar had taken him by surprise. "Would you believe that the majority of these people here, forgetting both their general obligations to France and the services specifically rendered by the fleet, let smoldering prejudices flare up again and speak as if they had been abandoned, almost betrayed?" And so he continued in page after page of adolescent fury. The only way he saw out of the mess was for France to promise the Americans a corps of 6,000 to 10,000 French soldiers "destined for the conquest of Canada next year." He never would understand that neither the French government nor Washington wanted to invade Canada. Nor did he realize that he appeared to be taking the French side in a competition, rather than an alliance, between the two countries.

Nevertheless, Lafayette remained steadfastly loyal to his adoptive father. The admiral must recognize, he said, that offending Sullivan and the people of New England "need not mean falling out with General Washington and Congress, the two great movers of all our undertakings. I would only fear seeing them prejudiced by people who explain away their own stupidities by blaming them on the fleet." He said sourly that he would prefer that France won the war alone as a lesson to the American upstarts, but that was impractical, because Washington was the only man for the job.[27]

Having gotten all that off his chest, the boy general calmed down and answered Sullivan's request for opinions on what his army should do. He advised retreating to the northern end of the island, and gave Sullivan "a public assurance upon my honor" that he would be happy to go anywhere and do anything "which will be deem'd useful to my native country and this country for whom I may venture to say I have given proofs of zeal." He asked permission to rejoin meetings of the general officers, but his outbursts had caused some of them to observe that his French nature had overwhelmed his claim to being three-quarters American. As Greene told Washington, "The Marquis' great thirst for glory and national attachment often runs him into errors."[28]

Lafayette was hurting, as lonely and unhappy as he had been in Albany. Again he unloaded on Washington. His reason for not writing the same day the French fleet went to Boston, he began, was that he "did not choose to trouble your friendship with the sentiments of an afflicted, injur'd heart, and injur'd by that very people I came from so far to love and support. Do'nt be surpris'd, my dear general, the generosity of your honest mind would be offended at the schoking sight I have under my eyes. . . . Now, my dear general, I am going to hurt your generous feelings by an imperfect picture of what I am forc'd to see. Forgive me for it. It is not the commander in chief, it is to my most dearest friend General Washington that I am speacking. I want to lament with him the ungenerous sentiments I have been forc'd to see in many american breasts."

The marquis reviewed the uproar after the French fleet left. "You ca'nt have any ideas of the horrors which were to be heard in that occasion," he said. "Frenchmen of the highest characters have been expos'd to the most disagreable circumstances, and me, yes, myself the friend of America, the friend of General Washington, I am more upon a warlike footing in the american lines, than when I come near the british lines at Newport." He expected Sullivan to order him to Boston and asked Washington to write to that place to get help for the fleet. He was afraid d'Estaing would feel put upon by "the behaviour of the people on this occasion. You ca'nt conceive how distress'd he was to be prevented from serving this country for some time."

Torn between his French loyalties and his love for Washington, the unhappy adolescent showed how much he missed his adoptive father. "Farewell, my dear general; when ever I quit you I meet with some disappointement and misfortune. I did not want to desire seeing you as much as possible." He closed on a positive note, however, saying that he had received a letter from Greene "very different from the expressions I have right to complain of, and that he seems there very sensible of what I feel."[29]

Sullivan's outbursts reached Congress in Philadelphia and Washington in New York on August 28, 1778, before Lafayette's letter. Congress "*[o]rdered,* that General Washington take every measure in his power that the protest of the officers of General Sullivan's army against the departure of Count d'Estaing not be made public." The commander in chief was already trying to limit the damage, writing to generals and politicians in Boston, New York, and Rhode Island, stressing that it was important to "palliate and soften matters." He reminded each that "prudence dictates that we should put the best face upon the matter and, to the world, attribute the removal [of the fleet] to Boston, to necessity. The reasons are too obvious to need explaining," the main one being to prevent America's enemies from turning the dispute between allies into a "serious rupture."[30]

The commander in chief had a separate message for the owner of the Irish temper on Rhode Island. "I will just add a hint," he told Sullivan. "Should the expedition fail, through the abandonment of the French fleet, the officers concerned will be apt to complain loudly." He wanted that squelched.[31]

It was too late, according to Greene, who had been working to undo the effects of Sullivan's undisciplined mouth and pen. "People censure the admiral with great freedom," he advised Washington, and they condemned the French nation as well as d'Estaing. "General Sullivan very imprudently issued something like a censure in general orders. Indeed it was an absolute censure. It opened the mouths of the army in very clamourous strains." Sullivan had also written obnoxious letters to the government of Rhode Island, but native son Greene kept them from being read to the legislature.[32]

Washington did not yet know about Greene's actions, but he knew the man would do the right thing. He advised Greene that he depended on his "temper and influence" to soothe the wounded feelings separating Americans from Frenchmen in the American army. Lafayette had "spoken kindly" of Greene's letter to him on this subject. The marquis would "therefore take any advice coming from you, in a friendly light, and if he can be pacified, the other French gentlemen will of course be satisfied as they look up to him as their head." Washington could not be there to calm Lafayette down and relied on the sensible Greene to look after him.[33]

Lafayette was not under Greene's eye as those letters galloped back and forth in the saddle pockets of couriers. He was in Boston. Then he was back in Rhode Island. Then he was in Boston again.

I THINK MYSELF HAPPY IN BEING LINKED TO YOU IN BONDS OF STRICTEST FRIENDSHIP

*S*ullivan sent Lafayette to Boston to make peace between America and the French navy. Sullivan's outburst reached the Massachusetts city ahead of d'Estaing, and when the fleet dropped anchor in the harbor, rioting broke out. There were brawls between Americans and French sailors, and a French officer was killed by a mob. Lafayette and Hancock restored calm, and soon the admiral and his captains enjoyed dinners in their honor. State officials placated the allies, the dead officer was buried in King's Chapel, and the legislature voted funds for a statue of him. Hancock, said Lafayette, "did much distinguish himself by his zeal on the occasion," and reported to Washington that he had the pleasure to inform him that "the discontent do'nt appear so much."[34]

During a banquet, Lafayette learned that there had been renewed fighting on Rhode Island. "That there has been an action fought where I could have been and where I was not," he told Washington, "is a thing which will seem as extraordinary to you as it seems so to myself." The young general rode relays of horses eighty miles in less than eight hours. Not having slept in several days, he was exhausted, but as Sullivan told Congress, "[h]e was sensibly mortified that he was out of action."[35]

The Americans were retreating from the island. Abandoned by his militia, Sullivan had withdrawn the remaining 1,500 men from the Newport lines on the night of August 28. Pigot was right on his heels, and they fought a hard battle at the northwest end of the island on the twenty-ninth. The Americans were dug in, outnumbered almost four to one, but Greene stopped the first enemy attack in the morning. British ships began bombarding the American right during the fiercely hot afternoon. Pigot launched several assaults on that flank, but skilled musketry and artillery drove back one after another. A new Rhode Island battalion of African American soldiers showed "desperate valor," according to Sullivan, in repelling three "furious assaults" by Hessian regulars. The

British general stopped trying, although sniping and bombardment by land and naval artillery continued until nightfall.[36]

Pigot pulled all his artillery up from Newport, and Sullivan made a show of preparing to meet a renewed attack. On the night of August 30, 1778, he withdrew his troops, ferrying them to Providence. Lafayette arrived when only a rear guard remained on the island, and insisted on taking command of it, Sullivan reported, and "not a man was left behind nor the smallest article lost."

Lafayette was the last man off the island, leaving about two in the morning. Afterward, he returned Sullivan's praise. "By what I have heard from sensible, and *candid* french gentlemen," he told Washington, "the action does great honor to Gal. Sullivan." The American had in fact mounted a masterly defense and retreat. Lafayette thought that the whole affair was equally honorable to the Americans and "schamefull for the british generals and troops. They had indeed so fine chances as to cut us to pieces."[37]

The next morning a British fleet arrived, landing 5,000 troops at Newport. D'Estaing's captains had been right to leave Narragansett Bay before they were trapped. Lafayette had stopped whining about American attitudes and wanted to close the rift between the two nations. He told d'Estaing that the solution was to propose joint actions against Canada, the West Indies, and other places. The general-admiral had no intention of doing so, but the marquis confessed "that I impatiently await the responses to the requests that you are going to make to Congress and even to General Washington." For once, he showed some discretion, saying that he would not write about these subjects, "even in confidence to my acquaintances in Congress or to the general, unless I receive your instructions, for fear that my measures would not be coordinated with yours."[38]

Lafayette headed back to Boston and sent his adoptive father a long account of what had happened, closing more happily than he had earlier. "I long my dear general, to be again with you," he said, "and the pleasure of cooperating with the french fleet under your immediate orders will be the greatest I may feel. Then I am sure every thing will be right."[39]

Washington had been too busy to answer Lafayette's earlier letter. He was trapped in his headquarters, looking for signs of movement among the enemy in New York, bearing a heavier burden for supply with Greene absent, and blocking an end run to Congress by Steuben, who wanted a command in the line.[40]

On September 1, Washington offered the boy general some fatherly advice about what cause they were fighting for. He sympathized with Lafayette's torment, saying that he felt "every thing that hurts the sensibility of a gentleman; and, consequently upon the present occasion, feel for you & for our good & great allys the French." He felt hurt also "at every illiberal, and unthinking reflection which may have been cast upon Count d'Estaing, or the conduct of the fleet under his command. And, lastly for my country." America was a land of free speech, he explained, and if d'Estaing's fleet had been an American one, the complaints would have been even louder. He begged Lafayette to "take no exception at unmeaning expressions . . . but in a free & republican government, you cannot restrain the voice of the multitude. Every man will speak as he thinks, or more properly without thinking." This was a matter not just of national differences but of human nature. "It is the nature of man, to be displeased with every thing that disappoints a favourite hope," and too many people were inclined to criticize without knowing the facts.

There were greater things at stake here, and Lafayette had a part to play. "Let me beseech you therefore my good Sir," Washington pleaded, "to afford a healing hand to the wound that, unintentionally has been made. America esteems your virtues & yr. services and admires the principles upon which you act. Your countrymen, in our army, look up to you as their patron. The count and his officers consider you as a man high in rank, & high in estimation, here and in France; and I your friend, have no doubt but that you will use your utmost endeavours to restore harmony, that the honour, glory, and mutual interest of the two nation's may be promoted and cemented in the firmest manner."[41]

For a man who had no children of his own, this was a masterly performance, fatherly in every way. Washington's love and sympathy for the youngster came through, he addressed him as an adult, and he appealed to Lafayette's better nature, gently reminding him of his responsibilities. By giving him the duty of healing the breach between the two countries, he boosted the marquis' ego and stopped him from focusing on himself. It had the desired effect, as Washington knew it would. When Lafayette received it, he sent a copy to d'Estaing. He had been "extremely pleased with General Washington's response," he told his cousin; "in it he shows all the sensibility and the delicacy that one could desire." The letter had been dictated by "the honesty of his soul. I admit that I greatly value recognizing on this occasion the heart of a man to whom I am tenderly devoted."[42]

Washington wanted to gain d'Estaing's confidence. "The adverse element [weather], which robbed you of your prize," he told him, "can never deprive you of the glory due to you. Though your success has not been equal to your expectations, yet you have the satisfaction of reflecting, that you have rendered essential services to the common cause." He lamented "the least suspension of harmony and good understanding between the generals of allied nations." At Washington's request, Congress resolved that d'Estaing "hath behaved as a brave and wise officer, and that his excellency and the officers and men under his command have rendered every benefit to these states." Also at Washington's urging, other generals apologized for what had happened. Greene graciously begged d'Estaing not to judge other American generals by the tone of Sullivan's letter. He assured the admiral "with the greatest sincerity of the respect and veneration that your reputation has inspired in them; permit me to add that no one feels this more deeply than I."[43]

Congress commended Sullivan for his conduct of the retreat from Rhode Island. In particular, the members "[r]esolved [t]hat Mr. President be requested to inform the Marquis de la Fayette, that Congress have a due sense of the sacrifice he made of his personal feelings in undertaking a journey to Boston with a view of promoting the interest of these states at a time when an occasion was daily expected of his acquiring glory in the field, and that his gallantry in going on Rhode Island when the greatest part of the army had retreated and his good conduct in bringing off the pickets and out sentries deserves their particular approbation."[44]

Washington had to curb Sullivan's unruly tongue. He had been gentle with Lafayette, but he addressed the older general bluntly, putting the responsibility for the commotion on the man who started it. The disagreement between the army in Rhode Island and the French fleet had given him "very singular uneasiness," he said. He pointed out that "the continent at large is concerned in our cordiality, and it should be kept up. . . . In our conduct towards them we should remember that they are a people old in war, very strict in military etiquette. . . . Permit me to recommend. . . the cultivation of harmony and good agreement, and your endeavours to destroy that ill-humour which may have got into the officers."[45]

Concern for d'Estaing's wounded feelings turned out to be exaggerated. As Lafayette discovered when he returned to Boston, d'Estaing and his officers were having a good time. The admiral and Hancock had become the best of friends. The governor had rounded up every available shipwright and fitter, and repairs went forward while the admiral and his senior officers ate at the governor's house every night. Hancock spoke French, but not very well. Once he invited d'Estaing and thirty officers to breakfast, and the count brought up almost all of the officers of his fleet, midshipmen included, Mrs. Hancock recalled. He was embarrassed, and invited her to visit his fleet along with all her friends. She led 500 ladies to the waterfront.

The fun ended early in November, when the fleet sailed over the horizon. Americans had learned that the mere fact that France had joined their struggle did not end the war.[46]

Lafayette tried to talk d'Estaing and Washington into adopting his plans to strike at the British everywhere. He wanted to get back into the fight, but nobody could figure out what the British were up to, unless it was nothing. The marquis was "very much afraid" that his spies had been hanged, he told d'Estaing in September, because he had ceased to hear from them. "Such an accident, rather common in that profession, would force me to take other measures, but I do not yet despair."[47]

The campaign season in America was coming to an end anyway. If the marquis could not find a fight in Washington's command, he wanted to get into battle in the French service, and expected the next scene of action to be in Europe. D'Ayen had told him that he did not think anything would happen there, but he replied that he wanted to rejoin the French army. He told Adrienne and d'Estaing the same.[48]

The question remained how he would be received if he went back to France. There, he knew, he was a celebrity, but he was also a fugitive. What he did not know was that other Frenchmen in America were already preparing a welcome for him. "I cannot help saying," the minister to the United States, Gérard, told Vergennes, that "the conduct of M. de Lafayette, equally prudent, courageous, and amiable, has made him the idol of Congress, the army, and the American people." D'Estaing gave the minister of marine an effusive account of the marquis' record in

America. Exaggerating the hardships of serving in the New World, and especially of dealing with impertinent republicans, he said, "It is his knowing how to turn all that to advantage, to put it in its place and remain in his own that has most impressed me in the difficulties M. le Marquis de Lafayette has overcome. As well as he can, he restrains the indiscretions of the Frenchmen in the American army who are not exactly subordinate to him; at the same time he helps them with his credit, his purse, and his table."[49]

Lafayette had been welcomed in America because American officials thought he was influential in France. He just might be welcomed in France because French officials thought he was influential in America. Before he left, however, he did not want his adoptive father to think that he was abandoning him.

He received Washington's letter of September 1 on the twenty-first. "My love for you is such, my dear general," he answered from Boston, "that I did enjoy it better (if possible) in a private sentimental light than in a political one. Nothing makes me happier than to see a conformity of sentiments between you and me upon any matter whatsoever, and the opinion of your heart is so precious to me, that I will ever expect it to fix mine. . . . I long much, my dear general, to be again with you. Our separation has been long enough, and I am here as inactive as any where else."[50]

Washington replied, "The sentiments of affection & attachment which breathe so conspicuously in all your letters to me, are at once pleasing & honourable; and afford me abundant cause to rejoice at the happiness of my acquaintance with you. I think myself happy in being linked with you in bonds of strictest friendship." He was especially grateful for Lafayette's "endeavours to cherish harmony" among the allies, which he said "deserves & now receives, my particular, & warmest thanks." After inviting Lafayette and his wife to Mount Vernon after the war, he gave his blessings to the marquis' immediate desires, as if he had read his young mind. If he had been thinking about visiting home this winter, he assured him, "but waver on acct. of an expedition into Canada, friendship induces me to tell you, that I do not conceive that the prospect of such an operation is so favourable at this time as to cause you to change your views." He would be very happy to have Lafayette with the Main

Army again, "but the present designs of the enemy are wrapped in such impervious darkness, that I scarce know what measures to pursue to counteract them."[51]

Lafayette had written several letters, strictly business, in recent weeks, always mentioning that he needed to see Washington on a personal matter. After that warm blessing, he made his concerns clear. "The news I have got from France, the reflexions I have made by myself, and these which have been suggested to me by many people," he said, made him ask for his adoptive father's advice on what to do. He went on nervously, "You may think my dear general, that I do'nt ask what I never ask'd in my life, a leave of quitting the post I am sent to, without strong reasons for it. But the letters I have receiv'd from home make me very anxious of seeing you."[52]

The young Frenchman had signed all his earlier letters to Washington "the Marquis de Lafayette." This and all later ones he signed simply "Lafayette," a token of intimate familiarity he showed to no one else, not even his wife. This small change of style carried major connotations in their relationship. It was the way a noble son signed letters to his noble father.

Before he could leave for France, Lafayette had unfinished business in America. One matter involved the British peace commissioner, Lord Carlisle. The other was, as Washington knew, his cherished project to invade Canada, making up for his earlier failure.

I FLATTER MYSELF THAT GENERAL WASHINGTON WILL NOT DISAPPROVE OF THIS PROPOSAL

On August 26, 1778, Carlisle issued a "manifesto" regretting that Congress refused to hear his appeals. His commission had been sent to America to keep the rebels from ratifying the treaty with France. Having failed in that, the emissaries offered several warnings about France's unreliability as an ally. It "has ever shown itself an enemy to all civil and religious liberty." She intended to "prolong the war" and make "these colonies the instrument of her ambition."[53]

The marquis decided that a rebuke to France was an insult to him. He told d'Estaing that he would challenge Carlisle to a duel, adding, "I flatter myself that General Washington will not disapprove of this proposal." He told Washington the same.[54]

Washington and d'Estaing both were appalled. The general-admiral twice asked Washington to talk the boy out of it. The American needed no prompting. "The generous spirit of chivalry, exploded by the rest of the world," he told Lafayette, "finds a refuge—my dear friend—in the sensibility of your nation *only*. But it is in vain to cherish it, unless you can find antagonists to support it." Carlisle would hide behind his position and "turn a virtue of such ancient date, into ridicule." Even if he accepted the challenge, the outcome of duels depended more on chance than bravery. He would not have Lafayette's life, "by the remotest possibility, exposed, when it may be reserved for so many greater occasions." He could have ordered the marquis to back off, but instead he appealed to his reason.[55]

That mature advice arrived too late, because Lafayette had already sent a "*billet doux*" (love letter), as he described it, to Carlisle in New York. It offered a challenge in florid, roundabout language that contained only one direct statement: "I do not deign to deny it, milord, but I wish to chastize you." The thirty-year-old, baby-faced lord rejected it. "I confess I find it difficult to return a serious answer," he sneered. He declined because the manifesto was not a private one to Lafayette but a public expression of the king's representatives. Washington had been correct.[56]

The boy general had made himself look ridiculous, although he did not see it like that. Lord Carlisle had made him "a very tardy reply, in which he escapes by means of diplomatic prerogatives." He told Washington that Carlisle "conceals himself behind his dignity." The silly business was concluded.[57]

The idea of a joint French-American invasion of Canada was an even greater obsession with Lafayette. It was also a greater fool's errand. In his first greeting to d'Estaing in July, he said that as soon as the French flag was seen near Canada, half the *habitants* and Indians would "declare themselves for us." He kept hammering at his cousin until d'Estaing issued a "Declaration in the king's name to all former Frenchmen of North America." It told the "inhabitants and savages" that they were born French, and had never ceased to be French.[58]

The marquis revived the idea of invading Canada as a way to heal the breach between the allies opened by Sullivan. D'Estaing issued the decla-

ration just to get the boy off his back. He knew that the French government had no interest in the project. Lafayette should have known also,
because Minister Gérard told him to knock off his agitation. Vergennes
had long since scotched any such notions. The American war had already
cost his government plenty, while Britain's resources required to maintain its hold on Canada drained its power in Europe. If the war came out
favorably for the allies, the foreign minister believed, a continuing British
presence in Canada would bind the United States closer to France. If his
government wanted any territorial gains, it looked toward the West
Indies.[59]

Lafayette was undeterred. On September 3, 1778, he told
Washington that he ought to move against Canada, "for as long as you
fight I want to fight along with you, and I much desire to see your
Excellency in Quebec next summer." The commander in chief, as he had
pointed out the flaws in the marquis' many proposals for more than a
year, explained the facts of this case. "Many circumstances, and events
must conspire," he said, "to render an enterprize of this kind practicable
and advisable." The enemy must withdraw from New York and Newport
before he could detach an expedition. Moreover, a wintertime invasion
of the north would present a monumental logistical challenge. "In a
word," conditions were "so much against the undertaking" that the marquis could take a furlough.[60]

Lafayette pressed ahead anyway. Except for some diehards in
Congress, nearly all American officials were opposed to a Canadian expedition. Washington explained that if they marched north, Americans no
longer would be fighting for independence but would look like conquerors. He did not tell Lafayette that he also harbored suspicions about
France's ambitions. John Laurens did. As he wrote to his father, he hoped
that "the marquis will be thanked for his good intentions, and his offers
waived."[61]

Lafayette went to Philadelphia in October to arrange a leave of absence and to lobby for his Canada project. Washington, asked by
Congress for his opinion, concluded that the marquis had put the whole
thing into the lawmakers' minds. So did Henry Laurens, who worried
that the naive Frenchman was becoming mired in republican politics.
Lafayette assured Washington that all he had done was to answer questions. "The idea was not suggested by me," he claimed, "and I acted in the

affair a passive part." That was probably an honest answer, because there were members who loved the idea of conquering the north.[62]

Lafayette was sick in bed for much of November, and Washington visited him often. He explained to him repeatedly the logistical objections against marching north. The marquis jotted them down and passed them on to Congress with his own answers. He did not know that his adoptive father had already told the lawmakers that he did not trust America's ally. France was "the most powerful monarchy in Europe by land," he said, able to "dispute the empire of the sea" with Great Britain, and if Spain joined her, the French would certainly be superior to the British. He did not want the United States to face a foreign rival holding "New Orleans on our right, Canada on our left, and seconded by the numerous tribes of Indians in our rear." He concluded with what would become the guiding principle of his own foreign policy later. "[I]t is a maxim founded on the universal experience of mankind, that no nation is to be trusted farther than it is bound by its interests."[63]

Washington trusted Lafayette, but he trusted no foreign power, even America's ally. The marquis was undeterred. He sent his chief spy in Canada some questions he wanted answered. He also forwarded a proclamation to be read to "my children the savages of Canada," promising the Indians that American and French forces would liberate them yet.[64]

Washington's judgment prevailed in Congress, and early in January 1779 the new president, John Jay, told Lafayette that the members had voted against any expedition to Canada. The United States must liberate itself, he advised, before it liberated others. The project would also disserve France by drawing it into a campaign whose outcome would be "very uncertain & might be very ruinous." Lafayette did not receive that until May, when he was in France conspiring with Franklin to mount an invasion that both their governments opposed.[65]

DO'NT FORGET AN ABSENT FRIEND

Canada was just an interruption in Lafayette's plans to return home. Washington advised that he ask Congress for a leave of absence, which would let him retain his commission and preserve his freedom to return to the American army—and to Washington's side. The general explained to the lawmakers that he preferred Lafayette's "being absent on this footing, if it depended on me."[66]

In October 1778 the marquis formally applied for leave. The sentiments that bound him to his country, he told the president, "can never be more properly spoken off [*sic*], than in presence of men who have done so much for theyr own. As long as I thought I could dispose of myself, I made it my pride and pleasure to fight under american colours in the defence of a cause, which I dare more particularly call ours, because I had the good luck of bleeding for her." Now that France had joined the war, he was compelled by his "duty as well as by patriotic love" to present himself before the king. He asked Congress to grant him the liberty of going home for the winter as a soldier on furlough.[67]

The lawmakers were won over by that, especially the mention of his wound, but legislatures never do anything by simple, direct means. The members debated how to thank the marquis, what presents to send back with him, instructions to him and to their agents in France, and a pile of other details. He considered Philadelphia "a tiresome prison," Lafayette complained to d'Estaing, "and if I were staying here only for my business I would soon have escaped." Republican government remained a mystery to him. "IF THEY WOULD BUSY THEMSELVES LESS WITH INTRIGUES AND MORE WITH BUSINESS, EVERYTHING WOULD BE FINISHED," he roared.[68]

Congress granted a "furlough for your return to France to be extended at your own pleasure," authorized its agents in France to have a sword made and presented to him, and thanked him for his "zeal in promoting that just cause in which they are engaged and for the disinterested services you have rendered to the United States of America." Best of all, Congress sent a letter to King Louis XVI: "Great, faithful and beloved friend and ally: The Marquis de la Fayette having obtained our leave to return to his mother country we could not suffer him to depart without testifying our deep sense of his zeal, courage and attachment. We have advanced him to the rank of a major general in our armies, which, as well by his prudent and spirited conduct he hath manifestly merited. We recommend this young nobleman to Your Majesty's notice as one whom we know to be wise in council, gallant in the field, and patient under the hardships of war. His devotion to his sovereign hath led him in all things to demean himself as an American, acquiring thereby the confidence of these United States, Your Majesty's good and faithful friends and allies, and the affection of their citizens."[69]

That just might be a ticket out of the royal doghouse for the fugitive from the king's warrant. There was other help for him, including a favorable report from Minister Gérard and another from William Carmichael, former secretary to the delegation in Paris. Lafayette hired him to be his chief of intelligence while he was gone and gave him a bottomless bank account to go with the job. In return, Carmichael advised Franklin to personally present all the resolutions of Congress at court. "I am sure all the consequence he can derive from the influence of his family or from his own merit," he suggested, "will be exerted for our interests because he thinks them blended with those of his nation, & I know that personally he ardently desires to cultivate your friendship & your esteem."[70]

Washington, Henry Laurens, and others also sent letters of introduction. The commander in chief's long message to Franklin ended on a personal note. "Coming with so many titles to claim your esteem," he said, "it were needless for any other purpose than to indulge my own feelings to add that I have a very particular friendship for him." Even the scruffy pamphleteer Thomas Paine put his oar in. The marquis, he told Franklin, returned "with the warmest thanks from this country." His "amiable and benevolent manners" were "a living contradiction to the narrow spirited declarations of the British commissioners. He happily returns in safety, which, considering the exposures he has gone thro', is rather to be wondered at."[71]

Lafayette took off for Boston to catch a ship Congress provided for him. He rode horseback through constant rain and was treated in every town to receptions at which he drank too much. At Fishkill, New York, eight miles from Washington's camp, he collapsed into bed on November 2, 1778. Washington sent his personal physician to attend to him and visited as often as he could. Despite the best efforts of eighteenth-century medicine—bleeding—he recovered in about three weeks. Meanwhile he acquired a pile of letters from well-wishers. Morgan was frightened at his condition and thought that he would be gone for good. All the generals in the army liked the marquis, he said. He was "very far from leaving the american service," Lafayette reassured him, and had "merely a furlough from Congress." He was confident that he would return to America in the spring.[72]

Lafayette was aboard ship by late December, but his departure was repeatedly delayed by Congress' dilatory forwarding of various instructions and messages. His adoptive father sent a heartfelt farewell. "I am persuaded, my dear marquis," he told him on December 28, "there is no need of fresh proofs to convince you either of my affection for you personally, or of the high opinion I entertain of your military talents and merit." He concluded, "The interest I take in your happiness cannot but make me desire you may be equally dear to your own. Adieu, my dear marquis, my best wishes will ever attend you."[73]

The general thought that the next time he heard from Lafayette would be after he reached France. Yet his ship did not sail. On January 5, 1779, the marquis wrote, "To hear from you, my most respected friend, will be one of the greatest happiness I may feel. The longer letters you'll write the more bless'd with satisfaction I schall think myself. I hope you will not refuse me that pleasure as often as you can." Once again, his hand and his English shook. "I hope you will ever preserve that affection which I do return by the most tenderest sentiments. How happy, my dear general, I would be to come next spring, principally as it might yet be propos'd I need not say."

Lafayette continued, "Your first letters will let me know what I am to depend upon on that head, and I flatter myself the first from me will confirm you that I am at liberty and that most certainly I intend to come next campaign." He regretted leaving his adoptive father, even if it was to be temporary. "Farewell, my most beloved general, it is not without emotion I tell you this last adieu before so long a seperation. Do'nt forget an absent friend and believe me for ever and ever with the highest respect and tenderest affection der. general your most obed. serv. and affectionate friend Lafayette." Five days later he added a postscript, saying that he hoped to sail the next day. "I hope I am right and I hope to hear soon from you. Adieu; my dear and for ever belov'd friend, adieu."[74]

Washington could not help being touched by such devotion. There was one more, written on January 11. "The sails are just going to be hoisted, my dear general, and I have but the time of taking my last leave from you. . . . Farewell, my dear general, I hope your french friend will ever be dear to you, I hope I schall soon see you again, and tell you myself with what emotion I now leave the coast you inhabit, and with what affection and respect I'll for ever be, my dear general, your respectfull and sincere friend Lafayette."[75]

After the long goodbye, Lafayette could not get the man he loved and admired so much off his mind. "Even those enemies who accused that great man of insensitivity," he wrote when he was back in France, "acknowledged his tenderness for M. de Lafayette. And how could his disciple have failed to cherish him who unites all that is good with all that is great and whose nobility springs even more from his virtues than from his talents? If he had been a simple soldier, he would have been the bravest one; if he had been an obscure citizen, all his neighbors would have respected him. With a just heart and a just mind, he judged all matters impartially. In creating him expressly for that revolution, nature did great honor to herself."[76]

I Love Him as My Own Son

(JANUARY 1779-MARCH 1780)

If one trusts solely to brave generals who love fighting, this will cause trouble. If one relies solely on those who are cautious, their frightened hearts will find it difficult to control the situation.

—SUN SHENG

Lafayette crossed the ocean on a new American frigate, *Alliance.* He was seasick most of the time, and the trip was rough. A storm tore away the main topmast and left her shipping water. The ship's crew included some British deserters and prisoners. "In order to encourage crews to mutiny," according to Lafayette, "His Britannic Majesty had made the rather immoral declaration that a crew would receive the value of any *rebel* ship it brought into an English port. Such an act could be accomplished only by the massacre of the ship's officers and those who opposed the mutiny."

The English crewmen hatched a plot to take the ship, but one of them had a careless mouth. The officers and passengers stormed the forecastle, and by the end of the day thirty-three men were in irons, at which point the officers ran out of irons. *Alliance* sailed into Brest on February 6, 1779, and the prisoners received the hospitality of the port authorities, who threw them into a dungeon.[1]

I WOULD WILLINGLY HAVE SOLD OFF THE FURNITURE OF VERSAILLES

*L*afayette and the American Revolution transformed French patriotism, redefining it in terms of "liberty." This new passion inflamed the younger generation in prominent noble families, including the Noailles and the Ségurs. No longer a callow provincial boy, Lafayette became a paragon of modern French chivalry, his leaving against the king's wishes underscoring the difference between the new patriotism and moldy old tradition. Because his homeland had entered the war, he was vindicated.

The marquis also was wrapped in the magical aura of George Washington, who had become venerated in France. He seemed to embody republican virtue as the model of the citizen-soldier, father and fatherland combined. In France, Lafayette was "the friend of Washington." But despite his later claims, he was not yet a republican. He had not thought much about slavery and was not interested in the conflicts between different groups in America. But he liked Americans and their liberty. Above all, he loved and worshiped Washington. This great man was a modern King Arthur, fighting to establish an ideal republic. To show his devotion, Lafayette wanted to help him build his Camelot.[2]

He galloped as hard as he could toward the capital and reached Versailles in the middle of the night of February 11. His uncle (and former colonel) the prince de Poix was holding a midwinter ball at his palace, and Lafayette burst in, wearing his American uniform. He knew he had to present himself at court. He also carried dispatches from America for the various ministers, so the next morning the prince escorted him to the palace, where he visited with Prime Minister Maurepas, Foreign Minister Vergennes, and the rest of the government. They listened to his tales from the American war and argued about what to do with him. The king would not receive him without some sort of penance. He was "questioned, complimented, and exiled," the marquis recalled; but it was to Paris he was sent, "and the confines of the Hôtel de

Noailles were thought preferable to the honors of the Bastille, which was first proposed." The royal doghouse would not be so flea-ridden after all, although the house of his father-in-law had its drawbacks. D'Ayen's father, the *maréchal*-duc de Noailles, would be his jailer. There he was to stay for ten days, in "internal exile," after which he would be chastised enough to present to the king. He left for Paris that afternoon.[3]

Lafayette had deserted Adrienne for nearly two years, and she had suffered through the death of one daughter and the birth of another without him, but she still adored him. That was rare enough among noblewomen, but she was so emotional about it that her mother thought she should break the news gently that her wandering husband had returned. She did not fall into a faint, as her mother feared, but threw herself on him as he walked in the door.

Her joy was "easy to credit, but impossible to describe," Adrienne wrote his aunt and grandmother at Chavaniac. "Monsieur de La Fayette has come back to me as modest and as charming as when he went away. . . . When I reflect on my good fortune in being his wife, I am truly grateful to God." She thought herself unworthy of him. "The knowledge that I am very far from being as good and gracious as he is makes me sad, and then I hope that my affection may make up for my shortcomings."[4]

She sold herself short, as Lafayette himself would realize years later. It was his responsibility to let his own family know that he was back, but he tossed that duty onto her. He was too busy being a celebrity, living the dream of the resentful adolescent who vows that he will become famous someday, showing all that they had been wrong about him.

Because Lafayette was young, he needed guidance. Vergennes, who took an immediate liking to him, saw that. Like Laurens and Greene before him, the foreign minister became the young man's "uncle" when he was far from Washington. And when the marquis met Franklin, he found something that he had never known in his life—a wise grandfather who could explain the world to him.[5]

The *maréchal*-duc imposed the terms of the marquis' confinement. He could see nobody but relatives, with a few exceptions such as important Americans. Because of intermarriage among the French nobility, almost everybody with a title was at least a cousin, so he met a stream of visitors, and he had no hesitation about sneaking out of the house. On his second night he visited John Adams, and the next day he dined at the home of a relative.[6]

Lafayette was no longer a country bumpkin. He was balder, and he stood erect, made small talk with ease, told interesting stories about America, and had turned into a brilliant conversationalist. A journalist reported on his "sensitive and polished intelligence . . . a lively unaf-

fected power of describing the famous persons he had met." It was not just his countrymen who were impressed. The affable Franklin and even the grumpy Adams were won over. Everyone was fascinated by his close relationship with the legendary Washington.[7]

The marquis was on a mission for his adoptive father, and to that end he wanted to meet Franklin immediately. The "Doctor" lived some distance away, at Passy, so Lafayette could not sneak out to his place without sneaking out of the city. He invited Franklin to the Hôtel de Noailles, and then asked Vergennes for instructions, to confirm that Franklin was so fascinating to the French that nobody

John Adams, by C. W. Peale, 1791–94. Adams never approved of Lafayette, or anybody else for that matter, but he did acknowledge Lafayette's contributions to American interests in diplomatic and trade negotiations, especially his role in getting the French army and fleet sent to Washington's side. (INDEPENDENCE NATIONAL HISTORICAL PARK)

would object to Lafayette's receiving him. While he was at it, he warned the foreign minister that rumors were spreading about his Canada project, but they were not his fault. There were loose lips in Congress, although rumors were not such a bad thing. "The truth can remain hidden only if it is lost in a mass of false intelligence," he said.[8]

Canada was one of the things Lafayette wanted to talk to Franklin about, but first he needed to regain his freedom of movement. His father-in-law, d'Ayen, and d'Ayen's father, the *maréchal*-duc de Noailles, no longer his critics, were now his boosters. They helped him write a suit-ably contrite letter to the king begging forgiveness and offering to per-form whatever service His Majesty required for him to "absolve" himself. "The misfortune of having displeased Your Majesty," he began, "produces such a deep sense of sorrow that I am encouraged not to try to excuse an action of which you disapprove but to present the real motives that in-spired it. Love of my country, the desire to witness the humiliation of her enemies, a political instinct that the last treaty would seem to justify: these, Sire, are the reasons that governed the part I took in the American cause." He had thought the royal warrant against his leaving had reflected "the solicitations and tender concern of my family" rather than an act of state. "Persuaded that I was blameless, sir, I fought for my country with a calm heart."

He had not returned to France after she entered the war because he was needed to help d'Estaing in America. In any event, "I would not think, Sire, of daring to justify before Your Majesty an act of disobedience of which you disapprove and for which I should repent." He blamed his errors on his youth, giving Louis an excuse to forgive him. It was an oily, almost smarmy performance.[9]

It had "happy results," as the marquis put it. The king granted him an audience "to receive a mild reprimand [*réprimande douce*], and when my freedom was restored I was advised to avoid those places where the pub-lic might consecrate my disobedience. On my arrival I had enjoyed the honor of being kissed by all the ladies. . . . They spoke well of me in all circles." He enjoyed "what I would have chosen: popular favor and the af-fection of the people I love."[10]

The young general was the lion of Paris and Versailles. He went riding with the king, attended the salons, and met enthusiastic applause wher-ever he appeared. When he and Adrienne were at the Comédie Française, the master of ceremonies roared from the stage, "Behold this youthful courtier . . . his mind and soul inflamed!" The crowd roared back its approval. The queen arranged his return to the army and promotion from *capitaine réformé* to *mestre de camp* (cavalry colonel) commanding a regiment of the King's Dragoons. This honor cost him 80,000 livres for the commission.[11]

Lafayette discovered that fame could be a source of political power. In America, power arose from the people, exercised by elected representatives and influenced by famous individuals such as Washington. In absolutist France, in principle all power descended from the king. But Louis was a weak king, swayed by his ministers and increasingly by public opinion. Lafayette was the greatest celebrity in the country, among the nobility, the common people, and the growing bourgeoisie. At first unconsciously, later deliberately, he put his fame to work.

In "the midst of the various whirlwinds" that tossed him about, Lafayette claimed later, he "did not lose sight of our revolution, the final success of which was still very uncertain." Accustomed as he was to seeing "great causes sustained by slender means," he often pointed out that the cost of one banquet would have reequipped Washington's army. The prime minister charged that "to clothe it I would willingly have sold off the furniture of Versailles."[12]

Lafayette shuttled between Paris, Versailles, and Passy, where Franklin was often laid up with gout. Over the following months, the marquis became the most important and effective agent Franklin ever had, reviving the court's devotion to American independence. France's chief aim in getting into the war had been to weaken England, but after Newport and the fall of Savannah, Georgia, in December 1778, it appeared that the war was going badly. It was also draining the treasury.

Being famous could be a drag when he tried to help the American agents. Often the marquis postponed meetings because he was summoned to a levée by the king or required to join the queen on a ride. "In our kingly countries," he told Franklin, "we have a foolish law call'd *Etiquette* that any one tho' a sensible man, must absolutely follow." After he saw the ministers, he would have the pleasure of telling Franklin "what is the matter at Versailles."[13]

Lafayette used his influence, in concert with Franklin and Adams, to get additional grants and loans, French fleets, and French troops to support Washington. He besieged the ministers, often speaking for the Americans, and he traded ideas with his newfound friends. He told Adams that England was stretched thin, and a fleet and just 5,000 troops could blast her out of the Western Hemisphere. Adams liked that ambition. The plan, he said, "must infallibly succeed." He would be happy "to have further conversations with you, Sir, upon those subjects." But Maurepas in particular resisted such grand schemes. The taking of Senegal in January made him and the other ministers more inclined to favor limited actions, such as raids on the English coast.[14]

Franklin had long favored such diversions, to drain resources from Britain's campaigns in America. Lafayette, if he could not talk the ministry into sending an army to join Washington's, decided that Franklin's ideas, which soon came across as his own, were worth pushing. Besides, they offered a chance to realize his ambition of a joint French-American operation. As for who should command the ships, Franklin had the man for the job—John Paul Jones, who had just returned from a raid in English waters.

Ten years older than Lafayette, Jones had been born the son of a Scottish gardener as John Paul Jr. Going to sea at the age of thirteen, he fought his way up from belowdecks to become second mate on a slave ship, then master of his own merchantman. He changed his

John Paul Jones, by C. W. Peale, 1781–84. Jones and Lafayette cooperated on an expedition to raid English ports, although Franklin feared the two proud fighters would go after each other. The campaign was cancelled before it began.

(INDEPENDENCE NATIONAL HISTORICAL PARK)

name to John Paul Jones when he fled a murder charge in the West Indies, and he became an American. His little "Continental Navy" was a branch of Washington's army, although nobody but Franklin could ever tell him what to do. He was a ruggedly handsome ladies' man and a notoriously aggressive fighter on land and sea. He also was vain, plagued by inner doubts, arrogant, abrasive, and pugnacious, with a thin skin, loud voice, and quick temper. For all his faults, he was a born sailor who instinctively went "in harm's way," as he put it.[15]

Lafayette set out to sell the ministers on the idea of a raid on England, with himself in charge of the land forces and Jones the ships. For someone so young, he enjoyed remarkable access to the highest levels of government, thanks to his celebrity. He was also not above complaining about the ministry's decision not to send troops or any more money to America. So he allowed rumors to circulate that he was organizing an army to join Washington, as a cover for what he was really badgering the government about.

After talking to Vergennes, in March 1779 Lafayette approached the prime minister, Maurepas. "I grant, Monsieur le Comte, that it is not so much for the sake of America but even more for that of France that I am vexed at the impossibility of aiding the Americans," he declared. Despite the minister's belief, the Americans were not losing dedication to their own war, and public opinion among them would favor bold action on the part of France. He believed he had learned what made the greatest impression on them, and "it is this experience that induces me to venture to share with you some ideas on a favorite expedition."

This American major general wanted to lead 1,500 French soldiers in a flotilla to raid the ports of England and Ireland, paying for it by exacting tribute from the targeted towns, which would be burned if they did not pay. The benefits from such an expedition were so obvious, he claimed, and his own knowledge of the Americans made the expedition seem so valuable, that he concerned himself "only with the degree of possibility" it offered. While the prime minister chewed on that, he went hunting with the king, and talked him into calling a meeting of the cabinet to discuss it.[16]

Franklin was impressed by Lafayette's energy and zeal and told him so. He also thought the proposed raid could bring in a pile of loot. "Much will depend, on a prudent & brave sea commander who knows the coasts, and on a leader of the troops, who has the affair at heart," he said, chucking both Jones and the marquis under the chin. The plan could succeed if the egotistical commanders could get along.[17]

Lafayette bounced Franklin's attitude off Maurepas. "It pleases him immensely," he said, "and his knowledge of England makes him see all its advantages." He recommended as naval commander "Captain Jones, an excellent sailor, they say, who knows all the coasts thoroughly and whom M. de Sartine [the minister of marine] seemed inclined to employ as head of the naval part of the expedition." Franklin, he said, would bring the proposal up with Vergennes personally. Meanwhile, the foreign minister was warming to the idea and asked him for more details. By the first of April 1779, hounded relentlessly by Lafayette, all the ministers had come around, provided the expedition did not cost too much.[18]

Lafayette spent the next month snarled in the knots of bureaucracy. The ministers had agreed to his project, but they did little to move it along. He pestered the ministers of war and of marine to hurry along the provision of everything from troops and cannons to ship stores and diplomatic cover. He picked up his old dream of invading Canada and thrust it at Vergennes. The idea of a revolution in Canada seemed "charming to every good Frenchman," he suggested. Besides the economic advantages from the fur trade, and the chance to "render liberty to our oppressed brothers," he slyly suggested that a liberated Canada would be a "fourteenth state, which will always be attached to us." The foreign minister still wanted no part of any such fantasy.[19]

Lafayette and Jones got together, under Franklin's roof, late in April. Giving Jones his sailing orders, the Doctor worried that the temperamental officers would go at each other's throat rather than the enemy's. He told them that the campaign was an audition both for them and for future French-American cooperation. "There is honour enough to be got for both of you if the expedition is conducted with a prudent unanimity." The proud fighters exchanged promises of mutual respect and cooperation. "Be certain, my dear sir," Lafayette told Jones, "that I'll be happy to divide with you whatever share of glory may expect us, and that my esteem and affection for you is truly felt, and will last for ever."[20]

Lafayette turned to Jacques-Donatien Leray de Chaumont, a French entrepreneur, to cut through the red tape and get the expedition outfitted. The latter's home was headquarters for the American delegation in Paris, and he had used his connections to forward clothing and other supplies to Washington. Not even he, however, could overcome problems such as the fact that most of the cannons provided to Jones were substandard. In addition, the finance minister kicked up a fuss over what the whole business was costing.

Lafayette and Jones offered a revised—and larger—proposal to extend their expedition to invade Ireland and stir up a rebellion there, then go on to America, either to invade Canada or to fight beside Washington. That was too much. Vergennes and Maurepas told Lafayette that an expedition to America was "impossible for the present." Maurepas said, "We shall have to wait and see what will result from the operations already determined upon." The marquis had no idea what the minister was talking about. [21]

The political situation had changed. On April 12, France and Spain had ratified the Aranjuez Convention, bringing the Iberians into the war. The Spanish minister objected to the cost of the Lafayette-Jones project but suggested that the two countries might combine on a bigger expedition—an invasion of Great Britain. Without telling either of the officers why, on May 22, 1779, the government cancelled their raid and ordered Lafayette to rejoin his regiment at Saintes. Lafayette gave Jones the bad news, saying that "political and military reasons have occasion'd that alteration." Jones demanded an explanation but instead he was told to chase the British navy out of the Bay of Biscay. [22]

Lafayette left for Saintes, afraid that the end of his project meant the end of French support for the United States. He felt exiled from Versailles, from his adoring public, and from Adrienne, who was pregnant again. He was a regimental commander at twenty-one, more than most men could have wished for. But he had been a major general in Washington's campaigns, as well as commander of an invasion of Canada and lately of the aborted raid against England. Now the boredom of garrison life loomed before him. When rumors circulated that a new army was being formed to go to America, he worried that it would leave without him.

DON'T FORGET ME, MY DEAR GENERAL

*L*afayette's regiment moved from Saintes to nearby St. Jean d'Angély before he reached it. The unit's discipline and maneuvers were not good, so he stepped up its training. Mostly, he fretted. He had returned to France hoping that the odds of getting into battle were higher there than in America. He decided that he had made a mistake, and missed his adoptive father, because he had not heard from him. Washington had written him several times, but the British blockade intercepted most of his messages.[23]

The marquis wrote Vergennes on June 1, 1779, saying that Congress had cancelled his Canada proposal, and on the tenth to complain about the way he had been treated. "I should be lacking in candor," he fumed, "if I did not admit that my blood boils a little in my veins. . . . Don't forget that I love the trade of war passionately, that I consider myself born especially to play that game, that I have been spoiled for two years by the habit of having been in command. . . . After all that, Monsieur le Comte (since I do not speak to you as the king's minister), judge whether I have the right to be impatient."[24]

When Lafayette learned that Anne-César, chevalier de La Luzerne, had been appointed minister to the United States, replacing Gérard, he poured out letters to send across the ocean with him. They included two written on June 12, one to Congress and the other to Washington, so long that they threatened their carrier with a hernia. "I desire to return again to that country of which I shall ever consider myself as a citizen," he told the president of Congress. He went on for page after page, saying how devoted he was to America, and how much he wanted to serve again in her army. Then he said something curious. "I shall frankly tell you, sir, that nothing may more effectually hurt theyr interests, consequence, and reputation in Europe, than to hear of some thing like dispute or division betwen whigs. Nothing could urge my touching this delicate matter, but the unhappy experience I every day make on that head, since I may hear myself what is said on this side of the Atlantic, and the arguments I am to fight against."[25]

Lafayette sent a copy of this letter with the one he wrote to Washington, who interpreted it as a complaint about noises in Congress. "The propriety of the hint you have given them must carry conviction," he told him, "and I trust will have a salutary effect," but he thought Congress had become far less quarrelsome in recent months than it had been before. That should make a good impression in Europe.[26]

What really bothered the marquis was the war between the American commissioners in France. Arthur Lee and Franklin could not get along, and they dragged other Americans in Europe into their feud. Adams complained that "their violence had arisen to such rancour" that whenever he agreed with one side, the other blistered him. This constant catfighting upset Lafayette. Congress had already had a belly full of these quarrels and resolved on April 20, 1779, that the "suspicions and animosities" were "highly prejudicial to the honor and interest of these United States." Lafayette's fears had already been addressed, but the problem continued.[27]

The marquis opened his letter to Washington with an outburst of adoration. "My dear general, here is at length a safe occasion of writing to you," he began, "here I may tell you what sincere concern I feel for our separation. There was never a friend, my dear general, so much, so tenderly belov'd, as I do love and respect you. Happy in our union, in the pleasure of living with you, in that so charming satisfaction of partaking any sentiment of your heart, any event of your life, I had taken such an habit of being inseparable from you, that I can't now get the use of absence and I am more and more afflicted of that distance which keeps me so far from my dearest friend." He imagined that Washington's army was on the march, which made not being by the general's side all the more painful. He was also consumed by a growing fear that Washington could be disabled or killed, and "the american army, the american cause itself would perhaps be entirely ruin'd."

As Lafayette and Franklin labored to get more money for the American cause, it was not congressional debates that troubled him so much as what was going on in Paris. "For God's sake," he pleaded, "prevent theyr loudly disputing together. Nothing hurts so much the interests and reputation of America than to hear of theyr intestine quarrels. On the other hand there are two partys in France—MMs. Adams and Lee on one part, Doctor Franklin and his friends on the other. So great is the concern which these divisions give me, that I can't wait on these gentlemen as much as I could wish, for fear of occasioning disputes, and bringing them to a greater light."

The fact that Lafayette had not heard from his adoptive father he blamed on "winds, accidents, and deficiency of occasions, for I dare flatter myself General Washington would not loose this [occasion] of making his friend happy. In the name of that very friendship, my dear general, never miss any opportunity of letting me know how you do." He repeated his worries about Washington's health and the dangers the general exposed himself to. "Those you possibly may laugh at and call woman-like considerations, but so, my dear friend, I feel, and any sentiment of my heart I never could, nay I never wanted to conceal."

The young man digressed to deliver personal and political news, to brag about his celebrity, and to criticize his government's failure to act decisively. Always he returned to how much he wanted to rejoin Washington. He described himself as "I, an american citizen," a marked change from the French boy who had blown up at Sullivan's remarks a year before.

Lafayette then said, oddly, "I have a wife, my dear general, who is in love with you, and any affection for you seems to me so well justified that I can's oppose myself to that sentiment of her's." He also invited Washington to "come to see us in Europe, and most certainly I give you my word, that if I am not happy enough as to be sent to America before the peace, I shall by all means go there as soon as I may escape." He renewed his invitation, not for the last time. "All Europe wants so much to see you, my dear general," he pleaded, "that you ca'nt refuse them that pleasure."

Above all, Lafayette missed his adoptive father. "I most instantly entreat you, my dear general, to let me hear from you," he begged. "Write me how you do, how things are going. The minutest detail will be infinetly interesting for me. . . . Adieu, my dear general, I can't leave the pen, and I enjoy the greatest pleasure in scribling you this long letter. Don't forget me, my dear general, be ever as affectionate for me as you have been—those sentiments I deserve by the ardent ones which fill my heart." He added a postscript. "For God's sake," he cried, "write me frequent and long letters and speak most chiefly about yourself and your private circumstances." His loyalties were no longer divided. He might be French by birth, but he loved Washington above all else.

The next day Lafayette added yet another postscript. He had just received an express message, with orders to report immediately to Versailles. There he was to meet "Mr. le comte de Vaux lieutenant general who is appointed to the command of the troops intended for an expedition." Lafayette would serve as *aide maréchal général des logis,* "which is in our service a very important and agreable place." He promised to keep his adoptive father informed of everything, and ended, "assuring your excellency again of my profond respect and tenderest friendship. Farewell my dear general and let our mutual affection last for ever and ever."[28]

The marquis had been sprung from his exile thanks to his old commander, General de Broglie. With Spain about to enter the war, de Broglie had drawn up plans to invade England with 30,000 soldiers carried in a combined French-Spanish fleet. By spring he had moved much of that army to Le Havre, where it would embark. He proposed his older brother, Victor-François, comte de Broglie, to command the invasion. Instead, command went to Noël de Jourda, comte de Vaux, the oldest soldier in the army, age seventy-four. Once that decision was made, on June 16, 1779, Spain presented its declaration of grievances to the British government and laid siege to Gibraltar.[29]

Lafayette spent the next ten days shuttling between Versailles and Paris, with side trips to consult Franklin. He would go ashore leading a regiment of grenadiers in the first wave, and when his dragoons landed, he would take command of them. Before that, he would be busy with logistical arrangements, his immediate superior told him. He also met with Vergennes and Maurepas, pressing them on a plan for the future—to send a French army to fight under Washington. This time, the foreign minister showed interest. At his request the marquis gave him maps of the British positions in America.[30]

The marquis was at Le Havre by July 1, busy with his duties but not too busy to pester Vergennes. Early in the month he recommended an attack on Halifax, because it was an important British supply base. By the eighteenth he had expanded his proposal. He wanted to lead 4,300 men to recapture Rhode Island, New York, the Virginia coast, and other places, before moving on to Halifax to prepare a revolution in Canada. This time, he struck a chord. Vergennes and other ministers, seeing the invasion of England delayed endlessly, began to agree with Lafayette. France's major efforts ought to be directed toward America, rather than England.[31]

Along with the rest of de Vaux's army, Lafayette kept looking seaward, hoping to spot the combined fleet under Lieutenant General (Rear Admiral) Louis Guillouet, comte d'Orvilliers, its sixty-nine-year-old commander. The fleet was delayed by bad weather and bureaucratic incompetence, and the admiral was demoralized by the recent suicide of his son. Smallpox and scurvy ravaged his men.

Lafayette fretted, because he had only himself to blame for not returning to Washington's army. He had repeatedly told the French government that he really wanted to fight in its army, but that was getting him nowhere. His project with Jones had been cancelled, and the present campaign was sitting on the beach, feeding sand fleas. On July 30, 1779, he pushed Vergennes again. Because his presence would be "less profitless" in America than in France, he volunteered to return to Washington's army on his own authority. If sending a larger force had to be postponed, he wanted to lead 2,000 or 3,000 men to join Washington. That would prop up the failing United States currency, provide a source of information about the enemy in Canada, and energize the American army.[32]

He was correct in believing that he would see no glory invading *l'Angleterre.* D'Orvilliers arrived on August 6, a month late. He had so many sick or dead from disease, and his supplies were so low, that he could do nothing, and not enough transports had been rounded up to take the army across the English Channel. The admiral advised cancelling the whole thing. Instead, he was ordered to blockade Plymouth. He stayed there for three days until a storm blew his fleet out of the channel. A small British flotilla challenged him, and he spent another three days chasing it, until it escaped into Plymouth. Since it was too close to the fall storm season to go ahead, the government postponed the invasion. The only good news for Lafayette was that he received a favorable reaction to his latest proposal from Vergennes, although an expedition could not be arranged until the following spring.[33]

There was something else nice to hear about. Franklin announced that the sword that Congress had authorized for Lafayette had been completed, and sent his nineteen-year-old grandson William Temple Franklin to present it. Made by the Parisian cutler Liger at a cost of 4,800 livres, it was a wonder to behold. An ornately engraved and encrusted gold hilt displayed the marquis' battles. One side of the blade showed the young warrior Lafayette slaying the British lion; the other depicted America released from chains and handing him an olive branch. This generated great publicity, and Lafayette appointed William as a volunteer aide-de-camp in the Continental Army. It carried no military rank, he said, and if

Congress objected, he took full responsibility, avowing that Washington would not disapprove anything he had done, "because friendship betwen my respected, belov'd General and myself, gives me the right of taking his name whenever I please."[34]

WE WILL TALK OF THIS MATTER
& FIX OUR PLANS

W ashington had been having a mixed year in Lafayette's absence, watching Clinton in New York. The British commander surprised him in June 1779 by seizing Fort Lafayette and Stony Point, guarding the two ends of Kings Ferry on the lower Hudson. Expecting a move against West Point, twelve miles upstream, he shifted most of his army to New Windsor. Clinton did not advance, however, so in July Washington sent Wayne and his 1,200-man light infantry brigade to retake Stony Point. In a predawn bayonet charge, Wayne and his men stormed the place and captured its garrison. The victory was a tremendous morale booster, but it had no strategic significance because Washington failed to attack Fort Lafayette.

The war was moving to the South, where the commander in chief had no real military authority. The British took Savannah in December 1778, moved on to the Georgia state capital at Augusta, then headed for Charleston, South Carolina. Major General Benjamin Lincoln, a waddling, ineffective, but popular leader, moved out to meet the enemy. They did an end run around him, but he made it back to Charleston in time. Citizens sent a frantic appeal to d'Estaing in the West Indies, and he joined the fight in September 1779. After a bungled French-American attack on Savannah in October, the enemy held their ground. D'Estaing, wounded and fearing the hurricane season, headed back to France. The British prepared an all-out move against Charleston for early 1780 and abandoned Rhode Island.[35]

Washington's real troubles were not on any battlefield. He was in an endless struggle to try to keep his army together, fed, and supplied. The states were not doing their part, and neither was Congress. Money, as always, was short, American credit had disappeared, and help from France had slowed to a trickle. He looked to Franklin, Adams, and Lafayette to turn the logistical faucet on again.

Washington missed Lafayette, and the younger man's absence caused him visible pain. He had expected, or at least hoped, that the marquis would return in the spring. That had not happened, nor had he heard from him. Then the new minister, La Luzerne, arrived in his camp early in September, accompanied by his secretary François, marquis de Barbé-Marbois, who brought the letter written by Lafayette in June. The general said that he was "drinking the health of the marquis de Lafayette," Barbé-Marbois told a friend, "and asked me if I had seen him before my departure. I answered that I had, and added that he spoke of him with the tenderest veneration. I said that the conduct of M. de Lafayette in America had made him generally esteemed, and had caused him to deserve the distinctions and favor granted him by the king. Washington blushed like a fond father whose child is being praised. Tears fell from his eyes, he clasped my hand, and could hardly utter the words: 'I do not know a nobler, finer soul, and I love him as my own son.' "36

Washington answered Lafayette with one of the longest letters he ever wrote. The young man's words, he said, filled him "with equal pleasure and surprize. The latter at hearing that you had not received one of the many letters I had written to you, since you left the American shore." He poured out his blessing in an enormous paragraph. "It gave me infinite pleasure to hear from yourself of the favourable reception you met with from your Sovereign, & of the joy which your safe arrival in France had diffused among your friends," he began. "I had no doubt that this wou'd be the case. To hear it from yourself adds pleasure to the acct." He congratulated him on his new position in de Vaux's army, "which I shall accompy. with an assurance that none do it with more warmth of affection, or sincere joy than myself. Your forward zeal in the cause of liberty— your singular attachment to this infant world—your ardent & persevering efforts not only in America but since your return to France to serve the United States—your polite attention to Americans—and your strict & uniform friendship for *me,* has ripened the first impressions of esteem & attachment which I imbibed for you into perfect love & gratitude that neither time nor absence can impair."

Washington hoped to see Lafayette again soon, as a general leading either French or American troops. But if circumstances postponed their reunion until after the war, he would welcome him "in all the warmth of friendship to Columbia's shore; & in the latter case, to my rural cottage, where homely fare & a cordial reception shall be substituted for delicacies & costly living." He extended the invitation to include "the Marchioness" (Adrienne). "My inclination & endeavours to do this cannot be doubted when I assure you that I love every body that is dear to you—consequently participate in the pleasure you feel in the prospt. of again becoming a parent & do most sincerely congratulate you and your lady on this fresh pledge she is about to give you of her love." And that was just the first paragraph!

The general continued for page after page, summarizing the events of the year, news of mutual friends, and the disputes among Americans Lafayette had complained about. Then he answered the marquis' invitation to France. To meet him anywhere would give him the greatest pleasure, but he reminded his young friend that he did not speak French. He was "too far advanced in years to acquire a knowledge of it—and that to converse through the medium of an interpreter upon common occasions, especially with the *ladies* must appr. so extremely awkward—insipid—& uncouth—that I can scarce beat it in idea. I will therefore hold myself disengaged for the *present* and when I see you in Virginia—we will talk of this matter & fix our plans."

Lafayette would renew his invitation often, and every time Washington turned it aside with similar excuses. As long as the war continued, there was no question of his leaving the country. After the war was not feasible, either. The general knew how the British dealt with rebels. If they ever got their hands on him, his head would decorate a pike on London Bridge. He did not have the heart to tell the young man that.

Washington continued, and continued, until he said, "But to conclude—you requested from me a long letter. I have given you one. But methinks, my dear Marquis, I hear you say there is reason in all things—that this is too long. I am clearly in sentiment with you & will have mercy on you in my next. But at present must pray your patience a while longer, till I can make a tender of my most respectful compliments to the Marchioness."

Answering Adrienne's expressions of love, as relayed by Lafayette, Washington revealed a playfulness and self-mocking humor that no one else ever drew out of him: "Tell her (if you have not made a mistake, & offered your *own love* instead of *hers* to me) that I have a heart susceptable of the tenderest passion, & that it is already so strongly impressed with the most favourable ideas of her, that she must be cautious of putting love's torch to it; as you must be in fanning the flame. But here again methinks I hear you say, I am not apprehensive of danger—my wife is young—you are growing old & the Atlantic is between you. All this is true, but know my good friend that no distance can keep *anxious* lovers long asunder, and that the wonders of former ages may be revived in this. But alas!" Difference in their years might stand between the old Washington and the young Adrienne, "[y]et, under the encouragement you have given me I shall enter the list for so inestimable a jewell."

Finally winding down, he said, "When I look back to the length of this letter, I am so much astonished & frightened at it myself, that I have not the courage to give it a careful reading for the purpose of correction. You must therefore receive it with all its imperfections—accompanied with this assurance . . . there is not a single defect in the friendship of my dear Marquis." Like Lafayette, he would not "leave the pen," but finally, exhausted, he could pour out no more.[37]

The marquis would not receive this letter for some months. He pounded Vergennes with plans and revisions of plans and revisions of revisions, all about sending a French army to join Washington. Much of his verbiage reflected diplomatic concerns that the Americans would not welcome such help. On August 13, 1779, he suggested making up most of the expeditionary force by assigning tall and disciplined grenadiers who would appeal to the allies, because "country people, understand waging war in the woods better than any other European corps, and if I ask for a larger proportion of them it is because . . . we must show some good moral and physical specimens of our nation."

Lafayette worried about advice from Gérard and others that France should not send an expedition until the Americans asked for it formally. The marquis objected, claiming to speak for Washington and Americans in general. By the middle of September, Vergennes was worn down. He did not know what could be done regarding America, the foreign minister told him. "It is obvious that the concern for America's welfare requires that troops be sent, but that alone would not be doing enough. If it is possible, one must take even longer views." News of Stony Point had heartened him, along with that of French victories in the West Indies. He invited Lafayette to Versailles, to talk about it all with the government.[38]

The continued delays in the invasion of England—it would not be formally abandoned until November 1779, when d'Orvilliers went completely insane, and no other high officer wanted to touch the undertaking—had persuaded Vergennes that the best use of French forces would be in the Western Hemisphere. So had Lafayette's badgering.

The foreign minister had been influenced by propaganda celebrating the valor of American militia, alleged high spirits and unity in the thirteen states, the determination of the Continental Army, and the genius of Washington. Lafayette's reports had given him some realism to temper the fantasy, however. Vergennes saw that the American army and its cause were on the verge of disintegration. The only solution was what Lafayette had proposed—send money, supplies, troops, and ships. Not everyone in the French government agreed. Some ministers and high officers rejected any intelligence that came from Lafayette because he was "Americanized." Vergennes had decided to go along with the marquis, but a decision and plan from the whole government were some months away.[39]

So Lafayette returned to Le Havre and fretted. In early October he sent a formal report to Congress. Beyond thanking the members for his sword, he did not have much to say. He wanted to be recalled to America, to serve "under American colours, among my fellow soldiers, and take orders from our great and heroïc general."[40]

Lafayette also wrote to Washington, frustration and loneliness bleeding from his pen. "How unhappy I am to find myself so far from you . . . you will easely conceive," he wailed. His "impression of sorrow" was no longer relieved by his earlier belief that he would be more useful to the United States in France than in America. Regretting that he had stayed in France, in other words, he wanted Washington's approval for decisions that had turned out wrong. "I hope, my dear sir, you will agree in opinion with me."

What Lafayette most wanted was to return to Washington's side. "But permit me to tell you again, how earnestly I wish to join you. Nothing could make me so delighted as the happiness of finishing the war under your orders." He asked his adoptive father to get him a formal recall.

"However happy I am in France . . . I have taken such an habit of being with you, and am tied to you . . . by such an affection, that the moment where I will sail for your country, shall be one of the most wished for and the happiest in my life."

The marquis concluded, "Oh, my dear general, how happy I would be to embrace you again! With such an affection as is above all expressions any language may furnish I have the honor to be very respectfully my good and beloved general your affectionate friend Lafayette."[41]

The republican principles Washington was fighting for were beginning to sink into Lafayette's outlook. When King Louis freed the serfs on his royal domains in September 1779, he urged the nobles to follow his lead. The marquis did not know if he owned any such people, vassals bound to the soil and subject to the will of their lords (as opposed to tenant farmers, who paid rent and could leave). He asked his lawyer to check it out. There were none on his lands in Brittany or Touraine, but he could learn nothing about the estates in Auvergne. However vaguely, there was something about this relic of feudalism that troubled the young marquis.[42]

In November, after hearing about unrest in the Irish Parliament among the feudal overlords of that British province, Lafayette told Franklin, "Nobility is but an insignificant kind of people for revolutions. They have no notions of equality betwen men, and they want to govern, they have too much to looze—good Presbiterian farmers would go on with more spirit than all the noblemen of Ireland." He deplored France's unwillingness to help the Irish. "My military countrymen don't know how to manage republican interests."[43]

This was his first denunciation of aristocrats. He was talking about Ireland, but his concerns applied to the United States, France's republican ally. There was a change under way in Lafayette's worldview. He saw republics on their own terms, no longer as tools for serving French interests. Most important, he no longer assumed that the French government could manage any situation involving a republic, so long as French soldiers carried out its orders.

Not giving up on the idea of sending a French army to America, in the fall of 1779 Lafayette threw his weight behind Franklin's request for loans to buy clothing and munitions. He leaned on Vergennes to approve the request, wanting Washington to get the resources to fight his war with or without French troops. When he learned of the disastrous attack on Savannah, he predicted that Americans would be dissatisfied with France's contributions to the war. The news, he told the foreign minister, would have a "bad effect on America." Franklin had his money by the end of the month.[44]

Lafayette received some happy news on the day before Christmas 1779. He had hardly seen Adrienne for months, except when he visited Paris, as she suffered ill health and a difficult pregnancy. On December 24 she wrote him with cold formality, announcing that he had a son. "Accept my compliments, Monsieur le Marquis," she began. "They are very sincere and very real. America will celebrate with illuminations, and I think Paris should do the same. The number of persons who resemble you is so small that it is public good fortune to see it increase. . . . M. le Maréchal [her grandfather] will no longer say that we give him only girls."[45]

Lafayette was at Passy. Chastened by his wife's tone, he headed to Paris to spend a few days with her. Before he left, he sent birth announcements to Franklin and Adams. "I don't loose any time in informing you," he crowed. "The boy shall be call'd *George,* and you will easely gess that he bears that name as a tribute of respect and love for my dear friend Gal. Washington." George-Washington Lafayette he would be.[46]

I SHALL TELL YOU FRANKLY THAT WE ARE WASTING PRECIOUS TIME

Once the loan to America was approved, Lafayette requisitioned muskets and powder to add to clothing already purchased for shipment. That set off a row between Vergennes and the war minister, the prince de Montbarey, with the foreign minister supporting the marquis' case. Lafayette still thought sending an expeditionary force across the Atlantic was the best idea. He resumed shuttling among the various ministers and Adams and Franklin, reminding one and all that a British fleet in American waters threatened French possessions in the West Indies. He got the guns and powder, but he had made an enemy of Montbarey.[47]

Lafayette spent January 1780 making himself the pest of Versailles. Whenever he went to talk to the prime minister, Maurepas was too busy to see him. Only Vergennes was on his side, so Lafayette sent Maurepas a long letter, reminding the prime minister that the previous summer "I was asked for my view on a new campaign in America," adroitly interpreting the minister's refusal to receive him as a request for further advice. Reviewing the failure to invade England and other setbacks, he said these events could further damage American finances. Enemy raids could make everything worse, with the British navy roaming without challenge. French assistance could double the force and strength of Washington's army, he claimed. "Nevertheless . . . since you approve of assistance of this kind, I shall tell you frankly that we are wasting precious time and that military preparations should have begun already."

That was cheeky, almost insubordinate, but Lafayette was so famous that he thought he could get away with anything. And he did, as usual for page after page, demolishing all objections to sending an expeditionary force to America. He outlined a plan to send troops, with himself in command, wearing either an American uniform or a French one. There his corps would be "a part of the American army" under Washington's command. He told Vergennes that the situation in America was serious. Although there were divisions in Congress, all its members agreed that more help was needed from France.[48]

This amazing performance swept away the last objections among the ministers. They had their own reasons for wanting to send an army and navy to America, but Lafayette talked them into doing it. They must have worried—America was an uncertain ally. They were about to risk major parts of their army and navy at a great distance on the word of an excitable, annoying upstart, as many officers viewed him. Some wondered whether he was arguing in his own interest rather than France's. Some also wondered whether, if the marquis commanded the French troops, he would march them into a disaster.

Vergennes told Lafayette that he had won, and asked him to set some issues down in writing before they all got together to work out the details. He wanted him to set forth arguments whether he should lead the French detachment, or retake command of an American division. He favored the first. If he was in command, Vergennes promised, the ministry could "proceed in complete security because the Americans know me too well for my presence to prompt any false anxieties" regarding French intentions. To answer fears in the war ministry that he was just angling for high rank in the French army, Vergennes suggested giving him a rank good only in America, or none at all "in order to put the ministry at ease."

As for the second choice, it was necessary first of all to forestall the bad effect that he said the arrival of another commander would produce in America. The idea that Lafayette was unable to lead this detachment "would be the last to present itself over there." He would simply explain to Americans, therefore, that he preferred to command an American division. He ended with, "*Conclusion.* 1. I believe that it is better to give me this corps. 2. If it is not given to me, I must leave immediately with the resources I request. In either case, unfortunately, it is necessary to reveal this secret to me and to set to work promptly."[49]

Lafayette could not lose, because either choice would send him back to serve under Washington, and he wanted to get back to him on any terms. He was not in the least unhappy when he learned that someone else would get the job, nor even that some officers refused to go along if he was in command. He was going to be with Washington again, and that counted the most.

There were several more experienced candidates for the command. De Broglie presented himself, but the Americans would not trust him. De Vaux was senior to everybody, but he was slowed by age. Then there was Jean-Baptiste-Donatien de Vimeur, comte de Rochambeau. He was fifty-five years old, had been in the army since 1740, and carried many scars from many battles. He was a legendary combat leader but always had been under someone else's command. Montbarey recommended him for the first independent command of his career. Since the war minister had lost so many recent arguments, the other ministers bowed to his wishes.

Ruddy-faced, with a stocky figure, Rochambeau was the sort of battle-scarred veteran who had a habit of reminding others that he was a battle-scarred veteran. But his face always wore a placid, wise expression. He never quarreled, never plotted, and was firm without being stubborn or tyrannical. He got along with everybody, because he had the instincts of a born diplomat. Unlike d'Estaing, he was the perfect man for the American assignment and readily agreed to place himself under Washington's orders. In return, the war ministry promoted him to the rank of lieutenant general so that he would outrank all French and American officers except Washington.

Rochambeau had known Lafayette since the marquis was a baby, and liked him. But when the young general visited him to tell him how to get along in America, the older general remembered something else—the boy had a tendency to ruffle his feathers. Still, they got along, and both hoped they would continue to do so on the far side of the ocean.[50]

Lafayette was a whirlwind for the rest of February. He specified American uniforms for Franklin to purchase, sent his spies to answer questions posed by Adams, and belabored the minister of marine on how to organize the fleet that would take Rochambeau to America. He reminded the minister that Americans were sensitive about prestige, so he should tell his officers that "more honor should be shown to the uniform of an Amer-

Jean-Baptiste-Donatien de Vimeur, comte de Rochambeau, by C.W. Peale, 1782. Commander of the French army in America, he lost his temper over Lafayette's behavior, but the marquis turned on his charm and they remained lifelong friends. (INDEPENDENCE NATIONAL HISTORICAL PARK)

ican general or the dignity of a state governor than would be shown to Imperial or Prussian officers of like rank." French officers should be polite to citizens, respect civil officials, and give presents to the Indians. The minister agreed to it all.[51]

Lafayette told Franklin that he expected to sail from Rochefort in early March 1780, in a frigate. He could take clothing for 4,000 men with him, and asked him to forward 15,000 stand of arms with accoutrements. He should be able to send clothing for another 6,000 men on other ships, and he had sent Vergennes specifications for winter clothing to be sent later. Franklin was happy to hear all that, but he was running out of money because Congress had spent most of the latest French loan. Moreover, Montbarey told him that the war ministry could not meet all his requests.[52]

"There is armament preparing with the greatest expedition," Adams advised Henry Laurens, "and to consist of eight or ten ships of the line and frigates . . . with several thousand men; all numbers are mentioned from six to ten thousand." The French were likely to be drawn into the American seas in sufficient force to have "great advantages in carrying out the war."[53]

He was too optimistic. The orders to the army and navy on February 24, 1780, called for about 6,000 regular infantry. When Rochambeau left on May 2 in seven ships of the line, two frigates, and other small armed ships, there was a shortage of transports. He left behind two regiments, part of his artillery, and part of the duc de Lauzun's legion, which would follow later as a "second division." Worse, Spain refused to cooperate. She was France's ally but would not become an ally of the United States, which she saw as a future rival for the Mississippi River.[54]

Lafayette spent the last few days of February in Paris, giving some attention to his neglected wife and children. He was not sneaking out of town this time, so he took better care of his finances. He had a new manager of his affairs, Jacques-Philippe Grattepain-Morizot, to whom he granted power of attorney. He gave similar power to Adrienne. Morizot was authorized to borrow against his property with her consent, although she would prevail in any disagreements. He told Morizot to draw 120,000 livres from his account so he could equip an American division. The steward warned him that he was buying glory at the expense of his fortune. He answered that glory was beyond price, Adrienne agreed, and he got the money.[55]

Dazzling in his American uniform, he took formal leave of the king and queen. He stopped in at Passy to see Franklin, who sent Washington a letter bubbling about Lafayette's "modesty" and "zeal for the honour of our country, his activity in our affairs here, and his firm attachment to our cause and to you." Without the marquis' efforts he would never have gained the full measure of French aid needed to win the war.[56]

Lafayette returned to Versailles for revisions of his instructions and those going to Rochambeau and to Charles-Henri d'Arsac, chevalier de Ternay, the commodore commanding the fleet. There were several bureaucratic issues he wanted made clear. He won on all points. New orders to Rochambeau told him to consider his command subordinate to Washington and his troops auxiliary to the American army. The American general would have the final say on all plans, although it was expected that he would consult with the French general, who should maintain good relations between the allies. Lafayette would go ahead of him to make arrangements, and a commissary, Dominique-Louis Ethis de Corny, would accompany him to handle finances.

Lafayette also got his status, and that of other French officers in American service, made clear. They were not to be treated as subordinates to generals in Rochambeau's force, but according to their American ranks, and their French commissions were suspended for the duration. He would be Washington's man and nobody else's. Most important, nobody but George Washington would command the war in America.[57]

Lafayette had been fighting to protect his adoptive father from challenges since the Conway Cabal. Now America's ally acknowledged that Washington was the supreme commander in the New World, even over French troops. Moreover, the commander in chief could dispose of Rochambeau's army without asking Congress' permission, as he still had to do with the Continental Army.

Lafayette's final instructions, issued March 5, 1780, began: "M. le Marquis de Lafayette, going to America, will hasten to join General Washington. He will inform him confidentially that the king . . . has resolved to send to their aid six ships of the line and 6,000 regular infantry troops at the onset of spring." Ternay's convoy would land at Rhode Island. It might go ashore elsewhere, however, so Lafayette should ask Washington to send French officers to other locations. They were to be given specified flag signals that the fleet would recognize, and even a password: *St. Louis et Philadelphie* (the patron saint of France and brotherly love, meaning both the American capital and the spirit of the alliance).

He was to tell the American that the French corps would be purely auxiliary, "and in this capacity" it would act only under Washington's orders. The French land general would take orders from the American commanding general "for everything that does not relate to the internal regulation of his corps." The "naval general" was "enjoined to support with all his power all operations in which his cooperation is required."

The instructions granted the utmost discretion to the American ally.

"Since operations must depend upon circumstances and local possibilities," the French government did not propose any. It was up to Washington and the council of war to decide which operations would be most useful. All the king wished was that the troops he sent to the assistance of his allies, the United States, "cooperate effectually to deliver them once and for all from the yoke and tyranny of the English." His Majesty expected that "the reciprocal attention that friends owe each other will ensure that General Washington and the American general officers see that the officers and the French troops enjoy all the amenities that are consistent with the good of the service."

There were practical details as well. Washington was asked to arrange for subsistence and for medical facilities for his French allies. This was the closest thing to a demand in the whole document, but it was one that Washington could live with.

After Lafayette had agreed with General Washington on all the measures to take with respect to the arrival of the French troops and to the security of their disembarkation, he should go to Congress, "but first he will decide with the American general to what extent he is to reveal to Congress the secret of our arrangements." Lafayette's subordination to Washington was emphasized, in other words, but that was what he wanted anyway. Once he reached Philadelphia, he was to report to La Luzerne, hand him this order and his agreements with Washington, ensure the minister's cooperation, and present himself to Congress. The last item granted the naval commander the freedom to cruise if his help was not needed by the land forces.[58]

Lafayette kissed Adrienne goodbye on March 6, 1780, and she promptly collapsed in grief. She remained in bed for two weeks, scarcely able to read the short notes he sent her daily, mostly about how "painful" it was for him to be away from her again. He reached Rochefort on the ninth and wrote longer letters to others. He asked the prince de Poix to send him a silver tea service as a gift for Mrs. Washington. He gave the officer who would replace him in his regiment detailed instructions, saying, "I resign all my rights in your favor until I return to take up French service."

The frigate *Hermione* sailed on March 11, picked up passengers at La Rochelle on the thirteenth, and headed west. On the fifteenth a stout headwind broke the mainmast, and she headed back to port with three

English cutters on her tail. On the eighteenth Lafayette wrote a last letter to Adrienne, saying, "Farewell, my dear, I embrace you, and tomorrow I shall give you my news at greater length." He did not. Just before *Hermione* weighed anchor on the twentieth, he complained to Franklin that the clothing he had wanted to take along had not arrived.[59]

The instructions Lafayette carried were his greatest gift to his adoptive father, elevating him above all other soldiers in America, and they were a gift to America, a positive message that the worst times were over. The Americans would have the muscle to contest Britain's control of the seas off their coast, without which the future of America was always in doubt.

I Am Considered Too American

(MARCH-DECEMBER 1780)

Here, the monster Hunger, still attended us; he was not to be shaken off by
any efforts we could use, for here was the old story of starving, as rife as
ever. . . . For several days after we rejoined the army, we got a little musty
bread, and a little beef, about every other day, but this lasted only a short
time and then we got nothing at all. The men were now exasperated beyond
endurance; they could not stand it any longer; they saw no other alternative
but to starve to death, or break up the army, give all up and go home.

—PRIVATE JOSEPH PLUMB MARTIN

Adrienne was not the only love Lafayette left behind in
France. After he landed in America he asked the prince de
Poix to send him "in great detail news of Mme de V——.
How is another young woman getting on? Tell that young
woman that in order not to frighten her I have gone to America, but that
on my return she will kindly not run away from me any more." Mme de
V—— was probably Henriette-Françoise Puget de Barbantane, comtesse de Vauban, wife of one of Rochambeau's officers. The other was her
sister, Aglaé d'Hunolstein. France was a happy hunting ground for the
lusty young marquis, but he had failed again to make Aglaé his mistress.[1]

Lafayette told his brother-in-law Noailles that a mutual friend "had
only some compliments for me from the charmer. . . . I often miss *Paris*
and those *ladies.*" Whether the "charmer" was Aglaé or another of his

dalliances is not apparent. "I hope, my dear vicomte, that our mistresses will never be so demanding as to prevent us from having supper with other girls, or we so stupid as to break up a party out of obedience. If I had a mistress," he sighed, "my feelings would be partly based on the delicacy or pride she would display in not showing jealousy and on the freedom I would have to do anything I wanted, even to neglect her without ever finding her demanding."[2]

"I beg you to place my homages at the feet of the queen," Lafayette told de Poix; "the fêtes at the Trianon and the trips to Maly seem to me now like those delightful dreams that leave a vivid impression and make one sorry to wake up. When I think about the time when I shall enjoy them again, I am like a saintly hermit meditating upon the bliss of the next world. If the divinity who dwells in yours (it is not because she is queen that I am so trite as to call her so, but because she is pretty and gracious) does not think now and then of my affection for her, I can only say that she is a poor judge of feeling." Whether he was reflecting on some past adventures with Marie-Antoinette or just flirting, it is impossible to say.[3]

The young general had other things to occupy him after he returned to Washington's side. The grand alliance between the French and the Americans, however, was not the great adventure he had thought it would be.

I EAT SEVERAL MEALS OF DOGG, AND IT RELLISH'D VERY WELL

As *Hermione* pounded across the Atlantic, the survival of the Continental Army and the Revolution was in doubt. It was the hardest winter of the century, the paper money was worthless, Congress had become a quarrelsome mob, the states resisted the central government, and the troops were starving. The army was camped in Jockey Hollow, outside Morristown, New Jersey. The men had moved into their huts in December 1779 and had been on half rations since the middle of November. "Those who have only been in Valley Forge or Middlebrook during the last two winters," de Kalb complained, "but have not tasted the cruelties of this one, know not what it is to suffer."[4]

The snow on the ground was about two feet deep and the weather extremely cold, reported the surgeon James Thacher early in the encampment. The soldiers lacked tents, blankets, shoes, and clothing. Tories refused to sell provisions, and patriots (as the American insurgents had begun to call themselves) demanded hard money. Rations shrank to one-eighth, then disappeared altogether in January. "Poor fellows!" Greene lamented. "A country overflowing with plenty are now suffering an army, employed for the defence of everything that is dear and valuable, to perish for want of food." The only reason the whole force did not desert, he believed, was because the roads were buried in snow.[5]

"We were absolutely, literally starved;—I do solemnly declare that I did not put a single morsel of victuals into my mouth for four days and as many nights," Private Joseph Plumb Martin remembered. He saw several men roast their old shoes and eat them, and officers kill and eat "a favourite little dog." That was not an exaggeration. "During our hungry time," Steuben's aide James Fairlie told a friend, "I eat several meals of dogg, and it rellish'd very well."

When the British besieged Charleston in February 1780, Congress ordered Washington to send troops there. He answered that only half his remaining 6,000 men were fit for duty, and they were too weak to travel. "The patience of the soldiery, who have endured every degree of conceivable hardship," he complained, "is on the point of being exhausted."[6]

Greene built sleds and hauled food to Jockey Hollow in mid-January 1780. The worst starvation was over, but the winter was not. The men were restless, and small mutinies broke out. Washington sent Steuben to lobby Congress to do something about supplies, but all he got was a promise to send a committee to see him. The inspector general was discouraged. Congress would not or could not finance the army; Major General Lincoln was playing "a hardy game" against the British at Charleston, about to put his head into a noose; Pennsylvania and Virginia were threatening to go to war over "their pretended rights" to western lands; there were feuds among the army's officers; and the staff departments were a mess.[7]

Hermione put into Marblehead on April 27, 1780, to pick up a pilot for Boston Harbor. "Here I am, my dear general," Lafayette declared, "and in the mist of the joy I feel in finding myself again one of your loving soldiers," he had affairs "of the utmost importance" that he should communicate to Washington alone. He did not know where Washington was, but "I beg you will wait for me [until I] join my belov'd and respected friend and general."[8]

Hermione fired a thirteen-gun salute as she hove into Boston, a fort returned the favor, and state and local officials met Lafayette on the waterfront. They treated him to banquets, fireworks, parades, and flattering speeches. He told Vergennes that "the reception that they have given me here and the inexpressible signs of goodwill that the American people have deigned to heap upon me have helped to increase my enthusiasm." It all reflected, he thought, public opinion in favor of France.[9]

The marquis made slow progress because of bad roads, receptions in every town, and enemy cavalry prowling for him. Washington received his note on May 7 at his headquarters in Morristown, the Ford House, a large, elegant pile of timber lent to him by a wealthy patriot. He read it "with all the joy that the sincerest friendship could dictate—and with that impatience which an ardent desire to see you could not fail to inspire." He sent out a troop of cavalry to escort his young friend to Morristown. He promised to "embrace you with all the warmth of an affectionate friend when you come to head qrs.—where a bed is prepared for you."[10]

Lafayette rode into Morristown on the tenth. Washington went out to meet him and, Hamilton remembered, his "eyes filled with tears of joy . . . a certain proof of a truly paternal love." The young man threw his arms around his adoptive father and kissed him on both cheeks. "After the first pleasure of meeting was over," Lafayette recalled, he and Washington went into a private room to talk over the state of affairs. "It was then that I told the commander-in-chief what had been arranged and the help he could now expect."[11]

They spent the next three days plotting actions with the army's top leaders. Lafayette and Hamilton worked out a protocol for greeting the French fleet. Not knowing where it would land, they sent French officers to places all along the coast. Lafayette consulted with Greene and the surgeons to coordinate supplies and medical care with Corny and La Luzerne's agents, and hired spies behind enemy lines.[12]

Washington and Lafayette discussed the marquis' dream of invading Canada. The young man did not object when his adoptive father said it would not happen, because the first target, when Rochambeau and

America's First Ally, *by Percy Moran. This is a dramatic representation of
Lafayette's arrival at Washington's home and headquarters in Morristown in
1780. Notice Washington extending his arms to embrace his adopted son.*
(LILLY LIBRARY, INDIANA UNIVERSITY)

Ternay arrived, would be New York. The British already knew that the
French were sending an expedition to America, but not where it was
headed. Washington suggested that Lafayette issue a proclamation to the
Canadians saying that liberation was on the way, to fool the enemy in
New York. It should be in his own name and "have as much as possible an
air of probability." He also thought "that something might be addressed to
the savages."

Lafayette prepared a windy bombast telling the peoples of the north
that the French were coming to help them throw off the English yoke. He
reassured La Luzerne "that in order to mislead the enemy," it was all a
sham. The document would be allowed to fall into enemy hands in New
York, and other copies would be "thrown in the fire on the arrival of the
French troops; thus I can say all that I please in a work destined never to
appear."[13]

Washington advised La Luzerne that Congress had promised to raise
an army of 25,000 men, and asked the ambassador to light a fire under

the legislature. Then he sent Lafayette to Philadelphia on May 14, 1780, with a letter of introduction. He was "perswaded Congress will participate in the joy I feel at the return of a gentleman who has distinguished himself in the service of this country so signally," he said. "The warm friendship I have for him conspires with considerations of public utility to afford me a double satisfaction in his return." He also declared, "The court of France has done so much for us, that we must make a decisive effort on our part."[14]

Lafayette reached the capital the next day and presented his orders to La Luzerne, after which he announced himself to Congress. "If from an early epoch in our noble contest, I gloried in the name of an American soldier, and heartily enjoyed the honor I have of serving the United States," he proclaimed, "my satisfaction is at this long wish'd for moment entirely compleat." The lawmakers could not match his grandiloquence, but they tried, resolving "[t]hat Congress consider the return of the Marquis de la Fayette to America to resume his command in the army, as fresh proof of the disinterested zeal and persevering attachment which have justly recommended him to the public confidence and applause."[15]

Anne-César, chevalier de La Luzerne, by C. W. Peale, 1781–82. La Luzerne was France's second ambassador to the United States and another "uncle" to the volatile Lafayette. (Independence National Historical Park)

Washington and Lafayette started an interesting shuffle in their relationship. The marquis planted himself close to La Luzerne, advising him on how to manipulate congressmen to raise men and supplies. He became the commander in chief's point man in all dealings with French officials. He also urged leaders in several states to contribute to the cause. Washington approved of these side-channel communications, exploiting the young general's popularity as a way to raise people and goods for his army, and it worked. La Luzerne wheedled lawmakers, Lafayette leaned on politicians, Washington put in his own digs, and Congress appointed a committee to raise provisions.[16]

Making separate arrangements for supplying two national armies presented complications that nobody had foreseen, and the loans from France were not large enough. Lafayette buried La Luzerne in complaints that demands exceeded resources. Corny had not brought along enough cash, and Lafayette had told the French government that he could not be involved in financial affairs. Asking the ambassador to help Corny buy livestock, he said, "As for me . . . I am only an American officer here." He was Washington's man, not the French government's.[17]

Thinking over their strategic talks at Morristown, Washington concluded that New York definitely should be the first target for the allied forces. He asked Lafayette to advise Rochambeau and Ternay to go to Sandy Hook, because the enemy's force included only about 8,000 regulars and about 4,000 refugees and militia. The Royal Navy had only one ship of the line and three or four small frigates in the harbor. Ternay's fleet could beat that, he believed. He told the marquis to "place these things in the fullest light to the French commanders by way of recommendation, leaving it to them to act according to the condition of the fleet and troops." Washington also asked him to write to the French naval commander in the West Indies, urging him to sail north. The need to encode and decode multiple copies of all messages was as new to the marquis as it was to the Americans.[18]

Lafayette wrapped up his business in Philadelphia on May 20 and that day advised Vergennes that he had carried out his instructions. Believing that Congress was "too numerous to act with discretion and dispatch," Washington had asked that a committee be formed to mobilize the nation's resources. Lafayette and La Luzerne had talked the lawmakers into implementing the proposal. As a result, he predicted, the Continental Army would have more stability and the French troops would not lack necessary provisions. The American army, he admitted, was very small, badly dressed, and poorly armed, all these problems being caused by the depreciation of the paper money, but he expected things to improve. If the French troops arrived in time, it was "a safe bet that New York is ours."

As for the man in charge, "Without being biased, sir, by the tender friendship I share with General Washington, I can assure you that the generals and French troops will have nothing but praise for his honesty, his delicacy, and that noble and frank politeness that characterizes him, at the same time that they will have to admire his great talents." Lafayette had told him that the French generals were as much under his orders as the Americans, but he did not intend to exercise his command in a "severe or arbitrary manner." The decision to send help to America was the right one: "my American friends hold, and Paris may rest assured that they will not abandon us."[19]

Lafayette received an express from Washington the same day. "Finish your business as soon as you can and hasten home," his adoptive father told him, "for so I would always have you consider head quarters and my house."[20]

WHAT M. DE LAFAYETTE HAS WRITTEN YOU IS PURELY A RESULT OF HIS ZEAL

From Rhode Island to Virginia, officers and signalmen skipped stones across the water, waiting for Rochambeau and Ternay. The British and Hessians in New York also wondered when the French would arrive. The Hessian general Knyphausen marched out of New York early in June and camped near Elizabethtown. Washington moved in the enemy's direction, but declined to fight, preferring to wait for his allies. Word arrived that Clinton had taken Charleston, and then Clinton himself reached New York with troops and ships. Knyphausen returned to the city, and Washington marched to Paterson, New Jersey. There he watched the enemy and wondered where the promised help from France was.

Lafayette wrote letters describing the American uniforms so that French officers could tell one rank from another. He sent out periodic updates on the military situation for Rochambeau to receive when he arrived. And he revived his dream of invading Canada, at least for La Luzerne's ears. The ambassador asked him to drop it, because there were more important things to do in the thirteen states. Lafayette had to admit that there was little support for his northward ambitions, but just in case, he told the ambassador, he was sending spies north, who, if they were captured, would "serve to put the enemy on the wrong scent." He loved being a spymaster as much as being a commander.[21]

It was as a commander that the young general received his greatest treat in July. Washington ordered all troops to wear red, white, and blue cockades, the colors representing the United States, France, and Spain. Lafayette had been discussing with him plans for a new Light Division, which he would command. On July 4 he asked the general's permission to deck his men out with black and red plumes, which he had imported for them to wear. Washington and Steuben had discussed a light infantry division for some time, and Lafayette had proven himself an able leader of such troops. On July 16, 1780, the commander in chief ordered each regiment to detail officers and enlisted men to the new division. "The men should be mostly of a middle size, active, robust, and trusty, and the first twenty must be all old soldiers." By the end of the month Lafayette had his division, plumes and all.[22]

The marquis and Washington talked about how to deploy the French forces. Writing to Rochambeau and Ternay at Cape Henry, where they were expected to put in first, Lafayette told them that the best way to attack New York would be to land French troops on Long Island, where they would be joined by the Americans. General Washington and he had "absolutely no doubt" that it could succeed. There were 7,000 Americans ready to march, "and, without boasting, I can vouch that they will be at least equal to the best troops that are opposed to them," while the enemy did not exceed 10,000 men. He interspersed his own comments "as a *private individual,*" especially about the need for clothing and other supplies. "There you have, gentlemen, what General Washington instructed me to add to my previous letters. He thinks that these proposals will be presented to you in clearer fashion in French."[23]

The French commanders arrived off Newport—not Cape Henry—on July 10, with a British fleet under Admiral Thomas Graves on their heels. They entered the harbor and began landing men the next day, and Graves blockaded the harbor entrance. The force was smaller than promised, and two months late because of bureaucratic incompetence during loading in France. The most important supplies for the Americans were not with them. Rochambeau forwarded a note from Vergennes, who told

Lafayette that the convoy carried "5,500 effectives; the shortage of transport ships did not permit us to send more men, and the season is too far advanced to send the rest immediately." What gave him "the greatest pain" was that clothing, arms, and ammunition for the American army were not aboard Ternay's ships. He did not know whom to blame for that.

Rochambeau told the people of Newport that his force was just the "first division" and that a "second division" was expected soon. That cheered the natives, who rang all the church bells in town, while the French occupied the old British works. Rochambeau had so many men sick that he did not think he could march for at least two months.[24]

With only rumors in the air that the allies had arrived, Lafayette and Hamilton refined the plan to take New York, in the form of another letter to the French commanders. Washington had heard that Graves was in American waters, and that gave him pause. He asked the marquis to revise his letter, and Lafayette overreacted, thinking that the commander wanted to abandon the plan altogether, while he wanted to storm the city. "Such are, my dear general, the ideas which I gave out in our last conversation."[25]

Washington patiently explained his reasoning. The marquis had "totally misconceived" his meaning if he thought he would "relinquish the idea of enterprizeing against New York till it appears obviously impracticable from the want of force, or means to operate," he said. What he had in mind by discouraging the first draft of the letter to the French commanders was, "1st . . . I thought we ought not to give them more than information of Greave's [*sic*] arrival, & 2dly. not to hold up *strong* ideas of success . . . because I never wish to promise more than I have a moral certainty of performing."[26]

Washington guided Lafayette's revised letter, which included a warning to the French that Graves had been sighted off New York. The draft had said that "we believe" that this should not change plans for an attack on the city. The message as sent said, "You can judge better than we what we can expect from your naval situation, and you will decide how far it will be prudent to follow the plan proposed by General Washington." Ternay declared that he could not cross the bar at Sandy Hook and preferred to fight the enemy at sea.[27]

The French commanders wanted to meet Washington. Because he could not leave camp, he sent Lafayette as his liaison. Washington armed him with a private document, for his eyes only, to provide a basis for discussions. There were eight points, the first of which was the need for naval superiority. Second, the advantages of taking New York Harbor were "so obvious, as not to need recapitulation." Number seven showed some distrust of the allies. "It must be clearly understood and agreed between the parties," Washington explained, "that if any capital operation is undertaken, the French fleet and land forces will at all events continue their aid until the success of the enterprize, or until it is mutually determined to abandon it."

The American commander softened that with the last item. "In all matters . . . the marquis (in behalf of the United States) will consult the convenience and wishes of the count and chevalier" and assure them that Washington intended "to make every thing as agreeable to them as possible" owing to "the high sense I entertain of their merits and of the generous aid they have brought us." He sent Lafayette off to negotiate, with letters of commendation. "As a general officer," Washington told his new allies, "I have the greatest confidence in him; as a friend he is perfectly acquainted with my sentiments and opinions; he knows all the circumstances of our army and the country at large; all the information he gives and all the propositions he makes, I entreat you will consider as coming from me."[28]

Washington had boundless confidence in Lafayette, but he was sending a boy to do a man's job. He did not realize that the marquis was not as popular in the French army as in America. He had also acquired a bad attitude toward Rochambeau's enterprise, especially when he learned that the clothing and other materials he had bought were not in Ternay's convoy. He had reached a private conclusion that the French general intended to sit in Newport and let the war go on without him. He may have been right about that, because on July 16, 1780, Rochambeau advised the minister of war to send him more troops, ships, and money, "but do not count on these people or on their resources; everyone here is without money and without credit." He thought the French army would have to fight the British on its own, and he would not do that without reinforcements.[29]

Lafayette left for Rhode Island on July 19 and reassured his adoptive father, "But I dare say they will be satisfied with my coming." He recruited militia and supplies as he rode through New England, and was happy to learn that Americans and Frenchmen were getting along well at Newport. The closer he got to his destination, however, the more he grumbled about the shortage of gunpowder in the French convoy. Still, he told Washington, he had "great hopes of succès," especially after a French ship docked in Boston with a cargo of powder.[30]

Washington answered as often as he could. On the twenty-second he bowed to Ternay's judgment that his ships could not cross the bar at New York, asked the marquis, "however painful it is to abuse the generosity of our friends," to press them for arms and powder, and told him to beg off again on a personal meeting with the French commanders. When Lafayette reached Newport, he found Rochambeau paralyzed by reports that Clinton and Graves planned to attack him, and he relayed Rochambeau's request for a diversion. In response, Washington moved troops to Kings Ferry, and Clinton hunkered down in New York.[31]

Rochambeau and Ternay were determined to sit still until their second division showed up. "*Don't fear by any means* theyr acting *rashly,*" Lafayette sneeringly told Washington, "and be assur'd that you may very far depend on theyr *caution.*" He said he had told Rochambeau that he thought fears of an attack from Clinton were baseless and "that if the second division comes we must attack. That in all cases if we are masters of the water we may attack." He claimed that the French soldiers and sailors all wanted to join up with Washington's army, but their leaders were dragging their feet. Fearing that he would miss an attack on New York, Lafayette pleaded for permission to rejoin the Main Army. He left on August 3 without waiting for the local commander's approval and before receiving that of the commander in chief.[32]

Washington suspected that Lafayette was not behaving diplomatically. The marquis should not press the French general and admiral to undertake "anything to which they show a disinclination," he advised. "Should they yield to importunity and an accident happen either there or here they would lay the consequences to us. . . . Our prospects are not so flattering as to justify our being very pressing to engage them in our views."

As for Lafayette wanting to rejoin the Main Army, Washington would have attacked New York if Clinton had gone to Rhode Island, but he had not thought an action was likely, and in fact the redcoats had pulled back into the city once he demonstrated. The marquis was more useful at

Newport, and besides, he could not have reached New York in time for a sudden battle.[33]

A letter from Vergennes was on its way to Lafayette, offering excuses for why the second division and its supplies would not be on their way soon. He had come to that conclusion on his own, and when he reached Washington's camp on August 7, 1780, he began a memorandum to Rochambeau and Ternay, which he sent on the ninth. Since he was asking for feedback before he prepared a final report to the commander in chief, he did not show it to Washington. If he had, the elder man would have edited it. Consequently, he learned too late that his young friend lacked diplomatic talent and the deference a junior officer should show to a senior.[34]

Lafayette summarized, point by point, what he had told the French commanders, emphasizing early action against New York. His most galling statement was, "In proposing that you send your stores to Providence, I told you that Rhode Island was useless to the Americans but that it was valuable for the aid coming from France, provided, however, that it did not need an army to guard it." If the English made the mistake of seizing Rhode Island, "a superior fleet with help from the mainland would always be able to take it back." This was a direct challenge to Rochambeau and Ternay's judgment, even their competence. Not only was he insulting, but he was wrong. A sizable French force on that island was a strategic sword pointed at Clinton's side.

The marquis next summarized, point by point, how they had answered him. He could be nasty. "The assistance sent to the United States was anything but provisional," he claimed they had said; "the second division should have left shortly after you, and we might expect it at any moment." He quarreled with Ternay on whether his fleet could control the channels around New York or cross the bar at the harbor mouth. His tone was abrasive, and he strayed into the political effects of French inaction, an area beyond his official competence. He made his points sound like orders from him to the French commanders. "It is very clearly settled that as soon as the French attain naval superiority, they must not lose a single day in beginning the joint effort." Urging an early reply correcting any misstatements, he said that "since America's fate appears to depend on your activity or inactivity during the rest of this summer, I place the greatest importance on representing your ideas perfectly. . . . I shall wait here eagerly, gentlemen, for your reply to this letter."

Lafayette was not done yet. He assured the general and commodore that it was "important to act during this campaign [year]. All of the troops that you may expect from France next year, as well as all of the plans for which you may hope, will not make up for the fatal harm of our inaction. Without American resources, no amount of foreign aid can accomplish anything in this country." He declared that it was very important to "take advantage of the times when you find an opportunity for cooperation here. Without it you can do nothing in America for the common cause."[35]

Lafayette sent a copy of this diatribe to La Luzerne. He had "tried to destroy these gentlemen's false ideas on some points," he said, "for I admit I do not share their opinion on many things." He was especially critical of the decision to sit tight at Newport. "I am considered too American not to be suspected of partiality," he admitted. He claimed to have superior knowledge of American public opinion, which he feared could be turned into a belief that there would be no second division. Tories were already claiming that, and asserting that France's policy was to prolong the war.

Lafayette charged that Rochambeau was "too attached to this post on Rhode Island." Another thing that "humiliated" him was that "M. de Ternay refused *under any circumstances* to force the harbor of New York, and I slightly changed the construction of the account I gave on that subject." Although Lafayette was "not happy with M. de Ternay," he respected Rochambeau, except that the general always yielded to Ternay. He asked La Luzerne to give the general "some good advice . . . of the necessity of acting as soon as possible."[36]

Rochambeau had written to Washington on August 10, before he received Lafayette's memorandum. He declared, "I do not think we can make any attempt on New York and Long Island without naval superiority" through the second division from France, or the French fleet from the West Indies, or if Clinton sent part of his troops and ships out of New York. That was the end of that.[37]

The French general received Lafayette's screed two days later. Rochambeau was famous for not getting angry about anything, but the impertinent marquis worked him into a raging lather. He sent a cold reply, brushing the young man off. He referred to his letter to Washington and declared, "I restrict myself, therefore, to awaiting his latest orders and to asking him the favor of a meeting, so that the commodore and I may go and verbally receive from him in conversation a definitive plan." He disagreed that French possession of Rhode Island was "of no use to the Americans." It might have been what caused Clinton to withdraw into New York, and it forced the enemy fleet to watch it, so "your American coasts are peaceful, your privateers take very advantageous prizes, and your maritime commerce goes on in complete freedom."[38]

Rochambeau vented his spleen to La Luzerne. Lafayette, he roared, "after having agreed with us here on all of our basic principles, wrote me on his return to his army a dispatch of twelve pages in which, surely at the instigation of some hotheaded persons, he proposes extravagant things to us, like taking Long Island and New York without a navy." Lafayette had overstepped his bounds, giving Rochambeau "political inducements: the wishes of the Americans, the efforts they have made in this campaign," and the obstacles they faced if they delayed a campaign. "Not a word, an order, or even an opinion from Mr. Washington." He and Ternay were "entirely satisfied" with the general's dispatches and "could not be more grateful for them." They would henceforth ignore messages from "some young and ardent persons" whom he saw around the American commander, and he would always address himself directly to his commander to receive his orders. "Tell me if I have guessed correctly about this sort of cabal that I think is surrounding our general and to which his good sense keeps him from surrendering." The "cabal" was Lafayette alone.[39]

There was an international uproar brewing, and La Luzerne had to calm it down. He received unexpected help from Lafayette, who was stunned by Rochambeau's icy response and apologized to the French leaders on August 18, 1780, saying, "Allow me to acknowledge here that I explained myself very awkwardly." Among other things, he would "forgo in the future" bringing up political matters. He promised to do everything he could to urge Washington to meet them between the two camps, but that might not be possible soon. "Any time you have orders to give me, regard me as a man who (you can be sure of it) loves his country with a singular passion, and who joins to that interest, which is foremost in his heart, the respectful affection with which I have the honor to be your very humble and obedient servant."[40]

The marquis turned on his boyish charm in a private note to Rochambeau. "[P]ermit me to address myself to you with all the confidence of that tender friendship, that veneration I have felt for you and have tried to show you since my tenderest youth. Although the expressions in your letter show your usual kindness to me, I noticed some items there that, without being addressed to me personally, show me that my last epistle displeased you." His heart could not "help but be affected at seeing you give my letter such an unfavorable interpretation . . . If I have offended you, I ask your pardon for two reasons: the first is that I love you; the second is that my intention is to do here all that may please you." He ended with a postscript. "My error was in writing officially with passion what you would have excused to my youth had I written it as a friend to you alone. But I acted in such good faith that your letter surprised me as much as it grieved me, and that is saying a good deal."[41]

Lafayette asked La Luzerne to help mend fences. He hoped the ambassador did not disapprove of his letter to the French generals, he said. "The letters I enclose here will show you that people are unhappy with me. . . . You will see by my replies that, without being at fault, I ask for pardon; I would even go on my knees if they wish and I think I would let myself be beaten. I could not keep myself from letting it be known, however, that they were a bit mistaken." He asked for the ambassador's support in confidence. "As for me, I shall not meddle in politics anymore."[42]

Before he received that, on August 19 La Luzerne answered Lafayette's missive of the eleventh, thanking him for "the confidence with which you opened your mind to me" and advising him not to get too worked up over public opinion. "Do you not think that if M. de Ternay judges that it is in fact impossible for him to force the harbor of New York," he asked bluntly, "it is essential to inform your general of this without concealment?" Besides, it was "better in every way to defer than to run overly large risks."

Interrupted by other business, the ambassador resumed on the twenty-third after he had received the marquis' latest. "Far from disapproving of your letter to our generals," he assured him, "I rediscover in it your zeal and your patriotism, and even the impatience you display seems to me a laudable sentiment. But the confidence you show in me makes me hope you will be grateful to me for being equally frank." He asserted that the experience of the French commanders made him side with their views. He especially thought Rochambeau's desire to meet with Washington was "full of sense" and the best way to establish a plan of operations. In closing, he was very pleased with Lafayette's "determination to end this little dispute by showing total deference to M. le Comte de Rochambeau." He could not make "a wiser and more honorable decision."[43]

La Luzerne mollified Rochambeau, agreeing that he should correspond directly with Washington to avoid confusing his opinions with "those of the young people full of ardor and the desire to do well, who are impatient with a necessary delay." Washington's subordinates were "young people full of good intentions, but . . . if one imparts to them an impatience that they do not really have, I believe I can assure you that it would not pass on to their commander." He was therefore inclined to believe that "what M. de Lafayette has written you is purely a result of his zeal and of a courage that experience will moderate."[44]

Rochambeau cooled off. He had boys of his own and told Lafayette, "Allow an old father, my dear marquis, to reply to you as a cherished son whom he loves and esteems immensely. You know me well enough to believe that I do not need to be roused to action; at my age, when we have made a decision based on military and political considerations . . . no possible instigation could make me change without a direct order from my general." Moreover, Washington "tells me in his dispatches that my ideas accord substantially with his own."

Lafayette had claimed that French troops were "invincible." Rochambeau let him in on "a great secret based on forty years' experience. There are no troops easier to defeat when they have lost confidence in their commander, and they lose that confidence immediately when they have been put in danger because of private or personal ambition. If I have been fortunate enough to keep their confidence thus far, I owe it to the most scrupulous examination of my conscience, in that, of the nearly 15,000 men who have been killed or wounded under my command in the various ranks and in the most murderous actions, I need not reproach myself that a single one was killed for my own advantage."

After that stunning statement, the old soldier concluded, "Be well assured, therefore, of my warmest friendship and that, if I have pointed out to you very gently the things in your last letter that displeased me, I concluded immediately that the warmth of your feelings and your heart had somewhat overheated the calmness and prudence of your judgment. Preserve this last quality in the council, and keep all of the first for the moment of action. This is still the old father Rochambeau speaking to his dear son Lafayette, whom he loves and will continue to love and esteem to his last breath." Lafayette had made a hash of his assignment but saved himself by winning the affection of even those he had offended.[45]

The young officer learned from the experience, which reminded him that he was Washington's agent and not an independent actor. If he had consulted his adoptive father before sending his memorandum, the whole thing could have been avoided. He talked with the general about it after he got Rochambeau's first response. Washington did not straighten the mess out for him but advised him on how to do that on his own, and he came out of the episode well. The controversy blew over, and the alliance was probably strengthened. Lafayette and Rochambeau remained lifelong friends.

Washington had learned that there were limits to the duties he could hand even to Lafayette. The war continued, and he would need him for things the young general did have the talent for.

WHOM CAN WE TRUST NOW?

The war in the South was a parade of disasters. Washington had sent de Kalb with a division of Continentals to relieve Charleston in April 1780. This was the first command worthy of his considerable abilities as a fighter, but he was not supported by the states he force-marched his 2,000 men through, and they were worn out and nearly starving in southern North Carolina when Charleston surrendered, on May 12. When General Benjamin Lincoln called for terms, Clinton humiliated the rebels, denying them the honors of war, meaning they surrendered with their colors cased. This gross insult was not forgotten on the American side.

In July 1780, against Washington's wishes, Congress sent Gates to take command of the Southern Army, which he restyled a "Grand Army" when he superseded de Kalb on July 25. The latter's force had dwindled to about 1,200 men and was in no condition to march without resupply. Gates ordered an immediate advance into South Carolina anyway. Instead of swinging west through country where supplies and patriots were plentiful, he headed straight for Camden, through barren country inhabited by Tories.

By the time he and his force of nearly 4,000—over half militia— approached Camden, his army was scattered and disorganized, and almost every man broke ranks often to answer the call of diarrhea, thanks to green rations. Cornwallis had concentrated on Camden to guard the stores and 800 sick he had at the place. The resulting battle on August 16, 1780, was the most complete defeat ever suffered by the Americans during the war. The militia stampeded at the first shot, and only de Kalb stood firm on the right. His horse shot from under him, bleeding from several wounds, the gallant Prussian refused to retreat and mounted a stunning counterattack. Without support, he was overwhelmed, and his body was later retrieved with eleven wounds in it. The Grand Army was annihilated.

Gates rode sixty miles to the rear that day and kept going, abandoning southern North Carolina. "But was there ever an instance of a general running away," snorted Hamilton, "as Gates has done, from his whole army? And was there ever so precipitate a flight? One hundred and eighty miles in three days and a half. It does admirable credit to the activity of a man at his time of life." His friends in Congress defended him, but Gates was disgraced and out of the war. So were South Carolina, Georgia, and much of North Carolina.[46]

Washington could do nothing about the South for the moment, because Congress had placed it outside his command. Instead, he was tied down around New York, where he and Clinton probed at each other without a major engagement.

The force nearest the enemy was Lafayette's Light Division, at outposts radiating from the "light camp." He gave his officers uniforms, swords, cockades, and epaulets, which he had brought with him from France. He had no uniforms for the 2,000 enlisted men, however. Each light infantry battalion was distinguished by the black and red plumes. He told his brother-in-law Noailles that he would "prefer that it were distinguished by a uniform or a good pair of shoes, but our skin is exposed, and we are sometimes barefoot, not to mention that the inside is often no better provided for than the outside." Lafayette bought a big white horse, like Washington's, on which to lead his men. He enjoyed a close relationship with his soldiers, whose morale was the highest in the army, according to surgeon James Thacher. "They were the pride of his heart, and he was the idol of their regard."[47]

The chevalier de Chastellux, French tourist and sometime aide to Rochambeau, also was impressed. "We found all his troops in order of battle on the heights to the left, and himself at their head," he reported, "expressing, by his air and countenance, that he was happier in receiving me there, than at his estate in Auvergne. The confidence and attachment of the troops, are for him invaluable possessions, well acquired riches, of which nobody can deprive him." As for the marquis, what was "still more flattering for a young man of his age, is the influence, the consideration he has acquired amongst the political, as well as the military order." That made him think about the future. "On seeing him," he remarked, "one is at a loss which most to admire, that so young a man as he should have given such eminent proofs of talents, or that a man so tried, should give hopes for so long a career of glory."[48]

Lafayette concluded that nothing was going to happen in the north until the French provided more help, so he looked south. Washington called for his generals' views, and the marquis said that the Continental Army ought to try to recover the southern states if Ternay would supply transportation. He had given up for the moment on a direct assault on New York. "Indeed sir, our ressources of every kind are so precarious that unless we depend on a more firm bazis, it is impossible to fix on any operation."[49]

The state of the Revolution was so low that Congress considered giving Washington dictatorial powers. Lafayette confided in La Luzerne about this, though he had learned his lesson about interfering in politics. He did not know whether, as Washington's friend, he ought to desire it for him, he said, but he understood "very certainly that I must neither speak of it nor ever appear to wish for this measure, which nevertheless seems immensely important to me." If Washington was in charge of everything, the French government might be more forthcoming with material aid. But the cause his adoptive father fought for was altering his outlook. His "republican and even entirely democratic principles," he said, should make him oppose such a measure. He also would not approve of it if he did not know the man and if he did not think the dictatorship "necessary to the public safety." Congress rejected the proposal, but the choice between democracy and dictatorship would linger in the marquis' mind for many years to come.[50]

On September 8, 1780, deciding that nothing would happen in his absence, Washington asked Rochambeau and Ternay to meet him at Hartford, Connecticut. His party rode out on the seventeenth. Lafayette, Knox, and an engineer went along with him. Six aides and an escort of twenty-two dragoons completed the procession. They stopped for lunch at West Point on the eighteenth, hosted by the commander of the fortifications, Benedict Arnold, who ferried them over the river in the early afternoon. Hamilton remained behind to receive dispatches.[51]

Major General Arnold was one of the most famous soldiers in the army, thirty-nine years old, formerly a druggist. He had a large head on a bull neck, with a high brow, fierce eyes, and a thrusting chin. He was a born fighter, wounded in the Quebec and Saratoga campaigns severely enough that he could not again command in the field. Arnold had become military governor of Philadelphia after Clinton abandoned the place, and Pennsylvania president Joseph Reed drew up a list of charges against him. His tenure had been dishonest, but the state's case was faulty. Congress cleared him of most of the charges but ordered a court-martial on four. In January 1780 the court cleared him of all but one. His sentence was a reprimand from the commander in chief, which Washington wrote as almost a commendation, but Arnold seethed with resentment. He harbored old grudges on various accounts and was vain, resentful, greedy, and quarrelsome.

In April 1779 Arnold had married Margaret Shippen, daughter of a prominent loyalist family. Peggy Shippen was nineteen years old, pretty, vivacious, rich, and well connected. With her help he began secret negotiations with the British. Pointing to his wounds, he talked Washington into assigning him to West Point, whose fortifications blocked the Hudson River, denying it to the British. He aimed to sell it to the enemy. Nobody in Washington's party knew that, of course, and the lunch was delightful. The commander in chief enjoyed flirting with pretty young women, and Peggy was an expert in that department.[52]

Washington and his group rode into Hartford on September 21. When they met their French opposite numbers, the tall, courtly

Washington overwhelmed them. Chastellux called him "the greatest and the best of men. The goodness and benevolence which characterize him, are evident from every thing about him; but the confidence he gives birth to never occasions improper familiarity; for the sentiment he inspires . . . [is] a profound esteem for his virtues, and a high opinion of his talents."

Rochambeau's aide Hans-Axel, comte de Fersen, was awestruck. "I had the opportunity of seeing this man, the most illustrious, not to say unique, in our century," he said.

Benedict Arnold, engraving after an earlier portrait. Arnold's attempt to sell West Point to the enemy has made his name a synonym for traitor.
(AUTHOR'S COLLECTION)

"His face handsome and full of majesty, but at the same time kind and honest . . . he looks like a hero; he seems to be very distant, speaks little but is polite and gentlemanly. His countenance is overcast with sadness, but this becomes him perfectly."[53]

Rochambeau, Ternay, and Washington spent September 22 together, with Lafayette as translator and secretary. They agreed on everything. New York was the "first and foremost object we can have on this continent," but to take it they needed more troops, ships, and money from France. Lafayette wrote the ten points of agreement in parallel French and English versions, and together the allied commanders asked King Louis for more help. "They separated quite charmed with one another, at least they said so," as one of Rochambeau's aides put it. The French commander sent his son, the vicomte de Rochambeau, to France with the message.[54]

The Americans headed back toward West Point, through hills ablaze with fall colors, to inspect the fortifications. Washington sent aides ahead to tell the post commander and his wife to expect them for dinner. While the aides enjoyed breakfast, Arnold received a message that visibly upset him. He rushed upstairs and said something to Peggy, who shrieked. Arnold then left the house. Sometime later, Hamilton received a package of dispatches, which he assumed were routine returns. He handed it to the commander in chief when he arrived in the afternoon.

The officers scattered to their assigned bedrooms to clean up, wondering where Arnold was. A servant told them that Mrs. Arnold was "indisposed." Lafayette had hardly begun to arrange his clothes when Hamilton broke in and told him to go to Washington at once. He rushed into the front room, where he found his adoptive father standing in the middle, the papers Hamilton had given him shaking in his hand. He was in tears. "Arnold has betrayed us!" he cried. "Whom can we trust now?"[55]

Lafayette and Hamilton took the documents and learned what had happened. Militia had stopped a horseman near the British lines and found messages in Arnold's handwriting, outlining his plan to sell West Point to the enemy. Another paper revealed that the captive was Major John André, Clinton's acting adjutant general. Washington confronted Peggy, who became hysterical. She was such a good actress that she fooled them all into believing that she knew nothing of her husband's plot. In fact, she had been in it up to her lovely neck.

After Washington ordered Wayne's troops to secure the forts, and put Greene in command of the district, the party sat down to the meal they had been looking forward to. "Never was there a more melancholy dinner," Lafayette recalled. "The general was silent and reserved, and none of us spoke of what we were thinking. . . . I have never seen General Washington so affected by any circumstance."[56]

Lafayette put the best face on the situation. "You will shudder at the danger we have run. You will wonder at the miraculous chain of accidents and unforeseen events that has saved us," he told La Luzerne. "We are all shocked by this vile conspiracy and amazed at the miraculous manner in which it came to our knowledge," he told Rochambeau, assuring him, "It is the first case of treason in our army . . . but the instance grieves us as much as it disgusts us." He told Vergennes, "This whole affair proves only the greed of Arnold and has no other consequences than to the abhorrence inspired by his sordid conduct." Rochambeau replied that he was "overcome with dismay and with delight at its exposure," while Vergennes said, "It seems that this signal mark of Providence's protection, which alone caused this detestable plot to fail, should be an encouragement for the United States." Lafayette could relax—France would not take Arnold's betrayal as a sign of weakness on the American side.[57]

Having covered Washington's flank, Lafayette worked up a lust for revenge against Arnold. The man had betrayed his country and its cause, but most of all he had betrayed Lafayette's adoptive father, and that made it personal with him. Conway, Gates, Mifflin, Lee—all paled in comparison. Lafayette had entered this war looking for glory and vengeance against the despised *Anglais,* but they were abstractions. There had been one individual he would have aimed for specifically if he could find him. Now Arnold the traitor joined Phillips the gunner as Lafayette's personal enemy.

Arnold's confederate André was in custody. Greene summoned a court-martial on September 29, 1780, seating Lafayette, Knox, Stirling, and eleven other generals to try the British officer. There was no doubt about the outcome, and the verdict was unanimous. He had been captured under a false name, in civilian clothes, and carrying incriminating documents. That made him a spy, not a prisoner of war, so he was condemned to death. He asked to be shot but was turned down. He would be hanged, as befitted a spy. Hamilton argued in his favor, and citizens in the neighborhood begged for mercy, but the decision stood.

André was twenty-nine years old but looked much younger. Baby-faced, with soft features and dark, liquid eyes, he was friendly, a good conversationalist, and a talented artist and poet. It was impossible not to like him, and Lafayette and Hamilton made the mistake of getting to know him before he was hanged on October 2. Seeing death on the battlefield had not prepared them for the horror of watching a young man strangle to death, his feet off the ground. They were both shaken.

"Poor André suffers to-day," Hamilton wrote his fiancée. "Every thing that is amiable in virtue, in fortitude, in delicate sentiment, and accomplished manners, pleads for him; but hard-hearted policy calls for a sacrifice. He must die." Distraught, he tried to justify his own part in the proceedings. "When André's tale comes to be told, and present resentment is over, the refusing him the privilege of choosing the manner of his death will be branded with too much obstinacy." He wrote an even more tormented letter to John Laurens.[58]

Lafayette was torn up over his role. "Arnold's baseness and villainy surpass in their details all that I have ever read about that sort of thing," he told Noailles. "But what has truly afflicted me is the necessity of hanging . . . a charming man who conducted himself throughout, and died, like a hero. This severity was necessary. . . . [T]his man's death, although inevitable in my opinion, left me with a feeling of sadness and respect for his character. I truly suffered in condemning him."[59]

The marquis even unburdened himself to Adrienne, in an exception to his usually boastful letters laced with loving platitudes. "He was a charming man," he told her. "He conducted himself in a manner so frank, so noble, so delicate that, during the three days that we held him, I had the foolishness to let myself acquire a true affection for him. In strongly stating my opinion in favor of sending him to the gallows, I could not prevent myself from regretting it deeply."[60]

HE MADE IT A RULE TO FOLLOW
GENERAL WASHINGTON IN EVERYTHING

*T*he appointment of Gates was Congress' last major intervention into the military conduct of the war. When Washington proposed sending Greene to replace him in September, the lawmakers agreed. He sent Steuben along with him. Before they started south, word arrived of an American victory at Kings Mountain, South Carolina, on October 7, 1780, when frontier riflemen whipped a corps of British regulars and Tory partisans, taking hundreds of prisoners and about 1,400 stand of arms. Cornwallis pulled back into middle South Carolina.[61]

Lafayette poured out letters to France, begging for more aid. When he learned that Henry Laurens, on his way to Paris to plead the American case, had been captured at sea by the British, he asked Adrienne to see Vergennes about getting him freed. She tried, but Laurens finished the war in the Tower of London, accused of "high treason."[62]

On October 7, 1780, the Light Division raided Bergen, New Jersey, bagging fifteen prisoners without losing a man. Lafayette and Hamilton drew up a plan for a larger raid on Staten Island; Lafayette also recommended his friend for a line command, but Washington turned that down. They marched out in the dark of October 27, but the quartermasters did not show up with the promised boats. Lafayette called it off, blistering the quartermasters for their "many blunders." "I confess, my dear general," he raged, "that I cannot reconcile my feelings to the idea that by this neglect I have lost a most happy opportunity." He felt frustrated not only on his own account but also "for all the officers and men who had promis'd themselves so much glory on the occasion."[63]

Lafayette looked for other ways to take a shot at glory, and almost daily he and Washington discussed taking the offensive. On October 30, he proposed an assault on Fort Washington, at the northern end of Manhattan. The French court had often complained to him about the inactivity of the American army, he said. Washington cooled him off. He wanted to do something, but with the French idle at Newport there was no support for the attack. "It is impossible my dear Marquis," he told him; "we must consult our means rather than our wishes, and not endeavour to better our affairs by attempting things, which for want of success may make them worse."[64]

Washington asked his generals how to help Greene in the South, and Lafayette proposed that he lead his Light Division in that direction. When his spies told him that Clinton might leave New York, he renewed the proposal; failing that, he wanted to take a stab at Staten Island again. He kept pressing for action, but the Main Army lacked the resources to match his ambitions. The heaviest blow fell on November 26. Preparing to go into winter quarters, Washington disbanded the Light Division, returning its men to their home regiments.[65]

When Washington asked his generals to recommend someone for adjutant general, Hamilton approached Lafayette for help getting the job. Restive on the commander's staff, he looked for any way out. He asked the marquis to write in his behalf, but specifically not to speak to Washington in person. Lafayette agreed, saying that he knew "the generals friendship and gratitude for you, my dear Hamilton, both are greater than you perhaps imagine." But his letter arrived too late; Washington had already appointed someone else. Hamilton was in Albany at his own wedding, and Lafayette wrote him, "I have been angry with you for not permitting my speaking immediately to the general on your affair. This curs'd way of a letter you have insisted upon" meant that Washington "had innocently put it out of his own power to oblige you." He saw the strain growing between Hamilton and Washington, but he could not do anything about it.[66]

The Frenchman's personal finances were in a mess, again. Morizot had begged him to economize, but his only concession was to take two of his own servants with him so that he need not hire help in America. On November 28, Morizot complained to Lafayette's aunt that bills arriving in France had overdrawn his account by 12,000 livres because he had bought two carriages and incurred "expenses stemming from an independent command." He asked Mademoiselle du Motier to help "extricate us from this embarrassment. It would be horrible, if Monsieur the Marquis' obligations should return to America without having been honored here."[67]

Still Lafayette emptied his pockets to hire spies and to entertain a mob of French officers who left Rhode Island on leave to visit him. They wanted to get into action and applied to Lafayette and Washington for commissions. The commander in chief treated them to a dinner and a tour of West Point but declined their offers unless they got leave from Rochambeau. When Ternay died suddenly, of an undiagnosed fever, in mid-December, Lafayette snorted that it was of mortification over his idleness.[68]

The marquis got Washington to send him to Philadelphia as his agent, to lobby for supplies and action to relieve Greene. Partisan warfare had broken out in the South, and British raiders operated with uncommon savagery. "I hate the idea of being from you for so long a time," Lafayette told his adoptive father. "But I think I ought not to stay idle." He took his French friends with him, enjoyed a round of parties and battlefield tours, and was elected to the American Philosophical Society. He kept his superior informed of everything, including negotiations with the new Spanish minister in Philadelphia. Spain had entered the war in America, and Lafayette pressured the minister to attack the British in Florida, until Washington told him to drop it. The young general filled his commander in on the latest news from France, renewed his efforts to rouse Rochambeau to action, and begged King Louis for men, ships, and money.[69]

When Lafayette again asked for permission to join Greene, his adoptive father put the matter in his hands and prepared letters of introduction to southern officials. "In all places, and at all times, my best wishes for your health, honor & glory will accompany you." Everyone Lafayette talked to advised him to stay with Washington. "I am more than ever puzzled, my dear general, to know what to do," he wrote. "I also candidly confess that private affection for you makes me hate the idea of leaving the man I love the most in the world to seek for uncertainties at a period when he may want me." Washington returned his affection, but he had "already put it absolutely in your choice" to go or stay. The young man was torn. He asked Greene for an invitation, then retracted the request, deciding to stay with Washington. As he told Hamilton, "He is going to be alone, you know how tenderly I love him, and I don't like the idea of abandonning him."[70]

When Congress decided to appoint another delegate to France to beg for new loans, Lafayette was asked for his recommendation. He knew how frustrated Hamilton had become after four years as an aide-de-camp, so he recommended him, and so did John Laurens. The lawmakers chose Laurens instead and directed him to consult with Washington, the French commanders, and Lafayette before he left. "I am by order of Congress to have a conference with him," the marquis told Washington, "and intend giving him many letters for France. As in your instructions to Laurens the presence of one who knows these people may be agreable to you, I shall set out for head quarters."[71]

"One might say that he made it a rule to follow General Washington in everything," Virginia commercial agent Philip Mazzei observed of Lafayette. It was not hard for anyone who saw them together to understand why. Rochambeau's aide the comte de Dumas delivered messages to Washington that winter and spent time at headquarters. He was "particularly struck," he said, "with the marks of affection which the general showed to his pupil, his adopted son the marquis de la Fayette. Seated opposite to him, he looked at him with pleasure and listened to him with manifest interest." Dumas joined Washington's party on a tour of West Point. After they visited the forts and reviewed the garrison, "as the day was declining, and we were going to mount our horses, the general perceived that M. de la Fayette, in consequence of his old wound, was very much fatigued. 'It will be better,' said he, 'to return by water; the tide will assist us in ascending against the stream.'" When the boat got into trouble in rough weather, Washington took the helm and guided it through rocks and ice to shore—all this to relieve the tired Lafayette from having to take a horseback ride.[72]

Washington loved the young man so much that he pampered him. Still, the time might come when he had to send him into danger once again. Arnold had landed in Virginia.

The Boy Cannot Escape Me!

(JANUARY-JULY 1781)

Now the method of employing men is to use the avaricious and the stupid,
the wise and the brave, and to give responsibility to each in situations that
suit him. Do not charge people to do what they cannot do.

—CHANG YÜ

afayette and Laurens set out for Washington's headquarters
at New Windsor, and on January 1, 1781, they learned that
2,500 Pennsylvania troops of the Continental Line had mutinied, killing two officers. The military mob headed
toward Philadelphia to present its grievances to Congress and the state
government. The complaints were real enough. The soldiers were unfed
and unclothed, they had not been paid in fifteen months, and their enlistments had been arbitrarily extended for a year. Lafayette, Laurens, and
General Arthur St. Clair rode to meet the mutineers. The marquis told
La Luzerne that "it must be admitted that some of them have a right to
complain about the interpretations put on their enlistments as well as the
manner in which some of the officers received their protests."[1]

He was "the only one for whom they admitted having a depth of friendship," Lafayette said. "I preach peace, and unless I were sure I could kill all of them if I wanted, I would not fire a single shot." The mutineers met with him at Princeton, and he urged them to go back to camp, but their blood was up. They told him that they would die to the last man under his orders but that he did not know all they had suffered, and they would "see to it that their country does them justice."[2]

The marquis was inclined to recommend harsh measures, but as he said, it would be "frightening to spend one's winter killing each other." Although he thought the men had been led astray by a few hotheads, he was sympathetic to them because of their sufferings over four years, and especially the "verified deception in their enlistments." The whole situation was "very unfortunate."[3]

Washington could not intervene because the state authorities stepped in. They negotiated back pay and promised food and clothing. When Clinton sent an emissary from New York to invite the mutineers to go over to the British, the Pennsylvanians seized him, and he was later hanged as a spy. It was all over by the seventeenth of January. The republican Washington explained to the royalist Lafayette and Rochambeau that since the civil powers had taken over the dispute "there would have been an impropriety in my interfering in their conciliatory measures, which would not have suited the principles of military discipline."[4]

The New Jersey Line rose at Pompton, New Jersey, over the same grievances, and Washington asked the state to let him handle it. He surrounded the mutineers, arrested their ringleaders, and put two of them in front of a firing squad. No matter the complaint, troops who pressed it by mutiny or desertion had to be put down quickly and hard, or the army would fall apart. Already, half the Pennsylvanians had gone home.[5]

Lafayette could turn any disaster into an opportunity. "Let us inform Versailles in very strong terms," he urged La Luzerne, "without money we shall be unable to budge, and what is worse, there will be no means of bringing us food where we shall be staying." He sent his own pleas to several French ministers, asserting that more financial aid was essential to the survival of America and its Revolution. Everything now depended on Laurens' ability to get more out of the French government.[6]

YOU WILL REMEMBER THAT YOUR CORPS
IS A PART OF THIS ARMY

afayette gave Laurens a bale of letters, messages, and instructions
that included letters to all the king's ministers, d'Estaing, Franklin,
Adrienne, d'Ayen, and about a dozen others. When he learned that
Thomas Paine would accompany Laurens, he loaded him down also. He
asked Adrienne to help Laurens out. "If I were in France he would dine
often with me," he said, and he would introduce Laurens to important
people in Versailles. "In my absence I beg you to be so good as to take my
place."[7]

The young general also offered advice to his friend, whose fiery temper he knew well. "But I again repeat," he told Laurens, "that you will
there find great deal of willingness to help us. If they do but little, which
I think would be a great folly, it will, I believe, be because they won't [be]
thinking themselves able to do better—so that don't get angry, and be
sure that theyr intentions are good."[8]

Lafayette's letter to Adrienne mentioned somebody else: "Among the
general's aides-de-camp is a young man whom I love very much and
about whom I have occasionally spoken to you; that man is Colonel
Hamilton." Hamilton had grown increasingly frustrated in what he regarded as a servant's job, and wanted a fighting command. Lafayette,
Laurens, and Greene all believed Washington was holding him back.

On his way to deliver a letter to Tilghman on February 16, 1781,
Hamilton passed Washington on the stairs. "He told me he wanted to
speak to me. I answered that I would wait upon him immediately,"
Hamilton explained to his father-in-law. On the way back, Lafayette
stopped him and they "conversed together about a minute." Washington
met him at the head of the stairs and accused the aide of making him wait
ten minutes. Then the general said angrily, "I must tell you, sir, you treat
me with disrespect." Hamilton bristled and answered, "I am not conscious of it, sir; but since you have thought it necessary to tell me so," he
resigned his position. Washington accepted that and returned to his office. "I sincerely believe my absence," Hamilton claimed, "which gave so
much umbrage, did not last two minutes."

Washington's temper, and his disregard for the feelings of others except Lafayette, had gotten the better of him. He sent Tilghman to make

peace with the young aide, but Hamilton was too stubborn to budge, although he agreed to stay until Washington found a replacement. Lafayette, who felt guilty about his role, intervened without success. He ended up apologizing to Washington for the other's behavior, but the split was complete.[9]

Hamilton remained the rest of the winter, the air frosty whenever he and Washington were in the same room, but headquarters was too busy to nurse bruised egos. Something had to be done about Arnold in Virginia. When a storm wrecked a British squadron at Gardiner's Bay, Long Island, it gave the French naval superiority off the middle states. Washington urged the chevalier Destouches, the new naval commander, to sail to the Chesapeake, and Rochambeau to put a thousand troops on the ships. He would send about 1,200 men from his own army to cooperate with them. The French commanders promised to send a squadron.[10]

"Arnold, now a British general," Lafayette told Adrienne, "has disembarked in Virginia with a corps of that nation that seems quite content to serve under his orders. One must not dispute about matters of taste." With the savage hostility of a traitor, Arnold led 1,600 men to Richmond, the new state capital, on January 5, burned everything he could, then withdrew. His vandalism was aided by Governor Thomas Jefferson's failure to mobilize the state. Light-Horse Harry Lee snorted that it would "scarcely be credited by posterity" that the governor of the oldest state in the Union "was driven out of its metropolis . . . and that its archives, with all its munitions and stores, were yielded to the will of the invader."[11]

Greene put Steuben in charge in Virginia. Brigadier General Thomas Nelson Jr., a veteran of the Continental Army, commanded the state troops. On January 7, he told Steuben that he had only "a few tired militia" trying to keep in touch with the enemy, as most of his troops had been put out of action by heavy rain and a lack of arms. The next day, Arnold routed his forces at Charles City Court House. Jefferson occupied himself writing letters to Washington, praising Steuben. The Prussian had a dimmer outlook, because the militia ran at the first shot, and he could not raise men or supplies or obtain intelligence. It was impossible to describe the situation he was in, he complained, "in want of every thing; and nothing can be got from the state, rather for want of arrangement than any thing else." Arnold rampaged as freely as a weasel in a henhouse until he retired to Portsmouth.[12]

When news of the situation reached Washington early in February 1781, he reassembled the Light Division to send to Virginia under Lafayette. He detailed a masking force to make Clinton think that Lafayette was going to raid Staten Island. The marquis and 1,200 men slipped out and covered the 100 miles to Trenton in under a week. It was amusing to see them traveling, Lafayette told La Luzerne. "We haven't a sou, a horse, a cart, or a wisp of hay." He expected to get to Virginia and back by impressing horses, boats, and supplies without spending any money. Marching on the cheap, he was having a grand time.[13]

Once he heard that Destouches had detached a squadron to the Chesapeake, Washington gave Lafayette his orders. The marquis was to proceed "with all possible dispatch" to Head of Elk. Once he had transport and cover from the French he was to sail down the bay to Virginia. When he arrived at his destination he must act "as your own judgment and the circumstances shall direct," he told him, in a great departure from the orders before Barren Hill. If Rochambeau sent troops, he should cooperate with their commander appropriately. Above all, he was to do "no act whatever with Arnold that directly or by implication may skreen him from the punishment due to his treason and desertion, which if he should fall into your hands, you shall execute in the most summary way." Finally, he wished the young general "a successful issue to the enterprise and all the glory which I am persuaded you will deserve."[14]

As Lafayette's division slogged through rain and mud and swollen rivers, Washington alerted Greene, Steuben, and Jefferson that he was on the way. He sent an additional brigade of New Jersey Continentals to join him, and ordered a battalion of Wayne's Pennsylvanians to go along. He soon raised that to the whole force, about a thousand men, as soon as Wayne could get them organized. Meanwhile, the French squadron commander entered the Chesapeake, found the waters at its upper end too shallow, and returned to Newport. He had captured a smaller British vessel, which he planned to refit and return to the bay. His ships might not be able to escort Lafayette south from Head of Elk.[15]

On March 1 Washington told Lafayette that he had heard from the French commanders, who planned to take their whole fleet into the

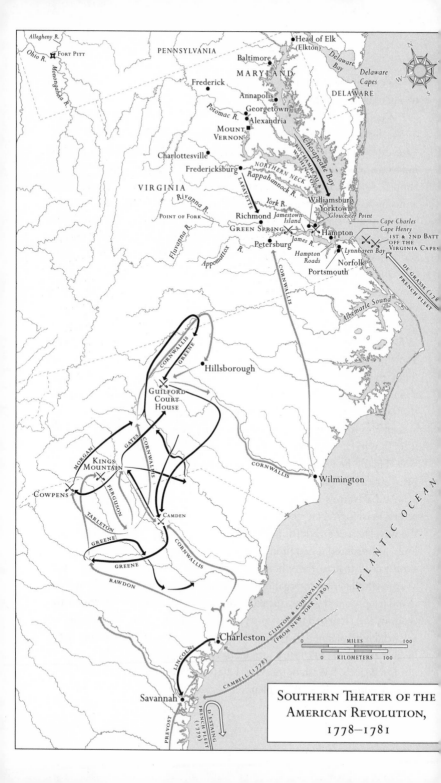

SOUTHERN THEATER OF THE
AMERICAN REVOLUTION,
1778–1781

Chesapeake, along with 1,100 troops. They expected to sail on March 5, and Lafayette should reach Head of Elk before them. The French admiral, however, seemed "to make a difficulty, which I do not comprehend about protecting the passage of your detachment down the bay."

Greene had reported that Cornwallis and 2,500 men were heading toward Virginia, and his army was too small to stop them. "This intelligence and an apprehension that Arnold may make his escape before the fleet can arrive in the bay," Washington told Lafayette, "induce me to give you greater latitude than you had in your original instructions." He granted the marquis freedom to move into North Carolina, cut Arnold off, intercept Cornwallis, and support Greene. This, he believed, should be a "secondary object" to be pursued only if Arnold retreated to New York, or if his works at Portsmouth were too stout to challenge. "There should be strong reasons to induce a change of our first plan against Arnold, if he is still in Virginia. . . . You will remember that your corps is a part of this army and let this idea have proper weight in your determinations."[16]

Lafayette began what became a lifelong friendship with Thomas Jeffer-

Thomas Jefferson, by C. W. Peale, 1791–92. As governor of Virginia, Jefferson was of little help to Lafayette's struggle with Cornwallis, but they became lifelong friends anyway, and conspirators in the early French Revolution. (INDEPENDENCE NATIONAL HISTORICAL PARK)

son, starting with an exchange of flattering letters. Lafayette made obeisance to the governor, then asked for help raising men and supplies.

Jefferson answered with praise for the "nobleman who has already so much endeared himself to the citizens of these states," then excused the state's not doing its part. He wrote Steuben on March 10 with a lame justification: "We can only be answerable for the orders we give, and not for their execution." He told Lafayette, "Mild laws, a people not used to war and prompt obedience, a want of the provisions of war & means of procuring them render our orders often ineffectual."

Lafayette answered, "Long since have I been used to those inconveniences that are so far compensated by the numberless blessings of a popular government." He did not "question the good intentions of the state." Utterances such as that caused Jefferson to sing Lafayette's praises as a defender of self-government for the rest of his life, but he did little to stave off the invader. Jefferson and his government were constitutionally incapable of meeting the demands of war.[17]

The marquis hurried on to Head of Elk, where his men arrived on March 2—ahead of schedule, as he boasted to Washington. They were mostly fed and clothed but short of shoes. The transports promised by the quartermasters were nowhere to be seen. The marquis appealed to Mordecai Gist, a Baltimore businessman, and to the governor and council of Maryland. Gist seized "everything that floats" in the Baltimore area, and a flotilla was ready by March 7. Governor Thomas Sim Lee rounded up provisions. When the French fleet failed to show, he looked for protection for the marquis' flotilla. Lafayette boarded his men and guns on the eighth, and the French sailed out of Newport the same day.[18]

Lafayette did not need a fleet to protect his little navy. Arnold wanted the Royal Navy to attack his transports, but he was rebuffed. He and Captain Thomas Symonds had fallen out over a division of prize money for some ships taken in the James River. Arnold complained to Clinton, making himself so obnoxious in his letters, accusing Symonds of cowardice, that the captain flatly refused to sail against Lafayette.[19]

The marquis also could be temperamental. With his men sitting in their boats and no French ships in sight, he fumed to Washington that it was all a plot. Rochambeau intended to steal his glory, fighting the enemy on his own, while he sat in the middle of nowhere. When Gist found him a twelve-gun sloop the next day, he decided to sail his troops to Annapolis, about halfway down the bay, while he went ahead with thirty men in a fishing boat armed with swivel guns. He reached Yorktown on March 14, 1781. Without naval support, the young general was discouraged. He ordered Wayne to go on to join Greene in North Carolina, and advised Washington that catching Arnold was a lost cause. When he heard that French ships had been sighted, however, he deployed Steuben's militia and prepared to bring his own troops from Annapolis for an assault on Portsmouth. It turned out that the ships were British, not French.[20]

Recommending that Washington recall the division to the Main Army, on March 23 Lafayette explained that he had gone ahead to Virginia to assess the situation firsthand and reduce the time required either to advance his detachment to Virginia or to send it back to New York. "I hope, my dear general, that my conduct will meet with your approbation, and it is the thing I the most heartily wish for." He faced a greater British force at Portsmouth than had been there a few days earlier. Not until the twenty-fifth did he learn that was because of something that had happened nine days earlier.[21]

Destouches had sailed from Newport on March 8, aiming for Chesapeake Bay. British admiral Marriot Arbuthnot took out after him, thirty-six hours behind, and beat him to the bay entrance. At the Battle off Cape Henry (First Battle off the Virginia Capes) on March 16, the fleets engaged for about an hour and a half. The furious cannonade tore up the sails and rigging on both sides. Destouches got the better of his opponent, but he decided that his damage was severe enough to abandon the expedition against Portsmouth, and he lit out for Newport. Arbuthnot limped into Lynnhaven Bay. With the seaway cleared, Clinton sent 2,000 troops under General William Phillips to reinforce Virginia and take command from Arnold. Lafayette's two personal enemies, the man who had killed his father and the one who had betrayed his adoptive father, stood before him, and he was not strong enough to tackle them. He decided to return to the Main Army.[22]

The marquis told Washington that the naval engagement had been in the French fleet's favor, and he was "sorry they did not pursue their advantage." British reinforcements scotched any hope of operating against Arnold, but if "the detachement from Newyork is strong that place must be weak, and it increases my desire to join your Excellency." Looking back, he wished he had not advanced his troops to Annapolis, "but the arrival of the french fleet could not then be questioned." He was afraid that he was exiled to a sideshow and that the main action would be against New York. He did not want to miss that.[23]

"I am truly unhappy that so much trouble, so many expenses have been the only result of our enterprise to relieve Virginia," Lafayette complained to Jefferson, and left for Annapolis after endorsing a plan circulated by Steuben to round up all available militia from Virginia. He would march them to North Carolina to help Greene contain Cornwallis. Greene, who had thumped the British at Guilford Court House on March 15, 1781, urged Lafayette to march south. He knew the Main Army was weak, he said, but if Washington understood "the critical situation of the southern states he would consent to your coming to our relief." It was too late. Lafayette had already headed north, leaving Steuben in Virginia, where the government would not let him take the militia out of state.[24]

The marquis was back at Head of Elk in early April, when he received worse news. Letters from Vergennes said that there would be no second division to join Rochambeau and Destouches. They were authorized to call on the West Indies fleet under Admiral François-Joseph-Paul, comte de Grasse, who might provide support later in the season. The French government would not guarantee a loan of 25 million livres requested by Laurens, but instead it had granted a subsidy of 6 million livres. "I have reason to believe," the foreign minister told Lafayette privately, "Mr. Washington will be satisfied with the efforts we are making for the support of the American cause and that he on his part will do everything in his power so that they will not be fruitless." Lafayette should assure the general that the French government had "complete confidence in his zeal, his patriotism, and his talents" and was sure he would win his war. "Some clothing for your troops is coming, and still more will come, I hope."[25]

This was discouraging news, and Washington, Lafayette, La Luzerne, and Rochambeau all were disappointed. The need for naval superiority was a main point that Washington had wanted Laurens to bring up when he went to France. Now it all depended on de Grasse's willingness to challenge the British fleet.[26]

Lafayette took it personally. Instead of reinforcements, his govern-

ment was sending clothes. Except for the idle Rochambeau and the ineffective Destouches, his adoptive father was alone. He wanted to return
to him.

IT IS PROBABLE I WILL BE IN THE SOUTHERN WILDERNESS UNTILL THE END

Washington wanted Lafayette back, and on April 5, 1781, he ordered him home. He wished the detachment would move "as
quickly as they can without injury to the troops." The next day he re-
versed himself, after hearing from Greene and Steuben. He ordered the
marquis to turn back and reinforce Greene, to block Cornwallis from
joining Arnold and Phillips. His generals agreed unanimously that this
was the best way to confront the expanding British campaign in the
South. "Your being already three hundred miles advanced, which is nearly
half way, is the reason which operates against any which can be offered in
favr. of marching that detachment back and forming another—A plan
which I once had in mind."

"I will now mention to you, in confidence," Washington continued,
"the reason which operated with me more than almost any other in favor
of recalling your detachment and forming another." He had received
complaints from regimental officers about Lafayette's taking French officers with his command, leaving Americans behind. Washington had pacified the gripers, but he expected the issue to come up again.[27]

Lafayette answered that he would prefer to be there with his light infantry if Washington attacked New York. "But I think with you that these
motives are not to influence our determination if this is the best way to
help General Greene." He told Hamilton that he feared that he was being
diverted to the South to draw attention from New York. "It is probable I
will be in the southern wilderness untill the end of the war—far from
head quarters, from the french army, from my correspondence with
France," he complained.[28]

Meanwhile, the governor and council urged Lafayette to keep some
troops in Maryland, because British ships were raiding the ports. He
could not do that, he told them, and worse, he was going to have to

requisition wagons, horses, and supplies from the people of the state. His troops were out of food and almost naked. He went to Baltimore to get supplies, spent his last £500 there, and signed a note for £1,550, secured against his estate in France. Congress promised to take care of that, but in the end it was another loss to him.[29]

This expedition was not starting well, the young general complained to Washington. When he issued orders to march southward, some of the troops rebelled. They were mostly New Englanders, already infested with southern mites, and they dreaded going south in the yellow fever season. After he crossed the Susquehanna, he caught three Tory spies in his camp and hanged one, then arrested some deserters. "But the idea of remaining in the southern states appears to them intolerable," he said, "and they are amazingly averse to the people and the climate. I shall do my best," but he feared desertion would continue to drain his corps of troops.[30]

"You surely know that I am leaving for the South," the marquis reminded La Luzerne. "Our officers and soldiers are not too happy about it." They had no money, clothing, or shoes, and in a few days they would be living on green peaches. Their feet were torn for lack of shoes, and their hands itched with scabies. Lafayette thought also that his personal baggage had been captured (it had been). But all that would not prevent them from marching "if we must."[31]

Washington sympathized with Lafayette's distress. He could not say what was really on his mind, because his letters could be intercepted. The youngster was not in a sideshow: he was about to become the star of the main event against the British. Washington did not tell Greene, Steuben, or Rochambeau, either. He wanted the enemy to think that he was planning to attack New York. He later told dictionary maker Noah Webster that his plan was "to misguide & bewilder Sir Henry Clinton . . . by fictitious communications, as well as by making deceptive provision of ovens, forage & boats in his neighborhood. . . . Nor were less pains taken to deceive our own army."[32]

The commander in chief sent out conflicting accounts of his plans, intended to fall into enemy hands. They baffled Lafayette, who alternately thought the New York attack was off and that it was on and he would be left out of it. But he solved his desertion problem, first by hanging a deserter, then by promising the troops that they would see action. If any of them did not want to follow him, he offered passes back to their home units. None took him up on it, and the desertion ended. Meanwhile, he heard from Steuben and Greene that the situation in Virginia and the Carolinas was growing worse by the day. Leaving his artillery and baggage to follow, commandeering horses and wagons so his men could alternately walk and ride on the forced march, Lafayette pressed into Virginia. He asked Jefferson to send him food, and sent an aide ahead to collect food and rum at Fredericksburg, which he reached on April 25, his men hungry and worn out.[33]

There the marquis received another message from Washington. "Though the situation of southern affairs would not permit me to recall your corps to this army," he told him officially, "yet it was with great reluctance I could resolve upon seeing you separated from head quarters. My friendship for you makes me desirous of having you near me." He would have summoned Lafayette back alone, he said, except that he was sure the young general would not want to turn his corps over to someone else, especially when there would not likely be a command for him in New York. Then Washington dropped a delicious hint. "I shall have one consolation, which is that from the present aspect of things it is perhaps most probable the weight of the war this campaign will be in the southern states, and it will become my duty to go there in person where I shall have the pleasure of seeing you again. Of this I would not have you to say anything. Adieu my dr. marquis wherever you are, assure yourself of my unalterable friendship & affection." In a separate, private letter, he affirmed, "The only cause of hesitation in my mind about sending your corps to the southward was a separation from you."[34]

Lafayette did not have time to figure out what his adoptive father was telling him. Phillips was marching on Richmond, leaving fire and destruction in his wake, and taunting the marquis. "The stile of your letters sir obliges me, to tell you," Lafayette replied, "that should your future favors be wanting in that regard due to the civil and military authority in the United States . . . I shall not think it consistent with the dignity of an american officer to continue the correspondence." Phillips became more polite, not because of that letter but because of something else that happened on April 30, 1781.[35]

Lafayette hustled most of his little army, about 800 men, to Richmond, which he reached on April 29. He planted his men and some militia on the heights overlooking the town and gazed south. Phillips approached the next day, but when he saw the American force, Lafayette told Greene, "he declined engaging." He marched down the James River to his transports and floated back to Petersburg. The British general had expressed "his surprise at the rapidity of our march. It is lucky we did so for my cannon and baggage could not leave Alexandria untill the 30th."[36]

"I request you will receive my affectionate acknowledgement for your kind letters," Lafayette began a report to Washington. "Every mark of friendship I receive from you adds to my happiness, as I love you with all the sincerity and warmth of my heart, and the sentiment I feel for you goes to the very extent of my affections." He explained that if he had not left his artillery behind and pushed forward, Richmond would have been lost. When Phillips "was going to give the signal to attack he recconnoitred our position Mr. Osburn who was with him says that he flew into a violent passion and swore vengeance against me and the corps I had brought with me."

He was uneasy, the marquis confessed, because he did not know what the public would think of his conduct. "The little dependance we put upon the militia I cannot expose in an official letter. I cannot say that no boats, no waggons, no intelligences, not one spy could be obtained." If Phillips had ever gained an advantage over him, "a defeat would have scattered the militia, lost the few arms we have and knocked down this handfull of Continental troops." Jefferson's government was still no help.

Washington had smartly maneuvered Lafayette into staying at his post, by hinting that he might see him in Virginia, and knowing that he would prefer a small command to none at all. "How happy I would be to see you I hope I need not to express," the young man gushed. "As you are pleased to give me the choice, I frankly shall tell my wishes. If you cooperate with the french against the place you know, I wish to be at head quarters. If some thing is cooperated in Virginia I wil find myself very happily situated." For the present, he would stay with his "separate and active command tho' it does not promise great glory." He admitted wistfully that he wished a French fleet would come into the bay. "Had I but ships my situation would be the most agreable in the world."[37]

Lafayette's situation was going to become more "agreable" than he could imagine. Greene welcomed him to Virginia with "a mixture of pain and pleasure." He gave him command of troops in the state, and authority to keep Wayne's Pennsylvanians in Virginia rather than send them on to the Carolinas. He added, "I have only one word of advice to give you (having entire confidence in your ability zeal and good conduct), that is not to let the love of fame get the better of your prudence and plunge you into a misfortune, in too eager a pursuit after glory. This is the voice of a friend, and not the caution of a general." Washington could not have put it better.[38]

IT IS NOT MY TONGUE THESE GENTLEMEN WILL CUT OFF

Washington knew that his young friend required constant reassurance. When he learned that Lafayette had resupplied his troops with his own credit, Washington said that it must entitle him to "all their gratitude & affection. . . . For my own part, my dear marquis, altho I stood in need of no new proofs of your exertions & sacrifices in the cause of America; I will confess to you, I shall not be able to express the pleasing sensations I have experienced at your unparallel'd & repeated instances of generosity & zeal for the service, on every occasion. Suffer me only to pursue you, with my sincerest wishes, that your successes & glory may always be equal to your merits."[39]

On May 1, Lafayette proclaimed victory in the battle that did not happen at Richmond, marched his men through the capital, and called on Jefferson to raise men, horses, wagons, and supplies. They had much in common, these skinny redheads with freckles. They talked in French and Latin, discussed philosophical matters, and got nowhere on having the state help fight the enemy. Lafayette had told his supply officers to impress horses and goods. Jefferson thought that kind of thing was tyrannical, but it did not mar their friendship.[40]

Lafayette knew that Virginia would do little to defend itself. He tried to change that by sending Steuben to lobby the legislature, the state's deputy quartermaster to buy or impress supplies, and Brigadier General George Weedon to recruit men for both the Continental Army and the militia. This exercise in frustration gave him an unsupported army of fewer than 1,000 men to face about 7,000 resupplied redcoats and

Hessians. When the state assembly lit out for Charlottesville at the middle of the month, with Jefferson in its wake, any hope for official cooperation vanished with it. Jefferson blamed the counties for not doing their part.[41]

As Phillips retired downriver, Lafayette shadowed him. When he learned that Cornwallis was on his way, he tried to beat the enemy to Petersburg, but he got there too late, lobbed a few cannonballs in Phillips' direction, and retired to the capital. "There is no fighting here unless you have a naval superiority or an army mounted upon race horses," he complained to Washington. "I am going to get beaten by both armies or each of them separately." He told La Luzerne that his situation was "a bit confining," with two British armies coming after him. "To complete the farce, I hear from all sides that General Clinton is coming to join the party. Thus I am proscribed by this triumvirate but, not being so eloquent as Cicero, it is not my tongue these gentlemen will cut off."[42]

Phillips died of a fever on May 13, leaving Arnold in command. The turncoat sent Lafayette a message requesting an exchange of prisoners; the marquis refused to answer it. Washington told him that his "conduct upon every occasion meets my approbation, but in none more than in your refusing to hold a correspondence with Arnold." When the enemy commander threatened to ship his prisoners to the West Indies, Lafayette reminded him that they could not arrange exchanges until Greene and Cornwallis set up a protocol. Arnold asked one of Lafayette's messengers, "What do you think the Americans would do with me if they should succeed in making me a prisoner?" That officer replied, "We should cut off the leg which was wounded in the country's service, and we should hang the rest of you."[43]

There were only two ways Lafayette could get out of his trap. One would be if Wayne arrived with his troops and supplies. The other would be for Washington to recall him. "I am not strong enough even to get beaten," he told his adoptive father. Until the Pennsylvanians arrived, "we are next to nothing" against so strong an enemy. Washington was too far away to help him, and still could not tell him why he was in Virginia. Worse, enemy reinforcements, about 2,000 men, had left New York for Virginia. "Your determination to avoid an engagement, with your present force, is certainly judicious," he reassured the young general. He hoped the Pennsylvanians had begun their march, but he had no news on that account. As for returning to New York, "it would be unnecessary for you to be here at present, and I am sure you would not wish to leave your charge while you are so near an enemy." He as much as said that the next main effort would aim at New York. That misled the British patrols he expected to intercept a copy of the letter; it also left Lafayette wondering what was afoot.[44]

The marquis sent frantic appeals to Wayne. "Should you arrive before Cornwallis," he told him, "I hope we may beat his army." If the Pennsylvanians force-marched the way he had made it to Richmond, the Americans might have a chance to keep Cornwallis from conquering Virginia. Lafayette complained to Washington that he had not heard from Wayne, and without reinforcement by the Pennsylvania troops he could not risk an engagement. Wayne was still at York, but finally he wrote, promising to march south on May 23.[45]

Mad Anthony had troubles aplenty. The men who had remained after the mutiny were in an uproar because they had not received their back pay, as promised. New troops were soon rebellious as well. They did not want to march south, because they believed that southern air was unhealthy for northerners, and had heard a yarn about Lafayette being warned that, with his thin hair, the Virginia sun could kill him. They mutinied, and Wayne had a dozen ringleaders shot. "The sight must have made an impression on the men," an officer observed; "it was designed with that view."

Wayne marched them out late in May but could not push them too hard, or they all might run off. Bad weather, muddy roads, and river crossings also held up progress, which was further delayed by too many hard-drinking officers who were hung over every morning. When they entered Virginia, they stepped up their griping. Wayne was on his way, but his brigade was not a bit happy about it.[46]

Lafayette had a mutiny of his own, among the militia of Hampshire County. He turned to his old friend Daniel Morgan, at home recuperating from illness. "I do very much want your assistance," he pleaded, because Morgan's influence could achieve more than orders from the governor. The Old Wagoner joined Lafayette in June, but he had as much trouble recruiting men as all others did in that state.[47]

On May 20, 1781, Cornwallis arrived in Petersburg and assumed command over Arnold. Lafayette pulled his tiny force of about 900

Continentals, with some reluctant militia, back into Richmond. The town was almost deserted, so he shipped its military stores upstream to Point of Fork, and put others on the road to Fredericksburg. If Cornwallis came after him, he would fade back, covering the stores. "For the love of God," the marquis pleaded with La Luzerne, "let me know what has become of the Pennsylvanians. . . . Their junction with us would make our little army a bit more respectable. We would be beaten but at least we would be decently beaten."[48]

Lafayette remained obsessed with his reputation. "If more is not known about our situation I fear I shall be judged severely, even unjustly," he wailed to Noailles. "I hope you will communicate what you know about [the situation] to our friends, so that if I am condemned, it will at least be only to the extent that I deserve it."[49]

The marquis told Greene that, "as I expect people . . . will find it very strange that I have not yet beaten the ennemy to pieces, my comfort will be in the approbation of the General, yours, and that of a few friends." He begged Hamilton to "write me if you approve of my conduct." He was so outnumbered that he had to suppress his own fighting instincts, he said.[50]

Nobody's approval meant more to Lafayette than his adoptive father's, and he begged for it again on May 24. "Had I followed the first impulsion of my temper, I would have risked some thing more—But I have been guarding against my own warmth." The fact that most of his manpower was unreliable militia meant that any engagement with the enemy would invite disaster. He would have risked attack only if the Pennsylvanians had joined him, but they had not. When Cornwallis marched upriver, Lafayette would be forced to abandon Richmond because he did not have enough men to defend it. "Was I any ways equal to the ennemy, I would be extremely happy in my present command—but I am not strong enough even to get beaten. Governement in this state [has] no energy, and laws have no force."[51]

The marquis received two replies from Washington. The first, after he had met with Rochambeau, told him that a campaign against New York "was deemed preferable to a southern operation as we had not the command of the water." He continued, "I shall advise you, every now and then of the progress of our preparations. It would be unnecessary for you to be here at present, and I am sure you would not wish to leave your charge while you are so near an enemy. . . . You will always remember my dear marquis that your return to this army depends upon your own choice." He let a copy of this letter fall into enemy hands.[52]

Then Washington sent Lafayette a secure letter, telling him that he would not attack New York. He had heard that Cornwallis' troops had marched themselves ragged on the way from the Carolinas, and he needed the marquis to hold the British general, but did not explain why. He told him to keep Cornwallis on the move but warned him not to hazard a general action unless he had "grounds to do it on. No *rational person* will condemn you for *not fighting* with the odds against you and while so much is depending on it. But all will censure a rash step if it is not attended with success."[53]

Washington could not have picked a better general for the risky operation in Virginia. Lafayette trusted Washington absolutely and followed his orders even when he did not know why they were put to him. Other generals, believing themselves exiled to a backwater, might have threatened to resign over the perceived insult to their pride, but the marquis would never do that to Washington.

Cornwallis crossed the river on May 26 and headed toward Richmond. The savage cavalryman Colonel Banastre Tarleton and 800 equally savage horse soldiers were in the van, looting, burning, killing, and raping. "I shall now proceed to dislodge La Fayette from Richmond," Cornwallis told Clinton when he set out, "and with my light troops destroy any magazines or stores in the neighbourhood." He was as obsessed with making a trophy of the marquis as Howe had been at Barren Hill. "The boy cannot escape me!" he crowed.[54]

THEY RETARDED AS MUCH AS POSSIBLE
THE ENEMY PROGRESS

*L*afayette led his 900 Continentals and about 2,000 militia north to Gold Mine Creek on the South Anna River. There he stood between Cornwallis and stores at Fredericksburg. Steuben with a few hundred militia and Continental recruits was northwest of Richmond at Point of Fork, where the Rivanna and Fluvanna join to form the James River. Lafayette begged Wayne to hurry, and told Steuben to move the stores from Point of Fork and head in his direction. Steuben, however, thought that Greene wanted him to go south to join up, because that was the last he had heard from him.[55]

When Lafayette evacuated Richmond, Virginians assumed that he had skedaddled, the way a timid man might leave a tavern just before a brawl. This made supply acquisition even more difficult. The militia mutiny in Hampshire had included attacks on supply officers, but Morgan put that down early in June. The most heartening development was the end of Jefferson's term as governor. He was replaced by General Thomas Nelson, who was more sympathetic to the need for the state to do its part, although responsibility for that rested with county lieutenants, and the state's coercive powers were nil.[56]

This was no skedaddle. Lafayette backed up while shielding Fredericksburg and Albemarle Old Court House, the two main supply depots. He also had to avoid a fight, because his militia would run away at the first shot, and Cornwallis outnumbered his Continentals by about six to one. He led the British on a grueling slog out of Richmond, burning bridges, felling trees across the roads, and sending small parties to snipe at the foe. He drew constant blood, wearing the enemy down. Early in June, however, he did not know just where Cornwallis was headed or what his intentions were. The redcoat commander wanted to take Virginia out of the war and struck out simultaneously at Charlottesville, Point of Fork, and Albemarle Old Court House.

The first blow fell on June 4, 1781. Tarleton made a long sweep to Cornwallis' left and descended on Charlottesville, aiming to capture the legislature. All but seven escaped him, and he sacked the town. He missed Jefferson, who had been warned. Redcoats helped themselves to souvenirs at Monticello, cleaning out the wine cellar.[57]

Next came Steuben's turn. He was isolated at Point of Fork, because British cavalry intercepted most communications. "No letters from General Greene or from you, my dear marquis, for six days," he complained on June 3. "I write everywhere, I send express messengers everywhere, but I get nothing. . . . It is as though I were in Kamchatka here." He did not know where either Lafayette or Cornwallis was. The baron still thought he was under orders to go to Greene when he had removed the stores from his post, because he had not received later orders canceling those instructions.[58]

On June 5, Lieutenant Colonel John Graves Simcoe approached Point of Fork with 100 cavalry and 300 infantry. Steuben sent the stores across the Fluvanna and lost only a thirty-man rear guard when the redcoats stormed in. Simcoe could not cross the river to chase him, because he lacked boats. Instead, he deployed his troops along the river and lit campfires to exaggerate his strength, and the baron concluded that this was the advance guard of the entire British army. The stores belonged to the state rather than to the Continental Army, so Steuben abandoned them to save his men from annihilation. He marched to Albemarle Old Court House, blocking Simcoe.[59]

At first, Lafayette was not too concerned about what had happened. Nothing had been lost "but what was left on the point," he told Steuben, and directed him to resume recruiting. But once the young man brooded on something he could work himself into a lather. He advised Washington, "The conduct of the Baron, my dear general, is to me unintelligible. Every man woman and child in Virginia is roused against him. They dispute even on his courage but I cannot believe their assertions." Lafayette thought Steuben had had enough troops to defend Point of Fork and the stores, but now both his militia and his Continental levies had deserted him. He also said that "every officer and soldier both in the regulars and militia are so much exasperated against the Baron and cover him with so many ridicules that after I have obtained a jonction with him I do not know where to employ him without giving offense."[60]

Steuben was the most unpopular officer in Virginia. He had been in the state since December, trying to raise men and matériel, but he lacked the political and diplomatic skills to succeed in the quarrelsome state. While his "goddams" echoed over the landscape, he alienated nearly everyone who should have supported him. It was not the state alone that carried the blame for his inability to raise men, arms, and supplies.[61]

Washington promised Lafayette that he would remove Steuben from "the quarter where he is so unpopular." But the marquis soon cooled off. His orders to the baron after Point of Fork were at first stiff, lacking the courtesies he had always paid him. Before long, he was sending him to round up men and supplies, had him in charge of training, and ended his orders with expressions of "sincere attachment." Steuben fell ill in early July and went on sick leave near Charlottesville. He was not too weak to get into a war with the state legislature, which investigated him for the loss of state property at Point of Fork. Lafayette defended him, and when Nelson presented formal charges, the marquis put him off.[62]

After Charlottesville and Point of Fork, Lafayette faced two highly mobile forces, Tarleton's and Simcoe's, on his right flank. He stepped up his "bush fighting," as it was called in Virginia, slowing Cornwallis down. He shifted westward, into the forested hills, off passable roads and onto narrow tracks. The hardwood forest, with islands of pines, contained a dense undergrowth that hampered the enemy cavalry.

It was a miserable campaign on both sides. Thorns and brambles tore the men's clothing, and poison ivy ruptured their skin. Chiggers, ticks, and mites feasted on American and redcoat alike, while stands of water hosted leeches and breathed out clouds of mosquitoes. The Americans backed up slowly, blocking every step of the way, riflemen sniping at the enemy. Tarleton lost track of Lafayette on June 13, telling Cornwallis, "I will immediately inform your Lordship if he does not keep a proper distance." Lafayette kept in touch, just not too closely. "The Americans retreated in such a manner," the marquis recalled, "that the front guard of the enemy arrived on the spot just as they quitted it, and . . . they retarded as much as possible the enemy progress."[63]

GOD GRANT THAT THE PUBLIC DOES NOT PAY FOR MY LESSONS

Wayne had finally connected with Lafayette on June 10, at the Rappahannock. On the fifteenth, Cornwallis cancelled the pursuit. Lafayette crowed to La Luzerne, "Lord Cornwallis seemed not to like this hilly terrain and withdrew toward Richmond. We make it seem we are pursuing him, and my riflemen, their faces smeared with charcoal, make the woods resound with their yells; I have made them an army of devils and have given them plenary absolution." The war was as much for public opinion as it was for the landscape, to deny Cornwallis' claims that the southern states belonged to Britain. To that end, "I try to let my movements give his the appearance of a retreat. Would to God there were a way to give him the appearance of a defeat."

Lafayette was so happy in Virginia that he was not sure he wanted to leave the state, even to attack New York. It was "so extraordinary," he gushed, "to command at my age anything honored by the name of an army that I shall remain in the South as long as I shall be opposed, as commander, to Lord Cornwallis." This was his way of repaying Washington for the confidence he had placed in him. Still thinking that the main scene of action would be New York, however, he planned to return to his adoptive father's side as soon as he had driven His Lordship out of Virginia.[64]

Cornwallis' army was footsore, ragged, demoralized by the sniping, and frustrated. Lafayette shadowed him to Richmond and onward when the redcoats left the capital on June 21, 1781, headed for Williamsburg. He advised Greene, "What Lord Cornwallis means I do not know but this retreat will not read well in newspaper. I follow and one would think I pursüe him." The fate of the southern states, the marquis believed, depended on the preservation of his own army. Accordingly, "I had rather loose some share of glory than to risk a defeat by which Virginia would be lost."[65]

Now that Lafayette appeared victorious, volunteers flocked to him, adding about 3,000 militia to his over 1,500 Continentals. Governor Nelson placed himself under the marquis' command at the head of the state troops, and Lafayette called him "the best that the state of Virginia could choose." He fired off a stream of orders to Wayne and Steuben to push on after Cornwallis, until late on the twenty-second Wayne protested that his men were worn out after covering twenty-two miles that day. The Pennsylvanians beat up Simcoe on the Chickahominy, keeping him from destroying stores and rounding up cattle; casualties were 160 British and 37 American. Wayne had "the best ground to believe that the [lads?] do not like our night manoeuvres," he told Lafayette.[66]

While Lafayette enjoyed himself in the fields and woodlots on the Virginia Peninsula, his adoptive father fretted because he had not heard from him lately. At the end of June he told his young friend that Rochambeau's army was approaching his, which he had moved to Peekskill to be nearer New York. "Be assured my dear marquis," he said, "that my anxiety to hear from you is increased by my sincere regard for you and by the interest I take in every thing which concerns you."[67]

News from Lafayette was already on its way. "The ennemy have been so kind as to retire before us," he said with a snicker. Twice Cornwallis had avoided a fight, bent on continuing his retreat. "Our numbers are I think exaggerated to them, and our seeming boldness confirms the opinion." He thought Cornwallis had about 4,000 men (the real figure was nearer 7,000), 800 of them mounted, and had just received 600 reinforcements, while the American side numbered about 4,000, mostly militia, only 1,500 regulars and 50 dragoons. Having driven the enemy about 100 miles, Lafayette claimed victory, because "His Lordship did us no harm of any consequence, lost an immense part of his former conquests and did not make any in this state." He thought it all would make a great impression on world opinion, unless Cornwallis turned on him.[68]

The redcoats occupied Williamsburg on June 25, and rested there. Lafayette closed up on the place two days later. He told Wayne to lighten his baggage to allow a quick move against any attempt by the enemy to board ship, although he did not think that likely. With harvest approaching, he was losing his militia. "Many and many men are daily deserting," he complained to Nelson. On July 4, 1781, the marquis informed Greene that he had fulfilled his orders. He had been told to hold his ground in Virginia, he reminded him. He not only had done that but had recovered all of the state except what was guarded by the guns of the Royal Navy. "We never encamp in a body, and our numbers are much exagerated." He had learned a lot since Barren Hill. Whenever Cornwallis sent troops to make a jab at the Americans, "a detachement marches against them and they generally retire. Children sing when they are affraïd."

Cornwallis had left Williamsburg, headed for Jamestown. Spy reports said he would send two regiments to New York and camp the rest at Portsmouth, across Hampton Roads. If the troops shipping out headed south, Lafayette promised Greene whatever aid he could give.[69]

Then the boy general pushed his luck, almost too far, when he marched out to follow Cornwallis, with Wayne and 500 men in the van. On July 6, 1781, Lafayette thought he might catch Cornwallis astride the James River, only partly embarked for Portsmouth. He caught up with Wayne early in the afternoon and received contradictory reports about whether most of the enemy or only a rear guard remained ashore. He ordered up the rest of the Continentals. While waiting for them to arrive, Wayne skirmished with Tarleton's outposts, his riflemen doing considerable damage. They were on the main road between Williamsburg and Jamestown, and Wayne did not realize that Cornwallis was drawing him into a trap. About a mile down the road, hidden behind some woods, was almost his entire army.

The reinforcements reached Green Spring Plantation at about five o'clock and would have to cross about 400 yards of marshy ground to join Wayne. Wayne still thought he faced only a rear guard, but Lafayette suspected that things were not as they appeared. He led three battalions and three guns across the swamp, keeping the rest in reserve at Green Spring. Wayne now had 900 men and deployed them for an attack. The marquis rode around his right to see, if he could, whether the main body of redcoats was still on the near side of the river. He saw them and rushed back to stop Wayne from getting drawn into a general engagement.

He was too late, and so was Cornwallis, who could have attacked earlier but waited until he had enough of Lafayette's corps in hand to make his blow decisive. Wayne sent a detachment to the left to capture an enemy gun, but it was repulsed and fell back. The noise persuaded His Lordship that Lafayette's main body was on the scene. He sprung his trap.

Wayne, seeing a tidal wave of redcoats about to sweep over him, faced what he later called "a choice of difficulties." If he retreated, it could turn into a panic. If he made a stand, his men would be slaughtered, because the enemy line overlapped both his flanks. That left just one thing to do. Mad Anthony charged with bayonets, storming straight at the enemy through a hail of grapeshot and musket fire. His troops made it to within seventy yards of the British line, stunning the redcoats. Lafayette galloped into the middle of the fight to salvage a situation he had failed to prevent. The marquis' horse was gutted by a cannonball, but the two generals steadied the line and conducted an orderly withdrawal.

As the Americans returned to Green Spring, they looked back and saw the smoke still hanging over the field, choking the British, who were swatting at swarms of insects and wondering what had happened to them. Cornwallis had underestimated "the boy" again. But it had been costly for both of them. Of his 900 men, Wayne lost twenty-eight killed, ninety-nine wounded, and twelve missing, along with two guns. The enemy lost seventy-five killed and wounded out of 7,000. It was too late to pursue Lafayette, so that was the end of the action.[70]

It had been what British generals called "a near-run thing." Lafayette issued a general order the next day giving entire credit to Wayne and his men for their spirited engagement. He sent an effusive report in the same line to Greene, with copies to the newspapers. Despite grumbling from Virginians that he had almost thrown away the whole campaign, Lafayette emerged as the greater hero.[71]

Green Spring was just an incident in an otherwise brilliant campaign, an amazing performance for a twenty-three-year-old. Lafayette had justified Washington's faith that he could handle an isolated command. Greene also felt vindicated in trusting him. Lafayette was celebrated on two con-

Charles, Earl of Cornwallis. He was the only man who ever inspired fear in Lafayette, who outfoxed him in Virginia. (AUTHOR'S COLLECTION)

tinents as the young hero who had run Cornwallis out of Virginia, although that was an exaggeration. Greene deserved credit for his strategic genius farther south, where he kept other British forces from combining with Cornwallis. Cornwallis and Clinton together contributed to the young general's triumph, the first by his contempt for "the boy." Clinton had opposed Cornwallis' Virginia campaign from the beginning, then bombarded him with contradictory orders to advance, withdraw, send men to New York or elsewhere, or expect reinforcements.

Whoever deserves partial credit, the whole thing would not have happened without Lafayette's persistence, boldness, imagination, and enthusiastic leadership. Rochambeau's chaplain said that for Americans the Virginia Campaign made the title "marquis" a "beloved symbol which rouses their admiration and gratitude."[72]

Lafayette sent Wayne across the river to keep an eye on Cornwallis in Portsmouth and pulled the rest of his army back to Malvern Hill, where he could cover all roads. Then he reported to Washington. "Agreably to your orders I have avoided a general action," he said slyly, "and when Lord Cornwallis's movements indicated it was against his interest to fight I have ventured partial engagements. His Lordship seems to have given up the conquest of Virginia." He was proud of himself and hoped his adoptive father also would be proud of him.[73]

Still, he had just had a close call. "This devil Cornwallis is much wiser than the other generals with whom I have dealt," he confessed to Noailles. "He inspires me with a sincere fear, and his name has greatly troubled my sleep. This campaign is a good school for me. God grant that the public does not pay for my lessons."[74]

TWELVE

The Fifth Act Has Just Ended

(JULY-DECEMBER 1781)

> *I see another snarl of men,*
> *A digging graves they told me,*
> *So tarnal long, so tarnal deep,*
> *They 'tended they should hold me.*
> *Yankey doodle keep it up,*
> *Yankey doodle dandy,*
> *Mind the music and the step,*
> *And with the girls be handy.*
>
> —EDWARD BANGS

As Cornwallis settled into Portsmouth, Lafayette heard from Vergennes. The French government was arranging a loan in Holland for 10 million livres, he said. Since the United States had no credit, King Louis had agreed to stand as the principal borrower. "I beg you not to let General Washington be unaware of that point." Louis' government could not afford any more grants or loans. "France is not inexhaustible," the foreign minister pointed out. He thought the Americans could be doing more to help themselves.[1]

Franklin said more positively that he thought "it was a wise measure to send Col Laurens" to France. His mission had been successful, although both would like to have wrung more money out of the French government. The Doctor agreed with Vergennes, however. "This court . . . does every thing it can for us," he observed. "Can we not do a little more for ourselves?"[2]

The most interesting news came from the marquis de Castries, the new minister of marine. He had advised Laurens that there would be a sizable French fleet in American waters later in the summer, but withheld details. He told Lafayette something that neither Washington nor Laurens knew—de Grasse's West Indies fleet was ordered to the Chesapeake. "If with such powerful assistance we maintain for a few months the naval superiority you desire," the minister pleaded, "we shall have no reproach to fear from you."

Although Laurens had not obtained everything he requested, he should be satisfied, Castries suggested, because he was going home with 20 million livres' worth of silver money and merchandise. This, the minister hinted, was more a result of Lafayette's incessant pleadings than of Laurens' mission.[3]

YOU WILL THEREFORE NOT REGRET
YOUR STAY IN VIRGINIA

Rochambeau also learned that de Grasse was under orders to sail north from the West Indies later in the summer, with a powerful fleet, a pile of hard money, and hundreds of troops. He did not tell Washington about that, but advised that they ought to get together. They met in Hartford, Connecticut, on May 21, 1781, then rode five miles south to Wethersfield, where they conferred the next day. It was a lovely place. One French officer said that "it would be impossible to find prettier houses and a more beautiful view."[4]

The generals circled each other like wary boxers. With the latest French naval commander, the marquis de Barras, unwilling to ferry troops to the Chesapeake, Washington focused on New York. Either the place would be conquered or the British would reinforce it with troops from the South, taking the pressure off Greene and Lafayette. Rochambeau agreed, or so it appeared. But if he left Newport, he asked, what would protect the fleet there, or the bulk stores at Providence? Washington replied that militia could guard the stores, and Barras could relocate to Boston. Rochambeau posed a hypothetical question: what if a

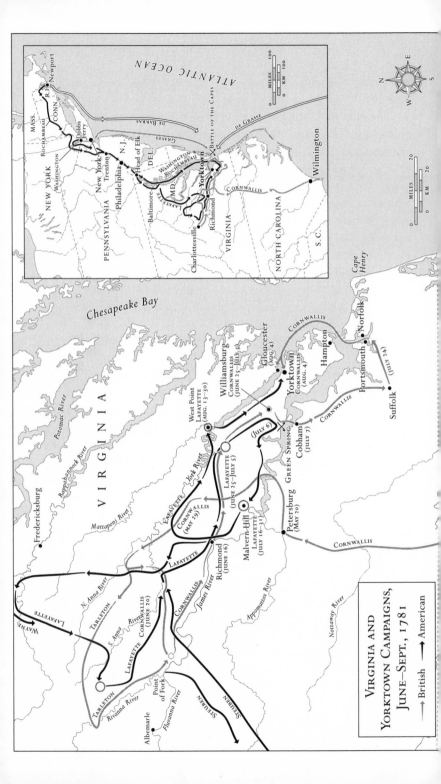

VIRGINIA AND YORKTOWN CAMPAIGNS, JUNE–SEPT., 1781

→ British → American

Inset map

ATLANTIC OCEAN

MASS.
CONN. R.
Newport
ROCHAMBEAU
NEW YORK
Washington
N.J.
New York
Trenton
Philadelphia
PENNSYLVANIA
Dobbs Ferry
Head of Elk
DEL.
Baltimore
MD.
WASHINGTON & ROCHAMBEAU
LAFAYETTE
Richmond
Charlottesville
VIRGINIA
Yorktown
DE BARRAS
GRAVES
Battle of the Capes
DE GRASSE
Cornwallis
Wilmington
NORTH CAROLINA
S. C.

MILES 100
KM 100

Main map

Chesapeake Bay

Cape Henry

Potomac River
Rappahannock River
VIRGINIA
Fredericksburg
Mattaponi River
N. Anna River
S. Anna River
York River
West Point
LAFAYETTE (AUG. 13–30)
Williamsburg
CORNWALLIS (JUNE 25–July 9)
LAFAYETTE (JUNE 25–July 5)
Gloucester (AUG. 4)
Yorktown CORNWALLIS (AUG. 4)
CORNWALLIS
Hampton
Norfolk
Portsmouth (JULY 14)
Suffolk
(July 6)
Green Spring
Cobham (JULY 7)
LAFAYETTE
CORNWALLIS (MAY 29)
Richmond (JUNE 16)
Malvern-Hill LAFAYETTE (JULY 16–31)
Petersburg (MAY 20)
CORNWALLIS
James River
Appomattox River
Nottaway River
TARLETON
LAFAYETTE
CORNWALLIS (JUNE 20)
LAFAYETTE
WAYNE
TARLETON
Point of Fork
Rivanna River
Fluvanna River
STEUBEN
Albemarle
MILES 20
KM 20

N W S E

superior French naval force became available on the American coast? Washington replied that it could help attack New York, or it might "be directed against the enemy in some other quarter as circumstances shall dictate." His mind was open, but Rochambeau thought he had a fixation on New York.

They compromised on the "Wethersfield Plan." The French army would march on New York, hoping to draw British troops from the South. The generals also agreed to write to de Grasse, urging him to sail north. On June 3, Clinton received an intercepted copy of the plan, which put him in a quandary. If the plan was real, he would have to withdraw troops from Cornwallis' army. If it was a deception, he could reinforce Cornwallis.[5]

Rochambeau began leaving Newport on June 9, content that New York was at least on the way to the South. On June 11 he appealed to de Grasse, because naval superiority was essential in either region. "I must not conceal from you, sir," he advised, "that these people are at the end of their means." De Grasse promised to help. By mid-August he would send twenty-nine warships, 3,000 soldiers including artillerymen and dragoons, ten cannons, siege guns, and mortars, and 1.2 million livres in silver.[6]

Washington sent Lafayette's former chief spy, Captain Allan McLane, to the Caribbean to find de Grasse. Rochambeau might think he was obsessed with New York, but in fact he had already considered moving south. McLane told the French admiral that he "could make it easy for Genl Washington to reduce the British army in the South" if he took his fleet and army to the Chesapeake. De Grasse agreed to sail north as soon as he could.[7]

Washington did not wait for Rochambeau; the French were slow, owing to a heat wave. By the time the lead elements of the French army arrived on June 21, he had pressed the Main Army in closer to Clinton's works. The whole allied force was together by July 6, 1781, and the French staged a grand review to honor the Americans, their white uniforms dazzling.[8]

"I admire the Americans tremendously!" said one of Rochambeau's aides. "It is incredible that soldiers composed of men of every age, even of children of fifteen, or whites and blacks, almost naked, unpaid, and rather poorly fed, can march so well and withstand fire so steadfastly." He credited that to "the calm and calculated measures of General Washington."[9]

Washington and Rochambeau agreed that an attack on New York would require siege operations, and they lacked the equipment and other resources for that. Without naval superiority, they could do nothing else, either. Washington gave up before he learned that Clinton had ordered Cornwallis to send troops to the city. On August 1, Washington wrote in his diary that with no hope of a move against New York, "I turned my views more seriously than I had before done to an operation to the southward." On August 14, he learned that de Grasse had sailed from Saint-Domingue (now Haiti), expected to reach the Chesapeake by September 3, and could stay until the middle of October. Washington began a march of 450 miles to where Lafayette awaited him. Masked by a covering force and phony camps, on August 20 the first troops crossed the river at Kings Ferry, and the last were over by the twenty-fifth. Clinton had no idea they were gone.[10]

Washington had been thinking about moving south for longer than he admitted. On July 13 he had told Lafayette that he would "shortly have occasion to communicate matters of very great importance" to the marquis. In the meantime, Lafayette should recruit a larger army and develop a cavalry force. Both were essential if the war continued in Virginia or shifted to South Carolina. Lafayette should send spies to the coast to detect if Cornwallis shipped any troops out. It was "more than probable" that if the British commander found it impossible to conquer Virginia, he would entrench at Portsmouth or Williamsburg and reinforce New York or South Carolina.[11]

Lafayette wanted to return to his adoptive father. "In a word, my dear general," he wailed on the twentieth, "I am home sick and if I can't go to head quarters wish at least to hear from there." As for the situation in front of him, Cornwallis, his spies told him, was "much disappointed in his hopes of command" over all British troops in America. The marquis hoped his adversary would go home to England. He was "a bold and active man, two dangerous qualities in this southern war."[12]

The young general enclosed a personal note, saying, "Certain I am you will do whatever you can for me that is consistent with your public duty. When I went to the southward you know I had some private objections." But when his troops became rebellious, he knew there was no one else who could get them to go to Virginia. Now, if Cornwallis sent troops to New York, the war in Virginia would become nothing more than minor skirmishing. "Would it be possible, my dear general, that in case a part of the British troops go to Newyork I may be allowed to join the combined armies[?]" He was not alone in thinking that New York was the next target. His spies advised him that Cornwallis assumed the marquis would return to the Main Army. "This induces me to think they believe you are in earnest in your preparations."[13]

Lafayette wrote yet a third letter the same day, July 20. His men had captured one of Tarleton's officers, who said that Cornwallis and Tarleton were definitely going to New York. He wanted to join Washington in any capacity, because "at all events, I would be with you, and of course would be very happy."[14]

On the twenty-sixth he reported that about 2,000 British troops were embarking at Portsmouth. There were rumors that Cornwallis was leaving with them, although he doubted that. They also had pilots aboard, so he sent spies out to watch all waterways in the Chesapeake area and tell him where they put ashore, if they did.[15]

Lafayette reported on July 30 that thirty transports full of troops were in Hampton Roads. "This state is so difficult to be defended that one false step involves the one that does not command the water into a series of inconveniences," he said. Cornwallis had taken on pilots for the Potomac River. "This, I suppose, is a feint, but a march south of James River throws me out of supporting distance for any thing that is north of it. A march to the north gives the ennemy command over everything south of the river."[16]

The next day one of the marquis' spies, a servant to Cornwallis, said that His Lordship, Tarleton, and Simcoe were still in Portsmouth but expected to move soon. Lafayette had sent Wayne toward Portsmouth to keep an eye on them. Should a French fleet enter Hampton Roads, he hinted, "the British army would, I think, be ours. I am litterally following Your Excellency's instructions, and shall continue to do so to the best of my power." Reflecting the unavoidable vagaries of military intelligence, on August 1 the young general said that he had received a report that the enemy fleet had sailed and was headed to Baltimore.[17]

Lafayette, in his confusion about the intentions of both Washington and Cornwallis, did not realize that his continual reporting on the situation in Virginia was of enormous value to the commander in chief, planning as he was to move the main effort to the South. To resolve part of his uncertainties, Washington sent him a private letter. The general could not tell his young friend that he was not relegated to a sideshow but was standing in what would soon become the next main theater of the war. He dropped a hint by way of some fatherly advice. "I am convinced," he said, "that your desire to be with this army arises principally from a wish to be actively useful. You will not therefore regret your stay in Virginia untill matters are reduced to a greater degree of certainty than they are at present, especially when I tell you, that" if part of the enemy's force did move from Virginia to New York, "it is more than probable that we shall also intirely change our plan of operations."

If Lafayette's information was correct, Washington said, the first part of the Wethersfield Plan had been accomplished, by forcing some of the enemy to withdraw from the South. American efforts "must now be turned towards endeavouring to expell them totally from those states if we find ourselves incompt. to the siege of N. Y." Then he delivered the clincher, to stop the boy general's pleas to return north. "Should your return to this army be finally determined," he warned him, "I cannot flatter you with a command equal to your expectations or my wishes," because there were too many generals for the number of troops in the army. He closed, "I however hope I have spoken plain enough to be understood by you."[18]

Once again Washington kept Lafayette on the job, hinting of great things to come in Virginia while suggesting that he would get no command in the Main Army. The situation had become critical. He had put the shift to the South in motion, and he expected much from the marquis. Still he could not tell him what was going on, so he placed his trust in the young man's absolute loyalty.

I HEARTLY THANK YOU FOR HAVING ORDERED ME TO REMAIN IN VIRGINIA

*L*afayette had had his hands full since Green Spring. There were three main challenges. One was to figure out what Cornwallis was going to do and where he was going to do it. The second was to get more help from the state. The third was negotiations under the protocol for feeding and exchanging prisoners.

Cornwallis' intentions remained undecipherable for some time. Lafayette assumed until the end of July that he planned to march into North Carolina. He promised Greene that he would send whatever assistance he could if that happened, and leaned on Governor Nelson to get the state to help out.

On July 9, Tarleton rode out of Suffolk, near Portsmouth, with orders to destroy American stores all the way to New London, 150 miles to the west. Lafayette at first interpreted this as cover for a larger move to North Carolina but soon decided he had been mistaken and fanned his troops out to cut off the raiders. Tarleton covered thirty to forty miles a day, despite the July heat. Since he outran all news of his location, he was never in danger. The raiders galloped through Petersburg, Amelia Court House, Prince Edward Court House, Charlotte, and New London to Bedford. There they camped for two days at the foot of the Blue Ridge Mountains, and rustled some of the finest horses in America. The militia was incompetent, even to stop the theft of horses that Virginians had refused to sell to the American army. Lafayette sent Wayne and his Pennsylvanians into Amelia County to intercept Tarleton's return. He posted Morgan with a strong detachment at Goode's Bridge, near Petersburg. Tarleton got word of the threat and returned by a more southerly route. He was back in Suffolk on July 24, his men and horses winded. He had outfoxed Lafayette, but it had hardly been worth it. The few stores destroyed did not compensate for his losses from the heat.[19]

Cornwallis finally made his plans clear in an unexpected way. When his transports left Portsmouth and sailed into Chesapeake Bay, Lafayette thought they were headed for Baltimore. On August 6, 1781, he learned that the fleet had turned into the York River, landing troops at Yorktown on the south bank and at Gloucester on the north. Clinton's oft-changing orders sent Benedict Arnold and part of the force to New York, leaving the rest to fortify a seaport on the York.[20]

Cooperation from Virginia was better under Nelson than it had been under Jefferson, but it produced more sympathy than real support. Lafayette repeatedly told the governor that if Cornwallis decided to march into the state, the shortages were so severe that he could have free run of the country.

The most serious shortage was of horses. Lafayette would never have cavalry to match Tarleton's, but he wanted enough horses to put a decent number of scouts out. Tarleton's raid caused the state assembly to grant Lafayette authority to impress 300 horses. Then it demanded a mountain of paperwork to document all impressments, account for arms in each county that had been plundered by the militia, and investigate the "misapplication" of horses previously furnished by the state. Legislative investigations accused Wayne of looting.

Tarleton's seizure of horses that the owners had refused to sell left Lafayette fuming. There had been a time when "private virtue and private exertions might have prevented the ennemy's getting such a large and excellent body of cavalry," he complained to the governor. That time was no more, "and unless public exertions give us an equality we are utterly ruined." This got him a few nags but little else. Even after Cornwallis returned to the Peninsula, Nelson mostly complained about Wayne's seizures of supplies.[21]

Lafayette found Cornwallis easier to get along with than Virginia officials. "I am going to send a flag to Lord Cornwallis," he told Washington. "I owe him the justice to say that his conduct to me has been peculiarly polite, and many differences between commissaries [of prisoner exchanges] very graciously adjusted by him to my satisfaction."[22]

The marquis did not believe that Cornwallis would stay at Yorktown, telling Washington on August 6 that he thought His Lordship planned to go to New York. Nevertheless, he advanced his troops carefully to watch the enemy, and his spies kept him well-informed. Yorktown was surrounded by the river "and a morass," he told Washington. Gloucester was a neck of land projecting into the river opposite Yorktown. A few British frigates and transports sat at anchor between the two locations. "Should a flet come in at this moment our affairs would take a very happy turn."[23]

On August 11, having heard from Washington, Lafayette replied, "Be sure, my dear General, that the pleasure of being with you will make me happy in any command you will think proper to give." He agreed that he should remain in Virginia so long as Cornwallis did, "and circumstances may happen that will furnish me agreable opportunities in the command of the Virginian army." His adoptive father had talked him into staying where he was.

"I have pretty well understood you, my dear general," Lafayette continued, "but would be happy in a more minuted detaïl which I am sensible cannot be intrusted to letters." Cornwallis had begun entrenching at York and Gloucester. "The sooner we disturb him the better," the marquis suggested, but that was impossible without French naval support. When Washington read that he was delighted, because it meant that Cornwallis was digging himself into a hole. But not all was happy in Virginia, Lafayette told him, because of the state's incessant complaints about Wayne's foraging. "The Pennsylvanians and Virginians have never agreed but at the present time, it is worse than ever," he said. Wayne "thinks he and his people have not been well used."[24]

Another issue troubling Lafayette personally was what to do with slaves captured from the British. Nelson's secretary declared that the governor had directed that all slaves taken from the enemy must be returned to their former owners. "The principle on which it is supposed men fight," he explained, "at present is to protect and secure to themselves and fellow citizens their liberties and property." Most of Lafayette's spies were black, risking their necks for American liberty, and he was outraged that an object of the war was to return them to slavery. Nelson opened a wound in his conscience that never healed.[25]

Above all else, Cornwallis scared the marquis. "I would rather be rid of Lord Cornwallis than of a third of his army," he told La Luzerne. "He showers me with courtesies, and we wage war like gentlemen. . . . But after all this, in the end he will give me a thrashing." He admitted to Henry Knox, "To speak plain English I am devilish afraïd of him." He advised the prince de Poix, "If you knew Lord Cornwallis your concern would be even greater, but not greater than my own. . . . [I]t is Lord Cornwallis who is charged with the Britannic thunder."[26]

Face Cornwallis he must. Letting Lafayette know that de Grasse had sailed for the Chesapeake, and hinting (but not saying) that the allied armies were on the march, Washington ordered Lafayette to take a position where he could prevent a British retreat into North Carolina, which he predicted they would try once they realized what overwhelming force was bearing down on them. Then he said, "You shall hear further from me as soon as I have concerted plans and formed dispositions for sending a reinforcement from hence. In the mean time I have only to recommend a continuation of that prudence and good conduct which you have manifested thro' the whole of your campaign." He especially wanted Lafayette to conceal de Grasse's arrival in the hopes of catching the enemy aboard transports, "which will be the luckiest circumstance in the world. You will take measures for opening a communication with Count de Grasse the moment he arrives, and will concert measures with him for making the best uses of your joint forces untill you receive aid from this quarter."[27]

Lafayette sent Colonel Josiah Parker on a reconnaissance in force toward Portsmouth. His troops had some minor skirmishes with the enemy and took a few prisoners, but the outer works had been abandoned. The British soldiers were aboard ships in the harbor, along with some Tories. Contrary winds kept them from sailing, but they dared not return to land, because there was smallpox ashore. Parker retrieved twenty-five cannons that had been thrown into the river.[28]

The marquis ordered Wayne to start marching down the James River and told him the good news, that there was "great reason to hope for an immediate aid by water." He ordered the Pennsylvanians to take up "an healthy position" to block the route to North Carolina. He sent an officer to round up pilots for de Grasse. He had moved to Williamsburg with the main part of his army and sent troops across the York to threaten Gloucester.[29]

Lafayette had meanwhile told Washington that the British were fortifying Gloucester but not doing much at Yorktown. If they intended to evacuate, he observed, "at least they are proceeding with amazing slowness." He knew now to expect some sort of reinforcement from the north and said that he hoped the commander in chief himself would arrive at the head of the combined American and French armies. He would like to attack Cornwallis, but he could not do that without "great apparatus." On the other hand, when a French fleet controlled the bay and rivers and the allied land force became superior to Cornwallis', "that army must soon or late be forced to surrender." He closed, "Adieu, my dear general, I heartily thank you for having ordered me to remain in Virginia and to your goodness to me I am owing the most beautifull prospect I may ever behold."[30]

The troops headed south were in motion, Washington told him. "Our march will be continued with all the dispatch that our circumstances will admit." Lafayette could not have missed those first-person pronouns, although Washington remained vague. Again he emphasized how important it was for the marquis to keep the redcoats from escaping the trap closing on them. "The particular mode of doing this, I shall not at this distance attempt to dictate."

That was an amazing grant of freedom to so young an officer, but Washington knew he could handle it. Lafayette's "own knowledge of the country from your long continuance in it, & the various & extended movements which you have made—have given you great opportunity for observation; of which I am perswaded your military genius & judgment, will lead you to make the best improvement." Lafayette always wanted Washington's approval. There could be no doubt that he had it.[31]

The British had slowed down their fortification work at Gloucester, the marquis reported on August 24, 1781, and still had not started much at Yorktown. They did not "appear very much alarmed," he said. His skills as a spymaster were as sharp as ever. "I have got some intelligences by the way of this servant I have once mentioned," he reported the next day. The man told him that the British had finally begun fortifying Yorktown. The enemy was working mostly on the river side, but he had no doubt that they would do something on the land side. The works at Gloucester were finished, "some trifling redoubts across Gloster neck and a battery of 18 pieces beating the river." He estimated Cornwallis' strength at 4,500 men fit for duty.[32]

The "servant" was a slave named James Armistead. The marquis had first hired him in March, after he had already been hired by the British, and he became a double agent, feeding false information to the enemy. He also ran messages between Lafayette and other spies in Portsmouth, where he served in Cornwallis' household and kept his ears open. He moved to the Peninsula with his employer and walked in and out of Yorktown freely. He was the marquis' best source of information, and when the campaign was over Lafayette tried to have him freed. Rebuffed, he never forgot his debt to James.[33]

Washington wrote from Philadelphia on August 27, promising to forward supplies. He expected the reinforcements to reach Head of Elk soon. The speed of their further movement south depended on the arrival of de Grasse and whatever transportation he could furnish. Barras had been no help.[34]

Lafayette's corps was too weak to attack Yorktown, and probably to stand up against a sally out of the town, but Cornwallis again exaggerated

American strength. Tarleton had a better estimate and urged an attack. His Lordship, however, had received a message from Clinton promising relief. He let his men continue digging their earthworks and sat in Yorktown like a bug in a bottle. Then Admiral de Grasse showed up.[35]

Lafayette received a message on August 30, announcing the fleet's arrival in Chesapeake Bay. The admiral promised to send three frigates up the James to keep Cornwallis from crossing over. Those ships would also cover a landing of 3,250 men under the marquis de Saint-Simon, on Jamestown Island. Other frigates would close the York. To help destroy Cornwallis' army, de Grasse said, he could also land 1,800 marines and,

François-Joseph-Paul, comte de Grasse, commander of the French West Indies fleet. His arrival in the Chesapeake sealed Cornwallis' fate at Yorktown. (Skillman Library, Lafayette College)

if need be, companies of armed sailors. He hoped that "all this," he told the marquis, "will contribute to sustaining your glory and will enable you to spend a more peaceful winter."

Lafayette had been in the Virginia wilderness for so long, facing a superior enemy, that this was wonderful news. But it was premature, because an attack on Yorktown would require heavy guns and equipment, and more men. Besides, he wanted Washington to command it.

Saint-Simon was a *maréchal de camp,* de Grasse advised him, "and will serve under you as commander of an auxiliary troop. I flatter myself, sir, that you will not feel any repugnance toward this arrangement, as I was obliged to bring him." The troops with him were under his orders in Saint-Domingue and "were at the disposition of the Spanish, who were willing to lend them to me in view of the critical position in which the Americans appeared to be." The *maréchal* was agreeable enough. "I shall thus confine myself, M. le Marquis," Saint-Simon told Lafayette, "to expressing to you how pleased I shall be to serve with you and to be able to cultivate your friendship and contribute to the glory and success of the American arms." For the first time, Lafayette commanded a combined French-American force.[36]

The marquis told Wayne the good news. Cornwallis, he said, must either accept a siege or try to cross the James River that night. "Now that you are over I am pretty easy." Winds permitting, the frigates would close off that escape route. The following morning, Wayne watched the French ships enter the river and start the landings. Never did he behold "a more beautiful and agreeable sight," he said. He rowed across to get a closer look, and an American picket challenged him. Although he gave "the usual answer," the man put a musket ball through his thigh. He had his wound patched and "took a walk to take a view of the French troops, who make a very fine soldierly appearance."[37]

Cornwallis heard about the French frigates and was not worried. Clinton had promised to send him help with Admiral Thomas Graves. Still, he wondered, where was Graves?

Lafayette looked over the same scene and felt proud of himself. He had trapped the dreaded Earl of Cornwallis. Still, he wondered, where was Washington?

MAY THAT GREAT FELICITY
BE RESERVED FOR YOU!

*T*he allied armies reached Head of Elk on September 6, 1781. Washington could do little but fret until he heard that de Grasse was in the lower bay and Barras got through with the siege equipment and provisions. This was the commander in chief's greatest gamble. He was moving over 10,000 troops southward on wretched roads, not knowing if water transport would arrive to shorten the march. One French fleet was sailing north from the West Indies; another would sail south, past New York. British fleets could take after either French one. The whole complicated campaign had to come together on the Virginia Peninsula, where everything depended on an excitable young general's ability to keep Cornwallis in Yorktown.

Lafayette sent Washington two messages on September 1, reporting de Grasse's arrival and relaying the arguments they had been having. The admiral wanted to conquer Yorktown and sail back to the West Indies, while the marquis resisted hasty action because it would waste lives. Still, he was ecstatic. Thanks to Washington, he was "in a very charming situation and find myself at the head of a beautiful body of troops."[38]

Washington warned Lafayette that Graves' fleet had been reported heading for the Chesapeake, and he should alert de Grasse. He should also tell him that the allied armies were approaching as fast as they could. "Nothing, my dear marquis," he assured him, "could have afforded me greater satisfaction than . . . the measures you had taken and the arrangements you were making in consequence of the intelligence I had given you." He still thought he had to steady the boy general. They should hope for the best, he said. "Should the retreat of Lord Cornwallis by water, be cut off . . . I am persuaded you will do all in your power to prevent his escape by land. May that great felicity be reserved for you! You see, how critically important the present moment is. . . . Adieu my dear marquis!"[39]

A few days later Washington learned that de Grasse had arrived. He also had "an additional pleasure in finding that your ideas on every occasion have been so consonant to my own, and that by your military dispositions & prudent measures have anticipated all my wishes." Using the few transports he found at Head of Elk, he expected to board some troops and ship out on the eighth.[40]

Lafayette wrote twice on September 8 with a proposal. Knowing that Benjamin Lincoln—exchanged from his captivity at Charleston—would as senior major general receive command of the American part of the allied armies, Lafayette asked that the division he would command under Lincoln include his veterans of the Virginia Campaign. "This will be the greatest reward of the services I may have rendered, as I confess I have the strongest attachement to those troops."

The supply situation was still a mess. The governor did what he could, Lafayette admitted. "The wheels of his government are so very rusty that no governor whatever will be able to set them fiercely agoing." There were no provisions for the French troops, and he had been "night and day so much the quarter master collector and beef driver I have drove myself into a violent headake and feaver." He had failed to persuade de Grasse to move ships up the York River above Yorktown and Gloucester. And while the marquis continued to gather intelligence about Yorktown, he still believed his force was too weak to attack the place. His manpower had grown large enough, however, to stop Cornwallis if the redcoats tried to break out. Finally, de Grasse had sailed out when he learned that a British fleet was approaching the bay entrance. Lafayette had heard that there had been a battle, but nothing more.[41]

Graves left New York on August 31, and de Grasse went out to meet him. They collided on September 5, 1781, in the Second Battle off the Virginia Capes. The French did not win a clean victory, but they beat the British up, keeping them busy enough for Barras to slip into Chesapeake Bay on September 10. Washington had started some of his troops down the bay and marched the others to Baltimore and Annapolis, where Barras gave them a ride. Graves limped back to New York on the fourteenth, and de Grasse returned to the bay. Cornwallis' last hope of escape had sailed over the horizon.[42]

Everything came together, as Washington had bet it would. Troops and supplies began arriving at Williamsburg and Jamestown. Washington wrote to Lafayette from Mount Vernon during his first visit home in more than six years. He, Rochambeau, and others had ridden overland and expected to reach the marquis' camp on September 14.[43]

Down in Williamsburg, Lafayette was in bed, sick with his fever and headaches. Everyone else was giddy at the prospect of victory. "I have not been pleased with Madam Fortune for some time," Wayne told him, "& she has added to that displeasure in attacking you at this crisis with a caitiff [despicable] fever. Try my dear marquis, to shake it off, & I will endeavour to get clear of my complaint the soonest possible. We will then go hand in hand, & force her youngest daughters from the enemies arms!"[44]

The marquis heard on the fourteenth that Washington and his party were approaching town. He leaped out of his bed, into his clothes, and onto his horse, galloped full tilt toward his adoptive father, jumped off the saddle, and ran, his arms outstretched, toward the general. Virginia militia major St. George Tucker told his wife that the marquis "caught the general round his body, hugged him as close as it was possible, and absolutely kissed him from ear to ear once or twice . . . with as much

ardor as ever an absent lover kissed his mistress on his return." Reunited
at last, they were both in tears.[45]

THE ENGINEERS TROLL ABOUT LIKE
SORCERERS MAKING CIRCLES

*A*s soon as they reached Williamsburg, Washington and Rochambeau
wanted to talk to de Grasse. On September 17 they set off on a
sixty-mile cruise to the French anchorage at Lynnhaven Bay, near the
mouth of the Chesapeake. Washington took an instant dislike to the tall,
stout, crude admiral, who called him *"mon cher petit général"* (my dear little general) and treated him like a green lieutenant. He asked if the admiral's orders allowed him to stay long enough to support a siege at
Yorktown, rather than a *coup de main* (all-out assault). The first would be
slow, the second bloody. De Grasse said that his orders required him to
sail south on October 15, but he could stretch that till the end of the
month. When the American asked him to send frigates up the York above
Yorktown to cut off Cornwallis' last opening, he refused. He declined to
commit himself to other attacks after Yorktown fell, but he made more
men and cannons available for the siege.

Adverse weather kept Washington from getting back to Williamsburg
until the twenty-second. There he found an astonishing letter from de
Grasse, who planned to sail out to meet a British fleet said to be headed
for him. The commander in chief answered that if the French navy left, it
would produce disaster. Besides opening the door for Clinton to relieve
Cornwallis, it would leave no way to feed the troops on the Peninsula.
He sent Lafayette to see the admiral, who had already changed his mind
and decided to stay, mostly because his captains wanted him to. Leaving
two ships of the line and three frigates to block the mouth of the York, de
Grasse moved to the bay entrance to await the British, who did not challenge him.[46]

Washington and Rochambeau marched out of Williamsburg on
September 28, driving in enemy outposts and patrols as they neared
Yorktown. The country had been devastated. Fields were in weeds, and
houses stood empty, their doors and windows broken. The country was
flat, and in front of their works the British had turned a wide area into a

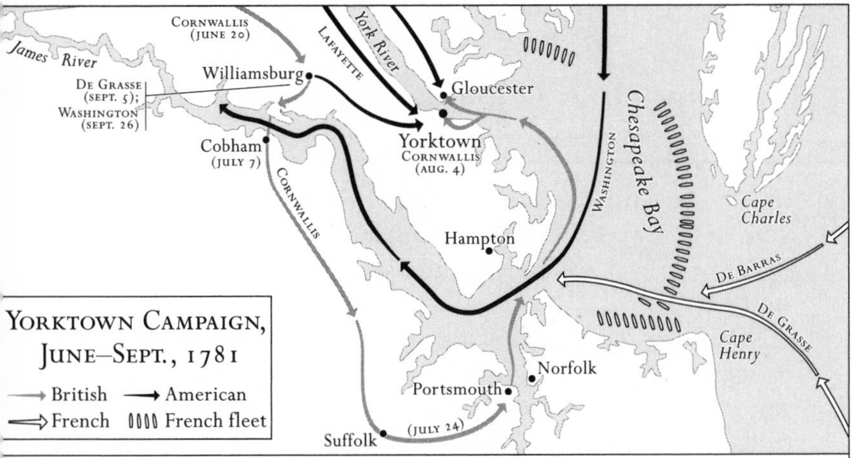
Yorktown Campaign, June–Sept., 1781
British
American
French
French fleet
James River
Cornwallis (June 20)
Williamsburg
De Grasse (Sept. 5); Washington (Sept. 26)
Lafayette
York River
Gloucester
Yorktown
Cornwallis (Aug. 4)
Cobham (July 7)
Cornwallis
Hampton
Washington
Chesapeake Bay
Cape Charles
De Barras
De Grasse
Cape Henry
Norfolk
Portsmouth
Suffolk
(July 24)

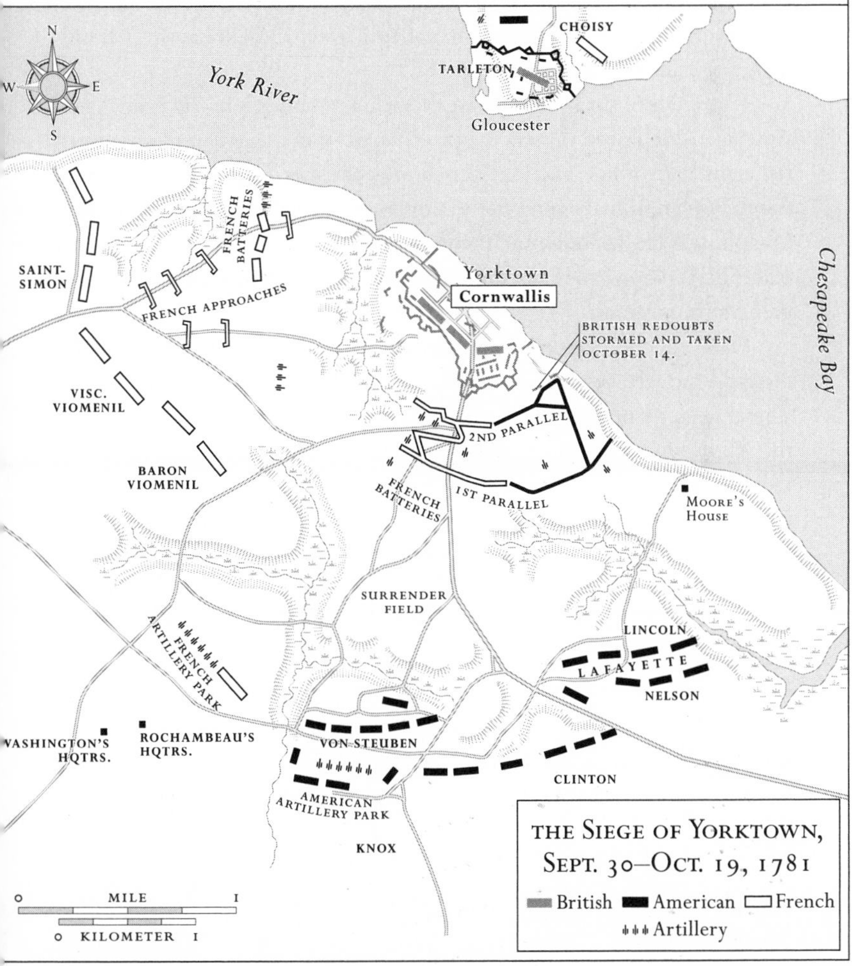
The Siege of Yorktown, Sept. 30–Oct. 19, 1781
British
American
French
Artillery
N
W
E
S
York River
Choisy
Tarleton
Gloucester
Chesapeake Bay
Saint-Simon
French Batteries
French Approaches
Yorktown
Cornwallis
British redoubts stormed and taken October 14.
Visc. Viomenil
Baron Viomenil
2nd Parallel
1st Parallel
French Batteries
Moore's House
Surrender Field
French Artillery Park
Lincoln
Lafayette
Nelson
Washington's Hqtrs.
Rochambeau's Hqtrs.
Von Steuben
Clinton
American Artillery Park
Knox
0 Mile 1
0 Kilometer 1

sandy desert. Yorktown was small, a main street and four cross-streets on a bluff overlooking the river. The redcoats had made the best of a bad situation, not having any high ground to build on. Their main defense was close to the town, less than 300 yards from the bluff and about 1,000 yards wide. It was a system of earthen parapets and ditches, zigzagged to connect a series of redoubts. Any attack would be shot at from the flank as well as the front.

The inner line housed sixty-five guns in fourteen batteries. The strongpoint, or "horn work," covered the road to Hampton, and forward of it were several outworks. The Fusiliers' Redoubt guarded Cornwallis' right, Redoubts Numbers 9 and 10 his left. Washington thought that between 5,000 and 6,000 enemy faced his nearly 20,000 men. In fact, Cornwallis had nearly 10,000 men at Yorktown and Gloucester, including sailors and marines.[47]

Washington was in command overall, and under him the French and Americans deployed in two wings. Rochambeau conceded the honor of the right to his allies, and the French took the left. To command the right wing, Washington assigned the senior major general, Benjamin Lincoln. Lincoln was fat, friendly, and incompetent, but Washington could not violate the pecking order any more than he could deny Lee's right to command at Monmouth.

Lafayette commanded the right of the American wing under Lincoln, Steuben the left, while Nelson led a second line of militia behind them. The arrangement did not satisfy the marquis, who wanted to command the whole right wing, forgetting his earlier message about serving under Lincoln. He thought he had earned the honor by leading the campaign that had trapped Cornwallis, and suggested sending Lincoln to Gloucester with an independent command. That "cannot hurt any body's pretentions or feelings," he claimed. Command of the right wing was the highest honor at Yorktown, and Lincoln would protest being deprived of it, so the junior general had to settle for the right end of the right wing.[48]

A siege was an engineering operation, and there were no American military engineers. There were, however, about a dozen highly skilled French *ingénieurs militaires* in the two armies. Rochambeau, veteran of a dozen sieges, was content to let this one be an American operation, because he knew it would be plotted by French specialists following French methods. Washington's chief engineer, Major General Louis Duportail, and his topographical engineer, Lieutenant Colonel Jean-Baptiste de Gouvion, were in charge.[49]

"The engineers troll about like sorcerers making circles around poor Lord Cornwallis," Lafayette laughed, "and the general officers train their spyglasses, awaiting the moment to take the trench." About a third of the soldiers were detailed to do the digging. Others went into nearby woods to make lumber for gun platforms, fascines (bundles of sticks to be dropped into

Benjamin Lincoln, by C. W. Peale, 1781–83. Captured at Charleston, Lincoln was exchanged for William Phillips, and by virtue of seniority deprived Lafayette of command of the right wing of the allied armies during the Siege of Yorktown. (INDEPENDENCE NATIONAL HISTORICAL PARK)

enemy trenches during an attack), gabions (large wood-and-brush baskets to be filled with earth and form the body of the fieldworks), and abatis (tree trunks sharpened to points, planted to face outward against attackers).[50]

Sappers and miners—troops who cleared the way for an assault on enemy fortifications—went out after dark on October 5 to transfer the engineers' designs to the landscape. One of them was Joseph Plumb Martin, of Lafayette's division. "It was a very dark and rainy night," he remembered. They followed the engineers and laid laths of pine wood end to end to outline where the troops would dig the trenches. A stranger approached and told them, in case they were taken prisoner, "not to discover to the enemy what troops" they were. The sappers were "obliged to him for his kind advice," but they already knew sappers and miners were denied quarter under eighteenth-century rules of warfare, and were not about to betray their own secret. The stranger was General Washington himself. Then the rain fell so hard that all were ordered back to the American lines. [51]

They went out again on the night of the sixth, while the British were distracted by Saint-Simon on the French left. His troops built a flying sap—a trench dug straight at the enemy, protected by pushing a gabion ahead of the diggers. Martin's gang laid out the rest of the outlines for the first American work. It was a parallel, a trench and parapet 2,000 feet long and about 600 to 800 yards from the enemy line, with a ditch in front. The line troops were ready with their tools to start digging but had to stand by, Martin recalled, until "after General Washington had struck a few blows with a pickaxe . . . that it might be said 'Gen. Washington with his own hands first broke ground at the siege of Yorktown.'" The ground was soft, and the work proceeded quickly. [52]

By dawn on October 7, the Americans had shoveled enough dirt to protect themselves in their trench and four redoubts. Saint-Simon had drawn fire during the night, but Cornwallis did not know about the American earthwork until morning. The redcoats moved up some field guns and lobbed a few balls at it. On the allied left, more favorable terrain allowed the French to avoid extended entrenchments. They threw up redoubts and began moving their guns forward. The first allied batteries were done on the ninth, and Washington gave Saint-Simon the honor of starting the show at three in the afternoon, on the far left. By the next morning four more French and American batteries were in action, bringing the total of guns at work to forty-six. By midmorning their fire was so effective that the British could answer with only about six rounds an hour. When a civilian came out of Yorktown under a flag of truce on the tenth, he reported that most British troops were huddled beneath the bluff over the river. That night, French guns set a British frigate afire and sank three or four other vessels.

The noise was tremendous, surpassing anything the Americans had ever heard. From great clouds of smoke, iron balls screamed into the enemy works, tearing holes in them. Where they were close enough, siege mortars added to the terror with exploding shells. The obese but energetic Knox was everywhere among the American artillery, amazing the British and the French alike. He had rounded up a siege train equal to that of the French, as if big guns and mortars could be picked up at country stores. Knox "scarcely ever quitted the batteries," the chevalier de Chastellux reported, awestruck. He observed that if the English "were astonished at the justness of the firing, and terrible execution of the French artillery, we were not less so at the extraordinary progress of the American artillery, as well as the capacity and knowledge of a great number of the officers employed in it."[53]

If Washington thought about his own ordeal at Fort Necessity as he watched hell fall onto the British lines, he told no one about it. Lafayette hardly saw him. He and the other major generals rotated in command of the American trenches, while Washington watched the work of the engineers. On October 11 the commander in chief agreed to open a second parallel closer to the British lines, reached by digging an approach trench, or zigzag, forward to where it would be. By that time, the marquis told La Luzerne, enemy return fire had fallen off almost to nothing. French and American officers champed at the bit, impatient with the slowness of the approach works. They wanted "to shorten the time by taking this point or that with drawn swords, but the general, who knows his success is assured, is determined to conserve the blood of his troops."[54]

The second parallel extended toward the British left anchored on Redoubts Numbers 9 and 10, which had to be taken. Washington decided to storm them at night. Number 10, beside the river, stood in Lafayette's sector, so he commanded the attack there. Number 9 went to Rochambeau, who assigned Colonel Guillaume, comte de Deux-Ponts, to lead 400 grenadiers against it. Saint-Simon would mount a diversion against the Fusiliers' Redoubt, at the opposite end of the enemy lines. The commander in chief ordered all artillery within range to hammer the other two redoubts beginning on October 11, and by the fourteenth they were smashed up enough to take by *coup de main.*

Washington had told the American and French officers to come up with a coordinated plan of assault. Attacking troops should not make a sound as they approached the redoubts, or the defenders would shoot them to pieces before they got there. In Europe, troops advanced with their muskets unloaded, and storming a fortified position with bayonets was the high mark of professional soldiering. When one of the French officers doubted whether the Americans were ready for that, Lafayette bristled. Another Frenchman recalled that he "assumed a lofty tone with his customary boast, declaring that with his men he was accustomed to taking all positions with the bayonet alone."[55]

Lafayette detailed 400 men, plus sappers and miners, to challenge Redoubt Number 10, putting his former aide Gimat, by then a colonel, in command. Hamilton commanded a battalion in Lafayette's division, and he protested, claiming seniority. When Lafayette refused to hear him, he went to Washington, who replaced Gimat with Hamilton on the grounds that he was scheduled to be first officer of the day. In reality, he went along with Hamilton because this should be an American operation. Lafayette concurred. Since Laurens also took part, all of His Excellency's boys were at risk.[56]

The redoubts were square, elevated earthen forts, about thirty feet on a side, open at the rear, bristling with abatis, and surrounded by ditches about eight to ten feet deep. The approach to them was made more difficult by shell craters, "sufficient to bury an ox in," according to Private Martin. The sappers would precede the assault to clear a way for the infantry, then stand aside to let the others storm over the parapet against men armed with muskets and cannons. There were 120 British and Hessians in Number 9 and about 45 in Number 10. The works were about 200 yards apart.

Saint-Simon started his demonstration on the allied left at six-thirty on the evening of October 14. Half an hour later six cannons fired in succession, the signal for Deux-Ponts and Hamilton to start crossing about 200 yards of open land to their objectives. Each force had gone about 120 yards when a sentry fired at the French column from Number 9. Another shot rang out from Number 10, and the Americans, like the French, picked up their pace. Lieutenant John Mansfield led the spearhead, known as a "forlorn hope," twenty men just behind the sappers and miners. He was followed by Gimat's lead battalion, with Hamilton close behind. Hamilton's own battalion, commanded by Nicholas Fish, attacked on Gimat's left, and another under Laurens swung around to the rear to close off the enemy's escape.

Just as the sappers reached the ditch, Number 10 exploded with musket fire. "I thought the British were killing us off at a great rate," Private Martin remembered. Before the sappers did their work, the forlorn hope and Gimat's men poured over the abatis, carrying the sappers along, while Laurens and his men stormed through the rear. As he mounted the parapet, Martin said, he "met an old associate hitching himself down into the trench; I knew him by the light of the enemy's musketry, it was so vivid." It was screaming, hand-to-hand combat, officers especially going down. One took a cannonball, another took two bayonets, and Gimat a ball in the foot. Lafayette reported that "the redoubt was stormed with an uncommon rapidity." The fort's defenders were overwhelmed, the survivors surrendering before they were all bayoneted. The whole thing had taken about ten minutes.[57]

Things did not go so well at Number 9. Unlike the Americans, who gamely ran over all obstacles and into the redoubt, the French followed the book. They waited for the sappers to clear a way, prolonging their time under fire before they crossed the parapet. Once they had done that, the garrison gave up. While Lafayette lost nine killed and twenty-five wounded, Deux-Ponts had fifteen killed and seventy-seven wounded. The enemy lost six officers and sixty-seven men captured; the rest were bayoneted. The redoubts were a ghastly mess of bodies and blood.[58]

Engineers and men armed with picks and shovels rushed into the redoubts to close up the open rears, which faced the British. Other parties extended the second parallel to the river, incorporating the redoubts. The Americans mounted two howitzers in each place, where they enfiladed the enemy trenches. After a few cannonballs had ricocheted that way, before dawn Cornwallis sent 350 men to spike the guns. They entered the second parallel where the Americans joined the French, killed a few sleeping Frenchmen and spiked their cannons, then pushed on toward the redoubts. Lafayette's brother-in-law Noailles rallied a battalion that drove them back into Yorktown, but not before they spiked the howitzers. They did not do much of a job of it, using bayonets as spikes, so the pieces were back in action in six hours.[59]

I PITY LORD CORNWALLIS

Cornwallis tried to break out on the night of October 16. He planned to cross over to Gloucester and fight his way out of the lines there, but he did not have enough boats, and a violent storm wrecked his last hope. On the morning of the seventeenth, the fourth anniversary of Saratoga, about a hundred guns and mortars erupted with a constant, terrible thunder. Shot and shell tore into the British works, and houses in the town took a beating. Governor Nelson offered his own house as a target, assuming that it was the enemy headquarters. Cornwallis, however, had moved to a cave called "the grotto," at the bottom of the bluff.

The British commander came out of his hole during the bombardment, looked out from the horn work, returned to the grotto, and sent an officer with a flag of truce. An American officer saw a drummer "mount the enemy's parapet and beat a parley, and immediately an officer, holding up a white handkerchief, made his appearance outside their works. The drummer accompanied him, beating." The allied batteries ceased fire. An American officer ran forward and met the redcoat, tying the handkerchief over the Englishman's eyes. He was led through the American works to a house in the rear.[60]

He carried a message from Cornwallis, proposing a surrender. He asked for twenty-four hours to submit his terms; Washington gave him two, and they arrived at about four in the afternoon. Both sides appointed commissioners to work up final terms the next day. Washington ordered that "[t]he same honors will be granted to the surrendering army as were granted to the garrison of Charles Town," meaning Lincoln's surrender at Charleston, when he was denied the honors of war. This set off a protracted wrangle, but by early on October 19, 1781, it had all been sorted out and signed by the commanders on both sides. Washington stood firm on the Charleston terms, but otherwise it was a generous surrender, to take place a mile and a half south of Yorktown at two o'clock that afternoon.[61]

While that little dance went on, another took place in the American lines. Steuben commanded the trenches when the truce flag came across. Later, Lafayette arrived to relieve the baron as scheduled. Steuben refused to give up command, saying that under European rules of war, the commander who received the flag had the right to retain command until the negotiations ended. Lafayette appealed to Washington, who consulted Rochambeau and other foreign officers, who told him that Steuben was in the right.[62]

French and American troops lined up along either side of the Hampton road. The surrender terms required that the enemy troops "shall march out, with colors cased, and drums beating a British or a German march." The redcoats and Hessians plodded along sullenly, their faces set straight ahead or toward the French side. They wanted to believe that they had been beaten by a professional army rather than by the ragged American rebels. A tradition invented in 1828 holds that their musicians played one song all through the ceremony, "The World Turned Upside Down." In fact, many tunes were played by bands, fifers, and drummers on both sides that day. There were several known by that title, one of them derived from "When the King Enjoys His Own Again," an old Jacobite serenade to Bonnie Prince Charlie. Since Charlie had rebelled against the king of England, the irony amused the redcoats, who had little enough to be happy about.[63]

Lafayette made his own musical contribution. Annoyed that the enemy refused to look at the Americans, he ordered a band to strike up "Yankee Doodle." As Light-Horse Harry Lee remembered, "the band's blare made them turn their eyes" to the American side. The redcoats had played it throughout the war to taunt captured rebels, although their own bands had played it at Saratoga.[64]

Cornwallis claimed that he was too sick to attend, so he sent his deputy, General Charles O'Hara, to surrender for him. O'Hara offered his sword to Rochambeau, who referred him to Washington. The Englishman apologized for his "mistake" and held the sword out. Washington would not accept surrender from a subordinate and handed him over to his American counterpart, Lincoln. The loser of Charleston took the weapon, then handed it back; O'Hara was entitled to keep it under the surrender terms. The enemy troops filed onto the field and grounded their arms and cased colors. Onlookers admired the spit-and-polish Germans but were annoyed at the redcoats, many of whom were drunk. Washington watched from a distance, gazing at the first surrender he had ever dictated.[65]

The American commander hosted O'Hara at dinner that night, and

Surrender of Cornwallis, *by the Spanish painter Vicente de Paredes. There have been thousands of depictions of the event since 1781, and this one is no more inaccurate than the others.* (LILLY LIBRARY, INDIANA UNIVERSITY)

soon former enemies at all levels were exchanging visits. Cornwallis invited Lafayette, and the marquis took along a map to review their mutual history. The next day the senior redcoat visited Lafayette at his headquarters. The marquis had always admired Cornwallis, and found him polite, even charming. He was well educated, a round-shouldered man with a wide, pleasant face and deep-set eyes, who showed honest respect for the balding redhead he had once dismissed as "the boy." The only rough patch came when the marquis rebuked the British for keeping Henry Laurens in the Tower of London. Cornwallis volunteered to be exchanged for him.[66]

Lafayette bragged to others about his part in the victory. "Our Virginia campaign has ended so well," he told Vergennes, "and my respect for Lord Cornwallis' talents makes his capture still more precious to me. After this attempt, what British general will take it into his head to come and conquer America?" He told the prime minister, "The play is over, Monsieur le Comte; the fifth act has just ended. I was a bit uneasy during the first acts, but my heart keenly enjoyed the last one." "I pity Lord Cornwallis, for whom I have a high regard," he admitted to Adrienne. He asked the prince de Poix, "As for me, my friend, judge whether my service has been agreeable. . . . As for the commander in chief, his genius, his greatness, and the nobility of his manners attach to him the hearts and veneration of both armies."[67]

Lafayette begged Washington to let him lead an expedition against the British supply post at Wilmington, North Carolina. The commander in chief agreed, provided de Grasse would donate shipping and an escort. The admiral wanted to get back to the West Indies, and sailed away on November 3. Washington sent troops overland to help Greene. Lafayette wanted to command them, but Arthur St. Clair outranked him.[68]

The Main Army trooped out to return to New York, and Washington planned to stop at Mount Vernon on his way back. He and Lafayette agreed that, with no campaign in prospect, the marquis could do the cause more good if he returned to France to lobby for more aid. Lafayette said farewell to Virginia and his troops at the end of October, telling Governor Nelson, "I cannot refrain from presenting your Excellency with the homage of my gratitude, and acknowledging the obligations which in a civil and military capacity, I owe to your Excellency's assistance." That oiled over his refusal to discuss the impressment and Point of Fork controversies.[69]

"In the moment the major general leaves this place," the marquis proclaimed to the Light Division, "he wishes once more to express his gratitude to the brave corps of light infantry who for nine months past have been companions of his fortunes. He will never forget that with them alone of regular troops, he had the good fortune to maneuver before an army . . . six times superior to the regular forces he had at that time."[70]

Lafayette rode out on November 1, and soon Washington headed for home. They had planned a reunion in Philadelphia, but the commander in chief was detained by military affairs and the funeral of Martha's son, John Parke Custis. "I owe it to friendship," he told the young Frenchman, "and to my affectionate regard for you my dear marqs. not to let you leave this country without carrying with you fresh marks of my attachment to you; and new expressions of the high sense I entertain of your military conduct, & other important services in the course of the last campaign."

Lafayette had asked about the next year's campaign, and Washington emphasized that without naval superiority and more money, he could do nothing. He ended, "If I should be deprived of the pleasure of a personal interview with you before your departure, permit me my dear marquis to adopt this method of making you a tender of my ardent vows for a propitious voyage—a gracious reception from your prince—an honorable reward of your services—a happy meeting with your lady & friends—and a safe return in the spring."[71]

Lafayette met tumultuous receptions in Baltimore and Philadelphia, which he reached on November 8. Congress granted his request for leave and appointed him an ambassador at large to advise the American delegates in Europe. They were told "to communicate and agree on everything with him." The members sent him off with an appeal for another hefty grant or loan, gushing resolutions of praise, a flowery letter to King Louis, and a pile of instructions and letters of recommendation. His last duty in the capital was to preside over a court-martial of two Tory spies caught stealing documents from Congress. They were sentenced to hang.[72]

The legislature offered Lafayette the frigate *Alliance,* docked at Boston, to carry him and his party back to France. On November 29 he sent a short note to Washington. "I will have the honor to write to you from Boston, my dear general," he said, "and would be very sorry to think this is my last letter. Accept however once more the homage of the respect and of the affection that render me for ever your most obedient servant and tender friend."[73]

The marquis and his group arrived in Boston on December 5, but his departure was delayed by weather and by receptions, parties, and tours in his honor. Superintendent of Finance Robert Morris had told the captain of the frigate to ensure that Lafayette arrived home safely. Captain John Barry sat in the harbor until the weather cleared, and when he sailed he would avoid engagements with British vessels.[74]

Still harbor-bound, on December 21 Lafayette wrote his farewell to his adoptive father, worried that the delays would make him miss the next campaign. On the twenty-third he added a postscript. "I beg your pardon, my dear general, to give you so much trouble in reading my scribles," he said, his hand shaking with emotion. "But we are going to sail, and my last adieu I must dedicate to my beloved general. Adieu, my dear general, I know your heart so well that I am sure not distance can alter your attachement to me. With the same candor, I assure you that my love, my respect, my gratitude for you are above expressions, that on the moment of leaving you I more than ever feel the strength of those friendly ties that for ever bind me to you, and that I anticipate the pleasure, the most wished for pleasure to be again with you, and by my zeal and services to gratify the feelings of my respect and affection."[75]

Alliance weighed anchor and headed out for France.

T H I R T E E N

Do Often Remember
Your Adopted Son

(JANUARY 1782-DECEMBER 1784)

They did not . . . sunder themselves from a parent fallen into decrepitude;
but with astonishing audacity they affronted the wrath of England in the
hour of her triumph, forgot their jealousies and quarrels, joined hands
in the common cause, fought, endured, and won. The disunited
colonies became the United States.

— Francis Parkman

News of Yorktown raced across the Atlantic. France was electrified, England stunned. The British prime minister, Lord North, cried, "Oh God! It is all over!" On March 4, 1782, Parliament voted to "consider as enemies to his majesty and the country all who should advise or by any means attempt to further prosecution of offensive war on the continent of North America." Except for skirmishing in the South, the guns fired no more.[1]

A pile of congratulations greeted Lafayette when he landed at Lorient in the middle of January. Vergennes told him, "The rejoicing is very lively here and throughout the nation, and you may be assured that your name is venerated here." The new minister of war said, "You have made a most glorious campaign, Monsieur le Marquis. Our old warriors admire you; the young ones want to take you as a model."

The king had promoted Lafayette to *maréchal de camp* (field marshal, the nearest equivalent to his American rank of major general). It would take effect after he left American service when a peace was signed, but it dated from October 19, 1781. At the age of twenty-four he had jumped two ranks, over the heads of many older officers. His colonelcy in the King's Dragoons went to Noailles, who paid him 60,000 livres. Since the post had cost him 80,000 livres, it was another loss.[2]

A newspaper said, "The general who contributed most to the success of this great enterprise, is without contradiction the Marquis de la Fayette. It is he who followed Cornwallis step by step, who harassed him unceasingly, who drove him back into Yorktown, and who prepared his downfall." He was the "Conqueror of Cornwallis" and the "Hero of Two Worlds."[3]

The title "Friend of Washington" pleased Lafayette the most. Their relationship had changed him. He had adopted an American directness and would not fawn on or defer to social superiors. Like Washington, he would treat everyone with respect and politeness, but only his adoptive father rated deference.

IN EVERYTHING I DO I FIRST CONSIDER WHAT YOUR OPINION WOULD BE

However happy he was to be in France, the marquis told Washington, he looked forward to returning to America and to the general's side. Washington, in "a remembrance from me, to you," sent him a resolution from the Virginia House of Delegates, praising the marquis and ordering that a bust be made of him. He had "a peculiar pleasure," he said, "in becoming the channel through which the just and grateful plaudits of my native state, are communicated to the man I love."[4]

Lafayette reached Paris on January 21 and found the streets mobbed. The king and queen were hosting a rally at the Hôtel de Ville (city hall) to celebrate the birth of the dauphin, the heir to the throne. Adrienne was there. News of his return spread through the crowd, so the queen put

Adrienne into the royal coach and headed for the Noailles palace. Marie-Antoinette got out, paid her respects to Lafayette, then presented his wife to him. Adrienne fainted dead away, and he carried her inside. The crowd went wild.[5]

The marquis was a greater celebrity than he had been the last time, and again he exploited it. He paid little attention to Adrienne, except that she was pregnant again by March. He was summoned to Versailles, and the court applauded as the king honored him. He danced with the queen, and although he was still awkward, everyone admired his grace.

Lafayette told Washington that the welcome he had received would "I am sure be pleasing to you." The king had praised the American general "in terms so high" that he could not "forbear mentionning it," and at a banquet for all the *maréchals* of France, Washington's "health was drank with great veneration."[6]

Lafayette planned to get more help for his adoptive father. He called on Franklin, who was delighted to see his "political aide-de-camp" again. The old printer had about given up asking for a new loan of 6 million livres. Lafayette, in his American uniform, hounded the ministers and raised the amount to 12 million. He met two responses: France could not afford it, and the Americans were not doing enough to help themselves. That did not faze him. The marquis, Franklin reported, had visited all the ministers, pushing them to grant more money for the United States, "and being better acquainted with facts he was able to speak with greater weight than I could possibly do."[7]

As Franklin's agent, Lafayette again made himself the pest of Versailles, and once again it paid off. On February 25, 1782, Vergennes told him that a loan of 6 million livres had been approved.[8]

The diplomatic waters were about to become more turbulent. Lafayette would have to "reconcile the French and American characters," his friend Ségur warned him, "deal tactfully with opposing interests, and fill the measure of your glory to overflowing by adding the olive branch to the laurel leaves." It would not be easy. He predicted that Lafayette would become "more revolted than ever at English arrogance, stupid Spanish vanity, French inconsistency, and despotic ignorance."[9]

Lord North resigned as prime minister on March 20, 1782. Parliament sent emissaries to Paris to get a separate peace with France, but Vergennes spurned them. Meanwhile, the Spanish would not recognize the United States and refused to receive the American minister, John Jay. The marquis fired his usual weapon—letters. He wrote Jay notes that he knew would be opened in transit, reminding the Spanish of their Bourbon heritage. Still, Spain saw the United States as a rival in the Mississippi Valley.[10]

As much as he wanted to return to his adoptive father, Lafayette decided that he could better serve the cause by staying in France. "I hope, my dear general," he begged, "you will approuve of my conduct." He explained that he needed to be on hand as diplomatic and political affairs sorted themselves out.[11]

Washington returned to his dwindling army in April 1782, and in the fall the Continental Army went into its last winter quarters, at New Windsor, where the soldiers erected over 700 timber huts and a large assembly building. Chastellux described the quarters as "spacious, healthy, and well built, and consist in a row of 'log-houses' containing two rooms, each inhabited by eight soldiers when full." It was a far cry from the smoky hovels of Valley Forge. There the army sat while in South Carolina Greene traded jabs with the British in Charleston.[12]

When French visitors gave Washington news of the marquis, they felt they were talking to a father about his absent son. The prince de Broglie visited headquarters that spring. When they drank a toast to the marquis, he said, Washington's face softened and shone with a benevolent smile.[13]

Lafayette conquered Aglaé d'Hunolstein at last, and she became his mistress, but he was so famous that they were denied the veneer of discretion that French nobles papered their frolics with. Their relationship became unusually scandalous. Her husband did not care, but her mother demanded that she break it off. It continued anyway, and soon the marquis paid court to Diane-Adélaïde de Damas d'Antigny, madame de Simiane, childless wife of the marquis de Miremont. Adélaïde was a beauty even more dazzling than Aglaé, and also Adrienne's friend. As usual, his wife swallowed any resentment and subordinated herself to him in everything.[14]

Lafayette got Henry Laurens released from British custody in April 1782. He had been let out of the Tower of London on bond in December, and the marquis demanded that he be allowed to go to France. While working up paroles for Cornwallis and his aides, he proposed exchanging Laurens for Cornwallis, whose many titles included Constable of the

Tower, in principle making him Laurens' jailer. The British allowed his friend to leave after Lafayette sent him a letter of credit to travel and live on. Ironically, Congress later disapproved his exchange, and he was traded for Burgoyne instead.[15]

The marquis was less successful with Spain. "The Spaniards don't like America," he warned Hamilton. He badgered the French ministers with his "outrage" and "disgust" over the Spaniards' refusal to receive Jay. It was doubly annoying because at The Hague Adams was making headway. In April the last of the United Provinces of the Netherlands recognized American independence, and work began on commercial and loan treaties. Franklin advised Jay to leave Madrid. He went to Paris to deal with the Spanish minister to France, the conde de Aranda. They nearly came to blows in Vergennes' antechamber, when the Spanish minister said that they could not exchange credentials because his government had not recognized American independence. Lafayette butted in, saying that it would not be "consistent with the dignity of France for her ally to treat otherwise than as independent." According to Jay, this crack appeared "to pique the Count d'Aranda not a little." Vergennes urged Jay to deal with the Spaniard anyway. The American refused. So long as the two countries disagreed on where the boundary between them should be—the Mississippi or the Appalachians—there was no getting them together.[16]

Lafayette fretted constantly that Washington would not approve his staying in France. He wrote him in April, again asking for his approval, and to say how much it hurt him to be on the wrong side of the Atlantic. He had not heard from him for so long that he was worried. At the same time, he feared that France would make a separate peace, and told Vergennes that it would not end the war. The only way to get Britain to recognize American independence was to beat her into it. He urged the minister to send a fleet and more troops to Washington, to capture New York, Charleston, and Canada.[17]

He was wasting wind. The presence in Paris of peace emissaries from London meant that the war was over, except for the paperwork. Regarding the British envoys, Franklin reported that Lafayette had asked about his dealings with them. "Agreeable to the resolutions of Congress, directing me to confer with him and take his assistance in our affairs, I communicated with him what had past." Lafayette offered to serve as an

American ambassador to any peace settlement, and Franklin said he "lik'd the idea."

At Lafayette's request, Franklin arranged a meeting with one of the Englishmen, and they "parted much pleas'd with each other." However, it took the marquis months to realize that his divided loyalties meant that neither the French nor the American envoys would trust him with everything. As he confessed to Adams, he had "no public capacity to be led into political secrets." He might as well have gone back to Washington.[18]

"The Marquis de Lafayette is of great use in our affairs here," Franklin reported in June, and since there was not likely to be military action in America, the Doctor wanted him to stay at least a few more weeks. John Jay echoed him. Lafayette told Washington about that and asked again for the general to approve his staying in Paris a little longer. He promised to sail for America in a month if he could.[19]

The British refused to talk to the Americans, the French refused to negotiate without them, and the two British envoys squabbled constantly. On June 17, 1782, Parliament passed an "enabling act," which the king signed on the nineteenth. It "enabled" the government to negotiate with the Americans. Then news arrived of the Battle of the Saints in the Caribbean, on April 12. De Grasse lost eight ships and was captured by British admiral George Rodney, whose government lost its enthusiasm for peace negotiations. "I am at a loss," Lafayette complained to Washington about this latest setback.[20]

Shrugging off that disappointment, the marquis reattached himself to the Freemasons, who received him enthusiastically. He was "seated in the east," the place of highest honor, although he was "not of high masonic rank." He let it be known publicly that he was a member of the order, which was still legally dangerous in France. It was his first open alignment with the egalitarian ideas of French liberals, many of them Masons.[21]

Lafayette brought Washington up to date near the end of June. He felt sorry for himself and wanted the elder man to feel sorry for him also, because he suffered "an insupportable degree of uneasiness" at not being with him. However, staying in France to help the American agents, he said, was a necessary sacrifice for the common cause. He reported Adrienne's pregnancy, hoping that Washington's godson George would soon have a brother. He ended with, "Adieu, my dear general . . . in every thing I do I first consider what your opinion would be had I an opportunity to consult it. I anticipate the happiness to be again with you."[22]

Lafayette looked forward to turning twenty-five on September 6, 1782. That would make him legally an adult, in full charge of his own affairs. He had been fairly unrestricted as an orphan anyway, but now he could buy and sell real estate. In addition, his fortune had grown while he was in America, thanks to an inheritance from a great-grandfather. It was time to get out of his in-laws' house.

The marquis spent 200,000 livres on a palatial mansion on the Left Bank, another 100,000 livres to remodel the place, and 50,000 more to decorate and furnish it in a mixture of Louis XV and rustic American. Characteristically, he dumped the whole responsibility for supervising the work on Adrienne. Perhaps because of the extra strain, she gave birth two months prematurely. Lafayette named the girl Marie-Antoinette-Virginie. He wanted "to present her as an offering to my western country," he told Franklin. "And as there is a good *Sainte* by the name of Virginie, I was thinking if it was not presuming too much to let her bear a name similar to that of one of the United States." Franklin observed, "And as we cannot have too many of so good a race, I hope you & Mde. de la Fayette will go thro' the Thirteen."[23]

Lafayette told Washington that, with little for him to do in the peace negotiations, "God grant, my dear general, I may be with you before you get this letter!" Nothing meant more to him than rejoining his adoptive father.[24]

But Franklin still needed him. The marquis shuttled between the Doctor and Vergennes, trying to iron out the "scruples" that were holding up peace negotiations. Vergennes urged that the British commissioners be empowered to negotiate a treaty with the Americans. The first article would renounce any British claims over the United States. That broke the logjam. In September 1782 British envoy Richard Oswald received a new commission authorizing him to treat with "the thirteen United States of America." That satisfied Franklin and the other American diplomats. However, Lafayette had conspired with Vergennes to send a French commissioner to London, arousing Jay's suspicions. He accused Lafayette of serving his own ambitions by posing as either American or French when it suited him. The marquis was stung.[25]

Negotiations bogged down again when the British defeated the

Spanish at Gibraltar. With time on his hands, Lafayette wrote his adoptive father on October 14. He needed another dose of approval.[26]

Washington always knew the right thing to say. "I approve, very highly," he assured him, "the motives which induced you to remain at your court, and I am convinced Congress will do the same." The allied armies had nothing to do but watch the British. "I had prepared a beautiful corps for you to command," he said. "It consisted of all the light infantry." That was just what his young friend wanted to hear.

There was also sad news to report. "Poor Laurens is no more. He fell in a trifling skirmish in South Carolina, attempting to prevent the enemy from plundering the country of rice. Genl. [Charles] Lee is also dead. . . . Your aid G. W. [George Augustine Washington, the general's nephew and Lafayette's aide in Virginia] has had an intermittant fever ever since April & by last acts. of him from Mount Vernon where he is, he was very low and weak." Washington ended with, "Adieu my dear marqs. Believe me to be, what I really am your sincere friend."[27]

Lafayette badgered Vergennes for a chance to drive the enemy off Washington's back. He wanted to assemble a big fleet and army, take Gibraltar, sail west to conquer Jamaica, then go north against wherever the British remained in North America. Vergennes could no longer deny the marquis anything, but that was too much for France to handle alone. He talked Spain into going along, with Gibraltar and Jamaica as reward. Together the two governments assembled an armada of sixty-six ships of the line and transports for 25,000 troops at Cádiz. D'Estaing was commander in chief, with Lafayette his second, commanding the land forces. He told Washington that although he would carry his field marshal's rank in the French army, he would wear his American uniform, as "an officer borrowed from the United States." Once he had Jamaica in hand, he would lead his army to Washington's side.[28]

Alarmed by news of the expedition, the British came around. On November 30, 1782, the British and American commissioners signed preliminary articles of peace, the first of which declared that the United States were "free, sovereign and independent states." King George relinquished "all claims to the government, property, and territorial rights of the same, and every part thereof." Three months later, Britain, France, and Spain signed their own preliminaries.[29]

Lafayette learned about the agreement after he sailed into Cádiz on

December 23, but he had other things on his mind. He sent Adrienne a typical letter saying how much he missed her. He wrote Aglaé about how devoted he was to her. He sent the prince de Poix a letter raving about Adélaïde, "so pretty, charming, engaging, noble, and sincere." He also mentioned a "dear princess," probably the princesse d'Hénin, another of his interests, to whose heart his reached out "with the most tender devotion." His appetites knew no bounds.[30]

The marquis' career as an American officer, however, had ended with the signing of the preliminary peace. His career as a field marshal also was cut short, because the expedition was canceled on February 1, 1783. Still, it was worth it, because his adoptive father had just won his war. Lafayette wanted to be the first to tell Washington the good news, and asked d'Estaing to give him a fast ship. He sent an aide instead, however, when he learned about another threat to Washington's country.

LET US UNITE IN PURCHASING A SMALL ESTATE

*B*ritish forces evacuated Charleston in mid-December 1782. In January 1783, Washington told Congress that he wanted to besiege New York, but the lawmakers objected. It was impossible, said Foreign Secretary Robert Livingston. Army officers had formed committees to demand back pay, and Congress had no money. If the war continued, Livingston told Lafayette, "we shall lean more upon France than we have done." Rochambeau had left on December 24, while his army went to the West Indies.[31]

The Americans did not know about the preliminary peace. Nor did they know that they faced a new threat from Spain, to which the British ceded Florida. Lafayette heard from Jay and from William Carmichael, American chargé in Madrid, in Jay's absence. Not only did the court there still refuse to receive him, it was rattling its sabers about the boundaries of the new republic. Lafayette did what he had done before— sent letters that he knew the Spanish secret service would intercept, expressing confidence that the Iberians would see the light.[32]

In February 1783, Vergennes asked Lafayette to go to Madrid. He agreed, saying he would "give the Spanish minister the opinion of a man who knows America and who, being French, will arouse his ill humor less." He warned Livingston, "Among the Spaniards we have but few well wishers, and as they at the bottom hate cordially the french, our alliance tho' a political, is not a sentimental consideration." He thought settlement of the boundaries of the United States was of crucial importance to the new nation. He also asked formally to be part of the American delegation that would take the final peace treaty to London, "in the capacity of an extraordinary envoy from the United States."[33]

Then Lafayette wrote a remarkable letter to his adoptive father. Two paragraphs stood out. One was a further expression of his devotion. "Were you but such a man as Julius Caesar or the king of Prussia, I should almost be sorry for you at the end of the great tragedy where you are acting such a part," he began. "But with my dear general I rejoice at the blessings of a peace where our noble ends have been secured." After reminiscing about their struggles at Valley Forge, the marquis gushed, "What a sense of pride and satisfaction I feel when I think of the times that have determined my engaging in the American cause!" He envied his own grandchildren "when they will be about celebrating and worshipping your name—to have had one of their ancestors among your soldiers, to know he had the good fortune to be the friend of your heart, will be the eternal honour in which they shall glory."

Out of the blue Lafayette offered a proposal that sounded like something John Laurens had outlined at Valley Forge. "Now, my dear general, that you are going to enjoy some ease and quiet, permit me to propose a plan to you which might become greatly beneficial to the black part of mankind," he said. "Let us unite in purchasing a small estate where we may try the experiment to free the Negroes, and use them only as tenants. Such an exemple as yours might render it a general practice, and if we succeed in America, I will chearfully devote a part of my time to render the method fascionable in the West Indias. If it be a wild scheme, I had rather be mad that way, than to be thought wise on the other tack."

Lafayette, French nobleman, had become a liberal republican who carried the ideas of liberty and equality further than most others were ready to go at that point. "Adieu, Adieu, my dear general," he began a long closing. "Had the Spaniards got common sense I could have dispensed with that cursed trip to Madrid. But I am called upon by a sense of my duty to America."[34]

Still in his American uniform, Lafayette reached Madrid on February

15, 1783. He called on the French minister, the comte de Montmorin, who presented him to King Carlos III. The king handed him off to his prime minister, the conde de Floridablanca, with whom he argued for several days. Lafayette despised the Spanish and rightly concluded that their chief concern was that the American Revolution could spread to their colonies. He also realized that they could not challenge Britain's agreement to fix the United States' western border on the Mississippi. He made overtures to other countries at a banquet of all the ambassadors and effectively isolated Spain. He sweet-talked the Spanish government into dealing directly with the new republic. By the time he left Madrid at the end of the month, the threats of war on the Mississippi had ended, and the government had agreed to receive Carmichael. Floridablanca dragged his feet on that, however, not accepting the American's credentials until August 23.[35]

John Jay, by unidentified, after John Trumbull, ca. 1875. He and Lafayette had their differences during the peace negotiations with Britain, but Jay admitted that the marquis did something he had tried and failed to accomplish—win Spain's recognition of the United States. They later shared an interest in the abolition of slavery.
(INDEPENDENCE NATIONAL HISTORICAL PARK)

It was an outstanding diplomatic performance. Carmichael was eternally grateful, and Montmorin was highly impressed. Lafayette was "your friend," he told Jay, "your adopted compatriot, and will be counted by posterity among the numbers who contributed most to the great revolution in which you were one of the principal actors." Lafayette boasted to Washington that he had "met with repugnances and prejudices." He was "by turns pressing and haughty," he "took care to engage them, and yet not to engage America," and he had acted "in the most private capacity." He had to go to Paris, and in about two months he would sail to America.[36]

Lafayette had grown up a lot under his adoptive father's guidance. No longer a self-centered teenager, he had learned to behave himself with tact and assurance in a delicate situation. Yet he was still a work in progress. His constant pleas for Washington's approval sounded like childish insecurity. He also neglected his responsibilities as a husband and father, and his military or diplomatic missions did not excuse that entirely. His chasing after other women exceeded the norm even among the French nobility, and it was downright juvenile. On the other hand, his irresponsibility caused Adrienne to stand on her own feet.

When he was in Madrid, the marquis received news that his aunt Madeleine had died, leaving his widowed aunt Charlotte alone. When he reached Paris, he learned that crop failures in Auvergne had produced famine throughout the province. Adrienne had ordered the steward at Chavaniac to open the Lafayette granaries to the peasants. She also told the district governor to establish a spinning and weaving mill and a school to teach the women how to make cloth from their husbands' wool. Lafayette was amazed at her independent action, approved of it all, and promised to raise money for her projects.

Then he set off for Chavaniac to see for himself. Adrienne had never visited the place, but Lafayette insisted on going alone. Aglaé had told him to leave Paris because she wanted to break off their affair. He was tired of their fights and her tantrums anyway, and there were always other women to conquer. He wrote her a long, self-pitying letter from Chavaniac, bowing to her wishes. At the same time he wrote Adrienne, describing things in Auvergne. The deprivation he saw around him was terrible. Although his stewards wanted to sell the remaining grain because the price was high, he ordered them to give it away. He learned that the reason for the high price was because the provincial Farmers General had pulled grain off the market to drive the cost up. His own people, he concluded, needed him as much as the Americans had. He withdrew his holdings from the monopoly, undermining it, and declared war on the Farmers General.[37]

France was a mercantilist economy, a system created in the seventeenth century to control all economic activity and produce income for the government. It worked through the monopolies in each province, called Farmers General, or just *la Ferme* (the Farm). Each Farm controlled production, distribution, and sale of everything made or grown in its province. It protected itself with tariffs at provincial or national borders, so commodities were taxed repeatedly as they moved across the country. The Farm paid the king a stiff royalty, which supported both the government and the wretched excesses at Versailles.[38]

Lafayette began his attack on the Farm as a way to help America, whose goods were priced out of the French market. The tariff on tobacco was especially annoying, but it was a general problem for American products. The United States needed to sell its goods abroad to pay its debts to France, he told the finance minister, Jean-François Joly de Fleury. France could claim all of America's trade or lose it to the *Anglais*. The marquis supported a petition by the merchants of Bayonne to make that town a free port, beyond the reach of the Farm. Joly de Fleury was looking for ways to reduce the national debt, but when he proposed to reduce the expenditures of the court and raise taxes, he lost his job. Lefèvre d'Ormesson replaced him.[39]

Lafayette remained under Congress' instructions to further American interests in Europe. He intervened in the cases of individual American merchants having difficulties in France, and he kept up his drumbeat on the ministers, haranguing them about anything that burdened American imports. He wanted a free-trade treaty between his two countries and urged both governments to move in that direction.[40]

The state of the French economy, and the resistance of the Farmers General, made the post of controller of finances a risky one. Charles-Alexandre de Calonne succeeded d'Ormesson in November 1783. He liked Lafayette's proposal and promised to take his ideas to the king. "The ideas upon commerce that are met with in this country are far from being allwaïs right," the marquis told Robert Morris. "To persuade people into their own interest is some times as difficult a matter as it would be to obtain a sacrifice." The Farm fought back fiercely, and "[t]hose opositions I have been every day combatting in the best manner I could."[41]

Opening a few seaports did not encourage more imports from America, because the Farm still controlled internal markets. It refused to carry American products, and priced French goods so high that Americans could not buy them. Lafayette published a manifesto exposing the way the Farm jacked up prices, condemning governmental protection of the system, and calling for open, competitive markets. "Here, then is a new source of wealth to revive our productions and our manufactures. It would be stupid to dry up this channel of commerce, since it is much easier to improve it," his broadside declared.

The marquis had gone over the Farm's head to forge an alliance between common Americans and Frenchmen, and it worked. Early in 1784 Calonne pledged "absolute" duty-free entry and distribution of American goods and ordered the Farm to give preferential treatment to American tobacco. In effect, the United States achieved most-favored-nation trading status. Moreover, he cancelled export taxes on French products going to America. Four ports were duty-free to American merchants.[42]

Morris told Congress that "the labors of that young nobleman" were of the utmost benefit to the United States. The marquis continued to battle the tangle of fees, regulations, and imposts hampering American trade, and jousted with the Farm. "The unexampled attention to every American interest," Morris proclaimed, "which this gentleman has exhibited cannot fail to excite the strongest emotions in his favor."[43]

HE HAS GAINED MORE APPLAUSE THAN HUMAN NATURE AT 25 CAN BEAR

Lafayette had received his country's highest military honor in the spring of 1783. The war minister nominated him for the Cross of St. Louis, created by Louis XIV in 1693. The king approved. His father-in-law, d'Ayen, who also wore the Cross, inducted him into the order.[44]

He enjoyed unexpected respect in military circles, especially when he bought the French army its first two batteries of horse artillery. His American experience contributed to other reforms. The army increased its light infantry to twelve regular battalions. The first light units were "legions" of infantry and cavalry, each including a dozen men with rifled carbines. Respect for light troops in both Washington's and the British armies drove the reforms, but it was Lafayette's experience that gave them their shape.

The trend to light troops would accelerate after the French Revolution in 1789, again under Lafayette's influence. One out of five infantry regiments became light, the rest line. They were organized alike, but the light troops quickly developed a tradition of dash and aggressiveness. They provided advance and flank guard service, rapid deployment, and expert skirmishing, and claimed the right to lead all attacks. Their mobile skirmishing tactics, worked out by Lafayette in America, helped make the Napoleonic army the terror of Europe.[45]

Lafayette had never had any sense when it came to his own money, but he had become an expert on commerce during his battle to open France to American trade. Congress resolved that its members were satisfied with his reasons for staying in Europe "and have a high sense of the new proofs he has exhibited of his zeal in the cause of the said states."[46]

The United States could not fulfill all Lafayette's wishes, however. When he received the marquis' request to be an American delegate to the signing of the final peace, Washington told Foreign Secretary Robert Livingston that if there were no reasons against it, he hoped "that Congress would feel a pleasure in gratifying the wishes of a man who has been such a zealous labourer in the cause of this country." Livingston advised against it because of distrust of the French in Congress. The "honor of the nation" required that it should be represented by a native. Washington withdrew his endorsement, adding that there was "no man upon Earth" he had "a greater inclination to serve" than Lafayette, but he had "no wish to do it in matters that interfere with, or are repugnant to, our national policy, dignity, or interest." Livingston gave Lafayette the bad news, saying, "Real obstacles present themselves." He thought the former American general deserved the honor, but factional politics stood in the way.[47]

Lafayette was Franklin's closest ally and his channel to Vergennes during negotiations with the British. But Franklin had enemies, and they resented his friend's efforts to participate in the peace talks. There was only one issue that they listened to him on, and that was Laurens' provision in the treaty draft that slaves behind British lines should be delivered to the Americans. Lafayette thought that that might result in their freedom. When the British commander at New York objected because the slaves had been granted their freedom, the marquis thought that was a ruse. "There is ten to one however," he told Henry Laurens, "those men are sent to West India markets" to be sold. Otherwise, Lafayette felt himself held at arm's length throughout the negotiations. He complained bitterly to his former aide James McHenry that he was even being denied credit for getting the loan of 6 million livres and for opening the markets.[48]

Lafayette's chief enemy in the American delegation was John Adams. The Massachusetts native was moody, felt homesick for his family, and detested Franklin and everyone associated with him. Lafayette was "an amiable nobleman," Adams told a friend, "& has great merit. I enjoy his friendship, & wish a continuance of it. But I . . . see in that youth the seeds of mischief to our country, if we do not take care. He was taken early into our service & placed in an high command, in which he has behaved well; but he has gained more applause than human nature at 25 can bear. It has enkindled in him an unbounded ambition, which it concerns us much to watch."

Adams worried that Lafayette could rise to the top of the American army while he was also rising in France. "This mongrel character of French patriot & American patriot cannot exist long," he declared, "and if hereafter it should be seriously the politicks of the French court to break our Union, imagination cannot conceive a more proper instrument for the purpose, than the marquis." When Lafayette got wind of this, he was shocked and hurt. Franklin consoled him and told the American foreign secretary that Adams was too suspicious by far.[49]

One issue that divided Lafayette from some of the Americans was the Society of the Cincinnati, organized at Washington's headquarters early in 1783. The general had accepted its presidency before he read its charter. It was to include all officers who had served in the army at least three years, and he thought it was a charitable organization. However, membership was hereditary, to pass down to firstborn sons into perpetuity. Announcement of the society's terms sparked an uproar among Americans, who feared it would be a counterrevolutionary aristocracy. Washington asked the membership to change the hereditary provision.[50]

The general also wanted Lafayette to organize a chapter in France, and sent an officer to Paris to give Lafayette the society's charter and to order manufacture of its badge in France. The marquis had the charter published and asked Vergennes for a waiver of the king's policy against membership in foreign orders. As he set out to recruit members, he kicked up a storm. Poor veterans could not afford to join, and liberals condemned it as a new military aristocracy. Lafayette sent Washington his proxy to vote against the hereditary provision.

Adams wrote Lafayette a letter about the group that the marquis interpreted as "very violent." The young man was hurt once again and called Adams an "honest man, because, altho' your opinion some times has seemed to me wrong your principles have ever been right and I greatly valüe your esteem." Adams denied that he had been "violent," but he was opposed to hereditary orders on principle.[51]

"A friendly letter I wrote you, and the one I receive is not so affectionate as usual," Lafayette shot back at Adams. It was all becoming an embarrassment. Thomas Conway, whose name was forever attached to the "cabal" against Washington during the Valley Forge days, wanted to join. The marquis advised Washington that he ought to be accepted, to keep him quiet. Lafayette would have been embarrassed further if he knew that Franklin also thought the hereditary order abominable. He connected with the comte de Mirabeau, a renegade noble, who published a blistering attack called *Considerations on the Order of Cincinnatus.*[52]

As that controversy simmered, the Lafayettes moved in to their new home, where they watched the fireworks, bonfires, and other festivities that followed the official end of the war on September 3, 1783. The Americans and British signed the Peace of Paris that day, after which the British, French, and Spanish diplomats signed the Peace of Versailles. The whole city celebrated the victory.

Adrienne emerged from her husband's shadow and became one of the most popular hostesses in Paris. When Abigail Adams arrived to join her grumpy husband, she hit it off immediately with Adrienne, and soon with the Noailles family. She described the marquise as "sprightly" and endearing. "You would have supposed I had been some long absent friend who she dearly loved," Abigail said of her first call at the Hôtel de Lafayette. "She is a good and amiable lady, exceedingly fond of her children . . . passionately attached to her husband!!!" She was amazed, and repeated, "A French lady and fond of her husband!!!"[53]

Monday open houses attracted Americans, serious-minded Frenchmen, and even Englishmen. The puritanical Adams acknowledged that the Lafayettes avoided the frivolous entertainments that most French nobles favored. He also admired the gilt-lettered copy of the Declaration of Independence hanging on the wall. He was there in October when William Wilberforce, founder of the British Anti-slavery Society, and William Pitt the Younger, future prime minister, arrived. Lafayette threw a big dinner party so that they could meet Franklin and other American notables. "Since we won the match," Lafayette told Adélaïde, he took "extreme pleasure in seeing the British."[54]

YOU WILL BE MY COMPASS, MY DEAR GENERAL

As Lafayette's stay in France extended, his correspondence with his adoptive father increased, and the British no longer intercepted their mail. Their exchanges were colored by the belief of both that the younger man soon would land in America.

Washington always patted the marquis on the back. He approved of his reasons for staying in Europe, and so advised Congress. He reminded his young friend "how much we all love & wish to embrace you" when they got back together. "The inhabitants of my humble cottage will salute you with the richest marks of grateful friendship wch . . . will be a greater feast than the luxuries of the East; the elegancies of Europe—or the ceremonies of a court can afford."[55]

Washington was somewhat pessimistic about the future of the United States, however. Americans "now stand an independent people," he said, "and have yet to learn political tactics. We are placed among the nations of the Earth, and have a character to establish; but how we shall acquit ourselves time must discover—the probability, at least I fear it, is, that local, or state politics will interfere too much with the more liberal & extensive plan of government which wisdom & foresight freed from the mist of prejudice would dictate." The country needed a stronger national constitution, and the effort to develop one would meet with his aid "as far as it can be rendered in the private walks of life," but he wondered if he would live to see it. For the first time, he mentioned his own mortality. Washington had already outlived his male ancestors, and he could see his own death coming. He wanted to await it at home, in peace.

The general also answered Lafayette's antislavery proposal. "The scheme, my dear Marqs. which you propose as a precedent," he said, "to encourage the emancipation of the black people of this country from that state of bondage in wch. they are held, is a striking evidence of the benevolence of your heart. I shall be happy to join you in so laudable a work; but will defer going into a detail of the business, till I have the pleasure of seeing you."[56]

After months of petitions to Congress about back pay, in March 1783 a near rebellion had arisen at Washington's headquarters at Newburgh. It focused on a list of "Addresses" that hinted at a march on the capital to impose a military dictatorship. In a dramatic appearance, Washington cooled the protesters off by reminding them of the self-government principles they had fought for. When the news reached France, it electrified the country. Here was a general who had been handed the chance to become a dictator and had gracefully turned it aside. "General Washington," Rochambeau later said, "with that noble and patriotic character which ever formed the basis of his conduct, used his influential power over the minds of his soldiers to bring them round to those feelings of generosity with which they had been animated in the whole course of the Revolution."[57]

When Lafayette heard about that—and about Washington's desire to resign his commission—he was carried away. "In every instance, my dear general, I have the satisfaction to love and to admire you," he cheered. "Never did a man exist who so honourably stood in the opinions of mankind, and your name, if possible, will become still greater in posterity. Every thing that is great, and every thing that is good were not hitherto united in one man. Never did one man live whom the soldier, statesman, patriot, and philosopher could equally admire." He ended with, "Adieu, adieu, my dear general, do often remember your adopted son." Washington's refusal to grab power burned into Lafayette's consciousness and stayed with him for the rest of his life.[58]

Washington delayed answering, because he had expected to see Lafayette in person. Awaiting the final treaty and the British evacuation of New York, "[t]ill I get home & have time to look into the situation of my private concerns . . . I can form no plan for my future life," so he could not accept the marquis' repeated invitations to France. He did want to tour the United States, and "there would be nothing wanting to make it perfectly agreeable" but Lafayette's company.[59]

So it continued, Lafayette's expressions of love and loneliness becoming ever more tearful. He compensated by sending gifts, including a portrait of the three Lafayette children—the first view the older man had of his godson and namesake. The commander in chief, meanwhile, began peacefully disbanding his army. On December 23, 1783, Congress accepted his resignation, and he headed home to Mount Vernon.[60]

Once settled there, Washington wrote to Lafayette. "At length" he had become a private citizen, he said with relief. He was "solacing" himself with "those tranquil enjoyments, of which the soldier who is ever in pursuit of fame—the statesman whose watchful days & sleepless nights are spent in devising schemes to promote the welfare of his own—perhaps the ruin of other countries, as if this globe was insufficient for us all—& the courtier who is always watching the countenance of his prince, in hopes of catching a gracious smile, can have very little conception."

Lafayette's adoptive father was everything that French nobles were not. He was "not only retired from all public employments," Washington rejoiced, "but am retireing within myself; & shall be able to view the solitary walk, & tread the paths of private life with heartfelt satisfaction." But he had a morbid outlook that frightened the young man. "Envious of none, I am determined to be pleased with all, & this my dear friend, being the order for my march . . . until I sleep with my Fathers."

Washington commended Lafayette for his work in Europe, "fresh evidence of your unwearied endeavours to serve this country." He begged him to "come with Madame la Fayette & view me in my domestic walks. I have often told you; & I repeat it again, that no man could receive you in them with more friendship & affection than I should do . . . with every sentiment of esteem, admiration & love."[61]

If Lafayette was going to see Washington again, he would have to go to Mount Vernon, so he redoubled his efforts to wind up his activities in Europe. They were many, involving both trade and the Society of the Cincinnati. He finally promised to sail to America in June. "You will be my compass, my dear general."[62]

At last, on May 14, 1784, he said, "To my great satisfaction, my departure is fixed upon the tenth of next month. . . . I do most feelingly anticipate the pleasure of our meeting at Mount Vernon." His biggest news was that he had found a cure for his *mal de mer*. "A German doctor called *Mesmer* having made the greatest discovery upon *magnetism animal,* he has instructed scholars, among whom your humble servant is called one of the most enthusiastic. I know as much as any conjurer ever did."[63]

Early in 1784, Lafayette had watched one of Dr. Friedrich (Franz) Anton Mesmer's performances, and swallowed the hokum about "animal magnetism." The Viennese charlatan prescribed a cure for seasickness. Let polar magnetic forces prevent it, he advised, by hugging the main-mast while facing north. When Mesmer's nonsense came under investigation by the king's government, Lafayette became an outspoken defender of the quack's theories.[64]

Like all Lafayette's sea voyages, this one did not go well. He left Adrienne and the children behind, not wanting any distractions when he hugged his adoptive father. She went to Chavaniac with the children, because that is where he wanted George to be raised. Washington lived on a country estate, and Lafayette had acquired a renewed interest in his own.

He wrote to Adrienne until he disappeared over the horizon, saying how hurt he would be to miss her. The first time the ship sailed out of Lorient, it was blown back by contrary winds. He tried the new seasickness remedy, but he noted that when Mesmer recommended that he "embrace the mainmast, Mesmer did not know, and I forgot, that it is coated with tar up to a certain height, and hugging it is absolutely impossible without getting tarred from head to foot." He left port on June 29 and was sick all the way across the Atlantic.[65]

THESE THINGS DARKENED THE SHADES & GAVE A GLOOM TO THE PICTURE

Lafayette and an aide landed at New York on August 4, 1784, to find the city decked out in bunting and wreaths in his honor. He soon discovered that the United States were not really united under the Articles of Confederation. There were rivalries of all kinds between the states, and in some cases shooting had broken out between state forces. There was only one point of agreement—the whole country loved Lafayette.[66]

He was overwhelmed by receptions, and New York's was typical. Crowds cheered him in the streets, old army friends greeted him, he could hear church bells and cannons, and he enjoyed banquets, rallies, and interminable speeches welcoming his return. He wanted to press on to Mount Vernon, but he could not resist the adulation that followed him to Philadelphia. "It is true, my dear heart," he told Adrienne, "that each step I take here brings me a new satisfaction." After addressing the American Philosophical Society on "the wonderful effects of a certain invisible power, in nature, called *animal magnetism,*" he pressed on. He reached Mount Vernon on August 17.[67]

The marquis and the general had a tearful reunion, then settled into a routine. "I am not just turning a phrase," Lafayette told Adrienne, "when I assure you that in retirement General Washington is even greater than he was during the Revolution. His simplicity is truly sublime, and he is as completely involved with all the details of his lands and house as if he had always been here." The typical day began with breakfast, after which the general and his guest chatted together for some time. "After having thoroughly discussed the past, the present, and the future," Washington went off to take care of his affairs, giving Lafayette things to read that had been written during his absence from America. When they reunited for dinner, they found Mrs. Washington with visitors from the neighborhood.

Washington and Lafayette at Mount Vernon, *1784, by Thomas Richard Rossiter and Louis R. Mignot. The indulgence of children represented here was one of a number of influences on Lafayette from this visit.* (LILLY LIBRARY, INDIANA UNIVERSITY)

The conversation at the table turned to "the events of the war or to anec-dotes that we are fond of recalling." After this "tea" they resumed their private conversations and spent the rest of the evening with the family.

They sat on the veranda overlooking the Potomac, sipping Martha's peach brandy. They ate Virginia ham and fried chicken. They talked about agriculture, and Lafayette fired off instructions to Adrienne on changes he wanted to make at Chavaniac, to turn it into another Mount Vernon.

His adoptive father's home life left a great impression. In France, children of nobles were usually out of sight. Here they overran the house and were present even at meals. He was taken with Martha's orphaned grandchildren, whom Washington had adopted. There were others as well, grandnieces and grandnephews and the offspring of neighbors. Washington was fond of them all and was delighted to read letters Lafayette had brought along from Adrienne and Anastasie. These were the strongest memories the marquis took home with him.[68]

They talked about slavery. Washington admitted he wanted to "get rid" of his slaves. Lafayette wanted to abolish the whole institution. But Virginia law would prevent the sort of freeman plantation he had pro-posed, let alone complete abolition of slavery.[69]

Washington told Lafayette that, expecting his arrival, he had post-poned a trip to his western lands, which had been invaded by squatters. They rode together to Alexandria and parted in tears on September 1, 1784, planning a reunion at Mount Vernon in a few weeks. The real rea-son for Washington's trip was to scout out his old dream of opening nav-igation between the Potomac and the Ohio, to link the West to the seaboard. The Spanish had closed the Mississippi to American shipping, and he thought his scheme would compensate for that. If his idea did not pan out, he feared that either the West would break away from the rest of the country or New York would replace Virginia as the gateway to that region by building its own canal.[70]

Lafayette went on to Baltimore and another round of grand recep-tions. There he met James Madison, a tiny man with a giant intellect, whom he had met briefly during the war. The son of a wealthy Virginia planter, he shared Lafayette's emerging interest in political philosophy, and he could speak French. He decided to tag along on the marquis' swing through New York and New England, all the while keeping his pa-tron Jefferson informed of everything.[71]

They spent four days in New York City, which declared Lafayette a "freeman and citizen," an idea that spread to other cities. Madison told Jefferson that he had "endeavored emphatically" to impress on Lafayette "that the ideas of America and of Spain irreconcilably clash—that unless the mediation of France be effectually exerted an actual rupture is near at hand." He feared that if war broke out, Britain would come in on the Spanish side. France, he told Lafayette, must lean on the Spanish government.[72]

Lafayette advised Vergennes, "The trade with England is owing to the surprising amount of credit that every American finds there. This abandon will bring about bankruptcies, and next winter will be favorable to us, provided our merchants consult the needs and tastes of the country." The population of the Ohio country was growing, the outlet for this whole area was the Mississippi, "and the prohibition of trade on the Mississippi will lead to disputes, later than is thought here but much sooner than is thought in Europe. The Americans like us, but they very genuinely hate Spain."[73]

James Madison, by James Sharples Senior, 1796–97. Madison and Lafayette became friends during the tour of New York and the negotiations with the Indians in 1784. (INDEPENDENCE NATIONAL HISTORICAL PARK)

Congress appointed commissioners to treat with the Six Nations and asked Lafayette to help out. He, Madison, the commissioners, another group from the state of New York, and the French chargé d'affaires François Barbé-Marbois set out for upstate. They detoured to a Shaker village, because Lafayette got the notion that they practiced something similar to mesmerism, a gross misreading of their beliefs. He tried Mesmer's methods on an injured man, but they did not work, and the disillusioned marquis lost faith in the Austrian quack.

The party continued onward through a war-ravaged landscape, freezing in rain and early snow. To Barbé-Marbois, the whites appeared to live much like the "savages," and he could scarcely tell the houses of one from the other. Lafayette took three casks of brandy with him to Oneida Castle, the meeting site. That earned him a big welcome, but the chiefs remembered Kayeheanla fondly anyway. They passed late September and early October in a round of drunken feasts, speeches, and dancing. It all ended with a treaty recognizing Indian sovereignty in western New York and American sovereignty between Lake Erie and the Ohio River. Lafayette and Barbé-Marbois also worked out an agreement to establish a French-run fur trade in New York to draw Indian business away from Canada, but the plan was later pigeonholed in Versailles.

Lafayette had a grand time. The balding marquis told the prince de Poix that he could not lose his scalp among the Iroquois, "because one does not lose, says the proverb, what he does not have." He told Adrienne that his "personal credit with the savages—who are as much friends as enemies—has proved to be much greater than I had supposed." He left with Peter Otchikeita, the twelve-year-old son of a chief, promising to have the boy educated in Paris.[74]

Madison told Jefferson that Lafayette had become involved with the commission because the Indians were still attached to France and to the marquis. "The commissioners were eclipsed," however. "All of them probably felt it." Arthur Lee complained to Madison about being upstaged by the French interloper. Lafayette "was not insensible of it but consoled himself with the service which he thought . . . he had rendered to the United States." Madison observed slyly "that the transaction is also pleasing to him in another view as it will form a bright column in the gazettes of Europe."

As the trip continued, Madison and Lafayette became friends. "The time I have lately passed with the M. has given me a pretty thorough insight into his character," Madison continued. "With great natural frankness of temper he unites much address; with very considerable talents a strong thirst of praise and popularity. In his politics he says his three hobby-horses are the alliance between France and the United States, the union of the latter and the manumission of the slaves. The two former are the dearer to him as they are connected with his personal glory. The last does him real honor as it is a proof of his humanity." Madison took the marquis to be "as amiable a man as his vanity will admit and as sincere an American as any Frenchman can be; one whose past services gratitude obliges us to acknowledge and whose future friendship prudence requires us to cultivate."[75]

In America as in France, Lafayette was too popular to be ignored by those in power. He was also compulsively helpful. When he learned that Jefferson would become minister to France, he offered not only his congratulations but his and Adrienne's hospitality when he reached Paris. He extended the same favors to Jefferson's secretary, David Humphreys, and told Adrienne to look out for both of them.[76]

Lafayette went on to Hartford, where he and his family became honorary citizens of Connecticut. In Boston he became an honorary citizen of Massachusetts and an honorary doctor of letters at Harvard. He continued to Providence and more celebrations. He returned to Boston, where the French frigate *Nymphe* awaited him, to cruise to Virginia for his reunion with Washington. He landed at Yorktown and went on to more celebrations in Williamsburg and Richmond, where his adoptive father awaited him.[77]

The marquis reached Richmond on November 18 and had an unexpected reunion with a slave who called himself James Armistead Lafayette. His former spy had petitioned the Virginia Assembly for his freedom as reward for his service during the war. Lafayette advised the lawmakers that James had "perfectly acquitted himself with some important commissions I gave him and appears to me entitled to every reward his situation can admit of." It was hard to say no to the Conqueror of Cornwallis. The Assembly eventually emancipated James and granted him a pension.[78]

Washington and Lafayette left Richmond on November 22 and spent two days on the road talking about personal and political matters. After they reached home, Washington told Lafayette about his plans for a Potomac canal. Without that connection, he said, the western part of the country would sooner or later break away, whatever the Spanish did. In fact, opening the Mississippi to American shipping might accelerate the split in the country. Lafayette always agreed with his adoptive father and told Madison that he had changed his mind on opening the western river. "Many people think the navigation of the Mississippy is not an advantage," he declared.[79]

Washington gave him a packet of letters to take back to France. One was to Adrienne. The pleasure he had received "in once more embracing my friend could only have been increased by your presence," the general told her. "The Marquis returns to you with all the warmth and ardour of a newly inspired lover. We restore him to you in good health crowned with wreaths of love and respect from every part of the Union." He also answered Anastasie's letter, sending the girl a kiss "which might be more agreeable from a pretty boy."[80]

The marquis had stops scheduled in Annapolis, Philadelphia, and New York, where his ship awaited him. The whole Washington household was in tears, and the general could not bear to part. He decided to accompany Lafayette and his party all the way, but the extended reception in Annapolis was too much for him. On December 1, 1784, they rode in their carriages side by side to Marlboro, where they hugged, tears rolled down their faces, and they separated.[81]

Lafayette sadly proceeded to Philadelphia, then on to Trenton, the temporary national capital. Congress gave him an elaborate greeting, then loaded him down with flowery resolutions, commendations to Louis XVI, and letters, along with British colors taken at Yorktown. He addressed the lawmakers, roaring, "May this immense temple of freedom ever stand a lesson to oppressors, an exemple to the oppressed, a sanctuary for the rights of mankind!" He cancelled a planned side trip to Boston and headed to New York.[82]

The state governor, the French consul, and a mob of dignitaries escorted their distinguished visitor on a decorated barge out to *Nymphe*. Lafayette hugged Greene, Hamilton, and Knox and climbed aboard. His party now included the orphaned son of a Continental Army officer, while the Indian boy had gone to Quebec, to follow him to France later. The French ship fired a thirteen-gun salute, answered by a fort on shore. She weighed anchor and promptly ran aground.

Before the marquis boarded, he received a letter from Washington, written after their parting. It was a final farewell. "In the moment of our separation upon the road as I travelled, & every hour since—I felt all that love, respect & attachment for you, with which length of years, close connexion & your merits, have inspired me," the general said. He had asked himself whether that was the last time they would see each other. "And tho' I wished to say no—my fears answered yes." His youth was long behind him, and he was "of a short lived family—and might soon expect to be entombed in the dreary mansions of my father's. These things darkened the shades & gave a gloom to the picture, consequently to my prospects of seeing you again: but I will not repine. I have had my day." He ended, "It is unnecessary, I persuade myself to repeat to you my dr. marqs. the sincerity of my regards & friendship—nor have I words which could express my affection for you, were I to attempt it."[83]

Lafayette refused to accept what Washington had said, and with the ship stuck in the mud, he argued back. "No, my beloved general," he cried, "our late parting was not by any means a last interview. My whole soul revolts at the idea—and could I harbour it an instant, indeed my dear general, it would make me miserable." He realized at last that he would never be able to welcome Washington to his own home in France. "But to you, I shall return, and in the walls of Mount Vernon we shall yet often speack of old times."

The marquis did not understand that his adoptive father spoke with the wisdom of years. The future was for the young, the general knew. Lafayette could imagine a future where the two of them were together again, but Washington knew better.

"Adieu, adieu, my dear general," the young man concluded, "it is with unexpressible pain that I feel I am going to be severed from you by the Atlantick—every thing that admiration, respect, gratitude, friendship, and filial love can inspire, is combined in my affectionate heart to devote me most tenderly to you—In your friendship I find a delight which words cannot express—Adieu, my dear general, it is not without emotion that I write this word—Altho' I know I shall soon visit you again—Be attentive to your health—Let me hear from you every month—Adieu, Adieu. L.f." He was too overcome even to sign his name.[84]

His adoptive father was at the Maryland legislature, lobbying for his Potomac canal project. When the lawmakers made the marquis and his male heirs citizens of Maryland, he fired off a quick note to let him know about it. It was too late. *Nymphe,* freed from her trap, put out to sea on the twenty-third.[85]

Once again, a seasick Lafayette sailed away, heartbroken over what his adoptive father had said. Back at Mount Vernon, George Washington wept openly at his dinner table whenever he talked about his love for Lafayette.[86]

FOURTEEN

Vive La Fayette!

(JANUARY 1785–DECEMBER 1791)

Our friend La Fayette has given in to measures as to the Constitution which
he does not heartily approuve, and he heartily approuves many things which
experience will demonstrate to be injurious. He left America, you know,
when his education was but half-finished. What he learnt there he knows
well, but he did not learn to be a government maker.

—GOUVERNEUR MORRIS

afayette was saddened by Washington's belief that he would
die before they could meet again, but he returned to
France energized. He was called *"le Vashington français"* (the
French Washington). His adoptive father was idolized in
France. To conservatives, he was the valiant soldier who had fought the
British enemy. To liberals, he was the leader of a struggle to establish a re-
publican order. Conservatives feared, and liberals hoped, that Lafayette
would transfer the American Revolution to Europe.[1]

The former major general in Washington's army was a powerful force
to reckon with. Soldiers were more likely to follow him than any general
sent against him, but the struggle ahead would not likely be a civil war.
His adoptive father had taught him that an indirect approach was the better one. He had also explained that self-government could be messy,

because the people would not always agree with one another. Moreover, the American Revolution had been less a military campaign than a struggle over an idea—"that all men are created equal." The English royalists had misjudged the American rebellion. They failed to understand the war of ideas, and treated it as a struggle for power. They lost. Lafayette's challenge, like Washington's, was to engineer an outcome in which power was subordinated to the idea.

THE HERO OF AMERICA HAS BECOME MY HERO

*L*afayette landed at Brest on January 20, 1785, and reached home near the end of the month. John Edwards Caldwell, the orphan, was with him, and Peter and another Indian boy joined the household later. Over the next few years, the sons of other Americans enlarged the mix. Young George spent the week with his tutor, and the other boys attended boarding schools, but they were all home for the weekends. Lafayette and Adrienne also adopted two African children. The place was overrun. He had turned his home into another Mount Vernon, and his sudden indulgence of the children caused chatter among other nobles. It simply was not done.[2]

The house was open to Americans, and Lafayette appointed himself guardian to any who were in Paris. He lent some money, found jobs for others, and bailed a few out of jail. They mixed with the children every Monday night. "He is returned fraught with affection to America and disposed to render every possible service," Jefferson told Madison. "I thought I was in America instead of Paris," another visitor said of the Hôtel de Lafayette.[3]

The onetime boy general became steadily balder. After combing his hair forward, during the late 1780s he began wearing a toupee, in the tousled Alexander the Great style coming into fashion. He also appeared to be more domesticated than he had been, but he took up where he had left off with Adélaïde de Simiane. When her husband committed suicide, Jefferson did not know "whether to condole with or congratulate the marquis."[4]

A visiting American writer said of Lafayette that year, "He has planted a tree in America and sits under it at Versailles." He meant Lafayette's efforts to improve trade between France and the United States. The Farm had reasserted its tobacco monopoly, and Lafayette fought back. He won concessions for whale oil and fish products, and talked the government into buying naval stores and timber from the Carolinas. One by one, American products gained access to French markets. Jefferson called Lafayette his "most powerful auxiliary and advocate." He was so effective that annual American exports to France increased by 1 million livres.[5]

George Washington, by Robert Edge Pine, 1785–87. The effects of the war had told on Washington, making him more conscious of his own mortality. (INDEPENDENCE NATIONAL HISTORICAL PARK)

Lafayette encouraged other European nations to open trade with the United States. Washington told him that his actions had "tended very much to endear you to your fellow citizens on this side of the Atlantic." He had a question, however. "But let me ask you my dr. marquis, in such an enlightened in such a liberal age, how is it possible the great maritime powers of Europe should submit to pay an annual tribute to the little piratical states of Barbary?"[6]

Adams, Franklin, and Jefferson inspired that question when they asked Congress for money to negotiate with the pirate states of North Africa and pay tribute. They also asked Lafayette if he could find out what other maritime powers paid to the Barbary pirates to protect their shipping. He gave them a list of what bribes were handed over, even by naval powers such as Britain and France. It was more than the United States expected or could afford to pay. They passed this on to Congress, wondering at Lafayette's "means of access to the depositories of this species of information."

"There is between Mr. Jefferson and Mr. Adams a diversity of opinion respecting the Algerines," Lafayette told Washington. Adams wanted to pay protection; Jefferson "finds it as cheap and more honourable to cruize against them." The marquis agreed with Jefferson and proposed forming an alliance with all Mediterranean powers, to "distress the Algerines into any terms." Congress dithered, and affairs between the United States and the Barbary pirates would not be settled until after the War of 1812.[7]

Another American diplomatic interest was Spain. At first Lafayette bowed to Washington's belief that opening the Mississippi to American navigation could make the West break away. General Washington thought it would "weaken America, and transform the back country people into Spaniards," he told Carmichael. Lafayette changed his mind when the Spanish began to grumble about war again, and he leaned on the French government to pressure the other kingdom. In 1790 his adoptive father, with his canal plans going nowhere, asked him and the American chargé in Paris, William Short, to urge the French government to persuade Spain to open New Orleans to American vessels. Lafayette advised Jefferson to foment an independence movement in Louisiana.[8]

These continuing services to American interests were noticed in the new nation. The Virginia Assembly ordered busts of Lafayette and Washington, for the statehouse and Paris, and Jefferson gave the commission to Jean-Antoine Houdon. The French set was ready in September 1786, for display in the Hôtel de Ville. At the dedication ceremony, Jefferson praised Lafayette's war record and his assistance to the American delegates in France. "In truth," he said, "I only held the nail; he drove it." He was at the peak of his international glory.[9]

Relations between France and the United States, and the need for a better American constitution, were two of Lafayette's hobbyhorses. The third was slavery. Before he climbed on that, however, he added a fourth—religious liberty. When he enrolled the orphaned Caldwell boy in a Catholic boarding school, he had a battle with the Benedictine monks who ran the place. The youngster was Protestant, and the marquis wanted him excused from daily Catholic services, which the monks maintained were mandatory.[10]

Lafayette decided to widen the fight for religious toleration. Protestants in France were "under intolerable despotism," he told Washington. "Altho' oppen persecution does not now exist, yet it depends upon the whim of king, queen, parliament, or any of the ministers. Marriages are not legal among them. Their wills have no force by law. The children are to be bastards. Their parsons to be hanged." Lafayette had decided "to be a leader in that affair, and to have their situation changed." He planned to tour Protestant congregations around the country, then appeal to the king to correct the injustice. "It is a work of time, and of some danger to me," he said. "But I run my chance."[11]

Lafayette met Huguenot leaders, pledging to champion their cause. "The hero of America has become my hero," one of them exclaimed. He promised that "with patience and care, just causes win." It did take time. He told his adoptive father in February 1788, "The edit [edict] giving to the *non catholic subjects of the king* a civil estate has been registered." He proudly boasted that he had introduced to the king's ministers "the first Protestant clergyman who could appear at Versailles since the Revolution of 1685," meaning the Nantes revocation.[12]

That left slavery. Shortly after he returned to France, Lafayette heard from the Swiss-French abolitionist the marquis de Condorcet, author of a notorious refutation of all justifications for slavery. "No one on our continent has helped more than you," he told Lafayette, "to break those chains with which Europe endowed America. Perhaps the glory of overthrowing the slavery that we have imposed on the unfortunate Africans is also demanded of you." That would make him "the liberator of two of the four parts of the world." Coming from the most famous and highly regarded abolitionist in the world, this was a flattering appeal.[13]

Lafayette asked Hamilton about the New York Society for Promoting the Manumission of Slaves, but Hamilton never responded; to him it was just one of those things that a lawyer had to join. Thanks to the abolitionist John Jay, Lafayette became a member in 1788. He had tried to talk the ministers and the king into abolishing slavery in France and its colonies but failed. So in June 1785, he shelled out 125,000 livres to buy a sugarcane plantation in Cayenne (French Guyana). There, he told Washington, he would "free my Negroes in order to make that experiment which you know is my hobby horse."[14]

Once Lafayette had bought his plantation, he left its operation to

Adrienne, as usual. She hired a manager and talked some priests into serving as teachers. Washington applauded him. The goodness of his heart, he said, "displays itself in all circumstances, and I am never surprised when you give new proofs of it." The Cayenne plantation was "a generous and noble proof of your humanity. God grant that a similar spirit will animate all the people of this country! But I despair of ever seeing that happen."[15]

Lafayette's adoptive father had become an abolitionist, but a cautious one. There was "not a man living" who wished more sincerely than he did "to see a plan adopted for the abolition of it," he told Robert Morris, "but there is only one proper and effectual mode by which it can be accomplished, & that is by legislative authority: and this, as far as my suffrage will go, shall never be wanting." He told another friend he would never again "possess another slave by purchase." Moreover, the general would support any plan "by which slavery in this country may be abolished by slow, sure, & imperceptible degrees."[16]

In May 1791 Lafayette backed a measure to grant the decision on emancipation to the French colonies, and he was afraid that British agents might try to prevent acceptance of the decree. He had voted according to conscience, "not to policy," he told Washington. "Should the British take advantage of my honesty, I hope you will influence the colonies to submit to a decree so conformant to justice."[17]

KINGS ARE GOOD FOR NOTHING
BUT TO SPOIL THE SPORT

*L*afayette wrote as often as he could to Washington. There was a change in his letters, however. He still professed his love and said how much he missed the elder man. "Adieu, my dear general, think often of your bosom friend, your adopted son, who loves you so tenderly," he typically said. He usually called himself an adopted son, but there were no more childish pleas for approval. They sent each other gifts—hunting dogs, seeds and birds, breeding asses, and presents from the children sailed west, while seeds and birds, gifts from Martha and the children, and a barrel of Virginia hams went the other way. The elder man did give advice to the younger one. He offered his best wishes for his undertakings, he told him, but he should remember that "it is a part of the military art to reconnoitre and *feel* your way, before you engage too deeply."[18]

Advice could go both ways. After Washington talked Maryland and Virginia into chartering his navigation projects on the Potomac and James Rivers, Virginia granted him fifty shares in each of the corporations. He did not know whether to accept them. Lafayette advised him to take the stock as a reward for his services. Washington had told him that the king of Spain had promised him two Spanish jacks to breed to his mares, but they never showed up. Lafayette called that "a farther proof that kings are good for nothing but to spoil the sport." He sent some Maltese jacks to Mount Vernon.[19]

Lafayette made a grand tour of the German states in the summer and fall of 1785. He had been invited by Frederick the Great to join an international mob of generals at the annual maneuvers of the Prussian army. Among them were Cornwallis and the Duke of York, heir to the British throne. Frederick seated him between them at the nightly banquets, and directed all his questions to the Frenchman. "My reception," Cornwallis complained, "was not flattering; there was a most marked preference for La Fayette."[20]

The marquis told Washington all about it in one of the longest letters he ever wrote, in February 1786. He had met many German veterans of the American war. "Ancient foes ever meet with pleasure," he observed. Great Frederick had gone to seed. He "could not help being struck by that dress and appearance of an old, broken, dirty corporal, covered all over with Spanish snuff, with his head almost leaning on one shoulder, and fingers quite distorted by the gout."

The Prussian army was larger than any Lafayette had ever seen. For eight days, he watched over 30,000 troops perform with mechanical precision. After the demonstrations, he toured several battlefields. Wherever he went, he told his "dear general," he "had the pleasure to hear your name pronounced with that respect and enthusiasm which altho' it is a matter of course . . . never fails to make my heart glow with unspeackable happiness. . . . And to be your friend, your disciple, and your adopted son was . . . the pride of my heart." Despite their admiration for Washington, Frederick and other royalists baited Lafayette on his republican beliefs. They believed the United States was a weak, quarrelsome rabble, and his tour became a constant argument. He ran into the same problem when he met Emperor Joseph II in Vienna.[21]

Washington was overwhelmed by the wealth of detail, which made him wax philosophical. "To have viewed the several fields of battle over which you passed," he mused, "could not, among other sensations, have failed to excite this thought, here have fallen thousands of gallant spirits to satisfy the ambition of, or to support their sovereigns perhaps in acts of oppression or injustice! melancholy reflection! For what wise purposes does Providence permit this?"[22]

They discussed what to do about the British, who refused to give up their military posts in the Northwest. Lafayette advised resuming the war; Washington was more patient. The young man was shaken when he learned that Greene had died. Washington told him that "in him you lost a man who affectionately regarded and was a sincere admirer of you." He was happier to report that Shays' Rebellion, a tax- and debt-relief uprising in Massachusetts that had threatened the national armory at Springfield, had ended peacefully.[23]

America and France entered times of trial in 1787. Washington left Mount Vernon in the spring to preside over the Constitutional Convention. Lafayette was appointed to the Assembly of Notables, summoned by the king because his government faced bankruptcy and he hoped the Notables would find a peaceful way to bail him out. Lafayette, one of thirty-six nobles there, became a leader of upper-class intellectuals who believed France must cease to be a "despotism" and adopt the principles of the American Revolution. The king called them to order in February, and they met into early May.[24]

The finance minister, Calonne, recommended big cuts in government spending, meaning the excesses of the spendthrift queen. He wanted to limit the king's access to state funds, and he wanted tax reform. Crowds filled the streets outside the Assembly, and the whiff of revolution was in the air, so there would be no further taxes on the poor, but new ones on the nobility, who had been exempt. He also wanted to eliminate the Farm. Lafayette was impressed, but his fellow nobles dug in. The Assembly started as an appeal to patriotism. It turned into a near brawl.

Lafayette was at first optimistic, he told Washington. He planned to push for fundamental reforms, including "a kind of House of Representatives in each province," and an overhaul of taxes, spending, and the government. Inquiry into the government's finances soon exposed corruption, causing an open confrontation between Lafayette and Calonne. The marquis called for a National Assembly. This was going too far—an elected legislature would mean the end of royal absolutism. Calonne demanded that Lafayette be arrested, but instead the king banished the marquis from court and fired the finance minister. The proposal for a National Assembly was diverted into a call for the Estates General, a gathering of the country's leading lights last summoned in the early seventeenth century.

Lafayette told Washington he had "made a motion to inquire into bargains by which, under pretence of exchanges, millions had been lavished upon princes and favourites . . . M. de Calonne went up to the king, to ask I should be confined to the Bastille. An oratory battle was announced betwen us for the next meeting and I was getting the proofs of what I had advanced, when Calonne was overthrown from his post, and so our dispute ended, except that the king and family . . . don't forgive me for the liberties I have taken." He was proud of himself. [25]

Lafayette thought he was doing as his adoptive father would have done. Others had already noticed that in him. The wily French bishop and politician Talleyrand concluded that it was as if somebody was telling him what to do, although he did not know who. Madame de Staël, witty chronicler of the French Revolution, said that it was "an extraordinary phenomenon, that a character like M. de Lafayette should have developed among the highest ranks of the French nobility." She concluded that the only explanation was his devotion to Washington. He had received liberal ideas from his adoptive father, but he entirely forgot the elder man's discretion and practicality. [26]

The debates in the Assembly spilled into the streets, and agitators ranted on every corner. For the first time, Frenchmen shouted about such ideas as liberty, equality, and representative government. Mobs filled Paris, calling for the heads of the king and all aristocrats, and France began its slide into anarchy. As Jefferson told Adams, "The king long in the habit of drowning his cares in wine, plunges deeper and deeper; the queen cries but sins on." He saw the end coming for royalism. [27]

Lafayette became known in court as "the most dangerous man of all."

When Marie-Antoinette urged the king to cancel Lafayette's commission, the marquis resigned from the army. No longer welcome at Versailles, he lost his attachment to the court and its system. Restrictions on the provincial assemblies did not improve his outlook. "We made loud complaints," he told Washington in October 1787, referring to his participation in the Auvergne Assembly. It rejected any new taxes without reform of royal spending. Some assemblies sent delegates to Versailles, and they were tossed into prison.

The king of France was "all mighty," the marquis complained. He had "all the means to enforce, to punish, and to corrupt." His ministers had "the inclination, and think it their duty to preserve despotism." But he was optimistic that his country would follow the American example. Washington sent him a copy of the new Constitution of the United States, telling him that it was "now a child of fortune, to be fostered by some and buffeted by others. What will be the general opinion on, or the reception of it" was not for him to decide. Lafayette declared it "a bold, large, and solid frame for the Confederation." He had only two objections: it needed a bill of rights, and he thought the office of president had too much power, although he took comfort that Washington could not refuse being elected president. The solution to France's problems, he decided, was to adopt a constitution on the American model.[28]

Washington worried about his adopted son's safety. A French abolitionist visited him at Mount Vernon early in 1788. "He spoke to me of M. de la Fayette with the greatest tenderness," the visitor reported. "He regarded him as his child; and foresaw, with a joy mixed with inquietude, the part that this pupil was going to act in the approaching revolution of France."[29]

"I hope and trust the political affairs in France are taking a favorable turn," Washington told Lafayette in February 1788. It gave him "great pleasure to learn that the present ministry of France are friendly to America; and that Mr. Jefferson and yourself have a prospect of accomplishing measures which will mutually benefit and improve the commercial intercourse between the two nations."[30]

One of those nations was sliding toward chaos, and the weakness began at the top. King Louis suffered bouts of depression and fell into prolonged silences. When he was worried, he stuffed himself with food and wine until he collapsed. The queen dominated him, and as the months passed he became increasingly isolated. Meanwhile, "clubs" and "societies" sprang up all over Paris, and Lafayette organized one called the Club of Thirty. After Washington sent him the American Constitution, he invoked it so often that they became known as "Constitutionalists," "Americans," or "Fayettistes." Eventually they called themselves "Patriots," like the American rebels.

They met often, and Jefferson was usually there, although he did not participate. "This party comprehended all the honesty of the kingdom," he told a friend. He saw it as the best hope for France's future. But Jefferson did not know where Lafayette got his ideas for running its meetings. When he hosted one of them, he was "a silent witness to a coolness and candor of argument, unusual in the conflicts of political opinion; to a logical reasoning, and chaste eloquence, disfigured by no gaudy tinsel of rhetoric or declamation . . . the Patriots all rallied to the principles thus settled." That could have described Washington's councils of war.[31]

The clubs planned to compete for power in the National Assembly that Lafayette had proposed, but they had to settle for an Estates General. The provincial assemblies met again in February 1788 but were denied freedom of debate and fell apart. The one in Auvergne voted to split into two provinces, and within months other separatist movements arose in almost every province, followed by riots in cities across France. Bowing to pressure from his ministers, on September 23, 1788, Louis called for the first meeting of the Estates General since 1614, for the following spring. He summoned a second Assembly of Notables in November to decide how the Estates General should be assembled.

There were three Estates—the clergy, the nobility, and everyone else. The king would appoint half the first two, which would elect the rest from their own members. The Third Estate excluded most commoners, because of limited suffrage and a high poll tax. Each Estate had one collective vote, so the first two could outvote the Third. Lafayette proposed that the Notables expand entry to the Third Estate and give it two votes to balance the vested interests. He lost.[32]

The affairs of France had "come to a crisis," the marquis admitted. Washington warned him, "Little more irritation would be necessary to blow up the spark of discontent into a flame that might not easily be quenched. . . . Let it not, my dear marquis, be considered as a derogation from the good opinion that I entertain of your prudence when I caution you . . . against running into extremes and prejudicing your cause."[33]

In the fall of 1788, a rumor that Lafayette had been imprisoned in the Bastille threw a scare into Washington. He told the marquis that he hesitated to say anything in his letters that might endanger the young man. Since that time, he said, he had "been made happy by hearing, that public affairs have taken a more favourable turn in France," a reference to the Estates General.[34]

When Washington received a letter from Lafayette in January 1789, it put him at ease. As for his own situation, he was still reluctant to accept the American presidency, but he would if he had to. While Europeans were quarreling among themselves, he observed, his young friend need not doubt that Americans would "continue in tranquility."[35]

The year 1789 would see big changes in both countries and in the separate roles of Washington and Lafayette. The strong bond between them guided the American's response to what happened across the ocean. He saw the events through Lafayette's eyes, hoping that his adopted son would achieve the success he desired. What actually happened took both of them by surprise.[36]

HE IS SENSIBLE HIS PARTY ARE MAD

Early in 1789 Washington sent Gouverneur Morris to France as a trade representative and as his confidential agent. A former congressman who had supported Lafayette during the aborted Canadian campaign in 1778, Morris was a gigantic man, as tall as Washington, who wore a peg leg because of a carriage accident a few years earlier. He had a ringside seat at France's unraveling and gave Washington candid reports on what his adopted son was up to.[37]

After Lafayette was elected to the Estates General from Auvergne, Morris told Washington that it was because "[h]e was too able for his opponents. He played the orator with as much *éclat* [brilliance] as ever. He acted the soldier and is at this moment as much envied and hated as his heart could wish. He is also much beloved by the nation for he stands forward as one of the principal champions for her rights." Lafayette and the other liberals were friends of the United States, but the other members of the Estates showed "extreme rottenness." The nobles were thieves and liars, and the people had "no religion but their priests, no law but their superiors, no moral but their interest." The first use they made of liberty was "to form insurrections everywhere."[38]

The government answered unrest by sending troops to shoot into crowds. Earlier, in the summer of 1788, a colossal hailstorm had flattened crops in the central part of the country. That followed two years of drought, and the worsened food shortages caused more riots. The court had lost its financial credit, so it issued paper money, backed by nothing. Nobody would

Gouverneur Morris, by Edward Dalton Marchant, after Thomas Sully, 1873–74. A man of biting wit, Morris had a ringside seat at the French Revolution and gave Washington candid reports about what his adopted son was up to. He also helped to save Adrienne's life, and resented Monroe's claiming full credit for that.
(INDEPENDENCE NATIONAL HISTORICAL PARK)

accept it. The Farm doubled its duties on foodstuffs, prices soared, markets crashed, and factories closed, laying off 200,000 workers. By 1789, leaflets papered the cities, accusing the court of trying to starve the country into submission.[39]

Lafayette was the champion of the Third Estate, but he had been elected to the Second with warnings to defend his own class' interests. He was torn. Early in May 1789 he went to Jefferson's house to ask for advice. Morris was there, and they both urged him to wait until things became clear before he played his hand. Jefferson told Washington that he was "in great pain for the M. de Lafayette." He told the marquis, "As it becomes more and more possible that the noblesse will go wrong, I become uneasy for you. Your principles are decidedly with the *tiers état* [Third Estate], and your instructions are against them." He cautioned against giving "an appearance of trimming between the two parties which may lose you both." He expected Lafayette to go over to the Third eventually, and warned him that he was playing in a dangerous game.[40]

The king opened the Estates General at Versailles in May and told the three bodies to meet separately. The Abbé Sieyès, one of Lafayette's Club of Thirty, proposed that they all meet together, with every member voting on his own, instead of the three collective votes. The Third naturally went along with that, and Sieyès talked the poorer clergy in the First into agreeing. Lafayette could get only 46 of 234 nobles in the Second to agree. Not much happened until the dauphin died a month later and the king retired with his ministers to mourn. The "court party" was leaderless, and the Fayettistes gained more converts in the First. Sieyès talked them into converting the Estates General into a National Assembly, ending 500 years of absolutism.

When the members tried to enter their meeting hall the next day, they were barred by troops. Inside, the remaining members of the First and the majority of the Second voided all resolutions of the Assembly. Lafayette's ally Sylvain Bailly of Paris led the assemblymen to the royal tennis court, where he declared that the Assembly was going to prepare a constitution, restore public order, and uphold the principles of a limited monarchy. The members swore the "Tennis-Court Oath," pledging to stick together. They reassembled in a church, their membership including the whole of the Third, 150 clergy, and two nobles.

Lafayette was at home working on a document that he hoped would resolve everything. He showed up the day after the oath, when the king ordered the Assembly to adjourn and reassemble as separate Estates. Bailly and the pugnacious comte de Mirabeau (critic of the Society of the Cincinnati) defied him. "A nation assembled does not accept orders," Bailly roared. The delegates cheered, then voted to end absolutism once and for all. "The National Assembly will now concern itself," Bailly declared, "without distraction or rest, with the regeneration of the realm and the public welfare."[41]

Morris told Lafayette that a people who had known nothing but tyranny could not become republicans overnight. The marquis, he confided to his diary, "tells me I ignore the cause, for that my sentiments are continually quoted against the good party. I seize this opportunity to tell him that I am opposed to the democracy from regard to liberty. That I see they are going to destruction and would fain stop them if I could. . . . He tells me he is sensible his party are mad, and tells them so, but is not the less determined to die with them." Morris suggested that "it would be quite as well to bring them to their senses and live with them."[42]

All through June and into July, Paris and Versailles rumbled like awakening volcanoes. Nobles were in terror, abandoned by the king, who did nothing. Soldiers in Paris joined the mobs in drinking and rioting, and let prisoners out of jail. There were 30,000 troops at Versailles to protect the king, but he was afraid to order them into action.

Inspired by the American Constitution and Declaration of Independence, Lafayette had worked since January on "the First European Declaration of the Rights of Man and of the Citizen." He showed his drafts to Jefferson, but it was mostly his own work. On July 10, 1789, he introduced it to the Assembly as a preamble to a constitution. It said that "all men are created free and equal" and abolished social classes. All men also were "born with certain unalienable rights, including life, liberty, property, and the pursuit of happiness, the right to work, the right to hold and express opinions and religious beliefs, and the right to defend their persons, their lives, and their honor." People possessed "natural rights," which were those that did not interfere with the rights of others. Other articles established a constitutional monarchy with three branches and called for "clear, precise and uniform laws for all citizens." The legislature must approve all spending.[43]

Jefferson liked it. Morris was cynical. "Our American example has done them good," he groused, "but like all novelties, liberty runs away with their discretion, if they have any. They want an American Constitution . . . without reflecting that they have not American citizens to support that Constitution." He doubted that democracy stood a chance in France, "unless the whole people are changed."[44]

The Declaration provided the "irritation" that Washington had warned about. Paris exploded, as street-corner ranters used it to whip crowds into a frenzy. The people were equal to the king and nobility, so they had the right to tear the latter two down. On July 12 a combination of food riots, anarchist uprisings, and looting consumed the city. Troops at the Tuileries Palace fired on the crowd. Other troops defied orders to shoot. The Third Estate of Paris, led by Bailly, formed a government and a Bourgeois Guard to restore order. It did not.

On the evening of the thirteenth, rumors spread that the queen had demanded that the king send troops to arrest the National Assembly, which voted to stay in session through the night. On the evening of July 14, 1789, the members learned that the Paris mob had taken the Bastille, the prison fortress on the city wall. The rioters had been looting arsenals all day, acquiring arms but no powder, which was stored in the Bastille. After the guards there killed 175 protesters, troops who had joined them dragged up a cannon and blew the doors in, freeing all seven prisoners. The mob spread out, killing, hanging, and beheading many.

Louis XVI. He was a waddling argument against the divine right of kings, but in a bow to tradition Lafayette wanted him to become the first head of a French constitutional monarchy. (SKILLMAN LIBRARY, LAFAYETTE COLLEGE)

All of Versailles was horrified. The king visited the Assembly on July 15 and bowed to its authority. He asked for help in restoring order. "And here, again," Jefferson remembered, "was lost another precious occasion of sparing to France the crimes and cruelties through which she has since passed. . . . The king was now become a passive machine in the hands of the National Assembly, and had he been left to himself, he would have willingly acquiesced in whatever they should devise as best for the nation. . . . But he had a queen of absolute sway over his weak mind and timid virtue." He was correct. Marie-Antoinette was plotting to reverse everything that had happened.[45]

Assuming that Louis' capitulation meant that the French Revolution was over, Lafayette led a delegation of the Assembly to Paris. What they found there was appalling. Bailly asked him to take command of the Bourgeois Guard, so he donned his *maréchal*'s uniform, commandeered a big white horse, and reined in the militiamen roaming the streets. He renamed them the National Guard of Paris and assigned officers for each district. He sent convoys to escort food into the city, and ordered the Bastille demolished. He attacked lynch mobs, and by the end of the month the city began to calm down. When Morris asked him if the troops would always obey him, he replied that they

Marie-Antoinette, Louis' queen. She represented everything that was worst about the wretched excesses of Versailles. "The queen weeps, but sins on," Jefferson said. If she had trusted Lafayette, she might have saved her and Louis' lives. (SKILLMAN LIBRARY, LAFAYETTE COLLEGE)

might not do guard duty in the rain, but they would follow him into action. Morris predicted that Lafayette would have "an opportunity of making the experiment." He thought Lafayette was trading wholly on his popularity. "If the sea runs high, he will be unable to hold the helm."

There were two kinds of ambition, "the one born of pride, the other of vanity, and his partakes most of the latter."[46]

On July 17 Lafayette summoned the king, who arrived with members of the Assembly. Lafayette met him at the city gates and conducted him to the Hôtel de Ville, where Bailly presented Louis with the key to the city and a red and blue cockade, symbol of the Revolution. The king confirmed the city's status as self-governing and Lafayette's as commander of the National Guard. Nobles began to flee the country that night. Morris told Washington that Lafayette "had his sovereign during the late procession to Paris completely within his power. He had marched him where he pleased, measured the degree of applause he should receive as he pleased, and if he pleased could have detained him prisoner."[47]

The center of Paris was calm, but everywhere else the city was overrun with savagery. Lafayette had seen nothing like it in America. He had naively thought that achieving liberty would be simple, but now he had the duty of taming the chaos. He learned how to be a labor negotiator, arbitrator, militia commander, and domestic diplomat. In the process he filled the vacuum left by the royal government, and by the fall he was known as *père nourricier* (father-provider) of the city. Between them, he and Bailly established the credibility of the revolutionary government, whose main instrument was the National Guard. A new "patriotism" emerged in France. Instead of king or country, it was love for a political ideal embodied in the people, but its hero was Lafayette.[48]

Four factions emerged during the disorder. The royalists wanted to restore the absolute monarchy under Louis. The Orléanists were populists who wanted to replace Louis with his cousin the duc d'Orléans, who had renamed himself Philippe Égalité (equality). Lafayette's club favored a constitutional monarchy with Louis on the throne. The Jacobin Club (named for an old monastery that served as its headquarters), led by lawyer and agitator Maximilien Robespierre, wanted to overthrow the monarchy and establish a dictatorship of the "common will."

Lafayette threatened to resign early in August if he did not get enough support for his efforts to restore order. The Paris government made him military dictator of the city, provided money for the troops, and offered him a hefty salary and expense allowance. Citing Washington's example, he declined the latter two. Enlisting trustworthy officers, he made the

Guard a force of 50,000 men, outfitted in uniforms of red, white, and blue that he designed. He seized weapons, banned street demonstrations, and arrested rabble-rousers. Like his adoptive father, he promised to return to private life once his work was done.[49]

The Assembly, which Lafayette seldom attended, adopted the Declaration of Rights on August 26, 1789, but it was no longer the document he had drafted. His definition of individual responsibility and provisions for universal suffrage, abolition of slavery, equality between the sexes, and free trade were gone. There were new provisions granting absolute freedom of speech and the press, and a universal right to resist "oppression," which each citizen could define for himself. It was a recipe for anarchy.

Violence continued to erupt. The Declaration's grant of unfettered freedom of speech and the press made things worse, because new demagogues and thousands of pamphlets and broadsides flooded Paris. They accused the royal family of living in luxury while the people starved, and demanded that the king move into the city. Lafayette and his Guard grew increasingly busy as September advanced. France seemed to be going insane, and even Jefferson was worried. Civil war was "much talked of and expected," he said.[50]

Mob rule was the greater danger, as the resistance from the king was not strong enough to force the moderates to band together and fight back. On the first of October a regiment of royal troops summoned by the queen entered the gates of Versailles, and the next day the king rejected the Declaration of Rights. Orators were soon working the Paris mobs. On October 5, thousands of women, finding the bakeries empty, marched on the Hôtel de Ville. It was before opening time, but somebody rang the emergency bell, which drew mobs armed with pikes. They broke into the place and looted it, then set off for Versailles to raid the palace bakery. Guardsmen joined them, to protect them from the royal troops. The horde expanded into many thousands, armed with a variety of weapons and even three cannons. When Lafayette reached the city hall, six Guard companies demanded that he lead them to Versailles. He agreed, on condition that they stood by their oaths to protect the royal family. He marched them to the head of the mob and reached Versailles at about midnight.

The Guard commander was greeted by a message from the frightened king, who "regarded his approach with pleasure" and had just accepted the Declaration of the Rights of Man. Lafayette led a weird torchlight procession through Versailles, then went to the palace, where he presented the crowd's demands for bread and for the king and government to move to Paris. By three in the morning, everyone was exhausted, so he went to the Noailles mansion and collapsed in sleep. He had asked that his Guard take over from the royal troops, but Marie-Antoinette objected. She did not trust him.

Lafayette was awakened before dawn by news that the mob had crashed the palace gate, overwhelmed the soldiers, and beheaded two of them. Grabbing a horse and waving his sword, he charged into the crowd, his guardsmen behind. The throng scattered, surrounding the palace. By ten o'clock he had talked the king into going to Paris and harangued the crowd from a balcony. The people called for the queen's head, so he took her out and kissed her hand. Madame de Staël, from inside, heard shouts of *"Vive La Fayette!"*

The mob set off for Paris, trailed by wagons carrying the royal flour. Behind them rode the royal family, surrounded by guardsmen. It took until the seventh to make the trip, which ended with a procession through hooting crowds. When the royal family reached the Hôtel de Ville, Bailly greeted them and thanked them for giving bread to the people. It ended with the king and family waving to cheering masses from the front steps. According to William Short, the American chargé, Lafayette was called "the guardian angel of the day."[51]

The "October Days" of 1789 were another triumph for Lafayette, but he failed to follow through. The royal family was confined to the Tuileries, while mobs roamed the streets to prevent their escape. The Assembly moved to Paris and voted to impose martial law. The Guard put down riots, brought food into the city, and arrested those whose hobby was beheading people. The country called Lafayette its "protector," but when the Assembly offered him its presidency, he declined because he was too busy putting down trouble.

Lafayette coasted along on his popularity, but he acted with no real authority. His ally Mirabeau observed, "The multitude is totally ignorant of the dictatorship which La Fayette exercises so maladroitly . . . and if it knew the sort of ministry without responsibility he wished to arrogate to himself, his public credit would be ruined." Louis offered Lafayette the marshal's baton, the constable's sword, even the position of lieutenant general of the kingdom, but he turned them down. Other generals thought he should accept these offers. If he feared for his popularity, he should take command of all National Guards in the country, disband or reform the army, and establish the constitutional monarchy. He stayed with the Paris Guard, making a point of refusing greater power, because that is what Washington had done, as he saw it.[52]

THE SCENE OF THE ONE ACTION WAS IN HEAVEN, THE OTHER IN HELL

The fall of the Bastille and the king's capitulation made the world think that France had completed a peaceful revolution. The news reached America early in the fall. Hamilton congratulated his friend Lafayette, although he feared "much for the final success of the attempts, for the fate of those I esteem who are engaged in it." He felt a "foreboding of ill" over what would happen, especially to Lafayette.[53]

Washington, since April 30, 1789, president of the United States, complained that he had not heard from his young friend in some time. There had been "a long interval of silence between two persons whose habits of correspondence have been so uninterruptedly kept up as ours," he told Lafayette, "but the new and arduous scenes in which we have both been lately engaged will afford a mutual excuse." He was mystified by the news from France. "The revolution, which has taken place with you, is of such magnitude and of so momentous a nature that we hardly yet dare form a conjecture about it. We however trust, and fervently pray that its consequences may prove happy."[54]

Privately, Washington told Morris that the revolution going on in France was "of too great a magnitude to be effected in so short a space, and with the loss of so little blood." On the other hand, he told a friend in January 1790, he would "sincerely rejoice to see that the American Revolution has been productive of happy consequences on both sides of the Atlantic." The "agency of the Marquis de la Fayette" was "in a high degree honourable to his character."[55]

Washington was ambivalent, because while he hoped for the best, he dreaded the consequences for his adopted son. He had reason to worry, because with the king a prisoner of the Assembly, the country's fate rested in the hands of its members. The royalists had fled the country, leaving three factions—the remaining nobles, the liberals, and the *enragés* (madmen). In January 1790, the lunatics took over the asylum. Lafayette was too often absent keeping the peace to organize resistance to them. Shouting the moderates into silence, the radical Jacobins abandoned the attempt to write a constitution and grabbed power through a supreme governing council, a Jacobin caucus that lorded it over the Assembly. They revoked the last of the king's authority and abolished the Catholic Church. Disagreement with them was declared treasonous. They extended their political control over the country by dividing it into districts, cantons, and communes, each run by a prosecutor. They were in total control by spring.

Once they had power, the radicals appropriated the lands of the king, church, and *émigrés* (nobles who had left the country) and issued 400 million livres in bonds, secured by the seized properties, which went up for sale. Their hatred for the old order was so intense that it inspired prolonged savagery all over France. Mobs looted unguarded mansions in the cities, while peasants did the same to country homes. The army started to fall apart, as commoner soldiers slaughtered officers. The establishment of a civil-service church touched off the mass butchery that only religion can inspire. Many of Lafayette's in-laws fled the country, but Adrienne stood by him, and her mother stood by her.[56]

"How often, my beloved general, have I wanted your wise advices and friendly support!" Lafayette cried to his adoptive father. Adrienne also wrote to Washington. "Monsieur, in the midst of the agitations of our revolution," she told him, "I have never ceased to share in Monsieur de La Fayette's happiness at having followed in your footsteps, in having found in your example and your lessons a means of serving his country."[57]

They had grounds for optimism early in 1790, because Lafayette retained his popularity. In a process called "Caesarism," strongmen took over in many provinces, but there was only one national figure— Lafayette. He was so popular that 1790 was for many months called the "Year of Lafayette." It appeared that he had persuaded the king to go along with the revolution, and he escorted the monarch into the Assembly in February to say so. But the queen and king were both plotting against him, and he did not know it.

Hoping to restore a liberal faction to counter the radicals, in the spring Lafayette formed a partnership with Mirabeau, and they organized the Club of 1789. "Your great qualities need my force," Mirabeau told him, "and my force needs your great qualities." He warned him that nobody can be popular all the time. Lafayette had strong principles, but not much practical political sense. Still, he had to be reckoned with. As long as the National Guard of Paris was behind him, he was invincible. This could not have been more different from the Washington of the Newburgh Addresses.[58]

The revolution was "getting on as well as it can with a nation that has swalled [sic] up liberty all at once," Lafayette told Washington in March, "and is still liable to mistake licentiousness for freedom——The Assembly have more hatred to the ancient system than experience on the proper organization of a new and constitutional governement——The ministers are lameting [sic] the loss of power, and affraïd to use that which they have." Because everything had been "destroïed and not much new building is yet above ground, there is much room for critics and calomnies."

If Lafayette had one political talent, it was for the symbolic gesture. "Give me leave, my dear general," he said, "to present you with a picture of the Bastille just as it looked a few days after I ordered its demolition, with the main kea [key] of that fortress of despotism." He presented it as a tribute which he owed "as a son to my adoptive father, as an aide de camp to my general, as a missionary of liberty to its patriarch." The key symbolized people fighting for liberty. He knew Washington would think of it that way, and when it arrived, the general gave it a place of honor in his parlor at Mount Vernon. It is still there.[59]

Washington was proud of Lafayette, loved him, and wanted him to do the right thing. Always he assumed that he had. "Nor is it without the most sensible pleasure I learn," he told former ambassador La Luzerne, "that our friend the Marquis de la Fayette, has in acting the arduous part which has fallen to his share, conducted himself with so much wisdom and apparently to such general satisfaction." He told Lafayette, "How much, how sincerely am I rejoiced, my dear marquis, to find that things are assuming so favorable an aspect in France! Be assured that you always have my best and most ardent wishes for your success."[60]

The American president accepted the Bastille key as "the token of victory gained by Liberty over Despotism . . . In this great subject of triumph for the New World," he continued, "and for humanity in general, it will never be forgotten how conspicuous a part you bore, and how much lustre you reflected on a country in which you made the first displays of character." Washington knew that other European powers threatened to intervene in France and would try to involve the United States. It was his government's policy "to keep in the situation in which nature has placed us," he said, "to observe a strict neutrality." America would remain "unentangled in the crooked politics of Europe."[61]

Washington's adopted son staged his most theatrical gesture on the first anniversary of the Bastille's fall. Talleyrand proposed a celebration, and Lafayette hijacked the idea to make himself the star, using the event to pressure the Assembly to cease tearing the country apart. He summoned delegations from National Guards all around France; workers converted the Champ de Mars, beside the Seine, into a gigantic stadium; and the city's population swelled. On July 10, 1790, 14,000 guardsmen from the provinces, representing over a million colleagues, declared themselves the Assembly of the Federation and elected him president. The next day he led them to the National Assembly and told it to finish the Constitution. The armed force behind him was a quiet threat. He marched his army to the Tuileries and presented it to the king, who received the troops gratefully. On the twelfth, he rode his white horse into the stadium to greet the royal family at one end, the Assembly at the other, while 160,000 spectators rimmed the place. America was represented by John Paul Jones and Tom Paine. Talleyrand led prayers as Lafayette stood beside him at the base of a pyramid where the royal family sat. Talleyrand thought it was all a joke. "For pity's sake," he whispered to Lafayette, "don't make me laugh!"

The *Fête de la Fédération* (Festival of the Federation) went on through July 14. William Short told Morris, "The marquis de Lafayette seemed to have taken full possession of the 'fédérés.' When I left Paris he was adored by them—that moment may be regarded as the zenith of his influence—but he made no use of it, except to prevent ill." He predicted that the time would come when the marquis would "repent not having seized that opportunity of giving such a complexion to the revolution, as every good citizen ought to desire." Lafayette again had been offered command of all National Guards but turned it down. No one, he said, should command outside his own city or province. This was a great error, because the Guard was his trump card.[62]

Replacing power with show turned out to be a trap. Lafayette's dream of a constitutional monarchy was all but dead, and he was the last to realize it. In refusing to accept national military power he had given up his last chance to salvage the situation. The king threw away the popularity he had regained by retreating to the Tuileries, and Lafayette's confinement to the Paris Guard created a political vacuum that was filled by the Jacobins. They flooded the country with lies about him and organized political clubs everywhere. They wanted to subvert all local governments, as well as the army and navy.

Thomas Paine, attributed to Bass Otis, after Thomas Thompson, from the William Sharp engraving after a painting by George Romney, ca. 1859. Lafayette used Paine and John Paul Jones as American stage props during the Festival of the Federation in 1790. (INDEPENDENCE NATIONAL HISTORICAL PARK)

Lafayette was the king's chief defender, but Louis let him down when radicals stirred up mutinies in several army and navy units. Louis' government, what there was of it, wanted the uprisings put down, and Lafayette urged the commandant at Metz to "strike a great blow" against the nearby Swiss Regiment. He did, hanging or torturing to death thirty-one soldiers and sending the rest to slave galleys. The king publicly congratulated the general for the massacre, and Lafayette's role became known. A Jacobin leader asked out loud, "Is it still possible to doubt that the great general, the hero of the Old World and the New, the immortal restorer of liberty, is the leader of the counterrevolutionaries, and the instigator of all the plots against the fatherland?" Mirabeau warned the king, "Popular outbreaks are the ruin of Monsieur de La Fayette. He will one day fire on the people. By that act alone, he will deal himself a mortal wound."[63]

Lafayette thought the French Revolution was over with the festival, but it was just beginning, and he was trapped in the storm he had unleashed. The country was "disturbed with revolts among the regiments," he complained to Washington in August. He said he was "constantly attaked on both sides by the aristocratic and the factious party" and did not know "to which of the two we owe these insurrections. Our safeguard against them lies with the National Guard. . . . and my influence with 'em is as great as if I had accepted the chief command." He ended on an ominous note, however. He had lost some of his "favour with the mob, and displeased the frantic lovers of licentiousness," because he was "bent on establishing a legal subordination."

The *émigrés* enlisted the other powers of Europe on their side. The kings and emperors loathed and feared the revolution, which they called the "French disease," a term formerly applied to syphilis. They blamed Lafayette for importing revolution from America, but they could not organize a plan of action. It was "not out of the heads of the aristocrats to make a counter revolution," he told Washington. But he thought their plans would be "either abandonned or unsuccessfull." He wanted to follow his adoptive father's example even as his popularity faded. He hoped "our business" would "end with the year—at which time this so much blackened Cromwell, this ambitious dictator, your friend, shall . . . become a private citizen." The people were becoming "a little tired with the Revolution and the Assembly," he admitted sadly.[64]

Lafayette did not know it, but his former ally Mirabeau had sold out to the queen and turned on him. Each thought himself the protector of the royal family, but because Marie-Antoinette feared Lafayette and trusted Mirabeau, the latter had the royal ear. He wanted to undermine Lafayette's domination of the city to pave a way for the king's escape. The result was another increase in violence. In January 1791, a great riot broke out in the suburb of La Chapelle. While Lafayette was putting it down, the Assembly more than doubled the duty on American whale oil. He was losing his grip.[65]

So long as the National Guard commander was busy keeping order, he could not throw his weight around in the Assembly. In March Lafayette complained to Washington that it had slapped a duty on American tobacco. One by one, the trade favors he had won for the United States were being repealed. Whatever expectations he "had conceived of a speedy termination to our revolutionary troubles," he complained, he was "tossed about in the ocean of factions and commotions of every kind." It was his "fate to be on each side, with equal animosity attacked." He begged for guidance. Washington was too far away, and as president he could not meddle in French affairs. The distance that separated them, he advised, "suspended" his opinion on what was going on in France. He was careful even in how he addressed his letter, for the first time writing "Monsieur de la Fayette." The National Assembly had abolished titles of nobility, so to call him "my dear marquis" instead of "my dear sir" could endanger him.[66]

Lafayette and the Guard spent most of the spring of 1791 putting down one uprising after another. Trying to please both sides, he angered both. He saw himself as the protector of the royal family, but they saw him as their jailer. On Easter Monday, April 18, the king and his family decided to go to their estate at Saint-Cloud. Word got out, a crowd gathered, and they were blocked at the gates of the Tuileries. Lafayette showed up with the Guard and ordered the troops to clear the way. They refused, the king and his family went back inside, and the mob screamed that Lafayette had tried to help the king escape.

Lafayette was an outcast even in the National Guard. He submitted his resignation but, as Morris drolly observed, "found afterwards various reasons for not doing it. This is like him." Bailly talked him into withdrawing the resignation. The restored commandant required all officers and men to sign a new oath and purged those who would not. The ones he ousted went over to the radicals. In May 1791 the Assembly created a High Court to try crimes against the state, and in June Robespierre became the chief prosecutor. Lafayette and the king both appeared defenseless.[67]

Lafayette more than ever wanted to escape from public life. He wished it was in his power to give Washington an assurance that the troubles were at an end, he said in May. "The rage of parties, even among the patriots, is gone as far as it is possible, short of blood shed." All factions were against him, he said. When the Guard disobeyed him at the Tuileries and neither the Assembly nor the king would back him up, he "stood alone in defense of the law." Before he could bring his fellow citizens "to a sense of legal subordination," he "must have conducted them through the fear to loose the man they love," meaning himself.[68]

The commander of the Paris National Guard still thought he was the indispensable man a month later. He wanted to visit America, but France was "not in that state of tranquillity which may admit" of his absence. Foreign armies and *émigrés* were at the borders, disorder was in the streets, and he was needed to overhaul the army and navy. "The United States and France must be one people, and so begin the confederation of all nations who will assert their own rights," he declared. The French Washington expected to lead a world revolution.[69]

Lafayette had lost control over his own revolution, however, and the king betrayed him again. Prodded by Marie-Antoinette and aided by Mirabeau, he had been plotting his escape from France since the Easter incident. At midnight on June 20, 1791, the royal family set out for Metz, headed for the Austrian border. When their disappearance was discovered at dawn, Lafayette fanned the National Guard out in every direction. As he rode through the streets, crowds condemned him as a traitor. When he reached the National Assembly, he faced more denunciations from the Jacobins, who wanted his head.

The king and family were stopped 150 miles northeast of the city on June 22. Three days later Lafayette and guardsmen led the royal carriage through howling mobs to the Tuileries Palace. He felt let down by the man he had tried to protect. "Sire," he told Louis, "your majesty knows my loyalty to the crown; but I must tell you that if the crown separates itself from the people, I will remain at the side of the people." He asked the king if he had any orders. Louis answered sadly, "It seems to me, that I am more subject to your orders than you are to mine."[70]

After the royal family was recaptured, the queen's brother, Emperor Joseph of Austria, called upon all European monarchs to vindicate the king's honor "and to limit the dangerous extremes of the French Revolution." Robespierre used that as an excuse to seize power, and the

Assembly called for 100,000 volunteers to guard the Austrian frontier. On July 14 the radical clubs assembled a great mob at the Champ de Mars to call for the overthrow of the king. Lafayette talked Bailly into once again declaring martial law, and led what was left of the Paris Guard to the scene. When he told the crowd to disperse, they outshouted him and began throwing stones. He ordered the troops to fire, and somewhere between thirteen and fifty rioters fell dead, with hundreds wounded. Mirabeau's prediction had come to pass.[71]

Lafayette followed that confrontation by trying to stomp out the radicals, driving many of them from the city. Only Robespierre and his crew remained. With some of their allies summarily hanged by the Guard, the Assemblymen resumed writing the Constitution, and the king approved it on September 13, 1791. Washington had warned Lafayette, "The tumultuous populace of large cities are ever to be dreaded. Their indiscriminate violence prostrates for the time all public authority, and its consequences are sometimes extensive and terrible." He was worried about the younger man. He saw "the critical situation" in which Lafayette stood, and advised him that he would never have a greater occasion to show his "prudence, judgment, and magnanimity."

It appeared that peace was at hand. The Assembly went home on September 30, and the next day the first elected Parliament convened. Lafayette claimed victory, having established an American-style government, although the licentious Constitution was nothing of the sort. Emulating Washington, he resigned as commander of the Guard on October 8 and prepared to go to Chavaniac. The radicals returned to Paris.[72]

The new Constitution was "good for nothing," Morris grumbled to Washington. "The truth is that instead of seeking the public good by doing what was right, each sought his own advantage." Every day, the Assembly committed "new follies, and if this unhappy country be not plunged anew into the horrors of despotism it is not their fault." He declared that "America in the worst of times was much better because at least the criminal law was executed, not to mention the mildness of our manners."[73]

Lafayette saw the defects in the Constitution and in his own behavior. Without Washington to guide him, he had bungled. He also realized that Morris had been correct when he said that France was not America. He told William Short dejectedly, "Our American Revolution, had left my mind as it were in a state of maidenhead. It was not acquainted with the ways of man as it is now. I have fought the same battles for the same cause with the same spirit and success at the head of the right angels against the wrong ones. But the scene of the one action was in Heaven, the other in Hell."[74]

The French Washington went to his country estate, expecting his nation's call to return to its service, just as had happened with his adoptive father. He did not have to wait long.

FIFTEEN

The Lament of Washington
(JANUARY 1792–DECEMBER 1799)

To arms, oh citizens!

Form up in battalions!

March on, march on!

And soak our fields

With their evil blood!

—"LA MARSEILLAISE"

Lafayette set out for Chavaniac, which had so far escaped looting. Without the National Guard around him, he was not safe in Paris, nor was Adrienne, whose father was an *émigré.* Adrienne's mother and one of her sisters followed them. The first thing he did at his "place of retirement" was to write to Adélaïde, telling her that he was happy to have "no role to play but that of a plowman," like his adoptive father at Mount Vernon. He began remodeling, hired an overseer, and imported breeding stock. He sold some land to finance it all, and Adrienne handled the details. She told his financial manager, Morizot, that they lived "in a world of profound peace. Monsieur de La Fayette revels in its delights as though he had never known a more active existence." Only a war against the *émigrés* could tear him away from the place, she said.

Before he left Paris, Lafayette had stamped one more American im-print on his native land. He had clothed the National Guard in red, white, and blue, the colors he had marched under in America. When the govern-ment called out volunteers, it ordered them to wear something blue. What was left of the royal army wore white. Red was the symbol of the French Revolution. Lafayette combined the colors into a new national flag—the red, white, and blue Tricolor, which still flies over France.[1]

HIS CIRCLE IS COMPLETED

With Lafayette gone from Paris, the Jacobins had the upper hand. The moderates were not strong enough to resist them and begged Lafayette to return to command the Paris Guard, but he refused. The Jacobins ignored the country's famine and fiscal crisis and abandoned the Constitution. They concentrated on the things that political fanatics thought important. They adopted beheading by the guillotine to replace hanging for executions, so common criminals could die like nobles. They changed the number and names of the months. Old titles of courtesy (*sieur, madame*) were outlawed, replaced by *citoyen* (citizen) and *citoyenne* (citizeness). Anybody who did not conform was an "enemy of the people."[2]

The *émigrés* thought they saw a chance to retake their country and as-sembled a small army in Austria, on the French border. Soon Austria and other German nations supported them. The Assembly had condemned to death any *émigrés* who did not return to France before the start of 1792, and rattled its sabers at Austria. It expected to put together three armies of 50,000 men each, volunteers and regulars, to face the enemy.

The minister of war recommended three generals to command the new forces. Rochambeau would lead the Army of the North on the Belgian border; a Prussian veteran of the Seven Years' War, Nicolas Baron von Luckner, the Army of the Rhine on the right; and Lafayette the Army of the Center, at Metz. The king objected to Lafayette. The minister told him that whatever his preferences, public opinion would force him to ap-point Lafayette. Besides, giving him an army would keep him out of Paris. The conqueror of Cornwallis left Chavaniac at the end of December 1791.[3]

Lafayette and the others folded the old military order into the new regime. The regulations of the royal army were still mostly in effect, and many regimental officers remained in place. But the Jacobins were hostile to anything left from the old days and wanted to replace the army with the "Nation at Arms." Lafayette had handed them the means to that with the National Guard, and it became the nucleus of a new People's Army.[4]

The volunteers were unruly, and the regulars remained mutinous. Generals were accused of betraying the soldiers by putting them where they might be shot at. When General Théobald Dillon confronted an Austrian contingent at Tournai early in the spring, his advance met some artillery fire, and the whole French force stampeded in panic. After they caught their breath, the soldiers hunted Dillon down, butchered him, and hanged his remains from a lamppost in Lille. Rochambeau narrowly escaped similar treatment.[5]

Lafayette formed his infantry brigades with one regiment of regulars and two battalions of volunteers, to combine the steadiness of the former with the enthusiasm of the latter. Instead, the regulars lost their steadiness, while the volunteers were explosive. The veteran of Washington's army introduced to the French army clouds of skirmishers to mask the main body of the army in attack, a larger version of his American tactics. He built on Knox's field artillery system, which grew into massed artillery as the revolutionary army became the Napoleonic one. Along with the rapid assembly of divisions through the *corps d'armée* (army corps), these measures allowed the French army to dominate Europe until 1815.[6]

The disaster at Tournai, followed by a similar one at Mons, reflected what Lafayette could see in his own troops. The volunteers were riddled with agitators, hostile to any hierarchy. They were disobedient to their generals, who in turn feared that they might suffer Dillon's grisly fate at the smallest setback. Led by Rochambeau, many commanders resigned. Those who remained, including Lafayette, decided that military survival required reestablishing order in the army and in Paris. By May, he was ready to march on the capital with his most reliable troops. He sent a message to the Austrian ambassador proposing a truce, so he could deal with the Paris militants, but he failed to act.[7]

Lafayette wrote Washington when he arrived at Metz in January

1792, and outlined his situation. He found only about half the army he had been promised. He was short of officers, the regulars were sullen, and the volunteers were undisciplined. He thought he was the only French general popular enough to impose discipline on this unruly mob. As for why he had taken the command, it was to defend French liberty and the new Constitution from foreign invaders and counterrevolutionaries, and because the people asked him to. He promised to keep Washington fully informed, "for I alwaïs consider myself, my dear general, as one of your lieutenants on a detached command."[8]

Lafayette and the remaining moderates were not ruthless enough to compete with the Jacobins, who were better propagandists. There was a common joke that winter that if Lafayette gave bread to the poor, the radicals would accuse him of trying to bribe the masses. When the second volume of Thomas Paine's *The Rights of Man* appeared, with a dedication to Lafayette on the opening page, it set the stage for his downfall, despite the differences between their beliefs.[9]

Lafayette warned Washington in March not to accept any false accounts about events in Europe, particularly news from England. There was no doubt that liberty and equality would be preserved in France, but on the other hand, "you well know that I will not if they fall survive them." Still he thought war unlikely. "The danger for us lies with our state of anarchy owing to the ignorance of the people."[10]

Washington sympathized with the younger man's being pulled away from his home, but "[i]n the revolution of a great nation we must not be surprized at the vicissitudes to which individuals are liable," and the demands on Lafayette equaled the weight of his public importance. The American was too far away to understand what was happening, so uncertainty bothered him. He was anxious for Lafayette's personal safety, and he had "yet no grounds for removing that anxiety."

Still, Washington had "the consolation of believing that, if you should fall it will be in defence of that cause which your heart tells you is just. And to the care of that Providence, whose interposition and protection we have so often experienced, do I chearfully commit you and your nation," hoping that all the turmoil would work out for the best. Washington had never been outwardly religious, and allusions to Providence had only recently entered his letters to Lafayette, who was a nonbeliever. It was a sign of aging. Not wanting to end on that note, he added that the Frenchman's friends in the United States were interested in his welfare, and asked about him "with an anxiety that bespeaks a warm affection." Lafayette was still popular in America, if not so much in France.[11]

The younger general never received that letter, because his world turned upside down before it reached him. On April 20, 1792, the Assembly declared war on Austria and sent the center and left armies into Belgium. They were up against 150,000 German regulars, and at the first shot both undisciplined French armies disintegrated. "War was therefore undertaken with all possible disadvantage," Jefferson's agent in France reported. A Prussian-Austrian army under Duke Ferdinand of Brunswick marched toward Paris. The Assembly called up all the National Guards and more volunteers; 600,000 flocked to the country's banner. That gave the enemy pause.[12]

This armed mob handed the Jacobins enough muscle to overwhelm all opposition. At its heart were several battalions of provincial National Guardsmen, selected for their revolutionary fanaticism and stationed in Paris. The Assembly declared an emergency, suspended all civil liberties, made itself the government in perpetuity, and began ordering arrests. It demanded that the king disband his personal guard, 6,000 strong, stationed around the Tuileries. He agreed, shedding the last protection he owned. Trading a strong card for a weak one, the king exercised his power of veto against some Assembly measures. When the radicals demanded that he retract the vetoes, he showed rare backbone and refused. Lafayette applauded him, promising that "all the friends of liberty and all good Frenchmen" would rally around the throne to defend it against "rebel plots and factions." Lafayette would be with them, upholding his oath to defend the nation, the law, and the king.[13]

Lafayette complained to Washington about Gouverneur Morris being appointed ambassador to France. He was a friend, he said, but his allegedly aristocratic and counterrevolutionary principles made him unfit to be the representative of "the only nation whose politics have a likeness with ours, since they are founded on the plan of a representative democracy." Yet he admitted that all cabinet posts had gone to Jacobins, and France was anything but a representative democracy.[14]

Lafayette sent an open letter to the Assembly, a tirade against the Jacobins. He naively assumed that the majority of the Assembly was against them, so it should rise and toss the rascals out. Knowing the royal family was under threat from mobs, he tried to call out the National Guard. It did not respond. When an armed horde invaded the Tuileries Palace and forced the king to put on the red cap of revolution, he offered to help the royal family escape. Marie-Antoinette spurned him.

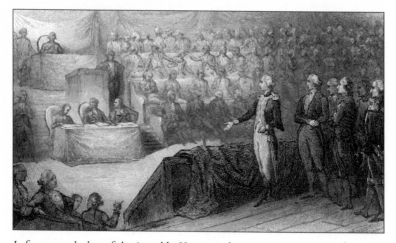

Lafayette at the bar of the Assembly. His empty harangue, not backed by force, set the stage for his downfall in 1792. (LILLY LIBRARY, INDIANA UNIVERSITY)

On June 28 Lafayette stormed into the Assembly and harangued the members, demanding that they shut down the Jacobin Club and restore order. At first many thought that he was there to announce a coup, but without any force to back him up, he just looked silly. When members asked why he had left his command without authority, he had no answer, and returned to his shattered army in Alsace. A regular artillery officer in Paris at the time disapproved of Lafayette's unauthorized presence and empty threats. It was perhaps necessary, he told his brother, "but it was very dangerous for the public liberty." He was considering how he might have handled the situation better. His name was Napoleon Bonaparte.[15]

Paris became an armed camp, or two of them. Hordes of volunteers, radical fanatics all, flooded the city. On the other side were the National Guard of Paris and the king's remaining defenders, the 600 men of the Swiss Guard. After three years in which politicians had threatened violence to get their way, the most violent of the bunch, the Jacobins, had won out. On August 10, 1792, volunteers attacked the Tuileries to seize the king, slaughtering the guards and 200 servants. Fighting continued in the streets for days, but the Paris Guard was outnumbered or deserted, and a general massacre of dissidents got under way. The Legislative Assembly, as it had restyled itself, declared the royal family traitors and sent them to prison. Further resolutions condemned Lafayette, also as a traitor, and sentenced him to death.[16]

"What a folly!" cried an American. He thought it absurd to claim that Lafayette, a champion of liberty, was a traitor to his country. The Assembly, thoroughly dominated by the Jacobins, offered a reward to anyone who brought in Lafayette or put him to death. "Thus, his circle is completed," Morris told Jefferson. "He . . . is crushed by the wheel he put in motion. He lasted longer than I expected."[17]

Lafayette summoned his officers and swore them to a new oath upholding the Constitution and the king. He toyed with the idea of marching on Paris, but once again he failed to act. He decided to run for it, and on August 21 he told Adrienne what he was doing. He would go to England, he said, and wanted his whole family to join him. "Let us resettle in America, where we will find the liberty that no longer exists in France."[18]

"I was dismissed and accused, that is to say an outlaw," Lafayette explained later. His "defense would have been bloody, but it would have been useless and the enemy was in position to profit from it." He wanted to attack in order to be killed, he claimed, but he saw no military advantage in that, so he stopped himself. "*I wanted to go die in Paris.* But I feared that such an example of popular ingratitude would only discourage future promoters of liberty. So I left."[19]

Lafayette led several dozen of his officers and others, who felt themselves threatened by the same forces that had condemned him, across the Belgian border into the Austrian Netherlands. The Austrians released some of them, transferred others to a military prison, and handed three to the Prussians. They were Lafayette, his aide Jean-Xavier Bureaux de Pusy, and a general, César, comte de La Tour-Maubourg. La Colombe, who had been with him since South Carolina, got away and went to New York. The king of Prussia ordered that the three Frenchmen be kept indefinitely in prison and sent them to Nivelles. Lafayette appealed to the Austrian emperor's uncle, who told him he was detained not as a prisoner of war, a citizen, or an *émigré* but because he had fomented the revolution that overturned France, put his king in irons and deprived him of all rights and legitimate powers, and was "the principal instrument of all the disgraces that overwhelmed that unfortunate monarch." It was fitting that Lafayette be confined until Louis was restored to power. The legitimate king of France would then determine the criminal's fate.[20]

The French Washington, who wanted to be loved by everyone, had become the most hated man in Europe. He who took revolution to France was its declared enemy. On the same grounds, he was an enemy to its real opponents, the crowned heads of Europe.

That revolution had turned into a national bloodbath, as the first guillotine went to work in Paris at about the time Lafayette crossed the border. Mobs rounded up suspects and butchered them by the thousands in the September Massacres. Looting, vandalism, and mass murder spread across the country. Every nation in Europe broke relations or declared war. The conflict would last for twenty-three years, but it got it off to a bad start for the allies. On September 20, 1792, at Valmy, a French army of 36,000 (mostly regulars) took on 34,000 men under Brunswick. The Prussians had outrun their supply lines, the weather was wretched, and the battle was mostly an artillery duel. The French gunners outmatched the enemy, and Brunswick retired over the border. The revolution was secure.[21]

I HAVE ASSOCIATED YOU WITH
STORMY DESTINIES

On August 26, Lafayette appealed to the American ambassador at The Hague, William Short. He was no longer French, he said, but an American citizen and an American officer. He asked for help. Short was sympathetic but did not know what to do, and asked Morris in Paris and Ambassador Thomas Pinckney in London. The prisoner's treatment was known to be brutal from the outset. Pressured by Madame de Staël to do something, Morris approached the Austrian chancellor, warning that the United States would feel "great concern" if Lafayette "should be in want."

Lafayette's American citizenship had had great value to him earlier in the French Revolution. The American people were bound to rise in out-rage over his savage treatment. On the other hand, America was an ally of France, and to the French government he was a deserter. In the end, Morris, Pinckney, and Short agreed that there was not much they could do. Morris sent his own money to a Dutch banker to make sure that the prisoner at least would not starve. The ambassadors asked Washington for instructions.[22]

Adrienne appealed to everyone of influence, begging for help for her husband. On September 10, 1792, an army headed by a Jacobin official invaded Chavaniac and sacked the place. She had a governess take ten-year-old Virginie to a safe place, but the mob had already spied Anastasie, age fifteen. George, twelve, was in hiding with his tutor, Félix Frestel. Adrienne, Anastasie, and Lafayette's aunt Charlotte were arrested and hauled to Le Puy for trial. There Adrienne defied the court and, along with Anastasie and Charlotte, was returned to Chavaniac on the grounds that there was no case against her. The Assembly declared her husband an émigré and confiscated the family property.[23]

Adrienne ordered Frestel to find a way to smuggle George out of the country. As Lafayette's son and heir, he was bound for execution if the Jacobins got their hands on him. Her husband had been moved to Wesel, near the Dutch border, where he was tossed into a small stone cell alone. The foul air, rancid food, and filth told on him, and his health declined. The prison doctor demanded that he be moved to better quarters, but the king refused—unless Lafayette revealed French military secrets. He did not.

On Morris' advice, Adrienne appealed directly to the king of Prussia. "I have always hoped, Sire, that Your Majesty would feel respect for virtue, irrespective of opinions, and would in this set a glorious example to all of Europe," she told him, and begged for the "happiness of giving to Your Majesty the joy of restoring me to life" by freeing her husband. She might as well have talked to a stone. Morris lent her 100,000 livres to pay her debts and feed her family.[24]

In October, Adrienne sent a tearful plea to the president of the United States. "In this abyss of grief," she cried, she hoped for "every thing from the goodness of a people with whom he has set an example of that liberty of which he is now the victim." She asked Washington to send an envoy to reclaim Lafayette, "in the name of the Republic of the U.S."

Once her husband was safe at Washington's side, she could bear the pain of separation "with more courage."[25]

News of Lafayette's captivity reached America along with that of mass executions taking place in France—the Terror, which took the head of the king early in 1793 and later that of the queen. Americans had first reacted favorably to the French Revolution, but as the bodies piled up, admiration turned to puzzlement, then to disgust. France seemed to be eating itself. Lafayette, however, remained popular, and by early 1793 he was the object of a national cult. A fashion for offering toasts to him spread across the country, and hundreds of them were published in newspapers. "The Marquis de La Fayette!" went a typical one. "May the gloom of a despot's prison be soon exchanged for the embraces of his father Washington, in the land of freedom!" People wanted him returned to the United States. One foreigner said that "to cherish and commiserate Fayette seems to be a sort of religious duty in this country."[26]

Americans sang songs and recited poems with titles such as "Sonnet to General Lafayette" and "Fayette in Prison, or Misfortunes of the Great—A Modern Tragedy." Washington, as president, could not act officially out of his private feelings. After discussing the problem with his two chief advisers, Secretary of State Jefferson and Secretary of the Treasury Hamilton, late in January 1793 he hit upon a solution. Washington sent his own funds to an American commercial agent in Holland, telling him to spend the money to benefit Lafayette and his family. That kept the United States government out of it. He also sent a carefully worded letter to Adrienne, saying that the money was the least he owed Lafayette for his services. He "could add much," he concluded, "but it is best perhaps that I should say little on this subject. Your goodness will supply my deficiency."[27]

Then Washington received Adrienne's letter of the previous October. "Enclosed is a letter from poor Madam La Fayette!" he told Jefferson. "How desirable it would be, if something could be done to relieve that family from their present unhappy situation." He, Jefferson, and Hamilton continued to debate what official position the government could take. The president suggested that Jefferson instruct Morris "to neglect no favourable opportunity of expressing *informally* the sentiments and wishes of this country respecting the M. de la Fayette." He also asked him to draft a letter to Adrienne, offering "all the consolation I can with propriety give her consistent with my public character and the national policy."[28]

On March 15, 1793, the secretary of state gave the American ambassadors in Europe the official position of the United States: "The interest which the president himself, and our citizens in general take in the welfare of this gentleman, is great and sincere, and will entirely justify all prudent efforts to serve him." Jefferson asked them to take every opportunity to work for Lafayette's freedom, through informal means if possible. They should find out who held Lafayette and how badly they wanted to keep him. If formal measures proved necessary, the diplomats were authorized to state the American government's "lively interest in his welfare." His liberation should be presented as a "mark of consideration and friendship for the United States, and as a new motive for esteem and a reciprocation of kind offices towards the power to whom they shall be indebted for this act."[29]

A private letter from Washington to Adrienne went out the next day. Hearing from her, he said, relieved his anxiety, because she was not as destitute as he had feared. "But I have still to sympathize with you on the deprivation of the dearest of all your resources of happiness. . . . I do it in all sincerity of my friendship for him, and with ardent desires for his relief; in which sentiment I know that my fellow-citizens participate."

Washington's position limited his freedom to act, he explained, but he assured Adrienne that he was doing everything he could to free her husband. Knowing that his letter might be intercepted by French agents, he proclaimed that his affection for both France and Lafayette was "unabated." He thought it was unfortunate that affairs had come between them, and remained "confident that both have been led on by a pure love of liberty." Accordingly, he expressed his earnest hope to "see them reunited in . . . their virtuous enterprise." This was a veiled invitation to the French authorities to liberate Lafayette. He did not understand that if they did so, they would kill him.[30]

Adrienne learned that Lafayette had been moved to Magdeburg. Other wives of *émigrés* had divorced their husbands to protect themselves and their children from the Terror. She refused to do that, and sold the little property remaining to her. Then she received Washington's financial support. "If I ever see and am reunited with my husband again," she answered, "it will be thanks only to your goodness and that of the United

States." She could do nothing for Lafayette and had no way to communicate with him. "That is the situation I now suffer."[31]

She told a friend that she felt herself "possessed of a courage which is not far removed from stupidity." It enabled her to "judge sensibly and calmly." Adrienne had never recognized her own strength. Over the coming months she would prove herself a strong, resourceful young woman who challenged France's enemies, France itself, and the Terror. Her husband was helpless. She became the valiant knight of the Lafayette family.[32]

France was in chaos, invaded over every border, the Terror spreading its reach. By the fall of 1793 the last of the liberals, Bailly, had gone to the guillotine. Yet the French armies beat back all invaders and put down counterrevolutions. Washington offered Adrienne further consolation, but still he could do nothing officially. Letters from citizens piled up, demanding that his government do something. The president prodded the secretary of state, who prodded the ambassadors in France, England, and Holland. They approached other diplomats but gained nothing.[33]

Jefferson gave the president a progress report. A legal problem had arisen when the ambassadors used, for the prisoner's relief, funds not appropriated for the purpose. He suggested that Washington ask Congress to appropriate Lafayette's back pay from the war by retroactively not accepting his offer to serve without compensation. Washington agreed, and in March 1794 Congress granted $24,424 to Lafayette. As Jefferson observed, the legislation provided a fund to cover both past expenditures and future relief. It did so in a way "which can give offence to nobody," because Congress had merely paid a debt.[34]

Adrienne finally heard from her husband. One of her letters had gotten through, and when he learned of her efforts to free him he felt "a need to thank you. I have associated you with stormy destinies which have turned out sadly," Lafayette apologized, "but I know that you find some satisfaction in the knowledge that your love and esteem are the happiest memories of my life."[35]

The Prussians moved Lafayette to Neisse, near the Polish border, early in 1794. He had become an embarrassment to King Frederick William II, who wished to be seen by the world as an enlightened ruler. Prussian courts had never charged Lafayette with a crime, and the government held him only as a favor to Austria, so he insisted that the empire take custody of him. The Austrians moved him to Olmütz, in Moravia, the worst place yet. The prison extended over a river that served as the town sewer, and his cell was filled with its stench, and with bedbugs, roaches, and other pests. His two friends were in the same place, but none of them knew that. They were chained in solitary cells, wearing rags, wallowing in their own filth.

As the Terror turned into the Grand Terror, Jacobin authorities arrested Adrienne and hauled her to a prison in Brioude, to await transportation to Paris, where she would be tried and executed. Her mother, grandmother, and sister Louise de Noailles were already lined up for the guillotine. George and Frestel were in hiding. Aunt Charlotte and the girls remained at Chavaniac, under house arrest. In June 1794 Adrienne landed in a Paris house converted to a women's prison.

Young George's resourceful tutor, Frestel, looked up Morris, who went to the authorities with a strong protest, pointing out that Lafayette was much beloved in America. The execution of his wife would "much impair" the friendly feelings between the two countries. France's only ally was the United States, so his words carried weight, and his protest saved her life. Robespierre kept her name off the condemnation lists. Her mother, grandmother, and sister, however, lost their heads, along with almost all other nobles still in the country. If there was any consolation, it was that Robespierre's own head bounced into a basket in July 1794.[36]

Those of his Jacobin allies followed, and two years of Terror came to an end, having claimed over a million lives. Moderates took control of the government, outlawed the Jacobins, and released most political prisoners, including the surviving aristocrats. Rochambeau got out, but Adrienne did not.

Washington and his cabinet had been all along discussing what to do about both Lafayettes. He considered writing a personal appeal to the king of Prussia, but the transfer to Austrian control ended that. The ambassadors had continued their informal advances to other diplomats, still getting nowhere. Before the Jacobin government fell, word reached Washington that it had declared Morris persona non grata and demanded his recall. At Jefferson's urging, Washington sent James Monroe to France with a plan to get American citizens and Adrienne out of prison.[37]

Monroe got along with the five-man Directory better than Morris had with its predecessors. He got Tom Paine and other Americans set loose, but Adrienne was not an American citizen. Legally, she was the wife of a French deserter. He approached the authorities about her case, and they moved her from place to place. He found her and sent his

James Monroe, attributed to Felix Sharples, ca. 1807–11. Monroe and his wife saved Adrienne from the guillotine. Later, he gave Lafayette the good news about his Louisiana land grant, and even later invited him to tour the United States as "the nation's guest." (INDEPENDENCE NATIONAL HISTORICAL PARK)

wife, Elizabeth, to visit her in prison. The scene was "most affecting," he recalled. News of the visit flashed across Paris, raising sympathy for the prisoner. Monroe soon joined his wife, their frequent visits embarrassed the authorities, and Adrienne's liberation soon followed, on January 22, 1795.[38]

Her husband had not been so fortunate. While Monroe had been working to get her out of jail, a group of Lafayette fans in London hatched their own daring plot. Two of them, a young German doctor named Justus-Erich Bollman, and Francis Huger, son of Lafayette's first host in South Carolina, went to Olmütz. They learned that the prison doctor had ordered the guards to take Lafayette on a carriage ride

into the country every day. The two swashbucklers stopped the carriage and told Lafayette to go. He misunderstood them, and in the confusion all three were captured. The Frenchman returned to his cell, while a sympathetic magistrate freed the other two.

Adrienne decided that if anybody was going to get her husband out of his hellhole, it would have to be herself. Like her countrywoman Joan of Arc, she set off on a righteous crusade.[39]

COURAGE, CHILD OF WASHINGTON!

*A*drienne asked Monroe to arrange American passports for herself, her daughters, George, and Frestel. George received papers under the old family name of Motier, while Frestel traveled under his own name. He and George headed to the coast to find passage to America, carrying a letter from Adrienne to Washington. "Monsieur, I send you my son," she began. With "deep and sincere feeling" she placed George "under the protection of the United States . . . and under the especial care of their president, the nature of whose sentiments toward my husband I so well know." She wanted the boy to live obscurely, resume his education, and fulfill "the duties of a citizen of the United States."[40]

Adrienne was an arsenal of energy and determination. She went to Chavaniac to pick up the girls, and to ensure that Lafayette's aunt retained her home, she dipped into the loan from Morris and bought Chavaniac. Back in Paris, she retrieved something of her own. Neither she nor her mother had been *émigrés,* so she felt entitled to La Grange, a small estate and château in Brie, seventy-five miles east of Paris, as an inheritance from her mother. She won that case also. She dealt with creditors and secured more loans. Finally, Monroe gave her passports, stamped for America, so she and the girls could leave on an American ship. They sailed for Hamburg in September 1795.[41]

Washington described to her his sincere pleasure in learning that she had been released from confinement. He instructed Monroe on how to help her further, because he had no idea that she was doing well enough on her own. Meanwhile, the president had sent John Jay to London to negotiate a treaty with Britain and to ask the government there to help free Lafayette.[42]

Adrienne's passport identified her as Mrs. Motier of Hartford, Connecticut—the only American community that had granted citizenship to Lafayette's entire family. She pressed on to Vienna. Her grandfather had once been an ambassador there, so she gained an audience with

Emperor Francis II. She asked for permission to join her husband in his cell, with their daughters. The startled emperor agreed but warned her that it would not help gain his release. He also told her to write him directly if she had any complaints about conditions in the prison. He added that she would find Lafayette well fed and well treated. "I hope that you will do me justice," he begged, in what she said to others about him. She reached Olmütz in the middle of October and joined her husband in prison.

Lafayette was starving, practically naked, and swarmed over by insects. Adrienne protested to the commandant about his condition. He refused to answer her, and when she wrote to Vienna she was rebuffed there also. She and her daughters were confined to a cell next to Lafayette's, and saw him only a few hours a day. She heard beetles clicking in the walls and prisoners being tortured in a nearby courtyard. For all the horror of the place, however, she was happy, because she was with her husband. The guards made the mistake of letting her and the girls keep their books and writing materials, and let them send letters to anywhere except America. The world soon learned about conditions at Olmütz.

Adrienne's brave and dramatic gesture—a theatrical stroke worthy of a Lafayette—set off an international scandal. It was not enough that this heroic woman had joined her persecuted husband, but two young girls also were subjected to the frightful conditions. Plays, newspaper articles, songs, and poems celebrated the noble "Prisoners of Olmütz." Debates erupted in the French, American, and British legislatures. Those in Congress were choked off because of the country's neutrality in France's wars with its neighbors. In the House of Commons, the unforgiving William Pitt the Younger declared, "Those who start revolutions will always be, in my eyes, the object of an irresistible reprobation. I take delight in seeing them drink to the dregs the cup of human bitterness that they have prepared for the lips of others."

The story became more dramatic when the world learned that Adrienne had become sick. She developed a fever, her arms and legs swelled, and she broke out in blisters. The prison doctor wanted to send her to Vienna for treatment. When she asked the emperor for permission, he granted it on condition that she and the girls would not be allowed to return to Olmütz. She refused to be separated from her husband again.[43]

Lafayette and his family in prison, engraving by John Jeffreys, based on an earlier picture, 1805. Schmaltz ran thick and sticky for the Prisoners of Olmütz.
(LILLY LIBRARY, INDIANA UNIVERSITY)

The international uproar spilled over to America. A French traveler reported that he heard everywhere "the same language expressive of attachment to France, of hatred and especially of distrust in regard to England, and of affection for M. de la Fayette," except in seaport cities dominated by commerce with Britain.[44]

Newspapers and taverns were filled with stories, songs, and poems about the Prisoners of Olmütz. The papers also carried illustrations of their plight, ranging from hopelessly romantic to horribly graphic. Schmaltz flowed thick and sticky. When the new attorney general, William Bradford, saw Washington weep at the mention of Olmütz, he composed "The Lament of Washington," which was set to music and sung or recited everywhere:

As beside his cheerful fire,
Midst his happy family,
Sat a venerable sire,
Tears were starting in his eye,
Selfish blessings were forgot,

Whilst he thought on Fayette's lot,
Once so happy in our plains,
Now in poverty and chains.
CHORUS:
Courage, Child of Washington!
Though thy fate disastrous seems,
We *have seen the setting sun*
Rise and burn with brighter beams.
Thy country soon shall break thy chain
And take thee to her arms again.[45]

These outcries added to Washington's burdens. Relations between the world's two revolutionary powers had deteriorated ever since Edmond-Charles-Edouard Genêt had arrived as French ambassador in May 1793. "Citizen" Genêt wore out his welcome quickly. He castigated Washington for not doing enough to pay the American debt to his country, and subsidized newspapers, pamphlets, and broadsheets accusing the government of favoring the British side in the war. He bought a ship, outfitted it as a privateer, and announced that it would sail to the West Indies to raid British shipping. A neutral power could not tolerate that, so Washington had him recalled.

Genêt left behind a network of Democratic Societies, which agitated against the central power of the United States, playing on the country's divided attitudes toward the French Revolution and its wars. The societies became the Democratic-Republican Party, the country's first, which was soon opposed by the Federalists. The latter supported neutrality in the European conflict, but favored better relations with Britain. American merchants wanted to trade with both sides, but the Royal Navy commanded the seas, and seized neutral ships supplying France.

As Washington sent John Jay to London to work out a treaty, calling for neutral rights and evacuation of the forts in the Northwest, the country broke into a sectional conflict. The West mistrusted the central government anyway, and when it imposed an excise tax on whiskey, the region exploded in the Whiskey Rebellion. Troops put it down, and the tax was later repealed, but resentment lingered.

In 1795 Jay returned with a treaty that included few concessions from Britain, the main one being a promise to abandon the western forts.

Fearing public reaction, Washington hesitated to ask the Senate to ratify it, but to get the redcoats off American soil he had to send it over. Then Ambassador Thomas Pinckney sent his own treaty from Spain in February 1796. He had won free navigation of the Mississippi and fixed the southern boundary of the United States on Spanish Florida's border. The British evacuated the western posts and stopped raiding American shipping, Anthony Wayne defeated the Indians in the Northwest, and East and West both calmed down.

The behavior of France next aggravated American factionalism, however. The French wildly misinterpreted the Jay Treaty, seeing it as an alliance against France, so early in 1797 President John Adams sent a delegation to Paris to negotiate a treaty of amity and commerce and restore peace between the two revolutionary powers. At first rebuffed, in October 1797 the American delegates met with a demand for loans to France and a bribe for three French agents identified as "X, Y, and Z," although the intended recipient was known to be Foreign Minister Talleyrand. By that time, American and French privateers were raiding each other's shipping, and the two countries were locked in what became known as the Quasi War. The XYZ Affair, as it was called in America, set a new low in Franco-American relations. With talk of a real war between the United States and France in the air, the Federalists gained the upper hand, authorized the United States Navy, began fortifying ports, and enlarged the army.[46]

Into this political thicket walked George-Washington Lafayette. He and Frestel landed at Boston in late August 1795 and wrote to the boy's godfather, forwarding Adrienne's letter. Washington wanted nothing more than to throw his arms around the fifteen-year-old, but his cabinet advised him to back off. The boy's presence in the United States could be interpreted as hostility to France, which had condemned his father. French agents might try to kill him on American soil, or retaliate against Adrienne. The British might decide that he favored the other side if he took the French youngster into his home.

The president needed time to think, so he asked a friend in Boston, Senator George Cabot of Massachusetts, to stall George and Frestel. He told him to enroll the boy in Harvard, and sent money to cover the cost. "Let me in a few words," he said, "declare that I *will be his friend.*" At that point he could not even write to George directly, so he asked Cabot to talk to him, and offer "the most unequivocal assurances of my standing in the place of and becoming to him a *father, friend, protector,* and *supporter.*" He should explain that, as president, he could not make his feelings public, and asked Cabot to explain to George and his tutor, in the clearest terms, why he could not take them into his house just yet. Washington's love for George's father was undiminished, "and my inclination to serve the son will be evidenced by my conduct."[47]

Washington left for Mount Vernon, assuming that George was in college, but the more he thought about it, the more he wanted to put the youngster under his own roof. He bombarded his advisers, asking how to do that without causing a diplomatic crisis. In October he learned that George and Frestel had gone to New York, where they stayed with La Colombe. He wrote to Hamilton, once again a New York lawyer, asking his advice on whether to take him in. He was sure that the boy felt abandoned in a strange land. Hamilton advised him not to see George, but suggested that it would be all right to write to him.[48]

Back in Philadelphia, the president did. Considerations "of a political nature," he told his godson, meant that he should remain "incog" for the time being, but he could rest assured that his own affection for George's father, Washington's "friend and compatriot in arms," extended "with not less warmth" to his son. He therefore should not ascribe presidential silence to "a wrong cause." He asked George and Frestel to see Hamilton, whom he had authorized to look after their well-being. Besides, Hamilton "was always in habits of great intimacy" with the boy's father. He could not predict how long circumstances would keep them apart, but he looked forward to embracing George "with fervency" as soon as he could.

Washington sent this letter unsealed to Frestel, asking him to explain the situation. He sent both letters to Hamilton, to read and take to the tutor. He would follow his advice on how to handle the matter, because he was "distrustful of my own judgment in deciding on this business lest my feelings should carry me further [than] prudence (while I am a public character) will warrant." Washington had "indirectly" sounded out the French ambassador, Pierre Adet, "on the coming over of the family of Fayette *generally,* but not as to the *exact* point." The diplomat answered that "as France did not make war upon women and children he did not suppose that their emigration could excite any notice." The case might be different, however, if one of them moved into the presidential household. Washington proposed a half-measure, moving George and Frestel to a suburb of Philadelphia.[49]

The president heard nothing from George, Frestel, or Hamilton. By December 1795 he was frantic. The boy's case gave him pain, he told Hamilton, "and I do not know how to get relieved from it." In January 1796, he asked James Madison what he could do to fulfill the obligations of friendship and his own wishes "without involving consequences." In February, he threw caution to the wind and asked Hamilton to tell George and Frestel to come to Philadelphia. He next sent his invitation directly to George, and in March he tried unsuccessfully to talk Congress into officially providing for the boy's care in the president's house. George finally arrived on his doorstep in early April.[50]

Their meeting was like a tearful reunion between the elder man and his adopted son, because Washington adored the boy at first sight. George and Frestel wanted him to pressure the Austrians into releasing Lafayette. He had, after all, abandoned caution to take them into his home and had gotten away with it. Washington asked Thomas Pinckney to go from Madrid to London to tell the Austrian ambassador that releasing Lafayette was "an ardent wish of the people of the United States, in wch I sincerely add mine." He asked Hamilton whether it would be a good idea for the president to write a private letter to the Austrian emperor explaining his and the American people's wish that Lafayette be set free to return to the United States.[51]

Washington did not wait for a reply. Nothing in his time as president tore at his heart more than his inability to do anything officially about Lafayette's situation. The time for restraint had passed, and he wrote to the emperor on May 15, 1796. "It will readily occur to your Majesty," he began, "that occasions may sometimes exist, on which official considerations would constrain the chief of a nation to be silent and passive in relation even to objects which affect his sensibility, and claim his interposition as a man. Finding myself precisely in this situation at present, I take the liberty of writing this *private* letter to your Majesty; being persuaded, that my motives will also be my apology for it."

He described America's gratitude to Lafayette and his own affection for him. He asked His Imperial Majesty to consider whether Lafayette's long imprisonment, the confiscation of his estate, and the poverty and scattering of his family did not "form an assemblage of sufferings, which recommend him to the mediation of *Humanity*? Allow me, Sir! on this occasion to be its organ; and to entreat that he may be permitted to come to this country" on such terms as the emperor might "think it expedient to prescribe."[52]

Washington knew that if he hesitated, the politicians around him would object to the letter. He sent it to Pinckney, asking him to find a way to deliver it to Vienna. His anxiety over Lafayette's situation, he said, was increased by young George's distress, "grieving for the unhappy fate of his parents." Seeing that compelled him to take such a bold step as to address the Austrian ruler directly. His message ended up on the mountain of unanswered mail piling up at the Austrian court, hundreds of letters from America and England appealing for Lafayette's release.[53]

Washington folded his godson into his family and took him to Mount Vernon when Congress adjourned for the summer. He had the boy resume his studies under Frestel's guidance, took him on his rounds, and mixed him in with the other children in the house. He loved him unabashedly. Visitors to Mount Vernon were amazed by the scene at dinner. "A few jokes passed between the president and young Lafayette whom he treats more like a child than a guest," one of them said. Washington urged Lafayette's friends in Europe to organize a campaign to free him, making it clear that he wanted him in the United States.[54]

It was to no avail, and Lafayette, Adrienne, and the girls remained in prison. But what the president of the United States could not accomplish, Napoleon did. He smashed the Austrian armies in Italy in the spring of 1797 and marched on Vienna. The hills were alive with the sound of "La Marseillaise," and the emperor sued for peace, abandoning his ally the king of Great Britain, whose navy mutinied. Things then became more complicated.

Talleyrand had escaped the Terror by going to America. He had returned to France in 1796 and became foreign minister. He demonstrated something that Lafayette never figured out—that it is possible to play both sides in a game, but only one of them at a time. Also back in France was Madame de Staël, and the two of them hatched a plot to free Lafayette and his friends La Tour-Maubourg and Bureaux de Pusy. The latter two were no problem, but the former commander of the Paris National Guard was still a loaded subject in France. Nevertheless, the

Directory urged Napoleon to make Lafayette's freedom part of the peace negotiations, assuming that he would go to America. Napoleon went along but stipulated that on his release Lafayette could go to America or anywhere else—except France. The Austrian chancellor sent his chamberlain to Olmütz to negotiate, and living conditions there suddenly improved. The Austrian told Lafayette that his release depended on his signing an oath swearing that he would never again set foot on Austrian territory. He replied that his sovereign was the French people and he would go wherever they sent him. He remained true to his principles, but they almost cost him his freedom.

The French and Austrian parties to the various negotiations soon reached one point of agreement—all Europe would be better off without Lafayette. They decided to move him to Hamburg and hand him over to the American consul. The Prisoners of Olmütz set out on September 19, 1797, in a closely guarded caravan. Once he was out of the gates, Lafayette heard that Napoleon had engineered a coup in Paris two weeks earlier, establishing a new three-man Directory. The prisoner thought that betrayed the revolution. He also learned about the condition barring him from France. He might be loved in America, but he was hated in his native land. He was determined to get back there, to win back its lost love.

The caravan reached Hamburg on October 4, and the Austrian consul handed the prisoners over to the American consul, Samuel Williams, "with much dignity," according to Gouverneur Morris. Washington's adopted son was free.[55]

THIS AFFAIR HAS MADE ME VERY UNHAPPY

Rumors that Lafayette was free reached the United States before he really was. George wanted to go back to France. Washington tried to talk him into waiting until there was definite word, because his family might be on the way to America. The boy insisted and left Mount Vernon on October 12 with $300 in his pocket and a letter from Washington to his father. His godfather told all his friends that George had left against his advice, sounding like every parent who has raised a child until he was old enough to make his own mistakes. "I said all I could, with decency," he told La Colombe as he did the others, to talk George into waiting until he received verified information, but the boy's eagerness to see his parents "was not to be restrained." His frustrated sighs were almost visible in his handwriting. Now he had two Lafayettes to miss.[56]

The letter George carried from Washington asked Lafayette to have his son tell him about how he had tried, "though ineffectually," to gain his release. He congratulated his adopted son on regaining his freedom, saying no one else could do it "with more cordiality, with more sincerity, or with greater affection." He explained why he had not been more public in his attempts to get him out of prison. As for his godson, "[h]is conduct . . . has been exemplary in every point of view, such as has gained him the esteem, affection, and confidence of all who have had the pleasure of his acquaintance." He also praised the boy's tutor. "No parent could have been more attentive to a favourite son," he said. Washington concluded, "Having bid a final adieu to the walks of public life," meaning that he had left the presidency the previous March, "I shall refer you to Mr. Frestal and George . . . to give you a general view of our situation, and of the party, which in my opinion, has disturbed the peace and tranquillity" of the United States. The "party" was France, because of the XYZ Affair and the Quasi War. He invited the whole Lafayette family to America.[57]

Washington soon received the first definite news that Lafayette had reached Hamburg. Warmly giving his blessings to both the boy and his tutor, in December 1797 he sent them another letter to take to his adopted son. He did not know whether Lafayette had returned to France or had left for America. If the latter was the case, "of all the numerous friends which you will find here none will greet you, Madam Lafayette and your daughters with a more sincere and cordial welcome than myself and all parts of this family would do." They all had grieved for his suffering and rejoiced at his liberation.[58]

Where Lafayette would go was up in the air. From Hamburg on October 6, 1797, he wrote a flowery letter to Napoleon, honoring "the services he has rendered to the cause of liberty and of our country. The gratitude which we delight in owing him is graven forever on our hearts." Although he proclaimed his patriotism and loyalty, he made no secret of the fact that he viewed the coup of September 4 as a betrayal of the revolution. He so told the French ambassador, who informed him that he could return to France if he signed an oath of loyalty to the new government. He refused. His stiff-necked principles meant that he remained an exile. He and his family moved to Holstein, in Denmark.[59]

Before Lafayette left, he wrote an affectionate letter to his adoptive father, "to express to you the feelings of my filial heart. . . . With what eagerness and pleasure I would hasten to fly to Mount Vernon, there to pour out all the sentiments of affection, respect and gratitude which ever bound me and more than ever bind me to you." He wanted more than anything to take his whole family to Mount Vernon at once, but Adrienne was still sick and could not face an ocean crossing in the stormy season. They would go to America the following spring if they could.[60]

Lafayette was not being entirely honest, because he wanted to retrieve the love of France before he dipped into that of America. He wrote Washington again in late December 1797, after he heard about the poor reception of the American peace commission in Paris, the start of the XYZ Affair. "I need not [be] telling you that this affair has made me very unhappy," he said. "I never thought I should live to see such an event, which has very much damped the pleasure of my return to this world."[61]

The Lafayettes were living on the charity of Adrienne's family, at her aunt's estate; sympathetic Americans also chipped in. Adrienne's health improved, then declined, then improved again. She traveled to France when she could, to straighten out their affairs and lobby for her husband's return. George arrived in Paris looking for his family, to find their home a burnt-out ruin. Some Fayettistes asked for an audience with Napoleon, who was away on campaign, but his wife, Joséphine, gave George a grand reception, and told him, "Your father and my husband must make common cause." Napoleon wanted to cloak his ambition in Fayettiste republicanism and was willing to use the boy's father as a prop. George made it to Holstein in February 1798, bearing Washington's letters.[62]

There might be hope for Lafayette yet. He would let the Directory use him if it restored him to favor in his native land.

I HOPED THIS WOULD NOT HAVE HAPPENED

*L*afayette's two countries seemed about to go to war in 1798—at least, so claimed the Federalists, who controlled Congress and the White House and were generally hostile to France, less so to Britain. The

Federalists authorized a "provisional army" of 10,000 men, later doubled (but never called up). Other measures to suppress sedition (meaning criticism of Federalist politicians) and to drive foreign (meaning French) agents out of the country aroused the Democratic-Republicans to fury. The United States split into two hostile camps, although Washington was everyone's choice to command the army. He agreed, on the condition that he not show up until there really was a war. He resented the idea that he might be jerked away from Mount Vernon once again, because of French stupidity. Hamilton, who engineered all this, became acting commander.[63]

Lafayette was confined to Holstein, working on his memoirs. Adrienne spent months in France after Anastasie's marriage in the spring, alternately taking the cure at spas and lobbying to secure the Noailles estate and liberate her husband. Lafayette told Washington that spring that she remained too sick to take a sea voyage, but he should expect a visit from him and George by September. He also hinted that he hoped to heal the differences between the two countries. He had in fact been negotiating with the Directory, which wanted to end the crisis set off by the XYZ Affair, while Napoleon concentrated on an invasion of England. Rumors circulated that Lafayette would be appointed minister plenipotentiary to the United States. When those stories hit America, the Federalists objected because they thought Lafayette's presence would suggest a favorable attitude on the part of the Directory toward the United States. Lafayette asked Hamilton what he thought. He advised him to stay away.[64]

In August 1798 Lafayette told Washington about Hamilton's advice. In any event, he said, he could not go to America until Adrienne's health improved. "How painful these delays are to me!" he cried. He looked toward "the beloved shores of America as the natural place of my retirement" and wanted nothing more than to own a small farm in Virginia. For the first time, he told Washington that he might go to America to work on a reconciliation between his "native and adoptive countries."[65]

Three weeks later, after Lafayette heard about the provisional army, he advised Washington that the Directory was bent on keeping the peace with the United States. When he received that information, Washington told the secretary of state that he did not think France would attack America as long as it was at war with Britain. But he had also received a news clipping saying that his adopted son and godson were on their way to see him. He dreaded that they would be dragged into American politics. "On public, and his own private account," he said, "I hoped this would not have happened while matters were in the train they are at present." When a visitor who had returned from Europe showed up at Mount Vernon in November, Washington grilled him about Lafayette and was told that he was safe at Hamburg.[66]

That information was out of date. Washington expected to see Lafayette at any time, but he learned in December 1798 that he had not sailed after all. Warning him to stay out of the partisan feuding in the United States, he assured him that his friendship had "undergone no diminution or change" and said that no one in America would receive Lafayette "with more ardent affection than I should after the differences between this country and France are adjusted" and peace was restored. Until that happened, he said candidly, it would be best if the younger man stayed in Europe.

Washington explained that if Lafayette walked onto the American scene while tensions were running high—or, worse, if a full-scale war broke out—he would find himself "in a situation in which no address or human prudence" could free him from embarrassment. "In a word you would lose the confidence of one party or the other, perhaps both, were you here under these circumstances." Congress had repealed all treaties with France, and the naval Quasi War had grown hotter. Washington said that the hostility toward France in the United States arose from the subversive activities of French agents, which had backfired. He was furious. "You mentioned that the Directory is disposed to resolve our differences," he snorted. "If that is the case, let them prove so with deeds!"[67]

Lafayette was shocked and hurt. The revolution he had started had come between him and his adoptive father. He had been rejected by both his countries, and he was an orphan again, for the first time since 1777. He had to face the fact—he could not go to Mount Vernon.

Hamilton confirmed it. "I join with you in regretting the misunderstanding between our two countries," he told Lafayette sympathetically. "And you may be assured that we are sincere." It was up to France to put an end to the dispute, "by reparation to our merchants for past injury" at the hands of her navy. If Lafayette went to America, he would end up torn between the two contending political factions. He should therefore "stand aloof."[68]

Lafayette received both messages in May 1799 and told Washington that he still wanted to go to America. But after hearing of the divisions in the United States over the conflict with France, learning that his native country was at fault, and finding himself unable to influence events, he had reached the same conclusions as presented in Washington's "candid and affectionate letter," as well as "a hint from Hamilton."

Lafayette had sworn off politics, but he had no asylum in either the Old World or the New, and was broke and at a loss what to do. He remained, however, an obedient son and would not sail for America until his adoptive father told him to. "Your opinion however my dear Gal has with me, as it ever had, an immence weight—I know you long to fold me to your paternal heart, yet you advise me against your own satisfaction & mine—you are better informed, & your judgement I am used to submit."[69]

Lafayette did not know it, but those were the last words he would ever direct to the one person he loved most. But then there was Adrienne, struggling through her illness to assemble an estate for them, battling bureaucrats and politicians to return him to France. She was an amazing woman, and the longer she was gone the more he missed her. He finally fell in love with the brave lady who had joined him in prison and managed his business affairs ever since. Sitting in a little cottage in Holland, where he had moved in January, he wrote her almost every day. They were real love letters. "I was just thinking very sadly but very tenderly of you, my dear Adrienne," he began one. He wanted to repay her for all she had done for him, and had been planning a farm for her, "either in the beautiful valley of the Shenandoah . . . or in the prairies of New England." It was a wistful dream.[70]

Across the ocean, Washington fretted. He had not received Lafayette's promise to obey his wishes, so he assumed that his adopted son was on his way to the United States. He asked those going to France to talk him into staying there if he had not left. His letters echoed those that described how George had left despite his best advice. He need not have worried. Lafayette would do as his adoptive father told him, just as he had during the Virginia Campaign of 1781. Sadly, the two of them parted forever with a misunderstanding between them.[71]

Lafayette had moved to Holland after a Fayettiste revolution there, but he was not safe, because an Anglo-Russian army had invaded the country. In October 1799, Adrienne confronted Napoleon directly. The two of them hit it off, he admiring her drive and intelligence, she his magnificent appearance and thoughtful expression. "Your husband's life is bound up with the preservation of the Republic," he told her. Interpreting that as a declaration against monarchy, she told Lafayette to write him a flattering letter. Since she commanded the family, he did as he would have if the order had come from Washington.

On November 9, 1799, Napoleon suspended the Constitution and replaced the government with a three-man Consulate, with himself as First Consul. This stroke came with a blare of noise about liberalism, speeches that sounded as if Lafayette had written them. It caused confusion in the ministries—Talleyrand, as usual, was the only holdover from the previous government—and Adrienne saw her chance. She told her husband to come to Paris at once, under an assumed name. When Lafayette arrived, she urged him to write the First Consul to announce his presence and promise to retire to La Grange. He did, but in an annoying way. He arrogated to himself the authority to end his exile and reminded the new dictator of the republican principles they both were supposed to represent.

Napoleon had seriously considered offering Lafayette a marshal's commission in the army, but at Lafayette's letter he exploded in rage, telling him to leave the country. Adrienne calmed the First Consul down. She had other allies in the government, and one of them shuttled back and forth between the two stubborn generals. When Adrienne pointed out that Napoleon had not *ordered* him to leave but had *advised* it, Lafayette saw an opening. He told the delegate that he had *voluntarily* decided to leave Paris, but not the country. "I confined myself to saying that I was little disposed to take notice of Bonaparte's threats, but that I felt myself to be bound by his advice," he recalled.

Everyone's honor was satisfied. Lafayette and his family set out for Fontenay-en-Brie, a château near La Grange, which was not then in habitable condition. He would have preferred Chavaniac, where his aunt still lived, but that would have been pushing his luck too far. He and Adrienne had their little farm at last.[72]

At Mount Vernon, Washington went about his rounds and worried about his adopted son and his godson. He had no other confidential friend, and he missed that kind of intimate companionship, even at long distance. On December 12 he rode out into a cold rain and returned soaking wet. The next day he complained of a sore throat and went to

bed. Doctors were summoned and bled him excessively. Near midnight on December 14, 1799, he spoke his last words, " 'Tis well," and died. He was buried in the vault at Mount Vernon, in a Masonic funeral.[73]

Knowing that the death he had long predicted was on its way, Washington had prepared a twenty-nine-page handwritten will in July. In a long list of small personal bequests, just after Lord Fairfax and ahead of two sisters-in-law, he wrote, "To General de la Fayette I give a pair of finely wrought steel pistols, taken from the enemy in the Revolutionary War."

George Washington near the end of his life, attributed to Ellen Sharples, after James Sharples Senior, ca. 1796–1810. (INDEPENDENCE NATIONAL HISTORICAL PARK)

There was something else. Washington freed his slaves, on his wife's death, and provided for their support in the only way Virginia law would let him. He was the only American Founding Father to do that. Whether intentionally so, or simply in answer to his own conscience, this act can be seen as Washington's last and fondest gift to his adopted son, Lafayette, who had started him on the road to emancipation.[74]

Le Vashington Français
(JANUARY 1800-MAY 1834)

Such characters should live to posterity,

when kings and the crowns they wear

must have mouldered into dust.

—CHARLES JAMES FOX

ews of Washington's death reached France early in February 1800. "This great man fought against tyranny; he established the liberty of his country," Napoleon proclaimed. The American's memory, he predicted, would always be dear to the French people, and especially to French soldiers, who, like Washington, fought for liberty and equality. The First Consul ordered that all flags and guidons in the republic be draped in crepe for ten days, and that a statue of Washington be erected in Paris.

Napoleon held a funeral ceremony at the Temple of Mars (Hôtel des Invalides) on February 8. The grieving Lafayette and Adrienne were not allowed to attend. A member of the Consulate delivered a eulogy, an endless rant praising France for praising Washington, rather than any tribute to the general himself. Napoleon was a new, improved version of Washington, thundered the orator.

La Grange, Lafayette's home after his release from prison. (LILLY LIBRARY, INDIANA UNIVERSITY)

The great American had been reclaimed as a French hero after being a villain since the Jay Treaty. As early as 1797 Bonaparte had proposed having himself officially described as the Washington of France. That title, *le Vashington français,* had belonged to Lafayette before 1792. He wanted it back.[1]

THE SOUL HAS DISAPPEARED FROM LA GRANGE

*T*hat honor might better have gone to Adrienne, who implemented her husband's plans for La Grange. She traveled ceaselessly to recover Lafayette estates seized during the Terror or to press for restitution where she could not regain the land. She also worked the family out of debt. After picking up a half-million francs (as livres had been renamed) for lost Noailles properties, in 1803 she told Gouverneur Morris that she would repay his 100,000-livre loan from 1793—with 53,000 francs, just over half the amount she owed him, without interest. She said she was obeying a new law converting debts incurred during revolutionary inflation. He did not believe that, but he let it go. "I only wish them a clear conscience," he sighed. The Lafayettes had lost a friend, but they were nearly solvent.[2]

Adrienne searched out the mass grave where her mother, grandmother, and sister rested among 1,300 other victims of the guillotine, near a ruined convent at Picpus. She established a private cemetery for the victims, with a chapel and memorial plaques. She wanted to be buried there.

Adrienne also continued her campaign to remove her husband from the list of *émigrés*, restoring his citizenship and freedom of movement. Lafayette was stuck at La Grange, and he wanted to go to Paris, "if only for a pair of boots and a wig," he said. He also hoped to visit an American peace delegation, recently arrived in the capital. On March 1, 1800, the First Consul granted him reprieve. The two of them met later at the Tuileries, where France's dictator had installed himself. Lafayette claimed in his memoirs that Napoleon offered him the ambassadorship to the United States, but he turned it down. That seems unlikely, because Bonaparte

Adrienne after prison. She worked herself to death for her husband, and it showed. (Skillman Library, Lafayette College)

viewed Lafayette as his chief rival and excluded him from all offices. He allowed him to buy a townhouse in Paris, however.[3]

On October 1, 1800, France and the United States signed a peace treaty, ending the Quasi War. Napoleon threw a grand celebration at his brother Joseph's luxurious estate, Mortefontaine, and made the mistake of inviting the Lafayettes. They were the center of attention in the crowd, and stole the First Consul's thunder, so he banned them from all future public events. The tense standoff between the two generals persisted, and intensified after Napoleon was elected Consul for Life in 1802. Nearly 4 million people favored that, with 9,000 opposed. Lafayette publicly denounced Napoleon's betrayal of everything Washington had stood for.[4]

La Grange looked more like Mount Vernon every day. Besides agricultural experiments, it filled up with grandchildren. George married, and so did Virginie and Anastasie. When George and the sons-in-law were away in Napoleon's armies, the women stayed in the château with their broods. After failing to preserve the freedom of the former slaves on his seized plantation in Cayenne, in 1802 Lafayette quit-claimed the property and received 140,000 francs. Then calamity hit.

In February 1803 Lafayette slipped on the ice in Paris and broke his femur. Surgeons gave him a choice between reduction of the fracture, which would leave him a cripple, or forty days of excruciating pain in a new device, which would heal him. He chose the pain. When the instrument of torture was removed, he had lost part of his thigh and his foot was crushed. More painful weeks of normal healing followed, and he came out of it needing a cane to hobble around.[5]

As Lafayette struggled with his injury, the Consul for Life made him a rich man, without meaning to. France had reacquired Louisiana from Spain in 1800, and in 1802 Napoleon advised the United States that he might sell the territory. His brothers objected, but he had sound reasons. France had lost Saint-Domingue to the Haitian slave revolt, and the Royal Navy had been beating up the French one. He could use 60 million francs to pay for his military campaigns. Besides, sale to the Americans would deny the territory to Britain and make the United States potentially a great maritime rival to the detested *Anglais.* The American government agreed to pay him the asking price ($12 million) in installments, and another 20 million francs ($4 million) to pay off its debts in France.

James Monroe visited Lafayette on his way to complete the Louisiana Purchase in 1803 and delivered an act of Congress granting him 11,520 acres of western lands as a bounty for his service during the American Revolution. President Jefferson, Secretary of State Madison, and

Treasury Secretary Albert Gallatin together had been trying to relieve Lafayette's financial problems, and took Congress' grant as an opportunity to solve them once and for all. The lawmakers had assumed that the lands would be in the Ohio country, where the best lands had already been taken. Jefferson got authority to select the lands for the Frenchman and handed him property in Louisiana after Lafayette sent him a blank power of attorney. It took four years of locating, assaying, and selling, but it cleared his debts; lots in New Orleans alone sold for $200,000, almost as much as he had spent in the American Revolution. He was no longer a fugitive from debt collectors, including Gouverneur Morris, whom he paid off at last.[6]

Jefferson urged Lafayette to move his family to Louisiana, and once the Purchase was complete, he offered him the governorship. The president said that he would rather have Lafayette in Louisiana than "an army of 10,000 men." He thought the former marquis would immediately win the loyalty of the territory's French inhabitants to himself and to the United States. Lafayette turned the offer down, because Adrienne was too sick to travel, his aunt was nearing the end of her days, and he could not simply unload his affairs in France. With his son and both sons-in-law in the service, he might endanger them if he gave up his French citizenship to become an American official.[7]

Lafayette presided over La Grange as Washington had at Mount Vernon, receiving a steady stream of visitors. His leg hampered his movements, and he could no longer sit a horse, so his slight frame took on padding. In 1804, Napoleon crowned himself emperor and made a final attempt to win Lafayette's favor, awarding him the Legion of Honor and appointing him a Peer of the Realm. The French Washington declined both, claiming that he wanted to stay in retirement. He said privately that he would have taken the office under a democratic regime, but not this one. That was not the only unhappiness in the household. Lafayette's brother-in-law Noailles died in Haiti, and Hamilton died in a duel. But after Napoleon's victories over the Austrians, the Prussians, and the Russians late in 1805, George and the sons-in-law came home.[8]

Then Lafayette's world fell apart. In August 1807 he and George went to Chavaniac. Shortly after he left, Adrienne came down with fever and vomiting. She had been literally working herself to death for him, and it finally caught up with her. Anastasie moved her to Paris and sent for

Lafayette. She lingered for weeks, often delirious, sores and blisters breaking out all over. He was at her bedside constantly, holding her hand, talking during her lucid spells.

Adrienne had always been devoutly religious, but told Lafayette that she had come to terms with his lack of belief. She repeatedly expressed her love for him and asked for assurance that he loved her in turn. "How grateful I am to God," she cried, "that so violent a passion should also have been a duty! How happy I have been, in having had the wonderful good fortune to be your wife." When he told her how much he loved her, she replied, "Is that true? Is that really true? How good you are! Say it again, for to hear it gives me pleasure." He was devastated, watching his wife disintegrate before his eyes. All his neglect of her came back to him, overwhelming him with guilt. She asked him, "Have you any grudge against me?" He answered, "What grudge could I have, my dearest? You have always been so sweet, so good." She whispered, "So I have been a pleasant companion for you?" He reassured her that she had. "Then bless me," she begged.

It was apparent by December 25 that Adrienne was near death. The family assembled, and a priest delivered the last rites. Lafayette held her hand throughout the day. "What joy! How happy I am to belong to you!" she told him near the end. Then she breathed her last. *"Je suis toute à vous"* (I am entirely yours), she said, and then said no more.[9]

Anastasie wrote her last words down, and Lafayette carried that paper the rest of his life. With it in his wallet was another, in his own hand, saying:

> *This thinking spark,*
> *This vibrant thing and pure,*
> *Which lives on after I am dead,*
> *Wants still to follow where you lead.[10]*

Lafayette buried his wife in Picpus cemetery and returned to La Grange, where he walled up the entrance to Adrienne's bedroom and built a secret door for himself. Whenever he was there, on certain anniversaries that he explained to nobody, he went into the room to commune with Adrienne. When he was not there, he dedicated part of every morning to thinking about her. "Before this blow," he told Jefferson, also a widower,

"I did not know what it was to be unhappy. . . . Pity me, my dear Jefferson."[11]

"I am more unhappy than I believed I could bear," Lafayette cried to Madame de Staël. Part of himself had died with Adrienne, he said. "I recognize the impossibility of lifting the weight of this pain." When she read that, she said, "The soul has disappeared from La Grange."[12]

HE HAS NOT RETREATED AN INCH

Lafayette relieved his grief by basking in his family and concentrating on his agriculture. His animals won ribbons at country fairs, and his estates prospered. He dictated his memoirs to his son, George, revising his early life to make it appear that he had always been a dedicated republican, even altering old documents. He wrote letters supporting revolutionary and antislavery movements wherever they appeared. His last close friend in America was Jefferson, and they exchanged letters and gifts.

Adélaïde moved into La Grange and stayed for a while, but she kept to her own room. He had cut off his relationship with her when she remarried some years earlier. Lafayette developed strong bonds with other women, most of them active in the arts, letters, and politics. The first was with Madame de Staël, whom he had known since she was a little girl. He kept up a close friendship with the witty social commentator until her death in 1817. As with the others, however, evidence of a sexual partnership is not clear. Out of belated loyalty to Adrienne, outwardly Lafayette appeared to become a faithful husband at last, although in later years his passes at young women earned him a reputation as a dirty old man.

As long as Napoleon remained triumphant, Lafayette kept his head down. His aunt Charlotte died at the age of eighty-two in 1811, and he inherited Chavaniac and other properties from her, becoming even richer. That was followed by the bloodbath between French troops and the *guérilleros* (guerilla fighters) and their British allies in Spain, and then by Napoleon's disastrous retreat from Moscow in 1812. Resistance to French domination erupted all over Europe. The empire was shrinking, but Napoleon still believed his victory was inevitable. "The whole world has become readjusted," he claimed, "with the single exception of Lafayette. He has not retreated an inch. He may *seem* quiet and peaceful enough, but mark my words, he is quite capable of starting all over again."[13]

In 1814, as the allies closed in on Paris, Lafayette was there, and he broke into tears when the enemy invaded the city. Napoleon's rump legislature opened secret negotiations, and the agile Talleyrand declared him deposed as emperor, proclaiming the restoration of the monarchy. The boy-king Louis XVII had disappeared during the Terror, but his uncle the comte de Provence survived in England. Hideously fat and obnoxious, he entered Paris as Louis XVIII on the heels of the allied armies. Napoleon retreated to Fontainebleu, where he abdicated on April 6, going to exile on Elba, an island off the southern coast.

Lafayette had only one satisfaction—the new Louis would be a constitutional monarch, something he had aimed at since 1789. But the Constitutional Charter granted the king's "divine right" to be "supreme head of state." There were a few concessions to liberal sentiments, but essentially absolutism had been restored. Europe was at peace, but in France the usual range of factions were at each other's throats. They were joined by *émigrés* who returned to demand back their lands, which were in the hands of peasants. The former marquis attended the king's first audience, then left for La Grange.

Lafayette told Jefferson that he had been glad to see Napoleon head off to Elba, but he was sympathetic to the deposed emperor because they shared a love for military glory. Otherwise, the man was a despot, and Lafayette wished he had been overthrown by popular revolt instead of foreign armies. He wanted no part of the Bourbon Restoration. Jefferson blamed all the bad news on those who had destroyed the limited monarchy Lafayette had tried to establish in 1789. They had pressed for self-government too fast, he said, and ended up with "the unprincipled and bloody tyranny of Robespierre, and the equally unprincipled and manic tyranny of Bonaparte." The American had changed his outlook. Liberty, he said, was a mixed blessing for people not ready for it, and France would not be ready for another generation.[14]

The Bourbon government refused to pay Bonaparte his pension and confiscated his properties. Without income, he could not maintain his guard on Elba. Rumors of plots to assassinate him were in the air. Lafayette decided that the Bourbons were hoping to drive the former emperor into taking some desperate action that would destroy him. They got their wish.

On March 1, 1815, Napoleon landed at Cannes and began a triumphal march to Paris, his army reassembling in his wake. Louis XVIII fled to the nearest British army. Thus began the Hundred Days, the emperor's second reign. Early in May, he took a page from Lafayette's book, staging a big pageant on the Champ de Mars, where he swore to uphold the Constitutional Charter. In balloting held to implement that document, Lafayette was elected to the Chamber of Deputies from Brie, and his son, George, from Auvergne.

The British and Prussian armies had assembled in Belgium, preparing to march on Paris, and on June 12, 1815, Napoleon trooped out to meet them. Two days after the crows settled on the corpses of his soldiers at Waterloo, on the twentieth he was back in the city, where his whole government had turned against him. Lafayette, backed by Bonaparte's former chief of police, Joseph Fouché, demanded that he step down. He was too exhausted to fight back, and abdicated on the twenty-second, naming his son Emperor Napoleon II. Lafayette tried to negotiate passage to America for the outgoing emperor, but Fouché sabotaged the talks behind his back. Fouché wanted a permanent end to the Bonaparte problem as much as the British did.

Napoleon ended up on St. Helena, a cold, windswept rock in the South Atlantic, where he died in 1821. In his last will and testament, he declared that the two allied invasions of France in 1814 and 1815 had been "due to the treason" of Lafayette, Talleyrand, and others. He never knew that it was his old friend Fouché who had engineered his downfall, using Lafayette as a front. Neither did Lafayette.[15]

The Chamber of Deputies named Napoleon II as emperor, appointed a five-man Directory to run the country, and sent Lafayette at the head of a delegation to stop the allied armies marching on Paris. He failed. The conquerors dictated a punitive peace and left behind an army of occupation, which remained until 1818. The Bourbons, back in the saddle, began the White Terror, slaughtering Jacobins, Bonapartistes, and Liberals until the occupying armies put a stop to it. Lafayette was secure in his properties because he had friends among the British.

In 1816 Lafayette performed another service for the United States, which was looking for a foreign expert to head up the army's Corps of Engineers. President Madison asked Lafayette for a recommendation, and he proposed General Simon Bernard. He had been a military engineer under Napoleon and kept his commission during the first Restoration. He served as an aide to Napoleon during the Hundred Days, so the king fired him. On Lafayette's recommendation he was allowed to emigrate to America, where he started the republic's "Third System" of coastal fortifications, in the process giving birth to pork-barrel politics (the trading of public-works appropriations in Congress).[16]

Lafayette became a leader of the "liberal" or "independent" wing of the Chamber of Deputies. In 1817 he and others founded a semisecret society—those were popping up again, political clubs drawn from Masonic lodges—to pay fines for liberal journalists. It became the Liberal Party. He agitated for American ideas such as a free press, individual liberties, and the right of all taxpayers to vote—a direct challenge to Bourbon repression. The Lafayette house in Paris became a meeting place for revolutionaries, and in 1820 he organized a mass march through the streets to protest the government's harsh measures. That earned him a formal condemnation, but he was too popular to put down. He never wavered in his republican principles. As Madame de Staël had said, "Since the departure of M. de la Fayette for America 40 years ago, it is impossible to cite either an action or a word from him which has not been [pointed] in the same direction." He remained stubborn and afraid of no one.[17]

As the government became more repressive, Lafayette became more outspoken. He loved the applause that followed his speeches, preaching his religion of popular sovereignty and constitutional government. If that took a revolution to bring about, he was all for it. It had worked for his adoptive father. In the early 1820s he helped organize the Charbonniers, a French version of the Carbonari (charcoal makers), nationalist plotters in Italy. They were accused of conspiring to overthrow King Louis, so the secret police arrested thousands and shut down the press. Fearing to arrest Lafayette, it rigged the election of 1823, and he lost his seat in the Chamber of Deputies. Once again he had failed to import American liberty to his homeland.[18]

Lafayette had meanwhile fallen into a strange, intense relationship with Fanny Wright, a Scots-born American writer, promoter of republican virtues, and enemy of slavery. She met him in 1821, when she was twenty-six years old, and latched on to him, calling herself his adopted daughter and asking him to adopt her legally. His real daughters put a stop to that. They were together whenever she was in France, and during his visit to America in 1824 she attached herself to him again. He helped finance her project for a freed-slave plantation in western Tennessee, similar to his old dream. It failed in 1828, and she returned to France, partly separated herself from him, and married another Frenchman. Lafayette gave the bride away.[19]

When the fiftieth anniversary of the American Declaration of Independence approached, Congress and President Monroe invited Lafayette to visit the United States as "the Nation's Guest." He was happy to go, and took George and some servants with him. The Bourbon government got the idea that it was all part of a plot to conquer the French Caribbean colonies and install Lafayette as governor, so troops broke up crowds who cheered him on his way to Le Havre.

Once Lafayette reached America in August 1824, what was planned as a short visit to major cities turned into a thirteen-month, 6,000-mile procession through all the states. The hysterical receptions were much alike. He entered a town escorted by militia, through victory arches decorated with boughs and bunting; endured speeches by local dignitaries and greetings from Revolutionary veterans and the Society of the Cincinnati; received poems and flowers from children; and made the rounds of dinners, Masonic banquets, schools, and anybody else who wanted to hear him. The nation went insane for the "last major general of the Revolution."

He left behind hundreds of places named Lafayette, Fayette, or La Grange. He also sparked a new interest in the Revolution, inspiring worshipful biographies of the struggle's leaders. He became a unifying, nonpartisan influence during the fierce election struggle between John Quincy Adams and Andrew Jackson, both of whom he met.[20]

Lafayette called at the White House when Monroe was still president, and again after Adams took over. Besides the last major general, only Jefferson and Adams remained of the major leaders of the Revolution. He found Jefferson "feeble and much aged," but his mind was still sharp. A witness at Monticello called them two ghosts from the great past, materializing one last time to inspire the new generation. After he spent an afternoon with Adams, according to family tradition the old man said when he left, "That was not the Lafayette I knew." Outside the door, Lafayette said, "That was not the John Adams I knew."

Time had caught up with all of them. The skinny boy who had become Washington's adopted son—a relationship the speeches mentioned routinely—had gained weight, struggled to walk with his cane, and carried a lumpy body topped by a pudding face crowned by the toupee. When he left the cornerstone ceremony for the Bunker Hill Monument to fill a bag with the battlefield's dirt for his own grave, somebody had to help him.[21]

The Nation's Guest received a grand reception when he visited Yorktown Battlefield, where he reviewed troops from Fort Monroe, who had been marched to Yorktown and encamped for the occasion. When that was over, the soldiers force-marched to beat him to Hampton Roads, where he reviewed them again in Bernard's great fortification. Lafayette pronounced himself "delighted" at the men's appearance in both places. He did not recognize that they were the same troops.[22]

The distinguished visitor also reviewed militia during his tour, what there was of it. It had never amounted to much in wartime, and in peace had nearly disappeared. In its place were fancy clubs of high-society dandies in the cities, who dressed themselves up in glorious uniforms to host balls and consume oceans of punches that they named for their units. When Lafayette visited the Silk-Stocking Regiment in New York, it renamed itself the 7th New York Regiment of National Guards, honoring his Paris National Guard of 1789. New York volunteer regiments in the Civil War adopted the term, and it became the fashion during efforts to revive militias in the 1870s. Legislation reorganizing the country's defense made it official in 1903.[23]

Lafayette left America in September 1825. When he got home, he took up where he had left off, spreading the lesson he had learned from Washington—that national independence opened the way for all other human rights. He involved himself in virtually every revolutionary and independence movement from the 1770s through the 1830s. Besides the United States and France, they included Spain, Latin America, and Greece during the 1820s and France (again), Belgium, and Poland in the 1830s. He also intervened for national movements in Ireland, Switzerland, Italy, and Germany. He fought the slave trade and became the world's foremost abolitionist. Always he argued that natural rights applied to all humans, and they included national self-determination.[24]

Lafayette's own country remained his greatest frustration. Louis XVIII had died while Lafayette was in America, and was succeeded by Charles X, a vengeful tyrant. Charles cracked down on all civil liberties but met resistance—the courts refused to enforce his decrees suppressing the press. As the next years passed, he viewed Lafayette as the cause of all his troubles, but he was afraid to attack him directly. When his enemy was elected to the Chamber of Deputies in 1827, he dissolved it and rigged new elections, but Lafayette returned anyway. He tried further repression, banning all forms of entertainment, even the opera, if they had

Lafayette after his tour of America, by Thomas Sully, from life, 1825–26. The artist was flattering, because most other portrayals by this time show Lafayette to be carrying a lumpy body topped by a pudding face, crowned with the toupee he had worn since the 1780s. Sully did justice to the elegant clothing—Lafayette was a lifelong clotheshorse. (INDEPENDENCE NATIONAL HISTORICAL PARK)

"revolutionary" themes. Gioacchino Rossini's opera *William Tell,* about a legendary Swiss rebel, closed before it opened.

Lafayette became increasingly outspoken, his speeches against despotism circulating despite the repression. He toured the country early in 1830 to address a series of Masonic banquets. Attendance was supposed to be limited to members of the lodges, but they attracted huge crowds of liberal opponents of the government, who heard Lafayette condemn Charles and everything he stood for. The king decided that Lafayette had engineered it all, because the same cities had refused to turn out for a recent tour by the dauphin.[25]

When the Chamber of Deputies assembled that winter, Charles opened it with a rebuke of the Liberals, in particular Lafayette. In return, the Chamber rebuked the king, and he dissolved it again. A new one assembled in July 1830, and the pattern repeated itself. This time the whole of Paris rose in outrage, screaming, "To the barricades!" Charles sent troops to put down the rebellion, but they were beaten back from the barricaded streets during the "Three Glorious Days of the Revolution." Lafayette organized a Commission to act as government and browbeat the Deputies into supporting the revolutionaries in the streets. The "man of the hour," as he was called—along with "the distinguished relic of 1789"—pulled the Bourbon flag down from the Hôtel de Ville and hoisted the Tricolor. The National Guard miraculously reassembled itself, and the Commission made him its commander. Putting on his old Guard uniform, he told Charles, "The Bourbons are finished!"

On July 29, 1830, the Commission, backed by the crowds, offered to make Lafayette dictator of the country, but he turned that down. Instead, he pushed the Deputies to write a republican constitution, but ran into resistance from conservatives. They wanted Louis-Philippe, duc d'Orléans, who had hereditary claims to the throne, to be king. Lafayette had favored a constitutional monarchy before, so he did again. He produced a draft Constitution, modeled on the American one, and grandly greeted the new "citizen king" as "the king we need." His Liberal friends were outraged, but he thought he had done the best he could for constitutional government. Charles abdicated, the Chamber of Deputies elected Louis-Philippe the new monarch, and work started to complete the new Constitutional Charter.

Once again, Lafayette had had a chance to take bold action and backed off. True to his principles, he would not become dictator, even by popular demand. If he led a republican movement with the disorganized Liberals, he would start a civil war and possibly invite foreign intervention. He had done what he thought Washington would have done.[26]

And it failed, because the "citizen king" soon showed his colors. He made Lafayette the commander of the National Guard of the Realm, a symbolic role but one that justified a trip to the tailors for a custom uniform. Louis-Philippe took the post away from him, however, when Lafayette spoke up in the Chamber calling for more liberal reforms, including the abolition of slavery. He also turned the body into a forum for revolutions and independence movements in other countries, and talked the Deputies into voting in favor of them. That brought outraged demands from other monarchs to put a lid on the troublemaker. Disowned by the king in the spring of 1831, Lafayette returned to La Grange. He was back in the Chamber in the fall but could not stop suppression of labor strikes and other authoritarian measures.

A cholera epidemic hit the country in 1832, and Louis-Philippe used it as an excuse to make himself his own prime minister and minister of the interior (chief of police). When a popular Liberal orator died of cholera, his funeral attracted thousands of mourners, who heard Lafayette give the main speech, condemning the oppression. The crowd roared, "To arms! To the barricades!" Within hours the rebels had taken control of central Paris, but a heavy rainstorm and an attack by police troops soon put an end to the uprising. The public duel between Lafayette and the equally stubborn king continued.[27]

Another woman had entered Lafayette's life in 1831. She was Christine Belgiojoso, twenty-two years old when he met her, a raven-haired beauty from Italy, with a startling alabaster complexion and great dark eyes. She was an outspoken revolutionary who had fled her native land. It was widely assumed that they were lovers. Like Fanny Wright, she called Lafayette her father, and when they were at La Grange his daughters made no secret of their disapproval. He doted on her, however. He climbed the five flights of stairs to her apartment every day after he left the Chamber of Deputies, and cooked the meals they ate together. It was his last female companionship outside his family.[28]

Early in 1834, at the age of seventy-six, the onetime boy general of the American Revolution was tired, his bones aching. He made his last speech to the Chamber on January 3, rebuking his country for not realizing the promise of American republicanism. It was a cold, nasty winter, and in February he collapsed at a funeral. He recovered in a few weeks, but another soaking in May put him to bed for the last time. His family assembled in the Paris house while crowds kept a vigil outside, day and night.

One of Lafayette's doctors saw him, whenever he was alert, kissing a picture he wore around his neck in a gold locket, a miniature of Adrienne. Around it he had engraved her last words, "I am entirely yours." On the back was another inscription: "So I have been a pleasant companion for you? Then bless me." He died quietly on May 20, 1834, and was buried at Picpus, beside his wife. George poured the dirt from Bunker Hill over him before the grave was sealed. In later years, French and American flags flew together above his resting place.[29]

Louis-Philippe made no public pronouncement about the man who had put him on the throne. Instead, he ordered a military funeral with the intent of keeping the public away. There were no speeches. Crowds protested, furious at being barred by troops. Newspapers compared the French government's imprisoning Lafayette in death to the way the Austrians had imprisoned him in life.

The French writer Stendhal said at the time, "I had the feeling, that Monsieur de La Fayette was quite simply a figure out of Plutarch. He took each day as it came, a man not overburdened with intelligence, who . . . dealt with each heroic situation as it arose, and in between times was solely occupied, in spite of his age, in fumbling at pretty girls' plackets, not occasionally but constantly, and not much caring who saw."[30]

Americans had no such ambivalence. Lafayette was, purely and simply, their hero, and a great man. When word of his death arrived, President Jackson called for the same honors that Adams had ordered for Washington thirty-five years earlier. Flags flew at half-staff, twenty-four-gun national salutes boomed out from every army post and navy ship, and officers wore crepe for six months. Congress passed resolutions of condolence to the Lafayette family, its chambers hung with black bunting. The lawmakers asked the whole country to wear mourning clothes for thirty days.

John Quincy Adams delivered the official eulogy to a joint session of Congress, with government officers and the diplomatic corps in attendance. "Pronounce him one of the first men of his age," he proclaimed, "and you have yet not done him justice. . . . Turn back your eyes upon the records of time; summon from the creation of the world to this day the mighty dead of every age and every clime—and where, among the race of merely mortal men, shall one be found, who, as the benefactor of his kind, shall claim to take precedence of Lafayette?"[31]

In England, which had lost thirteen colonies at the hands of Washington, Lafayette, and the others, philosopher John Stuart Mill was more thoughtful. "His was not the influence of genius," he said, "nor even of talents; it was the influence of a heroic character: it was the influence of one who, in every situation, and throughout a long life, had done and suffered everything which opportunity had presented itself of doing and suffering for the right. . . . It will be long ere we see his equal, long ere there shall arise such a union of character and circumstances as shall enable any other human being to live such a life."[32]

He was describing Lafayette. He could have been talking about Washington.

Greatness of Name in the Father Oft-Times Overwhelms the Son

He that will have his son have a respect for him and his orders,
must himself have a great reverence for his son.

—John Locke

I t is impossible to imagine the American Revolution turning out the way it did without either Washington or Lafayette. Its outcome, however, was not a result of their individual actions so much as those of the two of them together. The relation each had with the other was entirely unlike any he had with another person. They kept each other in the fight, through a bond forged in the Conway Cabal. They had no secrets between them.

Lafayette contributed the weight of his native country to Washington's struggle, along with his own fortune. He left home on a hunt for glory, and to defy his father-in-law. His daring departure fired the country's imagination and set off a chain of events that carried France into the war on the American side. When the marquis returned home the first time, he exploited his popularity and badgered his government into upping the ante against the British. He deserves credit for the decision to send more money and supplies, and an army and navy, to America. The alliance was a difficult one—as relations between the United States and France have been ever since—but it tipped the balance in the war.

Lafayette's best-known contribution to the struggle was the brilliant Virginia Campaign that ended at Yorktown. Washington had few generals to whom he would risk giving command of such a chancy operation. The commander in chief trusted the young man's unquestioning loyalty and filial obedience, as well as his skills as a campaigner. His constant, fatherly reassurance and approval kept Lafayette on the job.

Lafayette ended the Revolutionary War as the self-appointed arm of the adoptive father he revered. Not as well-known as Yorktown was his continuing service to his father's cause after the war. The French loans and trade concessions and his mediation with Spain were critical, keeping the United States alive long enough to adopt its Constitution and stand on its own feet.

Lafayette did not do these things because he was a dedicated republican. He did not do them for the new nation. He did them to serve his adoptive father.

Lafayette's love for Washington opened him to the human truths that the elder man had fought for. He became a liberal republican, and an advocate for enlightened government, religious freedom, and the abolition of slavery. In the last he opened his father's conscience. Washington was already troubled by slavery's contradiction to his principles, and the younger man prodded him along the road to abolition. He got there with his last act in life.

Lafayette tried to do everything as he thought Washington would, but he lacked his father's experience, wisdom, and sound political judgment. His decisions were often a superficial aping of the elder man and not actually a reflection of how Washington would have acted. He failed to reproduce the American Revolution in France and made the whole horrible situation there worse than it had to be.

So Lafayette made mistakes, misreading the lessons his adoptive father had taught him. But then, he was only human. His contributions to American history were important beyond measure. His contributions to world history, for all his errors, were also magnificent. Through six turbulent decades, he championed human rights, self-government, and the end of slavery. No one else came close to matching his record or his influence on events.

It is a pity that Lafayette is so little remembered on either side of the Atlantic. France has a great hole in its national memory where the revolutionary period should be. That country's revolution and Napoleonic years are a national embarrassment, not mentioned in public. Lafayette was a prominent figure during that period, so he is seldom mentioned either.

The small memory of Washington's best friend on the western side of the water, where the map is littered with places named in Lafayette's honor, is harder to explain. His tour of the United States in 1824 and 1825 can be compared only to those of some rock musicians in more recent times. The last surviving general of the Revolution, he was then the best-known of them all. Now Washington is the most famous, as he should be, and all the others, including Lafayette, have faded into the mist.

"Greatness of name in the father oft-times overwhelms the son," said playwright Ben Jonson, long before either Washington or Lafayette was born; "they stand too near one another. The shadow kills the growth."

The affection the two soldiers had for each other is their most touching lesson for our time. Americans today often think of Washington as the old sourpuss on the dollar bill and of Lafayette as a pigeon perch on a courthouse lawn. But they were not carved monuments in real life. They were people, with all the strengths and weaknesses of that species. They started out as children, as we all do. They grew up, and changed, and did some amazing things, and made mistakes.

Both were orphans, and that is where their connection began. Washington needed substitute fathers as he grew up, and he found them. Lafayette also longed for a father, and at the age of nineteen he found one in Washington and never let go. Washington was childless and naturally responded when the boy reached out to him. They supported and comforted each other through war and peace. Washington received from his adopted son the unquestioning loyalty and trust that he got from no one else. Lafayette received in return the reassurance, guidance, and approval that he craved. They loved each other, openly and without limits, for the rest of their lives.

Picture the commander in chief asleep on his cloak after Monmouth, with the boy general curled up beside him. That image reflects the enduring truth in their story. Who they were cannot be measured only by how much they shook the world.

N O T E S

Complete data on works cited in the chapter notes are presented in the Bibliography. Names of months are given standard three-letter abbreviations in the notes.

Abbreviations Used in Notes

adc	Aide-de-camp
Adr	Marie-Adrienne-Françoise de Noailles, marquise de Lafayette (Laf's wife)
AH	Alexander Hamilton
AW	Anthony Wayne
BF	Benjamin Franklin
Boatner	Boatner, *Encyclopedia of the American Revolution*
BTJ	Boyd, *Papers of Thomas Jefferson*
CIG	Clary, *Inspectors General* (3 vols.)
CW	Clary and Whitehorne, *Inspectors General*
Des	Charles-Henri-Théodat, comte d'Estaing
DM	Daniel Morgan
Duer	Duer, *Memoirs, Correspondence, and Manuscripts of General Lafayette*

FGW	Fitzpatrick, *Writings of George Washington*
FVS	Friedrich Wilhelm (Frederick William) von Steuben
GLW	Gottschalk, *Letters of Lafayette to Washington*
GM	Gouverneur Morris
GW	George Washington
GWD	Jackson and Twohig, *Diaries of George Washington*
GWL	George-Washington-Louis-Gilbert du Motier de Lafayette (Laf's son)
Heitman	Heitman, *Historical Register and Dictionary of the United States Army*
HG	Horatio Gates
HJM	Hutchinson, *Papers of James Madison*
HK	Henry Knox
HL	Henry Laurens
ILA	Idzerda, *Lafayette in the Age of the American Revolution, Selected Letters and Papers*
JA	John Adams
JH	John Hancock
JJ	John Jay
JL	John Laurens
JM	James Monroe
JMA	James Madison
JPJ	John Paul Jones
JS	John Sullivan
Laf	Marie-Joseph-Paul-Yves-Roch-Gilbert du Motier, marquis de Lafayette
LAH	Lodge, *Works of Alexander Hamilton*
Lasteyrie	Lasteyrie, *Vie de Madame de Lafayette*
LBF	Labaree, *Papers of Benjamin Franklin*
Luz	Anne-César, chevalier de la Luzerne
Memoirs	Laf, *Mémoires, correspondance et manuscrits du Général Lafayette*
nd	no date given
NG	Nathanael Greene
np	no place given
npub	no publisher given
NYC	New York City
OED	*Compact Edition of the Oxford English Dictionary*

PC	President of Congress
RM	Robert Morris
Roc	Jean-Baptiste-Donatien de Vimeur, comte de Rochambeau
SAH	Syrett, *Papers of Alexander Hamilton*
SD	Silas Deane
SGW	Sparks, *Writings of George Washington*
Smith	Smith, *Letters of Delegates to Congress*
Sparks	Sparks, *Correspondence of the American Revolution*
SS	Secretary of State
TJ	Thomas Jefferson
Tower	Tower, *Marquis de La Fayette in the American Revolution*
TP	Thomas Paine
Ver	Charles Gravier, comte de Vergennes
Wharton	Wharton, *Revolutionary Diplomatic Correspondence of the United States*

Chapter One

1. Bernier, *Lafayette*, 1–3. Biographers have argued about the correct form of Laf's name for two centuries. Gottschalk, *Lafayette Comes,* 153–54, points out that it was often written "Lafayette" before and after the American and French revolutions, sometimes "la Fayette." Laf himself wrote it as one word. It will be so presented here, except for quotations where it appears otherwise.

2. Bernier, *Lafayette,* 1–3; Gottschalk, *Lafayette Comes,* 7–9.

3. Gottschalk, *Lafayette Comes,* 7–11. Although the term "musketeer" means someone armed with a musket, the King's Musketeers evolved over the years to become four companies of household dragoons (heavy cavalry or mounted infantry), two each of "Grays" and "Blacks," after the color of their horses. They were armed with musketoons, heavy swords, and horse pistols.

4. Gottschalk, *Lafayette Comes,* 2–3.

5. Ibid. Laf offered variations on this "it's not my fault" routine in several letters and revisions of the Memoirs.

6. Anderson, *Crucible,* 378–80. The Battle of Minden followed a triumphant campaign by a French army commanded by the comte de Broglie, who had amassed huge territorial gains on the southern approaches to Hanover. Prussian Prince Ferdinand moved to counter de Broglie's successes by recapturing the town of Minden and its bridges across the River Weser, defended by an army under Marshal Louis, comte de Contades. Ferdinand regained most of Hesse and pushed Contades' shattered army back seventy miles to the River Lahn, a tributary of the Rhine. The two armies dug in there, ending the

French army's expensive and ultimately frustrated campaign. Ferdinand could have driven the French out of western Germany. Instead, he sent many of his troops to support Frederick II of Austria on another front.

7. Laf to unknown, nd, Lagrange Collection, quoted Maurois, *Adrienne,* 23.

8. Ibid.; Boatner, 865.

9. Gottschalk, *Lafayette Comes,* 3–4. In the feudal world, a family's wealth was figured not from the inherent value of property it possessed but from the expected income derived from the property, especially rents from tenant farmers. The *livre tournois* ("pound of Tours," after the city where it was minted), the French unit of currency before it was replaced by the franc in 1795 (*franc* had been slang for the livre before that date), was worth generally 19¢ (U.S.) or 9.4d (British pence) during the late eighteenth century. In the Americas, 5 livres equaled a Spanish "hard dollar" (*peso duro,* or "piece of eight"), and 25 livres bought a British pound. Three livres made a silver *écu,* or about 55¢. The *louis d'or,* commonly called the French Guinea in America during this period, was worth 12¢ less than the British Guinea in New York in 1784. (References to U.S. money reflect the system adopted by Congress in the 1790s.) Boatner, 714–15. Attempts to convert eighteenth-century moneys to modern dollar equivalents are futile.

10. Quoted Maurois, *Adrienne,* 25.

11. Bernier, *Lafayette,* 1–7; Gottschalk, *Lafayette Comes,* 5–6.

12. Laf later said that Marie's death in childbirth while he was in America in 1778 was "one of the greatest griefs" of his life. Laf, Autobiographical Notes III, ILA 2:231n (quotation); Gottschalk, *Lafayette Comes,* 5–6; Bernier, *Lafayette,* 1–7.

13. Laf, Memoir of 1779, ILA 1:6; marquis de Bouillé quoted Maurois, *Adrienne,* 26; TJ to JMA, JAN 30, 1787, quoted Gottschalk, *Lafayette Joins,* 328. JA described him as "panting for glory." Bailyn, *Faces,* 16.

14. Laf, Memoir of 1779, ILA 1:6; Gottschalk, *Lafayette Comes,* 12; Memoirs quoted Unger, *Lafayette,* 7–8. *La bête de la Gévaudan* has been a persistent varmint, still roaming the territory in 2006, according to a quick search of the Internet. Although the word "hyena" now refers to a particular African scavenger, the word is an old one, derived from the Greek for "hog." In medieval Europe it meant any of a number of large carnivores, which scavenged mostly at night. The broader meaning passed out of usage during Laf's lifetime, hence the "hyena" (*hyène*) of his earlier writings became a "beast" (*bête*) in his later, and in modern legends.

15. Gottschalk, *Lafayette Comes,* 6; Schama, *Citizens,* 32.

16. Laf quoted Maurois, *Adrienne,* 25. The interpretation that follows of what Laf absorbed from history, literature, and family tradition summarizes his later correspondence and the Memoirs; Gottschalk, *Lafayette Comes;* and Bernier, *Lafayette.*

17. See the comparative presentation of the two paintings in Anderson, *Crucible,* 366–67. Benjamin West (an American resident in London) and French painter Louis-Joseph Watteau helped to launch the Romantic Era with their dramatic paintings of major events.

18. Bernier, *Lafayette,* 7–10; Gottschalk, *Lafayette Comes,* 18–20.

19. Laf, Memoir of 1779, ILA 1:7; Gottschalk, *Lafayette Comes,* 13–15, 21–22.

20. ILA 1:12n; Gottschalk, *Lafayette Comes,* 18–20.

21. Laf, Memoir of 1779, ILA 1:7; another version of this story quoted Maurois, *Adrienne,* 27.

22. Gottschalk, *Lafayette Comes,* 21–22.

23. Ibid., 22–23; Laf quoted Maurois, *Adrienne,* 27.

24. Quoted Unger, *Lafayette,* 8–9.

25. Gottschalk, *Lafayette Comes,* 23–24.

26. The background to Laf's marriage follows Maurois, *Adrienne,* 28–31; Gottschalk, *Lafayette Comes,* 26–31; and Lane, *General,* 7–11.

27. Lasteyrie, 43–44. Gottschalk puts the dowry at 1.5 million livres, but where he got the figure is not clear. Unger says 200,000, without giving a source. He may have followed Maurois, who also gives no source for the 200,000. Either sum was considerable in its day.

28. Gottschalk, *Lafayette Comes,* 31–32.

29. Gottschalk, *Lafayette Comes,* 33–36, 38–40; Bernier, *Lafayette,* 10–22. The war ministry promoted Laf to captain effective MAY 19, 1774, but withheld the rank until he turned eighteen.

30. Maurois, *Adrienne,* 32–34, offers a fair sampling of these missives.

31. Gottschalk, *Lafayette Comes,* 40–45.

32. Ibid., 40–41. Laf did not receive "vaccination," a technique developed by Edward Jenner in England a few years later. Instead of direct inoculation with smallpox-bearing material, vaccination involves infecting the patient with vaccinia, the cowpox virus. Vaccination derived from Jenner's observation that people who handled dairy cattle and contracted cowpox were immune to smallpox. GW ordered inoculation of his troops during the Revolution.

33. Laf, Memoir of 1779, ILA 1:2, 6.

34. Maurois, *Adrienne,* 37–40; Gottschalk, *Lady-in-Waiting,* 12–15, 116; Bernier, *Lafayette,* 18–19; Ségur quoted ILA 1:13.

35. Laf, Memoir of 1779, ILA 1:6; Unger, *Lafayette,* 14–15.

36. Gottschalk, *Lafayette Comes,* 41–45; Bernier, *Lafayette,* 10–22.

37. Parkman, *Montcalm,* 545.

38. Levi, *Louis XIV,* 163–69, 193–222. In the fifth century the church began to stomp out "pagan" beliefs and customs, including the Olympic Games and the taking of baths. Until the late nineteenth century, Western Christians were generally the dirtiest people in the world.

39. Laf, Memoir of 1779, ILA 1:3.

40. Quoted Unger, *Lafayette,* 14.

41. Comte de Marck quoted Bernier, *Lafayette,* 18.

42. Gottschalk, *Lafayette Comes,* 37–38. Laf's height is given in English measures. The

French foot (not used since the adoption of the metric system during the French Revolution) was three-quarters of an inch longer than the English. Contemporary sources describe his height as five feet four or five inches, French measures.

43. Ibid., 46–48; Laf, Memoir of 1779, ILA 1:7. The situation also may have involved Lafayette's unsatisfied lust for Provence's mistress.

44. Gottschalk, *Lafayette Comes,* 48–52; TJ, *Autobiography,* 105.

45. Gottschalk, *Lafayette Comes,* 48–52; Maurois, *Adrienne,* 41–45.

46. Memoirs quoted Unger, *Lafayette,* 15.

47. Laf, Memoir of 1779, ILA 1:7.

48. Vovelle, *Fall,* 182–83; Schama, *Citizens,* 29. Saint-Jean de la Candeur can be freely translated as "Saint John of the Straight Talk." Masons in France, unlike in America, did not have minimum ages.

49. Unger, *Lafayette,* 15–16.

50. The best recent history of Freemasonry is Ridley, *Freemasons.* For a view from the inside, see also Coil, *Comprehensive View.* Modern Masonry grew out of two developments in the fourteenth century, after the Black Death wiped out a third of Europe's labor force. This raised the price of labor, so governments set limits on wages or contract prices that could be charged or paid for given services. To protect themselves from prosecution, trade guilds developed secret signs and codes. The other development was a tendency by late in that century for guildsmen to admit to their groups those who did not practice their craft, for political, social, or business reasons. These new members were known as "admitted" members, by the eighteenth century as "accepted" members, hence the "Free and Accepted Masons." By that time the Masons had lost all but a ritual association with their origins and were mostly clubs where tradesmen, gentlemen, and aristocrats could socialize outside their social classes. The "Freemasons" owe their name to "Freestone" masons, those who carved decorative stonework, in the medieval period. The social-equality beliefs of Masonry arose from horror at the mass slaughters in the name of religion that took place in the seventeenth century. Masons were therefore early believers in religious toleration and eventually Deism. The claim that revolutions were engineered by Masons is a myth. Masons and anti-Masons have been on all sides of most conflicts in the past two centuries.

Chapter Two

1. Biographies of GW are legion. The best are those of Freeman and Flexner; this account of GW's early life follows both. Recent biographies include Ellis, *His Excellency,* and Burns and Dunn, *George Washington.* On his military career, a recent account is Lengel, *General George Washington.* On the Indian and agricultural background of the Tidewater, see Clary, *Fortress,* 179, notes 1–5. GW's birthday was FEB 11 until 1752, when Britain adopted the modern calendar.

2. Flexner, *George Washington Forge,* 18–19.

3. Ibid., 19–20, demolishes the tendency of GW's early biographers to portray

Mary as the saintly mother of the plaster saint they offered as their version of GW. As his fame increased, she became jealous of him and claimed that he had left her to starve in Fredericksburg while he chased after glory. As Flexner observes, "[H]istory does not always draw noble men from noble mothers, preferring sometimes to temper her future heroes in the furnaces of domestic infelicity."

4. "Old Grog" acquired his nickname when he regularized the grog (daily rum) ration in the Royal Navy, a custom that endured until near the end of the twentieth century.

5. Flexner, *George Washington Forge,* 22–23.

6. Roberts, *George Washington Master Mason,* passim; Ridley, *Freemasons,* 94.

7. Quoted Flexner, *George Washington Forge,* 26.

8. GWD, quoted ibid., 35–36.

9. Quoted ibid., 54. The account of GW's mission to the French forts follows, besides the biographies, Anderson, *Crucible,* 43–49, and Parkman, *Montcalm,* 75–81. See also Lewis, *For King and Country.*

10. Both quoted Flexner, *George Washington Forge,* 55–56.

11. Quoted Parkman, *Montcalm,* 78. The English had called the French "frog-eaters" and "frogs" (from their presumed dietary preferences), and the French had called the English *rosbifs* ("roast beefs," from their habit of eating meat roasted instead of boiled) and *les goddams* (from their commonest word, at least as the French heard it), since early in the Hundred Years' War of the fourteenth and fifteenth centuries. During World War I American troops became known in France as *les sombiches,* for their favorite word.

12. Quoted Freeman, *George Washington* 1:326.

13. On the events leading up to the surrender at Fort Necessity, I follow Anderson, *Crucible,* 50–65, and Parkman, *Montcalm,* 81–93.

14. Parkman, *Montcalm,* 93–94. The bloody behavior of the Indians was usual in frontier warfare, and whites behaved the same way when they could. Grenier, *First Way,* suggests that this sort of thing produced a uniquely American style of warfare that persisted for centuries.

15. Flexner, *George Washington Forge,* 110–14; Anderson, *Crucible,* 66–68.

16. Ellis, *His Excellency,* 20.

17. Both quoted Parkman, *Montcalm,* 110–12. The account of the campaign and the Battle of Monongahela that follows relies on Anderson, *Crucible,* 94–107; Parkman, *Montcalm,* 118–34; and among the biographies, Flexner, *George Washington Forge,* 116–31, and Ellis, *His Excellency,* 20–24.

18. FGW 29:41–42, quoted Flexner, *George Washington Forge,* 120.

19. Quoted ibid., 127–28.

20. The event has also been called the Battle of the Wilderness and the Battle of Turtle Creek, after a tributary of the Monongahela. British troops would not suffer another defeat so lopsided until JAN 22, 1879, at Isandhlwana in the opening action of the Zulu War. Six companies of infantry, together with two guns and a small force of volunteers, were overwhelmed by Zulus armed with short spears and hard-charging tactics of assault and envelopment. Only a few men survived.

21. FGW 39:44, quoted Flexner *George Washington Forge,* 130.

22. FGW 39:44, quoted ibid., 131.

23. Flexner, ibid., 131n, points out that Braddock's orderly, Thomas Bishop, "attached himself to Washington" and served him as a valet and servant for more than thirty years.

24. Ibid., 137–38. This summary of GW's Virginia military career in the 1750s follows ibid., 136–87, and Ellis, *His Excellency,* 24–39. See also Clary, *Fortress,* 2–6.

25. Flexner, *George Washington Forge,* 137.

26. Quoted ibid., 148.

27. Quoted Ellis, *His Excellency,* 26.

28. Ibid., 31–32.

29. Both quoted Flexner, *George Washington Forge,* 222–23.

30. FGW 2:337, quoted ibid., 229. The summary of GW's life to 1775 that follows relies mostly on ibid., 227–345, and Ellis, *His Excellency,* 35–72.

31. Quoted Ellis, *His Excellency,* 55. On GW and the Potomac, see Achenbach, *Grand Idea.*

32. GW to George Fairfax, JUN 10–15, 1774, and GW to Bryan Fairfax, JUL 4, 1774, both quoted Ellis, *His Excellency,* 61–62. On the British side of the American Revolution and how the king's government blundered into it, see Weintraub, *Iron Tears.*

33. Quoted Flexner, *George Washington Forge,* 340–41.

34. Quoted ibid., 345.

Chapter Three

1. Quoted Risch, *Quartermaster Support,* 16; Clary, *These Relics,* 6–13, 292–300.

2. Quoted Weigley, *History,* 32.

3. Quoted CW, 12–13.

4. Orders and regulations for uniforms are in Ogden, *Uniform,* in chronological order. This was the first.

5. Flexner, *George Washington American,* 35; CW, 12n.

6. Ogden, *Uniform.* The blue frock-coat uniform first appeared officially for the artillery in 1777. In March 1779, Congress formally adopted European-style uniforms for all troops. The Continental Army gradually became more regular in appearance, but supply and cash shortages kept the enlisted men ragtag.

7. Weigley, *History,* 29–30; Ganoe, *History,* 2–9; Flexner, *George Washington American,* 29–43; Morton, "Origins"; Boucher, "Colonial Militia"; Spaulding, "Military Studies."

8. Lefkowitz, *George Washington's Indispensable,* 19–24; Boatner, 925–26; Heitman 1:37.

9. Lefkowitz, *George Washington's Indispensable,* 24–25; Boatner, 704–5; Heitman 1:708.

10. Weigley, *History,* 30, 44–45, 64–65; Forman, "Why the Military Academy," 17–18; Ganoe, *History,* 2–9. The lawmakers believed that military experience was important. Of thirteen general officers commissioned in 1775, eleven had had some war

service. Of seventy-three generals appointed during the war, sixteen had held commissions in European armies. Only twenty-one lacked any military background before 1775. But only a handful of the generals were thoroughly trustworthy, and some of the better ones had flawed characters. Lower down, there were too few good junior officers and sergeants.

11. Flexner, *George Washington American,* 17–18, 29; Boatner, 1161–2; Heitman 1:1000.

12. Higginbotham, *War,* 46; Flexner, *George Washington American,* 17–18; Gottschalk, *Lafayette Joins,* 204–5; Thane, *Fighting Quaker,* 23; Boatner, 605–7; John W. Shy, "Charles Lee: The Soldier as Radical," in Billias, *George Washington's Generals,* 22–53; Heitman 1:623.

13. Flexner, *George Washington American,* 18; Boatner, 902–4, 991–93; John H. G. Pell, "Philip Schuyler: The General as Aristocrat," in Billias, *George Washington's Generals,* 54–78; Heitman 1:810, 867.

14. Nelson, *General Horatio Gates;* Thane, *Fighting Quaker,* 23; Flexner, *George Washington American,* 18; George A. Billias, "Horatio Gates: Professional Soldier," in Billias, *George Washington's Generals,* 79–108; Heitman 1:449.

15. Weigley, *History,* 62; CW, 14–15; Wright, *Continental Army,* 45–56. Administrative and tactical organization would not take final form until after FVS arrived in 1778. Tactical formations between the battalion and the whole army did not become common in Europe until after the 1790s. Despite his original intentions, GW became a pioneer in tactical organization.

16. Maurer, "Military Justice"; CW, 15; Weigley, *History,* 63. The first articles of war limited whippings to the biblical maximum of thirty-nine strokes; Washington got Congress to raise that to a hundred a year later, but when he asked for a maximum of 500, the lawmakers refused. As the commander in chief gradually learned, American citizen-soldiers would not stand for being treated as if they were European regulars.

17. Weigley, *History,* 44–45, 51–61; CW, 14; Risch, *Quartermaster,* 1–73. "[O]ur hospital, or rather house of carnage," AW complained, "beggars all description; and shocks humanity to visit." Quoted Commager and Morris, *Spirit,* 828.

18. Quoted Ganoe, *History,* 13–14; Weigley, *History,* 52.

19. Flexner, *George Washington American,* 34–38.

20. Clary, *These Relics,* 6–13.

21. Riling, *Baron von Steuben,* 1–2. Lieutenant Timothy Pickering's manual for the Essex County, Massachusetts, militia offered some promise as a tactical standard. It was adopted as the official state manual in 1776 and was much copied in other American units. It offered simplified maneuvers, with original elements adapted to American conditions. It took FVS to straighten out this fundamental weakness in the Continental Army, as will be seen. HK thought he knew what the problem was. "The officers of the army," he said in 1776, "are exceedingly deficient in books upon the military art." HK to JA, MAY 13, 1776, quoted Forman, "Why the Military Academy," 18. Unfortunately, men did not become leaders through reading alone.

22. Weigley, *History,* 33–34.

23. GW to Reed, NOV 28, 1775, quoted Karsen, "American Democratic," 35.

24. Callahan, *Henry Knox;* North Callahan, "Henry Knox: American Artillerist," in Billias, *George Washington's Generals,* 239–59; Thane, *Fighting Quaker,* 10–11; Boatner, 586–87; Heitman 1:607. The performance of American artillery under HK's supervision amazed the French. The chevalier de Chastellux, who was in America in the early 1780s as both a tourist and a sometime aide to Roc, got to know HK at Yorktown and said, "As for General Knox, he belongs to the whole world by his reputation and his success. Thus have the English, contrary to their intention, added to the ornament of the human species, by awakening talents and virtues where they thought to find nothing but ignorance and weakness." He also said, "From the very first campaign, he was entrusted with the command of the artillery, and it has turned out that it could not have been placed in better hands." Quoted Chinard, *George Washington as French,* 53–54. HK was the one true American military genius of the war, and his field artillery tactical innovations, carried to France by Laf and others, profoundly influenced the development of artillery doctrine in what became the Napoleonic army, as will be seen. HK succeeded GW as commander in chief in 1783 and later became his secretary of war.

25. Boatner, 587–88; Higginbotham, *War,* 105. Three of the thirteen-inch siege mortars weighed over a ton each.

26. Higginbotham, *War,* 104–6; Flexner, *George Washington American,* 70–78.

27. Higginbotham, *War,* 16–15. On Arnold's part in the campaign, see Desjardin, *Through Howling.*

28. Weigley, *History,* 34–39, 62–63, GW quoted 34, 39. The recruiting difficulties were created when Congress, trying to standardize the size of regiments, abolished existing ones, depriving officers of their commissions, and authorized new units. The lawmakers tried to correct that when they restored state designations to Continental Army regiments but invited the states to review officer performance. Nobody wanted to reenlist because none knew who would be the new officers with the authority to recruit. By November, none had been selected.

29. This summary of the campaign of 1776 follows Fischer, *Washington's Crossing,* 66–114, quote at 114; and of the New York campaign, Schuster, *Battle.* See also McCullough, *1776.*

30. GW quoted Weigley, *History,* 37; Fischer, *Washington's Crossing,* 115–51.

31. FGW 8:247 quoted Flexner, *George Washington American,* 159–60.

32. Fischer, *Washington's Crossing,* 160–91; Weigley, *History,* 63.

33. Fischer, *Washington's Crossing,* 206–62.

34. Ibid., 263–345; Weigley, *History,* 39–40.

35. Murphy, "French Soldiers' Opinion," 191–98.

36. Higginbotham, *War,* 226–30.

37. Pachero, *French Secret Agents;* see also ibid., 230.

38. Corwin, "French Objectives"; Higginbotham, *War,* 231; Kapp, *Life of John Kalb,* 52–73; Boatner, 227–28, 1145–7. On French interest in and aid to America in the

1770s, see also Ketcham, "France and American Politics"; Meng, "Foot-note"; Rule, "Old Regime"; and Van Tyne, "French Aid."

39. Dull, *Diplomatic History,* 63–64; Higginbotham, *War,* 233; Boatner, 320–22; Stephenson, "Supply of Gunpowder"; Meng, "Foot-note"; Kite, "French Secret Aid"; Schoenbrun, *Triumph,* passim.

40. Perkins, *France,* 193–203; Kapp, *Life of John Kalb,* 94–95; Ver quoted Unger, *Lafayette,* 18–19.

41. Gottschalk, *Lafayette Comes,* 51–54, 157–58.

42. Gottschalk, *Lafayette Comes,* 66–76; de Broglie quoted Unger, *Lafayette,* 21–22; Laf, Memoir of 1779, ILA 1:8.

43. Quoted Kapp, *Life of John Kalb,* 94–95.

44. SD to Committee of Secret Correspondence, DEC 6, 1776, quoted Corwin, *French Policy,* 90–91.

45. Ibid.

46. Quoted Unger, *Lafayette,* 20–21.

47. Laf, Agreement with SD, DEC 7, 1776, ILA 1:17; Bill and Gottschalk, "Silas Deane's 'Worthless' Agreement."

48. Laf, Agreement with SD, DEC 7, 1776, ILA 1:17. Bendiner, *Virgin Diplomats,* 71, says that SD assumed Laf was close to the king, who winked at his defection to America, so he granted him his major general's commission. BF later fell into the same trap.

49. List of Officers . . . , ILA 1:18. SD, Laf, and de Kalb all signed this attachment.

50. Laf, Memoir of 1779, ILA 1:8.

51. Unger, *Lafayette,* 22–23.

52. Ibid., 23; M. Dubois-Martin to de Kalb, DEC 8, 1776, quoted Tower 1:28; Laf quoted Duer, 9–10.

53. Gottschalk, *Lafayette Comes,* 83–85, 117; Laf to Carmichael, FEB nd and 11, 1777, ILA 1:19–20.

54. Laf to Adr, FEB 20, 25, and 28, MAR nd and 7, 1777, ILA 1:21-27. French wives accepted their husbands' philandering but understandably did not enjoy having their noses rubbed in it.

55. Gottschalk, *Lafayette Comes,* 89–92; Laf, Memoir of 1779, ILA 1:9.

56. SD to JH, MAR 16, 1777, and Carmichael to Richard Henry Lee, MAR 17, 1777, ILA 1:33–36; Maurois, *Adrienne,* 49.

57. Laf to Adr, MAR 16, 1777, ILA 1:32.

58. Lasteyrie, 55–57.

59. Laf to d'Ayen, MAR 9, 1777, ILA 1:29–31.

60. Unger, *Lafayette,* 25–26.

61. Laf to de Broglie, MAR 23, 1777, ILA 1:37–38. Laf signed the articles of embarkation at Bordeaux as "Sieur Gilbert du Motier, chevalier de Chavaillac, age 20, tall, blond hair." Laf, Act of Embarkation, MAR 22, 1777, ILA 1:37. He usually signed himself as "Marquis de Lafayette," and he was indeed Gilbert du Motier, chevalier (knight, or

more broadly gentleman) of Chavaniac (Chavaillac was an older spelling). Travel incognito was common among nobles, and well advised in this case.

62. De Kalb to SD, MAR 25, and to Pierre de Saint-Paul, NOV 7, 1777, ILA 1:38–40, 145–59; Laf, Memoir of 1779, ILA 1:9–10; BF and SD to Committee of Secret Correspondence, APR 9, 1777, Wharton 2:286–90. De Kalb knew that Lafayette had jeopardized de Broglie's project. He would change his attitude in coming months, but for the moment he wanted Lafayette to return. "If he had not been aboard the ship and under way," he wrote his wife, "I think he would have gone home and, in my opinion, it would have been the right thing to do." De Kalb to Mme de Kalb, APR 1, 1777, quoted Unger, *Lafayette,* 26.

63. Isaacson, *Benjamin Franklin,* 334–35; Bernier, *Lafayette,* 34–38; SD to GW, APR 5, 1777, quoted Gottschalk, *Lafayette Comes,* 111; SD to Joseph-Matthias Gérard de Rayneval (Ver's secretary), APR 2, 177, ILA 1:40–41; SD to Ver, APR 5, 1777, quoted Unger, *Lafayette,* 27; Gottschalk, *Lafayette Comes,* 125–27; Lord Stormont to Lord Weymouth, APR 2 and 5, 1777, ILA 1:41–43. For further self-defense, see Carmichael to Charles Dumas, APR 21, 1777, and to John Cadwalader, OCT 8, 1777, Ammon, "Letters of William Carmichael."

64. Marquis de Noailles to Maurepas, APR 8, 1777, quoted Unger, *Lafayette,* 27.

65. Ver to Marquis de Noailles, APR 15, 1777, quoted Unger, *Lafayette,* 28; Stormont to Weymouth, APR 9, 1777, quoted Gottschalk, *Lafayette Comes,* 117.

66. Unger, *Lafayette,* 26–28; Corwin, *French Policy,* 92; Duer, 13.

67. De Kalb to SD, APR 17, 1777, and Laf to Carmichael, APR 19, 1777, ILA 1:46, 50–51.

68. Laf to Adr, APR 19, 1777, ILA 1:47, 49.

69. For an account of the voyage by the captain of the ship, see Chinard, *When Lafayette.*

70. BF to GW, MAY 15, 1777, cited Gottschalk, *Lafayette Comes,* 129.

71. BF and SD to Committee of Foreign Affairs (and to GW), MAY 25, 1777, ILA 1:51. Also in Wharton 2:324, and LBF 24:73–77.

72. SD to RM, MAY 26, 1777, ILA 1:52. By "avanturier" he meant *aventurier* (adventurer, meaning a sharp businessman). By living "in character," he meant as a nobleman should.

Chapter Four

1. GW to PC, FEB 20, 1777, FGW 4:327.

2. Quoted Ganoe, *History,* 41. See also CW, 17–21; Forman, "Why the Military Academy."

3. Boatner, 602–3; Walker, *Continental Army,* 130–33; Heitman 1:390; Walker, *Engineers,* 8–17; Schoenbrun, *Triumph,* 90–93. Duportail ended the war a major general and continued to rise in rank back home. He became friendly with Laf in America, then an

ally during the French Revolution. GW thought him one of the few foreign officers useful to his cause, ranking him with Laf and FVS. Freeman, *George Washington* 4:540, 567.

4. GW to Richard Henry Lee, MAY 17, 1777, FGW 4:423.

5. CIG 1:2–20, 52–59; CW, 20–21; Bodinier, *Dictionnaire,* 403–4; Heitman 1:329; Boatner, 1117–8; Wright, *Organization,* 205 (Duportail's role); Flexner, *George Washington American,* 195; "Coudray's Observations"; Sanger, *Inspector-General's Department,* 228; Laf, Memoir of 1779, ILA 1:12 (quotation). Tronson du Coudray's highest rank in French service had been equivalent to major. These appointments were the first use of the term "inspector-general" in America. CIG 1:5–20, 52–54.

6. Laf to Adr, MAY 30–JUN 15, 1777, and Memoir of 1779, ILA 1:10, 56–60.

7. Memoir by vicomte de Mauroy, ILA 1:53–56.

8. Tower 1:171; Memoirs 1:13 quoted Unger, *Lafayette,* 31–32.

9. Memoir by the chevalier Dubuysson, ILA 1:73–74. Dubuysson later became adc to de Kalb.

10. Ibid.; Gottschalk, *Lafayette Joins,* 3–7; Laf, Memoir of 1779, ILA 1:10.

11. Laf to duc de Mouchy, JUN 22, 1777, and to Adr, JUN 19, 1777, ILA 1:60–65.

12. Laf to Adr, JUN 19, 1777, and to Monsieur Duboismartin, OCT 23, 1777, ILA 1:61, 130. Duboismartin was de Broglie's secretary. Laf's slave is discussed below.

13. Laf had bought the ship with a down payment of 40,000 livres and still owed 72,000, the note due in JUN. ILA 1:84–85, and de Kalb to Pierre de Saint-Paul, NOV 7, 1777, ILA 1:145–49.

14. Memoir by chevalier Dubuysson, ILA 1:73–84.

15. Journal of du Rousseau de Fayolle, ILA 1:68–72.

16. Laf, Memoir of 1779, and Laf to Adr JUL 17 and 23, 1777, ILA 1:11, 66–68; Gottschalk, *Lafayette Joins,* 10–12.

17. Memoir by chevalier Dubuysson, and Journal of du Rousseau de Fayolle, ILA 1:68–83.

18. Gottschalk, *Lafayette Joins,* 14–23; Bernier, *Lafayette,* 42–43; Laf, Memoir of 1779, ILA 1:11–12.

19. Resolution of JUL 31, 1777, ILA 1:88. When de Kalb got his commission in SEP, the resolution was typical: "Resolved, that another major general be appointed in the army of the United States; the ballots being taken, the Baron de Kalb was elected." ILA 1:88n.

20. Gottschalk, *Lafayette Joins,* 30–37, 40–42. A native of Gascony, born in either 1743 or 1747, Gimat was a highly rated first lieutenant when he accompanied Laf to America. SD had promised him a commission as a major, and Congress granted that when he became Laf's adc. He returned to France with Laf in JAN 1779, and back to America with him in 1780. In FEB 1781 GW promoted him to command of a light infantry regiment, and he accompanied Laf to Virginia. He was wounded in the attack on Redoubt Number 10 at Yorktown. In JAN 1782 he returned to France on indefinite leave, and was discharged from American service NOV 1783. He rose to high rank in French service. Boatner, 433–34. La Colombe was born in Auvergne in about 1755, and his family had

connections to Laf's. He was a lieutenant on the reserve list, promised a lieutenancy by SD in the Continental Army. He served as adc to both Laf and de Kalb, often detached to line service in state regiments, until OCT 1779, having been promoted to captain in NOV 1777. He returned to France in NOV 1779 and rose slowly in rank until becoming a brigadier during the Revolution, in 1792, but he was dismissed and fled for his life. He protected GWL in New York during Laf's captivity, and later returned to France. He was wounded several times in both revolutions. Boatner, 248–49; ILA 1:112n.

21. HL to John Lewis Gervais, AUG 8, 1777, ILA 1:88n.

22. ILA 1:15n.

23. Laf, Memoir of 1779, ILA 1:91; Ségur in Chinard, *George Washington as French,* 36–37.

24. Flexner, *George Washington American,* 214–15; Gottschalk, *Lafayette Joins,* 28–29.

25. GW to Laf, SEP 30, 1779, quoted Gottschalk, *Lafayette Joins,* 28–29; Flexner, *George Washington American,* 4.

26. SGW 5:454.

27. "Family" was an Anglicization of *famille,* but as with other French loans to English after 1066, it did not make the jump with its parent meaning intact. According to OED, the original English meaning of the word was the servants of a household, the second the retinue of a nobleman, and the third the staff of a general. It was recorded first in 1545 to mean all people (including servants) inhabiting one household, and first in 1667 to mean a set of blood relations, its commonest meaning today, although since 1425 it has denoted those descended from a common ancestor. Laf learned the distinction within a few weeks, so that virtually every letter he wrote to GW ended with compliments to Mrs. Washington and also "to the family."

28. Chinard, *George Washington as French,* 44.

29. BF and SD to GW, AUG or SEP 1777, LBF 24:485.

30. Massey, *John Laurens,* 73; GW to JL AUG 5, 1777, and order of appointment OCT 6, 1777, in Townsend, *American Soldier,* 58–59.

31. Laf to JH, AUG 13, 1777, ILA 1:103.

32. De Kalb to PC, AUG 1, 1777, and additional material, ILA 1:149n. See also Journals of Congress, SEP 8, 1777, Tower 1:186–88.

33. De Kalb to de Broglie, SEP nd, 1777, quoted Kapp, *Life of John Kalb,* 127. One of the other officers with de Kalb had sent a letter to Congress exposing de Broglie's plot to become generalissimo. Comte Guillaume-Matthieu Dumas to Committee of Foreign Affairs, AUG 22, 1777, Wharton 2:377–78.

34. Memoirs, 1:19 (*pour apprendre et non pour enseigner*), rendered variously in Flexner, *George Washington American,* 215, and Unger, *Lafayette,* 41; Tower 1:184–85; Laf, Memoir of 1779, ILA 1:91 (second quotation). Almost nothing is known about Laf's slave except that he ran errands in Philadelphia for him in OCT 1777. HL to Laf, OCT 1777, ILA 1:126–28, and 128n. He was a gift from Edmund Brice.

35. GW to Harrison, AUG 19, 1777, ILA 1:104–5.

36. Harrison to GW, AUG 20, 1777, ILA 1:105–6.

37. Gottschalk, *Lafayette Joins,* 38–40.

38. Quoted ibid., 39.

39. Flexner, *George Washington American,* 214–15.

40. Laf, Memoir of 1779, ILA 1:91. Shorter men were put into the front rank so that taller men could fire over them. Regular armies often formed three ranks, and height was also graduated from one end to the other, tallest to shortest. What Laf saw reflected an absence of training in close-order maneuvers. Laf often described the men as "naked" (or more often "nacked"). He did not mean bare, but instead indifferently clad, not uniform.

41. Chinard, *George Washington as French,* 49–51. The nuts were hickory nuts.

42. Ibid., 65.

43. Lefkowitz, *Washington's Indispensable,* 64–66, 201–2; Boatner, 1108–9. Because of his loyal service, GW gave him the honor of bearing the official report to Congress announcing Cornwallis' surrender in 1781.

44. SAH 2:566, quoted Flexner, *Young Hamilton,* 138. Flexner's is the best of the many biographies of AH, especially for its concentration on the revolutionary years. The most recent, and more complete, is Chernow, *Alexander Hamilton.* Also useful are McDonald, *Alexander Hamilton,* Brookhiser, *Alexander Hamilton,* and two volumes edited by Morris, *Alexander Hamilton and Founding* and *Basic Ideas.*

45. Massey, *John Laurens;* Townsend, *American Soldier;* Flexner, *George Washington New,* 39–40. Huguenots were well represented in the American Revolution, including John Jay and Paul Revere.

46. McDonald, *Alexander Hamilton,* 14–15, and Flexner, *Young Hamilton,* 315–16. Taking such language out of context, modern minds think it homosexual, a term coined in the 1890s. It was not a burning issue in the eighteenth century, as it is today, and it is a fallacy to apply the attitudes of the present to the context of the past.

47. The letters between JL and HL on this subject appear in Townsend, *American Soldier,* 63–66. That Laf was responsible for this sudden vanity is my conclusion.

48. Martin, *Philadelphia Campaign,* 34–35. Laf's activities in 1789 are discussed below.

49. Boatner, 16–17; Heitman 1:157; Chinard, *George Washington as French,* 46; Freeman, *George Washington* 4:241ff. On Laf's affairs, see Gottschalk, *Lafayette and Close,* 427–30. On his relations with Catherine Alexander, see Laf to HL, FEB 7 and 9, and MAR 20, 1778, ILA 1:283, 286, 369. The "most charming *Miss Ketty*" was at York, the temporary capital, and Laf wanted HL to convey his compliments to her. She stayed with HL, "within very narrow bounds and without the smallest breach of decorum," HL said. HL to Laf, JUL 18, 1778, ILA 2:108–10.

50. Biographies include Greene, *General Greene;* Thayer, *Nathanael Greene;* Greene, *Nathanael Greene;* Thane, *Fighting Quaker;* and Golway, *Washington's General.* See also Theodore Thayer, "Nathanael Greene: Revolutionary War Strategist," in Billias, *George Washington's Generals,* 109–36; Boatner, 453–56; and Heitman 1:475.

51. De Kalb to Mme de Kalb, JAN nd 1778, quoted Perkins, *France in American,* 189–90.

52. The campaign of 1777 is summarized in Higginbotham, *War,* 175–203. See also Pancake, *1777,* and Martin, *Philadelphia Campaign.*

53. Quoted Golway, *Washington's General,* 133.

54. Laf, Memoir of 1779, ILA l:91–92.

55. Golway, *Washington's General,* 135; Laf, Memoir of 1779, ILA 1:92.

56. On the Battle of Brandywine in general, see Mowday, *September 11;* Martin, *Philadelphia Campaign,* 43–76; Higginbotham, *War,* 183–87. Accounts of individual Americans involved include Gottschalk, *Lafayette Joins,* 43–48; Flexner, *George Washington American,* 223–24; Freeman, *George Washington* 4:471–88; Golway, *Washington's General,* 134–40; Flexner, *Young Hamilton,* 171–75; Massey, *John Laurens,* 73–75. The handiest summary is Boatner, 104–10.

57. Laf, Memoir of 1779, ILA 1:94–95.

58. So he told HL, who repeated it, HL to John Lewis Gervais, OCT 8, 1777, quoted Massey, *John Laurens,* 75.

59. I suggest a rifle rather than a musket ball because of Laf's description of the wound. A musket ball in the .69- to .75-caliber range, typical for the British (Americans favored a bore around .60-caliber), would have caused much more damage if it had retained enough velocity to go through the leg. Rifles came in smaller calibers, around .30 to .40, and bullets moved at higher velocities.

60. Gottschalk, *Lafayette Joins,* 44–47; Flexner, *George Washington American,* 223–24; Laf, Memoir of 1779, ILA 1:95.

61. I believe this "Treat him as my son" line was Laf's invention, although I cannot be certain. It does not appear in the Memoir of 1779, although it is in Laf to Adr, OCT 1, 1777, ILA 1:114–19. Laf did not include the line in the account he wrote for Sparks in 1828, quoted ILA 1:101n. This is not the only area where Laf was contradictory about his history.

62. I base this conclusion on Laf's letters over the following months and years, in which he pointedly shrugs off the pain and takes every opportunity to mention that he had bled for the United States. See examples in the next chapter.

Chapter Five

1. AH to Hugh Knox, JUL nd, 1777, Morris, *Alexander Hamilton and Founding,* 31–32.

2. On Germantown, see Martin, *Philadelphia Campaign,* 99–120; Higginbotham, *War,* 186–87; Boatner, 426–30. JL was slightly wounded, at the stone house, during the battle. AH was not.

3. In Chinard, *George Washington as French,* 20. This answered GW's circular of APR 20, 1778. JL translated it into English.

4. GW to JH, SEP 11, 1777, SGW 5:59.

5. Laf to Adr, SEP 12, 1777, ILA 1:108, 110. Adr's letter to Laf has disappeared.

6. Maurois, *Adrienne,* 55, 58–63.

7. Laf, Memoir of 1779, ILA 1:96–97; Gottschalk, *Lafayette Joins,* 51–53. Over 30,000 letters written by Laf survive in one form or another. When Laf left the Moravian settlement OCT 18, the congregation's diary said: "The French Marquis de La Fayette left us to-day for the army. . . . We found him a very intelligent and pleasant young man." ILA 1:102n.

8. Laf to HL, SEP 25 and 27, 1777, ILA 1:110–13. The "proclamation" Laf referred to was an exercise in bombast Burgoyne had issued JUN 23, 1777. It appealed to Americans to remain loyal to the king, backed up by a threat to unleash thousands of Indians against those who rejected his demand. The message inspired both outrage and ridicule among Americans.

9. The best account of the Saratoga Campaign is Ketchum, *Saratoga.* Total surrendered, according to American returns, were 4,991—2,139 British, 2,022 Germans, and 830 Canadians. HG's terms under the surrender "convention" would have sent all of them home, but Congress overrode that, so only Burgoyne and two aides left. The rest of the "convention army" was interned near Boston, then over the years marched to other locations, most ending up near Charlottesville, Virginia. Escapes, death, paroles, and exchanges reduced the force by about half before the end of the war. See also Boatner, 275–76.

10. Laf to Adr OCT 1, 1777, ILA 1:114–19. He referred to a letter from GW, which has disappeared.

11. Laf to GW, OCT 14, 1777, ILA 1:121–24. The letter was all one paragraph, which I have broken up.

12. Laf to HL, OCT 18, 1777, ILA 1:124-26.

13. Gottschalk, *Lafayette Joins,* 63–65; NG to Mrs. Greene, NOV 20, 1777, quoted Greene, *Nathanael Greene* 1:514.

14. Amory, *Military Services;* Boatner, 1070–6; Charles P. Whittemore, "John Sullivan: Luckless Irishman," in Billias, *George Washington's Generals,* 137–62. On JS's campaign against the Iroquois in 1779, see Williams, *Year,* and Grenier, *First Way,* 166–69.

15. Laf to JS, and Certificate for JS, both NOV 1, 1777, ILA 1:139–40; Rossie, *Politics,* 181–83. Congress had already accepted the court's findings on OCT 20.

16. Callahan, *Daniel Morgan;* Higginbotham, *Daniel Morgan;* Boatner, 735–37; Don Higginbotham, "Daniel Morgan: Guerilla Fighter," in Billias, *George Washington's Generals,* 291–316.

17. Laf to Duboismartin, OCT 23, 1777, ILA 1:128–31.

18. Laf to Maurepas, OCT 24, 1777, ILA 1:131–34.

19. GW to PC, NOV 1, 1777, ILA 1:140–41. See also Thayer, *Nathanael Greene,* 187–88, and Flexner, *George Washington American,* 267.

20. De Kalb to Pierre de Saint-Paul, NOV 7, 1777, ILA 1:145–49. Saint-Paul was first secretary of the Ministry of War, investigating Laf's departure for America and his conduct after arrival.

21. Laf to Adr, NOV 6, 1777, ILA 1:142–45.

22. Laf to HL, NOV 18 and 20, 1777, ILA 1:152–55.

23. Gottschalk, *Lafayette Joins,* 80–85; Callahan, *Daniel Morgan,* 153–54; Laf, Memoir of 1779, ILA 1:100.

24. NG to GW, NOV 26, 1777, ILA 1:158–59; and in Greene, *Nathanael Greene* 1:527–28.

25. Laf to GW, NOV 26, 1777, ILA 1:156–58.

26. GW to PC, NOV 26, 1777, ILA 1:158–59.

27. Laf to HL, NOV 29, 1777, ILA 1:160–61.

28. PC to GW, DEC 1, 1777, and Laf, Memoir of 1779, ILA 1:100, 165; Journals of Congress, DEC 1, 1777, quoted Tower, 254; General Orders NOV 20 and DEC 4, 1777, FGW 10:88–89, 138. Stephen was dismissed on NOV 20.

29. Laf to HL, DEC 14, 1777, ILA 1:183–87.

30. Quoted Unger, *Lafayette,* 51.

31. BS, SD, and Lee to Committee of Foreign Affairs, DEC 18, 1777, Wharton 2:452–55.

32. Laf to d'Ayen, DEC 16, 1777, ILA 1:188–95.

33. Laf to Adr, JAN 6, 1778, ILA 1:222–26.

34. Laf to Adr, DEC 22, 1777, and JAN 9, 1778, ILA 1:198–99, 457–58; Laf to JA, JAN 9, 1778, Wharton 2:468; Adr to BF, AUG 3, and SEP 19 and 21, 1778, LBF 27:200–4, 427, 440–45.

35. Laf to RM, DEC 30, 1777, and JAN 9, 1778, ILA 1:201–2, 228–29; Moré de Pontgibaud, in Chinard, *George Washington as French,* 30–31.

36. HL to Laf, DEC 6, 1777, ILA 1:176–79.

37. Boatner, 704–5; NG to Jacob Greene, JAN 3, 1778, quoted Thane, *Fighting Quaker,* 120.

38. Risch, *Quartermaster Support,* 29–35; Trussell, *Birthplace.*

39. Laf, Memorandum on a winter campaign, DEC 3, 1777, ILA 1:173–76.

40. JL to HL, DEC 3, 1777, in Commager and Morris, *Spirit* 1:639.

41. Narrative attributed to James Sullivan Martin, ibid. 1:643.

42. Freeman, *George Washington* 4:565. The account of Valley Forge relies on Trussell, *Birthplace;* Risch, *Quartermaster Support,* 29–35; Clary, *These Relics,* ch. 1; Ganoe, *History,* 50–53; CIG 1:85–88. A recent reinterpretation is Fleming, *Washington's Secret War.*

43. Surgeon Albigence Waldo of the Connecticut Line recorded in his diary DEC 21, "Provisions scarce. . . . My skin and eyes are almost spoiled with continual smoke. A general cry thro' the camp this evening among the soldiers, 'No meat! No meat!' The distant vales echoed back the melancholy sound—'No meat! No meat!' Immitating the noise of crows and owls, also, made a part of the confused musick." He wrote on DEC 22, "My eyes are started out from their orbits like a rabbit's eyes, occasioned by a great cold and smoke. What have you got for breakfast, lads? 'Fire cake and water, Sir.' The Lord send that our commissary of purchases may live [on] fire cake and water till their glutted gutts are turned to pasteboard." Commager and Morris, *Spirit* 1:641–42.

44. Laf, Memoir of 1779, ILA 1:170; Pierre-Etienne Duponceau, aide to FVS, in Chinard, *George Washington as French,* 15.

45. Varnum to NG, FEB 12, 1778, and GW to PC, DEC 23, 1777, in Commager and Morris, *Spirit* 1:644, 650–51.

46. Laf to HL, JAN 2 and 15 (two letters), 1778, and to Henry, JAN 3, 1778, ILA 1:209–12, 236–38.

47. Laf, Memoir of 1779, Laf to Adr, JAN 6, 1778, to GW and to Adam Hubley, both JAN 20, 1778, ILA 1:169, 222–26, 238–41; Gottschalk, *Lafayette Joins,* 105–6.

48. Laf to GW, JAN 13, 1778, ILA 1:233–36.

49. Laf to GW, JAN 5, 1778, ILA 1:219–22.

50. Laf to Adr, JAN 6, 1778, ILA 1:222–26.

51. Boatner, 276–78; Bodinier, *Dictionnaire,* 105–6; Flexner, *George Washington American,* 262, 268; Weigley, *History,* 50–51; GW to Richard Henry Lee, OCT 17, 1777, FGW 9:388; AH quoted Flexner, *Young Hamilton,* 210. Besides Flexner's two books, the Conway Cabal is covered in Chadwick, *George Washington's War,* 261–67; CW, 22–31; CIG 1:61–85; Rossie, *Politics,* 188–202; Higginbotham, *War,* 216–22; Betz, "Conway Cabal"; and Brenneman, "Conway Cabal," among others. Wilkinson's part is covered in Jacobs, *Tarnished Warrior,* ch. 2; JL's in Massey, *John Laurens,* 89–92; and NG's in Golway, *Washington's General,* 154–57.

52. Gottschalk, *Lafayette Joins,* 67–72; HL to Laf, DEC 6, 1777, and Laf to HL, DEC 14, 1777, ILA 1:176–79, 183–88.

53. GW to Richard Henry Lee, OCT 17, 1777, FGW 9:387–89.

54. The documents on all this are reproduced in Sanger, *Inspector-General's Department,* 228–29.

55. Patterson, *Horatio Gates,* 216–19; Commager and Morris, *Spirit,* 1:651–52.

56. GW to Conway, NOV 9, 1777, FGW 10:29.

57. Commager and Morris, *Spirit* 1:651–52; Laf to HG, DEC 14, 1777, Laf to HL, DEC 18, 1777, Laf, Memoir of 1779, ILA 1:171–72, 182, 195–97.

58. Laf to HL, NOV 18, 1777, and HL to Laf, DEC 6, 1777, ILA 1:176–69.

59. Sanger, *Inspector General's Department,* 228–29; CW, 2–31; CIG 1:68–75; Wright, *Organization,* 195–96; AH quoted Kapp, *Life of Steuben,* 121–22.

60. See Francis Lightfoot Lee to Richard Henry Lee, DEC 15, 1777, and William Ellery to William Whipple, DEC 21, 1777, Smith 8:417, 453, as examples of thinking in Congress.

61. NG to HL, JAN nd 1778, Thayer, *Nathanael Greene,* 216–18; Flexner, *George Washington American,* 258–59, 262–63; Higginbotham, *War,* 218–20; JS and others to GW, DEC 31, 1777, and NG to PC, DEC 16, 1777, both quoted Gottschalk, *Lafayette Joins,* 100–1; JS to GW, DEC 30, 1777, ILA 1:208n.

62. Conway to HG, JAN 4, 1778, ILA 1:208n; GW to PC, JAN 2, 1778, FGW 10:249; GW to PC, JAN 3, 1778, quoted Palmer, *General von Steuben,* 133; Sanger, *Inspector General's Department,* 229.

63. Gottschalk, *Lafayette Joins,* 74–77, 90–91, 95–97.

64. Laf to GW, DEC 30, 1777, ILA 1:204–7. In Sparks 5:488 this was revised for clarity and so lost much of its charm.

65. GW to Laf, DEC 31, 1777, ILA 1:207–8.

66. Laf to GW, DEC 31, 1777, ILA 1:209.

67. See as examples Laf to HL, JAN 2, 1778, HL to Laf, JAN 12, 1778, Conway to HG, JAN 4, 1778, Laf to GW, JAN 5, 1778, Laf to RM, JAN 9, 1778, and others, ILA 1:209–33; NG to Jacob Greene, JAN 3, 1778, Greene, *Nathanael Greene,* 1:544; Tilghman to John Cadwalader, JAN 18, 1778, in Rankin, *American Revolution,* 173.

68. Abraham Clark to William Alexander (Lord Stirling), JAN 15, 1778, Smith 8:597.

69. Rossie, *Politics,* 188–202; NG quoted Rankin, *American Revolution,* 201–2; Massey, *John Laurens,* 90–92; AH quoted Flexner, *Young Hamilton,* 214.

70. Higginbotham, *War,* 220. Flexner, *George Washington American,* 271–77, suggests that the affair became known as the "Conway Cabal" because the phrase rings. Neither "Mifflin Cabal" nor "Gates Cabal" trips over the tongue.

71. De Kalb to de Broglie, JAN 5, 1778, quoted Kapp, *Life of John Kalb,* 137. De Kalb and Laf drew together during the crisis, and separated from other French officers. "He is an excellent young man," de Kalb told de Broglie, "and we are good friends. It is to be wished that all the Frenchmen who serve here were as reasonable as he and I. Lafayette is much liked; he is on the best of terms with Washington; both of them have every reason to be satisfied with me also."

Chapter Six

1. Many biographers have portrayed AH as an abolitionist. As Flexner, *Young Hamilton,* 39–40, 257–63, points out, the record will not support the claim except by selective citation of the documents. On JL's background in this area, see Townsend, *American Soldier,* 115–24.

2. HL to Laf, OCT 23, 1777, and Laf to BF, MAR 20, 1779, ILA 1:126–28, 2:241. Britain had taken Senegal from France in 1756 and held it under the treaty of 1763.

3. Quoted Higginbotham, *War,* 395; JL to HL nd spring 1776, quoted Townsend, *American Soldier,* 115–24 ; Flexner, *George Washington Anguish,* 116–17.

4. Quarles, *Negro;* Higginbotham, *War,* 394–97.

5. JL to HL, JAN 1, 1778, Townsend, *American Soldier,* 125.

6. AH to JJ, MAR 14, 1779, SAH 2:17–19.

7. JL to AH, JUL 14, 1779, and AH to JL, SEP 11, 1779, SAH 2:102–3, 165–69; GW to JL, MAR 22, 1782, Feinstone Collection, David Library; Massey, *John Laurens,* 128–53.

8. Ellis, *His Excellency,* 162–64, agrees that Laurens was the first person to affect GW's thinking on slavery but that Laf would have even greater influence. Both encouraged a natural trend in his own thinking.

9. On the origins of the expedition, see Nelson, *General Horatio Gates,* 171–75. Laf,

Memoir of 1779, ILA 1:245, states the case for conspiracy, and many authors have accepted his fantasies. For the Canadian side of the story, see Lanctot, *Canada and the American Revolution.*

10. Laf to GW, JAN 20, 1778, "a half past one," ILA 1:238–39.

11. HL to Laf, JAN 22, 1778, and Laf, Memoir of 1779, ILA 1:245. Stark was a tough old Indian fighter, a veteran of Rogers' Rangers during the French and Indian War, and the sort of character who generated legends in his own lifetime, many of them true. He served with distinction, mostly in the Northern Department, throughout the war. Boatner, *Encyclopedia,* 1052–3. Regarding his visit to HG's headquarters, in at least two versions of Memoirs, and separately in an 1829 letter to Jared Sparks, Laf claimed to have stopped in on his way to see Congress. After the party had drunk toasts to Congress and the United States, he embarrassed the others into drinking the health of GW. For the rest of his life he boasted of this as a triumph, but there is no contemporary evidence that the incident ever happened. Laf, Memoir of 1779, ILA 1:245, and discussion at 248n.

12. Laf, Memoir of 1779, HG to Laf, JAN 24, 1778, and HL to Laf, JAN 24, 1778, ILA 1:245, 249–50, 252.

13. Laf to HL, JAN 26, 1778, ILA 1:253–56.

14. GM to HL, JAN 26, 1778, ILA 1:256, 258; Gottschalk, *Lafayette Joins,* 113–14. Scotsman McDougall had commanded a privateer at the age of twenty-four during the Seven Years' War. A successful New York merchant, he served with distinction in the Hudson Highlands during most of the war. In 1779, at the age of forty-seven, he suffered an illness that kept him out of the Canada expedition. He was too much of a scrapper to stay out of the fight for long, however, and campaigned to the end of the war, after which he entered politics. Boatner, 690–91.

15. HL to Isaac Motte, JAN 26–30, 1778, ILA 1:256n.

16. Laf's suspicions lace his letters during the campaign, as will be seen. As for the board's motives in sending Conway, as also will be seen with HL's inquiries, he had become an embarrassment because of the backlash in the army over the Conway Cabal.

17. Laf to HL, JAN 27, 1778, ILA 1:258–60. Laf asked RM to get him £2,000 "because I want immediately ressources for the northern expedition." Laf to RM, JAN 29, 1778, ILA 1:263. Duer, born in 1749, was the son of a rich British family and a former army officer, adc to Clive in India in the 1760s. He visited New York as a timber buyer for the Royal Navy in 1768, and settled down there in 1773, becoming both richer and an American patriot, and served as an eloquent, hard-working delegate to Congress. He was not an enemy of GW. He rose from a sickbed to cast the deciding vote blocking nomination of a committee to remove GW from command. Laf's objection to him might have grown out of rivalry for the attentions of "Miss Ketty," whom Duer married in JUL 1779, GW giving the bride away. Duer prospered after the war, became a land speculator, and for six months in 1789 was AH's assistant secretary of the treasury. He was sued later for peculation in that position. He spent the last seven years of his life in debtor's prison, dying in 1799. Boatner, 339.

18. GW to Board of War, JAN 27, 1778, FGW 10:356.

19. HL to Laf, JAN 28, 1778, ILA 1:262–63. "Excellency" was the usual term of address to the commander of an army.

20. Laf to PC, and to HL (private), JAN 31, 1778, HG to Laf, JAN 31, 1778, with Instructions for the Marquis de Lafayette Major Genl. in the army of the United States of America and commanding an expedition to Canada, and Resolution of Congress, FEB 2, 1778, all ILA 1:263–73. His instructions were strange, considering it was a winter campaign. "You will constantly be in the woods at night, where the troops are so well acquainted with the mode of covering themselves, that you would find tents unnecessary and cumbersome." Once he had taken either St. Johns or Montreal, he was to publish a notice to all Canadian citizens, inviting them to join the cause against Britain. If they declined, he should burn all their vessels and seize all stores. If they wanted to sign on, he should tell them to send delegates to Congress. If he took Montreal, "which is a principal object of this expedition," he should seize all public arms, ammunition, stores, and so on. The instructions ended by saying the board "content themselves with suggesting, that the design of this expedition may not be misunderstood, that its grand object is to destroy, or possess the enemys vessels and stores of every kind upon Lake Champlain and in the city of Montreal; and all clothing and stores of every kind. . . . The consequences which may arise from success, are to be viewed in a secondary point of light, and therefore the holding the country or prevailing upon the inhabitants to confederate with the States, is not to be undertaken but with the greatest prudence, and with a prospect of durable success." That contradicted the original purpose of the undertaking. Why it was not cancelled outright is not apparent, unless it was to avoid the political embarrassment of admitting error.

21. HL to John Rutledge, FEB 3, 1778, HL to JL and JL to HL, both FEB 9, 1778, in Gottschalk, Lafayette Joins, 126–27; GW to Thomas Nelson, FEB 8, 1778, and to HG, FEB 9, 1778, FGW 10:432, 437–41; AH to George Clinton, FEB 13, 1778, SGW 5:508.

22. Laf to Adr, FEB 3, 1778, ILA 1:273–76.

23. Laf to HL, FEB 3 and 4, and HL to Laf, FEB 5, 1778, ILA 1:276–77, 279–81. HL answered Laf's reports, thanking him for the "pleasing accounts received from the spot from whence you are now wandering. If fretting or wishing, would rand the roads I would enter heartily upon so cheap a mode of scavaging—such as they are, may God conduct you, Noble Marquis, happily successfully, through them, that when, *You shall think it proper,* you may return & fill those tender breasts with joy which till that time will be the subjects of anxiety." HL to Laf, FEB 7, 1778, ILA 1:284–85. One wonders whether Laf's English grasped that "rand" meant melt, or that "scavaging" meant cleaning or clearing. Both terms were nearly obsolete by that time. No doubt he caught the reference to "tender breasts," meaning the ladies of York, especially Miss Ketty. NG's legendary sleeplessness, incidentally, was an effect of chronic asthma.

24. Troup to HG (two letters), FEB 6, 1778, ILA 1:282.

25. Laf to HG, FEB 7, 1778, ILA 1:283–84.

26. Laf to GW, FEB 9, 1778, ILA 1:287–88. Regarding the "neither-neither" usage,

French lacks English's contrasting "either-or," "neither-nor," and the like. Instead, repetitive "eithers" and "neithers" (or "ors" and "nors") are used for the same purpose. Also, "pompous" (cognate *pompeux*) was not then pejorative as it is now, although Laf's usage was facetious. It meant magnificent.

27. Committee of Conference to PC, FEB 11, 1778, ILA 1:271n. GM was on the committee.

28. Laf, Memoir of 1779, Laf to Moses Hazen, and Hazen to Laf, both FEB 18, 1779, McDougall to Laf, FEB 18, and to NG, FEB 28, 1778, and Laf to Albany Committee, FEB 19, 1778, ILA 1:246, 288–84, 293n.

29. Albany Committee to Laf, FEB 19, 1778, ILA 1:303–4.

30. Laf to Conway, FEB 19, 1778, ILA 1:294–85.

31. Conway to HG, FEB 19, 1778, and to Laf, FEB 20, 1778, ILA 1:301–2, 312.

32. Laf to HL, FEB 19, 1778, ILA 1:295–98.

33. Laf to GW, FEB 19, 1778, ILA 1:299–301.

34. Laf to PC, FEB 20, 1778, ILA 1:305–8.

35. Laf to HG, FEB 20 and 23, and to George Clinton, FEB 23, 1778, ILA 1:311, 313–17.

36. See Laf to HL, JAN 27, FEB 23, APR 14 and 26, and to RM, JAN 29 and FEB 23, 1778, in ILA 1 chronologically, and discussed at 1:317–18.

37. Laf to HL, FEB 23, 1778, ILA 1:318–20.

38. Laf to GW, FEB 23, 1778, ILA 1:321–22. He wrote a similar letter FEB 27, repeating a rumor that "John Adams spoke very disrespectfully of your excellency in Boston. I do not know if it is true. . . . Give me leave to say my opinion, my dear general; those ennemy's of yours are so low, so far under your feet, that it is not of your dignity to take much notice of 'em." ILA 1:325–27.

39. Gottschalk, *Lafayette Joins,* 139–42.

40. Resolution of MAR 2, 1778, and HL to Laf, MAR 4, 1778, ILA 1:331–34 and 134n.

41. HL to Laf, MAR 4, 1778, ILA 1:331–34.

42. HL to Laf, MAR 6, 1778, ILA 1:336–38. Laf had lobbied Governor Clinton for his New York ambitions. Laf to George Clinton, MAR 3, and Clinton to Laf, MAR 8, 1778, ILA 1:327–30, 339–42.

43. HL to Laf, MAR 7, 1778, ILA 1:338–39.

44. GW to Laf, MAR 10, 1778, ILA 1:342–43.

45. Laf, Memoir of 1779, ILA 1:246–47; Gottschalk, *Lafayette Joins,* 143–46.

46. Laf, Memoir of 1779, ILA 1:247.

47. Ibid.; aide quoted Gottschalk, *Lafayette Joins,* 143–6; Laf to PC, MAR 20, 1778, ILA 1:362–65. Laf was proud of his Indian name, but he never spelled it correctly, giving it variously as Kayenlaa and Kayewla. ILA 5:260n.

48. Laf to HG, and to PC, both MAR 11, 1778, ILA 1:3443–6. See also Tower 1:288.

49. Laf to HG, to PC, and to HL, all MAR 12, 1778, ILA 1:347–52.

50. HL to Laf, MAR 13, 1778, ILA 1:373n; Laf to GW, MAR 13, 1778, GLW 33–35.

51. Laf to GW, to HL, and to PC, all MAR 20, 1778, ILA 1:362–72.

52. GW to Laf, MAR 20, and Laf to GW, MAR 22, 1778, ILA 1:372–76.

53. HL to Laf, MAR 24, 1778, ILA 1:377–79.

54. Laf to GW, MAR 25, 1778, ILA 1:380–81.

55. Quoted Freeman, *George Washington* 5:39.

56. HL to Laf, MAR 27, 1778, postscript dated APR 1, ILA 1:383.

57. Laf to FVS, MAR 12, 1778, ILA 1:352–53, and Memoir of 1779, ILA 2:9. However, he also told a French agent in America, "He takes the greatest pains to instruct our troops, and, since he has their confidence, I am convinced that he will be of the greatest service to them." Laf to Lazare-Jean Théveneau de Francy, APR 10, 1778, ILA 2:20-22.

58. The best account of FVS' early years is Palmer, *General von Steuben,* 9–102. See also Chase, *Baron von Steuben;* Kapp, *Life of Steuben;* CIG 1:88–106; CW, 33–36.

59. JL to HL, FEB 1778, quoted FGW 11:329n. JL served as interpreter between GW and FVS.

60. Quoted Palmer, *Washington, Lincoln Wilson,* 47.

61. Quoted Kapp, *Life of Steuben,* 115–17.

62. Kapp, *Life of Steuben,* 123; Wright, *Continental Army,* 140–42.

63. Palmer, *General von Steuben,* 144–45; Palmer, *Washington, Lincoln, Wilson,* 48; Kapp, *Life of Steuben,* 126.

64. Palmer, *General von Steuben,* 140–48; Doyle, *Steuben,* 360; Walker quoted Scheer and Rankin, *Rebels,* 308; Flexner, *George Washington American,* 288.

65. Flexner, *George Washington American,* 288. See also Wright, *Organization,* 229–36.

66. CIG 1:121–22; Ganoe, *History,* 55; Kapp, *Life of Steuben,* 131.

67. Palmer, *General von Steuben,* 140–41; CIG 1:123–27.

68. Palmer, *General von Steuben,* 152–57; Weigley, *History,* 64.

69. Palmer, *General von Steuben,* 151–52.

70. Thane, *Fighting Quaker,* 127.

71. Gottschalk, *Lafayette Joins,* 105; Duponceau quoted Chinard, *George Washington as French,* 16; Golway, *Washington's General,* 158; Thayer, *Nathanael Greene,* 223–25.

72. Thayer, *Nathanael Greene,* 223–25; Laf to HL, FEB 9, 1778, and Memoir of 1779, ILA 1:245, 285–86.

Chapter Seven

1. Laf to de Francy, APR 10, Laf to HL, APR 26, and HL to Laf, MAY 3, 1778, ILA 2:20–22, 39, 45–46.

2. Laf to McLane, MAY 18, and as a typical example on widows, Laf to DM, APR nd, 1778, ILA 2:19–20, 55. Laf became a dedicated spymaster at GW's behest, and loved it, as will be seen. For GW's own espionage program, see a valuable recent account, Rose, *Washington's Spies.*

3. Memoirs quoted Unger, *Lafayette,* 70.

4. Laf to HL, APR 10, May 10 and JUL 23, to Adr, APR 14, and to Charles Lee, JUN nd, and HL to Laf, JUL 18, 1778, ILA 2:23–28, 29–30, 47–48, 62–64, 108–10, 112–13; GW to PC, JUL 14, 1778, FGW 12:225; Gottschalk, *Lafayette Joins,* 169–70.

5. Laf to GW, MAR 22, 1778, Laf to Adr, APR 14, and to HL, MAY 10, 1778, ILA 1:375, 2:29–30, 47–48, and 48n citing FGW 11:390–91.

6. Laf to HL, APR 21, 1778, ILA 2:30–33.

7. Higginbotham, *War,* 231–32; Isaacson, *Benjamin Franklin,* 344–49. For the French side of the story, see Corwin, *French Policy.* The queen looked down her royal nose at Americans in general and Franklin in particular. Requiring them to attend her took some of the shine off their diplomatic triumph.

8. BF and SD to PC, FEB 8, 1778, Wharton 2:490–91; Gottschalk, *Lafayette Joins,* 175–76. Changes in GW's behavior under Laf's influence were reflected in his farewell to his officers in New York in 1783. Whereas he had formerly been stiffly formal, on that occasion he hugged and kissed each one, tears flowing all around. Weintraub, *General Washington's Christmas,* 85–87.

9. GW to PC, MAY 1, 1778, FGW 11:332–33; Laf, Memoir of 1779, ILA 2:5.

10. Laf to PC, and to HL, both MAY 1, 1778, ILA 2:40–43.

11. Laf to de Francy, MAY 14, 1778, ILA 2:48–49; Gottschalk, *Lafayette Joins,* 178–82.

12. Laf to de Francy, MAY 2, 1778, ILA 2:44–45.

13. Laf to Adr, JUN 16, 1778, ILA 2:77–79.

14. GW quoted Palmer, *General von Steuben,* 163. In a tradition predating Alexander the Great, the best troops held the right end of the line, although by the eighteenth century this had become a point of honor or seniority. To head off complaints, GW arrayed the Continental Army left to right in the same order as their home states faced the Atlantic—New Englanders on the left, southerners on the right.

15. Palmer, *General von Steuben,* 162–65; Flexner, *George Washington American,* 289–91; Thayer, *Nathanael Greene,* 238; Gottschalk, *Lafayette Joins,* 181–82; RM to GW, MAY 9, 1778, SGW 5:357. JL's account of the review, in Townsend, *American Soldier,* 95, says that the "running fire" was followed each time by "loud huzzas."

16. Officer quoted Palmer, *General von Steuben,* 164; GW quoted Kapp, *Life of Steuben,* 139.

17. GW, Questions for the consideration of the general officers, APR 20, 1778, FGW 11:282–83; Laf to GW, APR 25, 1778, ILA 2:35–39; GW quoted SGW 5:360.

18. GW, Orders to Laf, MAY 18, 1778, ILA 2:53–54.

19. Laf, Memoir of 1779, ILA 2:6. Barren Hill is now called Lafayette Hill.

20. Leckie, *Wars,* 1:183; Laf, Memoir of 1779, ILA 2:7.

21. Boatner, 59–61.

22. Martin, *Narrative,* 103; Laf, Memoir of 1779, ILA 2:6–7.

23. Martin, *Narrative,* 103–5; Boatner, 60.

24. Laf, Memoir of 1779, ILA 2:7. Other accounts of Barren Hill include

Gottschalk, *Lafayette Joins,* 186–93; Martin, *Philadelphia Campaign,* 182–86; and Callahan, *Daniel Morgan,* 158–60.

25. Martin, *Narrative,* 106.

26. Laf to HL, MAY 25 and JUN 1, and HL to Laf, MAY 29, 1778, ILA 2:58–61, 64–65.

27. Palmer, *General von Steuben,* 169–70; Sunseri, "Friedrich Wilhelm von Steuben"; Higginbotham, *War,* 247.

28. Martin, *Narrative,* 118.

29. On light troop doctrine in the Continental Army, see Wright, *Continental Army,* 149, and Wright, "Corps of Light Infantry." Laf wasted no time pressing HL to support the new organization GW wanted. "With a great impatience I expect the arrangement of the army," he said, "and I think a corps of three thousand grenadiers and chasseurs selected among our troops, schall be the very soul of all our succès and prouve of an infinite advantage." Laf to HL, JUN 4, 1778, ILA 2:66–68. Grenadiers were veterans picked for their large size, originally to heave hand grenades. Those weapons had fallen out of use on land before Laf's time, but the designation remained. Chasseurs were infantry or cavalry equipped and trained for quick movement.

30. Laf to PC, and to HL, both MAY 25, and marquis de Bouillé to Laf, MAR 8, 1778, ILA 2:55–59.

31. Laf to HL, MAY 29, 1778, ILA 2:59–60.

32. HL to Laf, MAY 29 and 31, and Laf to HL, JUN 1, 1778, ILA 2:260–61, 264–65.

33. Laf to de Francy, JUN 12, 1778, ILA 2:73–74.

34. Laf to HL, JUN 12, and to Adr, JUN 16, 1778, ILA 2:74–79.

35. HL to Laf, JUN 19, and Laf to HL, JUN 23, 1778, ILA 2:82, 84.

36. HL to Laf, JUL 18, and Laf to HL, JUL 23, 1778, ILA 2:108–10, 112–13; GW to GM, JUL 24, 1778, FGW 12:226–28.

37. GW to GM, AUG 20, 1778, FGW 12:340.

38. GW to William Gordon, JAN 23, 1778, FGW 10:337; Laf to HL, JUN 1, 1778, and Memoir of 1779, ILA 2:9, 64–65; Gottschalk, *Lafayette Joins,* 204–6.

39. Accounts of the Monmouth Campaign and battle include Martin, *Philadelphia Campaign,* 197–243; Taafe, *Philadelphia Campaign,* passim; Higginbotham, *War,* 245–47; and Boatner, 716–26.

40. Freeman, *George Washington* 5:10; GW to general officers, JUN 16, 1778, FGW 12:75–78; Laf to GW, JUN 17, 1778, ILA 2:79–81.

41. Freeman, *George Washington* 5:14.

42. Ibid., 15–16. This council of war should not be confused with the one held earlier.

43. Memoirs, quoted Unger, *Lafayette,* 77; Lancaster, *From Lexington,* 349; Laf, Memoir of 1779, ILA 2:9–10.

44. Nelson, *Anthony Wayne,* 77–78; Laf, Memoir of 1779, ILA 2:10; NG quoted Thayer, *Nathanael Greene,* 244; AH quoted Boatner, 717; Gottschalk, *Lafayette Joins,* 206–9.

45. Laf to GW, JUN 24, 1778, ILA 2:85–86; Gottschalk, *Lafayette Joins,* 209–10.

46. Laf to GW, JUN 24, 1778, ILA 2:85–86.

47. GW to Laf, JUN 25, 1778, ILA 2:87.

48. AH to Elias Boudinot, JUL 5, 1778, in Scheer and Rankin, *Rebels and Redcoats,* 328–29; Lee to GW, JUN 15, 1778, ILA 2:95n. AH was present at the meeting. Lee had been ribbed by Lord Stirling when Laf got the command, and that probably goaded him into approaching GW.

49. GW to Lee, and Laf to GW, both JUN 26, 1778, FGW 12:119–20, 425–26; GW to Laf, JUN 26, 1778, and Laf, Memoir of 1779, ILA 2:10, 94–95.

50. Laf to GW, JUN 25 and 26, 1778, ILA 2:87, 89–90; AH to Laf, JUN 25, 1778, SAH 1:503–4. Regarding "spirits," eighteenth-century armies consumed quantities of alcohol that would amaze modern civilians. The only thing that would amaze modern soldiers was that in the old days the booze was issued, rather than bootleg. The Continental Army's ration provided a gill (four ounces) of spirits or a quart of beer a day for each enlisted man. He also got a pint of vinegar. The liquor was usually rum, sometimes the new American whiskey. It was usually diluted, sometimes with hard cider, the latter making what was called "stonewall." The beer could be either the thick malt brew of the day or spruce beer, made from green tips of spruce boughs. It tasted like turpentine, but the men got used to it; it prevented scurvy. Especially in New Jersey, soldiers enjoyed the local lightning, called "apple jack." Other favorites included hot buttered rum, Royal Navy grog, "gin horror," and makeshift punches. Beveridge, *Cups,* 3–8, 67–72. There were several reasons for the authorized consumption of alcohol. One was morale—regular soldiers had come to expect it for over a century. Another was that water supplies were notoriously unreliable and could flatten an army with "the soldiers' disease" (dysentery). Alcoholic drinks were also assumed to have medicinal value. An extra ration of liquor was a popular reward for good performance. And last, it was easier to send men into battle if they had a buzz on.

51. Martin, *Narrative,* 110; GW to Laf, JUN 27, 1778, FGW 12:121, and ILA 2:91–92.

52. Laf to GW (three letters), JUN 26, and GW to Laf, JUN 26, 1778, ILA 2:90–94; Gottschalk, *Lafayette Joins,* 213–15, including AH to GW, JUN 26, 1778.

53. Laf to GW, JUN 26, 1778, ILA 2:95; Gottschalk, *Lafayette Joins,* 2:95; Freeman, *George Washington* 5:18–20.

54. Participants in the Battle of Monmouth Court House left accounts so conflicting that it seems nobody on the scene really knew how it played out. This account follows, unless otherwise noted, Freeman, *George Washington* 5:10–44; Martin, *Philadelphia Campaign,* 197–243; Taafe, *Philadelphia Campaign,* passim; Boatner, 716–25; Leckie, *Wars* 1:182–86; Gottschalk, *Lafayette Joins,* 219–25; and Laf, Memoir of 1779, ILA 2:10–11.

55. Martin, *Narrative,* 114.

56. Ibid., 110–11. Martin, 115, also related one of the battle's most legendary tales: "A woman whose husband belonged to the artillery, and who was then attached to a piece in the engagement, attended with her husband at the piece the whole time; while

in the act of reaching a cartridge and having one of her feet as far before the other as she could step, a cannon shot from the enemy passed directly between her legs without doing any other damage than carrying away all of the lower part of her petticoat,—looking at it with apparent unconcern, she observed, that it was lucky it did not pass a little higher, for in that case it might have carried away something else, and ended her and her occupation." This was "Molly Pitcher," a name given to several women who hauled water to gun crews during the war; cannons had to be swabbed to dampen sparks and consumed a lot of water. This Molly was Mary Ludwig Hayes, wife of a private. Scheer and Rankin, *Rebels and Redcoats,* 333; Boatner, 710–11.

57. See the quotations and analysis of this incident in Scheer and Rankin, *Rebels and Redcoats,* 330–31, and Boatner, 722.

58. Laf never said anything of the sort in Memoir of 1779, ILA 2:11, where he quotes Lee as saying, "You know that all this was against my advice." He did later in Memoirs 1:26. AH's exchange with Lee is quoted in Flexner, *Young Hamilton,* 231, from the court-martial transcript. JL told his father, "The general expressed his astonishment at this unaccountable retreat. Mr. Lee indecently replied that the attack was contrary to his advice and opinion in council." JL to HL, JUN 30, 1778, in Townsend, *American Soldier,* 73. Scott's account created the legend that GW blew his stack. Asked years later whether he had ever heard GW swear, he said, "Yes, once. It was at Monmouth and on a day that would have made any man swear. Yes, sir, he swore on that day till the leaves shook on the trees, charming, delightful. Never have I enjoyed such swearing before or since. Sir, on that ever-memorable day, he swore like an angel from Heaven." Quoted Scheer and Rankin, *Rebels and Redcoats,* 330–31, which concludes that it is fiction.

59. AH to Elias Boudinot, JUL 5, 1778, in Morris, *Alexander Hamilton Founding,* 44.

60. Laf, Memoir of 1779, ILA 2:11.

61. McHenry to John Cox, JUL 1, 1778, in Scheer and Rankin, *Rebels and Redcoats,* 333.

62. Martin, *Narrative,* 112.

63. These figures are from Boatner, 725.

64. AW has acquired many biographies, including Nelson, *Anthony Wayne,* and Preston, *Gentleman Rebel.* See also Hugh F. Rankin, "Anthony Wayne: Military Romanticist," in Billias, *George Washington's Generals,* 260–90, and the sketch in Boatner, 1175–7.

65. GW to PC, JUL 1 and 3, and to BF, DEC 28, 1778, FGW 12:139–49, 13:459; William Watson to Rev. Joseph Lyman, JUL 11 (or 14), 1778, quoted Gottschalk, *Lafayette Joins,* 232.

66. Laf, Memoir of 1779, ILA 2:11.

67. Martin, *Narrative,* 115; General Orders, JUL 9, 1778, FGW 12:192.

68. Shy's article on Lee in Billias, *George Washington's Generals,* 45–47; Flexner, *George Washington American,* 311–16; and Boatner, 611–12.

69. AH's account of the duel with JL in Morris, *Alexander Hamilton Founding,* 45–47. He died in a boardinghouse, and the dogs really did mourn him. According to Postmaster General Ebenezer Hazard, "General Lee died . . . after a few days' illness, in some de-

gree his own physician and but badly attended, except by two faithful dogs, who frequently attempted in vain to awaken their dead master. They laid themselves down by his corpse for a considerable time, so long that it became necessary for new masters to remove them." He was buried in an Anglican churchyard with full military honors, despite his demand in his will that he not be buried "in any church or churchyard, or within a mile of any Presbyterian or Anabaptist meetinghouse. For since I have resided in this country, I have had so much bad company when living that I do not choose to continue it when dead." Scheer and Rankin, *Rebels and Redcoats,* 499–500.

70. Laf to HL, JUL 6, 1778, ILA 2:98–99.

Chapter Eight

1. All quoted Mahan, *Influence,* 371; see also 375, and Boatner, 349–50. In French measures, d'Estaing's oscillating height would have been about five-foot-ten to six feet. Under the *Ordonnance* of 1765, flag ranks in the French navy (followed by their British equivalents) were *amiral* (admiral), *vice-amiral* (vice admiral), *lieutenant-général des armées navales* (rear admiral), and *chef d' escadre* (commodore). Charles de la Roncière, *Histoire de la Marine Française* (1934), cited by Morison, *John Paul Jones,* 132n. Commanders of all these ranks figured in the American Revolution and associated conflict with Britain.

2. Higginbotham, *War,* 248; Gottschalk, *Lafayette Joins,* 236–40; Laf, Memoir of 1779, ILA 2:13; Des quoted Unger, *Lafayette,* 80.

3. Laf to Boudinot, JUL 15 and 25, 1778, ILA 2:107–8, 117.

4. Laf, Memoir of 1779, ILA 2:13. Laf did not admit in 1779 that he had used Des, but that is clear from the letters he wrote.

5. Laf to Des, JUL 14, 1778, ILA 2:102–6. JL was just two years older than Laf.

6. GW to Laf, JUL 22, 1778, ILA 2:110–11.

7. Laf to JS, JUL 22, 1778, ILA 2:111.

8. GW to Laf, and to PC, both JUL 22, 1778, FGW 12:204, 211; Laf to JS, JUL 22 and 24, and to Des, JUL 22 and 24, 1778, in Gottschalk, *Lafayette Joins,* 240–41. Laf to JS, JUL 22, and to Des, JUL 24 (quotation), are in ILA 2:111, 113–15. The second letter to Des was one of the first Laf ever did in cipher. "I beg you to excuse the clumsiness and the scribbling of my ciphers. I am new at this business, and I fear I have rendered them almost as unintelligible to you as to Mylord Howe." ILA 2:115.

9. Laf to JS, JUL 24, 1778, quoted Thayer, *Fighting Quaker,* 140; Laf to GW, JUL 25, 1778, GLW 53; Laf to JS and to GW, both JUL 28, 1778, ILA 2:119–21. Others in this period are in ILA 2:112–21.

10. GW to Laf, and to JS, both JUL 27, 1778, and Laf to GW, JUL 25 and 28, 1778, FGW 12:236–38.

11. Laf to GW, AUG 6, and GW to Laf, AUG 10, 1778, ILA 2:1320–33, 136–37.

12. Laf to JS and to Des, and Des to Laf, all JUL 30, 1778, ILA 2:122–27; Gottschalk, *Lafayette Joins,* 244–45; Freeman, *George Washington,* 5:65.

13. Quoted Tower, 1:439; Gottschalk, *Lafayette Joins,* 244–45.

14. JL quoted Gottschalk, *Lafayette Joins,* 246–48; Laf, Memoir of 1779, Laf to Des, AUG 5 and 8, 1778, ILA 2:14, 128–31, 134–45.

15. Amory, *Military Services,* 74; JL to HL, AUG 22, 1778, quoted Gottschalk, *Lafayette Joins,* 249.

16. Laf to Des, AUG 10, 1778, ILA 2:135–36.

17. Mahan, *Influence,* 362–63; Higginbotham, *War,* 248; Laf, Memoir of 1779, ILA 2:14.

18. Laf, Memoir of 1779, ILA 2:14.

19. Quoted Greene, *Nathanael Greene* 2:117; Gottschalk, *Lafayette Joins,* 250–52; Golway, *Washington's General,* 188–89.

20. Gottschalk, *Lafayette Joins,* 250-53; Golway, *Washington's General,* 188–89.

21. NG quoted Thane, *Fighting Quaker,* 146; Laf to Des, AUG 21, 1778, ILA 2:137–38.

22. JS and others to Des, AUG 21, 1778, ILA 2:141n.

23. Laf to Des, AUG 22, 1778, ILA 2:139. Major Perez Morton said that "one of our genl. officers in the course of the debates in council took occasion from the Count's conduct to reflect on the [French] nation at large. The Marquiss was very particular in enquiring his name, family; & rank and determines to call him to an account for it." Morton to James Bowdoin Jr., AUG 25, 1778, ILA 2:141n.

24. Tower 1:474–75, 478; Laf, Memoir of 1779, ILA 2:14–15.

25. Quoted ILA 2:154n.

26. Laf to Des, AUG 24, 1778, and Memoir of 1779, ILA 2:15, 141–42.

27. Laf to Des, AUG 24, 1778, ILA 2:142–46. See also Laf to Des, AUG 25, 1778, ILA 2:148–49.

28. Laf to JS, AUG 24, 1778, ILA 2:147–48; NG to GW, AUG 28, 1778, quoted Stinchcombe, *American Revolution and French Alliance,* 52, see also 50–53; Greene, *Life of Greene* 2:127.

29. Laf to GW, AUG 25, 1778, ILA 2:149–53. He repeated some of this, less personally, in letters to General William Heath, AUG 23, and to AH, AUG 26, ILA 2:154n, in both of which he asked for all to help Des' repairs. Laf to HL, AUG 26, ILA 2:156n, reproduced his statements to GW more fully. The letter from NG has disappeared. ILA 2:155n. Laf began a series of letters in French to AH, whom he called "cher colonel," repeating news that he told others in English. Laf to AH, AUG 26 and SEP 12, 1778, and from France SEP 12, 1779, SAH 1:537–43, 2:169–70.

30. Resolution of Congress, AUG 28, 1778, ILA 2:254n; GW to General William Heath (Boston), to Governor George Clinton (New York), and to JS, all AUG 28, 1778, FGW 12:364–69.

31. GW to JS, AUG 28, 1778, FGW 12:369.

32. NG to GW, AUG 28, 1778, quoted ILA 2:154n; Thane, *Fighting Quaker,* 148.

33. Laf to NG, SEP 1, 1778, FGW 12:386–87.

34. Higginbotham, *War,* 249; Laf to GW, SEP 1, 1778, ILA 2:162–64.

35. Laf to GW, SEP 1, 1778, and Memoir of 1779, ILA 2:15, 162–64; JS to PC, AUG 31, 1778, Tower 1:490.

36. JS to PC, AUG 31, 1778, Tower 1:490; Laf, Memoir of 1779, and to GW, SEP 1, 1778, ILA 2:15, 162–64; Boatner, 792–93. American losses on the twenty-ninth were 30 killed, 137 wounded, and 44 missing. Casualties among the British, Hessians, and Tories were 38 killed, 210 wounded, and 12 missing. Some losses on both sides were to heatstroke. Boatner, 793.

37. JS to PC, AUG 31, 1778, Tower 1:490; Laf, Memoir of 1779, and to GW, SEP 1, 1778, ILA 2:15, 162–64.

38. Laf to Des, AUG 31, 1778, ILA 2:156–60.

39. Laf to GW, SEP 1, 1778, ILA 2:162–64.

40. GW to GM, JUL 24, 1778, ILA 2:115–17; CW, 46–48.

41. GW to Laf, SEP 1, 1778, ILA 2:164–66.

42. Laf to Des, SEP 5, 1778, ILA 2:166–68.

43. GW to Des, SEP 11, 1778, SGW 6:57; Congress quoted Tower 1:494; NG to Des, SEP 23, 1778, quoted Unger, *Lafayette,* 85.

44. Resolution of SEP 9, and HL to Laf, SEP 13, 1778, ILA 2:172. Laf replied to HL, "Be so good, Sir, as to present to Congress my plain and hearty thanks, with the frank assurances of a candid attachement, the only one worth being offered to the representatives of a free people. The moment I heard of America, I lov'd her. The moment I knew she was fighting for freedom, I burnt with the desire of bleeding for her—and the moment I schall be able of serving her in any time or any part of the world, will be among the happiest ones in my life." Laf to PC, SEP 23, 1778, ILA 2:180. This hogwash impressed the members, who did not know he was looking for a way to return to the French army.

45. GW to JS, SEP 11, 1778, SGW 6:44.

46. Unger, *John Hancock,* 277; Higginbotham, *War,* 248.

47. Laf to Des, SEP 8, 1778, ILA 2:169–70.

48. Laf to d'Ayen, SEP 11, to Adr, SEP 13, and to Des, SEP 21, 1778, ILA 2:172–77.

49. Gérard quoted ILA 2:195n; Des to Sartine, NOV 5, 1778, ILA 2:202–3. Among the hardships: "One becomes accustomed to using a knife as a spoon, doing without napkins, drinking to the health of ten persons with each drop one swallows, quenching one's thirst with grog (a liquor composed of a little bad brandy, water, and sugar), keeping the most somber table in the world," and so on.

50. Laf to GW, SEP 21, 1778, ILA 2:177–79.

51. GW to Laf, SEP 25, 1778, ILA 2:182–85.

52. Laf to GW, SEP 28, 1778, ILA 2:185–86.

53. *Pennsylvania Packet,* SEP 12, 1778, quoted ILA 2:182n.

54. Laf to Des, SEP 13, and to GW, SEP 24, 1778, ILA 2:181–82.

55. GW to Laf, OCT 4, and Des to GW, SEP 25 and OCT 20, 1778, ILA 2:186–87.

56. Laf to Carlisle, OCT 5, and Carlisle to Laf, OCT 11, 1778, ILA 2:187, 189.

57. Laf to Des, OCT 20, and to GW, OCT 24, 1778, ILA 2:191–92, 195.

58. Laf to Des, JUL 14, 1778, ILA 2:102–6; Declaration quoted Unger, *Lafayette,* 91.

59. Dull, *Diplomatic History,* 114–15; Higginbotham, *War,* 249; Orville T. Murphy, "The View from Versailles: Charles Gravier Comte de Vergennes' Perceptions of the American Revolution," in Hoffman and Albert, *Diplomacy and Revolution,* 107–49.

60. Laf to GW, SEP 3, 1778, GLW 64; GW to Laf, SEP 25, 1778, FGW 12:502–3.

61. Quoted Townsend, *American Soldier,* 104.

62. GW to PC, SEP 12 and NOV 11, and to HL, NOV 14, 1778, FGW 13:223–44, 254, 257; GW to Laf, SEP 25, and Laf to PC, OCT 16, and to GW, OCT 24, 1778, ILA 2:182–85, 195, 196n.

63. Laf to PC, NOV 29, 1778, ILA 2:205–7; GW to PC, NOV 11, 1778, FGW 13:223–44.

64. Laf to Timothy Bedel, DEC 18, 1778, ILA 2:211–15.

65. PC to Laf, JAN 3, 1779, ILA 2:217; Gottschalk, *Lafayette Close,* 4.

66. GW to PC, OCT 6, 1778, FGW 13:40.

67. Laf to PC, OCT 13, 1778, ILA 2:190.

68. Laf to Des, OCT 20, 1778, ILA 2:191–92.

69. PC to Laf, OCT 24, Laf to PC, OCT 26, and Congress to King of France, OCT 21, 1778, ILA 2:193–94, 195n.

70. Laf, Instructions to William Carmichael, NOV-DEC 1778, and Carmichael to BF, OCT 30, 1778, ILA 2:199–200, 207–9. Before he left the country, Laf learned that Carmichael had been elected to Congress from Maryland. He still wanted to hear from him. Laf to Carmichael, DEC 30, 1778, ILA 2:215–16.

71. GW to BF, DEC 29 [28], 1778, FGW 13:459; TP to BF, OCT 24, 1777 [1778], LBF 27:618–20. Both letters were misdated in the originals. See also HL to Laf, DEC 6, 1778, ILA 2:209–10.

72. Gottschalk, *Lafayette Joins,* 304–6; Callahan, *Daniel Morgan,* 175–76; Laf to DM, NOV 28, 1778, ILA 2:204.

73. GW to Laf, DEC 28, 1778, FGW 13:459–61.

74. Laf to GW, JAN 5, 1779, ILA 2:217–19. On the seventh, he urged GW to ask the French to send an army to America, and "I also intreat your friendship not to forget writing to me . . . letters from you will make me extremely happy." Laf to GW, JAN 7, 1779, GLW 73. On the ninth he told Congress that "keeping a frigatte without sailing when she is ready does wrong to her and to the public." Laf to PC, JAN 9, 1779, ILA 2:220–21.

75. Laf to GW, JAN 11, 1779, GLW 73–74.

76. Laf, Memoir of 1779, ILA 2:18. This continued to appear in the later versions of the Memoirs.

Chapter Nine

1. Laf, Memoir of 1779, ILA 2:225–26; Allen, *Naval History* 2:439–40; Gottschalk, *Lafayette Joins,* 326. The prisoners were later exchanged for Frenchmen held by the British.

2. Schama, *Citizens,* 29–32, 40; Gottschalk, *Lafayette Joins,* 327–32.

3. Laf, Memoir of 1779, ILA 2:226; Gottschalk, *Lafayette and Close,* 1–3; Maurois, *Adrienne,* 74–75.

4. Adr to Mlle du Motier and Mme de Chavaniac, FEB 16, 1779, quoted Maurois, *Adrienne,* 75.

5. Laf wrote as many personal letters to Ver as official ones, and Ver was always indulgent. "Why should you reproach yourself, Monsieur le Marquis, for having written me about your affairs?" he began one letter. "I assure you that you could not have confided them to anyone whose interest in them would be more lively and genuine than my own. The only trouble they could cause me is that I am not always able to respond to your trust and contribute to your satisfaction as much as I would like." Ver to Laf, SEP 16, 1779, ILA 2:311–12. Ver knew, as the youngster did not, that politics is the art of the possible. Laf often asked BF to explain the mysteries of the planet. "You ask my opinion what conduct the English will probably hold on this occasion," BF began one reply, "& whether they will not rather propose a negotiation for a peace: I have but one rule to go by in defining of those people: which is, that whatever is prudent for them to do, they will omit; and what is most imprudent to be done, they will do it. This like other general rules, may sometimes have its exceptions; but I think it will hold good for the most part." BF to Laf, AUG 19, 1779, ILA 2:302–3. BF knew, as Laf did not, that people are not always consistent, but they make the world an interesting place. See also Hale and Hale, *Franklin,* 301–5.

6. Gottschalk, *Lafayette and Close,* 3–4; JA to Samuel Adams, FEB 14, and Mme du Deffand to Horace Walpole, FEB 17, 1779, ILA 2:231n.

7. Maurois, *Adrienne,* 76. The writer was Charles-Augustin Sainte-Beuve.

8. Laf to BF, FEB 13–14, and to Ver, FEB 14, 1779, ILA 2:228–30.

9. Laf to Louis XVI, FEB 19, 1779, ILA 2:232, 234.

10. Laf, Memoir of 1779, ILA 2:226.

11. Gottschalk, *Lafayette and Close,* 5–7, 77; Unger, *Lafayette,* 96–98.

12. Laf, Memoir of 1779, ILA 2:226.

13. Schoenbrun, *Triumph in Paris,* 238–75; Gottschalk, *Lafayette and Close,* 7–8; Laf to BF, FEB 21 and MAR 7, 1779, ILA 2:234, 237.

14. Laf to JA, and JA to Laf, both FEB 21, 1779, ILA 2:234–26.

15. Biographies include Morison, *John Paul Jones;* Thomas, *John Paul Jones;* and Thomson, *Knight of the Seas.* The phrase "in harm's way" was coined by JPJ. "I wish to have no connection with any ship that does not sail *fast,*" he wrote on NOV 16, 1778; "for I intend to go *in harm's way.*"

16. Laf to Maurepas, MAR 14, and to BF, MAR 20, 1779, ILA 2:238–41. Laf approached the Swedish ambassador about the loan of Swedish ships for the expedition; the Swedes agreed on the condition France would guarantee the costs. Laf to Ver, APR 26 and JUL 9, 1779, ILA 2:256–57.

17. BF to Laf, MAR 22, 1779, ILA 2:243–44.

18. Laf to Maurepas, MAR 23, to Ver, MAR 26 and APR 1, and to BF, MAR 31, 1779, ILA 2:244–53.

19. Laf to Montbarey, APR 14, to Sartine, APR 15–20, and to Ver, APR 26 and JUL 18, and Sartine to BF, APR 20, and to JPJ, APR 27, 1779, ILA 2:254–57, 255n.

20. BF to JPJ, and Laf to JPJ, both APR 27, and JPJ to Laf, MAY 1, 1779, ILA 2:258–62, 264; JPJ's letter book in the National Archives, JPJ to Laf and to BF, both APR 27, 1779, cited Morison, *John Paul Jones*, 188, and JPJ to Laf, MAY 1, 1779, quoted Thomas, *John Paul Jones*, 159, and Gottschalk, *Lafayette and Close*, 14; Allen, *Naval History* 2:439–88; Isaacson, *Benjamin Franklin*, 389–90.

21. JPJ to Leray de Chaumont, APR 30, Laf to BF, MAY 19, to PC, JUN 12, and to Ver, MAY 23 and JUL 1, 1779, ILA 2:263, 265, 268–69, 272–75, 284–87; Laf to Maurepas (quoting his earlier statement back to him), JAN 25, 1780, Tower 2:500; Gottschalk, *Lafayette and Close*, 9–10, 18–20.

22. Laf to JPJ, MAY 22, 1779, ILA 2:267; Gottschalk, *Lafayette and Close*, 18.

23. GW's letter to Laf on DEC 29, 1778, reached Boston after Laf sailed in JAN. GW enclosed duplicates in his to Laf of MAR 8 and again on OCT 20, 1779, the latter including a copy of one he wrote on SEP 30. He wrote on MAR 27 to introduce George Mason Jr., and on JUL 4 summarizing the military situation. There was also a short note on SEP 12, but the first letter Laf received was the one of OCT 20. FGW 13:459–61, 14:218–22, 15:369–70, 16:267–69, 491–94; ILA 2:381n.

24. Laf to Ver, JUN 1, 1779, ILA 2:270–71; Laf to Ver, JUN 10, 1779, quoted Gottschalk, *Lafayette and Close*, 24–25.

25. Laf to PC, JUN 12, 1779, ILA 2:272–75; see also Laf to HL, JUN 11–13, 1779, ILA 2:276n.

26. GW to Laf, SEP 30, 1779, FGW 16:371-72.

27. JA and Congress quoted ILA 2:281n. Lee tried to enlist Laf on his side in the disputes with BF and others, but Laf stayed out of it. Besides, he was friends with BF. Arthur Lee to Laf, JUL 9, 1779, ILA 2:289-90.

28. Laf to GW, JUN 12, 1779, ILA 2:276-81. As *aide maréchal général des logis,* Laf was assistant to the *maréchal général des logis,* Charles-Léopold Chazel, marquis de Jaucourt, who ranked as *maréchal de camp* (field marshal). The office combined some of the functions of quartermaster general in the American service with the duties of a topographical engineer. Jaucourt located camps, artillery parks, hospitals, and supply depots, quartered the troops and officers, and set up headquarters, and also selected the route of march. Regarding whether it was Congress or the emissaries Laf complained about, the copy in GW's papers substitutes the phrase "prevent the Congress from disputing" for "prevent theyr disputing." Whether the change was Laf's or the editor's is not clear. FGW 16:371n.

29. Gottschalk, *Lafayette and Close*, 22-30.

30. Ibid., 31-33; Laf to Ver, JUN 24, 1779, ILA 2:283-84. Luz congratulated him on his appointment as *aide maréchal,* which he thought would be good for allied relations. "I hope this campaign's operations will be active enough to enable you to consolidate in Europe the glory you have acquired in America," he said. "One means of consoling the Americans for the enormous loss they experienced when you left them will be to make

them see how usefully you are serving the cause in Europe." Luz to Laf, JUN 17, 1779, ILA 2:282–83.

31. Laf to Ver, JUL 1, 3, and 18, and to BF, JUL 12, 1779, ILA 2:284–88, 289n, 291–92; Gottschalk, *Lafayette and Close,* 37–38.

32. Laf to Ver, JUL 30, 1779, ILA 2:292–95.

33. Gottschalk, *Lafayette and Close,* 38–47.

34. BF to Laf, AUG 24, Laf to BF, AUG 29, and to William Temple Franklin, SEP 7, 1779, ILA 2:303–8; Isaacson, *Benjamin Franklin,* 385–86.

35. Higginbotham, *War,* 352–57; Boatner, 1062–7.

36. Letter of SEP 12, 1779, in Chinard, *Washington as French,* 77. Barbé-Marbois' journal has been published in Noel, "Our Revolutionary Forefathers."

37. GW to Laf, SEP 30, 1779, ILA 2:313–18, and FGW 16:369–73.

38. Laf to Ver, and Laf, Formation of Proposed Detachment to America, both AUG 13, Laf to Ver, AUG 16 and SEP 11, Laf to BF, AUG 17, BF to Laf, AUG 19, Laf to William Temple Franklin, SEP 14, and Ver to Laf, SEP 16, 1779, ILA 2:299–303, 309–12; Hale and Hale, *Franklin,* 301–5.

39. Orville T. Murphy, "The View from Versailles: Charles Gravier Comte de Vergennes' Perceptions of the American Revolution," in Hoffman and Albert, *Diplomacy and Revolution,* 107–49; Dull, *French Navy,* 154–56; Corwin, *French Policy,* 187–88; Bonsal, *When French,* 3–4.

40. Laf to PC, OCT 7, 1779, ILA 2:320–22. At about this time Laf heard rumors that there might be peace negotiations between the United States and Britain. He volunteered to serve as an American ambassador. There was nothing to the rumors, however. Laf to BF, OCT 11, and BF to Laf, OCT 19, 1779, ILA 2:325–27, 327n. BF liked the idea, which would reemerge later.

41. Laf to GW, OCT 7, 1779, ILA 2:232–25.

42. Gottschalk, *Lafayette and Close,* 52–53.

43. Laf to BF, NOV 2 and 9, and BF to Laf, NOV 10, 1779, ILA 2:334–35, 337–38, 339n.

44. Laf to BF, DEC 6, 1779, ILA 2:339; Laf to Ver, DEC 10, 1779, quoted Gottschalk, *Lafayette and Close,* 56; BF to Joshua Johnson, DEC 29, 1779, ILA 2:339n.

45. Adr to Laf, DEC 24, 1779, ILA 2:340. Adr erroneously dated this letter from Passy, which was where Laf was. Laf's letters to Adr during this period have disappeared. ILA 2:340n.

46. Laf to BF, and to JA, both DEC 24, 1779, ILA 2:341, 341n. He was baptized Georges-Louis-Gilbert-Washington du Motier, marquis de La Fayette, but he called himself George-Washington Lafayette.

47. Laf to Ver, and to BF, both JAN 9, 1780, ILA 2:341–42; Gottschalk, *Lafayette and Close,* 58–60.

48. Laf to Maurepas, and to Ver, both JAN 25, 1780, ILA 2:344–50.

49. Laf to Ver, FEB 2, 1780, ILA 2:350–52.

50. Whitridge, *Rochambeau,* passim and 70–74.

51. Laf, Observations on Military Clothing, FEB 12, JA to Laf, FEB 18, Laf to JA, FEB 19, and Laf, Observations on Matters Pertaining to the Navy for an Expedition to North America, FEB 21, 1780, ILA 2:353–57.

52. Laf to BF, FEB 24 and 29, BF to Laf, MAR 2, 1780, ILA 2:358–61, 360n. Laf departed from Congress' specifications for uniforms, sending his own to French suppliers, causing manufacturing problems. Jonathan Williams to BF, FEB 19, 1780, ILA 2:361n. A stand is a complete set of arms for one soldier (e.g., musket, bayonet, ramrod, flint, strap, etc.).

53. JA to HL, FEB 27, 1780, Wharton 3:524–26.

54. ILA 2:367n; Higginbotham, *War,* 235–36.

55. Maurois, *Adrienne,* 82; Gottschalk, *Lafayette and Close,* 67, 72–73.

56. BF to GW, MAR 5, and to PC, MAR 4, 1780, Wharton, 3:534–38.

57. Laf to Montbarey, MAR 4, 1780, and added material, ILA 2:363–64, 363n, 364n.

58. Ver, Instructions to Laf, MAR 5, 1780, ILA 2:364–67.

59. Maurois, *Adrienne,* 82–86, samples the letters; Laf to Adr, MAR 8 and 18, to prince de Poix, MAR 12, to Pierre-François Mareuil de Villebois, MAR 11, and to BF, MAR 20, 1780, ILA 2:373–80.

Chapter Ten

1. Laf to prince de Poix, MAY 4, 1780, ILA 3:6–8; Gottschalk, *Lady in Waiting,* 100–2, 128–29. Gottschalk bases his conclusion that Aglaé was the other young woman on Laf's letter to her of MAR 27, 1783. They connected after he returned to France the second time.

2. Laf to Noailles, OCT 3 and 23, 1780, ILA 3:180–86, 204–5.

3. Laf to prince de Poix, OCT 14, 1780, ILA 3:200–1.

4. De Kalb quoted Risch, *Quartermaster Support,* 62.

5. Both quoted Lancaster, *From Lexington to Liberty,* 380–81; Golway, *Washington's General,* 209–20.

6. Martin, *Narrative,* 248; James Fairlie to Charles Tillinghast, JAN 12, 1780, in Ryan, *Salute to Courage,* 178; SGW 4:50.

7. Golway, *Washington's General,* 209–20; Palmer, *General von Steuben,* 220–26; FVS to GW, MAR 28, 1780, Sparks 2:420–22.

8. Laf to GW, APR 27, 1780, ILA 3:3.

9. Laf to Adr, MAY nd and 6, to Ver, MAY 2, to prince de Poix, MAY 4, and to Massachusetts General Assembly, MAY 2, 1780, ILA 3:3–10, 10n. Samuel Cooper said, "As his arrival diffused a general joy, every expression of it was given here that circumstances would allow, and particular respects were paid by the government as well as the

people at large to this prudent and gallant young nobleman who keeps the cause of America so warm at his heart." Cooper to JA, MAY 23, 1780, ILA 3:10n.

10. GW to Laf, MAY 8, 1780, ILA 3:10–11.

11. AH and Memoirs quoted Unger, *Lafayette,* 114.

12. Gottschalk, *Lafayette and Close,* 86–88.

13. GW to Laf, MAY 19, Laf to Luz, and Laf, Proclamation to the Canadians, both MAY 25, 1780, ILA 3:24–25, 35–38.

14. GW to Luz, MAY 11, and to Laf, MAY 16, 1780, FGW 18:348, 369; GW to PC, MAY 13, 1780, ILA 3:11; GW to PC, MAY 13, 1780, SGW 7:50.

15. Laf to PC, MAY 16, and Resolution of MAY 16, 1780, ILA 3:13, 13n.

16. See GW to George Clinton, MAY 18, 1780, FGW 18:383–84; Wharton 3:683–84; ILA 3:25n. Typical appeals include Laf to Samuel Adams, MAY 30, and to Joseph Reed, MAY 31, 1780, ILA 3:41–44. Each letter was tailored to the recipient's personal vanity, to the history of his home state, and to the need for supplies. Mrs. Joseph Reed started a campaign in Philadelphia to raise money to clothe the soldiers, and Lafayette sent 100 guineas in Adrienne's name. "We are much less ashamed of our nakedness because it proves the virtue and patriotism of the American army; but since it does not speak highly of the public we are serving, you would be well advised to recommend to your friends in Congress to devise a way to cloathe the officers of their army." Laf to Esther De Berdt Reed, JUN 25, and to Luz, JUN 20, 1780, ILA 3:56–57, 61–62.

17. Laf to Luz, MAY 17 and 24 (three letters), and JUN 3, and Luz to Laf, MAY 28 and 31, 1780, ILA 3:20–23, 45–49.

18. GW to Laf, MAY 16, and Laf to Roc and Ternay, MAY 19, and to comte de Guichen, MAY 16–20, 1780, ILA 3:14–19, 16n. They used a substitution code.

19. Laf to Ver, MAY 20, 1780, ILA 3:26–29.

20. GW to Laf, MAY 20, 1780, FGW 18:398.

21. Laf to William Heath, JUN 11 (uniforms), to Roc, JUN 20, and to Luz, JUN 30, and Luz to Laf, JUN 5, 1780, ILA 3:52–56, 62–65. Luz told him, "It is surely not with the intention of subjecting Canada to the Thirteen States that you think of this expedition. Congress has no idea of that, and I am sure that it is even further from your mind." It would be immoral to promise liberation to the Canadians, then exchange Canada for the southern states at the end of the war, as Laf had proposed. Immediate attention should go to the British challenge in the South. "This is what I have explained to General Washington, and I have reason to believe he shares my opinion."

22. Bonsal, *When French,* 30; Laf to GW, JUL 4, and to FVS, JUL 16, 1780, ILA 3:67–69, 91; GW, orders of JUL 16 and 17, and AUG 1, 1780, FVS to GW, JUL 14, and GW to FVS, JUL 18, 1780, FGW 19:188–89, 191, 202–3, 303; Wright, *Continental Army,* 149–51.

23. Laf to Roc and Ternay, JUL 9, and to Luz, JUL 10, 1780, ILA 3:69–75, 76–77. On the shortage of clothing and pay, see Memorial of Grievances from the General Officers to Congress, with a postscript by Laf, JUL 11, 1780, ILA 3:78–80.

24. Higginbotham, *War,* 379–80; Gottschalk, *Lafayette and Close,* 94–99; Ver to Laf, JUN 3, Laf to Luz, JUL 14, William Heath to Laf, JUL 15, and Roc to Laf, JUL 16, 1780, ILA 3:96–97.

25. Kline, *Alexander Hamilton,* 81–83, 92–93; Notes of Council of War, JUL 15, 1780, FGW 18:482–85; Laf to GW, JUL 16, 1780, ILA 3:92–95.

26. GW to Laf, JUL 16, 1780, ILA 3:95.

27. Laf to Roc and Ternay, JUL 15, and Ternay to Laf, JUL 16, 1780, ILA 3:91, 97n.

28. GW, Memorandum for Concerting a Plan of Operations, JUL 15, 1780, ILA 3:88–89; GW to Roc, and to Ternay, both JUL 1780, FGW 19:185–88.

29. Whitridge, *Rochambeau,* 95–99; Gottschalk, *Lafayette and Close,* 101–6; Roc to Montbarey, JUL 16, 1780, ILA 3:39n.

30. Laf to Luz, and to Ver, both JUL 19, and to GW, JUL 21 and 22, 1780, ILA 3:100–5; Laf to GW, JUL 20 and 23, GLW 88–89, 92–93.

31. GW to Laf, JUL 22, 26 (two letters), 27, and 29, and Laf to GW, JUL 26, 1780, ILA 3:105–16.

32. Laf to GW, JUL 29 and 31, and AUG 1, GW to Laf, JUL 31 and AUG 1, Laf to William Heath, AUG 3, and Heath to Laf, AUG 3, 1780, ILA 3:113–26, 126n; GW to Roc, JUL 27, 1780, FGW 19:268–69. Heath commanded the Rhode Island militia and was senior American at Newport.

33. GW to Laf, AUG 3, 1780, FGW 19:314–15; GW to Laf, AUG 5, 1780, ILA 3:126–27.

34. Ver to Laf, AUG 5, 1780, ILA 3:127–30; Gottschalk, *Lafayette and Close,* 112–13.

35. Laf to Roc and Ternay, AUG 9, 1780, ILA 3:131–36.

36. Laf to Luz, AUG 11, 1780, ILA 3:137–39. Unaware that he had just thrown a cat at a hornet's nest, Laf pestered GW with plans to get his light division into action. Laf to GW, AUG 10, 1780, GLW 105–7; Laf to GW, AUG 14, 1780, ILA 3:142, 144.

37. Roc to GW, AUG 10, 1780, ILA 3:140n.

38. Roc to Laf, AUG 12, 1780, ILA 3:139–40.

39. Roc to Luz, AUG 14, 1780, ILA 3:141.

40. Laf to Roc and Ternay, AUG 18, 1780, ILA 3:144–46.

41. Laf to Roc, AUG 18, 1780, ILA 3:146–48.

42. Laf to Luz, AUG 18, 1780, ILA 3:148–49.

43. Luz to Laf, AUG 19–23, 1780, ILA 3:150–51. Luz told Ver that Laf's "ardor and courage" led him to complain about the lack of action. He told Roc that his arrival had raised American spirits, "but their zeal adjusts poorly to the delays that circumstances have made necessary. . . . M. de Lafayette has been able to tell you how they have reached this state of preparation with incredible difficulty and that the Congress is unable to maintain it beyond the end of this year." Luz to Ver, and to Roc, both AUG 21, 1780, ILA 3:139n.

44. Luz to Roc, AUG 24, 1780, ILA 3:142n.

45. Roc to Laf, AUG 27, 1780, ILA 3:155–56.

46. AH to James Duane, SEP 6, 1780, in Morris, *Alexander Hamilton and Founding,* 38–39; Edgar, *Partisans and Redcoats,* 48–121; Buchanan, *Road,* 44–172.

47. Laf to Noailles, SEP 2, 1780, ILA 3:156–58; Thacher quoted Gottschalk, *Lafayette at Close,* 156–57. See also Laf to GW, AUG 28 and SEP 2, 1780, GLW 109–11; Laf to prince de Poix, SEP 3 and OCT 14, and to Matthias Ogden, SEP 16, 1780, ILA 3:164–67, 173, 200–1.

48. In Chinard, *George Washington as French,* 48.

49. Gottschalk, *Lafayette and Close,* 124–25; GW, circular, SEP 6, 1780, FGW 20:5–9; Laf, Memorandum on Military Operations, SEP 20, 1780, ILA 3:171–73.

50. Laf to Luz, SEP 10, 1780, ILA 3:167–70.

51. Laf to Luz, SEP 10 and 17, 1780, ILA 2:167–70; Gottschalk, *Lafayette and Close,* 129–34.

52. Biographies include Decker, *Benedict Arnold;* Randall, *Benedict Arnold;* and, more even-handed than most, Martin, *Benedict Arnold.* The best account of his treason is Flexner, *Traitor.*

53. Both in Chinard, *George Washington as French,* 44, 62–63.

54. Summary of the Hartford Conference, SEP 22, 1780, ILA 3:175–78; aide quoted Scheer and Rankin, *Rebels and Redcoats,* 378; Gottschalk, *Lafayette and Close,* 129–34; Roc to Laf, OCT 4, 1778, ILA 3:192–93.

55. Flexner, *Traitor,* 371.

56. Quoted ibid., 372; Flexner, *Young Hamilton,* ch. 32; Randall, *Benedict Arnold,* 535–55.

57. Laf to Luz, and to Roc, both SEP 26, to Ver, OCT 4, Roc to Laf, OCT 4, and Ver to Laf, DEC 1, 1780, ILA 3:179–80, 180n, 186–90, 192–93, 238–39.

58. AH to Elizabeth Schuyler, OCT 2, and to JL, OCT nd, 1780, in Morris, *Alexander Hamilton Founding,* 53–61. Noose-and-drop hanging, which breaks the neck, did not come into general use until the mid-nineteenth century. Strangulation took about ten minutes. André was hanged from a gallows, a beam atop two posts set in the ground. He stood on his own coffin, on the tailgate of a wagon, which was driven out from under him. His arms were tied, and he wore a blindfold, which he put on himself. See the eyewitness accounts in Scheer and Rankin, *Rebels and Redcoats,* 386–88.

59. Laf to Noailles, OCT 3, 1780, ILA 3:180–86.

60. Laf to Adr, OCT 7–10, 1780, ILA 3:193–97. He also said, "General Washington was quite moved by what I told him for you; he charges me to present you with his respects and the homage of his most tender sentiments. He has many tender feelings for George and was very touched that we gave him his name. We speak often of you, and of the little family."

61. Greene, *General Greene,* 168–69; Buchanan, *Road,* 225–41; Edgar, *Partisans and Redcoats,* 117–21. NG and FVS reached HG's camp DEC 2, 1780. HG did not know that he had been relieved.

62. Laf to Ver, OCT 4, to Adr, OCT 7–10, to prince de Poix, OCT 14, and Adr to Ver, OCT 18, 1780, ILA 3:186–91, 193–96, 200–3; Massey, *John Laurens,* 165–66.

63. Laf to GW, OCT 7 and 27 (two letters), 1780, GLW 111–17; GW to Laf, OCT 12, Laf to Adr, OCT 7–10, to Lee, OCT 14, and to Noailles, OCT 28, 1780, ILA

3:193–97, 199, 199n, 206–7, 209–11; Flexner, *Young Hamilton,* 315–19. He kept up his spymaster activities during the fall, with his usual humor. "This evening I am expecting some gentlemen who are quite willing to be hanged owing to their friendship for me, and I shall know still more exactly the enemy situation." Laf to Noailles, OCT 23, 1780, ILA 3:204–5. He rebuked Henry Lee, who had groused about the condition of the army. Lee was "out of joking," suggesting things "dramatically opposed" to "republican principles." He did not yet understand that a free society involved free speech. Laf to Lee, OCT 19, 1780, quoted Royster, *Light-Horse Harry,* 32–33. He thought highly of Lee, however, calling him "beyond compare the best officer of light infantry . . . on this continent." Laf to GW, OCT 28, 1780, GLW 117; Laf to Luz (quotation), OCT 28, 1780, ILA 3:209n.

64. Laf to GW, and GW to Laf, both OCT 30, 1780, ILA 3:211–14.

65. GW, Orders, OCT 30 and NOV 24 and 26, 1780, FGW 20:272–73, 383–84, 401–3; Laf to GW, NOV 1, 8, 13, and 28, to Noailles, NOV 3 and 4, to NG, NOV 10, to BF, NOV 19, and to AH, NOV 22, 1780, ILA 3:214–34; Laf to GW, NOV 11, 14, 18, and 19, GLW 124, 127, 128–30.

66. Laf to GW, NOV 28, and to AH, NOV 28 and DEC 9, 1780, ILA 3:233–34, 234n, 250–53, 253n. See also Flexner, *Young Hamilton,* 320–21. The adjutant general's position went to Edward Hand.

67. Gottschalk and Sheldon, "More Letters." See also ILA 3:197n.

68. Gottschalk, *Lafayette and Close,* 143. Ternay died on DEC 15 of a fever that had not become critical until two days before. Boatner, 1093–4. Laf was more charitable later, calling Ternay's death "a great loss." Memoirs 1:384.

69. Gottschalk, *Lafayette and Close,* 163–65; Laf to GW, NOV 28, DEC 4, 5, 9, and 19, to Luz, NOV 27 (DEC 4–5), and to Ver, DEC 16, Ver to Laf, DEC 1, Francisco de Rendón to Diego Josef Navarro, DEC 5, GW to Roc and Destouches, DEC 15, and Roc and Destouches to GW, DEC 22, 1780, ILA 3:233–34, 238–39, 239n, 239–40, 241–44, 244n, 244–46, 247n, 247–48, 253–54, 258–63, 265–66, 268–71. Charles-René-Dominique Sochet, chevalier Destouches, replaced Ternay in command of the fleet at Newport.

70. GW to Laf, DEC 8 and 14, and to Sundry Gentlemen in Virginia, DEC 8, Laf to GW, DEC 9, 14, 16, to NG, DEC 25, and to AH, DEC 9, 1780, ILA 3:248–55, 258–60, 267–68, 272–76; GW to NG, DEC 8, 1780, FGW 20:438. NG advised Laf to stay away from the chaos and deprivation in the South. NG to Laf, DEC 29, 1780, ILA 3:274–76.

71. Laf to AH, DEC 9, and to GW, DEC 13 and 16, 1780, ILA 3:250–53, 257, 258n, 273–74; Massey, *John Laurens,* 171–72. JL was appointed "minister" rather than "envoy extraordinary," which was interpreted by many as a lack of confidence in BF. "Doctor Franklin has a party against him," Laf told GW on DEC 13. "I think it would be very wrong to recall him."

72. Both in Chinard, *Washington as French,* 40–42, 82. Mazzei was an Italian immigrant to America who served as TJ's agent for Virginia in Europe and saw Laf on both sides of the ocean.

Chapter Eleven

1. Laf to Luz, JAN 7, 1781, ILA 3:279–81; Van Doren, *Mutiny in January.*

2. Laf to Luz, JAN 4 and 7, 1781, ILA 3:276–81.

3. Laf to Luz, JAN 7 and 14, to Walter Stewart, to JL, and to GW, all JAN 7, St. Clair to GW, and JL to GW, both JAN 7, 1781, ILA 3:278–81, 283–89, 287n.

4. Laf to Luz, JAN 17, 1781, ILA 3:290–91; GW to HK, JAN 7, and to Roc, JAN 20, 1781, FGW 21:66–68, 120.

5. Laf to Luz, JAN 26, 1781, ILA 3:292–93.

6. Laf to Luz, JAN 17, to Castries, to Ver, and to prince de Poix, all JAN 30, 1781, ILA 3:290–91, 294–304, 300n.

7. Laf to prince de Poix, JAN 30, to BF, FEB 1, and to Adr. FEB 2, 1781, ILA 3:301–6, 309–14.

8. Laf to JL, FEB 3, 1781, ILA 3:314–15. JL also took along instructions from GW, GW to JL, JAN 15, 1781, FGW 21:105–10.

9. Laf to Adr, FEB 2, 1781, ILA 3:311; AH to Philip Schuyler, FEB 18, 1781, Morris, *Alexander Hamilton Founding,* 497–99; Flexner, *Young Hamilton,* 330–37; Chernow, *Alexander Hamilton,* 150–53; Chadwick, *George Washington's War,* 426–29; Gottschalk, *Lafayette and Close,* 186–87. Laf hesitated to bring the subject up again, but on APR 15, he asked AH, "Have you left the family, my dear Sir? I suppose so, but from love to the general for whom you know my affection ardently wish it was not the case." He wrote GW the same day: "Considering the footing I am upon with your excellency, it would perhaps appear to you strange, that I never mentionned a circumstance lately happened in your family. I was the first who knew of it, and from that moment exerted every means in my power to prevent a separation which I know was not agreable to Your Excellency. To this measure I was prompted by affection for you, but thought it was improper to mention any thing about it, untill you was pleased to impart it to me." GW answered, "The event, which you seem to speak of with regret, my friendship for you would most assuredly have induced me to impart to you in the moment it happened had it not been for the request of H—— who desired that no mention might be made of it: why this injunction on me, while he was communicating it himself, is a little extraordinary! But I complied, & religiously fulfilled it." Laf to AH, and to GW, both APR 15, and GW to Laf, APR 22 (second letter), 1781, ILA 4:32–34, 59–60.

10. Laf to Luz, FEB 7 and 15, Roc to GW, FEB 3, 1781, ILA 3:316–18, 320–21, 333n, and summary at 327–29. Ternay had died on DEC 15. Captain Charles-René-Dominique Sochet, chevalier Destouches, served as interim commander until May.

11. Laf to Adr, FEB 2, 1781, ILA 3:309–13; Lee quoted Ketchum, *Victory,* 126. See also Greene, *General Greene,* 168–76; Rankin, *War in Virginia,* 16–74; CW, 55–56; Clary, *Fortress,* 8–9.

12. Nelson in Ryan, *Salute,* 239–41; TJ to GW, JAN 10, and FVS to GW, JAN 11, 1781, Sparks 3:202–5. The state failed to hire or impress enough slaves to work in

construction or transport, while the British simply commandeered them. Quarles, *Negro,* 101–14.

13. Laf, Memorandum on Orders for the March, FEB 18, and Laf to Luz, FEB 19, 1781, ILA 3:329–33; GW to Roc, FEB 15, to Timothy Pickering, FEB 18, and to PC, FEB 26, 1781, FGW 21:229–32, 243, 300–2.

14. GW to Laf, FEB 20, 1781, ILA 3:334–36.

15. GW to FVS, FEB 20, to Arthur St. Clair, FEB 22 and 26, to TJ, FEB 21, to Elias Dayton, FEB 22, to Roc and Destouches, FEB 27, and to AW, FEB 26, 1781, FGW 21:256–58, 270–71, 272–73, 277–78, 294, 296–97, 311–14; Laf to FVS, FEB 21 and 24, to TJ, FEB 21, to Dayton, FEB 23, to GW, FEB 23, 24, and 25, to Pickering, and to St. Clair, both FEB 27, to Joseph Vose, FEB 28, GW to Laf, FEB 22, 23, 25, 26, and 27, to Elias Dayton, FEB 22, to Roc and Destouches, and to AW, both FEB 26, Roc and Destouches to GW, FEB 25, and Report of Board of War, FEB 28, 1781, ILA 3:336n, 336–41, 339n, 341n, 342, 344–56, 354n, 358n. The commander of the squadron detached by Destouches was Arnaud Le Gardeur de Tilly.

16. GW to Laf, MAR 1, 1781, ILA 3:357–58.

17. Malone, *Jefferson Virginian,* 344–46; TJ to Laf, MAR 2, 3, 6, 8, and 12 (two letters), and Laf to TJ, MAR 16, 1781, BTJ 5:43, 49–51, 74–76, 92–93, 129–31, 159–60; Laf to TJ, MAR 3, 8, 16, 19, and 24, TJ to Laf and to FVS, both MAR 10, and to Laf, MAR 14, 19, and 24, 1781, ILA 3:367–69, 387–88, 390–91, 391n, 396, 400–1, 402–5, 410–13. On Virginia politics during the war, see Eckenrode, *Revolution.*

18. Laf to GW, MAR 2 and 7, to Commanding Officer in Virginia, and to Gist, both MAR 3, to Thomas Sim Lee and Governor's Council, MAR 3, 5, 6, 7, and 8, to AW, MAR 4, Governor's Council to Laf, MAR 3 and 7, Gist to Laf, MAR 5 and 7, FVS to Laf, MAR 7, Laf to Luz, MAR 7, Laf to NG, MAR 8, and GW to Laf, MAR 8, 1781, ILA 3:359–65, 365n, 369–83, 385, 388; Laf to GW, MAR 3, 1781, GLW 153.

19. Ketchum, *Victory,* 126.

20. Laf to Luz, MAR 8, to GW, MAR 8, 11, 15, and 23, to Thomas Sim Lee, MAR 11, to FVS, MAR 14, to AW, MAR 15, NG to Laf, MAR 22, 1781, ILA 3:384–85, 385–86, 389, 392–93, 395, 397–99, 407–10; Laf to GW, MAR 9, 1781 (two letters), GLW 157–59; Palmer, *General von Steuben,* 256–61.

21. Laf to GW, MAR 23, 1781, ILA 3:408–10.

22. Laf to GW, MAR 25 and 26 (two letters), 1781, ILA 3:413–14, 416–18; Gottschalk, *Lafayette and Close,* 204–7; Boatner, 1151.

23. Laf to GW, MAR 26, 1781, ILA 3:417–18.

24. Laf to TJ, MAR 27, 1781, BTJ 5:262–62; FVS, Proposal for an Expedition against Cornwallis, with endorsements by Laf and others, MAR 27, NG to Laf, MAR 29, Lewis Morris to Laf, MAR 29, FVS to Laf, MAR 29, 1781, ILA 3:419–24, 424n. Laf later accused Destouches of bungling. "Had the French fleet come in Arnold was ours," he said, "the more certain it was, the greater my disappointment has been." Laf to AH, APR 10, 1781, ILA 4:16–17. Early in April, NG tried again to persuade Laf to go south, to prevent Cornwallis from joining Arnold. NG to Laf, APR 3, 1781, ILA 4:3–5.

25. Ver to Luz, MAR 9, and to Laf, MAR 10, 1781, ILA 3:391, 391n. On APR 19, Ver said that the king had decided to underwrite a loan of 10 million livres, making France's total contribution to America 20 million livres. "Mr. Laurens shows zeal," he also remarked, "but I tell you in confidence that he did not express it in a manner suited to the nature of his mission. We did not take offense, because we attributed his behavior only to his inexperience in public affairs. I think I should speak to you about this officer because it is possible that, because he was annoyed at not obtaining everything he asked for, or rather insisted upon . . . he may give a biased account to his chief. I feel I must prepare you to caution General Washington against the prejudices he could form." JL did not tell GW he had been treated unfairly. Ver to Laf, APR 19, 1781, ILA 4:47–48; JL to GW, APR 11, 1781, Wharton 4:356–57.

26. Dull, *French Navy,* 239–41.

27. GW to Laf, APR 5 and 6, 1781, ILA 4:6–9. Seven field officers of the Massachusetts Line complained through General William Heath that field commands of Massachusetts units in Laf's detachment had gone to officers outside the line. Specifically causing complaint were Gimat, once Laf's adc, now a colonel, and Major William Galvan. GW told the protestors that he had sent the most available officers without regard to seniority. James Mellen and others to Heath, FEB 27, and GW to Heath, MAR 2, 1781, FGW 21:342–44, 419–23; Laf to GW, APR 13, 1781, ILA 4:26–27.

28. Five days later he told AH, "If I go to exile, come and partake it with me." Laf to GW, APR 8, and to AH, APR 10 and 15, 1781, ILA 4:10–14, 16–17, 32.

29. Laf to Governor and Council APR 10 and 17, Governor and Council to Laf, APR 8 and 12, Laf to NG, APR 17, and to Board of War, APR 22, 1781, ILA 4:15, 17–19, 27–29, 35–41, 41–42, 53–54. On MAY 24, Congress resolved to assume responsibility for repayment, and on NOV 23 ordered the Superintendent of Finance to discharge the debt. The Baltimore merchants had sold Laf's promissory note to Dr. John Boyd, and when it fell due on JUL 1, 1783, Laf rather than Congress paid it. ILA 4:54n.

30. Laf to GW, APR 10 and 14, 1781, ILA 4:1924, 30–32; GW to Laf, APR 11, 1781, FGW 21:445–46.

31. Laf to Luz, APR 10, 1781, ILA 4:22–23. Laf lost his baggage to a British privateer.

32. GW to Laf, APR 14, 1781, FGW 21:455; GW to Webster, JUL 14, 1788, quoted Unger, *Lafayette,* 135.

33. FVS to Laf, APR 10 and 21, Laf to GW, APR 13, 15, 18, to NG, APR 17, to TJ, APR 21 and 25, to George Augustine Washington (Laf's new aide and GW's nephew), APR 21, to Luz, APR 22, to FVS, APR 25, and GW to Laf, APR 22, 1781, ILA 4:23–24, 29, 33–41, 43, 45, 46n, 48–51, 54–58, 62–64; Laf to GW, APR 13, 1781, GLW 179–80; FVS to GW, APR 15, 1781, Sparks 3:290–94.

34. GW to Laf, APR 21 and 22 (two letters), 1781, ILA 4:52, 56–60. There was another curious exchange during this time. Laf wrote GW on APR 23, "Great happiness is derived from friendship, and I do particularly experience it in the attachement which unites me to you. But friendship has its duties, and the man that likes you the best will be the forwardest in letting you know every thing where you can be concerned. When the

ennemy came to your house many Negroes deserted to them. This piece of news did not affect me much as I little value property—But you cannot conceive how unhappy I have been to hear that Mr. Lund Washington went on board the ennemy's vessels and consented to give them provisions." Lund was GW's cousin and manager of Mount Vernon. GW had already heard about the incident. He told Lund it would have been "a less painful circumstance to me" if he had let the British burn the place. He sent a copy to Laf as "proof of my friendship . . . The freedom of your communications is an evidence to me of the sincerety of your attachment—and every fresh instance of this gives pleasure & adds to the bands which unite us in friendship." Laf to GW, APR 23, and GW to Laf, MAY 4, 1781, ILA 4:60–61, 84–85; GW to Lund Washington, APR 30, 1781, FGW 22:14.

35. Laf to NG, APR 28, Phillips to Laf, APR 26, 28, and 29, and Laf to Phillips, APR 30, 1781, ILA 4:66–69, 71–73; Laf to Phillips, MAY 3, 1781, Lafayette Collection, Lilly Library.

36. Laf to NG (two letters), MAY 3, 1781, ILA 4:79–81.

37. Laf to GW, MAY 4, 1781, ILA 4:82–84.

38. NG to Laf, MAY 1, 1781, ILA 4:74–75.

39. GW to Laf, MAY 5, 1781, ILA 4:86–87.

40. Malone, *Jefferson Virginian,* 349–51.

41. Laf to Weedon, MAY 3, 15, 28, and 29, to Jethro Sumner, MAY 7, to FVS, MAY 10, 17, and 29, and to TJ, MAY 28, Richard Claiborne (deputy quartermaster) to Laf, MAY 2, 3, 21, TJ to Laf, MAY 14, 29, 30, and 31, Weedon to Laf, MAY 14, 19, and 22, and JVS to Laf, MAY 28, 1781, ILA 4:75–79, 81–82, 87, 91, 98–102, 104–8, 115–16, 119, 125–26, 136–46, 151–53. See also Poirier, "Three Elements."

42. Laf to GW, MAY 8, and to Luz, MAY 9, 1781, ILA 4:88–91.

43. Laf to GW, MAY 17, and to NG, MAY 18, and GW to Laf, MAY 31, 1781, ILA 4:108–14, 156n; Tower, 2:340. Laf had heard rumors of Phillips' death, and when Arnold's first emissaries arrived he asked them about it; they denied it. They returned the next day to admit the truth, and presented Arnold's message. Laf told GW, "The British general cannot but perfectly know that I am not to treat of partial exchanges and that the fate of the continental prisoners must be regulated by a superior authority to that with which I am invested." Laf to GW, MAY 17, 1781, GLW 192–93. Exchanges and paroles of prisoners were the most elaborate song and dance in eighteenth-century warfare. Neither Laf nor Arnold possessed authority in the matter until it was delegated to them.

44. Laf to GW, MAY 14, and GW to Laf, MAY 31, 1781, ILA 4:130–31, 153–56.

45. Laf to AW, MAY 15, to NG, MAY 18, and AW to Laf, MAY 19 and 20, 1781, ILA 4:102–3, 110–15, 116–17; Laf to GW, MAY 18, 1781, GLW 193–95.

46. Tucker, *Mad Anthony,* 192–93; Nelson, *Anthony Wayne,* 133–34; Denny, *Military Journal,* 34; Ketchum, *Victory,* 153–55.

47. Laf to DM, MAY 21, and TJ to DM, JUN 2, 1781, ILA 4:117–18, 119n; Callahan, *Daniel Morgan,* 249–50; Higginbotham, *Daniel Morgan,* 161–62.

48. Laf to Luz, MAY 22, 1781, ILA 4:120–21.

49. Laf to Noailles, MAY 22, 1781, ILA 4:121–25.

50. NG to Laf, MAY 23, and Laf to NG, MAY 24, 1781, ILA 4:126–29; Laf to AH, MAY 23, 1781, SAH 2:643–44.

51. Laf to GW, MAY 24, 1781, ILA 4:130–31.

52. GW to Laf, MAY 31, 1781, ILA 4:153–54.

53. GW to Laf, JUN 4, 1781, ILA 4:168.

54. Cornwallis to Clinton, MAY 26, 1781, Tower 2:238. Clinton wrote Lord George Germain, secretary of state for the colonies, on June 9, saying that Cornwallis had written that "the boy could not escape him." Cornwallis sent his first letter to Laf the same day, passing on the text of the cartel on prisoner exchanges. It was much more courteous than anything Phillips or Arnold had sent. Cornwallis to Laf, MAY 26, 1781, ILA 4:134–36.

55. Laf to AW, MAY 29, and to FVS, MAY 31, FVS to Laf, MAY 30, and Wayne to Laf, MAY 31 and JUN 1, 1781, ILA 4:141–42, 147–48, 150–51, 156–57; Palmer, *General von Steuben,* 273–82.

56. Weedon to Laf, JUN 1, 17 and 20, Laf to James Wood, JUN 3, to DM, JUN 12, to Weedon, JUN 16 and 21, to Thomas Sim Lee, JUN 25, and to Nelson, JUN 26 and July 1, Claiborne to Laf, JUN 13, to Thomas Pickering, JUN 14, and to Virginia Assembly, JUN 18, and Pickering to Claiborne, JUL 1, 1781, ILA 4:158, 160–61, 161n, 176, 180–81, 181n, 189–91, 201–2, 205, 210, 214, 228–31; Eckenrode, *Revolution,* 246–49. Throughout the campaign, Laf and Cornwallis continued their gentlemanly messages about prisoners. Cornwallis to Laf, JUN 4 and 28, Laf to Cornwallis JUN 20, and Laf to Captain Ewell, JUN 30, 1781, ILA 4:167–68, 196–97, 218–19, 221–22. On JUN 30 Laf appointed Charles Ewell as commissary of prisoners, also telling him to look after seven state legislators captured by Tarleton at Charlottesville.

57. Laf to AW, JUN 2, to FVS and to NG, both JUN 3, 1781, ILA 4:160–65; Malone, *Jefferson Virginian,* 356–58; Gottschalk, *Lafayette and Close,* 237–43.

58. FVS to Laf, JUN 3, 1781, ILA 4:166–67.

59. Laf to GW, JUN 3, and FVS to Laf, MAY 28 and JUN 5, 1781, ILA 4:139, 165–55, 170–71, 170n; Rankin, *War in Virginia,* 41–43, 66, 73–74; Boatner, 874–75. Simcoe found some canoes and sent men over to burn the stores.

60. Laf to JVS, JUN 13, to Luz, JUN 16, to NG, JUN 18, 20, and 21, and to GW, JUN 18, 1781, ILA 4:179–80, 182–83, 185–88, 191–95, 197–200, 202–4.

61. CIG 1:185–94.

62. GW to Laf, JUL 13, Laf to JVS, JUN 22, JUL 23 and 25, AUG 6, and 13, and OCT 26, and to Nelson, OCT 31, and NG to FVS, SEP 17, 1781, ILA 4:206–7, 247–48, 272–73, 276–77, 301–2, 320–21, 432–35; Palmer, *General von Steuben,* 286–87. FVS told the legislature that he would "be forced to expose the dastardliness of the government, the absurdity of the laws and the pusillanimity of those who should have executed them."

63. AW to Laf, JUN 4, 6, and 7, Laf to AW, JUN 7, NG to Laf, JUN 9, Tarleton to Cornwallis, JUN 13, 1781, ILA 4:169, 171–75, 178–79, 183; Memoirs quoted Unger,

Lafayette, 145. Regarding "bush fighting," see the comment of John Jacob Ulrich Rivardi: "Some would rather *bush fight* (as they call it) in case of a war, and the fact is, I fancy, that they had rather not fight at all." Rivardi to HK, JUL 20, 1794, quoted Clary, *Fortress,* 22–23. He wrote from Norfolk.

64. Laf to JVS, JUN 15, and to Luz, JUN 16, 1781, ILA 4:185–88.

65. Laf to NG, JUN 21, 1781, ILA 4:202–4.

66. Laf to Luz, and to Weedon, both JUN 16, to AW, JUN 21, 22, 25, and 26, to FVS, JUN 22, to NG, JUN 27, and to Nelson, JUN 28, AW to Laf, JUN 22 and 25, and NG to Laf, JUN 23, 1781, ILA 4:189, 205–9, 211–12, 215, 216–18.

67. GW to Laf, JUN 29, 1781, ILA 119, 121.

68. Laf to GW, JUN 28, 1781, GLW 203–4.

69. Laf to AW, JUN 30, to Nelson, JUL 1, and to NG, JUL 4, 1781, ILA 4:222–23, 228–34.

70. Laf to Charles Dabney, JUL 7, and to NG, JUL 8, 1781, ILA 4:235–38, 238n; AW to GW, JUL 8, 1781, quoted Gottschalk, *Lafayette and Close,* 266; Nelson, *Anthony Wayne,* 134–37; Boatner, 451–53. Only a few hundred men under Simcoe had crossed the river before AW approached.

71. Laf, General Orders, JUL 8, and Laf to Nelson, JUL 10, 1781, ILA 4:240, 242–43. As for "a near-run thing," that was a common description of a closely fought action for generations of British commanders, many of whom were fans of horse racing. The Duke of Wellington called the Battle of Waterloo (1815) "the nearest run thing you ever saw in your life."

72. Higginbotham, *War,* 374–75; Ketchum, *Victory,* 184–86; Gottschalk, *Lafayette and Close,* 268–71, Chaplain l'Abbe Claude Robin quoted 271. Laf and most historians believe that Laf convinced Cornwallis that his detachment was larger than it actually was. That worked for a while. Just after Green Spring, however, the British commander accurately put the marquis' strength at about 2,000. Cornwallis to Clinton, JUL 8, 1781, quoted ILA 239n.

73. Laf to GW, JUL 8, 1781, ILA 4:239.

74. Laf to Noailles, JUL 9, 1781, ILA 4:240–41.

Chapter Twelve

1. Ver to Laf, MAY 11, 1781, ILA 4:92–93. On JL in France, see Massey, *John Laurens,* 173–90.

2. BF to Laf, MAY 14, 1781, LBF 35:64–66.

3. Castries to Laf, MAY 25, 1781, ILA 4:132–34.

4. Probably Cromot du Bourg, quoted Freeman, *George Washington,* 5:286.

5. Flexner, *George Washington American,* 427–31; Ketchum, *Victory,* 135–42; Freeman, *George Washington* 5:296n; Higginbotham, *War,* 388n.

6. Roc to de Grasse, JUN 11, 1781, Tower 2:399.

7. Ketchum, *Victory,* 142–43.

8. Flexner, *George Washington American,* 434. French army uniforms were all white, except for colored lapel facings that distinguished regiments.

9. Baron Ludwig von Closen quoted ibid., 434–35.

10. GWD 2:241; Flexner, *George Washington American,* 436–37; Ketchum, *Victory.*

11. GW to Laf, JUL 13, 1781, ILA 4:247–48.

12. Laf to GW, JUL 20, 1781, ILA 4:255–57.

13. Laf to GW, JUL 20 (second of three), 1781, ILA 4:257–59.

14. Laf to GW, JUL 20 (third of three), 1781, ILA 4:259–61.

15. Laf to GW, JUL 26, and to George Weedon, JUL 27, 1781, ILA 4:210–11, 280–81.

16. Laf to GW, JUL 30, 1781, ILA 4:286–87.

17. Laf to GW, JUL 31, 1781, ILA 4:290–91; Laf to GW, AUG 1, 1781, GLW 214.

18. GW to Laf, JUL 30, 1781, ILA 4:288–90. GW's "public" letters of the same date, answering Laf's of JUL 8 and 20, are in FGW 22:431–32.

19. Laf to Allen Jones, JUL 10, to Nelson, JUL 12, to AW, JUL 15, 21, 23, and 25, to Thomas Burke (governor of North Carolina), JUL 16, to DM, JUL 16 and 17, to NG, JUL 23, to FVS, JUL 15, NG to Laf, JUL 22, AW to Laf, JUL 22 and 24, James Barron to Laf, JUL 31, 1781, ILA 4:241–44, 248–51, 251n, 253, 263–64, 266–70, 274–78, 292, 293n; Laf to GW, JUL 26, 1781, GLW 211; Boatner, 1089.

20. Laf to GW, AUG 1, 1781, GLW 214; Laf to Thomas Sim Lee, and to GW, both AUG 6, 1781, ILA 4:298–300.

21. Laf to Nelson, JUL 12, 13, 21, 22, and 29 (two letters), and AUG 7, to Thomas Tucker, JUL 19, to FVS, JUL 23, to William Davis, JUL 27, to Thomas Sim Lee, JUL 30, to AW, AUG 4, FVS to Laf, JUL 13 and AUG 6, Thomas Burke to Laf, JUL 16, Nelson to Laf, JUL 28 and 29, and AUG 3, AW to Laf, AUG 9 and 10, James McHenry to Nelson, AUG 8, 1781, ILA 4:243–45, 246, 254, 254n, 261–62, 264–66, 272–73, 278–86, 293–94, 296, 301–2, 307–8, 309, 311; Nelson, *Anthony Wayne,* 138–40. On AUG 9, AW provided Laf a return of all articles seized because they were "in danger of being all embezzled or destroyed, added to the distressed condition our people were in for want of shoes & overalls."

22. Laf to Cornwallis, JUL 19, to Nelson, JUL 23, to British Officer in Charge of the American Prisoners, JUL 25, and to GW, JUL 31, and Cornwallis to Laf, JUL 24, 1781, ILA 4:253–54, 254n, 271, 276, 290–91. When militia captured by the British were exchanged, Laf dumped the burden of their care onto the state.

23. Laf to GW, AUG 6, 1781, ILA 4:299–300.

24. Laf to GW, AUG 11, 1781, ILA 4:311–12.

25. Laf to Nelson, AUG 12, 16, 20, 26, 29, and 30, to FVS, AUG 13, to DM, AUG 15, to Weedon, AUG 15, to NG, AUG 25, Robert Andrews (quotation) to Weedon, SEP 26, William Davies to Laf, AUG 15, Thomas Burke to Laf, AUG 30, and David Jameson to Laf, AUG 31, 1781, ILA 4:314–15, 315n, 320–21, 323–29, 331–32, 336–37, 352–56, 361, 365–66, 369–73, 379.

26. Laf to Luz, AUG 14, to HK, AUG 18, to Adr, to Maurepas, and to prince de Poix, all AUG 24, 1781, ILA 4:321–22, 332–33, 342–49. These letters mostly bragged about himself. The one to Adr, the first in many months, said, "The vanity with which you credit me has perhaps been gratified by the grand role I have been compelled to play. . . . It was not rational to entrust such a command to me," on account of his youth. That was a common theme. He told Maurepas that "you must have been frightened by the danger-ous role entrusted to my youth. Five hundred miles from any other corps and without any resources whatsoever, I have been chosen to oppose the plans of St. James and the fortune of Lord Cornwallis."

27. GW to Laf, AUG 15, 1781, ILA 4:329–30.

28. Parker to Laf, AUG 19, 1781, ILA 4:334, 336.

29. Laf to AW, AUG 22 and 25, and to John Taylor, AUG 31, 1781, ILA 4:341, 359–60, 377.

30. Laf to GW, AUG 21, 1781, ILA 4:337–39.

31. GW to Laf, AUG 21, 1781, ILA 4:340.

32. Laf to GW, AUG 24 and 25, 1781, ILA 4:349–51, 356–59.

33. Wiencek, *Imperfect God,* 252–53; Quarles, *Negro,* 194–95. Information about James is fragmentary. His emancipation is discussed below.

34. GW to Laf, AUG 27, 1781, ILA 4:364–65.

35. Ketchum, *Victory,* 204.

36. De Grasse to Laf, and marquis de Saint-Simon-Montbléru to Laf, both AUG 30, 1781, ILA 4:373–76.

37. Laf to AW, AUG 31, and AW to Laf, AUG 31, 1781, ILA 4:378, 380; AW quoted Tower 2:431; Nelson, *Anthony Wayne,* 142–43.

38. Laf to GW (two letters), SEP 1, 1781, GLW 225–27.

39. GW to Laf, SEP 1 and 2 (quotations), 1781, ILA 4:383, 386–87.

40. GW to Laf, SEP 7, 1781, ILA 4:390.

41. Laf to GW (two letters), SEP 8, 1781, GLW 228–32. ILA 4:392–94 dates the second letter to the ninth, GLW to the eighth, making the one quoted the second of the day. I think GLW is correct. Laf to GW, SEP 10, 1781, GLW 232, repeated much of this. On supplies, see AW to Laf, SEP 2, Nelson to Laf, SEP 15, Laf to Nelson, SEP 4, 6, and 11, to Thomas Burke, SEP 6, to Luz, SEP 8, William Davies to Laf, SEP 7, and to Anthony Walton White, SEP 12, and Benjamin Harrison to GW, SEP 23, 1781, ILA 4:386–92, 398–401, 403. Laf told GW that he sent twenty letters a day on supplies, and received an equal number. Prisoner exchanges also continued. Cornwallis to Laf, SEP 15, and Laf to Cornwallis, SEP 25, 1781, ILA 4:400–1, 404.

42. Ketchum, *Victory,* 186–87; Mahan, *Influence,* 388–90; Boatner, 1237–9.

43. GW to Laf, SEP 10, 1781, ILA 4:397. See also Flexner, *George Washington American,* 445–47; Ketchum, *Victory,* 181–84; Wickwire, *Cornwallis,* 354–88.

44. AW to Laf, SEP 11, 1781, ILA 4:399.

45. Quoted Scheer and Rankin, *Rebels and Redcoats,* 476.

46. Tower 2:447; Observations by the comte de Grasse during his conference with

the marquis de Lafayette, SEP 26, 1781, and Laf to GW and to Luz, both SEP 30, 1781, ILA 4:405–10; Flexner, *George Washington American,* 448–51; Ketchum, *Victory,* 209–13.

47. Flexner, *George Washington American,* 451–52; Boatner, 1239, 1248. On the Siege of Yorktown, see Ketchum, *Victory;* Davis, *Campaign;* Walker, *Engineers;* Rankin, *War;* Clary, *Fortress,* 9–12 and citations; Higginbotham, *War,* 380–81; and Wickwire, *Cornwallis,* 354–88.

48. Laf to GW, SEP 30, 1781, ILA 4:411–12, 412n; Wright, *Continental Army,* 169–70.

49. Clary, *Fortress,* 10; Martin, *Narrative,* 198. Gouvion, an expert topographer, had plotted and mapped the routes of march from New York.

50. Laf to Luz (quotation), OCT 3, and to NG, OCT 6, 1781, ILA 4:413–14, 415n. On prisoners, see Laf to Cornwallis, OCT 3, 1781, ILA 4:412–13.

51. Martin, *Narrative,* 198–99.

52. Ibid., 199–200.

53. In Chinard, *George Washington as French,* 54n. Chastellux also said of Knox, "One cannot too much admire the intelligence and activity, with which he collected from all quarters, transported, disembarked and conveyed to the batteries the train destined for the siege, and which consisted of more than thirty pieces of cannon and mortars of a large bore." The French were absolutely amazed to find complete mastery of artillery in an American.

54. Laf to Luz, OCT 12, 1781, ILA 4:417–18.

55. Chevalier de Villebresme quoted ILA 422n. Laf said in his memoirs that his words were, "We are young soldiers and have only one way in these cases. That is to un-load our muskets and march right in with our bayonets." Quoted Gottschalk, *Lafayette and Close,* 319–22.

56. Flexner, *Young Hamilton,* 358–60; McDonald, *Alexander Hamilton,* 24–25.

57. Martin, *Narrative,* 202–3; AH to Laf, OCT 15, and Laf to Luz, OCT 16, 1781, ILA 4:418–21; Laf to GW, OCT 16, 1781, GLW 235–36; Flexner, *Young Hamilton,* 361–65.

58. Figures are from Boatner, 1245. For years a story circulated that Laf, with GW's approval, had ordered AH to "put to death all those of the enemy who should happen to be taken in the redoubt." AH flatly denied it. AH to editor of *Evening Post,* in Morris, *Alexander Hamilton and Founding,* 65.

59. Laf to Luz, OCT 16, 1781, ILA 4:420–21; GWD 2:267–68; Boatner, 1245–46; Flexner, *George Washington American,* 457.

60. Lieutenant Ebenezer Denny quoted Scheer and Rankin, *Rebels and Redcoats,* 490. The account of the surrender follows Scheer and Rankin, 490–95; Ketchum, *Victory,* 138–57; Flexner, *George Washington American,* 459–64; Martin, *Narrative,* 206–8; and Boatner, 1246–48.

61. GW to Cornwallis, OCT 18, 1781, FGW 23:237–38. Laf claimed later, in the Memoirs and letters, that the Charleston terms were his idea, and his biographers have generally accepted his claim. The record shows, however, that the stipulation was GW's

own, as retribution for the insult to American arms during Lincoln's surrender of that city. Besides, Laf's resentment of Lincoln at Yorktown makes his version unlikely.

62. Palmer, *General von Steuben,* 292; Thomas S. Jesup to William H. Denny, JUL 13, 1859, in Denny, *Military Journal,* 282–83. Jesup heard this story from Major William Croghan, who had been on Steuben's staff, and Laf's aide Colonel Richard Anderson.

63. Freeman, *George Washington* 5:388–89; Boatner, 1095.

64. Lee quoted Unger, *Lafayette,* 159; Boatner, 1230. They played it at Saratoga because they had been ordered to play "something light." There were countless versions, most of them obscene.

65. Freeman, *George Washington* 5:390–91. Of about 20,000 allied troops around Yorktown, casualties were less than 400. About 600 of Cornwallis' men fell during the siege, and he surrendered 8,081 at Yorktown and Gloucester. Boatner, 1248.

66. Gottschalk, *Lafayette and Close,* 329–31; Laf to Cornwallis, OCT 31, 1781, ILA 4:434. Cornwallis later became a highly successful governor-general of India, where he grew grossly fat.

67. Laf to Ver, to Maurepas, and to prince de Poix, all OCT 20, to Adr, OCT 22, and to Samuel Cooper, OCT 26, 1781, ILA 4:422, 422n, 424–26, 429–32.

68. GWD excerpt, OCT 21, Laf to GW, OCT 23, and de Grasse to GW, OCT 14, 1781, ILA 4:427–28; Gottschalk, *Lafayette and Close,* 332–35. The British left Wilmington on NOV 18.

69. Laf to Nelson, OCT 31, 1781, ILA 4:434–35.

70. Quoted Gottschalk, *Lafayette and Close,* 336.

71. GW to Laf, NOV 15, 1781, ILA 4:435–37.

72. Laf to PC, NOV 15 and 22, to NG, NOV 22; Resolutions of Congress, NOV 23, Congress to Louis XVI, NOV 29, 1781, ILA 4:437–43, 441n; PC to BF, JA, and John Jay, NOV 21, 1781, Tower 2:462–63; Gottschalk, *Lafayette and Close,* 336–47.

73. Laf to GW, NOV 29, 1781, ILA 4:443–44.

74. Barry's instructions, ILA 4:441n. Noailles was annoyed by the delays, telling a friend, "I think [it] more easy to take a British army than to have a frigate out of Boston harbour." Noailles to Molly Robinson, DEC 14, 1781, quoted Gottschalk, *Lafayette and Close,* 343.

75. Laf to GW, DEC 21–23, 1781, ILA 4:449–50.

Chapter Thirteen

1. Both quoted Higginbotham, *War,* 383.

2. Ver to Laf, DEC 1, and Ségur to Laf, DEC 5 (two letters), 1781, ILA 4:444–48; Gottschalk, *Lafayette and Close,* 350–51.

3. *Gazette de Leyde,* NOV 30, 1781, quoted Gottschalk, *Lafayette and Close,* 327.

4. Laf to GW, JAN 18, and GW to Laf, JAN 4–5, 1782, ILA 5:2–5.

5. Maurois, *Adrienne,* 101–2; Fraser, *Marie Antoinette,* 194; Belloc, *Marie Antoinette,*

135; Gottschalk, *Lafayette and Close,* 348–49. These accounts differ on details, but the gist is similar.

6. Laf to GW, JAN 30, 1782, ILA 5:9–11.

7. Ver to Laf, JAN 23, Laf to PC, JAN 18 and 29, to BF, JAN 22, and to JJ, JAN 30, and BF to RM, JAN 28, 1782, ILA 5:6–8, 7n, 10n.

8. Ver to BF, FEB 6, BF to Ver, FEB 15 and 16, Laf to Ver, FEB 16, to BF, FEB 12, 16, and 25, and MAR 15, and JA to Laf, FEB 20, 1782, ILA 5:10–15, 13n, 14n; Isaacson, *Benjamin Franklin,* 410.

9. Ségur to Laf, JUL 7, 1782, ILA 5:51.

10. BF to Robert Livingston, MAR 4, 1782, Wharton 5:214; Laf to Ver, MAR 20, to JA, MAR 27, to JJ, MAR 28, and to Livingston, MAR 30, 1782, ILA 5:15–21; Gottschalk, *Lafayette and Close,* 356–63. On Spanish interests in North America and border conflicts with the United States, see Weber, *Spanish Frontier.* Spain was fighting the British in the West Indies at the time.

11. Laf to GW, MAR 30 and 31, 1782, ILA 5:21–25.

12. Flexner, *George Washington American,* 476–77; Regulations for Hutting, NOV 1782, and Chastellux quoted Clary, *These Relics,* 11–13.

13. Laf to GW, APR 12, 1782, introducing de Broglie, GLW 250; Gottschalk, *Lafayette and Close,* 363.

14. Maurois, *Adrienne,* 103–4.

15. Laf to HL, APR 14 and AUG 20, and to BF, JUN 12, 1782, ILA 5:28–30, 39–40, 53–54; Massey, *John Laurens,* 188–89, 201, 211, 287n. BF noted in his journal on JUN 12 regarding Laf's conduct, "He appears very prudently cautious of not doing any thing that may seem assuming a power that he is not vested with." Quoted ILA 5:40n.

16. Laf quoted Lycan, *Alexander Hamilton Foreign,* 65–66; Morris, *Peacemakers,* 246–48; JA to Laf, APR 6, BF to Jay, APR 22, and Laf to JA, OCT 6, 1782, ILA 5:25–26, 37n, 60–62, 62n; JJ to Livingston, NOV 17, 1782, Wharton 6:45.

17. Laf to GW, APR 12, and to Ver, APR 18, 1782, ILA 5:26–28, 30–32.

18. Laf to JJ, APR 28, and to JA, OCT 6, and BF, Memorandum of Peace Negotiations, MAY nd, 1782, ILA 5:33–36, 36n.

19. Laf to BF, JUN 20 and 25, to Livingston, JUN 25, to GW, JUN 25, and to PC, JUN 29, ILA 5:540–49, 41n, 47n, BF quoted 43n; JJ to Livingston, JUN 28, 1782, Wharton 5:527.

20. Laf to GW, JUN 25, 1782, ILA 5:48–49, and account of British diplomatic maneuvers, 47n.

21. Minutes of the Assembly of JUN 24, 1782, of the Worthy Lodge of Saint John of Scotland of the Social Contract, ILA 5:41–42; Gottschalk, *Lafayette and Close,* 363–71.

22. Laf to GW, JUN 29, 1782, ILA 5:49–50.

23. Bernier, *Lafayette,* 148–50; Unger, *Lafayette,* 169; Laf to BF, and BF to Laf, both SEP 17, 1782, ILA 5:56–57.

24. Laf to GW, SEP 7, 1782, GLW 254.

25. Laf to Ver, SEP 10, and to BF, SEP 12 and 21, 1782, ILA 5:54–59; JJ to Laf, and

Laf to JJ, both SEP 21, 1782, Wharton 6:21, 29. JA announced that he had nearly completed a treaty of commerce with the United Provinces (signed OCT 8), together with loans of cash and credit. JA to Laf, SEP 29, and Laf to JA, OCT 6, 1782, ILA 59–62; JA to Livingston, OCT 8, 1782, Wharton 5:803–5.

26. Laf to Livingston, OCT 14, 1782, ILA 5:79n; Laf to GW, OCT 14, 1782, GLW 254–56.

27. GW to Laf, OCT 20, 1782, ILA 5:62–64. Congress also told him, "You need feel no anxiety on the score of an apology for yr. absence. Every body here attributes it to its true cause & considers it as a new proof of your attachment to the interests of America." Livingston to Laf, NOV 2, 1782, ILA 5:66–67. JL died in a skirmish at Combahee Ferry, South Carolina, AUG 27, Lee at Philadelphia, OCT 2. JL's death devastated AH, then in Congress. "You know how truly I loved him and will judge how much I regret him," he said. AH to Laf, NOV 3, 1782, quoted Chernow, *Alexander Hamilton,* 172. In the same letter he complained about how he looked forward to returning to private life. "You see the disposition I am in. You are condemned to run the race of ambition all your life. I am already tired of the career, and dare to leave it." Excerpted Morris, *Alexander Hamilton and Founding,* 577.

28. Laf to GW, OCT 24 and DEC 4, to the American Peace Commissioners, NOV 21, to Ver, NOV 22, to PC, DEC 3, to BF, DEC 6 and 8, and to JJ, DEC 26, 1782, ILA 5:64–65, 68–71, 69n, 72–76, 74n; Dull, *French Navy,* 317–24.

29. Higginbotham, *War,* 424–27. These arrangements violated the prohibition against separate peaces in the Franco-American treaty. But as Ver or BF would have been the first to say, diplomacy, like politics, is the art of the practical.

30. Quoted Maurois, *Adrienne,* 106.

31. GW to PC, JAN 20 and MAR 19, 1783, FGW 26:82–86, 237–38; Livingston to Laf, JAN 10, and to GW, FEB 16, 1783, ILA 5:78–79, 116n. Roc landed at Nantes on FEB 20. There was no crowd to welcome him, but he was content with the respect of the ministers. Whitridge, *Rochambeau,* 253.

32. JJ to Laf, JAN 19, and Laf to Carmichael, JAN 20 and 29, and FEB 2, 1783, ILA 5:79–83. Carmichael's letter has not survived. JJ was back on good terms with Laf.

33. Laf to Ver, to PC (two letters), and to Livingston, (two letters), all FEB 5, 1783, ILA 5:84–90. Ver's letter has disappeared.

34. Laf to GW, FEB 5, 1783, ILA 5:90–93.

35. Laf to JJ, FEB 15, to d'Estaing and to Ver, both FEB 18, to Floridablanca, FEB 19 (and Laf notes, FEB 22), and to Livingston, MAR 2, Floridablanca to Laf, FEB 22, Carmichael to Livingston, to JJ, AUG 23, 1783, ILA 5:95–106, 107n; Carmichael to Livingston, FEB 21, 1783, Wharton 6:268–70.

36. Montmorin to JJ, FEB 22, 1783, ILA 5:102n; Laf to GW, MAR 2, 1783, GLW 262–63.

37. Laf to Aglaé d'Hunolstein, MAR 27, 1783, quoted Maurois, *Adrienne,* 108–9; Laf to Adr, MAR 27, 1783, ILA 5:117–18, Bernier, *Lafayette,* 147–481; Gottschalk, *Lafayette and Close,* 417–19.

38. On this system and Laf's approach to it, see Gottschalk, "Lafayette as Commercial Agent"; Nussbaum, "Revolutionary Vergennes and Lafayette"; and Gottschalk, *Lafayette and Close,* 415–17.

39. Laf to Joly de Fleury, and to Ver, both MAR 19, 1783, ILA 5:110–13, 125n.

40. NG to Laf, JUN 10, 1783, and MAR 24, 1784, Laf to Ver, JUN 12 and 17, JUL 21, to PC, SEP 7, to BF, DEC 13, and Observations on Commerce Between France and the United States, DEC 13, Ver to Laf, JUN 29 and AUG 5, Calonne to Laf, DEC 18, 1783, ILA 5:133–35, 139–40, 144–45, 148–51, 178.

41. Calonne to Laf, DEC 15, and Laf to Ver, DEC 25, and to RM, DEC 26, 1783, ILA 5:182–84.

42. Laf, Observations on Commerce between France and the United States, DEC 13, 1783, and Calonne to Laf, JAN 9, 1784, ILA 5:382–88, 189. The most-favored-nation status grew out of Article Two of the 1778 Treaty of Amity and Commerce.

43. RM to PC, APR 16, 1784, Wharton 6:794; Laf to RM, JAN 10 and MAR 9, RM to PC, SEP 30, and to Laf, MAY 19 and SEP 30, Calonne to Laf, JAN 31, FEB 10 and 26, MAR 5 and 8, JUN 11 and 16, Laf to Calonne JAN 31, FEB 10 and 26, MAR 5, JUN 25, and to Ver, JUN 28 and OCT 12, Castries to Laf, JUN 17, 1784, ILA 5:190, 193–94, 198–200, 203–5, 218–19, 224–26, 232, 232n, 254–55, 269–70.

44. Recommendation of Lafayette for the Cross of Saint Louis, MAY 5, 1783, ILA 5:131; Gottschalk, *Lafayette Between,* 14–21, 66–68.

45. Elting, *Sword,* 15–16, 207–8.

46. Resolution of APR 10, 1783, ILA 5:90n.

47. GW to Livingston, MAR 29 and APR 16, 1783, FGW 26:267, 327; Livingston to GW, APR 9, and to Laf, MAY 1, 1783, ILA 5:93n, 128–30.

48. Laf to American Peace Commissioners, MAY 12 and JUL 22, to JA, JUN 16, to HL, JUL 6, to PC, JUL 20, and to McHenry, DEC 26, Barclay to Livingston, SEP 14, 1783, ILA 5:132–33, 133n, 136, 141–44, 147n, 150n, 184–86; GW, Memorandum of meeting with Sir Guy Carleton, MAY 6, 1783, FGW 26:402–5; Morris, *Peacemakers,* 274–81, 306–7. BF's son had remained a loyalist, which caused his enemies to claim that they colluded, each taking a side to protect the family interest whichever side won. The calumny spilled over against Laf, who earlier had talked BF into withdrawing his request to go home. A New York gossipmonger wrote that their relationship "led people to suspect that he meant only to retain a man that was perfectly subservient to his court." Wood, *Americanization,* 211. The true conspiracist can hold opposing ideas, in this case that BF was in cahoots with the British and the French.

49. JA to James Warren, APR 15, 1783, ILA 5:121–23; BF to Livingston, JUL 22, 1782, Wharton 6:582. BF told Livingston, "The instances he [Adams] supposes of their [French] ill will to us . . . I take to be as imaginary as I know his fancies to be that Count de Vergennes and myself are continually plotting against him."

50. Flexner, *George Washington American,* 513–14.

51. HK to Laf, JUN 16, GW to Laf, OCT 20, Laf to Ver, DEC 16, and to GW, DEC 25, Ségur (war minister) to Roc, DEC 18, 1783, Thomas Mullens to Laf, FEB 5, Laf to JA, MAR

8, to GW, MAR 9, and JA to Laf, MAR 28, 1784, ILA 5:137, 158, 176, 179–80, 180n, 196–97, 201–3, 205–7, 211–12; Laf to GW, MAR 9, 1784 (second letter), GLW 278–81.

52. Laf to GW, MAR 9, 1784, GLW 278–81; Laf to JA, APR 9, JUN 2 and 25, and JA to Laf, JUN 11, 1784, ILA 5:222–23, 227, 229, 229n; Doyle, *Oxford History,* 64 (on BF and Mirabeau).

53. Quoted McCullough, *John Adams,* 308–9.

54. Maurois, *Adrienne,* 115–16; Laf to BF, OCT 20, to unknown (probably Adélaïde), OCT 21, to Mme de Simiane (Adélaïde), OCT 21, to William Temple Franklin, NOV 19, 1783, and to Linguet, APR 20, 1784, ILA 5:157–59, 183–84, 382.

55. GW to Laf, MAR 23, 1783, ILA 5:113–16; GW, Memorandum of War Plan, MAY 1, 1782, FGW 25:237–38. The only letter that did not get through in this period was GW to Laf, DEC 15, 1782, FGW 25:433–35. GW's recommendation is GW to PC, MAR 23, 1783, FGW 16:250–51.

56. GW to Laf, APR 5, 1783, ILA 5:119–21. He also reported more deaths, including Lord Stirling's in January, and mentioned that Tilghman was getting married.

57. Laf to GW, APR 19 and JUN 10, and GW to Laf, JUN 15, 1783, ILA 5:124–25, 132–33, 135–36; Laf to GW, JUN 12, 1783, GLW 265; Flexner, *George Washington American,* 500–8; Roc in Chinard, *George Washington as French,* 35.

58. Laf to GW, JUL 22, 1783, ILA 5:145–46, answering GW to Laf, MAY 20, 1783, FGW 26:420–22, which enclosed newspaper accounts of the Newburgh Addresses. GW told Laf that he planned to resign. In JUN 1783 he sent a circular to all the states and to Congress announcing, "I am now preparing to resign it into the hands of Congress, and to return to that domestic retirement, which it is well known, I left with the greatest reluctance . . . it is yet to be decided, whether the Revolution must ultimately be considered as a blessing or a curse: a blessing or a curse, not to the present age alone, for with our fate will be the destiny of unborn millions be involved." FGW 26:4830–96. It was published in Europe in AUG and SEP, but GW had sent Laf an advance copy.

59. Laf to GW, SEP 8, and GW to Laf, OCT 12, 1783, ILA 5:151–57. He also wrote on OCT 30, to ask Laf to buy some plated tableware for Martha. He canceled the order on DEC 4, because he had found what he wanted in New York after the British evacuated. Laf had already bought it, and in April GW acknowledged receipt, and asked for the price so he could reimburse him. GW to Laf, OCT 30, 1783, ILA 5:159–61; GW to Laf, DEC 4, 1783, and APR 4, 1784, FGW 27:258–59, 384.

60. Laf to GW, NOV 11, 1783, and JAN 10, and to HK, JAN 8, 1784, ILA 5:162–64, 186–88, 191–92; Laf to GW, NOV 29, 1783, GLW 272. See also Weintraub, *General Washington's Christmas.*

61. GW to Laf, FEB 1, 1784, ILA 5:194–96.

62. Laf to GW (four letters), MAR 9, 1784, GLW 276–83. The third one is also in ILA 5:208–9.

63. Laf to GW, MAY 14, 1784, ILA 5:216–18.

64. Laf to BF, May 20, 1784, ILA 5:220–22; Isaacson, *Benjamin Franklin,* 426–27.

The king asked BF to join a commission of scientists and physicians looking into Mesmer's claims. One of Mesmer's pupils had split from him and offered a competing theory. Mesmer refused to appear before the commission, but the challenger did, treating Franklin without noticeable effect. The group decided that animal magnetism was nonsense that demonstrated "the power of imagination." Laf defended Mesmer and asked BF to give the quack another chance.

65. Laf to ADR, JUN 20, 25, and 28, 1784, ILA 5:226–27, 229–31. He sailed on the first ship to offer regular passenger service between France and the United States, *Courrier de New York.*

66. Shortly after his arrival, there was a gunfight between rival claimants and commissioners of Pennsylvania and Connecticut over disputed lands in the West. He used that news to urge TJ and others to proceed with a stronger constitution, although "it may be affirmed that this trifling affair is vanishing into nothing." Laf to TJ, OCT 11, 1784, ILA 5:266–67.

67. Laf to Samuel Adams, AUG 7, Address of the Committee of Officers of the Late Pennsylvania Line, AUG 9, Laf to the Committee, AUG 10, and to Adr, AUG 13, and Minutes of the American Philosophical Society, AUG 12, 1784, ILA 5:233–36, 236n; Laf to GW, AUG 10, 1784, GLW 284–85.

68. Laf to Adr, AUG 20, 1784, ILA 5:237–38; Laf to Adr, nd 1784, quoted Maurois, *Adrienne,* 120–21.

69. Wiencek, *Imperfect God,* 259–64; Ellis, *His Excellency,* 160–64; Flexner, *George Washington New,* 39–41.

70. Laf to Adr, AUG 20, 1784, ILA 5:237–38. On the Potomac plan, see Achenbach, *Grand Idea.* See also Ellis, *His Excellency,* 156–58, and Flexner, *George Washington New,* 72–75.

71. Address of the Citizens of Baltimore, and Laf reply, SEP 1, 1784, ILA 5:240–41.

72. JMA to TJ, SEP 7, 1784, ILA 5:241–42. Spain had closed all its ports in Europe, the West Indies, and America to American shipping, including New Orleans.

73. Laf to Ver, SEP 15, and JMA to TJ, SEP 15, 1784, ILA 5:243–44, 243n.

74. Barbé de Marbois' Journal of His Visit to the Territory of the Six Nations, Laf to the Commissioners of Congress, SEP 30, Laf, Account of Meeting with the Six Nations, OCT 3–4, Laf to Adr, OCT 4, to GW, OCT 8, and to prince de Poix, OCT 12, 1784, ILA 5:240–69; Lyon, *Man Who Sold,* 44–45.

75. JMA to TJ, OCT 17, 1784, ILA 5:271–74.

76. Laf to TJ, OCT 11, to Humphreys, OCT 31, and to Adr, OCT nd, 1784, ILA 5:266–67, 276–77.

77. Laf to GW, OCT 8, and to AH, OCT 22, 1784, ILA 5:264–65, 275–76; Laf to GW, OCT 22, 1784, GLW 287.

78. Laf, Recommendation for James, NOV 21, 1784, ILA 5:277–79, 279n. The emancipation was effected in JAN 1787.

79. Laf to JMA, DEC 15, 1784, ILA 5:285–87.

80. Both quoted Maurois, *Adrienne,* 123–24.

81. GW to Laf, DEC 8, 1784, ILA 5:279–80. This is quoted below. See also Maurois, *Adrienne,* 123–24.

82. Resolutions of Congress, DEC 9, 10, and 11, Laf, Address to the Continental Congress, DEC 11, Congress to Louis XVI, DEC 11, Richard Henry Lee to Laf, DEC 11, Laf to JJ and to PC, both DEC 12, to JMA, DEC 15, to GW, DEC 17, and to Samuel Adams, DEC 19, 1784, ILA 5:280–89, 281n, 282n, 285n.

83. GW to Laf, DEC 8, 1784, ILA 5:279–80.

84. Laf to GW, DEC 21, 1784, GLW 288–90.

85. GW to Laf, DEC 23, 1784, ILA 5:289–90.

86. Flexner, *George Washington New,* 414.

Chapter Fourteen

1. Faÿ, *Revolutionary Spirit,* 431–32.

2. Laf to Adr, JAN 23, to NG, MAR 16, and to Jeremiah Wadsworth, APR 16, 1785, ILA 5:292–93, 293n, 302–4, 318–19; Maurois, *Adrienne,* 125–28; Bernier, *Lafayette,* 148–50; Gottschalk, *Lafayette Between,* 162. The Indian boys stayed about three years.

3. TJ to JMA, MAR 18, 1785, quoted Adams, *Paris Years,* 73; Xavier de Schonberg quoted Unger, *Lafayette,* 208–9; Hawke, *Paine,* 175, 185; Bizardel, *First Expatriates,* 5–6; McCullough, *John Adams,* 326–27. Laf said, "I am more and more pleased with Mr. Jefferson. . . . He enjoys universal regard, and does the affairs of America to perfection." Laf to GW, JAN 1, 1788, GLW 334–36.

4. TJ to William Short, MAR 27, 1787, quoted Adams, *Paris Years,* 208.

5. John Ledward quoted Gottschalk, *Lafayette Between,* 267; Laf to JJ, FEB 8 and MAY 11, to NG, to Richard Henry Lee, and to JMA, all March 16, to JA, MAY 8, July 13, and DEC 13, to HK, MAY 11, to Pierre-Samuel du Pont de Nemours, MAY 30, to Patrick Henry, JUN 7, to Jeremiah Wadsworth, JUL 9 and DEC 3, to TJ, to Thomas Boylston, NOV 4 and 20, to Ver, NOV 16 and SEP 4, to James McHenry, DEC 3, and to marquis de Castries, DEC 29, Lee to Laf, JUN 11, TJ to JA, SEP 24, JA to Laf, DEC 13 and 20, all 1785, ILA 5:293–95, 302–4, 307–10, 308n, 320–22, 321n, 322n, 327–28, 331–35, 345–60, 349n; Laf to GW, MAY 24, OCT 8 and 15 (two letters), GLW 311–13, 332–33; TJ to JMA, JAN 30, 1787, quoted Gottschalk, *Lafayette Between,* 30; TJ, *Autobiography,* 76.

6. GW to Laf, AUG 15, 1786, FGW 28:518–22.

7. Laf to American Commissioners, APR 8, 1785, ILA 5:315–16, and related correspondence 316n; Laf to GW, OCT 16, 1786, and JAN 13, 1787, GLW 313–19.

8. Laf to Carmichael, MAR 10, to Patrick Henry and to Madison, both MAR 16, to GW and to HK, both MAY 11, JMA to Laf, MAR 20, 1785, ILA 5:300–2, 305–6, 309–14, 321–23; GW to SS, MAR 19, 1791, FGW 31:247; Laf to GW, JUN 6, GLW 355–57; Laf to TJ, JUN 7, 1791, BTJ 20:539–41; Flexner, *George Washington New,* 258; Lycan, *Alexander Hamilton,* 129.

9. Laf to GW, JUL 9, 1785, GLW 300; Gottschalk, *Lafayette Between,* 252; Malone, *Jefferson and Rights,* 44–46.

10. Gottschalk, *Lafayette Between,* 162.

11. Laf to GW, MAY 11, 1785, ILA 5:322–23.

12. Leader quoted Gottschalk, *Lafayette Between,* 179; Maurois, *Adrienne,* 127–28; Laf to Rabaut de Saint-Etienne, NOV 20, 1785, ILA 5:351–52; Laf to GW, OCT 26, 1786, and FEB 4, 1788, GLW 313–16, 337–39.

13. Condorcet to Laf, FEB 24, 1785, ILA 5:299–300, 300n. Marie-Jean-Antoine-Nicolas-Caritat, marquis de Condorcet (1743–1794), had authored *Réflexions sur l' esclavage des negres* (Reflections on the Enslavement of Negroes, published at Neufchâtel, 1781) under a pseudonym, though the author's identity became widely known. It answered a justification of slavery that had appeared in Paris in 1780, and aimed at refuting systematically all justifications for the institution, including the claim that it was necessary for colonial economies to succeed. The book was the most famous and influential antislavery tract of the eighteenth century.

14. Laf to AH, APR 13, 1785, and MAY 24, 1788, to HK, JUN 12, 1785, and to JJ, JUL 14, 1785, ILA 5:317–18, 318n, 329–30, 335–36; Laf to GW, FEB 6, 1786, GLW 303–10; Kramer, *Lafayette,* 217.

15. Maurois, *Adrienne,* 127–30; GW to Laf, JUN 8, 1786, FGW 28:456–57.

16. Quoted Ellis, *His Excellency,* 163–64.

17. Laf to GW, JUN 6, 1791, GLW 355–57.

18. Laf to GW, FEB 9, MAR 19, APR 16, JUL 14, and SEP 3, 1785, GLW 291–96, 300–2; GW to Laf, FEB 15, APR 12, MAY 12, JUL 25, SEP 1, and NOV 8, 1785, FGW 28:71–75, 132–33, 140, 205–10, 242–45, 308–9; Laf to GW, MAY 11 and 13, 1785, ILA 5:322–27; GWD 4:186.

19. GW to Laf, FEB 15, and MAY 13, 1785, ILA 5:322–27; GW to Laf, SEP 6, 1785, FGW 28:244; Laf to GW, FEB 7, 1786, GLW 303–10.

20. Cornwallis to Alexander Ross, OCT 5, 1785, quoted Gottschalk, *Lafayette Between,* 186.

21. Laf to GW, FEB 6, 1786, GLW 303–10.

22. GW to Laf, MAY 10, 1786, FGW 28:420–25.

23. Laf to GW, MAY 24 and OCT 16, 1786, JAN 13 and FEB 7, 1787, GLW 311–21; GW to Laf, JUN 8, AUG 15, and NOV 16, 1786, and MAR 25, 1787, FGW 28:456–57, 518–22, 29:74–75, 183–86; GWD 5:68, 73. Daniel Shays had raised a tax revolt in western Massachusetts, threatening the national armory at Springfield. This started a chain of events that led to the Constitutional Convention. NG died of sunstroke in Georgia, JUN 19, 1786.

24. Brinton, *Anatomy,* 73; Schama, *Citizens,* 238–47. TJ was at Laf's elbow from then on. See Ellis, *American Sphinx,* 106; TJ, *Autobiography,* 80–81; and TJ to Laf, APR 11, 1787, in Hazen, *Contemporary,* 19–20.

25. Laf to GW, JAN 13, FEB 7, and MAY 1 and 5, 1787, GLW 317–24; GW to Laf, MAR 25, 1787, FGW 29:183–86.

26. Quoted GLW vii–viii. TJ, *Autobiography,* 82, claimed that it was well-known that Laf and three other members were headed to the Bastille, and twenty others and two ministers to banishment, on Calonne's recommendation. "The king found it shorter to banish him."

27. TJ to JA, AUG 30, 1781, quoted Smith, *John Adams* 2:720.

28. Padover, *Life and Death,* 139–40; Brinton, *Anatomy,* 108; GW to Laf, JUN 6 and 30, AUG 15, and SEP 18, 1787, and FEB 7, 1788, FGW 29:229–30, 236–37, 258–60, 276–77, 409–12; Laf to GW, AUG 3, OCT 9 and 15 (two letters), 1787, JAN 1 and 2, and FEB 4, 1788, GLW 324–39.

29. Jean-Pierre Brissot-Warville in Chinard, *George Washington as French,* 87.

30. GW to Laf, FEB 7, 1788, FGW 29:409–12.

31. Hardman, *Louis XVI,* passim; Vovelle, *Fall,* 182–83; TJ to Richard Price, MAY 25, 1788, quoted Malone, *Jefferson and Rights,* 194–95; Ellis, *American Sphinx,* 108–9; TJ, *Autobiography,* 113–14.

32. Ibid., 292–304.

33. Laf to GW, MAR 6 and 18, and MAY 25, 1788, GLW 339–45; GW to Laf, APR 28, MAY 28, JUN 10 and 19, 1788, FGW 29:373–77, 475–82, 506–8, 522–26. No letters from Laf to GW between MAY 25, 1788, and JAN 12, 1790, have survived, although Laf mentioned in 1790 that he had written some. GLW xx, 345n. Specifically, there is no evidence of one he wrote on SEP 5, 1788, mentioned in GW to Laf, JAN 29, 1789, FGW 30:184.

34. Pendleton to JMA, OCT 6, 1788, and TJ to JMA, JAN 12, 1789, HJM 11:412–13, 17:529–30; GW to Laf, NOV 27, 1788, FGW 30:139–40. GW said he had written a long letter on SEP 15, but neither Laf nor anybody else has seen it since.

35. GW to Laf, JAN 29, 1789, FGW 30:184–87.

36. Sears, *George Washington and French,* 7–9, 13–14.

37. Bizardel, *First Expatriates,* 13; Brookhiser, *Gentleman,* 97–113.

38. GM to GW, APR 29, 1789, quoted Hazen, *Contemporary,* 61–62.

39. Schama, *Citizens,* 288–332.

40. Bizardel, *First Expatriates,* 28–30, quoting TJ to GW; TJ to Laf, MAY 6, 1789, BTJ 15:97–98. On Laf in the Estates General, see Gottschalk and Maddox, *Lafayette in French Through,* 46–70.

41. Quoted Gottschalk and Maddox, *Lafayette in French Through,* 70.

42. GM, JUN 23, 1789, *Diary* 1:121.

43. Summarized Unger, *Lafayette,* 234.

44. TJ to JM, AUG 9, 1789, quoted Malone, *Jefferson and Rights,* 193; GM to Carmichael, quoted Unger, *Lafayette,* 234–35.

45. TJ, *Autobiography,* 109–10. On the fourteenth the Bastille housed four forgers, a sexual deviant, and two lunatics.

46. Padover, *Life and Death,* 181; Laf quoted Gottschalk and Maddox, *Lafayette in French Through,* 122–23; GM quoted Brookhiser, *Gentleman,* 103, 114–15; GM, JUL 20, 1789, *Diary* 1:156.

47. Gottschalk and Maddox, *Lafayette in French Through,* 127; GM to GW, JUL 31, 1789, in GM, *Diary* 1:170–72.

48. Brinton, *Anatomy,* 91; Faÿ, *Louis XVI,* 317–29; Schama, *Citizens,* 449–53.

49. Schama, *Citizens,* 451–55.

50. TJ to JJ, SEP 23, 1789, quoted Gottschalk and Maddox, *Lafayette in French Through,* 287.

51. Gottschalk and Maddox, *Lafayette in French Through,* 330–34, Short quoted 385; Schama, *Citizens,* 458–70; Hardman, *Louis XVI,* 172–80; Lever, *Marie Antoinette,* 223–32; Belloc, *Marie Antoinette,* 226–27; Herold, *Mistress,* 89 (de Staël).

52. Gottschalk and Maddox, *Lafayette in French October,* passim; Mirabeau quoted Hardman, *Louis XVI,* 176–77.

53. AH to Laf, OCT 6, 1789, SAH 5:425; see also Kline, *Alexander Hamilton,* 223.

54. GW to Laf, OCT 14, 1789, FGW 30:448–49; Sears, *George Washington and French,* passim.

55. GW to GM, OCT 13, 1789, quoted Unger, *Lafayette,* 259; GW to Catherine MacAuley Graham, JAN 9, 1790, FGW 30:495–98.

56. Schama, *Citizens,* 472–513; Gottschalk and Maddox, *Lafayette in French October,* passim.

57. Laf to GW, JAN 12, 1790, GLW 346; Adr to GW, January 14, 1790, in Maurois, *Adrienne,* 179.

58. Vovelle, *Fall,* 122–24; Maurois, *Adrienne,* 180–81.

59. Laf to GW, MAR 17, 1790, GLW 347–48; Bizardel, *First Expatriates,* 40; Flexner, *George Washington New,* 313.

60. GW to Luz, APR 29, to Laf and to Adr, both JUN 3, 1790, FGW 31:39–41, 44–47. "I have never feared for the ultimate result," TJ said of the Revolution, "tho' I have feared for you personally. . . . Take care of yourself, dear friend." TJ to Laf, APR 2, 1790, BTJ 16:292–93.

61. GW to Laf, AUG 11, 1790, FGW 31:85–88.

62. Schama, *Citizens,* 509–13; Talleyrand quoted Orieux, *Talleyrand,* 93; Short quoted Bizardel, *First Expatriates,* 64–65.

63. Vovelle, *Fall,* 127–28, 132–37, Jean-Paul Marat quoted 128; Mirabeau quoted Unger, *Lafayette,* 270; Maurois, *Adrienne,* 186–87.

64. Laf to GW, AUG 23, 1790, GLW 348–50. Oliver Cromwell was "lord protector" (military dictator) of England in the 1650s. Laf was often called "Cromwell" by his enemies.

65. Schama, *Citizens,* 532–43; Laf to GW, JAN 25, 1791, GLW 351.

66. Laf to GW, MAR 7, 1791, GLW 352–53; GW to Laf, MAR 19, 1791, FGW 31:247–49.

67. Doyle, *Oxford,* 148; Schama, *Citizens,* 549–50; GM quoted Brookhiser, *Gentleman,* 123.

68. Laf to GW, MAY 3, 1791, GLW 353–55.

69. Laf to GW, JUN 6, 1791, GLW 355–57.

70. Schama, *Citizens,* 549–61; Laf and Louis quoted Unger, *Lafayette,* 273–74.

71. Doyle, *Oxford,* 154; Schama, *Citizens,* 566–68; Hardman, *Louis XVI,* 198–99. The statistics depended on which faction was doing the counting.

72. Vovelle, *Fall,* 144–45; GW to Laf, JUL 28, 1791, FGW 31:324–26; Bizardel, *First Expatriates,* 92. GW wrote Laf twice more that fall, praising his achievements and worrying about his situation. GW to Laf, SEP 10 and NOV 22, 1797, FGW 31:362–63, 425–26. He also urged him to take a break in America.

73. GM to GW, DEC 27, 1791, quoted Unger, *Lafayette,* 279.

74. Laf to Short, NOV 16, 1791, quoted Gottschalk, *Lafayette and Close,* 421–23.

Chapter Fifteen

1. Maurois, *Adrienne,* 196–99; Doyle, *Oxford History,* 112.

2. Brinton, *Anatomy,* 131–32; Schama, *Citizens,* 573–87.

3. Quoted Maurois, *Adrienne,* 200. Minister of War Louis Narbonne had been comte de Narbonne-Lara.

4. Goerlitz, *General Staff,* 10–11.

5. Elting, *Sword,* 32–33; Schama, *Citizens,* 599–600.

6. Elting, *Sword,* 32–33, 57–59; O'Connell, *Arms and Men,* 175. Napoleon and Moreau separately developed the army corps in 1800. It was a standing combination of divisions with its own staff, making it possible to assemble a massive force when an enemy army was located. Before 1800, in all armies the word "corps" was a general term for any body of troops.

7. Schama, *Citizens,* 600.

8. Laf to GW, JAN 22, 1792, GLW 358–60. He had written earlier from Chavaniac, but that letter has disappeared. He repeated its account of his country life in this one.

9. Brinton, *Anatomy,* 139–40; Hawke, *Paine.*

10. Laf to GW, MAR 15, 1792, GLW 360–62.

11. GW to Laf, JUN 10, 1792, FGW 32:53–55.

12. James Cole Mountflorence's Account of the French Revolution, transmitted with Mountflorence to TJ, FEB 1, 1793, BTJ 25:119–33, quotation at 122; Elting, *Sword,* 31–32.

13. Schama, *Citizens,* 604–5; Laf to King Louis, JUN 16, 1792, in Memoirs, quoted Unger, *Lafayette,* 281.

14. "Licentiousness under a mask of patriotism is our greater evil," Laf also groused. Laf to GW, JUN 15, 1792, GLW 360–62. TJ congratulated Laf, unaware that everything had fallen to pieces. "Behold you then, my dear friend, at the head of a great army, establishing the liberties of your country against a foreign enemy. May heaven favor your cause, and make you the channel thro' which it may power it's favors." TJ to Laf, JUN 16, 1782, BTJ 24:85–86.

15. Schama, *Citizens,* 609–10; Laf to Assembly, JUN 16, 1792, in Memoirs, quoted

Unger, *Lafayette,* 281; Hardman, *Louis XVI,* 218–20; Asprey, *Rise of Napoleon,* 60–66. "The Marquis Lafayette appeared at the bar of the National Assembly & denounced the Jacobin club, as the cause of all the evils under which the nation labours; it appears that he had a favorable hearing, and that notwithstanding violent attempts to impeach him &c., he had been permitted to leave Paris & rejoin the army, but without effecting his object." John Beckley to JMA, SEP 10, 1792, HJM 14:361–62.

16. Schama, *Citizens,* 610–18; Maurois, *Adrienne,* 205–7.

17. Mountflorence's Account, BTJ 15:128; GM quoted Brookhiser, *Gentleman,* 133.

18. Schama, *Citizens,* 610; Maurois, *Adrienne,* 207–8; Laf to Adr, AUG 21, 1792, in Memoirs, quoted Unger, *Lafayette,* 285–86.

19. Laf to Herr von Archenholtz, MAR 27, 1793, quoted Kramer, *Lafayette,* 51.

20. Duke of Saxe-Teschen, quoted Unger, *Lafayette,* 290.

21. Schama, *Citizens,* 619–41; Elting, *Sword,* 32–33.

22. De Conde, *Entangling Alliances,* 328–30; Sears, *George Washington and French,* 142–47; GM, *Diary* 2:552–55; Brookhiser, *Gentleman,* 133, 151–52.

23. Maurois, *Adrienne,* 207–26.

24. Quoted ibid., 229. See also GM, *Diary* 2:561.

25. Adr to GW, OCT 8, 1792, quoted Sears, *George Washington and French,* 147–48.

26. Ferling, *Leap,* ch. 11; quotations Hazen, *Contemporary,* 262–64.

27. Hazen, *Contemporary,* 220–21; GW to Nicholas van Staphorst, JAN 30 and 31, and to Adr, JAN 31, 1793, 32:321–33.

28. GW to SS, FEB 24 and MAR 13, 1793, FGW 32:355–56, 385–86.

29. GW to TJ, MAR 13, and TJ to GM and to Pinckney, MAR 15, 1793, BTJ 25:382, 387, and footnotes.

30. GW to Adr, MAR 16, 1793, FGW 32:389–90. The drafts and exchanges between TJ and GW are in BTJ 25:390–93.

31. Maurois, *Adrienne,* 236–39; Adr to GW, MAR 13, 1793, quoted Unger, *Lafayette,* 294.

32. Quoted Maurois, *Adrienne,* 233; see also pp. 213–315.

33. GW to Adr, and to GM, both JUN 13, to Nicholas van Staphorst, SEP 1, to SS, NOV 22, 1793, FGW 32:501–2, 33:77–78, 154; Pinckney to TJ, SEP 25, Enoch Edwards to TJ, OCT 28, TJ to GW, NOV 24, to Angelica Schuyler Church, NOV 27, to Pinckney, NOV 27, to John Barker Church, DEC 11, and to GW, DEC 30, 1793, BTJ 27:151, 275–77, 425, 433, 449–50, 502, 643–44; Malone, *Jefferson Ordeal,* 59–60.

34. TJ to GW, DEC 30, 1793, BTJ 27:643–44, 644n.

35. Laf to Adr, OCT 2, 1793, quoted Maurois, *Adrienne,* 239–40.

36. Ibid., 240–61; Schama, *Citizens,* 836–47.

37. Cabinet Minutes JAN 14, GW, Memorandum to State Files, JAN 16, and GW to James McHenry, APR 8, 1794, FGW 33:242n, 243n, 318–19; Pinckney to TJ, JUN 6, 1794, BTJ 28:97. McHenry offered to head a special commission to work for Laf's release.

38. JM, *Autobiography,* 70–71; GM, *Diary* 2:561n; Maurois, *Adrienne,* 258–62;

Ammon, *James Monroe,* 137–38. GM thought that JM took too much credit for Adr's survival, ignoring his own efforts.

39. Maurois, *Adrienne,* 262–64.

40. Quoted ibid., 266–67.

41. Ibid., 265–72.

42. GW to Adr, and to JM, both JUN 5, 1795, FGW 34:210–11; AH to William Bradford, JUN 13, and Bradford to AH, JUL 2, 1795, SAH 18:373–75, 393–97. Asking for British help was AH's idea.

43. Maurois, *Adrienne,* 275–301.

44. Quoted Hazen, *Contemporary,* 251.

45. Quoted ibid., 264. This was reportedly sung to another "plaintive air, composed on the execution of Marie Antoinette, which was current in Philadelphia after that melancholy tragedy."

46. This summary follows Ferling, *Leap,* ch. 11 and 12, passim. See also Freeman, *George Washington,* 7:521–34; Flexner, *George Washington Anguish,* passim; and De Conde, *Quasi War.* In the road-poor West, corn was more profitable distilled into whiskey, because it was easier to transport.

47. GW to Cabot, SEP 7, 1795, FGW 34:299–301.

48. GW to HK, SEP 20, to Acting SS, SEP 23, to AH, OCT 29, NOV 10 and 18, and AH to GW, NOV 19, 1795, FGW 34:310–13, 346, 362, 364, 364n.

49. GW to GWL, and to Frestel, both NOV 22, and to AH, NOV 23 and 28, 1795, FGW 34:367–69, 374–77.

50. GW to AH, DEC 22, 1795, and FEB 13, 1796, to Madison, JAN 22 and MAR 6, to GWL, FEB 28 and MAR 31, to Tobias Lear, MAR 27, and to HK, APR 11, 1796, and GWL to GW, DEC 25, 1795, FGW 34:404, 404n, 424–25, 462, 478, 485–87, 506–7, 35:8, 21; TJ to GWL, JUN 19, and GWL to TJ, JUL 29, 1796, BTJ 29:126, 159–60.

51. GW to Thomas Pinckney, FEB 20, and to AH, MAY 8, 1796, FGW 34:472–74, 35:38–43.

52. GW to Emperor of Germany, MAY 15, 1796, FGW 35:45–46.

53. GW to Thomas Pinckney, MAY 22, 1796, FGW 35:61–63.

54. Benjamin Latrobe quoted FGW 35:141n; GW to HK, JUL 11, to duc de la Rochefoucauld-Liancourt, AUG 8, to Charles Cotesworth Pinckney, DEC 5, 1796 ("I have used, and shall continue to use, every exertion in my power to effect this much desired object"), and JUN 24, 1797, to Gillaume-Mathieu, comte de Dumas, and to Laf's friend and fellow soldier Louis-Philippe, comte de Ségur, both JUN 24, 1791, FGW 35:133–34, 167–69, 308–9, 468–74.

55. Maurois, *Adrienne,* 302–13.

56. GW to AH, OCT 8, to La Colombe, and to William Vans Murray, both DEC 3, to C. C. Pinckney, to Frestel, and to John Marshal, all DEC 4, to GWL, and to Laf, both DEC 5, to Rufus King, DEC 6, to SS, DEC 11, 1797, FGW 36:39–42, 86–99, 104–6; GW to Samuel Williams, JAN 10, 1798, Feinstone Collection, David Library. GW ac-

companied them as far as "the Fedl. City," meaning the future Washington, D.C. GWD 6:261. Some of these letters mentioned a rumor that Laf had been on a ship that foundered off the New Jersey coast; also mentioned TJ to JM, DEC 27, 1797, BTJ 29:593–95.

57. GW to Laf, OCT 8, 1797, FGW 36:40–42.

58. GW to Frestel, DEC 4, to GWL and to Laf, both DEC 5, 1797, and to Samuel Williams, JAN 10, 1798, FGW 36:91–92, 95–98, 121–22.

59. Maurois, *Adrienne,* 313–15, including Laf to Napoleon, OCT 6, 1797.

60. Laf to GW, OCT 6, 1797, GLW 363–65.

61. Laf to GW, DEC 27, 1797, GLW 365–67.

62. Whitlock, *La Fayette,* 90–91; Maurois, *Adrienne,* 334–36.

63. CW, 73–77; Flexner, *George Washington Anguish,* 391–402.

64. Laf to GW, APR 26 and MAY 20, 1798, GLW 368–72; De Conde, *Quasi War,* 217; AH to Laf, APR 28, 1798, SAH 21:451.

65. Laf to GW, AUG 20, 1798, GLW 373–78.

66. Laf to GW, SEP 5, 1798, GLW 378–80; GW to Secretary of State, OCT 18, and Memorandum of an Interview, NOV 13, 1798, FGW 36:496–98, 37:18–20.

67. GW wrote to GWL the same day, knowing others would read the letter also. He told him that he had accepted the army command, "but I hope, and most ardently pray, that the Directory in your country will not, by a perseverence in the insults and injuries which they have heaped on this, make it necessary to resort to arms to repel an invasion, or to do ourselves justice." GW to Laf, and to GWL, both DEC 25, 1798, FGW 37:63–70.

68. AH to Laf, JAN 6, 1799, quoted Morris, *Alexander Hamilton and Founding,* 433; Lycan, *Alexander Hamilton,* 392.

69. Laf to GW, MAY 9, 1799, GLW 391–94. He had also written on APR 19, but only a small fragment survives in Memoirs 5:23–25. It discusses the military picture in Europe.

70. Laf to Adr, AUG 5, 1799, in Maurois, *Adrienne,* 363–64. Laf continued to write to Adélaïde, but Adr wrote to her more often.

71. GW to C. C. Pinckney, AUG 20, to William Vans Murray, OCT 26, and to SS, NOV 3, 1799, FGW 37:325–27, 399–401, 418–19.

72. Maurois, *Adrienne,* 379–81; Elting, *Sword,* 158–162.

73. Flexner, *George Washington Anguish,* 449–54.

74. GW, Last Will & Testament, FGW 37:275–303. Laf's pistols are at 286–87, the slavery provisions at 282–83. This has been published separately in Fitzgerald, *Last Will.* On Laf's influence, see Wiencek, *Imperfect God,* 260–64, 269, which concludes that the connection between Laf's antislavery views, as he expressed them to GW, and the emancipation terms of GW's will, is direct. Virginia law placed so many restrictions on emancipation that it made it nearly impossible. If a master succeeded in overcoming the obstacles, the newly freed slaves must leave the state immediately. A last will and testament, however, had a priority, descended from the Common Law of England, that

state legislatures hesitated to challenge, even on such grounds as not wanting to raise the number of free blacks in the state.

Envoi

1. A typical sentence in the oration was "Yea, your counsel will be heard, O Washington! O warrior! O legislator! O citizen without reproach! He [Napoleon], who still young surpassed you in battles, following your example will heal with his triumphant hands the wounds of the nation." Quotations in Chinard, *George Washington as French,* 127–38, which includes the entire eulogy by Louis, marquis de Fontanes. See also Faÿ, *Revolutionary,* 431–32, and Maurois, *Adrienne,* 389. The letter "W" began appearing in Western languages in the fifteenth century, replacing the Latin "V," which was assuming its modern pronunciations. It entered French in the eighteenth century, with inconsistent usage as it took hold.

2. Maurois, *Adrienne,* 385–91, 398–402; GM quoted Brookhiser, *Gentleman,* 170; Morgan, *True,* 394–96.

3. Maurois, *Adrienne,* 394–98; Memoirs quoted Unger, *Lafayette,* 329–30.

4. Asprey, *Rise of Napoleon,* 403; Schom, *Napoleon,* 224, 305; De Conde, *Quasi War,* 309; Maurois, *Adrienne,* 420–22.

5. Maurois, *Adrienne,* 415–16, 422–23.

6. Asprey, *Rise of Napoleon,* 451, 453n; Ammon, *James Monroe,* 213–15; Brant, *James Madison Secretary,* 244–46; Malone, *Jefferson President First,* 357.

7. TJ quoted Malone, *Jefferson President First,* 355–59; Maurois, *Adrienne,* 424.

8. Maurois, *Adrienne,* 424–37.

9. The chief account of Adr's death is a fifty-page, guilt- and grief-ridden letter Laf wrote in JAN 1808 to his friend, brother of his fellow prisoner, and son-in-law Charles-César-Fay de La Tour-Maubourg, in Maurois, *Adrienne,* 443–61, source of these quotations.

10. Quoted ibid., 462.

11. Laf to TJ, APR 8, 1808, Chinard, *Letters of Lafayette and Jefferson,* 272.

12. Laf to Mme de Staël, MAR 25, 1808, quoted Kramer, *Lafayette,* 150–51; de Staël quoted Maurois, *Adrienne,* viii.

13. Kramer, *Lafayette,* 137–84; Maurois, *Adrienne,* 463–65, Napoleon quoted 464.

14. Laf to TJ, AUG 14, 1814, and TJ to Laf, FEB 14, 1815, in Malone, *Sage,* 131–32.

15. Fouché called Laf "an old imbecile whom one can use like a . . . ladder which one throws down after one has used it." Elting, *Sword,* 638, 658–59, 733 (Fouché quotation); Schom, *Napoleon,* 761–63; Napoleon quoted Carr, *Napoleon Speaks,* 380. This had all been brought about, Laf told TJ, because of the outrages and looting committed by the Bourbons. They aroused patriotic anger, and allowed Napoleon "to reappear as a representative of the Revolution." TJ described Waterloo as the salvation of France. In 1815 Laf told TJ that his eleventh grandchild would receive "the friendly name of Thomas" in

his honor. Laf to TJ, OCT 10, 1815, and DEC 10, 1817, and TJ to Laf, MAY 17, 1816, in Malone, *Sage,* 133.

16. Clary, *Fortress,* 36–70.

17. Stewart, *Restoration,* 37–38, 42; Beard, *Charles X,* 160–61; Artz, *France,* 60–84; Mansel, *Paris,* 119–20, 173–74; de Staël quoted Kramer, *Lafayette,* 146–47.

18. Artz, *France,* 23–24, 59.

19. Kramer, *Lafayette,* 154–71.

20. Idzerda, Loveland, and Miller, *Lafayette Hero;* Kramer, *Lafayette,* 190–96.

21. Ellis, *American Sphinx,* 234; Malone, *Sage,* 402–8, 460; Brandon, *Pilgrimage,* passim; McCullough, *John Adams,* 637; Ammon, *James Monroe,* 541–51.

22. Weinert and Arthur, *Defender,* 51; Clary, *Fortress,* 62.

23. Millis, *Arms and Men,* 89; Hill, *Minute Man,* 29. Among these punches were Chatham Artillery Punch, Richmond Light Infantry Blues Punch, Charleston Light Dragoon Punch, and National Guard 7th Regiment Punch. Brief histories and recipes are in Beveridge, *Cups.*

24. Kramer, *Lafayette,* 253–73. "The state of slavery," he said, "is a most lamentable draw back on the example of independence and freedom presented to the world by the U. S." Laf to George and Clara Bomford, JAN 1, 1826, Feinstone Collection, David Library.

25. Beach, *Charles X,* 207, 243, 301–2; Ridley, *Freemasons,* 205. Freemasons organized several banquets for speakers to criticize the government in 1847, in a prelude to the Revolution of 1848.

26. Beach, *Charles X,* 377–91; Pinckney, *French 1830,* passim; Stewart, *Restoration,* 60–63; Artz, *France,* 36–37; La Fuye and Babeau, *Apostle,* 299; Schama, *Citizens,* 9–15; Kramer, *Lafayette,* 227–51.

27. Mansel, *Paris Between,* 273–75, 284–86.

28. Kramer, *Lafayette,* 171–84; ibid., 330.

29. Maurois, *Adrienne,* 468–69.

30. Quoted Maurois, *Adrienne,* 468.

31. Quoted Kramer, *Lafayette,* 3.

32. Mill, "Death of Lafayette," 1834, quoted ibid., 7.

CHRONOLOGY OF WASHINGTON AND LAFAYETTE

1732	February 22: Washington born
1743	April 12: Washington's father dies; Washington inherits land and slaves
1748	Washington becomes public surveyor
1751	Washington accompanies ailing brother Lawrence to West Indies, contracts smallpox
1752	July 26: Lawrence Washington dies; Washington executor of estate and residuary heir to Mount Vernon, which becomes his in 1761
	November 4: Washington joins the Freemasons
1753	Spring: French forces occupy Ohio Country
	Fall: Washington carries Governor Dinwiddie's ultimatum to the French
1754	Washington becomes lieutenant colonel of Virginia Militia
	April: Washington leads small force into French territory
	May 28: Washington defeats French at Jumonville Glen
	July 3: Washington surrenders at Fort Necessity; Seven Years' War (French and Indian War) begins
1755	July 9: Battle of the Monongahela
	August: Washington appointed commander in chief of Virginia
1757	September 6: Lafayette born
1758	Forbes-Bouquet Expedition against Ft. Duquesne (Pittsburgh)
	December: Washington resigns his commission
1759	January 6: Washington marries Martha Dandridge Custis
	August 1: Lafayette's father killed at Battle of Minden, Prussia; Lafayette inherits feudal holdings and title of marquis

September 13: Battle on the Plains of Abraham; deaths of Montcalm and Wolfe

September 17: Fall of Quebec

1760 April 5: Lafayette's sister born; dies three months later

1763 February 10: Treaty of Paris ends Seven Years' War

1770 April 3: Lafayette's mother dies

May: Lafayette inherits a great fortune from his grandfather

May: In Virginia House of Burgesses, Washington joins the radicals adopting a nonimportation agreement

1771 April 9: Lafayette becomes a sous-lieutenant in the King's Musketeers

1773 April 7: Lafayette becomes a lieutenant in the Noailles Dragoons

1774 April 11: Lafayette marries Adrienne de Noailles

May 19: Lafayette becomes a captain in the Noailles Dragoons

August 5: Washington appointed a delegate to the First Continental Congress

1775 April 19: Lexington and Concord

Summer: Lafayette stationed at Metz, comes under the influence of de Broglie, hears Duke of Gloucester's views on the rebellion in America

June 15: Washington becomes commander in chief of Continental forces; commissioned June 17

June 17: Battle of Bunker Hill

July 3: Washington takes command at Boston

December 15: Lafayette's daughter Henriette born

December 16: Lafayette joins the Freemasons

1776 Early: American campaign against Quebec fails

March 17: British evacuate Boston

Spring-Fall: New York campaign, Washington retreats to White Plains

June 11: Lafayette placed on reserve status

July 4: Declaration of Independence

November 16: British capture Fort Washington

December 7: Lafayette signs contract to serve in the Continental Army

December 26: Washington's victory at Trenton

1777 January 6–May 28: Washington establishes winter quarters at Morristown

February: Lafayette buys ship, visits London

February 3: Washington's victory at Princeton

April 20: Lafayette sails for America

June 13: Lafayette lands in South Carolina

July 1: Lafayette's daughter Anastasie born

July 27: Lafayette reaches Philadelphia, reports to Congress

July 31: Congress appoints Lafayette a "volunteer" major general

August 5: Washington and Lafayette meet, City Tavern

September 11: Battle of Brandywine; Lafayette wounded

October 3: Lafayette's daughter Henriette dies in Paris

October 4: Battle of Germantown

October 17: Burgoyne surrenders to Gates at Saratoga

November 25: Lafayette commands in skirmish at Gloucester

December 1: Congress appoints Lafayette to a line command

December 13: Congress appoints Conway as inspector-general; "Conway Cabal" begins

December 19: Continental Army goes into winter quarters at Valley Forge

December 30–31: Bond between Washington and Lafayette sealed

1778   January 23: Congress selects Lafayette to lead the "irruption" into Canada

February 6: Treaties of commerce and of alliance between France and the United States signed in Paris

February 19: Lafayette assumes command at Albany

February 23: Steuben arrives at Valley Forge

March 31: Lafayette leaves Albany for Valley Forge

May 4: Congress ratifies the treaties with France

May 18: Washington gives Lafayette command of a detachment

May 20: Lafayette's retreat from Barren Hill

June 18: Continental Army leaves Valley Forge

June 28: Battle of Monmouth Court House

July 4–August 12: Lee court-martial

July 11: D'Estaing arrives off New York

July 22: Washington sends Lafayette to Rhode Island

August 8–9: British evacuate works on northern end of Rhode Island

August 11–14: Storm scatters and damages British and French fleets; Howe withdraws to New York

August 21: D'Estaing sails for Boston; uproar begins in Sullivan's command

August 30–31: Lafayette joins evacuation from Rhode Island

September 14: Congress appoints Franklin minister plenipotentiary to France

October 5: Lafayette challenges Carlisle to a duel

October 13: Lafayette asks Congress for leave to return to France

December 23: British take Savannah

1779   January 11: Lafayette sails for France from Boston

February 6: Lafayette lands at Brest

February 12: Lafayette reaches Versailles; confers with ministers

February 12–19: Lafayette in "internal exile"

March 3: Lafayette becomes lieutenant commander of the King's Dragoons

March 14–31: Lafayette-Jones expedition argued and authorized

April 12: French-Spanish alliance confirmed in the Aranjuez Convention

May 22: Lafayette-Jones expedition abandoned; Lafayette commands King's Regiment of Dragoons

June 13: Lafayette appointed aide maréchal général des logis for French-Spanish campaign against England

June 16: Spain declares grievances against Britain, begins siege of Gibraltar

July 16: Wayne takes Stony Point

October 9: British defeat American and French forces at Savannah

November: Expedition against England abandoned

December 1: Continental Army goes into winter quarters at Morristown

December 24: George-Washington Lafayette born

December 26: Clinton sails from New York for Charleston

1780   January 8–16: British fleet captures Spanish convoy and blockading squadron

January–February: Lafayette presses French ministry to send expeditionary force to America

March 20: Lafayette sails for America from Rochefort; arrives Boston April 26

May 10: Lafayette rejoins Washington at Morristown

May 12: Americans surrender Charleston

June 22: Continental Army leaves winter quarters after worst winter of the war

July 10: Ternay and Rochambeau arrive off Newport

July 25–August 3: Lafayette confers with Rochambeau and Ternay at Newport

August 15: Lafayette assumes command of the Light Division

August 16: Battle of Camden; Gates defeated

September 21–22: Washington, Rochambeau, and Ternay confer at Hartford, with Lafayette as interpreter

September 25: Benedict Arnold's treason discovered

September 29–30: André court-martialed

October 2: André hanged

October 7: Battle of Kings Mountain

October 14: Washington appoints Greene to command the Southern Army

November 26: Washington disbands Lafayette's Light Division

December 15: Ternay dies

December 30: Benedict Arnold and his detachment arrive at Portsmouth

1781   January 4: Lafayette negotiates with Pennsylvania Line mutineers

January 5–7: Arnold occupies Richmond

January 17: Battle of Cowpens

January 20–27: Mutiny of the New Jersey Line

February 20: Washington appoints Lafayette to command Portsmouth Expedition

March 1: Articles of Confederation ratified

March 8: Destouche's squadron leaves Newport for Chesapeake Bay

March 15: Battle of Guilford Courthouse

March 16: Battle off Cape Henry (First Battle off the Virginia Capes); Destouche returns to Rhode Island

March 30–31: Portsmouth Expedition returns to Head of Elk

April 6: Washington orders Lafayette and his detachment to Virginia

April 21: Lafayette takes command of American troops in Virginia

April 24: British forces under Phillips and Arnold land at City Point; Cornwallis leads his command out of Wilmington to join Phillips

April 25: Lafayette arrives at Fredericksburg; Phillips enters Petersburg, burns warehouses; Greene's troops repulsed at Hobkirks Hill

April 29: Lafayette's detachment reaches Richmond ahead of Phillips

April 30: Phillips withdraws down James River

May 1: Greene orders Lafayette to remain in command in Virginia

May 6: Admiral de Barras arrives at Boston

May 9: Spanish capture Pensacola

May 10: British evacuate Camden

May 11: British surrender the fort at Orangeburg, South Carolina

May 12: British surrender Fort Motte, South Carolina

May 13: British troops sail from Staten Island to join Phillips; Phillips dies

May 15: British surrender Fort Granby, South Carolina

May 20: Cornwallis joins Arnold at Petersburg, takes command

May 20–25: Lafayette in camp at Richmond

May 22: Washington and Rochambeau meet at Wethersfield

May 24: Cornwallis leaves Petersburg, hoping to capture "the boy"

June 2: French forces under Admiral de Grasse capture Tobago

June 5: Steuben abandons Point of Fork

June 9–21: French army marches from Newport to join Washington in New York

June 10: Wayne and 1,000 Pennsylvanians join Lafayette

June 11–14: Lafayette maneuvers through the back country to shield Continental stores

June 15–16: Cornwallis occupies Richmond

June 19: Steuben joins Lafayette

June 21: After Charlottesville raid, Cornwallis gives up the chase, begins march to Williamsburg; Lafayette follows

June 25: Cornwallis occupies Williamsburg

June 27–July 4: Lafayette in camp near Williamsburg

July 4: Cornwallis abandons Williamsburg, marches toward Portsmouth

July 6: Skirmish at Green Spring

July 9–24: Tarleton's Raid

July 21–24: American and French armies demonstrate against New York

August 2: Cornwallis occupies Yorktown and Gloucester, begins fortifying

August 14: Washington learns that de Grasse is sailing for the Chesapeake

August 18: Cornwallis evacuates Portsmouth

August 19: American and French armies begin march to Virginia

September 2: De Grasse's fleet arrives at Yorktown; French marines placed under Lafayette's command

September 5: Second Battle off the Virginia Capes

September 10: De Barras' squadron arrives in the Chesapeake

September 14: Washington and Rochambeau arrive in Williamsburg

September 26: Lafayette visits de Grasse's flagship

October 3: Skirmish near Gloucester

October 6: Siege of Yorktown begins

October 9: Allied bombardment of Yorktown begins

October 14: Assaults on Redoubts Nos. 9 and 10; second parallel extended to river

October 16: Cornwallis attempts to cross York River, driven back by a storm

October 17: Cornwallis sends white flag to Allied lines

October 19: Cornwallis surrenders

November 4: De Grasse leaves the Chesapeake for the West Indies

November 8–10: Lafayette presides over court-martial of Tory spies

November 23: Congress instructs its ministers to confer with Lafayette

December 5: Lafayette promoted to maréchal de camp

December 23: Lafayette sails for France

1782   January 17: Lafayette lands at Lorient

January 21–22: Lafayette arrives in Paris during celebrations for the birth of dauphin; honored by the queen; pays respects to King Louis XVI

February 12: British surrender St. Kitts to the French

February 25: Vergennes endorses loan of 6 million livres to the United States

March 20: Lord North resigns as prime minister of Great Britain

March 27: Rockingham-Shelburne coalition replaces North's government

April: British emissary arrives in Paris for peace negotiations

April 12: British Admiral Rodney captures de Grasse at the Battle of the Saints

April 16: Last of the United Provinces recognizes American independence

April 18: Lafayette presents proposals for further French campaigns in America

June 17: British parliament passes Enabling Act

June 24: Lafayette received by Masonic lodge Saint-Jean d'Écosse du Contrat Social

July: Rockingham becomes British prime minister; peace negotiations begin in Paris

September: British lift Spanish siege of Gibraltar

September 7: French emissary leaves for England for secret talks with Shelburne

September 17: Lafayette's daughter Marie-Antoinette-Virginie born

September 24: British agent in Paris receives revised commission

October: Plans developed for Franco-Spanish expedition against the British West Indies; Lafayette becomes its land troops commander October 24

October 8: Commercial treaty between the United States and the United Provinces

November 30: Britain and the United States sign preliminary articles to peace

December 2: Lafayette joins Franco-Spanish expedition at Brest

December 14: British evacuate Charleston

December 23: Lafayette lands at Cádiz

December 24: Rochambeau's army sails for West Indies

1783   January 6: Petition from unpaid American soldiers read to Congress

January 20: Britain, France, and Spain sign preliminaries to peace

February 1: Franco-Spanish expedition cancelled

February 5: Lafayette writes Washington asking to be appointed as American representative at treaty ratification in London; proposes joint freed-slave plantation

February 14: Lafayette dispatches first news of preliminary peace to America

February 15: Lafayette arrives at Madrid

February 22: British House of Commons accepts peace but objects to details

February 24: Shelburne resigns

March: Washington puts to rest the Newburgh Addresses; American tobacco merchants complain to Lafayette about difficulties with the Farmers General

Mid-March: Lafayette returns to Paris, accepts rank of maréchal de camp

March 19: Lafayette begins negotiating trade concessions for the United States

March 23: Lafayette's word about the preliminary peace reaches Philadelphia

March 29: Lefévre d'Ormesson replaces Joly de Fleury as controller of finances

April 3: Fox-North coalition takes power in Britain

April 10: Congress passes resolution of approval and thanks for Lafayette's services to the United States in Europe

May 5: Lafayette recommended for the Cross of St. Louis

May 13: Society of the Cincinnati established at Fishkill, New York; Lafayette elected a charter member, later establishes a French chapter

June 28: *Arrêt du conseil* establishes regular packet service between France and the United States

July 2: British order in council prohibits trade between the United States and the British West Indies

August 22: Spain officially receives the American chargé

September: Peace of Versailles and Peace of Paris

October 29: Congress appoints Adams, Franklin, and Jefferson as commissioners to negotiate treaties with maritime powers of Europe

October 31: Congress receives minister from the United Provinces

November 3: Continental Army disbanded

November 4: Calonne replaces d'Ormesson as controller of finances

November 25: British forces evacuate New York City, board their fleet

December 4: British fleet sails out of New York; Washington bids farewell to his officers at Fraunces Tavern

December 13: Lafayette gives Calonne observations on American commerce

December 17: Fall of Fox-North coalition in Britain

December 23: Washington resigns as commander in chief; returns to Mount Vernon

1784   January 9: Lafayette informed of four free ports for American merchants in France

February 10: Lafayette approaches Calonne about restrictions on American trade

May 4: First general meeting of the Society of the Cincinnati, in Philadelphia

May 14: *Arrêt du conseil* proclaims Lorient a free port

May 19: Robert Morris requests Lafayette's help on further trade concessions

June 28: Lafayette sails for America

August 4: Lafayette arrives in New York City; received by State Assembly in Trenton

August 9: Lafayette arrives in Philadelphia

August 12: Lafayette addresses the American Philosophical Society

August 17–28: Lafayette visits Washington at Mount Vernon; as he leaves to resume his tour, Washington embarks on a trek into the wilderness that will lay the foundation for the Potowmack Company

August 30: *Arrêt du conseil* further reduces restrictions on American merchants

September 14: Lafayette receives the freedom of New York City

September 23: Lafayette arrives at Albany; decides to go to Fort Schuyler to negotiate with the Indians

September 29: Lafayette and the French chargé arrive at Fort Schuyler

September 30: Lafayette feted by Indians at Oneida Castle

October: Connecticut confers citizenship on Lafayette and his son

October 2: American commissioners arrive at Fort Schuyler

October 3: Lafayette addresses Indians

October 4: The Indians respond to Lafayette, and he departs; treaty negotiations between the Indian nations and American commissioners begin the next day; treaty negotiated October 22

October 7: Lafayette visits Saratoga battlefield

October 15: Lafayette arrives at Boston

October 19: Third anniversary of Yorktown victory; Lafayette honored by Boston merchants and by the Massachusetts State Assembly

October 20: Lafayette receives honorary degree from Harvard University

October 24: Lafayette honored at dinner of Rhode Island chapter of the Cincinnati

November 10: Commercial alliance between France and United Provinces

November 15: Lafayette arrives at Yorktown; goes on to Williamsburg

November 18–28: Lafayette petitions for James Armistead Lafayette's emancipation; meets Washington in Richmond, spends remaining time with him at Mount Vernon

December 1: Lafayette and Washington tearfully separate for last time

December 6–11: Lafayette visits Congress at Trenton

December 11: Congress praises Lafayette in a letter to Louis XVI; Lafayette takes leave of Congress with an appeal for national unity

December 18: Maryland House of Delegates grants citizenship to Lafayette and to his male heirs in perpetuity

December 20: Governor and other officials bid Lafayette farewell in New York

December 23: Lafayette sails for France

1785 January 20: Lafayette arrives in France

January 24: Lafayette addresses Provincial Estates at Brittany

January 25: First meeting of New York Society for Promoting the Manumission of Slaves

February 14: Congress authorizes $80,000 to treat with the Barbary States

February 24: Congress appoints Adams minister plenipotentiary to Great Britain

March 7: Congress accepts Franklin's resignation as minister to France

March 10: Jefferson appointed to replace Franklin

March 30: Lafayette asked to secure munitions for Virginia

May: Lafayette champions cause of Protestants in France

May 7: French government, prodded by Lafayette, agrees to buy American whale oil

June: Spanish chargé arrives in the United States

June 1: King George III receives Adams as American minister to his court

June 7: Lafayette begins purchase of estate in Cayenne to emancipate slaves

August: Lafayette urges French government to suppress Farm's tobacco monopoly

August–October: Lafayette tours German states, attends military exercises

November–December: Lafayette persuades Castries to purchase naval stores from the United States

November 17: Calonne tells Lafayette the government has reduced duties on American fish oils

1786 All year: Lafayette works for French trade concessions for United States

1787 February 22–May 25: Lafayette a member of the Assembly of Notables

May 24: Lafayette calls for toleration of Protestants and for reform of criminal law

Summer: Washington presides over Constitutional Convention in Philadelphia

1788 Lafayette joins New York Manumission Society

November 6–December 12: Lafayette attends Second Assembly of Notables

1789 March 26: Lafayette elected deputy to the Estates General from Auvergne

April 30: Washington becomes president of the United States

June 27: Lafayette joins with Third Estate, which constitutes itself as National Assembly

July 11: Lafayette presents draft Declaration of the Rights of Man and the Citizen

July 13: Lafayette elected vice president of the National Assembly

July 14: Fall of the Bastille

	July 15: Lafayette becomes commandant of the National Guard of Paris
	October 5–6: The "October Days"; king and royal family escorted to Paris
1790	June 19: Lafayette supports decree abolishing titles of nobility
	July 14: Festival of the Federation
1791	June 21: Flight of the king to Varennes
	July 17: National Guard under Lafayette's command fires on crowd at Champ-de-Mars
	October 8: Lafayette resigns as commandant of the National Guard of Paris
1792	Early January: Lafayette takes command of the Army of the Center at Metz
	May–August: Lafayette commands the Army of the Left
	August 10: Arrest of king and royal family
	August 19: Lafayette impeached by Convention; emigrates and is captured
	September 18, 1792–September 19, 1797: Lafayette imprisoned at Wesel, Magdeburg, Neisse, and Olmütz
1794	November 19: Jay Treaty concluded in London
1795	August 31: George-Washington Lafayette and Félix Frestel arrive in Boston
	October 24: Adrienne and her daughters join Lafayette in prison at Olmütz
1796	April: Washington welcomes George-Washington Lafayette and his tutor into his home in Philadelphia; later takes them to Mount Vernon
	May 15: Washington writes to the Emperor
	September 17: Washington gives his Farewell Address to the newspapers
1797	"Quasi War" breaks out between France and the United States
	March 4: Washington leaves the presidency, retires again to Mount Vernon
	September 19: Lafayette and family released from prison
	October 12: George-Washington Lafayette and tutor leave Mount Vernon
	October 18: XYZ Affair begins
	November: Lafayette moves to Lemkühlen, Holstein
1798	Washington appointed commander in chief of "Provisional Army"
	December 25: Washington writes last letter to Lafayette
1799	January: Lafayette moves to Vianen, Holland
	May 9: Lafayette writes last letter to Washington
	June: Washington signs his will, freeing his slaves
	November 9–10: Establishment of Consulate
	December 14: Washington dies at Mount Vernon
1800	January: Lafayette moves to La Grange
	February 8: Official French funeral for Washington; Lafayette excluded
	March 1: Napoleon removes Lafayette from list of *émigrés*
	September 30: France and the United States agree to new treaty
	October 1–3: Napoleon's treaty celebration at Mortefontaine
1802	Summer: Napoleoon elected Consul for Life; Lafayette opposes
1803	Spring: Congress grants western lands to Lafayette; Monroe arrives in France
	April 30: Louisiana Purchase concluded

1804   May: Napoleon crowned emperor

       Fall: Jefferson offers Lafayette governorship of Louisiana Territory; Napoleon
            awards Lafayette the Legion of Honor and appoints him as a Peer of the
            Realm; Lafayette declines both

1807   December 24: Adrienne dies; buried in Picpus Cemetery, Paris

1815   Napoleon returns; Lafayette begins first of several terms in Chamber of
            Deputies

       June 18: Battle of Waterloo

       June 22: Lafayette arranges Napoleon's abdication, negotiates with Allies

1823   Lafayette loses seat in Chamber

1824   August 16: Lafayette arrives in New York

1825   September 9: Lafayette sails for France

1830   July 28–30: "Three Glorious Days of the Revolution"

       August 16–December 26: Lafayette commands National Guard of the Realm

1834   May 20: Lafayette dies in Paris; buried beside Adrienne in Picpus Cemetery

ACKNOWLEDGMENTS

Being a historian is not a solitary occupation. The work depends absolutely on the dedicated staffs and volunteers who run the institutions that guard our documentary, material, and published heritage. Of the many who have been especially helpful to me during the course of this project, I wish to single out two (in alphabetical order): Rebecca Cape, of the Lilly Library of Indiana University at Bloomington, and Diane Windham Shaw, of the Special Collections and College Archives, Skillman Library of Lafayette College, Easton, Pennsylvania. I have dealt with many archivists and librarians over the years, but from now on the word "archivist" will bring to mind these two outstanding representatives of their profession.

Other research institutions (and especially helpful people in them) who contributed to the work include the Division of Rare and Manuscript Collections of Cornell University Libraries, Ithaca, New York (Elaine Engst): the Library of Congress, Washington, D.C.; the University of Virginia Libraries, Charlottesville (especially those who provide Internet access to the Washington Papers); the Mount Vernon Ladies Association, Mount Vernon, Virginia (Barbara McMillan); the Paul Horgan Library of the New Mexico Military Institute, Roswell (Jerry Klopfer and all the ladies at the desk who arranged so many interlibrary loans); the Roswell Public Library, Roswell, New Mexico; the Library of

Eastern New Mexico University at Roswell; the Golden Library of Eastern New Mexico University, Portales (Elisa Navarro and Ellen Jeane); the Zimmerman Library of the University of New Mexico, Albuquerque; the David Library of the American Revolution, Washington's Crossing, Pennsylvania (Richard Ryerson); the National Archives, Washington, D.C.; and the Office of the Curator, United States Senate (Amy Barton).

Historic places important to this project include Brandywine Battlefield Park, Pennsylvania (Jon Ford); the General Lafayette Inn and Brewery, Lafayette Hill, Pennsylvania (Jordanna Kelly); George Washington Birthplace National Monument, Virginia (Roberta Samuel); George Washington Masonic National Memorial, Alexandria, Virginia; Independence National Historical Park, Philadelphia, Pennsylvania (Andrea Ashby); Monmouth Battlefield State Park, New Jersey (Charles Sary); Morristown National Historical Park, New Jersey; Valley Forge National Historical Park, Pennsylvania; Washington Crossing Historic Park, Pennsylvania; Washington Crossing State Park, New Jersey; and Yorktown Battlefield, Colonial National Historical Park, Virginia (John Short).

A number of individuals also contributed advice, information, or other assistance. Bea Clary, Jim Donovan, John Flicker, Jay Miller, and Diane Shaw graciously agreed to read parts or all of an early draft of the manuscript, offered many useful comments, and helped keep me from making a fool of myself. Jack Frazier and Ian MacGillivray patiently answered my questions about the Freemasons without violating their oaths as members. Thanks to Jim Donovan, my agent, for making the project happen, and to my editor, John Flicker, who with his assistant Nina Sassoon turned it into what you hold in your hands. A special tip of the hat goes to Kristen Conner of the office of Senator Jeff Bingaman, who pointed me to an important source, and to the American Friends of Lafayette (Bill Kirchner and Al Oberst) for their interest, encouragement, and suggestions. And a bow of gratitude to Tracey and Ed Linneweber, who fed a lonely campaigner on his way from one battlefield to the next; visiting old friends is always a tonic.

I am grateful to Independence National Historical Park, the Lilly Library of Indiana University, the Skillman Library of Lafayette College, and the Office of the Curator of the United States Senate for their permission to reproduce illustrations from their collections.

As always, the fullest measure of credit belongs to my long-suffering but eternally patient quartermaster general, my wife, Beatriz Clary. This army of one could not begin to march without her, nor slog on through the struggle without her continuing support. She is really the one who keeps the guns in action.

Credit belongs to all of those good people for whatever is of merit in this book. Fault for whatever falls short is entirely my own.

BIBLIOGRAPHY

Note: Newspaper and newsletter articles are cited in the chapter notes only; the same is true of articles included in books listed in the bibliography.

Archival and Museum Collections

Libraries, archives, museums, historic sites, and other institutions consulted during research for this book are cited in the Acknowledgments.

The Papers of George Washington are housed mostly at the University of Virginia, with another substantial collection at the Library of Congress. The University of Virginia is nearing completion of a publication, in scores of volumes, of every surviving word that Washington wrote, with remarkable indexing and Internet access. His writings pertinent to this volume, however, are available in the earlier efforts of Sparks, Fitzpatrick, and Jackson and Twohig, cited below.

Lafayette's surviving papers are somewhat more scattered. The world's major collection, over 30,000 items, is housed at the Kroch Library, Division of Rare and Manuscript Collections, Cornell University, in the Arthur H. and Mary Marden Dean Lafayette Collection, acquired in the 1960s from the previous guardians in France.

Another significant collection is the store of manuscripts, publications, artifacts, illustrations, and memorabilia in the Special Collections and College Archives of the Lafayette College Library, Easton, Pennsylvania. The Library of Congress has a microfilm copy of the La Grange Collection of Lafayette family documents, the originals of which remain in France. The Lilly Library of Indiana University at Bloomington houses the Walter Gardner Collections of manuscripts, copies, publications, and illustrations related to Lafayette, while the Regenstein Library of the University of Chicago holds the papers of Lafayette expert Louis Gottschalk. Additional troves of Lafayette material include the Gilder Lihrman Collection at the Pierpont Morgan Library in New York, and a substantial Marquis de Lafayette Microfilm Collection in the Special Collections Department of the Cleveland State University Library, while others (mostly duplicated in the repositories) are scattered in several collections and in the autograph market. Many letters and documents pertinent to this book have been published in the various collections by Idzerda, Chinard, Duer, and Gottschalk, cited below.

Published Original Sources

Boyd, Julian P., and others, editors. *The Papers of Thomas Jefferson*. 30 volumes. Princeton: Princeton University Press, 1950–2003.

Boynton, Edward C., compiler and editor. *General Orders of George Washington, Commander in Chief of the Army of the Revolution, Issued at Newburgh on the Hudson, 1782–1783*. 1901. Reprinted Harrison, New York: Harbor Hill, 1973.

Brandon, Edgar Ewing, compiler and editor. *A Pilgrimage of Liberty: A Contemporary Account of the Triumphal Tour of General Lafayette Through the Southern and Western States in 1825, as Reported by the Local Newspapers*. Athens, Ohio: Lawhead Press, 1944.

Butterfield, C. W. *Washington-Irvine Correspondence: The Official Letters Which Passed Between Washington and Brig.-Gen. William Irvine and Between Irvine and Others Concerning Military Affairs in the West from 1781 to 1787*. Madison, Wisconsin: David Atwood, 1882.

Chastellux, le Marquis de. *Travels in North America in the Years 1780, 1781, and 1782*. 2 volumes. London, 1787. Translated by Howard C. Rice Jr. 2 volumes. Chapel Hill: University of North Carolina Press, 1963.

Chinard, Gilbert, editor and translator. *George Washington as the French Knew Him: A Collection of Texts*. New York: Greenwood, 1940.

———, editor. *The Letters of Lafayette and Jefferson*. Baltimore: Johns Hopkins University Press, 1929.

————, editor. *When Lafayette Came to America: An Account from the Dubois Martin Papers in the Maryland Historical Society*. Easton, Pennsylvania: The American Friends of Lafayette, 1948.

Cloquet, Jules. *Souvenirs sur la vie privée du Général Lafayette*. Paris: A. et W. Galignani, 1836. Also published as *Recollections of the Private Life of General Lafayette*. London: Baldwin and Cradock, 1835.

Commager, Henry Steele, and Richard B. Morris, editors. *The Spirit of "Seventy-Six": The Story of the American Revolution as Told by Participants*. 2 volumes. Indianapolis: Bobbs-Merrill, 1958.

Denny, Ebenezer. *Military Journal of Major Ebenezer Denny, an Officer in the Revolutionary and Indian Wars*. Philadelphia: Lippincott, 1859.

Duer, William A., editor. *Memoirs, Correspondence, and Manuscripts of General Lafayette*. New York: Saunders, 1837.

Fitzpatrick, John C., editor. *The Last Will and Testament of George Washington and Schedule of His Property*. Mount Vernon, Virginia: Mount Vernon Ladies Association of the Union, 1939.

————, editor. *The Writings of George Washington from the Original Manuscript Sources, 1745–1799*. 39 volumes. Washington: Government Printing Office, 1931–1944.

Fowler, David J. *Guide to the Sol Feinstone Collection of the David Library of the American Revolution*. Washington Crossing, Pennsylvania: The David Library of the American Revolution, 1944.

Gottschalk, Louis R., editor. *The Letters of Lafayette to Washington, 1777–1799*. Philadelphia: American Philosophical Society, 1944. Revised edition, 1976.

Hutchinson, William T., and others, editors. *The Papers of James Madison*. 17 volumes. Chicago: University of Chicago Press, and Charlottesville: University Press of Virginia, 1962–1991.

Idzerda, Stanley J., and others, editors. *Lafayette in the Age of the American Revolution: Selected Letters and Papers, 1776–1790*. 5 volumes. Ithaca, New York: Cornell University Press, 1977–1983.

Jackson, Donald, and Dorothy Twohig, editors. *The Diaries of George Washington*. 6 volumes. Charlottesville: University Press of Virginia, 1976.

Jefferson, Thomas. *Autobiography of Thos. Jefferson*. New York: Putnam Capricorn, 1959.

Knopf, Richard C., editor. *Anthony Wayne, A Name in Arms; Soldier, Diplomat, Defender of Expansion Westward of a Nation: The Wayne-Knox-Pickering Correspondence*. Pittsburgh: University of Pittsburgh Press, 1960.

Labaree, Leonard W., and others, editors. *The Papers of Benjamin Franklin*. 35 volumes. New Haven: Yale University Press, 1959–1999.

Lafayette, Marie-Joseph-Paul-Yves-Roch-Gilbert du Motier, marquis de. *Mémoires, correspondance et manuscrits du Général Lafayette, publiés par sa famille*. Compiled by George-Washington-Louis-Gilbert du Motier de Lafayette. 6 volumes. Paris: Fournier, 1837–1838. 6 volumes in 2. Brussels: Hauman, Cattoir, 1837. Republished as *Memoirs, Correspondence and Manuscripts of General Lafayette, Published by His Family*.

Partly translated and edited by William A. Duer. 3 volumes. London: Conduit Street, 1837. Volume one reprinted New York: Sanders, 1837.

Lasteyrie, Mme. de (Marie-Antoinette-Virginie Lafayette). *Vie de Madame de Lafayette par Mme. de Lasteyrie, sa fille, précédée d'une notice sur sa mère Mme. la Duchesse d'Ayen, 1737–1807.* Paris: Léon Techener Fils, 1868.

Lauber, Almon W., editor. *Orderly Books of the Fourth New York Regiment, 1778–1780; The Second New York Regiment, 1780–1783, by Samuel Tallmadge and Others, with Diaries of Samuel Tallmadge, 1780–1782, and John Barr, 1779–1782.* Albany: State University of New York Press, 1932.

Lodge, Henry Cabot, editor. *The Works of Alexander Hamilton.* 9 volumes. New York: Putnam, 1885–1886.

Maltby, Isaac. *The Elements of War.* Boston: Thomas B. Waite, 1811.

Martin, Joseph Plumb. *A Narrative of a Revolutionary Soldier: Some of the Adventures, Dangers, and Sufferings of Joseph Plumb Martin. The Memoir Previously Published as Private Yankee Doodle (1830).* New York: Signet, 2001.

Matthews, William, and Dixon Wecter. *Our Soldiers Speak, 1775–1918.* Boston: Little, Brown, 1943.

Monroe, James. *Autobiography of James Monroe.* Edited by Stuart Gerry Brown. Syracuse, New York: Syracuse University Press, 1959.

Morris, Gouverneur. *A Diary of the French Revolution.* Edited by Beatrix Cary Davenport. 2 volumes. Boston: Houghton Mifflin, 1939.

Morris, Richard B., editor. *Alexander Hamilton and the Founding of the Nation.* New York: Dial, 1957.

———, editor. *The Basic Ideas of Alexander Hamilton.* New York: Pocket Books, 1957.

Morse, Horace Henry, editor. *Lafayette Letters in the Bostonian Society.* Boston: Bostonian Society Publications, 1924.

Ogden, Henry A., compiler. *Uniform of the Army of the United States, Illustrated, from 1774 to 1889.* Washington: Quartermaster General's Office, 1889.

Padover, Saul K., editor. *The Washington Papers.* Norwalk, Connecticut: Easton, 1955.

Pickering, Timothy. *An Easy Plan of Discipline for a Militia.* Salem, Massachusetts: Samuel and Ebenezer Hall, 1775. Second edition, Salem: S. Hall, 1776.

Regulations for the Order and Discipline of the Troops of the United States. Philadelphia: Styner and Cist, 1779.

Smith, Paul H., editor. *Letters of Delegates to Congress, 1774–1789.* 8 volumes. Washington: Library of Congress, 1976–1981.

Sparks, Jared, editor. *Correspondence of the American Revolution: Being Letters of Earnest Men to George Washington, from the Time of His Taking Command of the Army to the End of His Presidency.* 4 volumes. Boston: Little, Brown, 1853.

———, editor. *The Writings of George Washington.* 12 volumes. Boston: Tappan and Dennet, 1834–1837.

Syrett, Harold C., and others, editors. *The Papers of Alexander Hamilton.* 26 volumes. New York: Columbia University Press, 1961–1979.

Tower, Charlemagne, Jr. *The Marquis de La Fayette in the American Revolution.* 2 volumes. Philadelphia: Lippincott, 1895, 1901.

Wharton, Francis, editor. *The Revolutionary Diplomatic Correspondence of the United States.* 6 volumes. Washington: Government Printing Office, 1889.

Books and Reports

Achenbach, Joel. *The Grand Idea: George Washington's Potomac and the Race to the West.* New York: Simon & Schuster, 2004.

Adams, Randolph G., and Howard H. Peckham. *Lexington to Fallen Timbers, 1775–1794.* Ann Arbor: University of Michigan Press, 1942.

Adams, William Howard. *The Paris Years of Thomas Jefferson.* New Haven: Yale University Press, 1997.

Alden, John R. *A History of the American Revolution.* New York: Knopf, 1969.

Allen, Gardner W. *A Naval History of the American Revolution.* 2 volumes. 1913. Reprinted Williamstown, Massachusetts: Conner House, 1970.

Ammon, Harry. *James Monroe: The Quest for National Identity.* New York: McGraw-Hill, 1971.

Amory, Thomas C. *The Military Services and Life of Major-General John Sullivan, of the American Revolutionary Army.* Boston: npub, 1868.

Anderson, Fred. *Crucible of War: The Seven Years' War and the Fate of Empire in British North America, 1754–1766.* New York: Vintage, 2001.

Artz, Frederick B. *France Under the Bourbon Restoration, 1814–1830.* Cambridge: Harvard University Press, 1931.

Ashburn, Percy Moreau. *A History of the Medical Department of the United States Army.* Boston: Houghton Mifflin, 1929.

Asprey, Robert. *The Rise of Napoleon Bonaparte.* New York: Basic Books, 2000.

Bailey, Ralph Edgar. *Guns over the Carolinas: The Story of Nathanael Greene.* New York: Morrow, 1967.

Bailyn, Bernard. *Faces of Revolution: Personalities and Themes in the Struggle for American Independence.* New York: Knopf, 1990.

Baldwin, Leland. *The Whiskey Rebels.* Pittsburgh: University of Pittsburgh Press, 1939.

Beach, Vincent W. *Charles X of France: His Life and Times.* Boulder, Colorado: Pruett, 1971.

Belloc, Hilaire. *Marie Antoinette.* Fifth edition. London: Methuen, 1923.

Bendiner, Elmer. *The Virgin Diplomats.* New York: Knopf, 1976.

Bernier, Olivier. *Lafayette: Hero of Two Worlds.* New York: Dutton, 1983.

Beveridge, N. E. (pseudonym of Harold L. Peterson). *Cups of Valor.* Harrisburg, Pennsylvania: Stackpole, 1968.

Billias, George Athan, editor. *George Washington's Generals and Opponents: Their Exploits and Leadership.* New York: Da Capo, 1994.

Bizardel, Yvon. *The First Expatriates: Americans in Paris During the French Revolution.*

Translated by June P. Wilson and Cornelia Higginson. New York: Holt, Rinehart and Winston, 1975.

Boatner, Mark Mayo III. *Encyclopedia of the American Revolution*. New York: David McKay, 1974. Third edition. Mechanicsville, Pennsylvania: Stackpole, 1994.

Bodinier, Gilbert. *Dictionnaire des officiers de l'armée royale qui ont combattu aux Etats-Unis pendant la guerre d'independance 1776–1783*. Vincennes: Bureau d'histoire, 1982.

Bolton, Charles Knowles. *The Private Soldier Under Washington*. New York: Scribner, 1902.

Bonsal, Stephen. *When the French Were Here*. Garden City, New York: Doubleday, Doran, 1945.

Bowman, Allen. *The Morale of the American Revolutionary Army*. Port Washington, New York: Kennikat, 1964.

Boyd, Thomas. *Light-Horse Harry Lee*. New York: Charles Scribner's Sons, 1931.

———. *Mad Anthony Wayne*. New York: Scribner, 1929.

Brackett, Albert G. *History of the United States Cavalry, from the Formation of the Federal Government to the 1st of June, 1863*. New York: Harper and Brothers, 1865.

Brant, Irving. *James Madison*. 6 volumes. Indianapolis: Bobbs-Merrill, 1941–1961.

Brinton, Crane. *The Anatomy of Revolution*. Revised and expanded edition. New York: Vintage, 1965.

Brookhiser, Richard. *Alexander Hamilton, American*. New York: Free Press, 2000.

———. *Gentleman Revolutionary: Gouverneur Morris, the Rake Who Wrote the Constitution*. New York: Free Press, 2003.

Buchanan, John. *The Road to Guilford Courthouse: The American Revolution in the Carolinas*. New York: Wiley, 1997.

Burns, James MacGregor, and Susan Dunn. *George Washington*. New York: Times Books, 2004.

Callahan, North. *Daniel Morgan: Ranger of the Revolution*. New York: Holt, Rinehart and Winston, 1961.

———. *Henry Knox: General Washington's General*. New York: Holt, Rinehart and Winston, 1958.

Carr, Albert. *Napoleon Speaks*. New York: Viking, 1941.

Chadwick, Bruce. *George Washington's War: The Forging of a Revolutionary Leader and the American Presidency*. Naperville, Illinois: Sourcebooks, 2004.

Charavay, Etienne. *Le Général La Fayette, 1757–1823, notice biographique*. Paris: Société de la Révolution Française, 1898.

Chernow, Ron. *Alexander Hamilton*. New York: Penguin, 2004.

Clary, David A. *Fortress America: The Corps of Engineers, Hampton Roads, and United States Coastal Defense*. Charlottesville: University Press of Virginia, 1990.

———. *The Inspectors General of the United States Army: A History, 1775–1903*. Report DAC-11. 3 volumes. Bloomington, Indiana: David A. Clary and Associates, 1983.

———. *These Relics of Barbarism: A History of Furniture in Barracks, Hospitals, and Guardhouses of the United States Army, 1800–1880*. Report DAC-7. Bloomington, Indiana: David A.

Clary and Associates, 1983. Republished Washington: Government Printing Office, 1985.

Clary, David A., and Joseph W. A. Whitehorne. *The Inspectors General of the United States Army, 1777–1903.* Washington: Government Printing Office for the Department of the Army, 1987.

Coil, Henry Wilson. *A Comprehensive View of Freemasonry.* 1973. Revised edition. Richmond, Virginia: Macoy, 1998.

Commager, Henry Steele, and Richard B. Morris, editors. *The Spirit of Seventy-Six: The Story of the American Revolution as Told by Participants.* 2 volumes. Indianapolis: Bobbs-Merrill, 1958.

Compact Edition of the Oxford English Dictionary: Complete Text Reproduced Micrographically. 2 volumes. New York: Oxford University Press, 1971.

Corwin, Edward S. *French Policy and the American Alliance of 1778.* Princeton, New Jersey: Princeton University Press, 1916. Reprint ed. Gloucester, Massachusetts: Peter Smith, 1969.

Cronau, Rudolf. *The Army of the American Revolution and Its Organization.* New York: Cronau, 1923.

Curtis, Edward E. *The Organization of the British Army in the American Revolution.* New Haven: Yale University Press, 1926.

David, Jay, and Elaine Crane, editors. *The Black Soldier from the American Revolution to Vietnam.* New York: Morrow, 1971.

Davis, Burke. *The Campaign That Won America: The Story of Yorktown.* New York: Dial, 1970.

Decker, Malcolm. *Benedict Arnold: Son of the Havens.* New York: William Abbott, 1932. Reprint ed. New York: Antiquarian Press, 1961.

De Conde, Alexander. *Entangling Alliance: Politics and Diplomacy Under George Washington.* Durham, North Carolina: Duke University Press, 1958.

————. *The Quasi War: The Politics and Diplomacy of the Undeclared War with France, 1797–1801.* New York: Charles Scribner's Sons, 1966.

Desjardin, Thomas A. *Through a Howling Wilderness: Benedict Arnold's March to Quebec, 1775.* New York: St. Martin's, 2006.

Dippel, Horst. *Germany and the American Revolution, 1770–1800: A Sociohistorical Investigation of Late Eighteenth-Century Political Thinking.* Translated by Bernhard A. Uhlendorf. Chapel Hill: University of North Carolina Press, 1977.

Dolph, Edward A. *"Sound Off": Soldier Songs from Yankee Doodle to Parley Voo.* New York: Cosmopolitan Books, 1929.

Doniol, Henri. *Histoire de la Participation de la France à l'Establissement des Etats-Unis d'Amérique.* 5 volumes. Paris: Imprimerie Nationale, 1886.

Doyle, Joseph B. *Frederick William von Steuben and the American Revolution.* Steubenville, Ohio: H. C. Cook, 1913.

Doyle, William. *The Oxford History of the French Revolution.* Second edition. New York: Oxford University Press, 2002.

Dull, Jonathan R. *A Diplomatic History of the American Revolution.* New Haven: Yale University Press, 1985.

————. *The French Navy and American Independence: A Study of Arms and Diplomacy, 1774–1787.* Princeton, New Jersey: Princeton University Press, 1975.

Dupuy, R. Ernest. *The Compact History of the United States Army.* Revised edition. New York: Hawthorn Books, 1961.

Dupuy, R. Ernest, Gay Hamilton, and Grace P. Hayes. *The American Revolution: A Global War.* New York: David McKay, 1977.

Eckenrode, H. J. *The Revolution in Virginia.* 1916. Reprint ed. Hamden, Connecticut: Archon Books, 1964.

Edgar, Walter B. *Partisans and Redcoats: The Southern Conflict That Turned the Tide of the American Revolution.* New York: Morrow, 2001.

Ellis, Joseph J. *American Sphinx: The Character of Thomas Jefferson.* New York: Knopf, 1997.

————. *His Excellency: George Washington.* New York: Knopf, 2004.

Elting, John R. *Swords Around a Throne: Napoleon's Grande Armée.* New York: Free Press, 1988. Reprint edition. New York: Da Capo, 1997.

Faÿ, Bernard. *Louix XVI, or, The End of a World.* Translated by Patrick O'Brian. London: W. H. Allen, 1968, and Chicago: Regnery, 1968.

————. *The Revolutionary Spirit in France and America.* Translated by Ramon Guthrie. New York: Harcourt, Brace, 1927.

Ferling, John. *A Leap in the Dark: The Struggle to Create the American Republic.* New York: Oxford Univeristy Press, 2003.

Fischer, David Hackett. *Washington's Crossing.* New York: Oxford University Press, 2004.

Fleming, Thomas. *Washington's Secret War: The Hidden History of Valley Forge.* New York: HarperCollins, 2005.

Flexner, James Thomas. *George Washington and the New Nation (1783–1793).* Boston: Little, Brown, 1970.

————. *George Washington: Anguish and Farewell (1793–1799).* Boston: Little, Brown, 1972.

————. *George Washington in the American Revolution (1775–1783).* Boston: Little, Brown, 1968.

————. *George Washington: The Forge of Experience (1732–1775).* Boston: Little, Brown, 1965.

————. *The Traitor and the Spy.* Boston: Little, Brown, 1975.

————. *The Young Hamilton: A Biography.* Boston: Little, Brown, 1978.

Foner, Jack D. *Blacks and the Military in American History: A New Perspective.* New York: Praeger, 1974.

Fraser, Antonia. *Marie Antoinette: The Journey.* New York: Doubleday, 2001.

Freeman, Douglas Southall. *George Washington.* 7 volumes. New York: Scribner, 1948–1957.

————. *Washington: An Abridgment in One Volume by Richard Harwell of the Seven-Volume George Washington.* New York: Charles Scribner's Sons, 1968.

Ganoe, William A. *History of the United States Army.* Revised edition. New York: Appleton-Century, 1942.

Gerson, Noel B. *Statue in Search of a Pedestal: A Biography of the Marquis de Lafayette.* New York: Dodd, Mead, 1976.

Goerlitz, Walter. *History of the German General Staff, 1657–1945.* Translated by Brian Battershaw. New York: Praeger, 1953.

Golway, Terry. *Washington's General: Nathanael Greene and the Triumph of the American Revolution.* New York: Holt, 2005.

Gottschalk, Louis R. *The Era of the French Revolution (1715–1815).* Cambridge, Massachusetts: Houghton Mifflin, 1957.

———. *Lady-in-Waiting: The Romance of Lafayette and Aglaé de Hunolstein.* Baltimore: Johns Hopkins University Press, 1939.

———. *Lafayette and the Close of the American Revolution.* Chicago: University of Chicago Press, 1942.

———. *Lafayette Between the American and the French Revolutions.* Chicago: University of Chicago Press, 1950.

———. *Lafayette Comes to America.* Chicago: University of Chicago Press, 1935.

———. *Lafayette in America, 1777–1783.* Arveyres, France: L'Esprit de Lafayette Society, 1975.

———. *Lafayette Joins the American Army.* Chicago: University of Chicago Press, 1937.

Gottschalk, Louis R., and Donald Lach, with the collaboration of Shirley A. Bill. *Toward the French Revolution: Europe and America in the Eighteenth-Century World.* New York: Charles Scribner's Sons, 1973.

Gottschalk, Louis R., and Margaret Maddox. *Lafayette in the French Revolution: From the October Days Through the Federation.* Chicago: University of Chicago Press, 1973.

———. *Lafayette in the French Revolution: Through the October Days.* Chicago: University of Chicago Press, 1969, 1973.

Greene, Francis Vinton. *General Greene.* 1893. Reprint ed. Port Washington, New York: Kennikat, 1970.

Greene, George Washington. *Nathanael Greene.* 3 volumes. Boston: Houghton Mifflin, 1871, 1900.

Grenier, John. *The First Way of War: American War Making on the Frontier, 1607–1814.* New York: Cambridge University Press, 2005.

Guthrie, Jas. M. *Camp-Fires of the Afro-American, or, The Colored Man as Patriot.* Philadelphia: Afro-American Publishing Co., 1899. Reprint ed. New York: Johnson Reprint, 1970.

Hale, Edward E., and Edward E. Hale Jr. *Franklin in France.* Boston: Roberts Brothers, 1887.

Hamersly, Thomas H. S. *Complete Army Register for 100 Years (1779–1879).* Washington: Hamersly, 1881.

Hardman, John. *Louis XVI.* New Haven: Yale University Press, 1993.

Hatch, Louis C. *The Administration of the American Revolutionary Army.* New York: Longmans Greene, 1904.

Hawke, Daniel Freeman. *Paine.* New York: Harper and Row, 1974.

Hazen, Charles Downer. *Contemporary American Opinion of the French Revolution.* Baltimore: Johns Hopkins University Press, 1897. Reprint ed. Gloucester, Massachusetts: Peter Smith, 1964.

Heitman, Francis B. *Historical Register and Dictionary of the United States Army, from Its Organization, September 29, 1789, to March 2, 1903.* 2 volumes. Washington: Government Printing Office, 1903.

————. *Historical Register of Officers of the Continental Army During the Wars of the Revolution, April, 1775, to December, 1783.* Revised edition. Washington: Rare Book Shop, 1914.

Herold, J. Christopher. *Mistress to an Age: A Life of Madame de Staël.* Indianapolis: Bobbs-Merrill, 1958.

Higginbotham, Don. *Daniel Morgan: Revolutionary Rifleman.* Chapel Hill: University of North Carolina Press, 1961.

————. *The War of American Independence: Military Attitudes, Policies, and Practice, 1763–1789.* New York: Macmillan, 1971.

————, editor. *Reconsideration of the Revolutionary War: Selected Essays.* Westport, Connecticut: Greenwood, 1978.

Hill, Jim Dan. *The Minute Man in Peace and War: A History of the National Guard.* Harrisburg, Pennsylvania: Stackpole, 1963, 1964.

Hoffman, Ronald, and Peter J. Abbot, editors. *Diplomacy and Revolution: The Franco-American Alliance of 1778.* Charlottesville: University Press of Virginia, 1981.

Huston, James A. *The Sinews of War: Army Logistics, 1775–1953.* Washington: Government Printing Office, 1966.

Idzerda, Stanley J., Anne C. Loveland, and Marc H. Miller. *Lafayette, Hero of Two Worlds: The Art and Pageantry of His Farewell Tour of America, 1824–1825.* Hanover and London: The Queens Museum, 1989.

Idzerda, Stanley J., and Roger E. Smith. *France and the American War for Independence.* np: Scott Limited Editions, nd.

Ingersoll, L. D. *A History of the War Department of the United States, with Biographical Sketches of the Secretaries.* Washington: Francis D. Mohun, 1880.

Isaacson, Walter. *Benjamin Franklin: An American Life.* New York: Simon & Schuster, 2003.

Jacobs, James R. *Tarnished Warrior: Major-General James Wilkinson.* New York: Macmillan, 1938.

Kapp, Friedrich. *The Life of Frederick William von Steuben, Major General in the Revolutionary Army.* Second edition. New York: Mason Brothers, 1859.

————. *The Life of John Kalb, Major-General in the Revolutionary Army.* New York: Mason Brothers, 1870.

Ketchum, Richard M. *Saratoga: Turning Point of America's Revolutionary War.* New York: Holt, 1999.

————. *Victory at Yorktown: The Campaign That Won the Revolution.* New York: Holt, 2004.

Kline, Mary-Jo, editor. *Alexander Hamilton: A Biography in His Own Words*. 2 volumes. New York: Newsweek, 1973.

Koenig, William J. *Americans at War, from Colonial Wars to Vietnam*. New York: Putnam, 1980.

Kohn, Richard H. *Eagle and Sword: The Federalists and the Creation of the Military Establishment in America, 1783–1802*. New York: Free Press, 1975.

Kramer, Lloyd. *Lafayette in Two Worlds: Public Cultures and Personal Identities in an Age of Revolutions*. Chapel Hill: University of North Carolina Press, 1996.

Kreidberg, Marvin A., and Merton G. Henry. *History of Military Mobilization in the United States Army, 1775–1945*. Washington: Department of the Army, 1955.

Lafayette in Virginia. Baltimore: Johns Hopkins University Press, 1928.

La Fuye, Maurice de, and Emile Babeau. *The Apostle of Liberty: A Life of La Fayette*. Translated by Edward Hyams. New York: Thomas Yoseloff, 1956.

Lancaster, Bruce. *From Lexington to Liberty: The Story of the American Revolution*. Garden City, New York: Doubleday, 1955.

Lanctot, Gustave. *Canada and the American Revolution, 1774–1783*. Cambridge: Harvard University Press, 1967.

Lane, Jason. *General and Madame de Lafayette: Partners in Liberty's Cause in the American and French Revolutions*. Lanham, Maryland: Taylor, 2003.

Leach, Douglas Edward. *Arms for Empire: A Military History of the British Colonies in North America, 1607–1763*. New York: Macmillan, 1973.

Leckie, Robert. *George Washington's War: The Saga of the American Revolution*. New York: HarperCollins, 1992.

———. *The Wars of America*. 2 volumes. New York: Harper and Row, 1968.

Lefkowitz, Arthur S. *George Washington's Indispensable Men: The 32 Aides-de-Camp Who Helped Win American Independence*. Mechanicsburg, Pennsylvania: Stackpole, 2003.

Lengel, Edward G. *General George Washington: A Military Life*. New York: Random House, 2005.

Lever, Evelyne. *Marie Antoinette: The Last Queen of France*. Translated by Catherine Temerson. New York: Farrar, Straus and Giroux, 2000.

Levi, Anthony. *Louis XIV*. New York: Carroll and Graf, 2004.

Lewis, Thomas A. *For King and Country: The Maturing of George Washington, 1748–1760*. New York: HarperCollins, 1993.

Lossing, Benson J. *The Pictorial Field Book of the Revolution*. 2 volumes. New York: Harper and Brothers, 1860.

Lumpkin, Henry. *From Savannah to Yorktown: The American Revolution in the South*. Columbia: University of South Carolina Press, 1981.

Lycan, Gilbert L. *Alexander Hamilton and American Foreign Policy: A Design for Greatness*. Norman: University of Oklahoma Press, 1970.

Lyon, E. Wilson. *The Man Who Sold Louisiana: The Career of François Barbé-Marbois*. Norman: University of Oklahoma Press, 1942.

Mahan, Alfred Thayer. *The Influence of Sea Power upon History, 1660–1783*. Twelfth edition. Boston: Little, Brown, 1918.

Malone, Dumas. *Jefferson and the Ordeal of Liberty.* Boston: Little, Brown, 1962.

————. *Jefferson and the Rights of Man.* Boston: Little, Brown, 1951.

————. *Jefferson the President: First Term, 1801–1805.* Boston: Little, Brown, 1970.

————. *Jefferson the Virginian.* Boston: Little, Brown, 1948.

————. *The Sage of Monticello.* Boston: Little, Brown, 1981.

Manceron, Claude. *The Wind from America, 1773–1781.* Translated by Nancy Amphoux. New York: Knopf, 1978.

Mansel, Philip. *Paris Between Empires, 1814–1852: Monarchy and Revolution.* London: Phoenix, 2001.

Martin, David G. *The Philadelphia Campaign: June 1777–July 1778.* New York: Da Capo, 2003.

Martin, James Kelly. *Benedict Arnold, Revolutionary Hero: An American Warrior Reconsidered.* New York: New York University Press, 1997.

Martin, James Kirby, and Mark Edward Lender. *A Respectable Army: The Military Origins of the Republic, 1763–1789.* Arlington Heights, Illinois: Harland Davidson, 1982.

Massey, Gregory D. *John Laurens and the American Revolution.* Columbia: University of South Carolina Press, 2000.

Maurois, André. *Adrienne, ou la vie de Mme de La Fayette.* Paris: Hachette, 1960. Translated by Gerard Hopkins as *Adrienne: The Life of the Marquise de La Fayette.* New York: McGraw-Hill, 1961.

McCabe, Lida Rose. *Ardent Adrienne.* New York: Appleton, 1930.

McCullough, David. *John Adams.* New York: Simon & Schuster, 2001.

————. *1776.* New York: Simon & Schuster, 2005.

McDonald, Forrest. *Alexander Hamilton: A Biography.* New York: Norton, 1979.

Merrill, James M., editor. *Uncommon Valor: The Exciting Story of the Army.* Chicago: Rand-McNally, 1964.

Miller, John C. *The Federalist Era, 1789–1801.* New York: Harper and Row, 1963.

Miller, Melanie. *Envoy to the Terror: Gouverneur Morris and the French Revolution.* New York: Brassey, 2004.

Millis, Walter. *Arms and Men: A Study in American Military History.* New York: Putnam, 1956. Reprint edition. New York: New American Library, nd.

Morgan, George. *The True Lafayette.* Philadelphia: Lippincott, 1919.

Morison, Samuel Eliot. *John Paul Jones: A Sailor's Biography.* Boston: Little, Brown, 1959. Reprint ed. Newport, Rhode Island: Naval Institute Press, 1990.

Morris, Richard B. *The Peacemakers: The Great Powers and American Independence.* New York: Harper and Row, 1965.

Morrisey, Brendan, and Adam Hook. *Yorktown 1781: The World Turned Upside Down.* London: Osprey, 1997.

Mowday, Bruce E. *September 11, 1777: Washington's Defeat at Brandywine Dooms Philadelphia.* Shippensburg, Pennsylvania: White Mane Books, 2002.

Myers, Minor, Jr. *Liberty Without Anarchy: A History of the Society of the Cincinnati.* Charlottesville: University of Virginia Press, 1982.

Nelson, Paul David. *Anthony Wayne: Soldier of the Early Republic*. Bloomington: Indiana University Press, 1985.

———. *General Horatio Gates: A Biography*. Baton Rouge: Louisiana State University Press, 1976.

Ney, Virgil. *Evolution of the United States Army Field Manual: Valley Forge to Vietnam*. Appendix B, Report of the Field Manual Review Board. Ft. Belvoir, Virginia: U.S. Army Combat Developments Command, 1966.

Nolan, J. Bennett. *Lafayette in America Day by Day*. Baltimore: Johns Hopkins University Press, 1934.

O'Connell, Robert L. *Of Arms and Men: A History of War, Weapons, and Aggression*. New York: Oxford University Press, 1989.

Orieux, Jean. *Talleyrand: The Art of Survival*. Translated by Patricia Wolf. New York: Knopf, 1974.

Padover, Saul K. *The Life and Death of Louix XVI*. London: Alvin Redman, 1965.

Palmer, John McAuley. *General von Steuben*. New Haven: Yale University Press, 1937.

———. *Washington, Lincoln, Wilson: Three War Statesmen*. Garden City, New York: Doubleday, Doran, 1930.

Pancake, John S. *1777: The Year of the Hangman*. Tuscaloosa: University of Alabama Press, 1977, 1992.

Parkman, Francis. *Montcalm and Wolfe: The French and Indian War*. 1884. Reprinted New York: Da Capo, 1984, 2001.

Parsons, John R., Jr. *History of Inspection in the Armed Forces*. Washington: Department of Defense, 1981.

Patterson, Samuel White. *Horatio Gates: Defender of American Liberties*. New York: Columbia University Press, 1941.

Penman, John Simpson. *Lafayette and Three Revolutions*. Boston: Stratford, 1929.

Perkins, James Breck. *France in the American Revolution*. Rochester, New York: University of Rochester Press, 1911. Reprint ed. Williamstown, Massachusetts: Corner House, 1970.

Pialoux, Paul. *Lafayette: Trois révolutions pour la liberté*. Brioude: Watel, 1989.

Pinkney, David H. *The French Revolution of 1830*. Princeton: Princeton University Press, 1972.

Pratt, Fletcher. *Eleven Generals: Studies in American Command*. New York: Sloane, 1949.

Preston, John Hyde. *A Gentleman Rebel: Mad Anthony Wayne*. Garden City, New York: Garden City Publishing, 1930, and Murray Hill, New York: Farrar and Rinehart, 1930.

Quarles, Benjamin. *The Negro in the American Revolution*. 1961. Reprint ed. New York: Norton, 1973.

Randall, Willard Sterne. *Benedict Arnold: Patriot and Traitor*. New York: Morrow, 1990.

Rankin, Hugh F. *The American Revolution*. New York: Putnam, 1964.

———. *The War of the Revolution in Virginia*. Williamsburg: Virginia Independence Bicentennial Commission, 1979.

Reinhardt, George C., and William R. Kintner. *The Haphazard Years: How America Has Gone to War*. Garden City, New York: Doubleday, 1960.

Ridley, Jasper. *The Freemasons: A History of the World's Most Powerful Secret Society*. New York: Arcade, 2001.

Riling, Joseph R. *Baron von Steuben and His Regulations*. Philadelphia: Ray Riling Arms Books, 1966.

Risch, Erna. *Quartermaster Support of the Army: A History of the Corps, 1775–1939*. Washington: Department of the Army, 1962.

Roberts, Allen E. *George Washington: Master Mason*. Richmond, Virginia: Macoy, 1976.

Rose, Alexander. *Washington's Spies: The Story of America's First Spy Ring*. New York: Bantam Dell, 2006.

Rossie, Jonathan Gregory. *The Politics of Command in the American Revolution*. Syracuse: Syracuse University Press, 1975.

Royster, Charles. *Light-Horse Harry Lee and the Legacy of the American Revolution*. New York: Knopf, 1981.

Ryan, Dennis P., editor. *A Salute to Courage: The American Revolution as Seen Through Wartime Writings of Officers of the Continental Army and Navy*. New York: Columbia University Press, 1979.

Sanger, J. P. *The Inspector-General's Department*. Appendix L to Annual Report of the Inspector General 1900, House Document 2, 56th Congress, 2nd Session, Volume 1, Part 3. Washington: Government Printing Office, 1900.

Schama, Simon. *Citizens: A Chronicle of the French Revolution*. New York: Vintage, 1989.

Schecter, Barnet. *The Battle for New York: The City at the Heart of the American Revolution*. New York: Walker, 2002.

Scheer, George F., and Hugh F. Rankin. *Rebels and Redcoats*. New York: World, 1957.

Schoenbrun, David. *Triumph in Paris: The Exploits of Benjamin Franklin*. New York: Harper and Row, 1976.

Schom, Alan. *Napoleon Bonaparte*. New York: HarperCollins, 1997.

Sears, Louis Martin. *George Washington and the French Revolution*. Detroit: Wayne State University Press, 1960.

Sedgwick, Henry Dwight. *Lafayette*. Indianapolis: Bobbs-Merrill, 1928.

Selby, John. *The Road to Yorktown*. New York: St. Martin's, 1976.

Shy, John. *Toward Lexington: The Role of the British Army in the Coming of the American Revolution*. Princeton: Princeton University Press, 1965.

Sichel, Edith. *The Household of the Lafayettes*. New York: Macmillan, 1900.

Six, Georges. *Dictionnaire biographique des généraux & amiraux français de la révolution et de l'empire (1794–1814)*. Paris: Georges Saffroy, 1934.

Smith, Page. *John Adams*. 2 volumes. Garden City, New York: Doubleday, 1962.

Smith, Richard Norton. *Patriarch: George Washington and the New American Nation*. Boston: Houghton Mifflin, 1993.

Sparks, Jared. *Life of Gouverneur Morris*. 3 volumes. Boston: Gray and Bowen, 1832.

———. *The Life of Washington*. Boston: Tappan and Dennet, 1843.

Spaulding, Oliver Lyman. *The United States Army in War and Peace*. New York: Putnam, 1937.

Steiner, Bernard C. *The Life and Correspondence of James McHenry, Secretary of War Under Washington and Adams*. Cleveland: Burrows Brothers, 1907.

Stewart, John Hall. *The Restoration Era in France, 1814–1830*. Princeton, New Jersey: D. Van Nostrand, 1968.

Stinchcombe, William C. *The American Revolution and the French Alliance*. Syracuse: Syracuse University Press, 1969.

Symonds, Craig L. *A Battlefield Atlas of the American Revolution*. Mount Pleasant, South Carolina: Nautical and Aviation Publishing Company of America, 1986.

Taafe, Stephen R. *The Philadelphia Campaign, 1777–1778*. Lawrence: University Press of Kansas, 2003.

Thane, Elswyth. *The Fighting Quaker: Nathanael Greene*. New York: Hawthorn, 1964.

Thayer, Theodore. *Nathanael Greene: Strategist of the American Revolution*. New York: Twayne, 1960.

Thomas, Evan. *John Paul Jones: Sailor, Hero, Father of the American Navy*. New York: Simon & Schuster, 2003.

Thompson, J. M. *Leaders of the French Revolution*. New York: Appleton, 1929.

Thomson, Valentine. *Knight of the Seas: The Adventurous Life of John Paul Jones*. New York: Liveright, 1939.

Townsend, Sara Bertha. *An American Soldier: The Life of John Laurens Drawn Largely from Correspondence Between His Father and Himself*. Raleigh, North Carolina: Edwards and Broughton, 1958.

Trussell, John B., Jr. *Birthplace of an Army: A Study of the Valley Forge Encampments*. Harrisburg: Pennsylvania Historical and Museum Commission, 1976.

Tucker, Glenn. *Mad Anthony Wayne and the New Nation*. Harrisburg, Pennsylvania: Stackpole, 1973.

Tuckerman, Bayard. *Life of General Lafayette*. 2 volumes. New York: Dodd, Mead, 1889.

Unger, Harlow Giles. *John Hancock: Merchant King and American Patriot*. New York: Wiley, 2000.

———. *Lafayette*. New York: Wiley, 2002.

Van Doren, Carl. *Mutiny in January*. New York: Viking, 1943.

Vovelle, Michel. *The Fall of the French Monarchy, 1787–1792*. Translated by Susan Burke. Cambridge: Cambridge University Press, 1984.

Walker, Paul K. *Engineers of Independence: A Documentary History of Army Engineers in the American Revolution, 1775–1783*. Washington: Corps of Engineers, 1981.

Ward, Harry M. *The Department of War, 1781–1795*. Pittsburgh: University of Pittsburgh Press, 1962.

Weber, David J. *The Spanish Frontier in North America*. New Haven: Yale University Press, 1992.

Weigley, Russell F. *History of the United States Army*. New York: Macmillan, 1967.

Weinert, Richard P., Jr., and Robert Arthur. *Defender of the Chesapeake: The Story of Fort Monroe*. Annapolis: Leeward Publications, 1978.

Weintraub, Stanley. *General Washington's Christmas Farewell: A Mount Vernon Homecoming, 1783.* New York: Free Press, 2003.

———. *Iron Tears: America's Battle for Freedom, Britain's Quagmire, 1775–1783.* New York: Free Press, 2005.

Whitlock, Brand. *La Fayette.* 2 volumes. New York: Appleton, 1929.

Whitridge, Arnold. *Rochambeau.* New York: Collier-Macmillan, 1965.

Wickwire, Franklin and Mary. *Cornwallis: The American Adventure.* Boston: Houghton Mifflin, 1970.

Wiencek, Henry. *An Imperfect God: George Washington, His Slaves, and the Creation of America.* New York: Farrar, Straus and Giroux, 2003.

Williams, Glenn F. *Year of the Hangman: George Washington's Campaign Against the Iroquois.* Yardley, Pennsylvania: Westholme, 2005.

Williams, T. Harry. *The History of American Wars from Colonial Times to World War I.* New York: Knopf, 1981.

Wood, Gordon S. *The Americanization of Benjamin Franklin.* New York: Penguin, 2004.

Woodward, W. E. *Lafayette.* New York: Farrar and Rinehart, 1932.

Wright, Constance. *Madame de Lafayette.* New York: Henry Holt, 1959.

Wright, Robert K., Jr. *The Continental Army.* Washington: Department of the Army, 1983.

Periodicals

Ammon, Henry, editor. "Letters of William Carmichael to John Cadwalader." *Maryland Historical Magazine* 44 (1949): 2–30.

Applegate, Howard L. "The Medical Administrators of the American Revolutionary Army." *Military Affairs* 25 (Spring 1961): 1–10.

Beard, William E. "The Castle of Rip Raps." *Coast Artillery Journal* 78 (1935): 44–48.

Benton, William A. "Pennsylvania Revolutionary Officers and the Federal Constitution." *Pennsylvania History* 31 (1964): 419–35.

Betz, I. H. "The Conway Cabal at York, Pennsylvania, 1777–1778." *Pennsylvanian German* 9 (1908): 248–54.

Bill, Shirley A., and Louis Gottschalk. "Silas Deane's 'Worthless' Agreement with Lafayette." *Prologue: The Journal of the National Archives* 4 (1972): 219–23.

Boucher, Ronald L. "The Colonial Militia as a Social Institution: Salem, Massachusetts, 1764–1775." *Military Affairs* 37 (December 1973): 125–30.

Brenneman, Gloria E. "The Conway Cabal: Myth or Reality?" *Pennsylvania History* 40 (April 1973): 169–77.

Call, Luther P. "The History, Organization, and Function of the Inspector General's Department." *Reserve Officer* 16 (October 1939): 11–13.

Carter, William H. "Bvt. Maj.-Gen. Simon Bernard." *Journal of the Military Services Institution of the United States* 51 (1912): 147–55.

————. "The Evolution of Army Reforms." *United Service*, Third Series 3 (May 1903): 1190–98.

Cooke, Jacob E. "The Whiskey Insurrection." *Pennsylvania History* 30 (1963): 316–46.

Corwin, Edward E. "The French Objectives in the American Revolution." *American Historical Review* 31 (1915): 33–61.

"Coudray's Observations on Forts for Defense of the Delaware, July 1777." *Pennsylvania Magazine of History and Biography* 24 (1900): 343–47.

Dennison, George M. "Martial Law: The Development of a Theory of Emergency Powers, 1776–1861." *American Journal of Legal History* 18 (January 1974).

Echeverria, Durand, and Orville T. Murphy. "The American Revolutionary Army: A French Estimate in 1777." *Military Affairs* 27 (Spring 1963): 1–7.

————. "The American Revolutionary Army: A French Estimate in 1777—Part II, Personnel." *Military Affairs* 27 (Winter 1963–64): 153–62.

Ekirch, Arthur A., Jr. "The Idea of a Citizen Army." *Military Affairs* 17 (Spring 1953): 30–36.

Ford, Worthington C. "Defenses of Philadelphia." *Pennsylvania Magazine of History and Biography* 18 (1894): 334–37.

Forman, Sidney. "Thomas Jefferson on Universal Military Training." *Military Affairs* 11 (Fall 1947): 177–78.

————. "Why the United States Military Academy Was Established in 1902." *Military Affairs* 29 (Spring 1965): 16–28.

Gottschalk, Louis R. "Lafayette as a Commercial Agent." *American Historical Review* 36 (1931): 561–70.

Gottschalk, Louis R., and Milancie Hill Sheldon, editors. "More Letters on the Management of an Estate During the Old Regime." *Journal of Modern History* 17 (1945): 148–52.

Karsten, Peter. "The American Democratic Citizen Soldier: Triumph or Disaster?" *Military Affairs* 30 (Spring 1966): 34–40.

Ketcham, Ralph L. "France and American Politics, 1763–1793." *Political Science Quarterly* 78 (1963): 198–223.

Kite, Elizabeth S. "French 'Secret Aid' Precursor to the French-American Alliance, 1776–1777." *French American Review* 1 (1948): 143–52.

Knollenberg, Bernhard. "John Adams, Knox, and Washington." *Proceedings of the American Antiquarian Society* 56 (October 1946, part 2): 207–38.

Lane, Jack C. "American Military Past: The Need for New Approaches." *Military Affairs* 41 (October 1977): 109–13.

Mahon, John K. "Anglo-American Methods of Indian Warfare, 1676–1794." *Mississippi Valley Historical Review* 45 (September 1958): 254–75.

————. "Pennsylvania and the Beginnings of the Regular Army." *Pennsylvania History* 21 (1954): 33–44.

Maurer, Maurer. "Military Justice Under General Washington." *Military Affairs* 28 (Spring 1964): 8–16.

Meng, John J. "A Foot-Note to Secret Aid in the American Revolution." *American Historical Review* 43 (1938): 791–95.

Morton, Louis. "The Origins of American Military Policy." *Military Affairs* 22 (Summer 1958): 75–82.

Murphy, Orville T. "The French Professional Soldier's Opinion of the American Militia in the War of the Revolution." *Military Affairs* 32 (February 1969): 191–98.

Nelson, Paul David. "Citizen Soldiers or Regulars: The Views of American General Officers on the Military Establishment, 1775–1781." *Military Affairs* 43 (October 1972): 126–32.

———. "Legacy of Controversy: Gates, Schuyler, and Arnold at Saratoga, 1777." *Military Affairs* 37 (April 1973): 41–47.

Noel, Percy, translator. "Our Revolutionary Forefathers: The Journal of François, Marquis de Barbé-Marbois." *Atlantic Monthly* 142 (1928).

Nussbaum, F. L. "The Revolutionary Vergennes and Lafayette Versus the Farmers General." *Journal of Modern History* 3 (1931): 599–613.

Poirier, Noel B. "Three Elements of Survival." *Journal of America's Military Past* 30 (Fall 2004): 21–33.

Quaife, Milo M., editor. "A Picture of the First United States Army: The Journal of Captain Samuel Newman." *Wisconsin Magazine of History* 2 (September 1918): 40–73.

Rule, John C. "The Old Regime in America: A Review of Recent Interpretations of France in America." *William and Mary Quarterly* 19 (1962): 575–600.

Shannon, Fred A. "The Federal Government and the Negro Soldier." *Journal of Negro History* 11 (October 1926): 563–83.

Spaulding, Oliver L., Jr. "The Military Studies of George Washington." *American Historical Review* 29 (July 1924): 675–80.

Stephenson, Orlando. "The Supply of Gunpowder in 1776." *American Historical Review* 30 (1925): 271–81.

Sunseri, Alvin R. "Frederick Wilhelm von Steuben and the Re-education of the American Army: A Lesson in Practicality." *Armor* 74 (1965): 40–47.

Todd, Frederick P. "Our National Guard: An Introduction to Its History." *Military Affairs* 5 (1941): 73–86, 152–70.

Trussell, John B. B., Jr. "The Role of the Professional Military Officer in the Preservation of the Republic." *Western Pennsylvania Historical Magazine* 60 (January 1977): 1–21.

Van Tyne, Claude. "French Aid Before the Alliance of 1778." *American Historical Review* 31 (1925): 20–40.

Weinert, Richard P., Jr. "Saga of Old Fort Wool." *Periodical Journal of the Council on Abandoned Military Posts* 8 (Winter 1976–1977): 3–14.

Wensyel, James W. "The Newburgh Conspiracy." *American Heritage* 32 (April–May 1981): 40–47.

Wright, John W. "Corps of Light Infantry." *American Historical Review* 31 (1926): 459–61.

Dissertations

Carp, E. Wayne. "Supplying the Revolution: Continental Army Administration and American Political Culture, 1775–1783." Ph.D. dissertation, University of California at Berkeley, 1981.

Chase, Philander D. "Baron von Steuben in the War of Independence." Ph.D. dissertation, Duke University, 1973.

Pachero, Josephine F. "French Secret Agents in America, 1763–1778." Ph.D. dissertation, University of Chicago, 1950.

Wright, Robert K., Jr. "Organization and Doctrine in the Continental Army, 1774–1784." Ph.D. dissertation, College of William and Mary, 1980.

INDEX

Page numbers of illustrations appear in italics.

A

Adams, Abigail, 360

Adams, John, xxi, 57, 58, 132, 133, 232, *232,* 234–35, 245, 250, 348, 349, 359, 360, 375–76, 381, 444

Adams, John Quincy, 443, 448–49

Adet, Pierre, 422

Alexander, Lady Kitty, 107

Alexander, William. *See* Stirling, William Alexander, Lord

Allen, Ethan, 57

American Colonies: attitudes toward the French, 73–84; Boston Tea Party, 56; expansion, 55, 56; food in, 89, 101–2; French spies in, 73; Intolerable Acts, 56, 57; King George III's Proclamation of 1763, 55–56; Lafayette's observations, 89–90, 92; marriage in, 170–71; mercantilism and England, 55; Ohio Company and, 35; prelude to revolution, 55–58; slavery in, 30, 31, 150–51; Stamp Act, 56

American Revolution: African Americans in, 215, 323, 325, 369; Battle of Barren Hill, 166, 179–84; Battle of Bemis Heights, 122; Battle of Brandywine, 111, *111, 112,* 113–17, *114, 116,* 169; Battle of Bunker Hill, 59, 62, 68; Battle of Camden, 64, 91, 276; Battle of Dorchester Heights, 68; Battle of Germantown, 119, 131, 169; Battle of Gloucester, 128–29; Battle of Green Spring Plantation, 311, 312, 320; Battle of Guilford Court House, 296; Battle of Kings Mountain, 282; Battle of Monmouth Court House, 1–3, 166; Battle of Princeton, 72; Battle of Rhode Island, 204–19, 234; Battle of Saratoga, 64, 122, 125, 131, 138, 140; Battle of Stony Point, 244, 247–48; Battle of Trenton, 72, 109; Boston, battle for, 63, 67–68, 108–9; British occupation of Philadelphia, 119; Canadian Expedition (irruption) of 1778, 152–62; casualties, 1, 2, 70, 129, 198, 311; European officers and, 73–74, 77–78, 84–88, 92–93, 173–74, 186; First Battle off the Virginia Capes, 295; French expedition to America (1780), 262–75; French financial support, 296, 314–15, 346; French fleet in, 203–19, 315; French support sought, 73–84, 94, 97–98, 131, 156, 173–79, 220; French treaty of alliance and, 186, 222–23, 225; Indian opposition, 122; invasion of Canada, 69–70; lack of funds and supplies, 234 (*see also* Continental Army); Lafayette in France raises funds, supplies, and an army (1779-1780), 234–54; Lafayette's importance in, 450–52; losses in the South, 275–77; map, Northern Theater, *66;* Monmouth Campaign, 174, 187–92, *193;* New Jersey, British occupation of, 72; New York City, British occupation of, 70–71, 95, 106; New York City, siege of, 70–71, 109; Peace of Paris, 360; prisoner exchange, 321, 328, 340–41, 347–48; Savannah, fall of, 234; Second Battle off the Virginia Capes, 329; Siege of Yorktown, 327–38, *331;* slaves captured in, 323; Spanish support for, 131, 175, 179, 238, 284; spies for, 173, 179; start of, 57; surrender at Yorktown, *340;* two-pronged British invasion of Northern New York, 95, 109–10; Virginia Campaign (1781), 174, 290–313, *292, 316;* war in the South, 282, *292,* 319–37, 344; Washington's importance in, 450–52; Wethersfield Plan, 317, 320; Yorktown, Siege of, 87; Yorktown Campaign (1781), 314–27, *316*

André, John, xxi, 280, 281–82
Arbuthnot, Marriot, 295
Armistead, James, xxi, 325, 369
Arnold, Benedict, xxi, 57, 69, 110, 122, 278–82, *279,* 286, 302; as British general, 290, 293, 294, 295, 297, 302, 303, 321
Arnold, Margaret Shippen "Peggy," 278, 280
Auvergne, France, 5, 7, 364; Château de Chavaniac, 7, *8,* 11, 355, 364, 401–2, 403–4, 405, 411, 431, 439; famine in, 355

B

Bailly, Jean-Sylvain, xxi, 386, 389, 390, 392, 399, 401, 414
Bangs, Edward, 314
Barbé-Marbois, François, marquis de, 245, 367–68
Barras, marquis, xxi, 315, 325, 327
Barren Hill, battle of, 166, 179–84
Barry, John, 343
Beaumarchais, Caron du, 166, 172
Belgiojoso, Christine, 447
Belvoir Plantation, 31, 34
Bemis Heights, Battle of, 122
Bernard, Simon, 442
Blanchard, Claude, 102
Boll, Justus-Erich, 416
Boston: battle for, 63, 67–68, 108–9; Boston Massacre, 68; killing of French sailor, 215; lack of cooperation, 65; Lafayette as honorary citizen, 369
Boudinot, Elias, 203
Bouquet, Henry, 51–53
Braddock, Edward, 42–47, 106

Braddock's defeat (Battle of the Monongahela), 42–47, 48–49, 59, 120
Bradford, William, 419–20
Brandywine, Battle of, *111,* 111, *112,* 113–17, *114, 116,* 169
British forces: Battle of Brandywine, 113–17, *114;* Battle of Monmouth Court House, 1–2, *193,* 194–98; Battle of Rhode Island, 208, 209; Battle of Saratoga, 138; Boston lost to Washington, 68; casualties, 1, 2, 71, 129, 198, 311; desertion from, 198; fleet, 70, 95, 109, 110, 179, 216; Gage as commander, 59; Howe as commander, 68; invasion of Northern New York, 95, 109–10; Monmouth Campaign, 187–92, *193;* Native American allies, 122, 162; in New Jersey, 72, 110; New York City, occupation of, 70–71, 95; Philadelphia and, 71, 72–73, 95, 110, 119, 179–80, 187; Siege of Yorktown, *316,* 327–38; size of, 70, 111; South Carolina campaign, 106; surrender, 338–41, *340;* Virginia Campaign, 290–313, 314–27, *316. See also* Hessians
Brunswick, Ferdinand, Duke of, 407, 410
Bunker Hill, Battle of, 59, 62, 68
Bureaux de Pusy, Jean-Xavier, 409, 424
Burgoyne, John, xxi, 109–10, 118, 122, 157, 348

C

Cabot, George, 421–22
Cadwalader, John, 165, 188, 189
Caesar, Julius, 7, 12, 15
Caldwell, John Edwards, 374, 376
Calonne, Charles-Alexandre de, xxi, 356, 357, 380, 381
Camden, Battle of, 64, 91, 276
Canada: American and French invasion sought, 122, 186, 212, 216, 221, 222–23, 224; American invasion fails, 69–70; as French colony, 14, 36, 53; Lafayette and Expedition of 1778, 152–62
Canadian Indians. *See* Native Americans
Carlisle, Lord, xxi, 186, 221–22
Carlos III, king of Spain, 354
Carmichael, William, xxi, 77, 80, 83, 226, 354, 376
Castries, marquis de, xxi, 315
Chang Yü, 287
Charleston, SC, 70, 89, 90–91; British attack, 244, 260; British forces evacuate (1782), 352; British occupation, 347; fall (1780), 265, 275

Charles X, King of France, 445–46

Chastellux, François-Jean de Beauvoir, chevalier de, xxi, 97, 102, 107, 277, 279

Chaumont, Jacques-Donatien Leray de, 237

Chavaniac, Marie-Catherine de, 9, 11

Clinton, Sir Henry, xxi, 70, 71, 80, 95, 106, 110, *193,* 194–98, 265, 269, 271, 272, 275, 276, 288, 291, 294, 298, 302, 317, 321, 327, 330; Battle of Barren Hill, 181–82; evacuation of Philadelphia, 179–80; Monmouth Campaign and, 187–92, *193*

Cochran, John, 117

Condorcet, Marquis de, 377

Continental Army: African Americans in, 150–51, 317; Battle of Monmouth Court House and, 198; commissioning of officers, 61, 62, 65, 67; creation of, 57–58; desertion from, 71, 72, 167, 288, 298–99, 310; discipline in, 64; Duportail as chief engineer, 87, *87;* European officers and, 73–74, 77–78, 84–85, 86–88, 92–93, 98, 121–22, 138–48, 166, 186; frontier riflemen, 60–61; generals of, 62–64, 106–9, 110; hardships and shortages, 59–60, 101, 133–36, 157–58, 159, 163, 167, 258, 259–60, 264, 276–77, 287–88, 298, 303, 317, 321–22; "Indian file" formation, 169; inspector-general for, 139–40, 141, 166–70; intrigues and betrayals against Washington, 71, 74–75, 134, 138–48, 154, 187, 281; irregulars vs. regular soldiers, 47; light troops, use of, 125, 184; light-troop tactics adopted by, 125; Main Army, 138, 152, 163, 164, 181, 206, 269, 283. 295, 296, 317, 319, 320, 341; medical services, 65; as militiamen, 61; mutiny (1781), 287–88, 303, 306; near-rebellion (1783), 362; New England troops, 65; organization, 101, 169; quartermaster general, 133–34; raising of, 70, 72; reluctance to fight in the South, 303; size of, 60, 70, 71, 111, 179, 188; Steuben's inspection system, 169–70; Steuben's training and regulations, 165–70, 184, 188; supply problems, 64–65, 127, 133–34, 244–45, 321–22, 328; training, 61, 67, 101, 139, 165–70, 184, 188; uniforms, 60–61, 101, 266, 317; Virginia Campaign (1781), *292, 316;* Washington appointed Commander in Chief (1775), 57–58; Washington organizes, 64–65; Washington's staff, 61–62; winter at Jockey Hollow (1779-1780), 259–60; winter at New Windsor (1782-1783), 347; winter at

Valley Forge (1777-1778), 135, 147, *147,* 149, 153, 156, 165–70; winter housing, 65

Continental Congress, 57; appointment of Gates to southern command, 275–76, 282; appoints Lafayette ambassador at large (1781), 342; back pay for soldiers, 362; Board of War, 139–40, 141, 143, 160, 161, 163, 164; British peace commission and, 186, 221; Canadian Expedition (irruption) of 1778 and, 152; commissioning of officers, 62, 98–99; Committee on Foreign Applications, 92–93; Continental Army created by, 57–58; dictatorial powers offered to Washington, 277–78; European officers and, 121–22, 186; French treaty of alliance ratified, 178; furlough granted to Lafayette (1778), 223–25; lack of financing for the army, 260; lack of funds and supplies, 244–45; Lafayette and, 93–94, 98; Lafayette given a command, 130; pardon for Lafayette sought, 225–26; promises to supply provisions, 262–63, 264; raising of the army, 70, 72; replacing Schuyler with Gates, 110; Sullivan-d'Estaing conflict and, 214; Washington and, 62; Washington appointed Commander in Chief (1775), 57–58

Conway, Thomas, xxi, 138–48, 163, 164, 165, 360; Cabal, 134, 138–48, 152, 154, 165, 255, 360, 450–52; Canadian irruption, 152–62

Copley, John Singleton, 93

Cornwallis, Charles, Earl of, xxi, 70, 71, 72, 113–15, *114,* 128–29, 276, 282, *312;* Battle of Monmouth Court House, 194, 195; desire to capture Lafayette, 305; Lafayette and, 322, 340–41, 379; as prisoner, 347–48; Siege of Yorktown, 327–38, *331;* surrender, 338–41, *340;* Virginia Campaign, 293–313, *316;* Yorktown Campaign, 314–27, *316, 331*

Corny, Dominique-Louis Ethis de, 255, 261, 264

Crane, Stephen, 118

Custis, John Parke "Jackie," 53–54; death of, 341

Custis, Martha Parke "Patsy," 53–54

D

d'Ayen, duchesse, 17, 18, 120, 231, 394

d'Ayen, Jean-Paul-François de Noailles, duc, xxi, 17–20, 24–25, 29, 75–76, 79, 80–81, 82, 83, 84, 89, 131–32, 219, 233, 357

Deane, Silas, xxii, 74, *76,* 77–78, 79, 80, 82, 83, 84–85, 86, 87, 88, 93, 97–98, 99, 131, 132, 138, 173, 175, 178, 203

Deane, Simeon, 175

de Broglie, Charles-François, duc, xxii, 25–26, 73, 79, 80, 81, 252; English invasion planned with, 242; plot to become generalissimo, 74–75, 77–78, 81–82, 83, 92–93, 99, 131, 148

de Broglie, Victor-François, comte, xxii, 26, 81, 242

Declaration of Independence, 70, 150, 360–61

de Francy, Lazare-Jean Théveneau, 172, 177, 185

de Grasse, François-Joseph-Paul, comte, xxii, 296, 315, 317, 318, 323, 324, *326*, 330, 341; Battle of the Saints and capture, 349; Siege of Yorktown and, 326–37

de Kalb, Johann "Baron," xxii, *76, 91,* 98–99, 164, 178, 259, 275–76; Canadian irruption, 155, 156, 160, 161, 162, 163; Conway Cabal and, 142, 148; death of, 276; de Broglie and, 73–74, 79, 91, 92–93; Lafayette and, 76, 80, 81, 82, 83–84, 89, 109, 127; at Valley Forge, 135, 165

de Staël, Madame, xxii, 381, 392, 410, 424, 439, 442

d'Estaing, comte, xxii, 202–3, 252; appeal to save Charleston, 244; Battle of Rhode Island and, 204–19; French-Spanish armada (1782), 351–52; Lafayette and, 222–23, 233

Destouches, chevalier, 290, 291, 295, 297

de Vaux, Noël de Jourda, comte, 241, 242

Dickens, Charles, 59

Dillon, Théobald, 405

Dinwiddie, Robert, 36, 37, 38, 40, 42, 49, 51

d'Ormesson, Henri-François de Paule Lefèvre, xxii, 356

d'Orvilliers, Louis Cuillouet, comte: commander, French fleet, 242–43, 248

Duer, William, 154, 155, 156

Dumas, Alexandre, 9

Duponceau, Pierre-Etienne, 167, 168, 169, 170

Duportail, Louis le Bègue de Presle, xxii, 87, *87,* 88, 119, 136, 189

E

England: American colonies, expansion of, 36–37; British invasion of Massachusetts, 57; British peace commission, 186, 221; British surrender at Yorktown and, 344; colonial troubles, French intervention in and, 27; French expedition to America and, 262; French hatred of, 13–14; French-Spanish invasion threat, 238; hostilities with France, 128, 179; Intolerable Acts, 56, 57; King George III's Proclamation of 1763, 55–56; mercantilism and the colonies, 55; peace negotiations, 348–49, 350–52; Peace of Paris, 360; prelude to revolution in the colonies, 55–58; reaction to Deane's recruitment of French nobles, 78–79, 81; reward for mutiny offered by, 229–30; spies for, 178; Stamp Act, 56; weakened state (1779), 234–35; West Indies and, 175, 179, 250

Epsewasson Plantation, 31

F

Fabius, 118, 119

Fairfax, George, 35, 56

Fairfax, Lord, 34

Fairfax, William, 34, 35, 47

Fairlie, James, 260

Fayon, Abbé, 12, 13, 15, 18

Ferdinand, Duke of Brunswick, 407, 410

Fersen, Hans-Axel, comte de, 279

Floridablanca, conde de, 354

Forbes, John, 51–53

Fort Duquesne, 39–47, 42, 51–52, 53

Fort Lafayette, 244

Fort LeBoeuf (Erie, PA), 37, 41

Fort Lee, 71

Fort Necessity, 39

Fort Niagara, 62

Fort Ticonderoga, 57, 62, 68

Fort Washington, 109

Fouché, Joseph, 441

France: American alliance and, 126, 131, 132, 173–79, 223, 225; American Revolution and, 27–29, 73–84, 94, 97–98, 131, 156; American Revolution and the cause of liberty, 230; American Revolution and the "noble savage," 73, 125; Aranjuez Convention ratified, 238; Assembly of Notables, 380; Black Musketeers, 16; Bourbon Restoration, 440–41; British surrender at Yorktown and, 344; cemetery at Picpus, 435, 448; Charbonniers, 442; constitutional monarchy, 440, 446–47; Dragons de Noailles, 17; egalitarian ideas in, 28, 349; Enlightenment philosophers, 121; Estates General (1788), 383–84; Farmers General and, 355–56, 380, 385; first foreign minister sent to America, 203; flag of, and Lafayette, 404, 446; fleet sent to America and Battle of Rhode Island, 179, 202–19; hatred of English in, 13–14, 27, 74;

history of, 7; hostilities with Britain, 128, 179; Jones-Lafayette plan to raid the British coast, 235–38; Lafayette raises funds, supplies, and an army for the American Revolution (1779-1780), 234–54; Lafayette's reputation in, 120, 123, 131–33, 155–56; "La Marseillaise," 403, 424; light-troop tactics adopted by, 357–58; loans to the United States, 296, 314–15, 346; loss of New World colonies, 14, 53, 131; map, 6; as mercantilist economy, 356; military influence of Lafayette, 405; monarchy, eighteenth century, 22–23; Mousquetaires du Roi, 9; Napoleonic rule, 424, 425, 431, 435–36, 439; Native American allies, 36, 44, 45, 53, 368; New World colonies, 36; nobility, eighteenth century, 23, 24; Passy, Franklin in, 233, 234, 250, 354; peace negotiations with England, 346–47; Peace of Versailles and Paris, 360; peace treaty with America (1800), 435–36; political clubs in, 383; prelude to Revolution, 380–88; Quasi War, 421, 426, 429, 435–36; refusal to help Ireland, 249; religious intolerance in, 150, 376–77; repression by Charles X and Lafayette's response, 445–47; Revolution, 388–402 (*see also* French Revolution); Rochambeau expedition to America (1780), 260–75; *sociétés de pensée,* 28; spies for, 73; trade with America, 355–57, 374, 399; United States relations with, 376; unrest (1788), 385; unrest (1789), 387–88; veneration of Washington in, 346, 372–73; Versailles, seat of court, 22–23, 81, 156, 230, 234, 250, 356, 388; Washington's death and, 433–34; West Indies and, 175, 248, 250; White Terror, 441; XYZ Affair, 421, 426, 427

Francis II, Emperor of Austria, 417–18

Franklin, Benjamin, xxii, 26, 43, *177;* Arthur Lee and feud, 239–40; expedition to raid English ports, Lafayette and John Paul Jones, 235–38; in France, peace negotiations and, 348–49; in France to raise support and supplies, 74, 82, 87–88, 131, 166, 245, 249, 252–53, 314–15; French treaty of alliance and, 175; invasion of Canada and, 224; Lafayette and, 84–85, 93, 97–98, 173, 177, 226, 231, 232, 233, 234–35, 242, 250, 253, 257, 348–49, 350, 358–59, 375; presentation sword awarded to Lafayette, 243; war strategy, 235

Frederick the Great, 379–80

Frederick William II, King of Prussia, 414–15

Freemasons, 26; Lafayette and, 26, 90, 349, 445–46; *sociétés de pensée* and, 28; Washington and, 26, 33–34

French and Indian War, 14, 125; Braddock's defeat (Battle of the Monongahela), 42–47; British casualties, 46; Dinwiddie and, 38, 42; Forbes' march on Fort Duquesne, 53; Fort Necessity defeat (1754), 40–41; French abandonment of Fort Duquesne, 53; irregulars vs. regular soldiers, 47, 51; massacre at Jumonville Glen (1754), 38–40; Native Americans in, 36, 44, 45, 51; Washington as Commander in Chief (1755), 49–53; Washington in, 38–41, 42–47; Washington's uniform, 49

French Revolution, 358; capitulation of Louis XVI, 388–89, 393; condemnation of Lafayette, 409; Declaration of Rights, 391; *émigrés,* 390, 394, 398, 403, 404–5, 435; factions emerging in, 390; Jacobins, 390, 394, 397–98, 404, 405, 406, 407–9, 415; Lafayette and prelude to, 380–88; Lafayette's role in, 388–402, 404–9, *408;* "La Marseillaise," 403, 424; Louis XVI and, 388, 390, 392–93, 394, 397–98, 399–401, 409; Marie-Antoinette and, 389, 398, 400; National Assembly and, 398, 399, 400–401, 404, 407–8, *408;* September Massacres, 410; storming of the Bastille, 388, 393; storming of the Bastille, anniversary, 396; "Tennis-Court Oath" and, 386; the Terror, 404, 410, 412, 413, 414, 415; war with Austria, 407, 410; Washington given key to the Bastille, 395–96

Frestel, Félix, xxii, 411, 415, 417, 421, 422, 423, 424, 426

G

Gage, Thomas, xxii, 59, 68

Gallatin, Albert, 437

Gates, Horatio, xxii, *64,* 68–69, 71, 110, 122, 140, 142, 146, 152, 154, 155, 156, 158, 159, 160, 165, 282; "Grand Army" of, 275–76

Genêt, Edmond-Charles-Edouard, 420

George II, King of England, 36–37

George III, King of England, 27, 80

Gérard, Conrad-Alexandre, xxii, 223, 226, 239, 247; first foreign minister to America, 203

Germantown, PA, 181; battle for, 119, 131, 169

Gimat, Jean-Joseph Sourbader de, xxii, 94, *116,* 116–17

Gist, Christopher, 37–38

Gist, Mordecai, 294

Gloucester, duke of, 26–27

Grant, James, 181–83

Graves, Thomas, xxii, 266, 267, 269, 327, 328, 329

Greene, Kitty, 170–71

Greene, Nathanael, xxii, 88, *108,* 108–9, 110, *111,* 111, 113, 124, 136, 157, 178; Battle of Brandywine, 115–16; Battle of Germantown, 119; Battle of Monmouth Court House, 2–3, 197, 199; Battle of Rhode Island, 205–6, 207, 209–10, 213–14, 215, 216–17; Conway Cabal and, 141–42, 146, 147; death of, 380; diplomacy of, 218; drafting of army regulations, 169; as "Dutch uncle" for Lafayette, 108, 156, 170, 214, 231; Lafayette and, 2–3, 127, 128, 129–30, 199, 261; Monmouth Campaign and, 188, 189–90; New York City, British occupation of and, 70–71; as Quaker, 2; supplying the troops, 260; Virginia Campaign (1781), 290–313, 321; war in the South and, 282, 283, 284, 341, 344, 347; Washington and, 2–3

Green Spring Plantation, Battle of, 311, 312, 320

Grey, Charles, 181

Guèrin, Charlotte, baronne de Chavaniac, 11, 411, 415, 417; death of, 439

Guèrin, Marie de, 11

H

Hamilton, Alexander, xxii, 102–6, *103,* 118–19, 138, 140, 141, 146, 149–50, 151, 190, 428; Battle of Monmouth Court House, 196, 197; court-martial and hanging of John André, 281–82; friendship with Lafayette, 282–84, 289, 297, 348, 393; George Washington Lafayette and, 422, 423; Lafayette and, 304, 377, 429–30; Lafayette's imprisonment and, 412; marriage of, 283; Monmouth Campaign and, 190, 191; at Morristown headquarters, 261; New York City offensive planned, 267; rift with Washington, 289–90; winter at Valley Forge (1777-1778), 168, 169

Hancock, John, xxii, *93,* 93, 205, 210, 211–12, 214, 215, 219

Hannibal, 118–19

Harrison, Benjamin, 99–100

Hartford, CT, 315, 369, 417

Henry, Patrick, xxiii, 57, 136

Hessians, 1, 2, 70, 71, 72, 109–10, *114,* 115–16, 129, 189, 198, 215, 302, 339

Houdon, Jean-Antoine, 376

Howe, Richard Lord, xxiii, 70, 72, 106, 203; Battle of Rhode Island, 209–10

Howe, Sir William, xxiii, 68, 72, 106, 110, 111, 113, 119, 127, 179, 305; Battle of Barren Hill, 181–82

Huger, Benjamin, 89

Huger, Francis, 416

Humphreys, David, 369

Hundred Years' War, 14; Poitiers, battle of, 13

Hunolstein, Aglaé, comtesse d', xxiii, 21, 120, 258, 347, 352, 355

I

Iliad (Homer), 13

Indians. *See* Native Americans

Iroquois nation, 162–63, 174, 181, 182, 367–68

J

Jackson, Andrew, 443

Jay, John, xxiii, 151, *354;* abolition of slavery and, 354, 377; as emissary to France, 349, 350, 354; Lafayette's imprisonment and, 417; as president of Congress, 224; Spanish negotiations and, 347, 348; treaty with Britain and, 420–21

Jefferson, Thomas, xxiii, 26, 296, 375; on the French Revolution, 381, 409; as governor of Virginia, 290, 291, 321; Lafayette and, 293, *293,* 299, 301, 374, 375, 383, 385–86, 436–37, 438–39, 440, 443–44; Lafayette's imprisonment and, 412–13; as minister to France, 369, 375–76, 382; Monticello sacked by British, 306

Johnson, Samuel, 150

Joly de Fleury, Jean-François, xxiii, 356

Jones, John Paul, xxiii, *235,* 235–38, 396

Jonson, Ben, 452

Joséphine, Empress of France, 427

Joseph of Austria, 400

Jumonville, Joseph-Coulon de Villiers de, 39–41

K

Knox, Henry, xxiii, 67–68, *69,* 72, 88, 107, 108, 115, 146, 170, 178, 323; Battle of Monmouth Court House, 196, 197–98

Knyphausen, Baron von, xxiii, 113, *114,* 116, 265

L

La Colombre, Louis-Sainte-Ange, chevalier Morel de, xxiii, 409, 422, 426

Lafayette, Anastasie, 130, 411, 415, 418–20, *419,* 428, 437–38, 443

Lafayette, Charles, marquis de, 8

Lafayette, Edouard, 8

Lafayette, George-Washington, xxiii, 250, 349, 364, 437; in America, 421–26; American passport for, 417; Empress Joséphine receives, 427; flight from Jacobins (1792), 411; flight from Jacobins (1794), 415

Lafayette, Gilbert de, II, 13

Lafayette, Gilbert de, III, *maréchal de France,* 13

Lafayette, Jacques-Roch, 8

Lafayette, James Armistead. *See* Armistead, James

Lafayette, Marie-Adrienne-François de Noaille, marquise de (Adrienne), xxiii; admiration for Washington, 246–47, 370, 433; American Revolution and, 132–33; appearance, 18, 19, *21, 435;* arrest of (1792), 411; arrest of (1794) and release, 415–16; buys back Chavaniac, 417; celebrity of her husband and, 233–34, 345–46, 360; cemetery at Picpus and, 435, 438, 448; at Chavaniac, 355, 364, 411; daughter Anastasie born, 130; daughter Henriette born, 28; daughter Marie-Antoinette-Virginie born, 350; death of her mother, grandmother, and sister, 415–16, 435; departure of Lafayette (1780), 256; final words and death of, 437–38, 448; as formidable manager and negotiator, 355, 377–78, 403, 411, 413–14, 417, 430, 431, 434; French Revolution and, 394; as hostess, 360; illness begun at Olmütz and, 418, 427, 428; Lafayette's arrest and imprisonment, 409, 411–12, 413–14, 418–20, *419;* La Grange and, 417, 431, *434,* 434, 436; loan from Gouverneur Morris and, 411, 434–35, 437; marriage to Lafayette, 17–20, 79, 80, 84, 120, 132, 231, 254, 347, 430; pregnancy, first, 22; pregnancy, fourth, 346, 349; pregnancy, third, 238; as prisoner at Olmütz, 418–20, *419,* 424, 425; role as Lafayette's representative, 132–33, 282, 289, 369; wedding ceremony, 19

Lafayette, Marie-Antoinette-Virginie, 350, 411, 415, 417, 418–20, *419,* 443

Lafayette, Marie-Joseph-Paul-Yves-Roch-Gilbert du Motier, marquis de, xxiii; appearance, 11, 15, *19,* 24, 25, 95, *97, 209,* 232, 301, 374, 444, *445;* baptismal name, 9; birth, 7; birthplace and family home, Château de Chavaniac, 7, *8,* 11, 355, 364, 401–2, 403–4, 405, 411, 431, 439; character and personality, 2, 3, 12, 15–16, 21–22, 23–24, 96, 97, 122, 126, 145–46, 158, 161, 163–64, 174, 175–76, 185, 187, 211, 213, 222, 232, 241, 294, 301, 345, 348, 351, 355; childhood, 9–17; clothing, fashion, and, 24, 99, 106, 254; commission in the King's Dragoons, 234; daughter Anastasie born, 130, 132–33; daughter Henriette born, 28; daughter Henriette dies, 178; daughter Marie-Antoinette-Virginie born, 350; education, 12–14, 15, 18; in England (1777), 79–80; English, attitude toward, 27, 177; Europe of his time, map, *6;* family history, 7–10, 13; father's death, 9, 10–11; Freemasonry and, 26, 28, 90, 349, 445–46; friends of, American, 102–6, 115, 121, 124–25, 149–50, 174, 177, 187, 198, 206, 282–84, 438–39, 440; friends of, French, 20–22, 28, 75–76, 312, 439; letters to Adrienne, 20, 79–80, 84, 88–89, 90, 120, 122, 128, 137, 155–56, 178, 186, 257, 282, 340–41, 352, 430; as letter-writer, prolific, 121; love affairs of, 20–22, 107, 120, 170–71, 258–59, 347, 352, 355, 374, 403; marriage to Adrienne Noailles, 16–20, 21, 22, 79, 80, 132, 231, 238, 250, 254, 345–46, 355, 430, 448; memoirs written by, 27, 96, 435, 439; mesmerism and, 363–64, 365, 367–68; military ability, 2, 277, 312, 405; military service, France, 16, 18, 19–20, 25–26, 28–29, 205, 238–39, 241–42, 243, 345; mother's death, 16; philosophy and social ideas, 26, 28, 104–5, 106, 121, 149–50, 230, 249, 345, 349, 362, 374, 376–77, 383, 387, 440, 442, 444–45, 451; place in French society, 23–24, 25; plantation in French Guyana, 377–78, 443; popularity of, 3, 25, 96, 109, 124, 277, 312, 372–73, 389, 392, 412, 442; reputation, 120, 123, 126, 131–33, 155–56, 158, 164, 185, 219, 304; seasickness and, 84, 88, 229, 363–64, 372; slaves and slavery, xxi, 90–91, 99, *116,* 149–50, 152, 230, 323, 325, 353, 358–59, 366, 369, 377–78, 443, 444–45, 451; smallpox inoculation, 20; son George-Washington born, 250; wards in care of and adoptions by, 368, 370, 374; wealth of, 9, 10, 14–15, 16, 24, 26, 84, 91, 350, 358, 434–35, 436–37; wedding ceremony, 19; writings by, style of, 12–13, 124

AMERICAN REVOLUTION AND: aides-de-camp
for, 94, 197; alliance with France
supported, 126, 131–32, 173–79;
American and French invasion of Canada
sought, 122, 186, 212, 216, 221, 222, 224,
232–33, 237, 261, 265–66; arrest warrant
in France issued for (1777), 81, 93, 131,
204, 219; Battle of Barren Hill, 179–84;
Battle of Brandywine, 111, *111,* 113,
115–17; Battle of Gloucester, 128–29;
Battle of Guilford Court House, 296; Battle
of Monmouth Court House, 2–3, *193,*
194–98, 452; Benedict Arnold's betrayal
and, 278–82, 302; Benjamin Franklin as
grandfather figure, 177, 231, 232, 233,
242, 253, 348–49, 350; Bergen, NJ raid,
282; British attempts to capture, 181–84;
Canadian Expedition (irruption) of 1778,
152–62; as celebrity, France, 231, 233–34,
238, 251, 346, 347; career as American
officer ends, 352; challenges Carlisle to a
duel, 221–22; as chief of "foreign affairs,"
173–74, 186; command of a Light
Division, 266, 276–77, 282–83, 291–313,
318–19; commands given to, 127–30, 136,
164, 178, 179–84, 204–19; command
sought by, 94–95, 99, 123–24, 125;
commissioning of French officers sought
by, 121–22; Conway and, 138–48,
152–62, 163; Cornwallis and, 305, 312,
313, 322, 323, 340–41; corps d'etrangers
formed by, 174; court-martial and hanging
of John André, 281–82; departs for France
(1781), 341–43; desertion problems in
troops, 298–99, 310; desire for glory in
France, 185; desire to join, 27–29, 75–84,
76; desire to return to America (1780),
248–49; divided loyalties of, 201, 204,
212–13, 219–28; drafting of army
regulations, 169; expedition to raid English
ports, with John Paul Jones, 235–38; in
France (1782), drumming up support for
America, 346; French expedition to
America (1780) and, 260–75, 284; French
fleet and the Battle of Rhode Island,
204–19; French rank granted, for America
only, 252; French-Spanish armada raised by
(1782), 351–52; horses, shortage of, 322;
house arrest in France (1779), 230–33;
Greene as "Dutch uncle," 108, 156, 170,
214, 231; as Kayeheanla and the Iroquois,

162–63, 174, 181, 182, 367–68; leaves
America for France (1778-1779), 219–28;
letters of introduction written for, 226;
light-troop tactics adopted by, 125, 184;
Monmouth Campaign and, 187–92, *193;*
mutiny dealt with (1781) and, 287–88,
303; New York City offensive and, 267,
269, 270; presentation sword awarded to,
243; raising French funds and French army
to fight, 234–54, 284, 288, 296, 315,
450–51; reception in America, 84–85,
88–95; reception in France (1779),
229–34; reception in France (1782),
344–46; recovery from wound, 119,
120–23, 124; restoration of standing in
France, 204; return to America (1780),
260–65, *262;* Robert Morris as his banker,
133; Rochambeau and, 252–53, 260–75;
Siege of Yorktown, 327–38, *331;* spending
personal funds on, 127–28, 133, 136,
157–58, 159, 163, 172–73, 203, 250, 252,
284, 298, 328; terms of service, 77–78,
85, 92–95, 255, 265; spies for, 173, 179,
203, 219, 261, 266, 317, 319, 325, 369;
surrender at Yorktown, 338–41, *340;*
Thomas Jefferson, friendship with,
293–94, 301; *Victoire* (ship), purchased,
used, lost, 79, 81, 82, 83–84, 89, 90, 91,
97, 128, 174; Virginia Campaign (1781),
291–313, *316,* 451; voyage to France
(1779), 229–30; West Indies pirate
recruitment proposal, 126, 138, 185; West
Indies proposed campaign against British,
126, 216; winter at Valley Forge (1777-
1778), *147,* 165, 169, 170–71, 174, 179;
wounding of, *112,* 115–17, *116;* Yorktown
Campaign (1781), 314–27, *316, 331,* 451;
war strategy, 134, 161

FRENCH REVOLUTION AND FINAL YEARS:
Assembly of Notables (1787), 380; arrest
and imprisonment, 409–25; in Chamber of
Deputies (1817), 442; in Chamber of
Deputies (1830-1831), 446–47; Christine
Belgiojoso and, 447; Club of Thirty, 383,
386; Commandant, National Guard of
Paris, 389–93, 396–401, 403, 404, 444,
446; Commandant National Guard of the
Realm, 447; crippling accident (1803), 436;
death of, 447–48; death of Adrienne and
grief following, 437–39; Declaration of the
Rights of Man and, 387; earth from

America for his grave, 444; Fanny Wright and, 442–43; French flag (Tricolor), and, 404, 446; French Revolution and, 388–402, 404–9, *408;* French Revolution, commander of People's Army, 404–5; grave of, 448; homelessness, post-release from imprisonment, 425–31; home life, 360–61; imprisoned in Olmütz, 415, 416; influence of, honors and accolades, 443–45, 448–49, 450–52; La Grange and, 431, 434, *434,* 436, 438–39, 439, 447–48; Liberal Party and political activism (1817-1823), 442; Louisiana Purchase and recouping of fortune, 436–37; Napoleon Bonaparte and, 426–27, 431, 434, 435, 439–41; October Days and, 391–93; as prisoner at Olmütz, 418–20, *419, 424*–25; refuses dictatorship, 446; release from Olmütz, 425; repression by Charles X and, 445–46; trip to America (1824-1825), 443–44; Three Glorious Days of the Revolution and, 446; U.S. Army Corps of Engineers and, 441–42; U.S. National Guard and, 444

Post American Revolution: as advocate for America, 375, 376, 451; awarded the Cross of St. Louis (1783), 357; as celebrity, America, 342, 364–69, 407, 412; denunciation of aristocrats, 249; Estates General (1788) and, 382–86; French Revolution, prelude to, 380–88; Germany tour (1785), 379–80; James Madison and, 366–67, 368–69; John Adams and, 359, 360; as *le Vashington français* (the French Washington), 373; light-troop tactics adopted by, 357–58; peace negotiations and, 358–59; peace negotiations with England and, 346–47, 348–49, 350–52; peace treaty, signing of, 358, 360; return to America (1784), 363–72; Spanish diplomacy by (1783), 352–55; "Tennis-Court Oath" and, 386; trade reforms and, 355–57, 374, 399

Washington and: absolute loyalty to, 305; admiration and awe for, 29, 95–96, 100–101, 142–44, 156, 197, 230, 240; death and, 433–34; father-son relationship with, 2, 3, 96–98, 100, 109, 117, 122–23, 128, 132, 136–37, 145–46, *147,* 148, 158, 159, 164, 199, 212–13, 216, 220–21, 227–28, 232, 241, 245–47, 248–49, 285–86, 299, 304, 318, 329–30, 351, 363, 370–72, 378–79, 400, 405–6, 427, 452;

final letter to, 430; first meeting with, 95–96; gives key to the Bastille, 395–96; influence on, 362, 365–66, 372–73, 390, 401; legacy left by, 432; letter from Washington (1779), 245–47; mentorship and military education by, 99–103, 444; proposal to free the slaves and, 353; response to his imprisonment, 411–13; return to America (1784) and, 363–72; return to American (1798) discouraged, 428–29; reunion with (1780), 260–65, *262;* "rule to follow in all things," 285, 430; Society of Cincinnati and, 359–60, 363; son, George-Washington Lafayette and, 421–26, 431–32 ; worry about separation from, 238–39, 240–42

Lafayette, Michel-Louis-Christophe-Roch-Gilbert du Motier, marquis de, 8–9, 10

La Luzerne, Anne-César, chevalier de, xxiii, 256, 261, *263,* 265–66; as "Dutch uncle" for Lafayette, 263, 308, 323; as minister to the United States, 239, 262–64, 271, 272–74, 280, 287, 288, 296, 298, 302, 395

"Lament of Washington" (Bradford), 419–20

Languedoc (ship), 209, 210

La Rivière, Marie-Louise-Julie, madame, 8–9, 11

La Tour-Maubourg, César, comte de, 409, 424

Laurens, Henry, xxiii, *121,* 223; capture of, 282, 340; as "Dutch uncle" for Lafayette, 121, 128, 158, 160–61, 172, 174–75, 183, 201, 231; as early supporter of Lafayette, 94; Lafayette arranges release, 347–48; peace negotiations and, 358–59; as president of Congress, 98, 130, 133, 136, 138, 140–41, 146, 152, 153, 154–55, 156, 165, 167, 176–77, 185, 186; slaves and slavery, 104, 150

Laurens, John, xxiii, 86, 98, 103, 104–6, *105,* 115, 134, 140, 146, 149–51, 153, 155, 166–67, 168, 183, 223, 281, 287–88; Battle of Rhode Island, 209; death of, 351; as delegate to France, 285, 289, 314–15; drafting of army regulations, 169; duel with Charles Lee, 201; emissary to d'Estaing, 204; slavery and, 106, 149–52

Lee, Arthur, xxiii, 131, 239–40

Lee, Charles, xxiii, 62–63, *63,* 64, 70, 71, 187; Battle of Monmouth Court House, 1, 2, *193,* 194–98, 199; court-martial and loss of command, 199–201; death of, 351; Monmouth Campaign and, 187–92, *193*

Lee, Light-Horse Harry, 290, 339

Lee, Richard Henry, 139

Lee, Thomas Sim, 294

Lincoln, Benjamin, xxiv, 244, 260, 275, 328, 338, 339

Livingston, Robert, xxiv, 352, 353

Louis XIV, King of France, 22, 23, 150

Louis XV, King of France, 16, 19, 22, 26

Louis XVI, King of France, xxiv, 22, 24, 74–75, 131, *388;* accolades for Lafayette, 345; arrest of (1792), 409; appoints d'Estaing as commander of French forces in America, 202–3; betrayal of Lafayette, 394, 397; capitulation of, 388–89; departure of Lafayette (1780), 354; frees the serfs, 249; French Revolution and, 388–89, 390, 392–93, 394, 399–401; Lafayette appeals to for supplies, 284; pardon for Lafayette sought from, 225–26, 230–31, 233; pre-Revolutionary period, 382–83, 386; reprimand of Lafayette, 233; spending of, 380

Louis XVII, King of France, 440

Louis XVIII, King of France, xxiv, 440, 445

Louis-Philippe, Citizen King of the French, 446–47; *see also* Orléans, Louis-Philippe, duc d'

M

Madison, James, xxiv, 366–67, *367,* 368–69, 374, 423, 436–37, 442

Marie-Antoinette, Queen of France, xxiv, 22, 24, 175, 259, 354, *389;* accolades for Lafayette, 345–46; as enemy of Lafayette, 382, 394; excesses of, 380, 389; French Revolution and, 389, 394, 398, 400; pre-Revolutionary period, 382–83

Martin, Joseph Plumb, xxiv, 182–83, 192, 195, 196, 199–201, 258, 260

Maryland: Lafayette and heirs made citizens of, 371; Lafayette's Light Troop in, 294; provisioning of the army by, 294; troops requested in, 297–98

Maurepas, comte de, xxiv, 131, 138, 230, 235; Lafayette's schemes and, 235, 236–38; support for America and, 250–51

Mazzei, Philip, 285

McDougall, Alexander, 153, 155, 157, 164

McHenry, James, 197, 359

McLane, Allan, xxiv, 173, 317

Mesmer, Friedrich Anton, 363–64

Mifflin, Thomas, xxiv, 61, 133, *134,* 140, 146, 152

Mill, John Stuart, 448–49

Mirabeau, Honoré-Gabriel Riqueti, comte de, xxiv, 360, 386, 392, 395, 398, 400

Monmouth Campaign, 174, 187–92, *193*

Monmouth Court House, Battle of, 1–3, 166, *193, 194*–98

Monongahela, Battle of. *See* Braddock's Defeat

Monroe, Elizabeth, 415–16

Monroe, James, xxiv, 117, 415–16, *416,* 417, 436, 443

Montbarey, Alexander-Marie-Léonor de Saint-Mauris, comte de, xxiv, 250, 254

Montcalm, marquis de, 14

Montgomery, Richard, 69

Montmorin, comte de, 354–55

Morel de La Colombe, Louis-Sainte-Ange, chevalier, 94

Morgan, Daniel, xxiv, 69, 122, *125,* 125, 191, 303, 306, 321; as "Old Wagoner," 125

Morgan's rifles, 122, 125, 128, 180, 188

Morizot, Jacques-Philippe Grattepain-, 254, 403

Morris, Gouverneur, xxiv, 153, 384, *385;* Adrienne's imprisonment and, 415; as ambassador to France, 407; in France (1789), 384; on Lafayette and the French Revolution, 386–87, 389, 390, 393, 396, 399, 401, 409; Lafayette's imprisonment and, 410, 411, 412, 425; loan to Adrienne, 411, 434–35, 437; as president of Congress, 186, 187; rescue of Adrienne and, 385

Morris, Robert, xxiv, 85, *173,* 343, 356, 357, 378; as Lafayette's banker, 133, 172

Morristown, NJ, 71; Washington's headquarters, 261, *262;* winter at Jockey Hollow (1779-1780), 259–60; winter quarters at, 72

Motier, Madeleine, mademoiselle du, 11

Murat, Abbé de, 9

N

Napoleon Bonaparte, xxiv, 64, 408, 424, 439; death of, 441; exile to Elba, 440; exile to St. Helena, 441; Hundred Days, 441; Lafayette and, 426–27, 431, 434, 435, 439–41; light troops, use of, 358; military influence of Lafayette, 405

Napoleon II, Emperor, 441

Native Americans: allied with the British, 51, 124, 162; allied with the French, 36, 44, 45, 53, 162; Battle of Barren Hill, 180, 182–83; of Canada, 162–63, 222, 224, 237, 262; Cherokees, 55; Delawares, 39; Fort Duquesne massacre and, 40; Iroquois, 162–63, 174,

180, 182, 183; King George III's Proclamation of 1763, 55–56; Lafayette and, 162–63, 174; Lafayette meets with the Six Nations (1784), 367–68; Pontiac's confederation, 55–56

Nelson, Thomas Jr., xxiv, 290; as governor of Virginia, 306, 309, 310, 321, 322, 328, 341; slaves captured in Virginia and, 323

New Jersey: British forces in America, 72, 110; militia, 188. *See also specific battles; specific cities*

Newport, RI,, 266–75, 283, 293, 294, 315, 317

New Windsor, 347

New York City: American offensive planned, 262, 264, 265, 266, 267, 269, 279, 297, 315, 318; battle for, 70–71, 109; British evacuation of, 362; British occupation of, 70–71, 95, 106; French fleet arrives at, 203–4; reception for Lafayette (1784), 364, 367

New York Society for Promoting the Manumission of Slaves, 377

Noailles, Louis-Marie, vicomte de, xxiv, 17, 81, 345; American Revolution and, 75–76, 78; Freemasonry and, 26, 28; Lafayette and, 20–22, 312; marriage to Louise de Noailles, 17, 18

Noailles, marquis de, 79, 82–83

North, Lord, 131, 344, 346

O

O'Hara, Charles, xxv, 339–40

Ohio Company, 35, 36; post at Forks, 38, 39, 41

Orléans, Louis-Philippe, duc d', xxv; *see also* Louis-Philippe

Oswald, Richard, 350

Otchikeita, Peter, 368, 374

P

Paine, Thomas, xxv, 226, 396, *397,* 406, 416

Parker, Josiah, 324

Parkman, Francis, 22, 41, 344

Peace of Paris, 360

Peace of Versailles, 360

Philadelphia, PA: attack on urged by Congress, 134, 178–79; British evacuation of, 179–80, 187; British forces in, size of, 179; British occupation of, 119; as British target, 71, 72–73, 95, 110; as Continental capital, 71, 91, 92, 223; Independence Hall, 92

Phillips, William, xxv, 10, 13, 281, 295, 297, 299, 302

Pigot, Robert, 208, 211, 215–16

Pinckney, Thomas, xxv, 410, 411, 421, 423

Pitt, William, 361, 418

Plato, 5

Plutarch, 1

Poix, prince de, xxv, 230, 256, 259, 323, 352, 368

Portsmouth, VA, 314, 318, 319, 324

Princeton, 189; Battle of, 72; Lafayette at, 288

"Prisoners of Olmütz," 418–20, *419,* 424

Pulaski, Casimir, 174

Putnam, Israel, 68

R

Raynal, Abbé Guillaume, 28

Reed, Joseph, xxv, 61, 67, 71, 278

Rhode Island: Battle of, 204–19, 234; British evacuation of, 244; French occupation of, 266–75, 315. *See also* Newport, RI

Richmond, VA, 299–300, 301, 304, 305, 306, 369

Riddle of the Sphinx, 30

Rights of Man, The (Paine), 406

Robespierre, Maximilien, xxv, 399, 400–401, 415, 440

Rochambeau, Jean-Baptiste-Donatien de Vimeur, comte de, xxv; as Commander of the French army in America, 252–55, *253,* 261–62, 284, 296, 297, 304, 315, 339; French Revolution and, 404, 405, 415; Lafayette and, reconciliation, 274–75; leaves America for France (1782), 352; strife with Lafayette, 267–75; surrender at Yorktown, 339; Virginia Campaign (1781) and, 291; Washington and, 278–79, 280–81, 329, 330, 362; Wethersfield Plan, 317, 320

Rodney, George, 349

Rogers, Robert, 50; Rangers, 50

Rossini, Gioacchino, 445

Rousseau de Fayolle, chevalier du, 92

S

Saint-Germain, Claude-Louis, comte de, xxv

Saint-Simon-Montbléru, marquis de, xxv, 326

Saratoga, Battle of, 64, 122, 125, 131, 138, 140, 175

Sartine, Antoine-Raymond-Jean-Gaulbert-Gabriel de, xxv, 237

Savannah, GA, fall of (Dec. 1778), 234, 244, 250

Schuyler, Philip John, xxv, 63, 69, 110, 162

Scott, Charles, 189, 194, 196

Ségur, Louis-Philippe, comte de, xxv, 20–22, 24, 78, 131; American Revolution and, 75–76, 96; Freemasonry and, 26, 28

Ségur, Philippe-Henri, marquis de, xxv

SevenYears' War, 26, 27, 49, 56, 63, 138, 202; Battle of Minden, 9, 10, 26. *See also* French and Indian War

Sharpe, Horatio, 42

Shays Rebellion, 380

Short, William, xxv, 376, 392, 396, 401, 410, 411

Sieyès, Emmanuel-Joseph, l'abbe, xxv, 386

Simcoe, John Graves, xxv, 307, 308, 309, 319

Simiane, Adélaïde, comtesse de Miremont, xxvi, 347, 352, 361, 374, 403

Slavery, 90–91, 149–52; British Anti-slavery Society, 361; emancipation of James Armistead, 369; John Laurens and, 104–5; Lafayette's anti-slavery proposal, 353, 361–62; Lafayette's slave(s), xxi, 90–91, 99, *116,* 150; Lafayette's views, 230, 323, 358–59, 366, 377–78, 444–45, 451; recruited for Continental Army, 150–51; tobacco and, 30, 31; Washington and, 32, 54, 57, 366, 378; Washington frees his slaves, 432

"Song of the Awkward Squad, The," 172

Spain: American Revolution, support for, 131, 175, 179, 238, 284; Aranjuez Convention ratified, 238; English invasion planned, 242; "Family Compact" with France, 175; Gibraltar and, 242, 350; Lafayette as emissary to, 352–55; Peace of Versailles, 360; refuses to help America, 254; as threat to the United States, 346–47, 348, 352–55, 376; U.S. treaty with, 421

Stainville, comte de, xxvi, 73–74

Stark, John, xxvi, 152, 157

St. Clair, Arthur, xxv, 287–88, 341

Stephen, Adam, 114, 119, 127, 130

Steuben, "Baron" von, xxvi, *166,* 338–39; celebration of French treaty and, 178–79; Charles Lee and, 201; command sought by, 186, 217; Continental Army and, 165–70, 184, 188; Lafayette's command of a Light Division, 266; lobbying Congress for supplies, 260; Monmouth Campaign and, 189; Virginia Campaign (1781), 290–313; war in the South and, 282

Stirling, William Alexander, Lord, xxvi, 106–7, *107,* 114, 115, 117, 136, 140, 142, 146, 178, 197, 200

Stony Point, Battle of, 244, 247–48

Stormont, Lord, 82, 83

Sullivan, John, xxvi, 88, 142, 146, *206;* Battle of Brandywine, 111, 113, *114,* 114–15; Battle of

Germantown, 119; Battle of Rhode Island, 204–19; capture of, 70; conflict with d'Estaing, 206–8, 209, 210–14, 215, 222–23; Lafayette and, 124–25, 205, 206–8

Sun Sheng, 229

Symonds, Thomas, 294

T

Talleyrand, xxvi, 100–101, 381, 396, 421, 424, 431, 440

Tarleton, Banastre, xxvi, 305, 306, 308, 310, 319, 326; horses stolen by, 321, 322

Temple, William, 243–44

Ternay, chevalier de, xxvi, 254–55, 262, 264, 265, 266, 267, 270, 271, 273, 278–79, 284

Thacher, James, 260

Three Musketeers, The (Dumas), 9

Tilghman, Tench, xxvi, 102–3, 146, 196, 289–90

Trenton, NJ, 71; Battle of, 72, 109, 117

Tronson du Coudray, 87–88, 92

Troup, Robert, 156

Tucker, St. George, 329

U

United States, 362; Articles of Confederation, 364; Barbary pirates and, 375–76; British holdings in the Northwest, 380, 420–21; Constitutional Convention, 380; death of Lafayette and, 448–49; declared a sovereign state, 351; expansion beyond the Mississippi, 367, 376, 421; first foreign minister sent to, 203; French loans to, 296, 314–15, 346; grants Lafayette back pay, 414; Jay Treaty, 420–21; Lafayette as celebrity in, 364–69; Lafayette as citizen of, 369, 410–11; Lafayette's imprisonment and, 411, 412, 414; Lafayette's trip (1824-1825), 443–44; Louisiana Purchase, 436; Peace of Paris, 360, 362; peace treaty with France (1800), 435–36; place names after Lafayette, 443; pork-barrel politics, 442; QuasiWar, 421, 426, 429, 435–36; relations with France, 420, 421, 426, 427–30, 435–36; repayment of Lafayette's debts and Louisiana Purchase, 436–37; Spain and, 376, 379, 421; Spanish threat to, 346–47, 367; trade with England, 367; trade with France, 356–57, 374; treaties with Native Americans, 368; Washington as president, 393, 412; Washington's pessimism about, 361; western border on the Mississippi, 354; XYZ Affair, 421, 426, 427

United States Congress. *See* Continental Congress

United States Constitution, 382, 383

U. S. Army Corps of Engineers, 87, 442

V

Valley Forge, PA, 135, 147, *147,* 149, 153, 156, 161, 163, 165, 174, 179, 183

Valmy, Battle of, 410

van Braam, Jacob, 37, 41

Varnum, James, 135

Vauban, comtesse de, 258

Vercingetorix, 7, 15

Vergennes, Charles Gravier, comte de, xxvi, 74, 78–79, 81, 82, 83, 131, 175, *176,* 223; American expedition supported, 242, 243, 247, 251–52; American supplies and, 249, 250–51, 314–15; Benedict Arnold's betrayal and, 281; as "Dutch uncle" for Lafayette, 176, 230, 231, 236, 239; Lafayette and, 264, 344–53; peace negotiations and, 344–45, 346, 348, 350–52; rejection of American expedition, 238; rejection of Canadian invasion, 237; second division not sent to America, 266–67, 270, 296; Society of Cincinnati and, 359–60

Vernon, Edward "Old Grog," 32

Villiers, Coulon de, 40–41

Virginia: accolades for Lafayette in, 345, 376; British force in, size of, 301–2; Campaign (1781), 174, 290–313, *292, 316;* disinformation from Washington and, 303, 305, 317, 319; First Battle off the Virginia Capes, 295; French and Indian War and, 49–53; Ohio Company and, 36–37; Second Battle off the Virginia Capes, 329; Siege of Yorktown, 327–38; seizure of horses in, 321–22; slavery laws, 366; slaves and slavery in, 30, 31; tobacco farming, 30–31, 55; uniform, Virginia Regiment, 49; Washington as "conscience of," 56; Washington family holdings in, 31; Yorktown Campaign (1781), 314–27, *316;* Virginia Campaign, 174

Voltaire, 131

von Luckner, Nicholas Baron, 404

W

Wadsworth, Jeremiah, 170

Walker, Benjamin, 168, 169

Ward, Artemas, 62, 68

Washington, Augustine "Gus," 31–32

Washington, George, xxvi; aging of, 406–7; ambitions and preference for luxury, 34, 50, 55, 101–2; appearance, *3,* 33, 95, *96,* 278–79, 375, *432;* birth, 31; birthplace, Popes Creek Plantation, 31; death of, 432; education, 32–33, 34, 47, 50, 61; establishes separation between American military and politics, 148; fame of, 48–49; family history, 31–32; family land and homes in Virginia, 31–32, 34, 54; father's death, 32; fox-hunting, passion for, 33; Freemasonry and, 26, 28, 33–34; horsemanship of, 33; lack of children, 54; Lawrence, half-brother and, 32–33, 35; marriage to Martha Dandridge Custis, 53–54; military ability, 42, 45–46, 48–49, 50, 51, 196–98, 318; Mount Vernon and, 32, 34, 35, 42, 53, 54, 67, 220, 329, 351, 363, *365,* 365–66, 371, 372, 422, 428, 431–32; philosophy and social ideas, 34, 65, 362; slavery issue and, 353, 361–62, 366, 378; slaves freed by, *432;* slaves owned by, 32, 54, 57; smallpox contracted by, 35; style of leadership, 106, 118–19; wealth of, 54–55

AMERICAN REVOLUTION: aides-de-camp, 61, 98, 285; as American Fabius, 118, 119, 128, 161, 179; appeals to Congress, 135–36; Battle of Brandywine, *111,* 111, 113–17; Battle of Germantown, 119; Battle of Monmouth Court House, 2–3, *193,* 194–98, 452; Battle of Princeton, 72; Battle of Rhode Island, 204–5, 216–18; Battle of Stony Point, 244; Benedict Arnold's betrayal, 278–82; character and personality, 33, 53, 58, 96, *96,* 176, 246–47, 278–79, 289–90, 318, 362; Commander in Chief (1775) of the Continental Army, 57–58; commissioning of officers and, 61, 62, 65, 186, 217; Continental Army, initial problems with, 60, 61, 67; Continental Army, organizing, 64–65, 67; Continental Army uniforms, 60–61; Conway and, 138–47; crosses the Delaware (Battle of Trenton), 72; d'Estaing and, 216–18; dictatorial powers offered to, 277–78; French expedition to America (1780) and, 262–75; French treaty of alliance and, 175–76; headquarters, 261, *262,* 287, 309, 362; inspector-general position proposed, 139–40, 141; intrigues and betrayals against, 71, 74–75, 134, 138–48, 154, 187, 281; invasion of Canada opposed by, 223;

Lee and, 195–96, 199–201; losses in the
south and, 276; Monmouth Campaign and,
187–92, *193;* New York City, retreat from,
70–71; New York City offensive, 262, 264,
265, 267, 269, 279, 297, 298, 304, 315,
318; rift with Hamilton, 289–90;
Rochambeau and, 252, 315, 317; Siege of
Yorktown, 327–38, *331;* spies for, 72, 173;
staff, 61–62, 98, 102–3, 105; Steuben's
training of the army and, 166–70; supply
problems, 244–45; surrender at Yorktown,
338–41, *340;* Virginia Campaign (1781),
290–313, *316;* war strategy, 118, 119, 128,
134, 161–62, 178–79; Wethersfield Plan,
317, 320; winter at New Windsor (1782-
1783), 347; winter at Valley Forge (1777-
1778), *147,* 165, 175; Yorktown Campaign
(1781), 314–27, *316, 331*

Early Years and Military Service:
childhood, 32–33; in Barbados, 35;
Braddock and military education, 42, 43,
47, 106; Braddock's defeat, 42–47, 48–49,
120; Commander in Chief (1755) of the
Virginia Regiment, 49–53; in Continental
Congresses, 57; Fort Necessity defeat
(1754), 40–41; Gist expedition to Ohio
(1753), 37–38; hemorrhoids and dysentery
(1755), 44, 46; massacre at Jumonville
Glen (1754), 38–40; Mississippi Land
Company and, 55, 56; as surveyor, 35; in
Virginia Assembly, 56

Lafayette: appreciation of efforts by, 358;
assigned to Washington, 85, 94–95; departs
from America (1781), 341–43; diplomatic
mission given to, 267–75; farewell letter to
(1784), 370–71; father-son relationship
with, 2, 3, 96–98, 100, 109, 117, 122–23,
128, 132, 136–37, 144–45, *147,* 148, 158,
159, 190, 199, 217–18, 220–21, 227–28,
285–86, 299, 309, 320, 329–30, 370–72,
378–79, 382, 426, 427, 431–32, 452; first
meeting with, 95–96; French Revolution
and worries over, 382, 384, 393–94, 400,
401, 406–7; George-Washington Lafayette
and, 421–26, 431–32; given a command,
127–28, 179–84, 190; imprisonment of,
411–13, 417, 419, 423–24, 426; legacy
left to, 432; long letter to (1779), 245–47;
mentorship of, 99–103; reunion with

(1780), 260–65, *262;* seeks a command,
123–24, 125; visit (1784), 363–72

Post-Revolution Years: busts and statues of,
376; Constitutional Convention and, 380;
French Revolution and, 395–96, 399;
Mount Vernon and retirement, 351, 363,
365, 365–66, 371, 372, 422, 428, 431–32;
post-war plans, 362–63, 365–66; Potomac
canal project, 369–70, 371, 376, 379; as
president of the United States, 393, 412;
refuses dictatorship, 362; Society of
Cincinnati and, 359–60, 363; veneration of
in France, 346, 372–73

Washington, George Augustine, 351
Washington, John, 31
Washington, Lawrence (grandfather), 31
Washington, Lawrence (half-brother), 32–35
Washington, Martha, 53–54, 58, 256, 341,
365–66
Washington, Mary Ball, 32
Watteau, Jean-Antoine, 14
Wayne, Anthony, xxvi, 170, *174,* 280; Battle of
Germantown, 119; Battle of Monmouth
Court House, 194–95, 197, 198; Charles Lee
and, 201; as Indian fighter, 421; Monmouth
Campaign and, 188, 189, 190, 191; Siege of
Yorktown, 327, 329; Virginia Campaign
(1781), 291–313, 319, 321, 322, 324
Webster, Noah, 298
Weedon, George, xxvi, 301
West, Benjamin, 14
West Indies, 73, 91; Battle of the Saints, 349;
French army in, 352; French fleet in, 296,
315; Lafayette's proposals for, 126, 138, 185,
216; slavery in, 149; struggle for control of,
175, 179, 223, 248, 250
West Point, 278–80
Whiskey Rebellion, 420
Wilberforce, William, 361
Wilkinson, James, 140
Williams, Samuel, 425
Wolfe, James, 14
Wright, Fanny, 442–43

Y

"Yankee Doodle," 314, 339
York, PA, 119, 135, 152, 155, 164, 303
Yorktown, VA, 295, 322, 324, 325, 326, 330,
331, 369; Siege of, 87, *316,* 327–38, *331*